2 The "deprivation [under "color of" law] of any rights, privileges, or immunities secured by the Constitution and laws"

3 "[S]ubjects or causes to be subjected . . . to the deprivation"

4 "[S]hall be liable to the party injured in an action at law": Damages

5 "[S]uit in equity or other proper proceeding for redress": Equitable Relief and "Procedural" Defenses

6 "Every person": Governmental Liability

7 "Every person": The Absolute Individual Immunity of Legislators, Judges, Prosecutors, and Others

8 Qualified Immunity for "Persons": An Affirmative Defense

Appendixes

Tables

Index

Introduction: History, Procedural Matters, and Attorney's Fees

1

§1.01   Summary

42 USC §1983,[1] the federal statute which is the subject of this book and whose history and purposes are sketched in this chapter,[2] is a powerful legislative "sword"[3] enacted by Congress pursuant to section 5 of the Fourteenth Amendment for the protection of certain rights "secured by the Constitution and laws" against infringement by the states. When these rights are violated, §1983 creates an action for damages and injunctive relief for the benefit of "citizens" and "other persons"[4] against those "persons"[5] responsible for the violations. An introductory series of comprehensive checklists, with appropriate cross-references to portions of this book,[6] sets out relevant legal issues which should be considered by §1983 plaintiffs who sue for damages or for declaratory and injunctive relief. Legal issues relevant to the defense of such actions are also presented in the checklists.

As with other civil cases, the Federal Rules of Civil and Appellate Procedure govern §1983 litigation.[7] However, the Supreme Court has put a unique gloss on FRCP Rule 12(b)(6) in cases involving pro se inmate claims under §1983.[8] Also of special importance for §1983 purposes is Rule 23, which sets out the requirements for class actions. The jurisdictional counterpart of §1983, 28 USC §1343(3), provides for federal jurisdiction without regard to jurisdictional amount, as does 28 USC §1331, the federal question jurisdiction provision.[9] Even where these statutes cannot be used, as, for example, with state-created claims, pendent jurisdiction may still be available.[10] Section 1983 plaintiffs also have the option of suing in state courts which are, in all likelihood, required by the Supremacy Clause to exercise concurrent jurisdiction.[11]

Jury trials are generally available to the parties in §1983 damages actions, but not in actions solely for injunctive relief.[12] However, where a §1983 plaintiff seeks both damages and injunctive relief, the legal claim must be tried first by a jury. Relevant jury findings bind the district court in its decision whether to grant or deny equitable relief.

---

[1] The text is set out at **§1.02.**

[2] *See* **§1.03.**

[3] In the sense of providing not only for injunctive relief but also for compensatory and punitive damages.

[4] *See* **§1.08.**

[5] *See* **§1.09.**

[6] *See* **§§1.05-1.07.**

[7] *See* **§1.16.**

[8] Haines v Kerner, 404 US 519 (1972). *See* **§1.15.**

[9] *See* **§1.10.**

[10] *See* **§§1.11-1.12.**

[11] *See* **§1.13.**

[12] *See* **§1.17.**

Attorney's fees, a matter of no small concern to litigants and lawyers alike, may be awarded to the prevailing party in §1983 cases under the Civil Rights Attorney's Fees Awards Act of 1976.[13] These awards are subject to the discretion of the court. There has been an explosion of litigation in the Supreme Court and the courts of appeals under this Act.

§1.02   Text of §1983 and Its Jurisdictional Counterpart, 28 USC §1343(3)

42 USC §1983 reads as follows:[14]

> Every person who, under color of any statute, ordinance, regulation, custom, or usage, of any State or Territory *or the District of Columbia*, subjects, or causes to be subjected, any citizen of the United States or other person within the jurisdiction thereof to the deprivation of any rights, privileges, or immunities secured by the Constitution and laws, shall be liable to the party injured in an action at law, suit in equity, or other proper proceeding for redress. *For the purposes of this section, any Act of Congress applicable exclusively to the District of Columbia shall be considered to be a statute of the District of Columbia.*

28 USC §1343(3) reads in relevant part as follows:[15]

> (a) The district courts shall have original jurisdiction of any civil action authorized by law to be commenced by any person: . . .
> (3) To redress the deprivation, under color of any State law, statute, ordinance, regulation, custom or usage, of any right, privilege or immunity secured by the Constitution of the United States or by any Act of Congress providing for equal rights of citizens or of all persons within the jurisdiction of the United States; . . .
> (b) *For purposes of this section—*
> (1) *the District of Columbia shall be considered to be a State; and*
> (2) *any Act of Congress applicable exclusively to the District of Columbia shall be considered to be a statute of the District of Columbia*

---

[13] *See* §§1.18-1.26.

[14] (Emphasis added to show 1979 changes.) §1983 was amended to include the District of Columbia. Act of Dec 29, 1979, Pub L No 96-170, §1, 93 Stat 1284. So, too, was 28 USC §1343(3).

[15] (Emphasis added to show 1979 changes.) *See* Act of Dec 29, 1979, Pub L No 96-170, §1, 93 Stat 1284. These amendments, in the words of §3 of Pub L No 96-170, "shall apply with respect to any deprivation of rights, privileges, or immunities secured by the Constitution and laws occurring after the date of the enactment of this Act [December 29, 1979]." *See* §§1.09-1.10 for further discussion.

§1.03   History and Purposes of §1983

Section 1983 is modeled on §2 of the Civil Rights Act of 1866,[16] which made criminal certain acts committed by persons "under color of any law, statute, ordinance, regulation, or custom."[17] Section 1983 and its jurisdictional counterpart, 28 USC §1343(3), specifically began as §1 of the Ku Klux Klan Act of April 20, 1871, which was enacted by Congress pursuant to section 5 of the Fourteenth Amendment in order to enforce that amendment.[18] This purpose is clear from the title of §1, "An Act to enforce the Provisions of the Fourteenth Amendment to the Constitution of the United States, and for other Purposes."[19]

In 1874 Congress codified existing law and, as a result, the substantive portion of §1 of the 1871 Act became a separate section identical to the present §1983. The section's coverage also was expanded beyond constitutionally secured rights, privileges, and immunities to include those secured by federal laws as well. Ultimately, the jurisdictional counterpart became 28 USC §1343(3).[20]

The Supreme Court broadly described the purpose of §1983 in the following terms:

> As a result of the new structure of law that emerged in the post-Civil War era—and especially of the Fourteenth Amendment, which was its centerpiece—the role of the Federal Government as a guarantor of basic federal rights against state power was clearly established. Section 1983 opened the federal courts to private citizens, offering a uniquely federal remedy against incursions under the claimed authority of state law upon rights secured by the Constitution and laws of the Nation. . . .
>
> The very purpose of §1983 was to interpose the federal courts between the States and the people, as guardians of the people's federal rights—to protect the people from unconstitutional action under color of state law, "whether that action be executive, legislative, or judicial."[21]

The Court has also indicated that §1983 is designed both to prevent the states from violating the Fourteenth Amendment and certain federal statutes and to compensate injured plaintiffs for deprivations of their federal rights.[22]

Section 1983 is directed not only at unconstitutional laws, but at affording protection of "a federal right in federal courts because, by reason of prejudice, passion, neglect, intolerance or otherwise, state laws might not be enforced and

---

[16] Adickes v Kress & Co, 398 US 144, 162-63 (1970).

[17] §2 of this Act is the predecessor of 18 USC §242, the criminal counterpart of §1983. *Id* 166 n 36.

[18] Monroe v Pape, 365 US 167, 171 (1961).

[19] 17 Stat 13 (1871).

[20] Lynch v Household Fin Corp, 405 US 538, 543 n 7 (1972).

[21] Mitchum v Foster, 407 US 225, 238-39, 242 (1972).

[22] Carey v Piphus, 435 US 247 (1978).

the claims of citizens to the enjoyment of rights, privileges and immunities guaranteed by the Fourteenth Amendment might be denied by the state agencies."[23]

§1.04 Policy Considerations in §1983 Litigation

It is obviously essential for lawyers, judges, and others involved in §1983 litigation to master the numerous and complex doctrines which are the subject matter of this book. However, it is also important to be aware of the policy considerations which have made §1983 litigation increasingly controversial. These considerations have a direct effect on the ways in which lawyers and judges, including Supreme Court Justices, interpret and evaluate §1983 and, hence, on the content of §1983 doctrines themselves.

Federalism

At the outset, there is considerable tension between the underlying purposes of §1983, which rather clearly reflect a distrust of state entities and state courts which was prevalent in 1871 when §1983 was enacted, and the current view of some of the Justices of the Supreme Court (and increasing numbers of federal judges) that many purported §1983 claims do not belong in federal courts but should instead be brought in state courts in the first instance, if at all. This view is based in part on an assumption that state courts are as competent as federal courts to decide such claims, whether on federal constitutional law grounds or state law grounds. Moreover, the assumption is typically accompanied by a conviction that federal courts ought to minimize their involvement in and supervision over state and local government matters. Analysis of Supreme Court decisions in Chapter 3 dealing with due process and in Chapter 5 involving the various ways of avoiding the merits in §1983 litigation supports these observations.

Overdeterrence and Overburdened Federal Courts

In addition, there is increasing sensitivity in the Supreme Court to the possibility that state and local government officials, often targets of §1983 plaintiffs, are thereby being improperly overdeterred in the performance of their government duties. This sensitivity is especially apparent, as shown in Chapters 7 and 8, in the Supreme Court's absolute and qualified immunity decisions. Further, the concern with overdeterrence and the previously mentioned federalism-based view that many purported §1983 cases do not belong in federal court are related to the perception of some that federal courts are in danger of being overwhelmed by many §1983 cases which are of questionable merit.

---

[23] Monroe v Pape, 365 US 167, 180 (1961).

Cutting Back the Scope of the §1983 Remedy

Implicit in these developing judicial attitudes is the position that the remedies provided by §1983 have become far too wide-ranging in scope and effect. It follows that those who hold this position will often use different techniques to cut back on the scope of the §1983 cause of action. These techniques range from limiting the constitutional right implicated—due process, as discussed in Chapter 3, is a prime example—through expanding the protections of absolute and qualified immunity, as discussed in Chapters 7 and 8, to prodefendant applications of the doctrines of standing, abstention, and preclusion discussed in Chapter 5.

Implications

Several important points emerge. Lawyers involved in §1983 litigation should be prepared to confront these judicial concerns head on and, if possible, to use them for the benefit of their clients. This will frequently be more comfortable for defense counsel than for plaintiff's counsel. Further, as demonstrated throughout this work, even though the major outlines of §1983 liability have already been articulated by the Supreme Court, it is to be expected that additional §1983 issues, even apparently trivial ones, will continue to splinter the Court. While some §1983 issues can be readily resolved by straightforward statutory interpretation techniques, many cannot be because of the lack of any real guidance in §1983's language and legislative history. Instead, such issues will be decided in large measure on the basis of policies which will often implicate the judicial concerns mentioned earlier.

The judicial concerns with federalism, overdeterrence, and overburdened courts may mask a deeply felt but not explicitly articulated *positivist* jurisprudential perspective which is in opposition to a *rights* perspective. Under the *positivist* perspective, the source of law is the state itself which, together with its officers, should not ordinarily be sued by its citizens even for claimed violations of constitutional rights. While this assessment is admittedly speculative, the judicial concerns with federalism, overdeterrence, and overburdened courts, whatever their source, are real. Consequently, they will continue to play a significant role in §1983 interpretation in the Supreme Court and other federal courts.

These judicial concerns are not illegitimate. But it is hoped that they do not become more significant than they deserve to be. Thus, with respect to federalism, one might observe that §1983 is a statute whose purpose is to vindicate the Fourteenth Amendment which was in fact expressly designed to bring about a profound change in federal-state relations and our constitutional structure. With respect to overdeterrence, it may be argued that because of the importance of Fourteenth Amendment compliance, we are better off running the risk of *over*deterring Fourteenth Amendment violations than the risk of *under*deterring them. And with respect to claims of overburdened federal courts, the protection of Fourteenth Amendment rights appears an appropriate and worthy use of scarce national resources. Indeed, it may even be suggested that the Forty-Second Congress took these very positions when it enacted §1983 in 1871.

§1.05   General Checklist

Those who may sue

Natural persons, corporate and other entities, and governmental bodies: **§1.08**

Those who may be sued

Natural persons, corporate and other entities, and governmental bodies: **§1.09,** Chapters 6 and 7

Causes of action

1. Fourteenth Amendment—due process and equal protection: **§§2.03, 3.08-3.11, 3.14**
2. Fourteenth Amendment—Bill of Rights violations: **§§2.03, 3.03-3.07**
3. Fourteenth Amendment—privacy and access to the courts: **§§2.03, 3.12, 3.13**
4. Federal statutory violations: **§2.12**
5. The requirement of state action and color of law: **§§2.04-2.10**

Choice of forum—federal or state

1. Federal jurisdiction over §1983 claims: **§§1.10, 2.12**
2. Federal jurisdiction over joined state claims: **§§1.10-1.12**
3. Federal venue: **§1.15**
4. State jurisdiction: **§1.13**
5. Removal: **§1.14**

Attorney's fees

1. When awarded: **§§1.18-1.22**
2. To and against whom awarded: **§1.24**
3. Computing the amount: **§§1.25-1.26**

§1.06   Damages Actions Checklist

Elements of the prima facie cause of action

1. Basis of liability: **§§3.01-3.14**
2. Cause in fact: **§§3.18, 4.02**
3. Proximate cause and duty: **§§3.16-3.17**

    4. Respondeat superior for individuals and governmental bodies: §§3.15, 6.05-6.16

Compensatory damages

    1. In general: §§4.01-4.03
    2. For particular causes of action: §§4.04-4.07
    3. Local government liability: §§6.05-6.16

Punitive damages

    1. In general: §§4.08-4.09
    2. For particular causes of action: §§4.10-4.13
    3. Local government immunity: §§6.17-6.19

Wrongful death and survival: §§3.19-3.20

Statutes of limitation: §§4.14-4.17

Governmental liability

    1. Political subdivisions of a state: §§6.05-6.19
    2. The state itself—the Eleventh Amendment: §§5.08, 6.20

Absolute individual immunity

    1. Legislators: §§7.02-7.05
    2. Judges: §§7.06-7.12
    3. Prosecutors: §§7.13-7.14
    4. Public defenders: §7.15

Qualified individual immunity

    1. The objective part: §§8.03-8.14
    2. The now eliminated subjective part: §8.15
    3. Burden of proof: §8.16

The Eleventh Amendment bar to damages relief against a state: §§5.08, 6.20

Forcing the plaintiff out of federal court and into state court

    1. Exhaustion of judicial and administrative remedies and federal habeas corpus: §§5.09-5.11
    2. Uncertainty of state law—*Pullman* abstention: §5.16
    3. Res judicata and collateral estoppel: §§5.17-5.20

§1.07 Declaratory and Injunctive Relief Checklist

Formal requirements

1. For declaratory relief: **§5.02**
2. For injunctive relief: **§5.02**

Statutory bars to injunctive relief: § 5.03

Justiciability requirements

1. Standing: **§5.05**
2. Ripeness: **§5.06**
3. Reviewability: **§5.07**
4. Others (including mootness): **§5.04**

The Eleventh Amendment bar to declaratory and injunctive relief against a state: §§ 5.08, 6.20

Forcing the plaintiff out of federal court and into state court

1. Exhaustion of judicial and administrative remedies and federal habeas corpus: **§§5.09-5.11**
2. Pending state criminal and other proceedings—the *Younger* rule: **§§5.12-5.15**
3. Uncertainty of state law—*Pullman* abstention: **§5.16**
4. Res judicata and collateral estoppel: **§§5.17-5.20**

Statutes of limitation: §§4.13-4.17

§1.08 Who May Be a §1983 Plaintiff

A §1983 cause of action for damages and declaratory and injunctive relief is given to "any citizen of the United States or other person within the jurisdiction thereof" who has suffered the deprivation of constitutional or certain federal statutory rights by virtue of the conduct of state officials. Interpreting the "citizen . . . or other person" language in conjunction with similar language in the Fourteenth Amendment, the Supreme Court has held that only natural persons can be citizens of the United States; corporations cannot be.[24] Thus, a corporation cannot assert a violation of the privileges and immunities clause of the Fourteenth Amendment in a §1983 case or, indeed,

---

[24] Grosjean v American Press Co, 297 US 233, 244 (1936); Hague v Committee for Indus Org, 307 US 496, 514 (1939).

in any case.[25] However, the Court has also held that "a corporation is a 'person' within the meaning of the equal protection and due process of law clauses,"[26] thereby indicating that a corporation, even if not a citizen, is still an *other person* for §1983 plaintiff purposes.

Federal courts dealing with corporate claims under §1983 have rather consistently concluded that a corporation—whether profit-making or not-for-profit—is not an *other person* for §1983 purposes so long as the corporation is suing in its own right.[27] However, a shareholder, even a majority or sole shareholder of a for-profit corporation, is not considered a proper §1983 plaintiff.[28] Although this in effect treats the shareholder as not being an *other person*, it is preferable to view the shareholder, where a natural person, as an *other person* or as a *citizen* but one who does not have standing.[29] Distinguishing between §1983 *other person* issues and standing is also important where a not-for-profit corporation sues under §1983. Such a plaintiff is an *other person*, but that *other person* similarly might not have standing. This latter question depends on whether the not-for-profit corporation is legitimately asserting either its own rights[30] or those of its members.[31]

Not only are corporations of all kinds, profit and not-for-profit alike, considered *other persons* for §1983 plaintiff purposes, but so are labor unions. The Supreme Court made this clear in *Allee v Medrano*,[32] a §1983 case where a party was a recognized labor union, when it said that "[u]nions may sue under 42 U.S.C. sec. 1983 as persons deprived of their rights secured by the Constitution and laws."[33] Furthermore, this assertion has also been applied to

---

[25] Hague v CIO, 307 US 496, 514 (1939).

[26] Grosjean v American Press Co, 297 US 233, 244 (1936).

[27] Des Vergnes v Seekonk Water Dist, 601 F2d 9 (1st Cir 1979) (profit); Advocates for the Arts v Thomson, 532 F2d 792 (1st Cir), *cert denied*, 97 S Ct 254 (1976) (not for profit); Adams v City of Park Ridge, 293 F2d 585 (7th Cir 1961) (profit and not for profit); Raymond Motor Transp Inc v Rice, 417 F Supp 1352 (WD Wis 1976), *revd on other grounds*, 434 US 429 (1977) (profit); Colorado Seminary v National Collegiate Athletic Assn, 417 F Supp 885 (D Colo 1976), *affd*, 570 F2d 320 (10th Cir 1978); Gentry v Howard, 365 F Supp 567 (WD La 1973) (profit); Mini Cinema 16 Inc of Fort Dodge v Habhab, 326 F Supp 1162 (ND Iowa 1970) (profit); DDB Realty Corp v Merrill, 232 F Supp 629 (D Vt 1964) (profit).

[28] Gregory v Mitchell, 634 F2d 199 (5th Cir 1981); Smith v Martin, 542 F2d 688 (6th Cir 1976), *cert denied*, 431 US 905 (1977); Erlich v Glasner, 418 F2d 226 (9th Cir 1969), a much-cited case on this issue; Gentry v Howard, 365 F Supp 567 (WD La 1973).

[29] *See* §5.05 on standing. A comparable standing issue arises in connection with §1983 wrongful death actions. *See* §3.20. Also, an assignee of a §1983 action for damages would in all likelihood not have standing, although he or she would clearly be a "person" for §1983 plaintiff purposes. *See* Carter v Romines, 560 F2d 395 (8th Cir 1977), *cert denied*, 436 US 948 (1978).

[30] Advocates for the Arts v Thomson, 532 F2d 792 (1st Cir), *cert denied*, 429 US 894 (1976); Adams v City of Park Ridge, 293 F2d 585 (7th Cir 1961).

[31] Sierra Club v Morton, 405 US 727 (1972); NAACP v Button, 371 US 415 (1963).

[32] 416 US 802 (1974).

[33] *Id* 818 n 13.

an unrecognized labor union.[34]

Again, however, all such *other persons* must still have standing, a separate consideration. Moreover, it clearly does not follow from the fact that a §1983 plaintiff is an *other person* that a §1983 cause of action is stated. This, too, is a distinct inquiry and goes to the merits. For example, whether a Fourteenth Amendment liberty or property interest is implicated in a §1983 case is a question on the merits and is essentially unrelated to the plaintiff's status as an *other person.*

While natural persons who are *citizens* are also *other persons* for §1983 plaintiff purposes, some natural persons, such as aliens, are not *citizens.* Yet, aliens may be §1983 plaintiffs because they are considered to be *other persons.*[35] In contrast, it was held, even before the Supreme Court's abortion decisions,[36] that an unborn fetus is neither a *citizen* nor a *person* for Fourteenth Amendment or §1983 purposes.[37] This conclusion is now clearly correct after those decisions.

Where the plaintiff, the decedent's administratrix, sued police officers alleging, among other things, that they conspired *after* decedent's death to cover up their wrongful shooting and killing of the decedent in violation of his Fifth, Sixth, Eighth, Ninth, and Fourteenth Amendment rights, the Ninth Circuit held that the cover-up claim was properly dismissed by the district court. The court said: "A 'deceased' is not a 'person' for the purposes of 42 U.S.C. §1983 . . ., nor for the constitutional rights which the Civil Rights Act serves to protect."[38] However, the decedent's §1983 challenge, through his administratrix, to actions committed *before* his death was distinguished by the Ninth Circuit as surviving under state law.[39]

Such a result can be avoided, even in a cover-up case, by framing the §1983 complaint to allege harm to the plaintiff, not the decedent. Thus, where it was claimed that defendants conspired to cover up the facts of the decedent's death, thereby depriving the decedent's estate and the individuals represented by the estate's administratrix of property—their cause of action for wrongful death—

---

[34] Memphis Am Fedn of Teachers v Board of Educ, 534 F2d 699 (6th Cir 1976). *Recognition* refers to a union's status as a collective bargaining representative as determined by the National Labor Relations Board.

[35] Graham v Richardson, 403 US 365 (1971).

[36] Doe v Bolton, 410 US 179 (1973); Roe v Wade, 410 US 113 (1973).

[37] *E.g.*, McGarvey v Magee-Womens Hosp, 340 F Supp 751 (WD Pa 1972), *affd*, 474 F2d 1339 (3d Cir 1973).

[38] Guyton v Phillips, 606 F2d 248, 250 (9th Cir 1979). In a similar Tenth Circuit case, a father sued a district attorney charging that the latter's refusal to prosecute the man who allegedly killed plaintiff's son resulted from prejudice against Saudi Arabians. Affirming the district court's dismissal of the complaint on various grounds, the Tenth Circuit reasoned that because the alleged discrimination was not directed against the plaintiff, he suffered no violation of his civil rights. It was also significant that the alleged discrimination occurred *after* the son's death, not before. The Tenth Circuit based its conclusion on both lack of standing and no cause of action. Dohaish v Tooley, 670 F2d 934 (10th Cir 1982).

[39] *See* **§3.19** on survival of §1983 actions.

in violation of due process, the Second Circuit[40] held that the administratrix had standing to sue under §1983 for the deprivation of the estate's due process rights.

In an apparent case of first impression, the Fifth Circuit held in *City of Safety Harbor v Birchfield*[41] that a city is not an *other person* for §1983 plaintiff purposes. Safety Harbor sought damages and injunctive relief in a §1983 suit against several Florida legislators and private persons for alleged constitutional violations in connection with certain annexation legislation. Concluding that Safety Harbor could not be a §1983 plaintiff, the court first observed, relying on *Monroe v Pape*,[42] that a municipality is not considered a person when it is sued as a defendant. It then emphasized the distinction in American jurisprudence between private persons and public entities.[43] Finally, it referred to portions of the legislative history of §1983 which indicated that the section was designed to provide a remedy for private parties only.

The Fifth Circuit's reliance on *Monroe v Pape* is now misplaced in light of *Monell v Department of Social Services*[44] which, in overruling this aspect of *Monroe*, held that a city is in fact a *person* which may, under certain circumstances, be sued as a defendant under §1983. However, the Fifth Circuit relied more heavily in its opinion upon the legal distinctions between private persons and public entities and on the legislative history of §1983. Thus, *Monell* does not necessarily undermine the result in *City of Safety Harbor.*

If a city may not be a §1983 plaintiff in its own right because it is not an *other person*, a state likewise may not sue in its own right under §1983.[45] However, several Pennsylvania district court decisions held that a state as parens patriae may in some circumstances be a §1983 plaintiff in seeking to vindicate the rights of its citizens. Specifically, the state of Pennsylvania was permitted as a §1983 plaintiff in actions brought on behalf of all its citizens in connection with a city's alleged racially discriminatory employment practices for police officers and firefighters.[46]

---

[40] Barrett v United States, 689 F2d 324 (2d Cir 1982). *See also* Bell v City of Milwaukee, 746 F2d 1205 (7th Cir 1984), holding that decedent's siblings and the estate of decedent's father could recover for due process and racial equality deprivations brought about by defendants' conspiracy to cover up the truth about decedent's shooting death.

[41] 529 F2d 1251 (5th Cir 1976).

[42] 365 US 167 (1961).

[43] "Such entities are creatures of the state, and possess no rights, privileges or immunities independent of those expressly conferred upon them by the state." 529 F2d at 1254.

[44] 436 US 658 (1978). *See* **ch 6.**

[45] Buda v Saxbe, 406 F Supp 399 (ED Tenn 1974).

[46] Pennsylvania v Flaherty, 404 F Supp 1022 (WD Pa 1975) (police); Pennsylvania v Glickman, 370 F Supp 724 (WD Pa 1974) (firefighters). *See also* Pennsylvania v Brown, 260 F Supp 323 (ED Pa 1966), *vacated in part on other grounds*, 373 F2d 771 (3d Cir 1967) (education). However, Pennsylvania was not permitted as a §1983 parens patriae plaintiff in Pennsylvania *ex rel* Rafferty v Philadelphia Psychiatric Center, 356 F Supp 500 (ED Pa 1973) involving a discharged nurse's suit against a state and federally funded psychiatric center alleging violations of her procedural due process and First Amend-

Similarly, in a police misconduct case, the Third Circuit[47] held that the Commonwealth of Pennsylvania could sue under §1983 for injunctive relief under a parens patriae theory. Among other things, the court, in an extensive discussion, emphasized Pennsylvania's "significant sovereign interests of its own in the prevention of future violations of constitutional rights of its citizens, in circumstances in which it cannot reasonably anticipate that private enforcement will achieve the protection of those sovereign interests."

These cases, which emphasize the health and welfare of the state's citizens, follow the lead of the Supreme Court which has said in a non-§1983 case that "a State may sue as parens patriae to prevent or repair harm to its 'quasi-sovereign' interests."[48] Such §1983 state-as-plaintiff cases do not, though, stand for the proposition that a state is an *other person.* Rather, they indicate only that a state has standing as parens patriae to assert the rights of its citizens who might have sued on their own under §1983. It is worth noting that a similar parens patriae approach was discussed by the Seventh Circuit in connection with a city's suit against the United States Attorney General and others for allegedly discriminatory enforcement of civil rights laws.[49] In that case, the court found that the city could show injury neither to its citizens nor to itself and hence did not have standing. However, the *other person* issue was not addressed at all.

§1.09   Who May Be a §1983 Defendant

Section 1983 makes actionable the conduct of "[e] very person" who, under color of law, causes constitutional or certain federal statutory deprivations. Who is a *person* under §1983 and the closely related issues of individual and

---

ment rights. The court found that the "public interest claimed here is . . . vague, speculative and remote, too remote to be encompassed by the doctrine of *parens patriae.*" *Id* 506.

[47] Pennsylvania v Porter, 659 F2d 306, 316 (3d Cir 1981) (en banc). *See also* New York *ex rel* Abrams v 11 Cornwell Co, 695 F2d 34 (2d Cir 1982), where, relying on the parens patriae test of Alfred L Shapp & Son v Puerto Rico, 458 US 592 (1982), the Second Circuit held that the state of New York had standing to seek the vindication of the constitutional rights of mentally disabled persons under 42 USC §1985(3). It found that New York's interest was "quasi-sovereign" in nature, that a substantial segment of its population was allegedly injured, and that a suit by mentally retarded persons themselves would fail for lack of standing. New York had sued property owners for their allegedly conspiratorial and wrongful refusal to sell to the state a residence to be used as a mental health facility.

In contrast, in United States v City of Philadelphia, 644 F2d 187 (3d Cir 1980), the Third Circuit held, after a lengthy analysis, that the United States does not have implied authority to sue a city and its officials for an injunction against alleged police violations of the Fourteenth Amendment rights of individuals.

[48] Hawaii v Standard Oil Co, 405 US 251, 258 (1972).

[49] City of Milwaukee v Saxbe, 546 F2d 693 (7th Cir 1976). This case is not, of course, a §1983 case since the defendants were federal officials who did not act under color of state law. *Id* 703.

governmental absolute immunity are discussed extensively in Chapters 6 and 7. Briefly, however, it is clear that all natural persons, corporate entities, associations, and the like are *persons* for §1983 defendant purposes.[50] It is also settled, after *Monell v Department of Social Services*,[51] that cities, counties, and other local government entities, whether general or special purpose, are suable as *persons* under certain circumstances. Despite *Monell*, however, states and their agencies may not be *persons* suable directly under §1983;[52] in any event the Eleventh Amendment operates to bar such §1983 suits in federal court.[53]

In 1973 the Supreme Court held in *District of Columbia v Carter*[54] that the District of Columbia was not a "State or Territory" within the meaning of §1983's "arising under" language. Hence, at the time, no §1983 cause of action could be stated against the district or its officials. However, as noted earlier,[55] Congress amended §1983 and 28 USC §1343, its jurisdictional counterpart, effective December 29, 1979, to allow suits in federal court against any person acting under the authority of the laws of the District of Columbia. The amendments also provided that "any Act of Congress applicable exclusively to the District of Columbia shall be considered to be a statute of the District of Columbia." According to the House Report, these amendments were "necessary in order to give citizens of the District of Columbia rights equal to those of citizens in the states and territories of the United States."[56] They were also in response to the Supreme Court's decision in *District of Columbia v Carter*, and to "the many changes that have taken place in the District of Columbia Government over the years."[57]

As a result of these amendments, District of Columbia officials are persons and may be sued under §1983 in both their individual and official capacities for damages and prospective relief. Also, the District of Columbia as a governmental body is a person suable under §1983 for damages and prospective relief. This is clear from the various references in the House Report to the liability of the District of Columbia. It also appears from the House Report that, as a matter of legislative intent, the district should fall within the ambit of the *Monell* case,[58] which held that local governments are suable persons under §1983. Further, only the District of Columbia, and not the United States government, is affected when a §1983 cause of action is brought challenging a district official's actions under authority of an Act of Congress,

---

[50] *See generally* **ch 6** on local government liability and **chs 7 & 8** on absolute and qualified individual immunity.

[51] 436 US 658 (1978).

[52] *See* **§6.20.** For a contrary view, *see* Justice Brennan's concurring opinion in Hutto v Finney, 437 US 678, 701-02 (1978).

[53] *See* **§§5.08, 6.20.**

[54] 409 US 418 (1973).

[55] *See* **§1.02.**

[56] HR Rep No 548, 96th Cong, 1st Sess 1, *reprinted in* 1979 US Code Cong & Ad News 2609.

[57] *Id* 2, *reprinted in* 1979 US Code Cong & Ad News at 2610.

[58] Monell v Department of Social Servs, 436 US 658 (1978), discussed in **ch 6.**

provided the Act of Congress is applicable *exclusively* to the district. This is because "many of the local statutes were passed as Acts of Congress to be applied by the District government."[59]

Section 1983 actions cannot ordinarily be maintained against either the United States or its officials,[60] although there may be conspiracy cases where a federal official is a proper §1983 defendant because he or she acted under color of state law.[61] Officials of the Commonwealth of Puerto Rico are proper §1983 defendants, but the Commonwealth may not be sued under §1983 in federal court because of the Eleventh Amendment.[62]

That a defendant is a suable *person* under §1983 does not, of course, go either to the merits of the §1983 claim asserted or to the existence of state action.

§1.10   Federal Court Jurisdiction Over Claims Brought Under §1983, Federal Statutes, and State Law

28 USC §1343(3), §1983's jurisdictional counterpart, provides in relevant part that federal district courts have jurisdiction over civil actions brought to

> redress the deprivation, under color of any State law, statute, ordinance, regulation, custom or usage, of any right, privilege or immunity secured by the Constitution of the United States or by any Act of Congress providing for equal rights of citizens or of all persons within the jurisdiction of the United States. . . .[63]

---

[59] HR Rep No 548, 96th Cong, 1st Sess 3, *reprinted in* 1979 US Code Cong & Ad News 2611.

[60] *E.g.*, City of Milwaukee v Saxbe, 546 F2d 693, 703 (7th Cir 1976); Gillespie v Civiletti, 629 F2d 637 (9th Cir 1980); Stonecipher v Bray, 653 F2d 398 (9th Cir 1981) (IRS and its agents). *But see* Pope v United States Parole Commn, 647 F2d 125 (10th Cir 1981) (per curiam) where the court erroneously asserted that an inmate's pro se complaint against the United States Parole Commission and its members alleging wrongful denial of parole "is cognizable under 42 U.S.C. §1983." Ultimately, however, the Tenth Circuit ruled against the plaintiff on the merits.

[61] *See* **§2.10.**

[62] Fernandez v Chardon, 681 F2d 42 (1st Cir 1982), *affd on other grounds sub nom* Chardon v Fumero Soto, 462 US 650 (1983). *See also* Examining Bd of Engrs, Architects & Surveyors v Flores de Otero, 426 US 572 (1976) in which the Supreme Court held that Puerto Rico district courts have jurisdiction over §1983 suits, but left open the question whether Puerto Rico is a state or territory for jurisdictional purposes.

[63] For the full text of §1343(3), *see* **§1.02.** §1343(3) jurisdiction and stating a claim under §1983 are different. As the Fifth Circuit recently put it, "When a defendant's challenge to the court's jurisdiction is also a challenge to the existence of a federal cause of action, the proper procedure for the district court is to find that jurisdiction exists and to deal with the objection as a direct attack on the merits of the plaintiff's case." Daigle v Opelousas Health Care Inc, 774 F2d 1344, 1347 (5th Cir 1985). Unlike dismissal for failure to state a claim, dismissal for want of jurisdiction does not have any preclusive effect on the merits. *See* **§§5.17-5.20** on preclusion.

There is no jurisdictional amount requirement.[64] According to the Supreme Court, whenever a §1983 claim alleges a constitutional violation, then §1343(3) confers subject matter jurisdiction upon the federal district court.[65] Constitutional rights, privileges, and immunities for §1983 purposes are thus the same as constitutional rights, privileges, and immunities for §1343(3) purposes. They include, the Supreme Court has held, both personal liberties and property interests.[66]

Until recently, however, it was not so simple where a §1983 claim based on a federal statute was asserted. Section 1983 refers to "laws" while §1343(3) refers, apparently more narrowly, to those federal laws "providing for equal rights of citizens" and others. In a given case, the question then became whether a §1983 cause of action was stated and, if so, whether §1343(3) conferred jurisdiction. This question, as discussed later,[67] split the circuits while the Supreme Court for a time refused to answer it.[68]

Previously, the §1983 plaintiff who sought to assert a federal statutory claim could avoid this "laws" problem and satisfy federal jurisdiction by meeting the now eliminated $10,000 jurisdictional amount requirement of 28 USC §1331[69] by finding another jurisdictional statute which did not require a particular amount,[70] or by asserting, together with the federal statutory claim, a

---

[64] Unlike 28 USC §1331, the general federal question jurisdiction provision, which previously had a jurisdictional amount requirement of $10,000, but no longer does.

[65] The Court has said: "Despite the different wording of the substantive and jurisdictional provisions, when the §1983 claim alleges constitutional violations, §1343(3) provides jurisdiction and both sections are construed identically." Lynch v Household Fin Corp, 405 US 538, 544 n 7 (1972).

[66] *Id.* However, where a §1983 plaintiff seeks prospective relief in certain circumstances, federal statutes like the Tax Injunction Act, 28 USC §1341, may preclude such relief in federal courts. *See* §5.03. Furthermore, the policies underlying such statutes may even have an impact on federal court jurisdiction over §1983 damages actions. Thus, in Fair Assessment in Real Estate Assn v McNary, 454 US 100 (1981), discussed at §§5.03 & 5.10, the Supreme Court held that "taxpayers are barred by the principle of comity from asserting §1983 actions [for damages] against the validity of state tax systems in federal courts." Four Justices concurred in the judgment and argued, among other things, that comity has a limited role in damage actions, unlike actions for prospective relief. They concluded: "It is thus entirely clear that as a jurisdictional matter, the federal courts have jurisdiction over claims seeking monetary relief arising from unconstitutional state taxation." 454 US at 133. These Justices preferred to treat the case as one in which exhaustion of administrative remedies was required by congressional policy underlying the Tax Injunction Act.

[67] *See* §2.12.

[68] *E.g.,* Hagans v Lavine, 415 US 528, 533-34 n 5 (1974).

[69] §1331 was so used by welfare recipients in Black v Beame, 550 F2d 815, 817-18 (2d Cir 1977).

[70] *E.g.,* Gomez v Florida State Employment Serv, 417 F2d 569 (5th Cir 1969), where the court mentioned as an alternative jurisdictional basis 28 USC §1337, which provides for federal jurisdiction over actions arising out of statutes regulating interstate commerce irrespective of the amount involved.

substantial §1983 constitutional claim.[71] This latter approach made use of the device of pendent jurisdiction, discussed later.[72] The Supreme Court used this device when it earlier sidestepped the difficult "laws" question.[73]

These end-runs are no longer necessary in light of several significant developments regarding federal court jurisdiction over §1983 laws claims. Through the Federal Question Jurisdictional Amendment Act of 1980,[74] Congress amended 28 USC §1331 by eliminating the previous $10,000 jurisdictional amount requirement for federal question jurisdiction. This amendment became effective December 1, 1980, and applies to any civil action pending on the date of its enactment. The Jurisdictional Amendment Act renders largely irrelevant the need to rely upon 28 USC §1343(3) or (4) for federal court jurisdiction over §1983 laws claims.

In addition, before the Jurisdictional Amendment Act became effective, the Supreme Court had resolved several important jurisdictional and laws questions associated with §1983 claims based on violations of federal statutes. In *Chapman v Houston Welfare Rights Organization*,[75] the Court in an opinion by Justice Stevens held that federal courts do not have jurisdiction under 28 USC §1343 over §1983 claims founded on asserted violations of the Social Security Act. According to the Court, neither §1983 nor the Social Security Act is a statute "providing for equal rights" under §1343(3) or a statute "providing for the protection of civil rights" under §1343(4). However, in *Maine v Thiboutot*,[76] the Court in an opinion by Justice Brennan held that §1983's laws language encompasses claims based on *all* violations of federal statutory law, including the Social Security Act. Thus, the scope of §1983's laws language is broader than that of §1343(3)'s equal rights language. Thereafter, though, the Court limited the apparently broad holding of *Thiboutot* in *Middlesex County Sewerage Authority v National Sea Clammers Association*.[77]

The implications of *Thiboutot* and *National Sea Clammers* for the laws aspect of the prima facie §1983 cause of action are considered elsewhere.[78] For present jurisdictional purposes, several observations may be made in light of *Chapman* and the Jurisdictional Amendment Act. Even though *Thiboutot* held that a §1983 cause of action may be based on violations of the Social Security Act, it is clear after *Chapman* that federal courts do not have jurisdiction under 28 USC §1343 to hear such claims. However, after the Jurisdictional Amendment Act, federal courts *do* have jurisdiction under 28 USC §1331 to hear such claims. As to §1983 claims based on violations of other federal statutes, it is apparent from *Chapman* that any such federal statutes which deal

---

[71] *E.g.*, Lynch v Philbrook, 550 F2d 793 (2d Cir 1977).

[72] *See* §1.11.

[73] *E.g.*, in Hagans v Lavine, 415 US 528 (1974).

[74] 28 USC §1331, Pub L No 96-486, 94 Stat 2369 (codified at 28 USC §1331).

[75] 441 US 600 (1979).

[76] 448 US 1 (1980), discussed at §2.12.

[77] 453 US 1 (1981).

[78] *See* §2.12.

solely with levels of subsistence for individuals—such as the Social Security Act—will not be considered by the Court to secure either equal rights within the meaning of §1343(3) or civil rights within the meaning of §1343(4). Here, too, there is no jurisdiction under §1343. However, after the Jurisdictional Amendment Act there *is* jurisdiction under §1331.[79]

In yet another important development,[80] Congress amended §1983 and 28 USC §1343 to permit §1983 suits in federal court against the District of Columbia and its officials for their violation of constitutional and federal statutory rights. While §1343(3) remains the same, §1343 was amended in relevant part to include the following:

(b)   For purposes of this section [§1343]—

(1)   the District of Columbia shall be considered to be a State; and

(2)   any Act of Congress applied exclusively to the District of Columbia shall be considered to be a statute of the District of Columbia

The House Report states: "[T]his change makes it clear that the Federal Courts shall have jurisdiction of Section 1983 actions against District of Columbia officials acting under authority of local laws, even if those laws were passed by Congress."[81]

This amendment to §1343 was significant in a District of Columbia Circuit case[82] where the plaintiff landlords challenged the operations of a District of Columbia agency (the Rental Accommodations Office) responsible for administering rent control laws, claiming numerous intentional violations of due process and of various statutes. The district court dismissed the §1983 action on several grounds, one of which was that Congress lodged exclusive jurisdiction over such complaints in the District of Columbia courts. Reversing, the Court of Appeals ruled that there was federal jurisdiction over plaintiffs' claim. The relief they were seeking was not available under the judicial review procedures of the District of Columbia Administrative Procedure Act (APA). Also, plaintiffs were challenging various agency actions "relatively unrelated to the formal decisional process." Most important, the District of Columbia APA should be accorded no more weight than that accorded a similar state statute. Just as a state statute, by providing a state remedy, could not preclude a §1983 action in federal court, neither could the APA.

In the circuits, and despite the broad jurisdictional grants of §§1331 and 1343, there are circumstances where federal jurisdiction is thought to be absent. Thus, federal courts have no appellate jurisdiction over state court

---

[79] *E.g.,* Tyler v Mmes Pasqua & Toloso, 748 F2d 283 (5th Cir 1984) (federal court jurisdiction under §1331 for claim brought under Food Stamp Act of 1974, 7 USC §2011 *et seq,* even though no jurisdiction under §1343.)

[80] *See* §1.09.

[81] HR Rep No 548, 96th Cong, 1st Sess 3, *reprinted in* 1979 US Code Cong & Ad News 2611.

[82] District Properties Assocs v District of Columbia, 743 F2d 21 (DC Cir 1984).

judgments with respect to modifying or vacating them.[83] Still, the Fifth Circuit[84] concluded that federal courts *do* have subject matter jurisdiction in appropriate cases to enjoin the enforcement of state court judgments. It ruled that the plaintiff class representative could challenge state parental termination proceedings as violative of due process and equal protection in federal court. Here, the plaintiff had sought a declaration that the challenged state court judgment was null and void and should be enjoined.

Federal court jurisdiction is also absent in certain cases involving attorney discipline. For example, in dismissing the plaintiff's §1983 claim seeking a mandatory injunction to expunge his conviction and disbarments from agency and state court records so that he might again practice law, the Ninth Circuit[85] in reliance on *Theard v United States*[86] stated:

> [I]t is well settled that United States District Courts lack subject matter jurisdiction to control or review final orders entered in state attorney disciplinary proceedings, and that a petition for writ of certiorari to the Supreme Court of the United States is the only method by which review may be had.

The same is true in certain bar admission cases. In a Fifth Circuit case,[87] the plaintiff, claiming that he was unconstitutionally denied admission to the Texas bar by reason of racial and religious discrimination, challenged the unappealed administrative decision of the state board of law examiners. The Fifth Circuit ruled that the district court did not have subject matter jurisdiction. Even though the challenged state decision was not, strictly speaking, a final judicial decision by a state court, the state board exercised the judicial authority of the Texas Supreme Court. Further, plaintiff should not be advantaged just because he deliberately bypassed the available state judicial review procedures. Thus, the plaintiff's claim came within the rationale of the Supreme Court's decision in *District of Columbia Court of Appeals v Feldman*[88] which, in the Fifth Circuit's words, "held that a federal district court lacks subject matter jurisdiction to review a state court's allegedly unconstitutional denial of admission to the bar. The basic reason was that the state court judgment was characterized as judicial

---

[83] Hagerty v Succession of Clement, 749 F2d 217 (5th Cir 1984) ("well-settled rule that a plaintiff may not seek a reversal of a state court judgment simply by recasting his complaint in the form of a civil rights action"); Rhoades v Penfold, 694 F2d 1043 (5th Cir 1983) (so interpreting Rooker v Fidelity Trust Co, 263 US 413 (1923)).

[84] Rhoades v Penfold, 694 F2d 1043 (5th Cir 1983).

[85] Silverton v Department of the Treasury of the United States, 640 F2d 214, 220 (9th Cir 1981).

[86] 354 US 278 (1957).

[87] Thomas v Kadish, 748 F2d 276 (5th Cir 1984).

[88] 460 US 462 (1983).

in nature, and final state court judgments may be reviewed only by the Supreme Court itself."[89]

In a §1983 case involving domestic relations,[90] the Fifth Circuit observed generally that a child custody dispute standing alone is not within the subject matter jurisdiction of federal courts. Nevertheless, the court went on to rule that the district court, instead of dismissing outright, should have retained jurisdiction over the plaintiffs' substantial claim that the defendants violated plaintiffs' Fourth Amendment rights by invading their home without a warrant. The court asserted: "The mere fact that a claimed violation of constitutional rights arises in a domestic relations context does not bar review of those constitutional issues."[91]

§1.11   Pendent Jurisdiction

Pendent jurisdiction is federal jurisdiction over either a *state-created claim*[92] or a *federally-created claim*[93] as to which there would otherwise not be federal jurisdiction. A federal court has the power to decide such claims where they are joined with a substantial federal claim over which the federal court has jurisdiction provided that the substantial federal claim and the joined state or federal claim "derive from a common nucleus of operative fact" and the plaintiff "would ordinarily be expected to try them all in one judicial proceeding."[94] Pendent jurisdiction is discretionary with the federal court and may be exercised even though the plaintiff is ultimately unsuccessful on the substantial federal claim.[95]

---

[89] 748 F2d at 277.

[90] Franks v Smith, 717 F2d 183 (5th Cir 1983).

[91] *Id* 186.

[92] *E.g.*, United Mine Workers v Gibbs, 383 US 715 (1966).

[93] *E.g.*, Rosado v Wyman, 397 US 397, 405 (1970), *affd*, 402 US 991 (1971).

[94] United Mine Workers v Gibbs, 383 US 715, 725 (1966) is currently the leading case. Early pendent jurisdiction cases include Hurn v Oursler, 289 US 238 (1933); Siler v Louisville & Nashville RR, 213 US 175 (1909); Osborn v Bank of United States, 22 US (9 Wheat) 738 (1824).

[95] The Supreme Court seemed to encourage the use of pendent jurisdiction and limit a district court's discretion to reject it in Hagans v Lavine, 415 US 528, 545-46 (1974) where it said: "[G]iven advantages of economy and convenience and no unfairness to litigants, [the doctrine] contemplates adjudication of these [pendent] claims." The pendent claim will frequently be dismissed where the federal claim is rejected prior to trial. On the other hand, the court may decide a pendent (nonconstitutional) claim first in order to avoid having to decide a §1983 constitutionally based claim. *See, e.g.*, Dunton v County of Suffolk, 729 F2d 903 (2d Cir 1984) (pendent jurisdiction over state claim improper despite jury verdict for the plaintiff on that claim; plaintiff's federal claims were "so insubstantial" that federal court did not have jurisdiction); Fox v Custis, 712 F2d 84 (4th Cir 1983) (pendent jurisdiction over state claim improper where federal claim dismissed on merits; issues presented by state claim were "relatively novel, complex and of great local importance" and should not have been decided by district court but rather by state courts in the first instance; Judge Hall dissented); McLaurin v Fischer, 768 F2d 98 (6th Cir 1985) (district court's dismissal of pendent state claim not an abuse of discretion; different proofs would be required for the federal and state

This device avoids forcing the plaintiff to institute a second proceeding in state court. It is therefore very useful for the §1983 plaintiff as well as for the §1983 defendant in some situations, since it saves a defendant from having to defend two suits in different forums. Before the $10,000 jurisdictional amount requirement for federal question jurisdiction was eliminated,[96] the plaintiff with a substantial §1983 constitutional claim was able to join a factually related federal statutory claim against the defendant. For example, a welfare recipient could challenge an aspect of a state welfare scheme both on constitutional grounds and on federal statutory grounds in a single federal proceeding.[97] Now, of course, the federal statutory claim may be brought independently in federal court.

More important currently, and frequently resorted to in damage actions especially, the §1983 plaintiff with a substantial constitutional claim can also assert a factually related state claim against the defendant. For example, a police officer accused of wrongfully using excessive force can be sued in federal court by a §1983 plaintiff for both an alleged Fourteenth Amendment violation and for assault and battery.[98] As a general matter, this use of pendent jurisdiction will be available to the §1983 plaintiff where the defendant has allegedly acted in a manner inconsistent not only with the Fourteenth Amendment but with state law as well.[99] However, there is an important restriction: the Supreme Court held in *Pennhurst State School & Hospital v Halderman*[100] that the Eleventh Amendment bars a pendent state claim for *injunctive relief* against state officials sued in federal court. Furthermore, to the

---

claims; there was also the possibility of jury confusion on damages issues); Bell v Sellevold, 713 F2d 1396 (8th Cir 1983) (district court's so-called pendent jurisdiction over forcible entry and detainer action in state court clearly improper; plaintiff asserted a federal claim in federal court, but the state claim, the forcible entry and detainer action, was not in the federal court at all, nor was it a "claim belonging to the plaintiff"; it was, instead, "a claim being asserted in a state court by the federal-court defendants"; here, the plaintiff had not pleaded in federal court that his eviction would violate state law; thus, the assertion of jurisdiction was an unauthorized "kind of involuntary removal" by the district court); Traver v Meshriy, 627 F2d 934 (9th Cir 1980) (pendent jurisdiction over tort claims of false imprisonment, assault, slander, and intentional infliction of emotional distress; §1983 claim against bank and its employees "tenuous but not frivolous"); Mendoza v K-Mart, Inc, 587 F2d 1052 (10th Cir 1978) (pendent jurisdiction over state claim proper because §1983 federal claim substantial even though dismissed by district court on state action grounds). *Cf* Uptown People's Community Health Servs Bd of Directors v Board of Commrs, 647 F2d 727 (7th Cir 1981) (no pendent jurisdiction over state claims because no substantial federal claim, despite the fact that some state claims had been heard in district court; record inadequate to make a determination and question not briefed on appeal).

[96] *See* §§**1.11, 2.12.**

[97] *E.g.*, Louise B. v Coluatti, 606 F2d 392 (3d Cir 1979); Williams v Wohlgemuth, 540 F2d 163 (3d Cir 1976); Almenares v Wyman, 453 F2d 1075 (2d Cir 1971), *cert denied*, 405 US 944 (1972).

[98] *See* §§**1.10, 2.12.**

[99] That is, ultra vires.

[100] 465 US 89 (1984). *See* §**5.08.**

extent that §1983 plaintiffs choose to litigate their §1983 claims in federal court and their related state claims in state court, troublesome res judicata and collateral estoppel problems may emerge.[101]

§1.12   Pendent Parties

It has been contended that "the doctrine of pendent jurisdiction is sufficiently broad to support a claim . . . against a person not a party to the primary, jurisdiction granting claim" so long as both claims arise out of a common nucleus of operative fact and the plaintiff would ordinarily be expected to try both in one proceeding.[102] Applying this approach, the Second Circuit concluded that a §1983 constitutionally based claim against a *city's* welfare commissioner conferred pendent jurisdiction upon a federal district court over a federal statutory claim against a *state's* welfare commissioner.[103]

The Supreme Court passed on the propriety of this expansion of pendent jurisdiction to include pendent parties in *Aldinger v Howard.*[104] In that case the §1983 plaintiff sued various state officials alleging constitutional violations in connection with her discharge from governmental employment and sought damages and injunctive relief. She also asserted a state claim against a county which could be sued under state law but not under §1983 because at that time a county was not considered a person.[105] The Ninth Circuit held that the federal district court had no jurisdiction over the state claim because a different party was involved.

Affirming, the Supreme Court first stated it would not "formulate any general, all-encompassing jurisdictional rule." It went on to observe that adding a new party is both factually and legally different from adding a new claim against a party already there, and then reasoned that "as against a plaintiff's claim of *additional* power over a 'pendent party,' the reach of the statute conferring jurisdiction should be construed in light of the scope of the cause of action as to which federal judicial power *has* been extended by Congress."[106] The Court consequently concluded that *pendent party jurisdiction* as to cities and counties was inappropriate because Congress had excluded them from the reach of §1983 by considering them not to be persons for §1983 purposes.

---

[101] *See* §§5.17-5.20.

[102] Almenares v Wyman, 453 F2d 1075, 1083 (2d Cir 1971), *cert denied,* 405 US 944 (1972). The Eighth Circuit reached the same conclusion in Schulman v Huck Finn Inc, 472 F2d 864 (8th Cir 1973).

[103] Almenares v Wyman, 453 F2d 1075 (2d Cir 1971), *cert denied,* 405 US 944 (1972).

[104] 427 US 1 (1976).

[105] Monroe v Pape, 365 US 167 (1961) *overruled in part,* Monell v Department of Social Servs, 436 US 658 (1978). *See* §1.09 & ch 6.

[106] 427 US at 17. In pendent party cases, the Court reasoned, the federal court must be persuaded "that Congress in the statutes conferring jurisdiction has not expressly or by implication negated pendent party jurisdiction's existence." *Id* 18.

Aldinger, with its reliance on congressional intent that §1983 exclude cities and counties from the person category, seemed at the time to undercut the use of the pendent party device in most, if not all, §1983 cases. However, the Supreme Court's subsequent decision in *Monell v Department of Social Services*[107] overruled earlier decisions that cities and counties were not persons for §1983 purposes, and instead concluded that they were. Thus, after *Monell*, cities and counties can be sued directly for damages and injunctive relief provided that their official policies or customs are shown to be causally responsible for the plaintiff's constitutional deprivation.[108] However, neither their liability nor that of an individual such as a supervisory official can be based solely on respondeat superior.[109]

In light of *Monell* and assuming the requirements for pendent jurisdiction[110] are otherwise satisfied:

1. A §1983 plaintiff asserting a constitutional claim against a city or county will be able to use the device of pendent jurisdiction and join a state or federal statutory claim against the city or county even where the state or federal statutory claim is based solely on respondeat superior

2. A §1983 plaintiff asserting a constitutional claim only against a city official or county official, but not against the city or county itself because of the absence of an official policy or custom, should be able to use the device of pendent party to join a state or federal statutory claim against the city or county even where the state or federal statutory claim is based solely on respondeat superior[111]

3. A §1983 plaintiff asserting a constitutional claim only against a subordinate city or county official, but not against a superior city or county official because of the absence of any causal involvement by the superior in the subordinate's allegedly unconstitutional conduct, should be able to use the device of pendent party to join a state claim, even if based on respondeat superior, against the superior official.[112]

---

[107] 436 US 658 (1978).

[108] *See* §§6.05-6.19.

[109] *See* §§3.15 & 6.05-6.19.

[110] *See* §1.11.

[111] But it is possible that even after *Monell*, the Supreme Court will interpret §1983 as showing congressional intent to preclude federal jurisdiction over all state claims against local governments on a respondeat superior theory. This approach was used in Kedra v City of Philadelphia, 454 F Supp 652, 682-83 (ED Pa 1978). *See also* the memorandum decision in a non-§1983 case, Symm v United States, 439 US 1105 (1979), where Justice Rehnquist, joined by Chief Justice Burger, dissented, and said: "*Monell* did not . . . disturb the jurisdictional analysis applied in *Aldinger*." *Id* 1110 n 4. *See also* Owen Equip & Erection Co v Kroger, 437 US 365, 372 n 12 (1978): "*Monell* in no way qualifies the holding in *Aldinger* that the jurisdictional questions presented in a case such as this one are statutory as well as constitutional. . . ."

[112] *Aldinger* does not appear inconsistent with (3) because *Aldinger* relied on the status of a county as a nonperson for §1983 defendant purposes while a city official or county official is clearly a person.

Recent circuit court decisions demonstrate some continuing uncertainty as to the scope of *Aldinger*. In a Seventh Circuit case,[113] plaintiffs sued various defendants, including a private party and law enforcement officers, for allegedly unlawful arrest and confinement. While the decision of the district court to dismiss the §1983 claims against the private defendant was affirmed by the Seventh Circuit, the court was split on the pendent party question of whether the pendent jurisdiction of the district court could reach the plaintiff's state law false arrest and imprisonment claims against the private defendant. Judges Posner and Gibson found *Aldinger* distinguishable on the ground that, unlike the pre-*Monell* policy regarding local governments, "[t]here is no similar policy of immunizing private individuals from liability under section 1983. They are 'persons' within the meaning of section 1983."[114] Judge Posner went on to characterize pendent party jurisdiction as a "great convenience" to the plaintiff, especially since "many civil rights plaintiffs anticipate a friendlier reception from the federal [than the state] court."[115] However, Judge Coffey disagreed, contending that *Aldinger* controlled. Since the private defendant could not in the case before the court be liable under §1983 because he did not act under color of law,[116] he could not "be brought into federal court solely on the coattails of another being sued in federal court."[117] This result was "a logical application of the *Aldinger* decision."[118]

In contrast to the Seventh Circuit's majority opinion, the Eleventh Circuit ruled the other way in a similar case.[119] Here, the plaintiff inmate sued various prison officials under §1983 for failing to prevent another inmate from beating him, in violation of the Eighth and Fourteenth Amendments. In the same action, the plaintiff also sued that inmate for assault and battery under state law. Holding that the district court properly ruled that it should not exercise pendent party jurisdiction over the state claim against the assaulting inmate, the Eleventh Circuit emphasized the discretionary nature of that decision, the "tenuous nature of pendent party jurisdiction," the legitimate concern that the state claim would interfere with the trial of the §1983 claims, and deference to state court resolution of the state claim.

---

[113] Moore v Marketplace Restaurant, 754 F2d 1336 (7th Cir 1985).

[114] *Id* 1359.

[115] *Id* 1361.

[116] *See* §§2.04-2.10 on state action and color of law.

[117] 754 F2d at 1354.

[118] *Id.* Note that Judge Gibson, who agreed with Judge Posner on the pendent parties issue, but disagreed with Judge Coffey on the same issue, disagreed with both on the question of whether the private defendant should have been dismissed out on the plaintiff's §1983 claims. He argued that the private defendant could ultimately be found liable under §1983. *Id* 1361-63.

[119] Williams v Bennett, 689 F2d 1370, 1379-80 (11th Cir 1982).

§1.13   State Court Jurisdiction Over §1983 Claims

Federal court jurisdiction over §1983 claims pursuant to 28 USC §1343(3) is not exclusive. Consequently, state courts are not precluded from exercising concurrent jurisdiction over §1983 claims and may hear and decide those claims.[120] Moreover, while the Supreme Court has not passed on the matter, it has been asserted that the Supremacy Clause of the United States Constitution *compels* state courts to hear and decide §1983 cases submitted to them.[121] This assertion is especially persuasive where there are state-created claims enforceable in state courts which are analogous to §1983 claims.[122] In any event, where §1983 claims are in fact submitted to and heard by state courts, it is clear that relevant §1983 substantive rules must be applied by those courts.[123] According to the Supreme Court in *Maine v Thibotout*,[124] this applies to the 1976 Civil Rights Attorney's Fees Awards Act as well.[125]

Even though state courts are generally available to §1983 plaintiffs, there is

---

[120] In Martinez v California, 444 US 277, 283 n 7 (1980), the Supreme Court indicated that state courts may hear §1983 claims, but reserved the question of whether they *must* do so. Some state cases which have exercised concurrent jurisdiction are: Perry v Apache Junction Elementary School Dist, 20 Ariz App 561, 514 P2d 514 (1973); Vason v Carrano, 31 Conn Supp 338, 330 A2d 98 (1974); Backus v Chilivis, 236 Ga 500, 224 SE2d 370 (1976); Alberty v Daniel, 25 Ill App 3d 291, 323 NE2d 110 (1974); Rzeznik v Chief of Police of Southampton 374 Mass 475, 373 NE2d 1128 (1978); Shapiro v Columbia Union Natl Bank & Trust Co, 576 SW2d 310 (Mo 1978) (en banc), *cert denied,* 48 USLW 3210 (S Ct Oct 1, 1979) which held, after canvassing relevant cases, that a §1983 action is cognizable in the state courts; Judo Inc v Peet, 68 Misc 2d 281, 326 NYS2d 441 (NY Civ Ct 1971); Williams v Greene, 36 NC App 80, 243 SE2d 156 (1978); Commonwealth *ex rel* Saunders v Creamer, 464 Pa 2, 345 A2d 702 (1975); Kish v Wright, 562 P2d 625 (Utah 1977). Grubb v Public Util Commn, 281 US 470, 476 (1930) referred to "the doctrine often sustained by this Court that the state and federal courts have concurrent jurisdiction of suits of a civil nature arising under the Constitution and laws of the United States, save in exceptional instances where the jurisdiction has been restricted by Congress to the federal courts." *See also* Gulf Offshore Co v Mobil Oil Corp, 453 US 473 (1981) (state courts may assume subject matter jurisdiction over federal claims unless there is either provision by Congress to the contrary or incompatibility between the federal claim and state court adjudication) *and* Aldinger v Howard, 427 US 1, 36 n 17 (1976) in which Justice Brennan in his dissenting opinion spoke of concurrent jurisdiction. *See generally* C. Wright, Law of Federal Courts 268-73 (4th ed 1983).

[121] *E.g.,* Williams v Horvath, 45 Cal App 3d 422, 119 Cal Rptr 413 (1975), *revd on other grounds,* 16 Cal 3d 834, ___ P2d ___, 129 Cal Rptr 453 (1976); Dudley v Bell, 50 Mich App 678, 213 NW2d 805 (1973); Lewis v Delta Loans Inc, 300 So 2d 142 (Miss 1974). Terry v Kolski, 78 Wis 2d 475, 254 NW2d 704 (1977). Chamberlain v Brown, 223 Tenn 25, 442 SW2d 248 (1969) is to the contrary and is probably wrong. *Cf* Testa v Katt, 330 US 386 (1947).

[122] Testa v Katt, 330 US 386 (1947).

[123] C. Wright, Law of Federal Courts 271-73 (4th ed 1983). These substantive rules include the elements necessary for the prima facie §1983 cause of action, *see* **chs 2 & 3,** and damages, *see* **ch 4,** as well as rules governing absolute and qualified immunity, *see* **chs 6, 7 & 8.**

[124] 448 US 1, 10 n 11 (1980).

[125] 42 USC §1988. *See* **§§1.18-1.26.**

no exhaustion of state judicial remedies requirement in §1983 cases which would force them to proceed in state court in the first instance.[126] They thus have the option of proceeding in either forum. As it turns out, although increasing numbers of §1983 suits are being filed in state courts, the overwhelming majority of §1983 plaintiffs sue in federal court. They are so motivated, rightly or wrongly, by factors such as a perceived sympathy for, and understanding of, §1983 claims by federal judges and a correspondingly perceived antipathy for, and lack of competence in connection with, such claims on the part of state judges.[127] Reinforcing the view of §1983 plaintiffs that state courts are unfavorably disposed toward them is the fact that many §1983 cases are either brought by so-called unpopular plaintiffs or raise controversial and politically sensitive matters or both. On the other hand, strategic considerations such as crowded federal dockets, the possibility of choosing a sympathetic state court judge, favorable procedural rules, and the likelihood of better treatment of pendent state claims could encourage a §1983 plaintiff to file in state court instead of federal court. The Eleventh Amendment's bar against suing a state in federal court could also be determinative.[128]

It should be noted that the Supreme Court's *Younger* Rule[129] and the doctrine of abstention[130] will frequently operate to force a §1983 plaintiff to resort to a state court.[131] In such cases there is obviously no choice of forum available and §1983 plaintiffs are told in effect to utilize their state judicial remedies.

§1.14   Removal

Where a defendant is in fact sued initially in a state court under §1983, the choice arises of whether to defend in the state court or remove the proceeding to federal court.[132] This choice is given the §1983 defendant by 28 USC §1441(b), which provides in relevant part that "[a]ny civil action of which the district courts have original jurisdiction founded on a claim or right arising under the Constitution, treaties or *laws of the United States* shall be removable without regard to the citizenship or residence of the parties."[133] The proper venue upon removal is to the district court "for the district and division

---

[126] *See* **§5.06.** For discussion of a de facto exhaustion of state judicial remedies requirement, however, *see* **§§5.09-5.12** on the *Younger* Rule and **§5.13** on *Pullman* abstention.

[127] Neuborne, *The Myth of Parity*, 90 Harv L Rev 1105 (1977).

[128] *See* **§§5.08, 6.20.**

[129] *See* **§§5.12-5.15.**

[130] *See* **§5.16.**

[131] In order to initiate a civil proceeding in state court or to defend in a state criminal proceeding.

[132] Section 1983 defendants frequently prefer the state courts because they perceive an advantage there. *See* **§1.13.**

[133] (Emphasis added.) The requirement is that the §1983 action could have initially been brought in federal court with 28 USC §1343(3) jurisdiction. *See* **§1.10.**

embracing the place where such action is pending,"[134] and the proper procedure for removal is set out in 28 USC §1446.[135]

While an extensive discussion of removal is beyond the scope of this chapter, a §1983-related removal case of apparent first impression should be mentioned. In *Sweeney v Abramovitz*,[136] the defendant had initially sued the plaintiff police officer and others under §1983 alleging First and Fourteenth Amendment violations. At trial, the jury returned a verdict for the defendants. The police officer thereupon sued the defendant in state court claiming malicious prosecution in that the §1983 action had been prosecuted without probable cause and with a malicious intent. This second suit was removed to a Connecticut federal district court by the defendant, and the plaintiff police officer then moved for remand to the state court.

The district court ultimately held that removal was proper. It first rejected the defendant's attempt to rely on 28 USC §1443, a special civil rights removal statute, because it did not consider §1983 to be a law providing for "equal civil rights" as required by that statute, "at least where sec. 1983 is not invoked to vindicate a racially motivated denial of equal protection."[137] However, it accepted the defendant's argument that §1441(b), with its "arising under . . . laws" language, permitted removal.

The court conceded that the plaintiff's complaint made no explicit use of federal law, but it reasoned that

> [w]hen [plaintiff] alleges that [defendant] brought suit "without probable cause," he is implicitly saying, "without probable cause to believe there existed a valid cause of action under 42 USC §1983." The meaning of §1983 and its application to the circumstances alleged in [defendant's] original suit are essential ingredients of [plaintiff's] claim. . . .
>
> Moreover, the potential for using state malicious prosecution suits to deter legitimate §1983 actions implicates important federal concerns.[138]

The court, after determining that the question of what constitutes probable cause to bring a §1983 suit should not be governed by state law, but rather by federal standards, then concluded that the malicious prosecution suit could be removed.[139]

---

[134] 28 USC §1441(a). *See* **§1.15** on federal venue generally.

[135] *See*, on removal and its procedures, C. Wright, Law of Federal Courts 209-37 (4th ed 1983).

[136] 449 F Supp 213 (CD Conn 1978).

[137] 28 USC §1443, a rather unique removal statute governing certain civil rights cases of both a civil and criminal nature. The Supreme Court passed on the use of this statute in Greenwood v Peacock, 384 US 808 (1966) and Georgia v Rachel, 384 US 780 (1966).

[138] Sweeney v Abramovitz, 449 F Supp 213, 215-16 (CD Conn 1978). *See generally* on the meaning of "arising under" C. Wright, Law of Federal Courts 90-98 (4th ed 1983).

[139] The court also observed that a federal forum should be available to guard against the possibility that malicious prosecution actions could deter the use of §1983.

§1.15   Federal Venue

Section 1983 actions may be brought only in the judicial district where all the defendants reside, or in the district in which the claim arose unless the defendants reside in different districts in the same state, in which case the suit may also be brought in any of such districts.[140] For federal venue purposes, a corporation may be sued in any judicial district in which it is incorporated, is licensed to do business, or is doing business.[141] For the convenience of parties and witnesses and in the interest of justice, a district court may transfer any civil action (including §1983 actions) to any other district or division where it might have been brought initially.[142] It may also, upon request of all of the parties, transfer any civil action from the division in which it is pending to any other division in the same district.[143] A district court may further order that a civil action be tried at any place within the division in which it is pending.[144]

§1.16   Procedural Rules, Class Actions, Three-Judge Courts, and Appeals

The Federal Rules of Civil Procedure[145] govern the trial of §1983 claims in federal district court. This is clear from Rule 1 which provides in relevant part that the Rules "govern the procedure in the United States district courts in all suits of a civil nature whether cognizable as cases at law or in equity. . . ." However, the Supreme Court put a special §1983 gloss on Rule 12(b)(6), which provides for dismissal on motion for failure to state a claim upon which relief can be granted.[146] Reversing the 12(b)(6) dismissal of a pro se inmate's §1983 damages action against prison officials in connection with his incarceration, the

---

[140] 28 USC §§1391(b) & 1392(a). *See generally* 28 USC §§1391-1407. According to the Eighth Circuit, a district court did not err in transferring plaintiff's §1983 case from the Eastern Division of the Eastern District of Missouri, where she resided, to the Southeastern Division of that District, where all the defendants resided. 28 USC §1391(a) provides that a civil action, not of a local nature, against a single defendant must be brought in the division in which the defendant resides. Hence, the court reasoned, "where multiple defendants reside in the same division they should be regarded as a 'single defendant' for purposes of venue under section 1391(a)." Rey v City of Fredericktown, 729 F2d 1171 (8th Cir 1984).

[141] 28 USC §1391(c).

[142] 28 USC §1404(a), which speaks of the convenience of parties and witnesses and the interest of justice. The Supreme Court interpreted the language "where it might have been brought" in Hoffman v Blaski, 363 US 335 (1960).

[143] 28 USC §1404(b).

[144] 28 USC §1404(c).

[145] *See* C. Wright, Law of Federal Courts 399-407 (4th ed 1983) for historical background. The Rules were amended in part in 1980 and 1983.

[146] Rule 12 deals generally with defenses and objections, how they are presented and when, and with motions for judgment on the pleadings.

Court in *Haines v Kerner*[147] set out the following test:

> We cannot say with assurance that under the allegations of the *pro se* complaint, which we hold to less stringent standards than formal pleadings drafted by lawyers, it appears "beyond doubt that the plaintiff can prove no sets of facts in support of his claim which would entitle him to relief."[148]

(*Text continued on page 31*)

---

[147] 404 US 519 (1972).

[148] *Id* 520, 521. In the circuits, *Haines* and related appointment of counsel issues arise with some frequency. Representative cases include:

The Haines Test

First Circuit

Gilday v Boone, 657 F2d 1 (1st Cir 1981) (pro se inmate complaint alleging constitutional deprivation by state prison officials should be treated as §1983 claim, even though §1983 not specifically mentioned).

Second Circuit

Robles v Coughlin, 725 F2d 12 (2d Cir 1983) (inmates' pro se complaints challenging conditions of confinement reinstated; "sua sponte dismissal prior to service of process is strongly disfavored in this circuit"; complaints should be liberally construed).

Bayron v Trudeau, 702 F2d 43 (2d Cir 1983) (sua sponte dismissal of pro se prisoner's petition before service of process is "strongly disfavored"; dismissal reversed where plaintiff alleged intentional deprivation of his property and the reading of his legal papers).

Anderson v Coughlin, 700 F2d 37, 43 (2d Cir 1982) (in forma pauperis pro se prisoner complaint may be dismissed as "frivolous" within the meaning of 28 USC §1915 "where the plaintiff is engaged in repeated litigation of issues already determined, the allegations of the complaint are 'beyond credibility,' the complaint fails to state a claim upon which relief may be granted, or there is little chance of success on the merits in light of various defenses which may be asserted").

Third Circuit

Ross v Meagan, 638 F2d 646 (3d Cir 1981) (per curiam) (district court's failure to permit amendment of pro se inmate complaint in order to correct lack of specific allegations found to be abuse of discretion).

Fourth Circuit

Boyce v Alizaduh, 595 F2d 948 (4th Cir 1979) (pro se inmate complaint dismissed as to all but one of the defendants; *Haines* test applied).

Fifth Circuit

Williams v Rhoden, 629 F2d 1099 (5th Cir 1980) (pro se inmate's complaint should not have been dismissed prior to service of process because (1) he did not proceed in forma pauperis and (2) in any event, his complaint when liberally construed stated a cause of action).

McGruder v Phelps, 608 F2d 1023 (5th Cir 1979) (materials filed by pro se inmate plaintiff should have been treated as a properly filed amendment to his complaint, even though not so characterized by plaintiff).

Seventh Circuit

Sisk v United States, 756 F2d 497 (7th Cir 1985) (where pro se inmate's damages action has survived various pretrial motions, it should not be dismissed thereafter for want of prosecution before district court considers other feasible alternatives for deciding the case on its merits).

Shashoua v Quern, 612 F2d 282 (7th Cir 1980) (complaint properly dismissed;

because it was drafted by a lawyer, the "rules of pleading are not as relaxed as they are for pro se complaints").

Ninth Circuit

Franklin v State of Oregon, State Welfare Div, 662 F2d 1337 (9th Cir 1981) ("weight of authority suggests that an in forma pauperis action should be processed unless it clearly appears that the action is so meritless that it cannot be corrected by amendment").

Stanger v City of Santa Cruz, 653 F2d 1257 (9th Cir 1980) (pro se inmate has right to have process issued and served, and to amend complaint to cure any defect unless it "clearly appears" that the defect cannot be cured by amendment).

Appointment of Counsel

First Circuit

Appleby v Meachum, 696 F2d 145 (1st Cir 1983) (per curiam) (after final judgment, a court of appeals may review denial of a 28 USC §1915 motion for appointment of counsel for abuse of discretion; however, an interlocutory appeal of such a denial may not be brought under the three-part "collateral order" test of Coopers & Lybrand v Livesay, 437 US 463 (1978).

Fifth Circuit

Robbins v Maggio, 750 F2d 405 (5th Cir 1985) (denials of in forma pauperis inmates' requests for appointment of counsel immediately appealable under collateral order doctrine).

Slavin v Curry, 690 F2d 446 (5th Cir 1982) (exceptional circumstances warranting appointment of counsel for pro se plaintiff under 28 USC §1915 include "exceedingly complex" cases or cases where the plaintiff is unable actively to investigate or pursue his or her claim; case-by-case determination is to be made by the district court).

Wright v Dallas County Sheriff Dept, 660 F2d 623 (5th Cir 1981) (denial of appointment of attorney for inmate reversed; district court to consider whether case before it was one of those in which "plaintiffs in §1983 cases need to have the assistance of counsel to be enabled to present their cases adequately").

Woodall v Foti, 648 F2d 268 (5th Cir 1981) (per curiam) (adopting "a two-stage procedure for processing a prisoner's *pro se* civil rights complaint filed in forma pauperis under 28 USC §1915").

Sixth Circuit

Henry v City of Detroit Manpower Dept, 739 F2d 1109, 1111 (6th Cir 1984) ("a citizen seeking to file a civil rights complaint [under Title VII and 1983] has a right of appeal from a denial of appointment of counsel"; extensive discussion of legislative history, case law, and policy).

Johnson v Hubbard, 698 F2d 286 (6th Cir 1983) (district court's refusal to pay witness fees for in forma pauperis plaintiff not improper under 28 USC §1915, even though filing fees and other preliminary court charges waived; plaintiff's right of access to the courts was similarly not abridged; moreover, the district court's dismissal of plaintiff's complaint for want of prosecution because plaintiff had failed to produce witnesses to prove the case was not an abuse of discretion; Judge Swygert dissented).

Seventh Circuit

McKeever v Israel, 689 F2d 1315 (7th Cir 1982) (district court's refusal to appoint counsel under 28 USC §1915 improper where it erroneously did not recognize its own authority to do so; Judge Posner dissented at length).

Carruth v Pinkney, 683 F2d 1044 (7th Cir 1982) (inmate has no constitutional right to appointed counsel in civil case; however, court has discretion under 28 USC §1915 to appoint counsel for party in civil action who proceeds in forma pauperis; factors to be considered include the merits of the case, the complexity of the legal and factual issues, and the litigant's ability to recognize and present the issues; a request for

Thereafter, in *Hughes v Rowe*,[149] the Supreme Court reversed a district court's $400 fees award to the defendant correction officers who had been sued by the plaintiff inmate. According to the Court, plaintiff's complaint was not groundless or without foundation. The Court added:

> Faithful adherence to the principles of *Haines v Kerner* dictates that attorney's fees should rarely be awarded against [uncounseled prisoner] plaintiffs. The fact that a prisoner's complaint, even when liberally construed, cannot survive a motion to dismiss does not, without more, entitle the defendant to attorney's fees. An unrepresented litigant should not be punished for his failure to recognize subtle factual or legal deficiencies in his claims.[150]

Although Rule 8 provides in effect that notice pleading is sufficient in the federal courts, the circuits uniformly require plaintiffs who allege §1983 conspiracies to set them out in some factual detail in order to avoid dismissal under Rule 12(b)(6).[151] This specificity has also been insisted upon where the defendants might be protected by absolute immunity.[152] In addition, some federal courts require §1983 plaintiffs who sue local governments to allege challenged official policies or customs with particularity in order to avoid 12(b)(6) dismissal.[153] These developments reflect judicial sensitivity to the §1983 caseload and a desire to eliminate nonmeritorious §1983 lawsuits on the pleadings. In this way, it is thought that scarce judicial resources will be conserved and defense costs of litigating will be minimized.

Another procedural development worth noting is the recent amendment to Rule 11 which imposes sanctions, including expenses and attorney's fees,

---

appointment of counsel should not be denied solely because an appointed attorney may not be paid for his work; where counsel not appointed, district court *not* required "to bring to the attention of the *pro se* litigant or to decide the *unraised* issues which were subsidiary to the claims actually presented").

Eighth Circuit

Manning v Lockhart, 623 F2d 536 (8th Cir 1980) (pro se inmate was entitled to appointment of counsel because "there is a question of credibility of witnesses and . . . the case presents serious allegations of fact which are not facially frivolous"; however, "we do not endorse the appointment of counsel in every §1983 case filed by a state prisoner").

Ninth Circuit

Nicholson v Rushen, 767 F2d 1426 (9th Cir 1985) (per curiam) (plaintiff arrestee represented by counsel in §1983 case has no constitutional right to effective assistance of counsel).

[149] 449 US 5 (1980) (per curiam).

[150] *Id* 15.

[151] *See* §2.10.

[152] *E.g.*, Elliott v Perez, 751 F2d 1472 (5th Cir 1985) (absolute immunity "requires the trial judge to demand heightened standards of pleading by plaintiffs in cases in which that doctrine comes into play"), also noted at §7.07. *See generally* **ch 7** on absolute immunity.

[153] *See* §6.07.

against attorneys and clients alike for its violation. Rule 11 in relevant part requires attorneys to sign all pleadings, motions, and other papers and thereby certify that after "reasonable inquiry, those papers are well grounded in fact" and warranted by existing law or good faith argument for extension, modification, or reversal of the law. For example, according to the Fifth Circuit,[154] Rule 11 "means that in a case ostensibly raising the probable question of immunity, counsel for the plaintiff is affirming that, after making reasonable inquiry, he believes in good faith that the defendant official cannot successfully show that he has the defense of immunity."

Rule 26 similarly was amended in relevant part to require an attorney to sign every request for discovery or response or objection thereto, thereby certifying after "reasonable inquiry," that it is warranted by existing law or a good faith argument for extension, modification, or reversal of existing law, that it is not interposed for an improper purpose, and that it is not unreasonable or unduly burdensome or expensive under the circumstances. Here, too, sanctions for violating Rule 26, which can include reasonable expenses and attorney's fees, may be imposed against attorneys and clients.

While the purposes of these amendments are laudable, Rules 11 and 26 should not be applied to §1983 litigation in a heavy-handed or discriminatory manner by federal judges. If federal judges were to do so, then the result would be an unfortunate and socially costly chilling effect on the willingness of both plaintiffs' and defendants' attorneys involved in §1983 cases to litigate creatively and imaginatively. For example, would Rule 11 sanctions have been imposed by the district courts against plaintiff's counsel in *Monell v Department of Social Services*[155] and against defense counsel in *Harlow v Fitzgerald*[156] for their imaginative and ultimately successful legal arguments dealing with local government liability and qualified immunity?

Many §1983 suits, typically those seeking declaratory or injunctive relief,[157] are brought as class actions pursuant to Rule 23 of the Federal Rules of Civil Procedure. The subject of class actions is highly complex and is well beyond the scope of this chapter.[158] Briefly, however, and to paraphrase Rule 23, an action may be brought by members of a class or against members of a class only where:

1.   Joinder of all members is impracticable because the class is so numerous

2.   There are common questions of law or fact

---

[154] Elliott v Perez, 751 F2d 1472, 1481 (5th Cir 1985).

[155] 436 US 658 (1978). *See* **ch 6.**

[156] 457 US 800 (1982). *See* **ch 8.**

[157] *See* **ch 5.**

[158] *See generally* H. Newberg, Class Actions (2d ed 1985). In a §1983 case dealing primarily with pendent parties, *see* **§1.12,** the Second Circuit permitted a pendent statutory claim to proceed as a class action even though the jurisdiction-granting constitutional claim did not proceed as a class action. Almenares v Wyman, 453 F2d 1075, 1084-86 (2d Cir 1971), *cert denied,* 405 US 944 (1972).

3. The claims or defenses of the class representatives are typical of those of the class

4. The representatives will fully and adequately protect the interests of the class

However, these requirements of Rule 23(a) are only conditions precedent. In order to be maintainable as a class action, the action must in addition fall into any one of the following three categories set out in Rule 23(b):

1. The prosecution of separate actions would create a risk of either inconsistent or varying individual adjudications as to class members or of individual adjudications which as a practical matter would adversely affect the interests of class members not parties to the individual adjudications

2. The party opposing the class has acted or failed to act on grounds generally applicable to the class, so that injunctive or declaratory relief is appropriate for the entire class

3. Questions of law or fact common to all class members predominate over questions affecting only individuals and a class action is, in the district court's opinion, better than any other method of fairly and efficiently adjudicating the controversy

Rule 23 further deals with notice to members of a class, judgment, actions partially conducted as class actions, what judicial orders may be made in the conduct of class actions, and the dismissal or compromise of class actions.

The use of three-judge federal courts in §1983 litigation has been severely limited by 28 USC §2284.[159] Section 2284(a) provides in relevant part that three-judge federal courts are to be convened only "when otherwise required by Act of Congress, or when an action is filed challenging the constitutionality of the apportionment of congressional districts or the apportionment of any statewide legislative body." Although Congress requires three-judge courts in connection with certain non-§1983 civil rights cases,[160] it has not done so for §1983 cases as such. Thus, the three-judge court requirement only applies to §1983 apportionment cases. However, §2284 only applies to actions commenced *after* the date of its enactment in 1976. The prior three-judge federal court statute, since repealed, still governs actions filed on or before that date.[161]

The Federal Rules of Appellate Procedure govern appeals from district court decisions to circuit courts of appeals.[162] Rules 3, 4, and 5 explain how and when

---

[159] Pub L No 94-381, 90 Stat 1119 (repealing 28 USC §§2281, 2282).

[160] Under the Civil Rights Act of 1964, 42 USC §§2000a-5(b) & 2000e-6(b) & 1971(g); under the Voting Rights Act of 1965, 42 USC §§1973b(a), 1973c & 1973h(c).

[161] *See generally* C. Wright, Law of Federal Courts 295-99 (4th ed 1983).

[162] *See id* 718-24 on the historical background. 28 USC §§1291-1294 set out relevant circuit court jurisdiction provisions. Certain provisions of the Federal Rules of Appellate Procedure have been amended effective July 1, 1986. *See* 54 USLW 4281.

one takes appeals as of right and by permission. General procedural provisions are set out in Rules 25-48. Supreme Court review of circuit court decisions is available through appeal, certiorari, and certification of questions, as set out at 28 USC §1254. Review of state court decisions by the Supreme Court is available through appeal and certiorari, as set out at 28 USC §1257. The Court's Rules of Procedure apply.

While ordinarily the denial of a defense motion for summary judgment is not immediately appealable, the Supreme Court held in *Mitchell v Forsyth*[163] that district court decisions denying defense motions for summary judgment which are based on claims of absolute or qualified immunity and which raise only issues of law are immediately appealable. The Court's explicit goal was to reduce the costs of defending against §1983 litigation as it had previously asserted in its qualified immunity decision in *Harlow v Fitzgerald.*[164] The First Circuit had reached the same result earlier[165] while the Eighth Circuit had ruled that denials of defense motions for summary judgment on qualified immunity grounds are immediately appealable even where injunctive relief is also sought.[166] However, the Court in *Mitchell* left open the question whether interlocutory appeals from denials of such defense motions are available in the latter situation.

§1.17   The Right to a Jury Trial

The Supreme Court has not expressly addressed the applicability to §1983 actions brought in federal court of the Seventh Amendment's guarantee of a jury trial "[i]n suits at common law, where the value in controversy shall exceed twenty dollars. . . ." However, it is clear by analogy from the Court's decision in *Curtis v Loether,*[167] a 1968 Civil Rights Act fair housing case,[168] that where a §1983 claim seeking only compensatory and/or punitive damages is brought in federal court,[169] both parties have a right to jury trial. Just as the Court in *Curtis* held the Seventh Amendment applicable to an action for damages based on the fair housing statute because such an action is in essence a tort action, a §1983 damages action similarly "sounds basically in tort" and "is analogous to a number of tort actions recognized at common law."[170] Also in *Curtis,* the

---

[163] 105 S Ct 2806 (1985), discussed at **§8.05.**

[164] 457 US 800 (1982). *See* **ch 8** on qualified immunity and *Harlow* which eliminated the subjective part of the qualified immunity test.

[165] Krohn v United States, 742 F2d 24 (1st Cir 1984).

[166] Tubbesing v Arnold, 742 F2d 401 (8th Cir 1984).

[167] 415 US 189 (1974).

[168] 42 USC §3612.

[169] *See* **ch 4** on damages.

[170] 415 US at 195.

Court described actual and punitive damages as "the traditional form of relief offered in the courts of law."[171]

It is similarly clear from Supreme Court and circuit decisions that where a §1983 plaintiff asks only for equitable relief,[172] with no request for retro-spective monetary relief of any kind, the Seventh Amendment is not applicable and neither party has a right to a jury trial.[173] Such equitable relief includes traditional injunctive relief, but also covers, several circuits have held, discharged employees' §1983 actions for reinstatement and back pay.[174] Significantly, though, declaratory relief pursuant to the Declaratory Judgment Act[175] is as such considered neither equitable relief nor legal relief for Seventh Amendment purposes. As the Supreme Court has observed, the Act "specifi-cally preserves the right to jury trial for both parties."[176] Where only declaratory relief is sought, and a party demands a jury, then the district court must use the three-pronged test set out in the paragraph immediately following in order to determine whether the issues presented are equitable or legal in nature.

Some complexity is introduced in cases where a plaintiff seeks both damages and equitable relief.[177] Two important Supreme Court cases, *Beacon Theatres Inc v Westover*[178] and *Dairy Queen Inc v Wood*,[179] stand for the proposition that where legal and equitable claims are joined, the right to jury trial on the legal claims may not be infringed by trying the legal issue incidentally to the equitable one, or by a prior court trial of a common issue existing between the claims.[180] At the jury demand of either party, the legal claim must be tried first by a jury and relevant jury findings will bind the district court in its decision whether

---

[171] *Id* 196. A pre-*Curtis* district court opinion held that there is no right to a jury trial even in §1983 damage action cases because such suits are not "suits at common law." Lawton v Nightingale, 345 F Supp 683 (ND Ohio 1972). *Curtis* rather clearly undercuts the reasoning in *Lawton. See* Van Ermen v Schmidt, 374 F Supp 1070 (WD Wis 1974).

[172] *See* **ch 5** on §1983 equitable relief.

[173] Ross v Bernhard, 396 US 531 (1970); Dairy Queen Inc v Wood, 369 US 469 (1962); Beacon Theatres Inc v Westover, 359 US 500 (1959).

[174] McFerren v County Bd of Educ, 455 F2d 199 (6th Cir), *cert denied*, 407 US 934 (1972); Harkless v Sweeney Indep School Dist, 427 F2d 319 (5th Cir 1970), *cert denied*, 400 US 991 (1971), a leading case; Smith v Hampton Training School for Nurses, 360 F2d 577 (4th Cir 1966) (en banc). The Supreme Court has not passed directly on the relationship between the Seventh Amendment and §1983 litigation. In a 1964 Civil Rights Act context, though, it did mention the reinstatement and back pay question but then cautioned that it expressed no views on the question. Curtis v Loether, 415 US 189, 196-97 (1974).

[175] 28 USC §§2201-2202. *See* **ch 5.**

[176] Beacon Theatres Inc v Westover, 359 US 500, 504 (1959).

[177] Rule 18, Fed R Civ P permits joinder of legal and equitable claims.

[178] 359 US 500 (1959).

[179] 369 US 469 (1962).

[180] So read in Ross v Bernhard, 396 US 531, 537-38 (1970).

to grant or deny equitable relief thereafter. In this connection, the Court said in *Ross v Bernhard*[181] that "[t]he Seventh Amendment question depends on the nature of the issue to be tried rather than on the character of the overall action,"[182] with the legal nature of an issue to be determined by the use of a three-pronged test. The relevant inquiries are:

1. The premerger history with reference to that issue
2. The kind of remedy sought
3. The practical abilities and limitations of juries[183]

While these Supreme Courtdecisions do not involve §1983 litigation, the rules they establish are in fact applied by the circuits to §1983 cases.[184]

It is usually not difficult to characterize an issue as equitable or legal for Seventh Amendment purposes. As noted, however, the Supreme Court cautioned in *Ross v Bernhard*[185] that simply calling an issue legal or equitable is not determinative. Thus, for example, according to the Fourth Circuit, a claim for back pay unaccompanied by a reinstatement claim will be characterized as a legal damages action if it is pressed against defendants in their individual capacities. However, the same claim pressed against defendants in their official capacities will be characterized as equitable.[186]

According to the Third Circuit,[187] a plaintiff is entitled to a jury trial where the pleadings so suggest. Thus, where the plaintiffs, discharged employees, sued state officials for political discrimination under §§1983 and 1985 and asked for compensatory and punitive damages as well as for equitable relief, the Third Circuit ruled that they were entitled to a jury trial. There was no requirement that claims for damages must be supported in order to entitle plaintiffs to a jury trial; it was sufficient that the pleadings indicated "an issue triable of right by a jury." Nevertheless, the district court's error in refusing a jury trial was harmless error[188] because the evidence was insufficient in any event to avoid a directed verdict against the plaintiffs.

The right to a jury trial will be deemed waived where neither party has filed

---

[181] *Id.*

[182] *Id* 538.

[183] *Id* 538 n 10. However, it has been asserted that "[f]or the most part the lower courts have ignored [this] *Ross* footnote, or cited it as a makeweight reference to support results that would have been reached had the footnote never been written." C. Wright, Law of Federal Courts 614 (4th ed 1983) (criticizing inclusion of third factor of FIL 22 7 4312 "complexity").

[184] *E.g.,* the Fourth, Fifth and Sixth Circuits. *See* note 174.

[185] 396 US 531 (1970).

[186] Burt v Board of Trustees of Edgefield County School Dist, 521 F2d 1201 (4th Cir 1975). At 1204 the court explained that "[p]rivate citizens are not empowered to reinstate or order back pay out of school board or county funds." Because the district court's order awarding back pay, inter alia, was ambiguous on this point, the Fourth Circuit was ambiguous on this point, the Fourth Circuit reversed and remanded.

[187] Laskaris v Thornburgh, 733 F2d 260 (3d Cir 1984).

[188] Judge Adams dissented on the harmless error issue, contending that a jury could possibly have found evidence of political motivation directed against plaintiffs.

a timely and otherwise proper demand pursuant to Rule 38 of the Federal Rules of Civil Procedure.[189] However, the Seventh Circuit was solicitous of a pro se §1983 plaintiff who, in connection with his suit against prison officials for damages and other relief, "buried" a demand for jury trial in his complaint, and did not object when the trial court proceeded without a jury.[190] Reversing and remanding for a jury trial, the court indicated that the prisoner may not have been aware of his right to object.

It has been suggested that plaintiffs in §1983 cases frequently do not want a jury trial because of a supposed jury bias in favor of public officials, and that defendants typically do want one for this very reason.[191] Whether or not this is true, the §1983 plaintiff who does not want a jury trial should strictly limit any claim to equitable relief. If the plaintiff asks for damages, then the defendant clearly has the right to a jury trial. If the plaintiff asks only for declaratory relief, then upon defendant's request for a jury trial, the district court will use the Supreme Court's three-pronged test mentioned earlier and may well conclude that the claim should be tried by a jury because some or all of the claims made are legal ones.

§1.18 The 1976 Attorney's Fees Awards Act: Introduction

In a significant amendment to 42 USC §1988—the amendment is called the Civil Rights Attorney's Fees Awards Act of 1976—Congress authorized federal courts to award attorney's fees in §1983 cases, among others, in certain circumstances.[192] Specifically, the Act provides on this subject that "[i]n any

---

[189] Rule 38(d) expressly discusses waiver. Waivers by plaintiffs were found in McCray v Burrell, 516 F2d 357 (4th Cir 1975) and Amburgey v Cassady, 507 F2d 728 (6th Cir 1974).

[190] Chapman v Kleindienst, 507 F2d 1246 (7th Cir 1974). *Compare* the Supreme Court's concern for pro se §1983 complaints filed by inmates in Haines v Kerner, 404 US 519 (1972). *See* **§1.16.**

[191] Van Ermen v Schmidt, 374 F Supp 1070, 1075 (WD Wis 1974); Comment, *Monetary Claims Under Section 1983—The Right to Trial by Jury,* 8 Harv CR-CL L Rev 613 (1973). Lawton v Nightingale, 345 F Supp 683 (ND Ohio 1972) used this jury bias factor as partial justification for its holding that parties in §1983 damage actions have no right to jury trial. The court asserted: "The person seeking to vindicate an unpopular right could never succeed before a jury drawn from a populace mainly opposed to his views." *Id* 684. However, *Lawton's* conclusion was undercut by Curtis v Loether, 415 US 189 (1974).

[192] The Amendment reads as follows:

In any action or proceeding to enforce a provision of sections ... [42 USC §§1981, 1982, 1983, 1985 and 1986] title IX of Public Law 92-318, or in any civil action or proceeding, by or on behalf of the United States of America, to enforce, or charging a violation of, a provision of the United States Internal Revenue Code, or Title VI of the Civil Rights Act of 1964, the court, in its discretion, may allow the prevailing party, other than the United States, a reasonable attorney's fee as part of the costs.

action or proceeding to enforce [section 1983 and other civil rights statutes] the court, in its discretion, may allow the prevailing party . . . a reasonable attorney's fee as part of the costs." The overriding purpose of the Act is "to encourage the private enforcement of civil rights laws in order to fully vindicate the federal rights involved."[193]

This Act was Congress's response to the Supreme Court's 1975 decision in the *Alyeska Pipeline* case[194] which held, relying on the so-called American rule, that federal courts have no power to award attorney's fees to litigants representing the public interest as private attorneys general absent express congressional authorization. While *Alyeska Pipeline* itself dealt with environmental litigation, it was clear from the Court's reasoning and its dictum that civil rights litigation was also comprehended by its decision.[195]

Neither *Alyeska Pipeline* nor the Act changed the pre-*Alyeska Pipeline* rule that federal courts do have the inherent power to assess attorney's fees against a losing party who engages in "irresponsible conduct," that is, litigation in bad faith, vexatiously, or for oppressive purposes.[196] As will be seen, however, the Act goes well beyond this rule both on its face and as applied by the federal courts.

Before the following sections are considered, it is crucial to distinguish between entitlement issues and computation issues. Entitlement issues include the standards for determining who is a prevailing party and when, the nature of the proceedings covered by the Act, and immunity from fees liability.[197] Computation issues are those dealing with the determination of a fees award after an entitlement thereto has been found, including the relevance of the extent of a prevailing plaintiff's success, how market rates are used, whether and when upward adjustments are allowed, and the impact of offers of judgment.[198] All these issues, and more, have been addressed by the Supreme Court and the circuit courts in an explosion of attorney's fees litigation.

§1.19   —Entitlement to Fees

The circuits uniformly have applied the attorney's fee amendment to 42 USC §1988 retroactively to pending cases,[199] including those on appeal, and the

---

[193] Sargeant v Sharp, 579 F2d 645, 648 (1st Cir 1978).

[194] Alyeska Pipeline Serv Co v Wilderness Socy, 421 US 240 (1975).

[195] *Id* 262-64.

[196] Runyon v McCrary, 427 US 160, 183 (1976). *See, e.g.,* Stolberg v Members of Bd of Trustees for State Colleges, 474 F2d 485 (2d Cir 1973).

[197] *See* §§1.19-1.24.

[198] *See* §§1.24-1.25.

[199] *E.g.,* Perez v Rodriguez Bon, 575 F2d 21 (1st Cir 1978); Fountila v Carter, 571 F2d 487 (9th Cir 1978); Simpson v Weeks, 570 F2d 240 (8th Cir 1978); Beazer v New York City Transit Auth, 558 F2d 97 (2d Cir 1977); Bond v Stanton, 555 F2d 172 (7th Cir 1977), *cert denied,* 438 US 916 (1978). In Corpus v Estelle, 605 F2d 175, 177 (5th Cir 1979), the Fifth Circuit rejected the interesting contention that "Congress lacked authority under Section 5 under the Fourteenth Amendment to provide awards under

Supreme Court approved this application in light of the clear legislative history on this point.[200] The Fifth Circuit considered a case to be pending for purposes of the Act even though the only issue on appeal was attorney's fees.[201] The First Circuit held that a case before a district court was pending even though the Act became effective after all proceedings before the district court were completed but before judgment had been entered.[202]

The Act covers fees incurred in obtaining both equitable and legal relief at the district court level by the *prevailing party,* who may be either the plaintiff or the defendant. It also encompasses fees on appeal.[203] Furthermore, the Act on its face covers all §1983 actions whether based on the Constitution or "laws."[204] The legislative history shows that Congress intended "that the standards for awarding fees be generally the same as under the fee provisions of the 1964 Civil Rights Act,"[205] which contains substantially similar language.

However, the standards are different for awards to plaintiff and defendant. A prevailing *plaintiff* "should ordinarily recover an attorney's fee unless special circumstances would render such an award unjust";[206] neither subjective bad faith[207] nor intentional conduct[208] is required. Special circumstances *do not*

---

the Act, in cases pending on the date of enactment, for services rendered before that date."

[200] Hutto v Finney, 437 US 678, 694 n 23 (1978).

[201] Rainey v Jackson State College, 551 F2d 672 (5th Cir 1977). *See also* David v Travisono, 621 F2d 464 (1st Cir 1980) (per curiam), where the court held that attorney's fees should be awarded to the prevailing plaintiffs even though the only issue still pending on the effective date of the Act was trivial and remotely related to the merits of the case itself; Sethy v Alameda County Water Dist, 602 F2d 894 (9th Cir 1979) (per curiam), which held the Act applicable to a case in which the Ninth Circuit's opinion affirming the district court's judgment was filed before the Act became effective but its mandate issued 15 days after the effective date.

[202] Perez v Rodriguez Bon, 575 F2d 21 (1st Cir 1978). Cf Escamilla v Santos, 591 F2d 1086 (5th Cir 1979) (per curiam), where the Act was held inapplicable to a case in which there were no issues at all, including fees, pending in the district court at the time the Act became law. The district court's memorandum opinion which followed an earlier consent decree was considered a final judgment and the district court thus retained no jurisdiction to award attorney's fees after denying them in its memorandum opinion. *See also* Taylor v Sterrett, 640 F2d 663 (5th Cir 1981).

[203] *Hutto,* 437 US at 694. Cf Fox v Parker, 626 F2d 351 (4th Cir 1980), where plaintiff, who withdrew his appeal, was not entitled to attorney's fees in pursuing his appeal. Although a prevailing party on the trial level, he was not a prevailing party on the appellate level.

[204] *See* Maine v Thibotout, 448 US 1 (1980) ("laws"); Bond v Stanton, 555 F2d 172 (7th Cir 1977) ("laws"), *cert denied,* 438 US 916 (1978); Lipson, *Beyond Alyeska - Judicial Response to the Civil Rights Attorney's Fees Act,* 22 St Louis ULJ 243, 250 n 44 (1978). *See generally* §2.10 on the federal statutory or "laws" aspect of §1983 causes of action.

[205] Brown v Culpepper, 559 F2d 274, 277 (5th Cir 1977), quoting from S Rep No 1011, 94th Cong, 2d Sess 4, *reprinted in* 1976 US Code Cong & Ad News 5908, 5912.

[206] Newman v Piggie Park Enters, Inc, 390 US 400, 402 (1968) (1964 Civil Rights Act case).

[207] *Id* 401.

[208] Brown v Culpepper, 559 F2d 274, 278 (5th Cir 1977).

include the following: defendants' good faith in enforcing an invalid state statute;[209] the losing party's reliance on advice of counsel;[210] the prevailing plaintiff's ability to pay;[211] the case involved "basically financial interests";[212] the prevailing plaintiff who successfully sued a law enforcement officer for the use of excessive force had been drunk and ill-mannered;[213] the prevailing plaintiff perjured herself at trial;[214] the uncertainty in the law;[215] the prevailing plaintiffs, represented by a public interest organization, undertook a successful fund-raising effort in connection with the case;[216] the prevailing plaintiff could have retained competent counsel without the prospect of attorney's fees;[217] the prevailing plaintiff was the primary beneficiary of the suit;[218] and the threat of attorney's fees responsibility would have a deterrent effect upon the defendant local government.[219] Furthermore, the prevailing plaintiff's recovery of nominal damages only is not a special circumstance,[220] although it may be relevant to the amount of the fees award.[221]

Conversely, a prevailing *defendant* may be awarded attorney's fees in the court's discretion only "upon a finding that the plaintiff's action was frivolous, unreasonable or without foundation, even though not brought in subjective bad faith."[222] This difference in standards is based on the Act's generally pro-plaintiff and pro-civil rights orientation and protects a defendant only from groundless litigation. In this latter regard, it should be emphasized that simply

---

[209] Johnson v Mississippi, 606 F2d 635 (5th Cir 1979).

[210] Davidson v Keenan, 740 F2d 129 (2d Cir 1984).

[211] International Socy for Krishna Consciousness v Collins, 609 F2d 151 (5th Cir 1980) (per curiam).

[212] International Oceanic Enters, Inc v Menton, 614 F2d 502 (5th Cir 1980).

[213] Hall v Hall, 738 F2d 718 (6th Cir 1984).

[214] Price v Pelka, 690 F2d 98 (6th Cir 1982) (Judge Merritt dissented).

[215] Northcross v Board of Educ, 611 F2d 624 (6th Cir 1979).

[216] McLean v Arkansas Bd of Educ, 723 F2d 45 (8th Cir 1983) (per curiam) (Judge Gibson dissented).

[217] Ackerley Communications v City of Salem, 752 F2d 1394 (9th Cir 1985); Sanchez v Schwartz, 688 F2d 503 (7th Cir 1982). However, the Second Circuit took a contrary approach. *See* Kerr v Quinn, 692 F2d 875, 877 (2d Cir 1982); Zarcone v Perry, 581 F2d 1039 (2d Cir 1978), *cert denied*, 439 US 1072 (1979). *Zarcone* was followed by the Ninth Circuit in Buxton v Patel, 595 F2d 1182 (9th Cir 1979).

[218] *Id.*

[219] Ackerley Communications v City of Salem, 752 F2d 1394 (9th Cir 1985).

[220] Fast v School District of City of Ladue, 728 F2d 1030 (8th Cir 1984) (en banc); Perez v University of Puerto Rico, 600 F2d 1 (1st Cir 1979); *But see* Huntley v Community School Bd, 579 F2d 738 (2d Cir 1978) (per curiam). Is a plaintiff who recovers only nominal damages a prevailing party? Justice White, dissenting from denial of certiorari in Moran v Pima County, 54 USLW 3328 (S Ct Nov 11, 1985), an Arizona case, contended that there is a dispute among the circuits on this issue. *Cf* City of Riverside v Rivera, 106 S Ct 2686 (1986), discussed at §§1.25-1.26.

[221] *See* §1.25.

[222] Christiansburg Garment Co v EEOC, 434 US 412, 421 (1978); *see also* General Camera Corp v Urban Dev Corp, 734 F2d 468 (2d Cir 1984) (per curiam) and Green v Ten Eyck, 572 F2d 1233, 1243 n 11 (8th Cir 1978).

because a defendant ultimately prevails, it does not follow that the §1983 claim was groundless at the outset. This post hoc approach is not appropriate under the Act because it would discourage plaintiffs from bringing §1983 claims whose outcomes are not certain.[223] Similarly, just because a plaintiff's suit is dismissed for want of prosecution, it does not necessarily follow that the suit was groundless.[224] Also, a prevailing defendant is not entitled to fees where there was "some slight legal support" for plaintiff's constitutional arguments.[225] In contrast, the prevailing defendants were entitled to fees where plaintiff's suit was preposterous and constituted a personal vendetta,[226] was a transparent attempt to bully the administration of justice,[227] and was not supported by even a scintilla of evidence.[228]

A plaintiff can be a *prevailing party* entitled to attorney's fees even though the litigation is terminated without formal judicial action or by consent decree.[229] The reason for this is set forth in the Act's legislative history: "A 'prevailing party' should not be penalized for seeking an out-of-court settlement, thus

---

[223] *See also* recently amended Rule 11 of the Fed R Civ P which requires attorneys to sign all pleadings, motions, and other papers and thereby certify that he or she has read them; that the papers are, to the best of his or her knowledge and after reasonable inquiry, "well grounded in fact" and warranted by existing law or a good faith argument for a change or extension in the law; and that the papers are not interposed for an improper purpose. If Rule 11 is violated, the court, on motion or even on its own, may impose on the lawyer and his or her client an "appropriate sanction," including expenses and attorney's fees. *See* §§1.16 & 1.24.

[224] Anthony v Marion County Gen Hosp, 617 F2d 1164 (5th Cir 1980).

[225] Vakas v Rodriguez, 728 F2d 1293, 1297 (10th Cir 1984).

[226] Munson v Friske, 754 F2d 683 (7th Cir 1985).

[227] Glick v Koenig, 766 F2d 265 (7th Cir 1985).

[228] Buford v Tremayne, 747 F2d 445 (8th Cir 1984). *See also* Steinle v Warren, 765 F2d 95 (7th Cir 1985) (fees awarded against pro se lawyer plaintiff who filed a §1983 suit knowing it was time-barred; fees also awarded against plaintiff for his "completely frivolous" appeal).

[229] Brown v Culpepper, 559 F2d 274 (5th Cir 1977). As reflected in the following cases, there is a threshold "catalyst" requirement:

First Circuit

Nadeau v Helgemoe, 581 F2d 275 (1st Cir 1978) (fees may be awarded in consent decree cases; the "key issue is the provocative role of the plaintiffs' lawsuit, not the motivations of the defendant").

Third Circuit

Ross v Horn, 598 F2d 1312 (3d Cir 1979) (fees may be awarded to a party even though no judgment entered in that party's favor where lawsuit was "the catalyst for the implementation of all or any of the reform measures" undertaken by defendants).

Fourth Circuit

DeMier v Gondles, 676 F2d 92 (4th Cir 1982) (plaintiffs were prevailing parties; they voluntarily dismissed their suit after defendant sheriff stopped his strip search policy and legislature passed new legislation dealing with the matter).

Bonnes v Long, 599 F2d 1316 (4th Cir 1979) (plaintiff may be a prevailing party even though consent judgment confers some benefit on defendant as well; case remanded for findings of fact and conclusions of law on whether particular plaintiffs were prevailing parties).

helping to lessen docket congestion."[230] In addition, a plaintiff can prevail without winning on all issues, although in such cases fees awarded may be proportionately reduced.[231] Furthermore, the Eighth Circuit[232] held that a

---

Fifth Circuit

Smith v Thomas, 725 F2d 354 (5th Cir 1984) (plaintiff a prevailing party: defendant sheriff agreed he had acted unconstitutionally in firing the plaintiff; this was responsible for plaintiff's continued employment, not the sheriff's loss of election).

Robinson v Kimbrough, 620 F2d 468 (5th Cir 1980) (plaintiffs, who obtained no formal judicial relief, were still prevailing parties; their lawsuit was a "significant catalyst" in achieving their primary objective of modifying the county's jury lists to reflect fairly the number of blacks and women) *opinion withdrawn*, 652 F2d 458 (5th Cir 1981) (no relevant findings by district court on prevailing party issue; parties *on remand* to submit additional evidence).

Harris v City of Fort Myers, 624 F2d 1321 (5th Cir 1980) (plaintiffs who obtained consent decree were prevailing parties even though defendant city argued that the consent decree only compelled it to do those things that it had already undertaken to do; a close case in which the court carefully reviewed the record).

Ward v Dearman, 626 F2d 489 (5th Cir 1980) (per curiam) (rejecting plaintiffs' argument that they had obtained the relief sought as a practical matter and were thus entitled to fees; there was no voluntary compliance by the *defendants* themselves stemming from plaintiffs' suit; rather the conduct of others had brought about the result).

Seventh Circuit

Dawson v Pastrick, 600 F2d 70 (7th Cir 1979) (plaintiffs in §1981 fair employment practices litigation leading to consent decree were prevailing parties where lawsuit "operated as a catalyst prompting the defendants to institute fair employment practices").

Eighth Circuit

Williams v Miller, 620 F2d 199 (8th Cir 1980) (per curiam) (plaintiffs could be prevailing parties even though they moved to dismiss suit without prejudice; relief sought was in substance obtained by defendants' voluntary compliance after suit was filed and suit may have been the "catalyst" that brought compliance about).

Ninth Circuit

American Constitutional Party v Munro, 650 F2d 184 (9th Cir 1981) (plaintiffs not prevailing parties; insufficient evidence introduced to show that lawsuit played a causal role in passage of a legislative amendment; a single legislator's affidavit, dated one year after the amendment, was entitled to no weight and in any event did not demonstrate that the lawsuit was a "material factor" in the legislative process).

Eleventh Circuit

Fields v City of Tarpon Springs, 721 F2d 318 (11th Cir 1983) (black plaintiffs' suit was a catalyst in bringing about changes in defendant's park and recreational services).

[230] HR Rep No 1558, 94th Cong, 2d Sess 8 (1976).

[231] *See* §1.25.

[232] Kimbrough v Arkansas Activities Assn, 574 F2d 423 (8th Cir 1978). The First Circuit reached the same conclusion in Lund v Affleck, 587 F2d 75 (1st Cir 1978) (§1983 claim was "substantial" and the successful pendent claim arose from "the same nucleus of facts"), as did the Second Circuit in Gagne v Maher, 594 F2d 336 (2d Cir 1979), *affd*, 448 US 122 (1980) ("substantial" §1983 claim and desirability of avoiding unnecessary decision of constitutional issues). *See also* Reproductive Health Servs v Freeman, 614 F2d 585, 600 (8th Cir 1980).

Where, however, a plaintiff lost on his §1983 claim and won on his pendent state

plaintiff was entitled to attorney's fees even though he obtained a preliminary injunction effectively terminating the litigation based on his non-§1983 pendent claim. The court found that his §1983 claim was "substantial."[233]

The argument was made that a plaintiff can be a prevailing party in an action for damages on making out a prima facie claim even though ultimately losing on qualified or absolute immunity grounds.[234] However, not only is this inconsistent with a common sense interpretation of the word *prevailing,* but the Supreme Court in *Hutto v Finney*[235] indicated rather clearly that such a plaintiff is not considered a prevailing party. Consequently, a defendant who successfully asserts an immunity or affirmative defense in an action for damages is the prevailing party under the Act.

In a series of important cases, the Supreme Court dealt with important entitlement issues. Thus, the Court in *Hanrahan v Hampton*[236] interpreted the Act's *prevailing party* language as applying only to a party who establishes entitlement to some relief on the merits of his or her claims, whether at the trial or appellate level. The district court had directed verdicts in favor of the various law enforcement officer defendants in connection with the §1983 claims against them. Reversing and remanding for a new trial, the Seventh Circuit also awarded substantial attorney's fees to plaintiffs' counsel for their successful appellate work. It relied on the following as support for its conclusion that plaintiffs had prevailed on appeal:

1. The reversal of the district court's judgment directing verdicts against the plaintiffs

2. The reversal of the district court's denial of plaintiffs' motion to discover the identity of an FBI informant

3. The direction to the district court on remand to consider allowing further discovery and to conduct a hearing on plaintiffs' contention that sanctions should be imposed on some of the defendants because of their conduct in response to the district court's discovery orders

The Supreme Court unanimously reversed the Seventh Circuit on this attorney's fees issue. It acknowledged that plaintiffs may sometimes be prevailing parties when they vindicate rights through a consent judgment or

---

claim, the Second Circuit ruled that the plaintiff was not entitled to attorney's fees. Russo v State of New York, 672 F2d 1014 (2d Cir 1982). The Third Circuit ruled the same way in Luria Bros v Allen, 672 F2d 347 (3d Cir 1982), as did the Eighth Circuit in Reel v Arkansas Dept of Correction, 672 F2d 693 (8th Cir 1982). To the same effect are two Fifth Circuit decisions, Raley v Fraser, 747 F2d 287 (5th Cir 1985) and McDonald v Doe, 748 F2d 1055 (5th Cir 1984).

[233] *See* §1.11 on pendent jurisdiction in §1983 cases.

[234] Lipson, *Beyond Alyeska - Judicial Response to the Civil Rights Attorney's Fees Act* 22 St Louis ULJ 243, 262-63 (1978).

[235] 437 US 678, 699 n 32 (1978) (dictum). This has been made even clearer by subsequent Supreme Court decisions, as discussed at §1.25.

[236] 446 US 754 (1980) (per curiam). Justice Stevens did not participate.

even without formally obtaining relief. The Court also noted the possibility in some cases of the award of fees pendente lite. However, "Congress intended to permit the interim award of counsel fees only when a party has prevailed on the merits of at least some of his claims."[237] Because plaintiffs had not prevailed on the merits of any of their claims on appeal but were, as a practical matter, in the same position in which they would have been had they defeated defendants' motion for a directed verdict at the trial level, they were not entitled to fees under the Act. While such procedural or evidentiary rulings may affect the ultimate disposition on the merits, they do not, according to the Court, render the party who obtains them as prevailing for the purpose of shifting counsel fees to the opposing party.[238]

There is still some uncertainty regarding the test for determining whether a party is prevailing for fees purposes. The Court denied certiorari in two cases[239] where the Fourth Circuit, in establishing a prevailing party test, focused "only on the factual question of whether the lawsuit caused a change favorable to the plaintiff." Justices Rehnquist and O'Connor dissented. They first asserted that the Fourth Circuit's factual approach to the prevailing party question conflicted with the First Circuit's approach in *Nadeau v Helgemoe*[240] which requires not only that the lawsuit in fact bring about some discernible benefit to the plaintiff, but that the benefit also have some basis in law. That is, under the *Nadeau* approach, "[i]f it has been judicially determined that defendants' conduct, however beneficial it may be to plaintiffs' interests, is not required by law, then defendants must be held to have acted gratuitously and plaintiffs have not prevailed in the legal sense."[241] Justices Rehnquist and O'Connor then argued that the *Nadeau* approach was the proper one because it reflected congressional intent in enacting the Attorney's Fees Awards Act. They concluded: "[U]nless an action brought by a private litigant contains some basis in law for the benefits ultimately received by that litigant, the litigant cannot be said to have 'enforced' the civil rights laws or to have promoted their policies for the benefit of the public at large."[242]

---

[237] *Id* 758.

[238] Similar reasoning was used both by the Third Circuit in Swietlowich v County of Bucks, 610 F2d 1157 (3d Cir 1979), which involved vacating a judgment solely because of error in instructions given to the jury, and by the Fourth Circuit in Bly v McLeod, 605 F2d 134 (4th Cir 1979).

[239] Bonnes v Long, 651 F2d 214 (4th Cir 1981) and Young v Kenley, 641 F2d 192 (4th Cir 1981) (Nos 80-2112 & 2153), *cert denied,* 50 USLW 3662 (S Ct Feb 22, 1982).

[240] 581 F2d 275 (1st Cir 1978).

[241] *Id* 281.

[242] 50 USLW at 3664. *Nadeau* has been followed in the District of Columbia, First, Fifth, Sixth, Seventh, and Tenth Circuits. Miller v Staats, 706 F2d 336 (DC Cir 1983); Ortiz De Arroyo v Barcelo, 765 F2d 275 (1st Cir 1985) (*Nadeau* reaffirmed); Hennigan v Onachita Parish School Bd, 749 F2d 1148 (5th Cir 1985) (central issue); Garcia v Guerra, 744 F2d 1159 (5th Cir 1984); Johnson v Jago, 691 F2d 283 (6th Cir 1982); Harrington v De Vito, 656 F2d 264 (7th Cir 1981); Anderson v Town of Erie, 767 F2d 1469 (10th Cir 1985).

More recently, though, in *Hensley v Eckerhart,*[243] an important computation case discussed later,[244] the Court, quoting *Nadeau,* described a "typical formulation" for determining whether a plaintiff is prevailing, as follows: "[P]laintiffs may be considered 'prevailing parties' for attorney's fees purposes if they succeed on *any* significant issue in litigation which achieves *some* of the benefit the parties sought in bringing suit".[245]

With respect to the timeliness of a prevailing party's request for attorney's fees, the Supreme Court held in *White v New Hampshire Department of Employment Security*[246] that such a request is *not* a "motion to alter or amend the judgment" subject to the 10-day requirement of Rule 59(e) of the Federal Rules of Civil Procedure. It thus reversed the First Circuit's contrary decision.[247] Emphasizing the "harsh and unintended consequences" of applying Rule 59(e) to postjudgment fee requests, the Court observed that a district court could exercise its discretion to deny fees where a fee request "unfairly surprises or prejudices the affected party." Also, district courts could adopt local timeliness rules for attorney's fees requests.[248] The Court expressly refused to address the question of whether fee requests are motions for "costs" within the meaning of Rules 54(d) and 58, which have no timeliness requirements.[249]

§1.20 —§1983 Statutory Claims

As noted earlier, fees are available to prevailing plaintiffs in both §1983 constitutional and laws cases. In *Maine v Thibotout,*[250] which ruled that §1983's laws language encompasses certain violations of federal law, including the Social Security Act violation before it, the Supreme Court also held that attorney's fees may be awarded under the Act to a party who prevails on a §1983 statutory claim, whether in federal or state court. The Court relied both on the plain language of the Act, which makes no exceptions for §1983 statutory actions, and on the Act's legislative history. Moreover, in affirming the decision of the Supreme Court of Maine that plaintiffs were eligible for attorney's fees under §1988, the Court stated that the Act's legislative history, the Supremacy

---

[243] 461 US 424 (1983).
The Court has granted certiorari in Hewitt v Helms, 780 F2d 367 (3d Cir 1986), *cert granted,* 54 USLW 3819 (June 17, 1986) to deal with the question whether an inmate is a prevailing party where his release from prison rendered his prospective relief claim moot and his damages claim was lost on immunity grounds.

[244] **§1.25.**

[245] 461 US at 433 (emphasis added).

[246] 455 US 445 (1982).

[247] White v New Hampshire Dept of Employment Security, 629 F2d 697 (1st Cir 1980).

[248] *E.g.,* Pitts v Freeman, 755 F2d 897 (11th Cir 1985) (ND Ga local rule: 15 days from final judgment).

[249] 455 US at 454 n 17. In Knighton v Watkins, 616 F2d 795 (5th Cir 1980), the court treated fee requests as such motions for costs.

[250] 448 US 1 (1980), also discussed at **§2.12.**

Clause, and federalism concerns all indicated clearly that the Act applies in state courts as well as federal courts.

In *Maher v Gagne*,[251] still another attorney's fees case, the Court asserted that where a §1983 statutory claim—here, too, as in *Thiboutot*, an alleged Social Security Act violation—is pendent to a substantial constitutional claim, attorney's fees may be assessed under the Act against state officials in their official capacities (and thus against a state) even though the case is settled without a determination that any constitutional rights were violated. After noting that plaintiff was the prevailing party, the Court first observed that its decision on the same day in *Thiboutot* held that the Act was intended to apply to §1983 cases involving federal statutory violations. The Court then rejected defendant's argument that the Eleventh Amendment precludes a federal court from awarding fees against a state in all cases involving a statutory, non-civil rights claim. It emphasized that plaintiff had raised substantial constitutional issues which remained in the case until settlement and that an award of fees in connection with a *pendent* §1983 federal statutory claim was an appropriate congressional means of enforcing the Fourteenth Amendment.

The Court in *Maher* expressly reserved the broader question of whether a federal court is prevented by the Eleventh Amendment from awarding attorney's fees against a state based *solely* on a §1983 federal statutory, non-civil rights claim.[252] It should be noted, though, that this reserved Eleventh Amendment question will arise only in those situations where *state* officials are successfully sued in their *official* capacities, but *not* where local government officials are successfully sued in their official capacities or where local governments are successfully sued for damages directly. Furthermore, the Eleventh Amendment applies only to federal courts and not to state courts.[253]

In *Smith v Robinson*,[254] the Court carved out an exception to *Maher* in cases involving suits under the Education of the Handicapped Act (EHA).[255] Plaintiffs, parents of a handicapped child, sued various city and state officials in federal court on different grounds, alleging violations of state law, the EHA, §504 of the Rehabilitation Act,[256] and, through §1983, due process and equal protection. Plaintiffs were ultimately successful on EHA grounds and sought attorney's fees in connection with various claims. Ultimately, the First Circuit held that plaintiffs were not entitled to fees and the Supreme Court, in an opinion by Justice Blackmun, affirmed.

At the outset, according to the Court, the EHA clearly did not provide for fees. Also, even though the plaintiffs' constitutional claims were substantial and nonfrivolous within the meanings of *Maher*, this was not enough: "[P]laintiffs may not rely simply on the fact that substantial fee-generating claims were

---

[251] 448 US 122 (1980).

[252] *Id* 130-31.

[253] *See* §§**1.24** & **5.08**.

[254] 104 S Ct 3457 (1984), also discussed at §**2.12**.

[255] 20 USC §1401 *et seq.*

[256] 29 USC §794.

made during the course of the litigation."[257] Their due process claims were not sufficiently related to their ultimate success[258] to support an award of fees for the entire proceeding. Their equal protection claim was identical to their EHA claim; however, Congress intended through adoption of the comprehensive EHA scheme that the EHA be the exclusive avenue for such equal protection claims, and that no independent constitutional claims be permitted. That is, the EHA in effect amended §1983 to exclude from its purview constitutional claims identical to those covered by the EHA. Otherwise, the EHA's administrative remedies could be circumvented. Finally, fees were not available under §504 of the Rehabilitation Act, even though that statute so provided. Congress intended that the EHA scheme be paramount to the more general scheme of the Rehabilitation Act.[259]

§1.21 —State Administrative and Judicial Proceedings

Another issue—now resolved—regarding entitlement to an award of attorney's fees was whether they could be awarded for participation in state administrative proceedings. If an exhaustion of state administrative remedies requirement were imposed upon some §1983 actions,[260] it was possible that the 1976 Act could authorize federal courts to award attorney's fees where the federal plaintiff prevailed at the state administrative level. This possibility was based on the Supreme Court's decision in *New York Gaslight Club Inc v Carey*[261] where it held: "[U]nder Title VII of the Civil Rights Act of 1964, a federal court may allow the prevailing party attorney's fees for legal services performed in prosecuting an employment discrimination claim in *state* administrative and judicial proceedings that Title VII requires federal claimants to invoke."[262]

In reaching this conclusion, the Court examined the language and history of the attorney's fees provision of Title VII, the nature of the state proceedings, and the relationship between those proceedings and Title VII's enforcement mechanisms. Like Title VII's attorney's fees provision, the 1976 Act covers "any action or *proceeding*." Also, the availability of an agency attorney under state law to present the case in support of the discrimination complaint at a public hearing was considered by the Court not to be a special circumstance justifying denial of a fees award to the plaintiff. In the Court's view, a private attorney was necessary throughout the administrative level to represent the

---

[257] 104 S Ct at 3467.

[258] That is, within the meaning of Hensley v Eckerhart, 103 S Ct 1933 (1983), discussed at §1.25.

[259] Justices Brennan, Marshall and Stevens dissented, disputing the Court's interpretation of the various statutes and their interrelation.

[260] *See* §§5.10-5.11.

[261] 447 US 54 (1980).

[262] *Id* 56 (emphasis in original).

plaintiff's interests; the agency attorney represented the state's interests.[263]

However, in *Webb v County Board of Education*,[264] the Supreme Court rejected the analogy between Title VII and §1983, inasmuch as exhaustion of administrative proceedings is not required for §1983. Thus, the word *proceeding* in §1988, unlike the same word in §706(k) of Title VII, does not include administrative proceedings which precede successful §1983 actions. Consequently, the plaintiff, a terminated teacher who had lost in an administrative proceeding but prevailed in court, was not automatically entitled to attorney's fees for the administrative proceeding. "Administrative proceedings established to enforce tenure rights created by state law simply are not any part of the proceedings to enforce §1983."[265]

The Court also went on to reject the plaintiff's argument[266] that he was entitled to fees for work performed in the administrative proceeding because that work was reasonably related to the subsequent successful §1983 action. Plaintiff did not show how any "discrete portion" of that work was useful and necessary for the §1983 litigation that followed. Thus, the district court did not abuse its discretion in refusing to award any fees for the administrative proceeding, especially given the "all or nothing" aspect of plaintiff's contention.

Justices Brennan and Blackmun agreed with the Court that attorney's fees for work in optional administrative proceedings were not automatically awardable and that such fees could be awarded only to the extent that the work was " 'useful and of a type ordinarily necessary' to the successful outcome of the subsequent litigation." However, they dissented as to the application of this standard to the case before them. In their view, the plaintiff showed that he was entitled to fees for at least some of the work relating to the hearings that were transcribed and relied on in litigating the §1983 action. Also, they contended that plaintiff did not in fact make an "all or nothing" fees argument.[267]

---

[263] Despite this possible analogy between Title VII and §1983, and even before the Court's decision in Webb v County Bd of Educ of Dyer County, 477 US 54 (1985), discussed in text, the Second Circuit held that attorney's fees were not available to a potential §1983 plaintiff who prevailed at the state administrative level. Blow v Lascaris, 668 F2d 670 (2d Cir 1982) (per curiam). To the same effect was Horacek v Thone, 710 F2d 496 (8th Cir 1983), which held that an attorney who represented a mentally retarded person at an administrative hearing was not entitled to fees under the Act. The *Gaslight Club* argument was rejected. *See also* Estes v Tuscaloosa County, 696 F2d 898 (11th Cir 1983), where the court rejected the fees claim of a plaintiff who had prevailed in an administrative proceeding before a county civil service board. Among other things, the Eleventh Circuit asserted that the Act did not create an action for damages independent of civil rights statutes such as §1983. *And see* Latino Project v City of Camden, 701 F2d 262 (3d Cir 1983), similarly ruling in a Title VI setting.

[264] 105 S Ct 1923 (1985).

[265] *Id* 1928.

[266] Pursuant to Hensley v Eckerhart, 461 US 424 (1983), discussed at **§1.25.**

[267] 105 S Ct at 1929-38.

Analogously, the Fifth Circuit[268] held that plaintiffs who were successful in a prior state *court* proceeding challenging taxing practices where they asserted state law grounds were not entitled to attorney's fees for that prior proceeding. In contrast, in a Ninth Circuit case,[269] attorney's fees were awarded for a state court proceeding, even though plaintiff was unsuccessful there, because that state proceeding was an essential part of the later federal proceeding (pursuant to *Pullman*[270] abstention) where plaintiff *was* successful.

§1.22   —Status of the Parties

The status of the parties[271] may be relevant to entitlement to an attorney's fees award. Thus, the plaintiff's status was significant in *Hughes v Rowe*[272] where the Court displayed special solicitude toward inmates who lose their §1983 suits when it reversed a district court's $400 fee award to the defendant correction officers who had been sued by the plaintiff inmate. Defendants' motion to dismiss for failure to state a claim had been granted with the Seventh Circuit agreeing that the suit was groundless. Among other things, the Court suggested that attorney's fees should "rarely" be awarded against an unsuccessful pro se inmate; such a litigant "should not be punished for his failure to recognize subtle factual or legal deficiencies in his claims."[273]

A defendant's status may also be relevant to the entitlement issue. In *Supreme Court v Consumers Union*,[274] the Supreme Court held that attorney's fees could not be awarded against the Virginia Supreme Court and its chief justice in the chief justice's official capacity in connection with challenged acts protected by absolute legislative immunity from suits for damages *and* injunctive relief. The Court stated that "[b]ecause the Virginia Court is immune from suit with respect to its legislative functions, it runs counter to that immunity for a district court's discretion in allowing fees to be guided by considerations centering on the exercise or non-exercise of the state court's legislative powers."[275] However, fees can be awarded against enforcement officials in their official capacities, including prosecutors successfully sued for prospective relief and

---

[268] Redd v Lambert, 674 F2d 1032 (5th Cir 1982). *See also* Greer v Holt, 718 F2d 206 (6th Cir 1983), where the court held that attorney's fees could not be awarded to the prevailing §1983 plaintiff for work done in successfully defending him in prior criminal proceedings, even though a victory in the criminal proceedings was considered necessary for the later §1983 action. According to the Sixth Circuit, the criminal proceedings were not a "proceeding to enforce" civil rights.

[269] Bartholomew v Watson, 665 F2d 910 (9th Cir 1982). *Bartholomew* was followed in Lampher v Zagel, 755 F2d 99 (7th Cir 1985) and Stathos v Bowden, 728 F2d 15 (1st Cir 1984).

[270] *See* §5.16.

[271] *See also* §1.24.

[272] 449 US 5 (1980) (per curiam). *See also* §1.16.

[273] *Id.*

[274] 446 US 719 (1980), also discussed at §7.12.

[275] *Id* 738-39.

state judges *exercising an enforcement role* who also are sued successfully for prospective relief. Because the Court did not reach the question of whether judges are absolutely immune from suit for prospective relief regarding their judicial acts, the related attorney's fees issue was not addressed beyond the observation that "the question of awarding attorney's fees against judges will not often arise."[276]

Thereafter, in *Pulliam v Allen*,[277] the Supreme Court, answering the question left open in *Consumers Union*, held that judges could be successfully sued for declaratory and injunctive relief in their official capacities for their judicial acts and could, moreover, have attorney's fees awarded against them under the Act in such suits.

The First Circuit held that a hearing was required on the question of fee entitlement and criticized the district court's procedures, saying: "[T]he summary disposition of the threshold question of entitlement in an informal unrecorded settlement conference followed by issuance of an order denying counsel fees without an adequate statement of the reasons for the order does not meet minimum standards of procedural fairness and regularity."[278] However, the court cautioned that it was not deciding that a formal evidentiary hearing is required whenever an award of attorney's fees is contested.[279]

§1.23 —Role 68 Offers of Judgment; Settlements and Ethical Issues

Rule 68 of the Federal Rules of Civil Procedure provides in relevant part that an adverse party may offer to allow judgment to be taken against him or her "with costs then accrued." If the offer is refused and the judgment finally obtained by the offeree is less favorable than the offer, "the offeree must pay the costs incurred after the making of the offer." If the offer is accepted, then the offeror must pay the costs accrued to the date of the offer. Because the Attorney's Fees Awards Act provides that attorney's fees are allowed "as a part of the costs," troublesome questions arise regarding the proper interpretation of Rule 68 and the Act.

---

[276] *Id* 735 n13.

[277] 466 US 522 (1984), also discussed at **§7.12**.

[278] Sargeant v Sharp, 579 F2d 645, 647 (1st Cir 1978). *See also* Iranian Students Assn v Sawyer, 639 F2d 1160 (5th Cir 1981) (entitlement to evidentiary hearing on prevailing party question: was plaintiffs' lawsuit a "significant catalyst"?).

[279] The propriety of a summary denial of fees is still open in the Supreme Court. In Consolidated Freightways Corp v Kassel, 456 US 1 (1982), the Supreme Court initially granted certiorari to decide the following question: "May a court, without articulating its rationale, summarily deny an application for attorney's fees under 42 U.S.C. §1988?" Thereafter it dismissed the writ as improvidently granted with Justice White dissenting on the ground that there is no per se rule prohibiting a court from summarily denying an application for fees. He therefore would have affirmed the decision of the Eighth Circuit.

In *Fulps v City of Springfield*,[280] for example, the defendants served an offer of judgment on two plaintiffs which specified dollar amounts for the plaintiffs and added "plus costs accrued to the date of this offer." The Sixth Circuit, relying in part on Justice Powell's separate concurring opinion in *Delta Air Lines v August*,[281] held that the defendants' offer to pay costs then accrued included reasonable attorney's fees. It stated: "[W]e conclude that Congress expressly characterized fees as costs [in the Act] with the intent that the recovery of fees be governed by the substantive and procedural rules applicable to costs."[282] The court went on to distinguish *Roadway Express Inc v Piper*[283] on the ground that in that case 28 USC §§1920 and 1927 were involved, while here the entitlement to "costs," including fees, arose from Rule 68. However, the court recognized that its interpretation could discourage Rule 68 offers in some cases "since attorney's fees are often a significant portion of the ultimate amount paid by defendants in civil rights actions."[284]

Another more important example is *Marek v Chesny*,[285] where the plaintiff rejected a Rule 68 offer of judgment of $100,000, including liability, costs, and attorney's fees of $32,000 then accrued. Thereafter, he obtained a jury verdict of $60,000 which, when added to the previously accrued costs and attorney's fees of $32,000, amounted to less than the $100,000 offer.[286] The Seventh Circuit addressed two questions: whether an offer of judgment including both liability and attorney's fees was valid, and, if it was, whether the prevailing plaintiff who rejected the offer could recover attorney's fees for work performed thereafter.

Answering the first question in the affirmative, the court observed that a different answer would render Rule 68 unusable in most cases involving statutes authorizing fee awards to prevailing plaintiffs, since many defendants would not want to run the risk of settling their cases in chief while leaving open the amount of fees. It also disagreed with the suggestion of Justice Powell in *Delta Air Lines v August*[287] that a Rule 68 offer including fees could create a conflict of interest between lawyers and clients in many cases.[288] The court

---

[280] 715 F2d 1088 (6th Cir 1983).

[281] 450 US 346 (1981).

[282] 715 F2d at 1093.

[283] 447 US 752 (1980) ("excess costs" under 28 USC §1927 do not include attorney's fees; §1927 was subsequently amended).

[284] 715 F2d at 1095.

[285] 105 S Ct 3012 (1985), *revg* 720 F2d 474 (7th Cir 1983).

[286] For a thoughtful discussion of how to apply Rule 68 in cases "which involve complex injunctive remedies rather than easily compared dollar damages," *see* Garrity v Sununu, 752 F2d 727, 731 (1st Cir 1984) (affirming district court's finding that judgment was more favorable than offer; latter was indefinite and ambiguous in some respects).

[287] 450 US 346 (1981).

[288] Several circuit courts earlier expressed concern or otherwise commented on the possible conflict of interest between lawyer and client when §1983 actions and attorney's fees claims are settled. Moore v National Assn of Secs Dealers, 762 F2d 1093 (DC Cir 1985); Jeff D v Evans, 743 F2d 648 (9th Cir 1934), *revd*, 106 S Ct 1531 (1986),

noted that such a potential conflict arises whenever a settlement offer is made where there is a contingent fee agreement. Thus, the settlement offer made by the defendants here was a valid one under Rule 68.

The Seventh Circuit also held, as to the second question, that the word *costs* in Rule 68 did not include attorney's fees where a statute authorized attorney's fees as costs recoverable by the prevailing party. Thus, the prevailing plaintiff here could get attorney's fees for work performed after the defendants' offer of judgment was rejected, even though it turned out that the offer was more favorable than what was in fact received ultimately. Emphasizing the policy of encouraging meritorious civil rights litigation underlying §1983, the court observed that if such attorney's fees could not be recovered,

> the plaintiff's lawyers would have either to collect an additional fee from the plaintiff, thus reducing his net recovery . . . , or to swallow the time they put in on the trial. Either way, the next time they are faced with a similar offer, they will have to think very hard before rejecting it even if they consider it inadequate. . . .[289]

In short, civil rights plaintiffs and their lawyers should not be placed in this "predicament," given the purposes of §1983.

However, the Supreme Court, in an opinion by Chief Justice Burger, reversed. It agreed with the Seventh Circuit that a Rule 68 offer was valid even if the offer did not itemize or separate damages and costs. This approach encouraged settlements because, otherwise, defendants would be reluctant to make settlement offers that did not represent their total liability.[290] As to whether attorney's fees were included in the costs covered by Rule 68, though, the Court rejected the Seventh Circuit's reasoning. The drafters of Rule 68 intended *costs* to include all the costs properly awardable in an action. Because §1988 provides that attorney's fees are awardable as costs to prevailing parties in §1983 and other civil rights litigation, attorney's fees are thereby covered by Rule 68 as well. Furthermore, not only was this Rule 68 policy neutral as between plaintiffs and defendants—because settlements were often in the best interest of civil rights plaintiffs—but Rule 68 was designed to encourage

---

discussed later in this section; White v New Hampshire Dept of Employment Sec, 629 F2d 697, 705 (1st Cir 1980), *revd on other grounds*, 455 US 445 (1982); Gagne v Maher, 594 F2d 336, 344 (2d Cir 1979), *affd*, 448 US 122 (1980); Nadeau v Helgemoe, 581 F2d 275, 281-82 (1st Cir 1978); Prandini v National Tea Co, 557 F2d 1015, 1021 (3d Cir 1977). *But see* Note, *Promoting the Vindication of Civil Rights Through the Attorney's Fees Awards Act*, 80 Colum L Rev 346, 361-63 (1980). Cf Committee on Professional & Judicial Ethics of New York City Bar Assn Op No 80-94, 50 USLW 2204 (Sept 20, 1981), which ruled unethical defense counsel proposals to settle civil rights litigation if plaintiff's counsel will waive statutorily authorized attorney's fees.

[289] 720 F2d at 478-79. The Seventh Circuit also contended that Fulps v City of Springfield, 715 F2d 1088 (6th Cir 1983), noted in the text, was not inconsistent: there, the issue was whether a settlement offer included attorney's fees, *not* whether Rule 68 might abrogate §1988's right to attorney's fees.

[290] *See* note 288 in connection with a possible conflict of interest between lawyer and client when settlements are being considered.

settlements by making parties "think very hard" about offers. Consequently, the prevailing plaintiff was not entitled to attorney's fees for work performed after the offer of judgment was rejected.[291]

In the circuits, questions have arisen regarding the interpretation of settlement agreements and the possible conflict between lawyer and client when §1983 actions are settled.[292] With regard to interpretation, according to the Third Circuit,[293] where the parties discussed and could not agree on attorney's fees during settlement talks, the fact that the settlement agreement was silent as to attorney's fees did not automatically deprive the prevailing plaintiff of fees. "[T]he burden is on the losing party to show that the settlement agreement clearly waived the statutory right to attorney's fees."[294] The Sixth Circuit[295] put the matter in intent terms when it observed that the omission in a settlement of any reference to fees does not necessarily mean that fees claims have not been settled. Rather, the Sixth Circuit stated, the proper question is "whether the parties intended to include attorney's fees in the settlement."

As to the ethical issues implicated in settlements, the Supreme Court recently decided *Evans v Jeff D*,[296] an important case involving the negotiated settlement

---

[291] Justices Powell and Rehnquist, concurring, joined in the opinion of the Court. Justice Powell had previously contended in *Delta Air Lines* that Rule 68 offers should itemize damages and attorney's fees, and Justice Rehnquist had previously argued, in the same case, that Rule 68 offers did *not* include attorney's fees as costs. Both, though, changed their positions on these issues in *Marek*.

Justices Brennan, Marshall, and Blackmun dissented. In effect, they adopted the position of the Seventh Circuit. They added, however, that the Court's approach was not at all neutral as between plaintiffs and defendants but rather favored defendants. Moreover, the Court's approach would not further the goal of uniformity because other fee-shifting statutes contained language different from that of §1988, which would therefore have to be separately interpreted for Rule 68 purposes. They also asserted that the Court's holding was inconsistent with *Roadway Express*.

[292] *See* also note 288 on this issue. The clearest case is one in which a defendant offers to settle the case in chief on terms highly favorable to the plaintiff on the condition that the plaintiff waive statutory attorney's fees. But the problem may arise whenever the case in chief and attorney's fees are considered together for settlement purposes.

[293] El Club Del Barrio Inc v United Community Corp, 735 F2d 98 (3d Cir 1984).

[294] *Id* 99.

[295] Jennings v Metropolitan Government, 715 F2d 1111, 1114 (6th Cir 1983). *Compare* Chicano Police Officers Assn v Stover, 624 F2d 127 (10th Cir 1980) (stipulated settlement which did not mention fees was ambiguous and should be construed on remand to ascertain the parties' intent; Judge Seth dissented, arguing against what he called improperly opening up a stipulated settlement) and Aho v Clark, 608 F2d 365 (9th Cir 1979) (consent decree did not mention fees; fees denied because an award of fees would alter the compromises that the parties had made, it would be unfair to the defendants, and defendants would not have agreed to the compromise had they believed plaintiffs would thereafter seek fees).

[296] 106 S Ct 1531 (1986) Justices Brennan, Marshall, and Blackmun dissented, arguing that permitting negotiated fee waivers was inconsistent with the congressional goal of attracting competent counsel. However, they agreed that simultaneous negotiation of fees and merits claims was permissible.

of a class action suit which granted prospective relief to the plaintiff class, where the defendants, Idaho public officials, insisted upon a waiver of attorney's fees as a condition of settlement. Plaintiffs' counsel resisted but, sensitive to the ethical implications of the matter, finally agreed to a waiver of fees only upon approval of the district court. The district court approved the settlement and thereafter denied fees based on the conditional waiver. Reversing, the Ninth Circuit held that the district court should not have approved the waiver of fees just because it was part of the settlement to which the parties had agreed. "[T]he [district] court has a duty to review the reasonableness of all the terms of class action settlement agreements, particularly those relating to attorney's fees."[297] This was especially true in light of the "clear public policy" of §1988 to award reasonable fees in civil rights cases. The Ninth Circuit mentioned that it generally "disapproved simultaneous negotiation of settlements and attorney's fees."[298]

The Supreme Court in turn reversed in an opinion by Justice Stevens. First, the Fees Act did not reflect congressional intent to bar "all fee waivers offered in connection with substantial relief on the merits." Second, the Court asserted, any such approach would adversely affect the vindication of civil rights in some cases "by reducing the attractiveness of settlement." In this regard the Court expressly approved the inclusion of attorney's fees in settlement negotiations regarding the case in chief. There was, in the Court's view, no ethical problem either with fee waivers in principle or with such simultaneous negotiations. The lawyer's ethical obligation is to serve his or her client loyally, not necessarily to seek a statutory fee award. Finally, according to the Court, the district court did not abuse its discretion by approving the settlement with the fee waiver. There was no indication that Idaho adopted a uniform policy of conditioning settlements on fee waivers or that defendants' conduct here was a vindictive attempt to discourage attorneys from representing civil rights plaintiffs.

The *Evans* issue is a troublesome one because of the interest on the one hand in encouraging settlements and the interest on the other—as reflected by §1988—in encouraging civil rights advocacy. The Court has now made clear under §1988 that negotiated fee waivers are not per se invalid and that simultaneous negotiation of fees and the merits is permitted. However one evaluates the Court's decision, at least some guidance to attorneys has finally been provided under the Fees Act. It remains to be seen, though, what effect *Evans* will in fact have on lawyers representing civil rights plaintiffs. This will depend in part on whether, despite the Court's decision, states determine *as a matter of state law* that the defense conduct involved in *Evans* is unethical.[299]

---

[297] Jeff D v Evans, 743 F2d 648, 650 (9th Cir 1984).

[298] *Id* 652.

[299] The dissenting Justices made this observation in *Evans* and further suggested that lawyers and their plaintiff clients might agree in advance and in writing that fees will not be waived.

§1.24 —For and Against Whom Fees May Be Awarded

Attorney's fees may be awarded according to appropriate factors even though the prevailing party is not charged for legal services received or is represented by publicly funded attorneys. The First Circuit stated: "Attorney's fees are, of course, to be awarded to attorneys employed by a public interest firm or organization on the same basis as to a private practitioner."[300] This rule was later announced by the Supreme Court in *Blum v Stenson*.[301] Further, fees can be assessed against a *state* or *local* governmental official sued successfully for damages in an individual capacity.

Until the Supreme Court's 1978 decision in *Hutto v Finney*,[302] it was not clear, because of the Eleventh Amendment,[303] whether fees could constitutionally be assessed under 42 USC §1988 against a *state* governmental official sued for declaratory or injunctive relief in an *official* capacity (where the state or state agency would have to pay those fees). However, the Court held in *Hutto* that the Eleventh Amendment is no bar to such an award under the Act even if the state itself is not a named party in the suit. Moreover, after the Court's decision in *Monell v Department of Social Services*[304] which held that local governmental

---

[300] Reynolds v Coomey, 567 F2d 1166, 1167 (1st Cir 1978). *See also* Mid-Hudson Legal Servs Inc v G&U Inc, 578 F2d 34 (2d Cir 1978); Torres v Sachs, 538 F2d 10 (2d Cir 1976). To the same effect are: Palmigiano v Garrahy, 616 F2d 598 (1st Cir 1980) (fees may be awarded to National Prison Project of the privately funded American Civil Liberties Union on the same basis as to private attorneys; court rejected the state's argument that a fees award was improper because the legal services organization was prohibited by the Legal Services Corporation's administrative guidelines from accepting "fee generating" cases); Watkins v Mobile Hous Bd, 632 F2d 565 (5th Cir 1980) (per curiam) and Oldham v Ehrlich, 617 F2d 163 (8th Cir 1980) (reduction in fees award to prevailing party simply because of representation by legal services association was in error); Leeds v Watson, 630 F2d 674 (9th Cir 1980) (fees award to prevailing plaintiffs not precluded by representation through legal services organization partially supported by public funds); Dennis v Chang, 611 F2d 1302 (9th Cir 1980) (prevailing plaintiffs entitled to fees from state even though they were represented by legal services organization funded in part by the state and providing services without cost; state's argument of "double payment" rejected).

[301] 465 US 886 (1984), discussed at §1.25. *See also* Shadis v Beal, 685 F2d 824 (3d Cir 1982) (holding void as against public policy contractual provisions forbidding a nonprofit legal services organization from requesting or accepting attorney's fees from Pennsylvania or its employees).

[302] 437 US 678 (1978). While some pre-*Hutto* cases held that the Eleventh Amendment did not bar attorney's fees against a state, *e.g.*, Rainey v Jackson State College, 551 F2d 672 (5th Cir 1977), others held the contrary, *e.g.*, Skehan v Board of Trustees of Bloomsburg College, 436 F Supp 657 (MD Pa 1977). In Maher v Gagne, 448 US 122, 130-31 (1980), discussed at §1.20, the Supreme Court reserved the question of whether a federal court can award attorney's fees under the Act against a state based solely on a §1983 federal statutory, non-civil rights claim.

[303] *See* §5.08 on the Eleventh Amendment.

[304] 436 US 658 (1978). *See* §1.09 on certain defendants as "persons" and **ch 6** on governmental liability.

entities are persons under §1983, fee awards may also be assessed against a local governmental official successfully sued for declaratory or injunctive relief in an *official capacity* (where the local government or its agency must pay the fees). That the Act is intended to allow fee awards against such defendants and thus against the relevant governmental entity as well is clear, as the Court noted in *Hutto*, because of the Act's broad language and its legislative history. The Court quoted from the Senate Report:

> [I]t is intended that the attorney's fees, like other items of costs, will be collected either directly from the official, in his official capacity, from funds of his agency or under his control, or from the State or local government (whether or not the agency or government is a named party.)[305]

It is important here, just as it is in a local government liability setting,[306] to distinguish carefully between individual or personal capacity suits and official capacity suits. As the court made clear in *Kentucky v Graham*,[307] liability on the merits and responsibility for fees go hand in hand. Hence, when an official is sued for damages in his or her individual or personal capacity, then that official is personally responsible for attorney's fees as well as damages if the suit is successful. Similarly, when a official is sued for damages in his or her official capacity, then, assuming the governmental defendant is a proper party, proper notice, and proof of an official custom or policy, that suit is in effect a suit against the governmental entity[308] and the latter is responsible for attorney's fees if the suit is successful. Accordingly, in *Graham* itself, where the federal damages action was found to have been directed against state employees in their individual capacities alone because of the Eleventh Amendment bar to

---

[305] *Hutto v Finney*, 437 US at 694 (1978), quoting from S Rep No 1011, 94th Cong, 2d Sess 5 (1976) (footnotes omitted), *reprinted in* 1976 US Code Cong & Ad News 5908, 5913. Suppose, however, that a state refuses to pay. In Gates v Collier, 616 F2d 1268 (5th Cir 1980), the Fifth Circuit, confronted with such a case, upheld the district court's order adding Mississippi's auditor and treasurer as defendants and directing the other defendants to submit a requisition to the auditor for the issuance of a warrant upon the treasurer to satisfy the attorney's fees award out of certain state funds. The court asserted that it could use any of the methods generally at its disposal in enforcing judgments to ensure compliance by state officials. To the same effect is Gary v Louisiana, 622 F2d 804 (5th Cir 1980), where Louisiana unsuccessfully attempted to rely on a provision of its constitution prohibiting the payment of judgments against it except from funds appropriated for that purpose by the legislature. *See also* Spain v Mountanos, 690 F2d 742 (9th Cir 1982) where the district court was found to have equitable authority under Rule 70 of the Federal Rules of Civil Procedure to order state officials to pay a fees award after the state legislature had refused to do so. Execution against state property or funds was not the exclusive avenue, even though the state controller against whom the order was issued by the district court was required to act in violation of state law.

[306] *See* §§6.04-6.07 & 6.14.

[307] 105 S Ct 3099 (1985).

[308] Brandon v Holt, 105 S Ct 873 (1985). *See* §§6.05-6.16 on the requirement of an unconstitutional official policy or custom for local government liability.

suing a state in federal court,[309] the Court ruled that the state could not be held liable for attorney's fees. *Hutto* was consistent, the Court asserted, because there the state defendants, prison officials, had been sued in their official capacities for injunctive relief, a suit seeking institutional changes which was in effect successfully brought against the prison itself.

Thus, the various defendants, individual and governmental, against whom fees may be awarded under the Act are as follows:

1. A state or local governmental official in an individual or personal capacity where plaintiff is successful in an action for *damages* against such official in that capacity

2. A local governmental entity where plaintiff is successful in an action for *damages* against that entity because an official policy or custom was proved, and where either the local government was sued directly or its official was sued for damages in an *official* capacity[310]

3. A local governmental entity where plaintiff is successful in obtaining *declaratory* or *injunctive relief* against that entity through proof of an official policy or custom, and where either the local government was sued directly or its official was sued for such relief in an official capacity. In this situation, fees are assessed in effect only against the governmental entity and not against the governmental official in an individual capacity; only where that governmental official litigates in bad faith is it appropriate to award fees against the official in an individual capacity. The Supreme Court emphasized this in *Hutto* when it said, referring to the Act's legislative history: "Awards against the official in his individual capacity, in contrast, were not to be affected by the statute; in injunctive suits they would continue to be awarded only 'under the traditional bad faith standard recognized by the Supreme Court in *Alyeska*' "[311]

4. A state or local government official in an individual or personal capacity where plaintiff is successful in obtaining *declaratory* or *injunctive* relief against the official in an *official* capacity but there is *no proof* of an official policy or custom. This result appears to follow from *Graham* with its assertion that fees liability follows merits liability

As noted earlier,[312] the Supreme Court held in *Supreme Court v Consumers Union*[313] that attorney's fees could not be awarded against the Virginia Supreme Court and its chief justice in his official capacity as to certain challenged acts

---

[309] *See* §§**5.08, 6.20.**

[310] Justice Brennan suggested in his concurring opinion in *Hutto,* 437 US at 701, that a state should be considered a person for §1983 purposes and could thus be sued for damages, because §1983 was intended by Congress to operate as a waiver of the states' Eleventh Amendment immunity from suit in the federal courts. *See* §**6.20.** *See generally* **ch 6** on governmental liability.

[311] 437 US at 701.

[312] §**1.22.**

[313] 446 US 719 (1980), also discussed at §**7.12.**

protected by absolute *legislative* immunity. However, fees could be awarded for other challenged acts of an *enforcement* nature which were unprotected by absolute immunity. This, too, demonstrates that a party's attorney's fees responsibility is premised on a finding of that party's liability on the merits. Similarly, in *Pulliam v Allen*,[314] the Supreme Court held that attorney's fees could be awarded against judges successfully sued for declaratory and injunctive relief in connection with their *judicial* acts. *Pulliam* was rather clearly an official capacity suit.[315] It might be thought, therefore, that the defendant magistrate in *Pulliam* was not personally responsible for the attorney's fees award: those fees were to be paid from government funds. However, governmental liability was not involved in *Pulliam;* the challenge was to the practice of the individual defendant magistrate although it was an official capacity suit. Also, while the Court did not make the matter clear, the implication of the *Pulliam* opinion is that the magistrate was to pay personally. If this is so, then a distinction must be drawn for fees purposes between injunctive relief official capacity suits which are directed against a governmental body and those which are directed only against the defendant officials. This would be consistent with the Court's assertion in *Graham* that fees responsibility accompanies liability on the merits.[316]

Attorney's fees under §1988 are awarded against the losing party and not against his or her attorney. However, attorney's fees awards are made against attorneys on other grounds. In *Roadway Express Inc v Piper*,[317] the Fifth Circuit had vacated the district court's order assessing attorney's fees against the Title VII plaintiffs' *attorneys.* Though it agreed with the district court's finding that plaintiffs' attorneys had acted in a "vexatious manner," it held that §1988 authorized fee awards only against unsuccessful *parties*, not their attorneys.

---

[314] 466 US 719 (1984), also discussed at **§7.12.**

[315] This is clear from the affirmed Sixth Circuit opinion, 690 F2d 376 (1982).

[316] Otherwise, every successful injunctive relief official capacity suit, regardless of whether the plaintiff proved an official policy or custom, would result in governmental liability for attorney's fees. This result appears foreclosed by *Pulliam* and *Graham.*

These issues are beginning to trouble the circuits. *See* Kolar v County of Sangamon, 756 F2d 564 (7th Cir 1985) (successful damages action against county sheriff in his official capacity was a suit against the county for fees purposes; to avoid future confusion, unless otherwise stated in the complaint, a suit against a government official will be considered an official capacity suit); Glover v Alabama Dept of Corrections, 753 F2d 1569 (11th Cir 1985) (damages award against state official in his individual capacity gave rise to fees award against state because defendant represented by state attorney general; this decision is no longer good law after *Graham*); Leggett v Badger, 759 F2d 1556 (11th Cir 1985) (damages award against state prison guard in his individual capacity gave rise to fees award against state because defendant represented by state attorney general; *Glover* followed; this decision, like *Glover,* does not survive *Graham*); Odum v Clark, 748 F2d 1538 (11th Cir 1984) (successful injunctive relief action against sheriff and deputy sheriff in their official capacities entitled plaintiffs to fees award against county under the rationale of *Hutto*; county attorney who represented defendants never argued that the defendants' conduct did not represent official county policy).

[317] 447 US 752 (1980), *affg* 599 F2d 1378 (5th Cir 1979).

Also, relying on 28 USC §1927 which at the time so provided, the Fifth Circuit had stated that, while there could be an assessment against plaintiffs' attorneys for the "excess costs" generated by their unreasonable and vexatious conduct, those "excess costs" could not include attorney's fees.

The Supreme Court affirmed the Fifth Circuit's interpretation of §§1927 and 1988. It remanded, however, for the district court to consider the question of whether plaintiffs' attorneys should be liable for attorney's fees under either Federal Rule of Civil Procedure 37(b), authorizing sanctions for failure to comply with discovery orders, or the district court's inherent power to impose sanctions for willful abuse of judicial processes. In response to *Roadway Express*, however, Congress amended §1927 in 1980 to provide explicitly that attorneys can indeed be personally liable for attorney's fees resulting from their conduct in multiplying the proceedings in any case "unreasonably and vexatiously."[318]

It should also be noted that Rule 11 of the Federal Rules of Civil Procedure authorizes district courts to impose sanctions upon attorneys and their clients for certain improper conduct relating to pleadings, motions, and other papers. These sanctions may include attorney's fees and other expenses. Rule 11 and related matters are discussed elsewhere.[319]

In the circuits, the emerging rule is that prevailing pro se plaintiffs who are not lawyers are not entitled to attorney's fees.[320] However, prevailing pro se parties who are lawyers have been allowed to recover fees.[321] The Fifth Circuit stated that attorneys may appeal from a denial of attorney's fees to their clients,[322] while the Second Circuit asserted that it is the prevailing party who has standing to make a fees claim; a lawyer can do so only with the client's consent.[323] An intervening party can be a prevailing party entitled to fees,[324] as can a state.[325]

---

[318] Pub L No 96-349, 33, 94 Stat 1156 (1980). Fees were awarded under this statute against attorneys in Hagerty v Succession of Clement, 749 F2d 217 (5th Cir 1984) and Limerick v Greenwald, 749 F2d 97 (1st Cir 1984).

[319] *See* **§1.15.** *See also* Chu by Chu v Griffith, 771 F2d 79 (4th Cir 1985) (Rule 11 sanctions ordered); Eastway Constr Corp v City of New York, 762 F2d 243 (2d Cir 1985) (Rule 11 sanctions ordered); Rodgers v Lincoln Towing Serv Inc, 771 F2d 194 (7th Cir 1985) (Rule 11 sanctions ordered).

[320] Turman v Tuttle, 711 F2d 198 (10th Cir 1983) (per curiam) (a "majority of the circuits" so hold); Owens-El v Robinson, 694 F2d 941 (3d Cir 1982); Cofield v City of Atlanta, 648 F2d 986 (5th Cir 1981) (put in terms of congressional purpose); Davis v Parratt, 608 F2d 717 (8th Cir 1979) (per curiam); *See also* Owen v Lash, 682 F2d 648, 649 n 10 (7th Cir 1982) (question left open).

[321] Duncan v Poythress, 750 F2d 1540 (11th Cir 1985) (prevailing plaintiff) *affd,* 777 F2d 1508 (11th Cir 1985) (en banc) (extensive policy analysis); Ellis v Cassidy, 625 F2d 227 (9th Cir 1980) (prevailing defendant).

[322] Lipscomb v Wise, 643 F2d 319 (5th Cir 1981) (per curiam).

[323] Brown v General Motors Corp, 722 F2d 1009 (2d Cir 1983).

[324] United States v Board of Educ, 605 F2d 573 (2d Cir 1979) (Title VII case).

[325] People of New York v 11 Cornwell Co, 718 F2d 22 (2d Cir 1983) (en banc) (Judge Lumbard dissented).

In a First Circuit case[326] dealing with the question of who should pay attorney's fees, plaintiffs had successfully sued city officials for declaratory and injunctive relief in their challenge to the constitutionality of certain state statutes regulating bars and restaurants. Affirming the district court's fees award against the city alone, the First Circuit rejected the argument that the state should pay fees because it was a state statute that had been held facially invalid. First, the city enforced the statute. Second, there would be serious practical problems involved in tracing the "cost dollar back to the most appropriate 'tax pot.' " Third, the state was not an indispensable party within the meaning of Rule 19(a) of the Federal Rules of Civil Procedure; complete relief—the award of fees—could be provided without the state. Finally, the state had not attempted to enforce the statute and had declined to intervene in the lawsuit.

Where the United States was successfully sued under §1983 for engaging in a conspiracy with a school board, the Fifth Circuit[327] held that it could be liable for attorney's fees under the Equal Access to Justice Act.[328] Section 2412(b) of that Act incorporated §1988, which in turn was the basis for the United States' fees liability here. However, postjudgment interest on §2412(b) fee awards was not authorized.

§1.25   —How Fees Are Determined

Circuit courts review district court fee awards according to the standard of abuse of discretion.[329] In cases arising shortly after the Act became effective, several circuits made clear the following:

1.   Attorneys seeking fees under the Act should file extensive work schedules with the relevant details set out[330]

2.   District courts should scrutinize such schedules and issue findings of fact and conclusions of law,[331] although "the inquiry into the adequacy of the fee [should not] assume massive proportions, perhaps even dwarfing the case in chief"[332]

---

[326] Venuti v Riordan, 702 F2d 6 (1st Cir 1983).

[327] Knights of the KKK v East Baton Rouge Parish School Bd, 735 F2d 895 (5th Cir 1984).

[328] 28 USC §2412 *et seq.*

[329] Henderson v Fort Worth Indep School Dist, 574 F2d 1210 (5th Cir 1978); Johnson v Georgia Highway Express Inc, 488 F2d 714 (5th Cir 1974) (1964 Civil Rights Act case).

[330] King v Greenblatt, 560 F2d 1024 (1st Cir 1977); Rainey v Jackson State College, 551 F2d 672 (5th Cir 1977).

[331] Fountila v Carter, 571 F2d 487 (9th Cir 1978).

[332] Lindy Bros Builders Inc v American Radiator & Standard Sanitary Corp, 540 F2d 102, 116 (3d Cir 1976) (a much-cited private antitrust case extensively discussing fee awards in general).

Even though the abuse of discretion standard of appellate review appears rather narrow and deferential, district courts are often reversed by their circuits because they did not use and properly evaluate the correct factors in determining a "reasonable" amount of fees to be awarded.

Fees may be awarded for work both at the trial level and the appellate level,[333] and can range from the hundreds of dollars[334] to the hundreds of thousands of dollars.[335] An early First Circuit decision stated that the reasonableness of fees under the Act should be determined using the same factors used in determining fees in other types of complex federal litigation.[336] Rejecting the low fee schedule of the Criminal Justice Act of 1964,[337] the First Circuit, relying on *Johnson v Georgia Highway Express, Inc,*[338] a much-cited Fifth Circuit Title VII decision, instead asserted that the following factors should be taken into account:

1. The time and labor required
2. The novelty and difficulty of the questions
3. The skill necessary to do the legal work well
4. The preclusion of other employment by the attorney because of work on the case
5. The customary fee
6. Whether the fee is fixed or contingent
7. Time limitations
8. The amount involved and the results obtained
9. The experience, reputation, and ability of the attorney
10. The "undesirability" of the case
11. The nature and length of the professional relationship with the client
12. Awards in similar cases[339]

Alternatively, a Third Circuit private antitrust case, frequently cited in civil rights fee litigation, suggested that a district court first determine fees in terms

---

[333] Hutto v Finney, 437 US 678 (1978); Kimbrough v Arkansas Activities Assn, 574 F2d 423 (8th Cir 1978); Green v Ten Eyck, 572 F2d 1233 (8th Cir 1978); Rainey v Jackson State College, 551 F2d 672 (5th Cir 1977).

[334] Kimbrough v Arkansas Activities Assn, 574 F2d 423 (8th Cir 1978) ($200 for appellate work).

[335] Pennsylvania v O'Neill, 431 F Supp 700 (ED Pa 1977) (almost $200,000, with approximately $150,000 to one firm), *affd,* 573 F2d 1301 (3d Cir 1978).

[336] King v Greenblatt, 560 F2d 1024 (1st Cir 1977), *cert denied,* 98 S Ct 3146 (1978).

[337] The Criminal Justice Act of 1964 provided for fee rates of $30 per in-court hour and $20 per out-of-court hour. 18 USC §3006A *et seq* (as amended 1984).

[338] 488 F2d 714 (5th Cir 1974) (1964 Civil Rights Act case), also relied upon by the Ninth Circuit in Fountila v Carter, 571 F2d 487 (9th Cir 1978).

[339] King v Greenblatt, 560 F2d 1024, 1026-27 (1st Cir 1977), *cert denied,* 98 S Ct 3146 (1978).

of hours worked and normal billing rates and then modify this *lodestar* amount by the contingent nature of success and the quality of the work done.[340]

These two methods of computation—the *Johnson* approach and the *lodestar* approach—are complementary and not in fact inconsistent with one another. This is reflected in the recent use by the Supreme Court in *Hensley v Eckerhart*[341] of the lodestar approach while at the same time noting that the *Johnson* approach is relevant to adjusting the lodestar amount. The lodestar approach has been used by the District of Columbia, First, Second, Third, Fifth, and Seventh Circuits.[342]

Using these approaches in cases decided prior to recent attorney's fees case law of the Supreme Court, circuit courts occasionally awarded premiums to attorneys because of the complexity of the litigation involved[343] and, conversely, refused to do so and reduced district court awards where the legal issues were few and simple, although the factual issues were complex.[344] Where a plaintiff prevailed on some but not all claims, some courts awarded fees covering the unsuccessful aspects of litigation as well as the successful ones.[345] Others adopted a rather rigid pro rata formula for apportioning fees such that, for example, a plaintiff who prevailed on one of four issues was entitled to an award of one-quarter of reasonable attorney's fees.[346] The latter approach was criticized not only for being unrealistic in terms of how attorneys prepare cases, but for discouraging plaintiffs' attorneys from being creative.[347]

The Third Circuit early rejected this rigid apportionment approach, saying: "We think experience in litigation teaches that there is no necessary percentage relationship between the number of claims and contentions presented in a

---

[340] Lindy Bros Builders v American Radiator & Standard Sanitary Corp, 540 F2d 102 (3d Cir 1976). For further elaboration of this approach, *see* Hughes v Repko, 578 F2d 483 (3d Cir 1978).

[341] 461 US 424 (1983), discussed later.

[342] Institutionalized Juveniles v Secretary of Pub Welfare, 758 F2d 897 (3d Cir 1985) (extensive discussion); Lynch v City of Milwaukee, 747 F2d 423 (7th Cir 1984); Riddell v National Democratic Party, 712 F2d 165 (5th Cir 1983); Wheatley v Ford, 679 F2d 1037 (2d Cir 1982); Copeland v Marshall, 641 F2d 880 (DC Cir 1980) (en banc) (several judges dissented); Furtado v Bishop, 635 F2d 915 (1st Cir 1980). *See also* Northcross v Board of Educ, 611 F2d 624 (6th Cir 1979) (a pre-*Hensley* case adopting an "analytical approach" and rejecting a "list of factors" approach).

[343] Pennsylvania v O'Neill, 431 F Supp 700 (ED Pa 1977) (almost $200,000 in fees), *affd*, 573 F2d 1301 (1978). *Compare* Hensley v Eckerhart, 461 US 424 (1983), discussed later.

[344] Beazer v New York City Transit Auth, 558 F2d 97 (2d Cir 1977).

[345] Guajardo v Estelle, 432 F Supp 1373 (SD Tex 1977), *affd on this ground,* 580 F2d 748 (5th Cir 1978) finding that fees in connection with a settlement ultimately not entered into were proper under the Act.

[346] Hughes v Repko, 429 F Supp 928 (WD Pa 1977), *revd,* 578 F2d 483 (3d Cir 1978).

[347] Lipson, *Beyond Alyeska - Judicial Response to the Civil Rights Attorneys' Fees Act,* 22 St Louis ULJ 243, 260 (1978). After *Hensley,* it is also not good law.

lawsuit and the lawyer time spent on each."[348] Instead, it concluded that district courts should consider the results obtained by the petitioning party on particular claims regardless of the number of parties, determine whether the party "essentially succeeded" on various claims, and then give the prevailing party "credit only for the hours of legal service reasonably supportive of such claims."[349] A somewhat broader approach was suggested by a California district court; considering whether the "legal work [is] reasonably calculated to advance . . . clients' interest."[350]

Extent of Plaintiff's Success

The Supreme Court in a series of significant decisions, recently dealt with these and other computation issues. In *Hensley v Eckerhart*,[351] the first of these cases, the Court ruled that "the extent of a plaintiff's success is a crucial factor in determining the proper amount of an award of attorney's fees under 42 U.S.C. §1988." Through their attorneys, the prevailing plaintiffs, involuntarily committed mental patients, claimed 2,985 hours worked and sought payment of approximately $150,000 at rates ranging from $40 to $65 per hour. They also sought a premium of 30 per cent to 50 per cent, for a total of $195,000 to $225,000. Defendants opposed the request and argued, among other things, that fees should not be awarded for time spent on unsuccessful claims. The district court awarded over $133,000, reducing one attorney's hours and refusing to grant plaintiffs a premium. The Eighth Circuit affirmed. Granting certiorari, the Supreme Court vacated and remanded. It stated:

> We hold that the extent of a plaintiff's success is a crucial factor in determining the proper amount of an award of attorney's fees under 42 U.S.C. §1988. Where the plaintiff has failed to prevail on a claim that is distinct in all respects from his successful claims, the hours spent on the unsuccessful claim should be excluded in considering the amount of a reasonable fee. Where a lawsuit consists of related claims, a plaintiff who has won substantial relief should not have his attorney's fee reduced simply because the district court did not adopt each contention raised. But where the plaintiff achieved only limited success, the district court

---

[348] Hughes v Repko, 578 F2d 483, 486 (3d Cir 1978). *See also* Familias Unidas v Briscoe, 619 F2d 391 (5th Cir 1980) (fees awarded to prevailing plaintiffs should be based only on work performed on issues on which they succeed, but where preparation for successful and unsuccessful claims overlaps, fees should be awarded for this work); Jones v Diamond, 594 F2d 997, 1026-27 (5th Cir 1979) (implicitly rejecting a rigid pro rata formula for apportioning fees); Brown v Bathke, 588 F2d 634 (8th Cir 1978) ("Attorney's fees for a claim which is reasonably calculated to advance a client's interests should not, however, be denied solely because that claim did not provide the precise basis for the relief granted").

[349] 578 F2d at 486-87.

[350] Stanford Daily v Zurcher, 64 FRD 680, 684 (ND Cal 1974), *affd,* 550 F2d 464 (9th Cir 1977) (cited with approval in S Rep No 11, 94th Cong, 2d Sess *reprinted in* 1976 US Code Cong & Ad News 5908, 5913), *revd on other grounds,* 436 US 547 (1978).

[351] 461 US 424 (1983).

should award only that amount of fees that is reasonable in relation to the results obtained.[352]

In its opinion the Court rejected any mechanical apportionment of fees based on the success or failure of particular issues. It also emphasized the importance of an attorney's filing time records, as well as the need for a district court, in the exercise of its discretion when awarding fees, to make clear that it has considered the relationship between the results obtained and the fee awarded. Because the district court in *Hensley* had not considered the question of what a reasonable fee was, given the plaintiffs' level of success, the case was remanded.

Chief Justice Burger concurred, asserting the importance to lawyers of extensive billing time records.[353] However, Justices Brennan, Marshall, Blackmun, and Stevens concurred in part and dissented in part.[354] They agreed that the extent of a plaintiff's success is relevant to determining what is a reasonable fee, but contended that several other factors, omitted in the Court's opinion, are also significant. These include the time-value of money (because of delays in payment to attorneys) and the prelitigation likelihood that claims which in fact did prevail would prevail. These Justices suggested that the proper approach to determining whether a fee is reasonable is to ask whether it would induce other attorneys to represent similarly situated clients seeking comparable relief. Further, they argued that the district court's award in *Hensley* was reasonable and should not be vacated. Otherwise, they suggested, this case and other fees litigation will be unduly prolonged to the detriment of prevailing civil rights plaintiffs in general.

Prevailing Market Rates and Upward Adjustments

In *Blum v Stenson*,[355] another important fees computation case, the Court held that Congress clearly intended that prevailing parties be awarded attorney's fees calculated by the use of prevailing market rates, regardless of whether such parties were represented by nonprofit legal service organizations or private attorneys. It rejected as contrary to the legislative history of §1988 the argument that fees should be calculated on a cost-based standard. However, the Court cautioned that "the burden is on the fee applicant to produce satisfactory evidence—in addition to the attorney's own affidavits—that the requested rates are in line with those prevailing in the community for similar services by lawyers of reasonably comparable skill, experience and reputation."[356] Because the Legal Aid Society of New York, which had successfully represented the prevailing plaintiffs, had established that its hourly rates ranging from $95 per hour to $105 per hour for the claimed 801.75 hours billed

---

[352] *Id* 440-41.

[353] *Id.*

[354] *Id.*

[355] 465 US 886 (1984).

[356] *Id* 896 n 11.

were reasonable, the district court did not err in calculating the "initial" fees award at $79,312.

The Court went on, though, to rule that the district court erred in providing a 50 per cent upward adjustment to the $79,312 amount on the grounds that "the issues were novel, the litigation was complex and the results were of far reaching significance to a large class of people [a statewide class of Medicaid recipients]."[357] For one thing, the novelty and complexity of the issues were "fully reflected" in the number of billable hours. Also, any special skill and experience were reflected in the reasonableness of the hourly rates. For another, there was no showing that plaintiffs' success was exceptional and the undertaking "risky." The fact that a large number of persons were greatly benefited was not shown to warrant an upward adjustment, especially since this consideration, according to the Court, would ordinarily be subsumed within other factors used to calculate a reasonable fee. In short, the plaintiffs failed to carry their burden of justifying an upward adjustment.

Justices Brennan and Marshall concurred, emphasizing that in their view "the risk of not prevailing, and therefore the risk of not recovering any attorney's fees, is a proper basis on which a district court may award an upward adjustment to an otherwise compensatory fee."[358] They also noted that the Court had expressly left this question open.[359]

Attorney's fees are not, as mentioned earlier,[360] available under §1988 for administrative proceedings. In *Webb v County Board of Education*,[361] the case so holding, the Supreme Court went on to observe that under the rationale of *Hensley* fees can be awarded for a "discrete portion" of such work to the extent that it was "useful and of a type ordinarily necessary" to the successful outcome of the later §1983 litigation.[362] The burden is on the prevailing plaintiff to make such a showing.

The fact that the Court has decided these and other attorney's fees cases in a relatively short period reflects its increasing sensitivity to the growing numbers of such cases in the district courts and the circuit courts of appeal with the consequent expenditure of a significant amount of judicial and private resources.[363] Confronted with a broadly phrased pro-civil rights attorney's fees statute, the Court has attempted to provide guidelines so as to avoid windfalls to attorneys. However, these guidelines must of necessity be generally articulated, with the result that most of the important attorney's fees decision making will take place in the lower federal courts.

---

[357] *Id* 898.

[358] *Id* 902.

[359] *Id* 893 n 17.

[360] **§1.21.**

[361] 105 S Ct 1923 (1985).

[362] *Id* 1929. In an opinion dissenting in part, Justices Blackmun and Brennan discussed the application of this standard in some detail.

[363] *See* Gabriele v Southworth, 712 F2d 1505 (1st Cir 1983) where the First Circuit lamented that "the fee part of this litigation has long since outdistanced the substantive part."

Damages and Fees Awards

In this connection, the *Hensley* approach is especially ambiguous. To be sure, *Hensley* made clear that a plaintiff who prevails on some but not all claims will have this taken into account in the fees award. But suppose a plaintiff, who seeks damages in a §1983 case, proves a constitutional violation but recovers only nominal damages and has substantial although reasonable attorney's fees. Is the prevailing plaintiff—or the plaintiff's lawyer, if the case was taken on a contingent fee basis—to recover very little, if anything, in the way of attorney's fees, or should the full amount of a reasonable attorney's fee be awarded? If the primary purpose of the 1976 Act was to promote the vindication of constitutional rights, then it would appear that the full reasonable attorney's fee ought to be awarded. On the other hand, *Hensley* indicates that the results obtained are relevant to the amount of fees awarded.

Clarifying the matter to some extent, the Supreme Court recently handed down *City of Riverside v Rivera*,[364] which dealt with the relation between damages and fees awards. Here, the Ninth Circuit had upheld a district court fees award of $243,343.75 where damages of only $33,500 were awarded. The Court similarly affirmed, although there was no majority opinion.

Justice Brennan, joined by Justices Marshall, Blackmun, and Stevens, found that the district court had properly applied the *Hensley* factors. They also ruled that *Hensley's* lodestar approach is appropriate even where its use in a monetary damages case results in fees that exceed damages recovered. They thus rejected the contention that fee awards in damages cases should be modeled upon the contingent fee arrangements commonly used in personal injury litigation. In their view, this was entirely consistent with the purposes of §1988, including the enforcement of civil rights laws through fee awards adequate to attract competent counsel. Such a result, moreover, would not result in a windfall for lawyers, because they are compensated at a reasonable rate and only for time reasonably expended. Justice Powell concurred in the judgment, observing simply that affirmance was required by the district court's detailed findings of fact. Justice Rehnquist dissented, joined by Chief Justice Burger and Justices O'Connor and White. After characterizing the plurality's interpretation of *Hensley* as "revisionist," they criticized the alleged failures of the district court to take account of "billing judgment" and to consider the "results obtained." Section 1988 was not, they maintained, designed to be a lawyer's "relief act."

After *City of Riverside*, it is clear that the Court is split on the application of the *Hensley* factors in certain damages cases. However, all of the Justices agree that the contingent fee model is inappropriate for the determination of fees.

The important question of the effect of Rule 68 offers of judgment on attorney's fees computation is discussed elsewhere.[365]

In the circuits, there has been an explosion of litigation dealing with

---

[364] City of Riverside v Rivera, 106 S Ct 2686 (1986), *affg* Rivera v City of Riverside, 763 F2d 1580 (9th Cir 1985).

[365] §1.23.

attorney's fees issues, including the computation issues considered here.[366] However, the following observations may be offered. After *Hensley*, it is clear that nominal damages may result in a reduction in the fee award,[367] but not necessarily in nominal fees.[368] The circuits, following *Blum*, have been confronted with the question of which market rates to use for determining fees awards, with the possibilities including normal versus community versus national,[369] plaintiff's home district versus forum district,[370] and historic or trial rates versus current rates.[371] Also after *Blum*, the circuits are wary of the use of premiums and multipliers for the benefit of prevailing plaintiffs, with upward adjustments currently the exception, not the rule.[372] For this purpose, total success does not equal exceptional success.[373] Similarly, a lawyer is not entitled to a premium or enhancement just because he or she was governed by a standard of perfection.[374] With respect to the *Hensley* requirement that a distinction must be drawn between time spent on unsuccessful *unrelated* claims and unsuccessful *related* claims, the Seventh Circuit stated that "an unsuccessful claim will be *un*related to a successful claim when the relief sought on the unsuccessful claim is intended to remedy a course of conduct entirely distinct and separate from the course of conduct that gave rise to the injury on which the relief granted is premised."[375]

---

[366] For a comprehensive analysis and application of *Hensley* and *Blum, see* Institutionalized Juveniles v Secretary of Pub Welfare, 758 F2d 897 (3d Cir 1985).

[367] Nephew v City of Aurora, 766 F2d 1464 (10th Cir 1985) ($12,500 fees award excessive where $2,000,000 damages award sought but only nominal damages were awarded).

[368] *Id;* Lynch v City of Milwaukee, 747 F2d 423 (7th Cir 1984); Perez v University of PR, 600 F2d 1 (1st Cir 1979). *See also* §1.25 on the relationship between nominal damages and prevailing party status.

[369] Laffey v Northwest Airlines, 746 F2d 4 (DC Cir 1984) (normal rates, not higher community rates); Louisville Black Police Officers Org Inc v City of Louisville, 700 F2d 268 (6th Cir 1983) (community rates used, not national rates).

[370] Polk v New York State Dept of Correctional Servs, 722 F2d 23 (2d Cir 1983) (choice of either plaintiff's home district or forum district).

[371] New York State Assn for Retarded Children Inc v Carey, 711 F2d 1136 (2d Cir 1983) (historic rates, not current rates, should be used for multiyear cases); Morgado v Birmingham-Jefferson County Civil Defense Corps, 706 F2d 1184 (11th Cir 1983) (same); Suzuki v Yuen, 678 F2d 761 (9th Cir 1982) (in light of inflation and time elapsed since trial, trial rates should not be used).

[372] *E.g.*, McKinnon v City of Berwyn, 750 F2d 1383 (7th Cir 1985); Garrity v Sununu, 752 F2d 727 (1st Cir 1984); Hall v Borough of Roselle, 747 F2d 838 (3d Cir 1984); *In re* Illinois Congressional Dists Reapportionment Cases, 704 F2d 380 (7th Cir 1983). On the other hand, the use of a "negative multiplier because the damage award is low is error if the award is typical of awards in the same type of case." Di Filippo v Morizio, 759 F2d 231, 236 (2d Cir 1985).

[373] Jones v Central Soya Co, 748 F2d 586 (11th Cir 1984).

[374] Grendel's Den Inc v Larkin, 749 F2d 945 (1st Cir 1984).

[375] Mary Beth G v City of Chicago, 723 F2d 1263, 1279 (7th Cir 1983). *Compare* Illinois Welfare Rights Org v Miller, 723 F2d 564 (7th Cir 1983), which applied *Hensley* in a rather unique combined summary judgment and settlement case.

§1.26   —Services Performed; Contingent Fee Agreements

Attorney's fees may be awarded for time spent by a plaintiff's attorney in postjudgment monitoring of a court order[376] and in litigating fees issues.[377] On the latter point though, the Seventh Circuit expressed some reservations when it affirmed a district court's denial of the prevailing plaintiff's claim for additional fees for time spent in litigating his original claim for fees following remand after his first appeal. It stated:

> For rather obvious practical reasons we are loath to disturb a ruling by a district judge on a request for second-round attorneys' fees. The consequence if we should reverse and remand for an award of additional fees is all too predictable: however little the plaintiff is awarded on remand he will move the district court to award him attorneys' fees for the time spent in prosecuting this appeal, and if the district court denies his motion he will be back up here. Every civil rights litigation will be like a nest of Chinese boxes. The outside box is the litigation of the civil rights issue itself. Within it is the litigation over the fees incurred in the litigation over the merits—ordinarily a lesser litigation, as our metaphor implies, though in this case the stakes in each of the two rounds of fee litigation have been greater, at least in monetary terms, than the stakes in the original civil rights litigation. Within the initial fee litigation will be another litigation—usually a smaller one, here again a bigger one—over the attorneys' fees incurred by the plaintiff in the initial fee litigation. And so on without necessary end.[378]

A reasonable attorney's fee includes "expenses of litigation that are distinct from either statutory costs or the costs of the lawyer's time reflected in his hourly billing rates—expenses for such things as postage, long distance calls, xeroxing, travel, paralegals, and expert witnesses. . . ."[379] And at least one circuit held, after extensive discussion, that the 1976 Act authorizes federal courts to add postjudgment interest to attorney's fees awards, although not to out-of-pocket costs.[380]

There has been considerable discussion in the circuits regarding the effect

---

[376] *E.g.*, Garrity v Sununu, 752 F2d 727 (1st Cir 1984).

[377] *E.g.*, Cruz v Hauck, 762 F2d 1230 (5th Cir 1985); Jones v Stack, 758 F2d 567 (11th Cir 1985) (where fee counsel is retained by the attorney who thereafter succeeds in obtaining fees for the initial proceeding, then the latter should supplement his or her own fee application to include costs incurred in retaining fee counsel; fee counsel lacks standing); Bagby v Beal, 606 F2d 411 (3d Cir 1979); Weisenberger v Huecker, 593 F2d 49 (6th Cir 1979).

[378] Muscare v Quinn, 680 F2d 42, 44 (7th Cir 1982).

[379] Heiar v Crawford County, 746 F2d 1190, 1203 (7th Cir 1984) (joining other circuits on the matter).

[380] Gates v Collier, 616 F2d 1268 (5th Cir 1980) (reliance for its "liberal approach" on legislative history and on cases interpreting the 1976 Act; Judge Hill dissented).

of a contingent fee agreement on attorney's fees computation. In a leading Tenth Circuit case, *Cooper v Singer*,[381] a panel initially ruled that the district court erred in denying fees to the prevailing plaintiffs because they had a contingent fee contract with their attorney. However, the agreed fee would serve as the maximum allowable fee under §1988 unless it was unreasonably high, in which case it should be reduced to a reasonable amount. Judge Holloway dissented, arguing that if a reasonable fee exceeded the agreed-upon amount, the plaintiff should be compensated up to the contractual amount, with the attorney getting the remainder. On rehearing en banc, the Tenth Circuit reversed the panel decision. Extensively discussing relevant case law and relying on the Supreme Court's decision in *Hensley*, the court ruled that "the existence of a contingent fee agreement should neither prohibit the fee award nor limit its amount. We also conclude that Congress intended that the section 1988 fee award would fulfill the plaintiff's fee obligations."[382] Thus, a contingent fee which was lower than a reasonable fee would not prevent an award of the higher fee. But a contingent fee which was higher than a reasonable fee would not be awarded; rather, the lower reasonable fee would be awarded.

While the Seventh and Eighth Circuits similarly agree that a contingent fee agreement is not an automatic ceiling on a fees award,[383] the Sixth Circuit[384] stated that absent extraordinary circumstances, an attorney's fees award should not exceed the amount that an attorney agreed to charge the client. The Eleventh Circuit[385] also treated the contingent fee as the limit on a fees award. And where the amount determined by the contingent fee agreement was greater than a reasonable attorney's fee, the Third Circuit[386] ruled that the plaintiff should pay the difference between the two fees. The Ninth Circuit held,[387] rejecting the apparent position of the Eleventh Circuit,[388] that the

---

[381] 719 F2d 1496 (10th Cir 1983) (en banc), *revg* 689 F2d 929 (10th Cir 1982). See also City of Riverside v Rivera, 106 S Ct 2686 (1986), discussed at **§1.25,** which ruled that the contingent fee model is inappropriate for the determination of fees awards.

[382] 719 F2d at 1503. In a Third Circuit case which addressed the effect of contingent fee agreements upon statutory fees awards, the court observed that many circuits had determined that the "statutory fee should be paid to plaintiff's lawyer with any lesser contingency fee considered satisfied." In the case before it, the court remanded for the purpose of awarding the greater of the statutory fee or the contingent fee. If the statutory fee turned out greater, the plaintiff would be entitled to his full damages award with his contingent fee obligation satisfied. If the contingent fee turned out greater, plaintiff would pay his attorney only the difference between the two. This was not a case warranting a dual fees award. Sullivan v Crown Paper Bd Co, 719 F2d 667 (3d Cir 1983).

[383] Sisco v JS Alberici Constr Co, 733 F2d 55 (8th Cir 1984); Lenard v Argento, 699 F2d 874 (7th Cir 1983). The Third Circuit took the same position. Sullivan v Crown Paper Bd Co, 719 F2d 667 (3d Cir 1983).

[384] United States v Slodov, 675 F2d 808 (6th Cir 1982).

[385] Pharr v Housing Auth, 704 F2d 1216 (11th Cir 1983).

[386] Sullivan v Crown Paper Bd Co, 719 F2d 667 (3d Cir 1983).

[387] Hamner v Rios, 769 F2d 1404 (9th Cir 1985). The Ninth Circuit went on to characterize the positions of the Second Circuit in Wheatley v Ford, 679 F2d 1037 (2d Cir 1982) and the Tenth Circuit in Cooper v Singer, 719 F2d 1496 (10th Cir 1983) (en banc) as treating the statutory fee as the ceiling on a fee award, even if the contingent fee amount would be greater. 769 F2d at 1408-09.

losing defendant must pay any difference between the statutory fee amount and the contingent fee. However, the Ninth Circuit emphasized that a district court has discretion to limit the attorney to the lower statutory award where performance is particularly bad or the contingent fee amount would constitute a windfall to the attorney.

In general, there appears to be a growing insistence upon the need for contemporaneous attorney's records for fees purposes.[389] Furthermore, the Eighth Circuit, obviously as weary as other circuits are of the increasing numbers of attorney's fees cases on appeal, asserted in its supervisory capacity that it would thereafter defer to the district court's exercise of discretion in awarding fees unless there was a misapplication of relevant legal standards. The court's well-taken warning is worth setting out fully:

> Our concern centers on the large number of cases on our docket alleging an abuse of the district court's discretion which are based simply on the amount of an attorneys' fee award. Such appeals often lack substance and hinder the prompt disposition of more meritorious appeals. The dockets of all federal courts are overcrowded. We suggest to the bar and to individual counsel that as officers of the court, lawyers have a responsibility in limiting litigation over attorneys' fees. Most fee cases can be processed through amicable negotiation and agreement; the district courts should not become the inevitable haven for adversary proceedings concerning attorneys' fees.
>
> Good faith negotiations do not always achieve a resolution satisfactory to all parties, and we do not criticize suits based on fee claims that cannot be resolved through mediation efforts. Appeal of the district court's fee determination should be taken only where the district court allegedly has misapplied the applicable law. Appeals contending that the district court abused its discretion in determining the amount awarded ordinarily do not require oral argument and will be decided without argument by a three-judge screening panel. If the court holds an appeal is frivolous and not brought in good faith, the court may properly exercise sanctions relating to costs and attorneys' fees.[390]

§1.27   Costs

Subject to the district court's discretion, costs are recoverable by the prevailing party in §1983 litigation just as in other federal litigation. Pursuant to federal statute, taxable costs include clerk and marshal fees, court reporters'

---

[388] Pharr v Housing Auth, 704 F2d 1216 (11th Cir 1983).

[389] E.g., Grendel's Den Inc v Larkin, 749 F2d 945 (1st Cir 1984); New York State Assn for Retarded Children Inc v Carey, 711 F2d 1136 (2d Cir 1983) (described as a prerequisite for a fees award).

[390] Moore v City of Des Moines, 766 F2d 343, 346 (8th Cir 1985).

fees, printing and some witness fees, copying fees, and certain docket fees.[391] A Pennsylvania district court decision also awarded expert witness fees as costs, although the award was not specifically authorized by federal statute, saying: "[T]here is an increasing body of decisional authority approving the award of additional costs in cases in which equitable principles warrant such an award . . . I am in agreement with these [collected] cases insofar as they award expert witness fees as costs."[392] Such fees can, of course, be substantial.

In *Roadway Express Inc v Piper*,[393] the Supreme Court held that 28 USC §1927, which authorizes federal courts to require attorneys who increase litigation costs unreasonably and vexatiously to "satisfy personally such excess costs," did not include attorney's fees in those "excess costs." However, in response to *Roadway Express*, Congress in 1980 amended §1927 to provide explicitly that attorneys can indeed be personally liable for attorney's fees when they increase litigation costs "unreasonably and vexatiously."[394]

Also, as discussed earlier,[395] Rule 11 of the Federal Rules of Civil Procedure authorizes the award of expenses as sanctions against attorneys and their clients for improper conduct relating to pleadings, motions, and other papers.

---

[391] 28 USC §§1920, 1923. *See also* Jones v Diamond, 594 F2d 997, 1028 (5th Cir 1979), where the court, exercising its discretion, refused to award to prevailing plaintiffs "costs incurred in late or dilatory tactics which contributed nothing to the appropriate resolution of the case."

[392] Pennsylvania v O'Neill, 431 F Supp 700, 713 (ED Pa 1977), *affd*, 573 F2d 1301 (3d Cir 1978); cases collected at 431 F Supp at 713. Th the same effect are Berry v McLemore, 670 F2d 30 (5th Cir 1982) and Walker v Robbins Hose Co, 622 F2d 692 (3d Cir 1980) (assumed *arguendo*). *Compare* Jones v Diamond, 594 F2d 997, 1028-29 (5th Cir 1979), which stated as a general rule that federal courts have no authority to award as costs expert witness fees in excess of the statutory per diem and mileage allowance set out in 28 USC §1821.

[393] 447 US 752 (1980) discussed at **§1.24.**

[394] Pub L No 96-349, §33, 94 Stat 1156 (1980).

[395] *See* **§§1.16 & 1.24.**

The "deprivation [under "color of" law] of any rights, privileges, or immunities secured by the Constitution and laws"

2

§2.01 Summary

42 USC §1983, enacted by Congress pursuant to section 5 of the Fourteenth Amendment,[1] creates an action for damages[2] and injunctive relief[3] against individuals[4] and governmental bodies[5] who deprive a plaintiff of rights, privileges, or immunities "secured by the Constitution and laws." In order to establish a prima facie §1983 cause of action based on a constitutional

---

[1] *See* §1.03.

[2] Damages are discussed in **ch 4.**

[3] Declaratory and injunctive relief are discussed in **ch 5.**

[4] Some individuals, however, are absolutely immune from §1983 damages liability, including state legislators, judges, and prosecutors. *See* **ch 7.**

[5] See **ch 6** on governmental liability.

violation,[6] the plaintiff must prove that the defendant's conduct was a cause in fact[7] of plaintiff's constitutional deprivation. Such constitutional deprivations may include violations of Fourteenth Amendment guarantees standing alone, as, for example, procedural due process and equal protection; violations of those provisions of the Bill of Rights which are incorporated by the due process clause of the Fourteenth Amendment and made applicable to the states; violations of constitutional rights, based on the due process clause, which are not explicitly mentioned in the Constitution, such as the rights of access to the courts and of privacy; and violations of the right to travel interstate which is protected by the privileges and immunities clause of the Fourteenth Amendment.[8] In order to establish a prima facie §1983 cause of action in connection with federal statutory rights or "laws," the plaintiff must similarly prove that defendant's conduct was a cause in fact of plaintiff's own statutory deprivation.[9] The Court has decided several important laws cases which take an intermediate position on the potential use of federal statutory violations as a basis for §1983 actions.

Whether a Fourteenth Amendment violation or a federal statutory violation is alleged, §1983 requires that the challenged conduct be "under color of law." This means that color of law is a condition precedent to stating a §1983 claim.[10] The color of law inquiry is so closely related to the Fourteenth Amendment's state action requirement that when state action is present, the color of law requirement is also met. It is relatively easy to find state action where the individual official clearly acted in an official capacity in a manner authorized by state law. It is somewhat more difficult to find, although the Supreme Court has already done so,[11] where the individual official acted in an official capacity but in a manner not authorized by state law. The hardest state action problems of all arise where private persons or entities act in a situation where government is also involved.

The Supreme Court has set out several tests to determine whether such nominally private conduct is to be treated as if it were state action.[12] Two of these tests, the symbiotic relationship test and the state function test, have been limited by the Court as reflected in its use of a so-called nexus test which increasingly dominates the Court's state action analysis. This has not escaped the attention of the circuits which, following the Court's lead, have begun to

---

[6] State of mind, or basis of liability, requirements for a prima facie §1983 constitutionally based claim are discussed in **ch 3.** Individual and governmental defenses and immunities are discussed in **chs 6, 7, & 8.**

[7] Cause in fact in connection with individual and governmental liability is discussed at **§§3.18 & 6.06,** respectively. *See also* **§4.02.**

[8] *See* **§2.03.** The Supreme Court has also approved the use of §1983 in connection with alleged racial discrimination in voting which violates the Fifteenth Amendment. Lane v Wilson, 307 US 268 (1939).

[9] *See* **§2.12.**

[10] *See* **§§2.04-2.10** on color of law and state action.

[11] Monroe v Pape, 365 US 167 (1961).

[12] *See* **§§2.04-2.07.**

cut back on findings of state action. One major exception to this trend are cases involving the private use of state enforcement schemes in certain circumstances.[13] Another is the Court's holding that a private person conspiring with an absolutely immune defendant acts under color of law.[14]

§2.02   Section 1983 and the Fourteenth Amendment: *Monroe v Pape*

Restrictive application of the state action doctrine,[15] a narrow reading of the Fourteenth Amendment's privileges and immunities clause,[16] a similarly narrow reading of §1983's jurisdictional counterpart,[17] and the Court's refusal to incorporate completely the provisions of the Bill of Rights[18] were jointly responsible for the dormancy of §1983 from the time of its enactment[19] to the year 1961. However, the picture began to change dramatically in that year, largely because of the broad scope given §1983 by the Supreme Court in *Monroe v Pape*.[20]

Monroe was a §1983 damages action brought against police officers[21] who allegedly entered plaintiff's home without warning and forced the occupants to stand naked while the entire house was ransacked. Plaintiff was thereafter arrested, but was released without being charged. Reversing the dismissal of this suit, the Supreme Court found that a §1983 cause of action was stated even though the police officers misused their authority in a manner inconsistent with state law. This behavior, according to the Court, still constituted action taken "under color of law." A Fourteenth Amendment violation was properly asserted because defendants had allegedly violated plaintiff's incorporated

---

[13] *See* Lugar v Edmondson Oil Co, 457 US 922 (1982) discussed at **§2.06.**

[14] Dennis v Sparks, 449 US 24 (1980). *See also* Tower v Glover, 467 US 914 (1984), discussed at **§7.15,** holding that public defenders accused of conspiring with other officials act under color of law.

[15] Civil Rights Cases, 109 US 3 (1883).

[16] Slaughter-House Cases, 83 US (16 Wall) 36 (1873), limiting clause to privileges and immunities of national, not state, citizenship. One such privilege and immunity is apparently the right to travel interstate. The Bill of Rights is not among the privileges and immunities of national citizenship. Twining v New Jersey, 211 US 78 (1908).

[17] Eisen v Eastman, 421 F2d 560, 563 (2d Cir 1969), *cert denied,* 400 US 841 (1970); Hague v CIO, 307 US 496, 531 (1939) (concurring opinion by Justice Stone).

[18] *E.g.,* Adamson v California, 332 US 46 (1947). Since then, however, selective incorporation of most of the provisions of the Bill of Rights has carried the day. *See* **§2.03.**

[19] *See* **§1.03.**

[20] 365 US 167 (1961).

[21] The City of Chicago was also a defendant, but the Court held that it was not a *person* under §1983. This holding in *Monroe* was overruled in 1978 in Monell v Department of Social Servs, 436 US 658 (1978). *See* **ch 6.**

Fourth Amendment rights.[22] The Court further held that specific intent to deprive a person of a federal right is not required in order to state a §1983 claim; rather, the "background of tort liability" must be taken into account.[23] Finally, a §1983 plaintiff need not first exhaust state judicial remedies before proceeding in a federal forum with a §1983 claim.[24]

Monroe meant that much official conduct previously thought not to be actionable under §1983 was now within its scope. Continuing this broadening trend, later Supreme Court decisions incorporated more and more provisions of the Bill of Rights into the Fourteenth Amendment,[25] held that §1983 and its jurisdictional counterpart covered deprivations of property rights as well as personal rights,[26] and asserted that exhaustion of state judicial and administrative remedies was not required for §1983 purposes.[27] Only recently has this trend been slowed considerably, if not altogether halted.[28]

The relation between §1983 and the Fourteenth Amendment is best described as very close. *Monroe* and early cases[29] indicate that the section makes Fourteenth Amendment violations actionable, whether for damages or injunctive relief. Consequently, Fourteenth Amendment interpretation significantly determines the scope of the prima facie cause of action under §1983 for claimed constitutional violations.[30]

§2.03   The Fourteenth Amendment

Fourteenth Amendment violations include violations of procedural due process and equal protection.[31] They also include violations of the due process-based rights of access to the courts[32] and privacy,[33] as well as the right

---

[22] *See* **§2.03.**

[23] The implications of this conclusion for §1983 actions are discussed in **ch 3.**

[24] *Monroe,* 365 US at 183. *See* **§§5.06-5.08** on exhaustion of state remedies generally.

[25] *See* **§2.03.**

[26] Lynch v Household Fin Corp, 405 US 538 (1972).

[27] McNeese v Board of Educ, 373 US 668 (1903). *See* **§5.07.**

[28] For example, absolute immunity has been extended to state legislators, judges, and prosecutors, see **ch 7;** actual damages probably have to be proved in all §1983 damage actions, see **ch 4;** respondeat superior cannot be used in §1983 cases, see **chs 3 & 6;** and numerous obstacles confront the §1983 plaintiff seeking declaratory and injuctive relief, see **ch 5.** On the other hand, local government bodies are now "persons" and thus amenable to suit under §1983, see **ch 6.**

[29] *E.g.,* Hague v CIO, 307 US 496 (1939). *See also* Lane v Wilson, 307 US 268 (1939) involving a §1983 action against government officials who discriminated on racial grounds in violation of the Fifteenth Amendment.

[30] *See* **ch 3.**

[31] The due process and equal protection guarantees appear on the face of the Fourteenth Amendment. See **§§3.08 & 3.11** on basis of liability for procedural due process and equal protection, respectively.

[32] *E.g.,* Boddie v Connecticut, 401 US 371 (1971). *Compare* Ortwein v Schwab, 410 US 656 (1973) (per curiam) and United States v Kras, 409 US 434 (1973), in which the Court limited the scope of the right of access to the courts. *See* **§3.10.**

to travel interstate which is apparently protected by the privileges and immunities clause.[34] Conduct which infringes upon these Fourteenth Amendment rights may be actionable under §1983. Furthermore, state or local official conduct which infringes upon certain provisions of the Bill of Rights may similarly be actionable under §1983, where the Fourteenth Amendment incorporates those provisions.[35] This, in effect, constitutes a kind of "double incorporation" approach:[36] §1983 incorporates the Fourteenth Amendment which in turn incorporates various provisions of the Bill of Rights and applies them to the states.

The Supreme Court has held the following provisions of the Bill of Rights to be applicable to the states through the Fourteenth Amendment, with the same constitutional standards governing the states as govern the federal government:[37]

1. Freedom of speech, press, assembly, and petition under the First Amendment[38]
2. Free exercise and establishment of religion under the First Amendment[39]
3. Protection against unreasonable searches and seizures under the Fourth Amendment[40]
4. Protection against double jeopardy and self-incrimination, and the right to just compensation, under the Fifth Amendment, but not the grand jury clause[41]

---

[33] *E.g.,* Roe v Wade, 410 US 113 (1973); Griswold v Connecticut, 381 US 479. *See* **§3.09.**

[34] Shapiro v Thompson, 394 US 618 (1969); Edwards v California, 314 US 160, 171 (1941) (concurring opinion).

[35] On their face, the provisions of the Bill of Rights apply only to the federal government. Applying some provisions to the states through due process incorporation means that such provisions are encompassed in the term "liberty" which appears in the due process clause.

[36] *See* Shapo, *Constitutional Tort: Monroe v. Pape and the Frontiers Beyond,* 60 N W UL Rev 277 (1965), where this term was coined.

[37] The only exception, *arising out of a split Supreme Court,* relates to the Sixth Amendment right to jury trial. A split Court held that while this right applies to the states in the same way it applies to the federal government, nonunanimous juries may convict in the states although only unanimous juries may convict in federal trials. Johnson v Louisiana, 406 US 356 (1972); Apodaca v Oregon 406 US 404 (1972).

[38] Hague v CIO, 307 US 496 (1939) (petition); De Jonge v Oregon, 299 US 353, (1937) (assembly); Near v Minnesota 283 US 697 (1931) (press); Fiske v Kansas, 274 US 380 (1927) (speech).

[39] Everson v Board of Educ, 330 US 1 (1947) (establishment); Cantwell v Connecticut, 310 US 296 (1940) (free exercise).

[40] Mapp v Ohio, 367 US 643 (1961); Wolf v Colorado, 338 US 25 (1949).

[41] Benton v Maryland, 395 US 784 (1969) (double jeopardy); Malloy v Hogan, 378 US 1 (1964) (self-incrimination); Chicago B&Q RR v Chicago, 166 US 226 (1897) (just compensation); Hurtado v California, 110 US 516 (1884) (grand jury clause not incorporated).

5.   Right to speedy, public, and impartial jury trial and right to notice, confrontation, compulsory process, and counsel under the Sixth Amendment,[42] but not the Seventh Amendment's guarantee of a jury trial in a civil case[43]

6.   Freedom from cruel and unusual punishment and from excessive bail under the Eighth Amendment[44]

§2.04   State Action in the Supreme Court

In order for the §1983 plaintiff to state a cause of action based on a Fourteenth Amendment violation, the challenged conduct must constitute both color of law and state action. This requirement stems from the section's "color of law" limitation as well as from the state action language of the Fourteenth Amendment itself. For all practical purposes, according to the Supreme Court, "color of law" and state action are the same where Fourteenth Amendment violations are involved[45] and mean that §1983 regulates state and local governmental conduct, as distinct from purely private conduct. This state action requirement has occasionally been referred to as jurisdictional,[46] but that designation is incorrect. Rather, state action is a necessary element of the prima facie §1983 cause of action, and goes to jurisdiction no more than any other finding in a §1983 case that no Fourteenth Amendment violation has occurred.[47]

The easy cases in which to find state action are those where a state employee acting on behalf of the state pursuant to state authority thereby brings about plaintiff's constitutional deprivation. Whether it is damages or declaratory or injunctive relief which is being sought, there is no serious question about the existence of state action in such cases. Somewhat more difficult to deal with are those cases in which misuse or abuse of the official position of a state employee occurs when the employee acts in a manner inconsistent with state authority. However, in *Monroe v Pape,* [48] the Supreme Court held that because

---

[42] Washington v Texas, 388 US 14 (1967) (compulsory process); Klopfer v North Carolina, 386 US 213 (1967) (Speedy trial); Pointer v Texas, 380 US 400 (1965) (confrontation); Gideon v Wainwright, 372 US 335 (1963) (counsel); Irvin v Dowd, 366 US 717 (1961) (impartial jury); *In re* Oliver, 333 US 257 (1948) (public trial and notice).

[43] Minneapolis & St Louis RR v Bombolis, 241 US 211 (1916).

[44] Schilb v Kuebel, 404 US 357 (1971) (excessive bail); Robinson v California, 370 US 660 (1962) (cruel and unusual punishment).

[45] Lugar v Edmondson Oil Co, 457 US 922 (1982), discussed at §2.06; Adickes v Kress & Co, 398 US 144 (1970). *See,* however, Justice Brennan's concurring opinion in the latter.

[46] *E.g.,* Robinson v Bergstrom, 579 F2d 401 (7th Cir 1978).

[47] *E.g.,* Carter v Norfolk Community Hosp Assn, 761 F2d 970 (4th Cir 1985) (state action goes to the merits).

[48] 365 US 167 (1961). *See* §2.02; *see also* Screws v United States, 325 US 91 (1945), also concerning ultra vires violation of due process rights of prisoner, held to be action under color of law; United States v Classic, 313 US 299 (1941), involving ultra vires

such conduct is state action, it constitutes action taken under "color of law" for §1983 damages purposes.

The hardest state action cases, though, are those in which a private person or entity acts with some governmental involvement. The question then becomes whether such private conduct ought to be treated *as if it were* governmental conduct. The answer is important not only because the requirements of the Fourteenth Amendment might then regulate such private conduct, but also because of the significance in our society of the distinction between the public and private sectors.

There are no hard and fast rules for determining the presence of state action. Indeed, the Supreme Court has emphasized repeatedly that the state action inquiry must be made on a case-by-case basis.[49] Despite this emphasis on individual cases, certain generalizations are still possible. State action exists (1) where the state and the private party or entity maintain a sufficiently interdependent or symbiotic relationship;[50] (2) where the state requires, encourages, or is otherwise significantly involved in nominally private conduct;[51] and (3) where the private person or entity exercises a traditional state function.[52] On the other hand, it is also true that extensive state regulation, funding, or subsidization of an otherwise private entity is not, without more, sufficient to render that entity's conduct state action. There must be a *nexus* between the challenged conduct and the state.[53] For the same reason, furthermore, a statute's giving a choice to a private person does not automatically convert that person's conduct into state action.[54] Moreover, only certain state functions, when delegated to and exercised by private persons, constitute state action.[55]

Occasionally, the Court has misapplied its own state action doctrines because of its concern with the policy implications of its decisions. For example, in *Martinez v California*, [56] the Court held that a claim by decedent's survivors that the defendant parole board officials were liable for damages for their negligent and reckless decision to release one Thomas, who killed decedent five months later, did not state a §1983 cause of action. In a short opinion by Justice Stevens, the Court stated, first, that it was not the state but rather Thomas who

---

interference by officials with the right to vote in a state congressional primary, held to be action under color of law; Home Tel & Tel Co v Los Angeles, 227 US 278 (1913) dealing with injunctive relief under the Fourteenth Amendment.

[49] "Only by sifting facts and weighing circumstances can the nonobvious involvement of the State in private conduct be attributed its true significance." Burton v Wilmington Parking Auth, 365 US 715, 722 (1961).

[50] *E.g.,* Burton v Wilmington Parking Auth, 365 US 715 (1961).

[51] *E.g.,* Lombard v Louisiana, 373 US 267 (1963).

[52] *E.g.,* Marsh v Alabama, 326 US 501 (1946); Smith v Allwright, 321 US 649 (1944).

[53] *E.g.,* Jackson v Metropolitan Edison Co, 419 US 345 (1974).

[54] *E.g.,* Flagg Bros v Brooks, 436 US 149 (1978).

[55] Burton v Wilmington Parking Auth, 365 US 715 (1961).

[56] 444 US 277 (1980). The Court probably did the same in Polk County v Dodson, 454 US 312 (1981). *See* **§2.08.**

had "deprived" the decedent of life. Thus, the requisite state action was absent. Second, the decedent's death was "too remote a consequence of the parole officers' action to hold them responsible under the federal civil rights law."[57]

The Court's brief mention of the absence of state action is somewhat misdirected. The challenged conduct in *Martinez* was the parole decision of the defendants, conduct which is clearly state action. Had the parolee Thomas been a §1983 defendant, then the reference to the absence of state action would have been appropriate. What the Court should have said more clearly was that, while the parole board's challenged decision was state action, that decision did not render the defendants accountable under §1983 for decedent's death. Put another way, the defendants' decision was not the *proximate cause* of decedent's death. In this light, *Martinez* is not a state action case but rather is essentially a §1983 proximate cause case. The Court so indicated by its description of decedent's death as "too remote a consequence" of defendants' action to hold them liable. This aspect of *Martinez* is discussed elsewhere.[58]

State action and color of law issues typically arise in connection with state and local governments. However, in *Lake Country Estates Inc v Tahoe Regional Planning Agency*,[59] the Court held that the officials of an interstate-compact planning agency created by California and Nevada, and approved by Congress, acted "under color of state law" in discharging their agency duties.

§2.05   The Symbiotic Relationship and Governmental Involvement Approaches

The leading Supreme Court decision using the interdependent or symbiotic

---

[57] 444 US at 285.

[58] *See* §**3.16.** Cf Arnold v IBM, 637 F2d 1350, 1356 (9th Cir 1981) where the plaintiff sued a corporation and several of its employees in connection with his arrest on charges of stealing corporate documents and trade secrets, and the search of his residence. Affirming the district court's grant of summary judgment in favor of the defendants, the Ninth Circuit first observed that the Supreme Court in *Martinez v California* was able to use a proximate cause approach to state action because

> [i]f the actions of the state officers are not the proximate cause of the plaintiff's injuries, then there is no state action.
>
> [But] [t]he similarity between proximate cause and state action often disappears when the defendants are private parties, rather than state officials. . . . Here, [plaintiff's] injuries were the result of state action. State officials performed the acts of arresting, searching and indicting about which [plaintiff] complains. [While] [s]ome circuits have examined the liability of private persons involved in police arrests in terms of state action . . . . [i]n this case, however, the question before us is whether there is any evidence that the private defendants . . . caused those acts to occur within the meaning of [§ 1983].

Finding no such evidence of proximate causation–defendants neither controlled the police nor directed them to take action against plaintiff—the Ninth Circuit ruled for the defendants.

[59] 440 US 391 (1979), also discussed at §**7.05** in connection with legislator immunity.

relationship approach is *Burton v Wilmington Parking Authority,*[60] which involved the refusal of a privately owned restaurant to serve a black. The restaurant was located in an off-street automobile parking facility owned and operated by a state agency, and was the agency's lessee. Finding state action, the Court emphasized the following factors:

1. Public ownership of the land and building
2. The leased areas constituted an important part of the state's plan to keep the unit self-sustaining
3. Upkeep and maintenance were the state's responsibility
4. Restaurant guests were provided a convenient place to park
5. Profits earned by discrimination were indispensable elements in the financial success of the state agency

The Court then concluded:

> Addition of all these activities, obligations and responsibilities of the Authority, the benefits mutually conferred, together with the obvious fact that the restaurant is operated as an integral part of a public building devoted to a public parking service, indicates that degree of state participation and involvement in discriminatory action which it was the design of the Fourteenth Amendment to condemn.[61]

A second and closely related approach to state action focuses on the extent of state requirement or encouragement of, or other involvement in, the nominally private conduct. Where, for example, a state requires private persons to discriminate on racial or religious grounds, then that private conduct is clearly state action for purposes of a Fourteenth Amendment (and §1983) challenge.[62] This may be an explanation of the leading and troublesome case of *Shelley v Kraemer,*[63] where the Court invalidated as violative of equal protection a state judicial decree enforcing a racially restrictive covenant against a white property owner who wanted to sell his property to a black. It should be emphasized, however, that *Shelley* has not been interpreted by the Supreme Court as rendering all private discrimination state action simply because it is enforced through judicial decree.[64]

Even extensive state regulation, however, is not sufficient under this approach to convert the regulated entity's conduct into state action. Thus, in

---

[60] 365 US 715 (1961).

[61] *Id* 724.

[62] Adickes v Kress & Co, 398 US 144, 170 (1970). The symbiotic relationship in *Burton* may be seen as an extreme case of governmental involvement under this second approach.

[63] 334 US 1 (1948).

[64] Cf Bell v Maryland, 378 US 226 (1964), one of a group of "sit-in" cases decided by the Court in 1963 and 1964. *See* J. Nowak, R. Rotunda & J. Young, Constitutional Law 510 (2d ed 1983).

Jackson v Metropolitan Edison Co,[65] the Court held that a public utility's termination of service to a customer without a final hearing was not state action even though the utility had monopoly status and was extensively regulated. Emphasizing that the regulatory body had not ordered the challenged practice, the Court observed: "[T]he inquiry must be whether there is a sufficiently close nexus between the State and the challenged action of the regulated entity so that the action of the latter may be fairly treated as that of the State itself."[66] Similarly, the Court held in *Moose Lodge v Irvis*[67] that the racially discriminatory policies of a private club were not attributable to the state even though the club had a liquor license which subjected it to state regulation.

In this connection, the Court in *Flagg Brothers v Brooks*[68] refused to find state action in a proposed sale by a warehouseman of goods entrusted to him for storage pursuant to state statutory authorization. Relying on *Jackson* and *Moose Lodge,* the Court noted that it

> has never held that a State's mere acquiescence in a private action converts that action into that of the State. . . . It is quite immaterial that the State has embodied its decision not to act in a statutory form. . . . Here, the State of New York has not compelled the sale of a bailor's goods, but has merely announced the circumstances under which its courts will not interfere with a private sale.[69]

Two recent Supreme Court state action cases, one dealing with schools and the other with nursing homes, demonstrate the Court's continuing insistence on a nexus and its resistance to expanding the scope of *Burton's* symbiotic relationship test. In *Rendell-Baker v Kohn,*[70] former staff members of a small, nonprofit school sued under §1983 claiming that their discharges were violative of the First Amendment. The school, organized as a nonprofit corporation under state law, was located on private property; was operated by a board of directors, none of whom was a government official or was chosen by any government or official; had students (with drug, alcohol, behavioral, or other problems) referred by various government bodies; was authorized to issue high school diplomas certified by a town's school committee; had received in recent years approximately 90 per cent of its funding from various government sources; was required to comply with various governmental regulations covering many aspects of operation as a condition of funding; and had received a state grant for a vocational program for students.

Finding no state action, the First Circuit rejected the plaintiffs' arguments that the state was "sufficiently intertwined" with the school, and that the state agency which had made the vocational grant under which one of the plaintiffs

---

[65] 419 US 345 (1974).

[66] *Id* 351.

[67] 407 US 163 (1972).

[68] 436 US 149 (1978).

[69] *Id* 164-166.

[70] 457 US 830 (1982), *affg* 641 F2d 14 (1st Cir 1981).

was hired had also approved her discharge, thereby converting at least that discharge into state action. Extensively canvassing the case law and various approaches to state action, the court first stated that the school's dependence on state funds "demonstrates only that the state has the potential to control the school's operations, not that it actually does so." It then found that despite the fact the school's "funding, regulations and function" showed a close relationship with the state, they were not enough to make the school's actions, especially its personnel actions relating to the plaintiffs, attributable to the state. Further, the plaintiff who had been hired under a state agency's vocational grant was not, for that reason alone, a public employee.

In an opinion by Chief Justice Burger, the Court affirmed. Holding that the school's challenged action was not state action, the Court found the school's receipt of public funds did not make its discharge decision action of the state. Also, the discharge decision was neither compelled nor even influenced by any state regulation. Further, the school was not performing a function which was the "exclusive province" of the state. The Court, moreover, rejected a symbiotic relationship argument, reasoning that "the school's fiscal relationship with the state is not different from that of many contractors performing services for the government."[71]

Similarly, in *Blum v Yaretsky*,[72] the Court, in an opinion by Justice Rehnquist, held that certain decisions by nursing homes to discharge or transfer patients without notice or hearing were not state action. It was not enough for state action that the state *responded* to these decisions by adjusting patient Medicare benefits. Also, the challenged decisions were based on medical judgments made by private parties according to professional standards. Further, state regulations did not dictate the challenged decisions, and the relationship between the state and the nursing homes was not a symbiotic one within the meaning of *Burton*, despite extensive regulation.[73]

§2.06 —State Action and Color of Law

In contrast to *Rendell-Baker* and *Blum*, the Court's decision in *Lugar v Edmondson Oil Co*[74] took a more expansive view of state action, albeit in a narrowly circumscribed setting. The Court also made explicit that challenged

---

[71] Justice White concurred in the judgment on the ground that there was no "allegation that the employment decision was itself based upon some rule of conduct or policy put forth by the state." Justices Marshall and Brennan dissented, contending that there was a sufficiently substantial nexus between the school and the state to render the school's discharge decision state action.

[72] 457 US 991 (1982).

[73] The Court also rejected plaintiffs' public function argument on the ground that nursing homes do not perform a function which is traditionally an exclusive prerogative of the state. Justice White concurred in the judgment while Justices Brennan and Marshall dissented.

[74] 457 US 922 (1982), *revg* 639 F2d 1058 (4th Cir 1981). *Lugar, Rendell-Baker*, and *Blum* were all handed down on the same day.

conduct which constitutes state action is thereby also conduct under color of law for §1983 purposes.[75] In *Lugar*, plaintiff alleged that private party debt claimants in a state court action, in violation of due process, had maliciously used state prejudgment attachment procedures which resulted in wrongful seizure of his property under a levy later set aside. Affirming the district court's dismissal of plaintiff's complaint, the Fourth Circuit described the issue as follows: "Whether the mere institution by a private litigant of presumptively valid state judicial proceedings, without any prior or subsequent collusion or concerted action by that litigant with the state officials who then proceed with adjudicative, administrative, or executive enforcement of the proceeding, constitutes action *under color of state law* . . . ."[76] In arriving at its conclusion of no color of law, the Fourth Circuit emphasized the following:

1.   State action and color of law, while "ordinarily" amounting to the same thing, "are separate, not necessarily congruent, but cumulative predicate elements of a prima facie §1983 claim"[77]

2.   In cases where the specific conduct alleged to have deprived the secured right is clearly official action, "the state action question is subsumed in the under color of law question, and the latter is seldom raised"[78]

3.   In cases where private actors alone are alleged to have engaged, at the "operational or enforcement level," in conduct that deprived the secured

---

[75] This became a live issue in part because of Polk County v Dodson, 454 US 312 (1981) which held that a public defender representing an indigent criminal defendant in a state criminal proceeding does not in so doing act under color of law. In what could have turned out to be an important footnote, *id* at 322 n 12, the Court also rejected the plaintiff's alternative color of law argument, based in part on *Burton*, that the state's funding of criminal defenses makes it a "joint participant" and thereby creates a "symbiotic relationship" with individual public defenders. The Court responded that *Burton* dealt with the *state action* issue, while here the issue was *color of law*, involving a public defender who was "concededly" a county employee. It then said:

> Although this Court has sometimes treated the questions as if they were identical [citing United States v Price, 383 US 787, 794 & n 71 (1966)] we need not consider their relationship in order to decide this case. Our factual inquiry into the professional obligations and functions of a public defender persuades us that [defendant] was not a "joint participant" with the state and that, when representing [plaintiff], she was not acting under color of state law.

It was not as clear from the Court's language as it should have been whether the Court simply avoided the state action issue entirely and held only that there was no color of law, or whether the Court also suggested by its rejection of the "joint participant" argument that the challenged conduct of the public defender could not be attributed to the state and thus was not state action as well. Cf Dennis v Sparks, 101 S Ct 183 (1980) and Adickes v Kress & Co, 398 US 144 (1970)—see §2.10—holding that private persons conspiring or jointly engaging with state officials in challenged conduct act under color of law. *See also* on the state action-color of law relationship two pre-*Lugar* cases, Herwald v Schweiker, 658 F2d 359 (5th Cir 1981) and Gresham Park Community Org v Howell, 652 F2d 1227 (5th Cir 1981).

[76] 639 F2d at 1061-62 (emphasis added).

[77] *Id* 1062.

[78] *Id* 1063.

right, state action may be found only by attribution to the state and here, too, "the under color of law question has been merged in the state action inquiry just as it is in offical act cases"[79]

4. In cases like *Lugar,* where "the conduct of a private action defendant is alleged to have combined with the acts of state officials at the enforcement or operational level" to cause the deprivation, state action and color of law are different and refer to different conducts; thus, state action may be present with respect to a private defendant's challenged conduct. In *Lugar,* according to the Fourth Circuit, because the challenged private conduct was not *jointly engaged* in with state officials, color of law was not present

In an opinion by Justice White, the Supreme Court reversed. After canvassing its earlier decisions on the state action-color of law relationship, the Court broadly concluded that challenged conduct constituting state action is also action under color of law. It relied as well on the legislative history of §1983 to demonstrate that §1983's color of law was not intended to *limit* those Fourteenth Amendment violations which could be redressed by §1983 actions. In short, "the under color of state law requirement does not add anything not already included within the state action requirement of the Fourteenth Amendment. . . ."[80]

On the state action-color of law merits, the Court ruled that, in a due process challenge to state attachment procedures, "invoking the aid of state officials to take advantage of state created attachment procedures . . . is sufficient when the state has created a system whereby state officials will attach property on the *ex parte* application of one party to a private dispute."[81] Because the plaintiff was challenging the constitutionality of these procedures and not merely alleging their misuse or abuse, plaintiff was deprived of his property through state action and the private defendants therefore acted under color of law. A two-part test was used and, according to the Court, satisfied:

> First, the deprivation must be caused by the exercise of some right or privilege created by the state, or by a rule of conduct imposed by the state, or by a person for whom the state is responsible. . . . Second, the party charged with the deprivation must be a person who may fairly be said to be a state actor because he is a state official, or because he has acted together with or has obtained significant aid from state officials, or because his conduct is otherwise chargeable to the state.[82]

Chief Justice Burger dissented. While he agreed that the state action and color of law inquiries were the same, he argued that the private defendants' use of the state attachment procedures was not conduct attributable to the

---

[79] *Id* 1064.
[80] 457 US at 935 n 18.
[81] *Id* 942.
[82] *Id* 937.

state. Justice Powell, with whom Justices Rehnquist and O'Connor joined, also dissented. Insisting that there were significant distinctions between state action and color of law, especially where private actors were involved, they contended that the private defendants' use of the state attachment procedures was neither state action nor action under color of law.

The *Lugar* majority's view of the state action-color of law relationship means that once a Fourteenth Amendment violation (with its state action requirement) is found, the §1983 plaintiff need not surmount a separate color of law hurdle. This is comparable to the Court's holding that §1983 has no independent state-of-mind requirement.[83] However, because §1983 applies to other constitutional and federal statutory provisions ("laws" actions) with no state action requirement, "the statutory concept of action under color of state law would be a distinct element of the case not implicitly satisfied by a finding of a violation of the particular federal right."[84]

Although §1983 speaks of "custom or usage," the Supreme Court held in *Adickes v Kress & Co*[85] that this language does not reach a purely private custom, however pervasive. Rather, some sort of state involvement in the custom is necessary for state action and §1983 purposes.[86] In *Adickes* itself, which dealt with the refusal of a privately owned restaurant to serve plaintiff because she, a white, was in the company of blacks, the Court observed that in order to establish state action, plaintiff had to prove that the restaurant refused her service because of a state-enforced custom of racial segregation. This state enforcement, according to the Court, was not limited to the use of the criminal trespass statute, but could also be found in police toleration of violence directed against plaintiff and others like her.

Adickes also stands for the rule that a private person can be liable under §1983 as a result of a willful participation in joint activity with the state or its agents.[87] In *Adickes*, the plaintiff was arrested for vagrancy immediately after she was refused service. The Court indicated that, if plaintiff could prove that the arresting police and the restaurant had reached an understanding to this effect or were otherwise involved in a conspiracy, then the refusal of the restaurant to serve plaintiff coupled with her later arrest would constitute sufficient state involvement to warrant a finding of state action.[88]

Similarly, and more recently, the Court held unanimously in *Dennis v Sparks*[89] that a private defendant who conspires with an absolutely immune state

---

[83] *See* **§3.02.**

[84] 457 US at 935 n 18. See **§2.12** on laws actions.

[85] 398 US 144 (1970).

[86] In this way the Court was able to avoid the difficult question of the power of Congress under section 5 of the Fourteenth Amendment to regulate purely private conduct. *See* United States v Guest, 383 US 745 (1966).

[87] 398 US at 152.

[88] The relationship between state action and conspiracy is discussed at **§2.10.**

[89] 499 US 24 (1980). See **§2.10** on conspiracy and state action.

judge acts under color of law. It also ruled in *Tower v Glover*[90] that public defenders accused of conspiring with state officials, including judges, act under color of law, even though the Court had earlier held in a nonconspiracy setting in *Polk County v Dodson*[91] that a public defender representing an indigent defendant in a state criminal proceeding does not thereby act under color of law. *Polk County* raises a different state action issue discussed later.[92]

§2.07   The State Function Approach

A third and very distinct approach to state action focuses on the nature of the activity engaged in by the private person or entity and asks whether it constitutes a traditional state function. The classic case is *Marsh v Alabama*[93] which involved a company-owned and operated town in which the plaintiff, a Jehovah's Witness, was arrested and convicted of trespass for distributing religious leaflets. Finding state action, the Court emphasized that the town had "all the characteristics of any other American town." It reasoned: "Ownership does not always mean absolute dominion. The more an owner, for his advantage, opens up his property for use by the public in general, the more do his rights become circumscribed by the statutory and constitutional rights of those who use it."[94]

The Court used a state function approach to find state action where a dominant political party excluded blacks from participating in its primary elections,[95] saying: "[S]tate delegation to a party of the power to fix the qualifications of primary elections is delegation of a state function that may make the party's action the action of the state."[96]

The Court also used this approach to bar the exclusion of blacks from the preprimary election of Texas's Jaybird Democratic Association, even though the record showed no state involvement whatever.[97] It noted that the Association's candidates almost always ran unopposed and won in both the regular Democratic primary and the general election. Thus the preprimary elections were the equivalent of state elections. Further, the Court implied in *Evans v Newton*[98] that park operation is similarly a state function subject to the requirements of the Fourteenth Amendment.

However, the Court apparently has become increasingly worried by the potential for expansion of the state function doctrine. For example, after some

---

[90] 467 US 914 (1984). See also **§7.15** on public defender immunity.

[91] 454 US 312 (1981).

[92] That is, the converse of the typical state action question: when does the conduct of a state employee become that of a private person for state action purposes?

[93] 326 US 501 (1946).

[94] *Id* 506.

[95] Smith v Allwright, 321 US 649 (1944), a Fifteenth Amendment case.

[96] *Id* 660.

[97] Terry v Adams, 345 US 461 (1953). There was, however, no majority opinion.

[98] 382 US 296, 301-02 (1966).

uncertainty as to the applicability of this doctrine to privately owned shopping centers and malls,[99] the Court held in *Hudgens v NLRB*[100] that the conduct of such centers and malls was not state action for First Amendment purposes. In *Jackson v Metropolitan Edison Co,*[101] the Court likewise refused to find state action in the termination of service without notice by a heavily regulated public utility with monopoly status. It distinguished earlier state function cases as involving the delegated powers "traditionally associated with sovereignty" and emphasized that "the supplying of utility service is not traditionally the exclusive prerogative of the State."[102]

The Court again focused on the feature of exclusiveness in *Flagg Brothers v Brooks,*[103] where it rejected the state function approach in the case of the sale by a warehouseman, pursuant to statutory authorization, of goods entrusted to him for storage. Responding to the plaintiffs' contention in this §1983 case that "the resolution of private disputes is a traditional function of civil government" delegated to the defendant Flagg Brothers,[104] the Court asserted that the state, by the establishment of its dispute resolution system, "can hardly be said to have delegated to Flagg Brothers an exclusive prerogative of the sovereign."[105] It suggested that "this entire field of activity is outside the scope of [the state function doctrine] . . . whether these commercial rights and remedies are created by statute or decisional law."[106] However, the Court expressly left open the question whether a state could avoid the applicability of the Fourteenth Amendment (and thus §1983) by delegating to private parties such noncommercial functions as education, fire and police protection, and tax collection.[107]

---

[99] *See* Lloyd Corp v Tanner, 407 US 551 (1972); Amalgamated Food Employees Union v Logan Valley Plaza, 391 US 308 (1968).

[100] 424 US 507 (1976), *overruling* Amalgamated Food Employees Union v Logan Valley Plaza, 391 US 308 (1968).

[101] 419 US 345 (1974).

[102] *Id* 353 (emphasis added).

[103] 436 US 149 (1978). The Court similarly rejected the state function approach in Rendell-Baker v Kohn, 457 US 830 (1982) (traditionally, education not an exclusive state function) and Blum v Yaretsky, 457 US 991 (1982) (traditionally, nursing homes do not perform an exclusive state function), both discussed at **§2.06.**

[104] 436 US at 157.

[105] *Id* 160.

[106] *Id* 162.

[107] *Id* 163. As to police protection *see* Griffin v Maryland, 378 US 130 (1964) where the Court found state action in connection with the conduct of a deputy sheriff employed as a private security guard. However, the defendant had "purported to exercise the authority of a deputy sheriff." *Id* 135.

§2.08   The Converse of the Typical State Action Question

The Supreme Court granted certiorari but then dismissed the writ as improvidently granted in *Stengel v Belcher*,[108] a case which might have posed a challenging state action question. The Sixth Circuit decision had to do with an off-duty, out-of-uniform police officer whose involvement in a barroom brawl resulted in his shooting several persons and killing two of them. The officer did not identify himself as such when he intervened. On the other hand, police department regulations imposed a continuing duty on police officers, even when off duty, to act in connection with any type of police or criminal activity. Also, the officer used mace issued by the department and he used a gun, similarly issued by the department, which he was required to carry at all times.

The district court submitted the state action issue to the jury which returned verdicts against the police officer. Affirming, the Sixth Circuit indicated that the officer was acting under color of law as a matter of law and that there was no need to have given this issue to the jury. It said:

> The fact that a police officer is on or off duty, or in or out of uniform is not controlling. "It is the nature of the act performed, not the clothing of the actor or even the status of being on duty, or off duty, which determines whether the officer has acted under color of law."[109]

Stengel, in contrast with the state action cases surveyed earlier where the question was whether concededly private conduct ought to be treated as if it were governmental conduct, seems to raise the converse, equally interesting question: when does a state employee whose conduct is usually considered to be state action become a private citizen for state action purposes?[110] The Court would probably have affirmed *Stengel* on the ground that the officer's conduct was not that of a private citizen under the circumstances. The officer apparently intervened because he was under an obligation to do so. His intervention was further made possible because of the mace and gun issued to him. This would likely have been found to be sufficient governmental encouragement of and involvement in the officer's conduct for state action purposes.[111]

---

[108] 522 F2d 438 (6th Cir 1975), *cert granted*, 425 US 910, *cert dismissed as improvidently granted*, 429 US 118 (1976).

[109] 522 F2d at 441 (quoting Johnson v Hackett, 284 F Supp 933, 937 (ED Pa 1968)).

[110] This question was addressed in Layne v Sampley, 627 F2d 12 (6th Cir 1980). *Layne* involved an off-duty police officer who had allegedly shot plaintiff in violation of plaintiff's constitutional rights. After stating that a police officer's off-duty status does not, standing alone, determine the issue of state action, the Sixth Circuit held that it was for the jury in the case before it, under proper instructions, to decide the state action issue. The court then reinstated the jury's verdict, which had in effect found that the defendant police officer's conduct constituted state action. *See* §2.09.

[111] That this result would have been likely appears from the comments of Chief Justice Burger, who explained in his concurring opinion, 429 US at 120, that the Court granted certiorari originally because the question posed limited the state involvement to the

The Court dealt with the same kind of question in *Polk County v Dodson*,[112] where it held that a public defender representing an indigent defendant in a state criminal proceeding had not acted under color of law in moving to withdraw as counsel on the ground that the plaintiff's claims were wholly frivolous. In an opinion by Justice Powell, the Court emphasized the following:

1. The public defender's assignment "entailed functions and obligations in no way dependent on state authority"; the relation between plaintiff and defendant "became identical to that existing between any other lawyer and client"[113]

2. A public defender's employment relation with the state does not mean that he or she acts under color of law:

    (a) a public defender owes "undivided loyalty" to the client and functions in an adversarial posture with respect to the state; a public defender is therefore not subject to the direction of the state with regard to representation of indigent defendants

    (b) the state has a constitutional obligation to respect the professional independence of its public defenders;

    (c) simply because public defenders making withdrawal decisions might be viewed by indigent prisoners as "hostile state actors" is not determinative

The Court went on to suggest that a public defender might act under color of law while performing certain administrative and investigative functions.[114] However, where a public defender performs a lawyer's traditional functions as counsel to a defendant in a criminal proceeding, he or she does not act under color of law. In such a case, the public defender is protected by the equivalent of absolute immunity.[115]

It remains to be seen whether *Polk County's* approach to color of law will ultimately be applied to other professionals employed by the state, such as doctors. Where such professionals have custodial or supervisory functions in addition to professional functions, then rather clearly, as the Court noted in

---

requirement that defendant wear a gun even while off duty. As it turned out, however, noted Chief Justice Burger, the defendant testified he intervened in order to arrest several of the plaintiffs, he used mace issued by the police department, and he intervened pursuant to a police regulation which required such intervention. The Chief Justice then emphasized that

> it is unclear what the result would have been had the only contemporaneous evidence of state action been the presence of the state-required gun. I wish to make it clear that the Court is not passing on that question today, because it is not presented by the record in this case.

[112] 454 US 312 (1981).

[113] *Id* 318.

[114] *Id* 323. *See* Chapman v Musich, 726 F2d 405 (8th Cir 1984) (post-*Polk County* case similarly leaving open this question).

[115] *See* §7.15.

Polk County itself, color of law may be present.[116] But even where there are no such custodial or supervisory functions, color of law might still be found. Unlike public defenders, the state has no *constitutional* obligation to respect the professional independence of nonlawyer professionals. *Polk County* might, thus, be limited to public defenders regarding whom, moreover, there are weighty policy considerations cutting in favor of absolute immunity.[117] Under this view, *Polk County* is an absolute immunity case masquerading as a color of law case.

It bears reemphasizing that none of the state action approaches used by the Supreme Court is exclusive of any of the others. Not only is there considerable overlap, but the Court itself frequently considers the applicability of all three in many state action cases.[118] Furthermore, the Court may in effect be using a balancing test in its state action cases.[119] If this is so, then the perceived importance of the §1983 plaintiff's constitutional claim will be a significant factor in the Supreme Court's state action determination. From this perspective, state action is not a unitary concept, but varies depending on the constitutional violation asserted.[120]

§2.09   State Action in the Circuits

Following the lead of the Supreme Court in state action cases, the circuits generally address each case on an individual basis[121] and use the three approaches discussed earlier: (1) the existence of an interdependent or symbiotic relationship; (2) governmental requirement or encouragement of, or involvement in, the nominally private conduct including the nexus inquiry; and (3) the delegation to private persons or entities of a state function.[122] The numerous circuit court decisions dealing with state action and color of law are set out in an extensive accompanying footnote[123] and are organized on the

(*Text continued on page 95*)

---

[116] Polk County v Dodson, 454 US at 320 (distinguishing Estelle v Gamble, 429 US 97 (1976) and O'Connor v Donaldson, 422 US 563 (1975), both involving §1983 actions against physicians, on this ground).

[117] *See* **§7.15.**

[118] *E.g., See* Flagg Bros v Brooks, 436 US 149 (1978); Jackson v Metropolitan Edison Co, 419 US 345 (1974).

[119] Glennon & Nowak, *A Functional Analysis of the Fourteenth Amendment "State Action" Requirement,* 1976 Sup Ct Rev 221.

[120] The Fifth Circuit took this position when it said: "Absent a charge of racial discrimination we are disinclined to press the state action doctrine and all that it entails into the internal affairs of a hospital." Greco v Orange Memorial Hosp Corp, 513 F2d 873, 882 (5th Cir 1975), involving a doctor's claim that the defendant hospital unconstitutionally prohibited the performing of elective abortions in its facilities. See also, to the same effect, Weise v Syracuse Univ, 522 F2d 397, 406 (2d Cir 1975) where the court said: "[A] consideration of whether there is state action necessarily entails a balancing process. . . . As the conduct complained of becomes more offensive, and as the nature of the dispute becomes more amenable to resolution by a court, the more appropriate it is to subject the issue to judicial scrutiny." However, the First Circuit has questioned such an approach. Lamb v Rantoul, 561 F2d 409, 411 (1st Cir 1977).

[121] Burton v Wilmington Parking Auth, 365 US 715 (1961).

[122] *See* **§§2.04-2.07**

123 **Administrators; court-appointed**

Loyd v Loyd, 731 F2d 393 (7th Cir 1984) (court-appointed estate administrator's sale of real estate not state action; he acted in a private capacity; also, the state probate scheme was not challenged on constitutional grounds).

(Athletic Associations)

Ponce v Basketball Fedn of Puerto Rico, 760 F2d 375 (1st Cir 1985) (basketball federation's suspension of plaintiff not state action).

Spath v NCAA, 728 F2d 25 (1st Cir 1984) (court avoided deciding whether NCAA a state actor in connection with by-law regulating athletic qualifications; *Rendell-Baker* and *Blum* cast doubt on affirmative answer).

Clark v Arizona Interscholastic Assn, 695 F2d 1126 (9th Cir 1982) (AIA's regulations, prohibiting boys from playing on girls' volleyball teams were state action; AIA significantly "intertwined" with the state).

Bar Associations

Keating v Martin, 638 F2d 1121 (8th Cir 1980) (per curiam) (recommendation of chairman of state bar association that disciplinary proceedings be instituted against plaintiff was not under color of law).

Educational Institutions, Facilities, or Associations

Krynicky v University of Pittsburgh, 742 F2d 94 (3d Cir 1984) (University of Pittsburgh and Temple University were state actors even after *Lugar, Rendell-Baker,* and *Blum; Burton's* symbiotic relationship test still viable; close interdependence between universities and Pennsylvania which affirmatively took responsibility for them).

Milones v Williams, 691 F2d 931 (10th Cir 1982) (private school's treatment of students was state action because of significant state involvement in placing students there, in the challenged behavior modification program, and in funding and overall regulation; *Rendell-Baker* distinguished).

Harris v Hubbert, 588 F2d 167 (5th Cir 1979) (Alabama Education Association not sufficiently involved with the state in plaintiff's transfer for state action purposes);

Braden v University of Pittsburgh, 552 F2d 948 (3d Cir 1977) (en banc) (still good law to this effect).

Foundations

Jackson v Statler Found, 496 F2d 623 (2d Cir 1974), *cert denied,* 420 US 927 (1975) (tax-exempt foundation might act under color of law depending on government aid, regulation, and approval of the challenged activity as well as the extent to which the foundation serves a state function and the existence of legitimate associational claims to be treated as private).

Guardians, Court-appointed

Taylor v First Wyoming Bank, 707 F2d 388 (9th Cir 1983) (conduct of court-appointed guardian in obtaining court order placing ward in convalescent home was not state action).

Housing Providers

Halet v Wend Inv Co, 672 F2d 1305 (9th Cir 1982) (where challenge was to private apartment complex's adults only policy, there was a symbiotic relationship alleged between the complex and Los Angeles County).

Insurance Companies

Life Ins Co of No Am v Reichardt, 591 F2d 499 (9th Cir 1979) (private insurance companies whose policies allegedly discriminated against women were not state actors; mere approval by California State Insurance Commissioner of those policies not enough).

Judges

Harris v Harvey, 605 F2d 330 (7th Cir 1979) (judge's conduct in engaging in racially motivated campaign to discredit plaintiff was state action; he used his power and prestige even though his conduct was extrajudicial).

Law Enforcement Officers On and Off Duty

Lusby v TG&Y Stores Inc, 749 F2d 1423 (10th Cir 1984) (off-duty police officer acting as private security guard at store acted under color of law in arresting plaintiffs; he identified himself as police officer, he later went to police station to finish his paperwork, and he used police documents to get information; even if he was a private person, the police followed a policy that allowed him to substitute his judgment for that of the police, and such cooperative activity was similarly action under color of law).

Bonsignore v City of New York, 683 F2d 635 (2d Cir 1982) (off-duty police officer who shot his wife with a police pistol and then committed suicide did not act under color of law).

Delcambre v Delcambre, 635 F2d 407 (5th Cir 1981) (per curiam) (on-duty police chief who assaulted plaintiff, his sister-in-law, did not act under color of law; this was a family and political dispute, and plaintiff was not threatened with arrest).

Layne v Sampley, 627 F2d 12 (6th Cir 1980) (off-duty police officer who shot plaintiff acted under color of law; he had authority to carry the weapon, the dispute between them arose out of performance of police duties, and police officer had a gun in company of other police officers).

Traver v Meshriy, 627 F2d 934 (9th Cir 1980) (off-duty police officer, employed by a bank as a private security guard, acted under color of law when he responded to another employee's call for help; he was part of a police department program, he was selected by the police department, and he owed his primary duty to the department).

Lawyers, Court-Appointed

Cornes v Munoz, 724 F2d 61 (7th Cir 1983) (court-appointed public defender did not act under color of law in representing plaintiff; *Polk County* governed).

Jackson v Salon, 614 F2d 15 (1st Cir 1980) (court-appointed counsel did not act under color of law in representing clients).

Lawyers, Private

Barnard v Young, 720 F2d 1188 (10th Cir 1983) (no color of law where private attorney employed subpoena duces tecum power of state of Oklahoma against plaintiff in child custody dispute; state officers did not significantly assist).

McCord v Bailey, 636 F2d 606 (DC Cir 1980) (private defense counsel who represented plaintiff at criminal trial did not act under color of law).

Henderson v Fisher, 631 F2d 1115 (3d Cir 1980) (per curiam) (although private lawyers are " officers of the court", their conduct is not for this reason state action).

Legal Service Organizations

Gerena v Puerto Rico Legal Servs Inc, 697 F2d 447 (1st Cir 1983) (discharge of lawyer by Puerto Rico legal services organization neither state nor federal action).

Graseck v Mauceri, 582 F2d 203 (2d Cir 1978) (dismissal of lawyer by Legal Aid Society of Suffolk County not state action).

Libraries

Chalfant v Wilmington Inst, 574 F2d 739 (3d Cir 1978) (en banc) (discharge of employee from library system was state action; extensive governmental support and involvement in operations of library; *Burton* governed).

Hollenbaugh v Carnegie Free Library, 545 F2d 382 (3d Cir 1976) (same).

Medical Institutions, Facilities, or Associations

Carter v Norfolk Community Hosp Assn, 761 F2d 970 (4th Cir 1985) (hospital's revocation of doctor's staff privileges not state action despite receipt of state funds).

Hicks v Southern Maryland Health Sys Agency, 737 F2d 399 (4th Cir 1984) (plaintiffs' discharge by SMHSA was neither state action nor federal action).

Crowder v Conlan, 740 F2d 447 (6th Cir 1984) (private hospital's restriction of doctor's staff privileges was not state action despite extensive government funding and regulation; there was no nexus shown).

Mendez v Belton, 739 F2d 15 (1st Cir 1984) (private hospital's revocation of doctor's staff privileges not state action).

Smith v North La Medical Review Assn, 735 F2d 168 (5th Cir 1984) (medical peer review organization established under federal law was a federal actor, not a state actor; there was extensive federal supervision; also, there was no nexus between the organization and Louisiana).

Lubin v Crittenden Hosp Assn, 713 F2d 414 (8th Cir 1983) (no nexus between county and private hospital's disciplinary action against doctor; *Burton* symbiotic relationship test should be limited to racial discrimination cases).

Loh-Seng Yo v Cibola Gen Hosp, 706 F2d 306 (10th Cir 1983) (private hospital's conduct in connection with doctor not state action because of no nexus);

Community Medical Center v Emergency Medical Servs of Northeastern Pennsylvania, 712 F2d 878 (3d Cir 1983) (claim that EMSNP discriminated against plaintiff not enough for state action; EMSNP a nonprofit corporation organized to coordinate emergency health care services which was recognized by state and United States as eligible to receive grants).

Morrison v Washington County Alabama, 700 F2d 678 (11th Cir 1983) (county hospital's allegedly wrongful discharge of decedent which resulted in his death was action under color of law; the discharge was based on administrative considerations, not medical ones, and the hospital had arranged for the decedent to be placed in police custody; this was not simply a medical malpractice action).

Finch v Mississippi State Medical Assn, 585 F2d 765, 778-79 (5th Cir 1978) (state action found because "[a] person or a professional society given the authority by state law to make the sole nominations for a state agency is, at least in performing the selection process, performing a state function").

Downs v Sawtelle, 574 F2d 1 (1st Cir 1978) (sterilization by community hospital was state action; symbiotic relationship because of extensive funding and regulation and because town appointed hospital's entire board of directors).

Mental Health Institutions, Facilities or Associations

McVarish v Mid-Nebraska Community Mental Health Center, 696 F2d 69 (8th Cir 1982) (state substantially involved in management and control of mental health center and in governing board's decision to discharge plaintiff employee).

National Guard

Schultz v Wellman, 717 F2d 301 (6th Cir 1983) (plaintiff's discharge from Kentucky National Guard by Guard's officers was action under color of state law because federal law provided that the authority to discharge enlisted personnel rested with the state).

Rowe v Tennessee, 609 F2d 259 (6th Cir 1979) (same as *Schultz*, even though discharged plaintiff technically an employee of the United States; overlapping state and federal authority did not preclude state action).

Nonprofit Corporations

Casias v City of Raton, 738 F2d 392 (10th Cir 1984) (plaintiff, who was terminated by defendant council, a nonprofit corporation devoted to alcoholism treatment, may have been a de facto employee of the city, given claim of extensive city involvment in the council).

Gilmore v Salt Lake Community Action Program, 710 F2d 632 (10th Cir 1982) (community action agency's discharge of plaintiff not state action; even though state was actively involved in the agency, the challenged conduct did not result from a "governmental rule, policy or decision").

Nursing Homes

Hoyt v St Mary's Rehabilitation Center, 711 F2d 864 (8th Cir 1983) (rejecting argument that for a patient, a nursing home is the equivalent of *Marsh's* "company town" for state function purposes; *Blum* followed).

Taylor v St Clair, 685 F2d 982 (5th Cir 1982) (private nursing home's discharge or transfer of Medicaid patients not state action; *Blum* controlled).

Cape Cod Nursing Home Council v Rambling Rose Rest Home, 667 F2d 238 (1st Cir 1981) (nursing home not required to provide access to service organizations).

Physicians, Court-appointed or Publicly Employed

Morrison v Washington County Alabama, 700 F2d 678 (11th Cir 1983) (physician at county hospital who allegedly wrongfully discharged decedent causing his death acted under color of law; his judgment was not medical but administrative, and he enlisted the aid of hospital staff and the county police; this was not simply a medical malpractice case).

Hall v Quillen, 631 F2d 1154 (4th Cir 1980) (court-appointed physician's examination of involuntarily committed plaintiff was not state action; Judge Winter dissented in this pre-*Polk County* case).

Physicians, Private

Calvert v Sharp, 748 F2d 861 (4th Cir 1984) (private physician who treated inmate did not act under color of law; physician had no custodial or supervisory duties; *Polk County* applicable).

Private Individuals or Entities Cooperating with State Officials or Using State Procedures

See note 124.

Racing Organizations

Roberts v Louisiana Downs, 742 F2d 221 (5th Cir 1984) (private race track's denial to horse trainer of stalling privileges was state action; extensive governmental involvement in day-to-day management).

Bier v Fleming, 717 F2d 308 (6th Cir 1983) (rejection of application for stall space was not state action; Third Circuit's decision in Fitzgerald v Mountain Laurel Racing Inc, 607 F2d 589 (3d Cir 1979), distinguished because there the private defendant had acted in concert with officials and had enforced a state rule).

Heflin v Kentucky State Racing Commn, 701 F2d 599 (6th Cir 1983) (Churchill Downs's rejection of plaintiffs' application for stall space was not state action; there was no nexus between the pervasive state regulation and the challenged conduct).

Fitzgerald v Mountain Laurel Racing Inc, 607 F2d 589 (3d Cir 1979) (expulsion

basis of the nature of the defendants. Although generalizations should be made cautiously in the state action-color of law area, several may be offered. More cases are raising *Lugar* issues where a private individual or entity has made use of state procedures or cooperated with state officials.[124] Also, it occasionally

(*Text continued on page 97*)

of trainer and driver by racing association was state action where there was a nexus between state and expulsion; Judge Adams dissented).

Towing Companies

Hinman v Lincoln Towing Serv Inc, 771 F2d 189 (7th Cir 1985) (private towing company's retention of a trespassing vehicle, removed from private property through the request of the landowner, until receipt of payment by vehicle owner, as permitted by state law, not attributable to the state; there was no significant state encouragement and the towing company performed no state function

Transportation

Bloomer Shippers Assn v Illinois Cent Gulf RR, 655 F2d 772 (7th Cir 1981) (suit against Illinois Central Railroad for failure to provide adequate service, discrimination, and improper line abandonment was properly dismissed on state action grounds; while the railroad was heavily regulated, there was insufficient nexus).

Unions

Jackson v Temple Univ, 721 F2d 931 (3d Cir 1983) (union's refusal to bring plaintiff's grievance to arbitration not action under color of law).

Utilities

Cobb v Georgia Power Co, 757 F2d 1248 (11th Cir 1985) (power company which obtained a temporary restraining order did not thereby act under color of law; also, the fact that it was heavily regulated did not mean that its conduct was state action; *Lugar* followed).

Kearson v Southern Bell Tel & Tel Co, 763 F2d 405 (11th Cir 1985) (telephone company's termination of service for nonpayment was not state action).

Vikse v Basin Elec Power Coop, 712 F2d 374 (8th Cir 1983) (that private electric cooperative acted under color of law was assumed where it exercised delegated eminent domain power against plaintiff condemnees).

Occhino v Northwestern Bell Tel Co, 675 F2d 220 (8th Cir 1982 (per curiam) (telephone company's termination of customer's service not state action).

Volunteer Fire Departments

Adams v Bain, 697 F2d 1213 (4th Cir 1982) (plaintiffs' removal as firefighters by volunteer fire department was state action; county officials acted together with the fire department; also, state function was being performed; symbiotic relationship test not relied on).

Janusaitis v Middlebury Volunteer Fire Dept, 607 F2d 17 (2d Cir 1979) (volunteer fire department's dismissal of fireman was state action; symbiotic relationship existed).

[124] **Private Individuals or Entities Cooperating with State Officials:**

Austen Oil & Gas Inc v Stream, 764 F2d 381 (5th Cir 1985) (allegation that lessor and state law enforcement officers acted together pursuant to plan was sufficient for color of law purposes; this went beyond claim that lessor simply requested official intervention).

Cruz v Donnelly, 727 F2d 79 (3d Cir 1984) (per curiam) (food store employee who asked police to search plaintiff suspected of shoplifting did not act under color of law; *Lugar* distinguished on ground that it involved an ex parte prejudgment attachment procedure.

Howerton v Gabica, 708 F2d 380 (9th Cir 1983) (state action where landlords, using self-help, evicted tenants with extensive police assistance).

Coleman v Turpen, 697 F2d 1341 (10th Cir 1983) (private wrecking company's selling of prisoner's property was state action because the company was originally called by the sheriff to take and store the property; when state allowed its sale, there was joint participation).

Goichman v Rheuban Motors Inc, 682 F2d 1320 (9th Cir 1982) (conduct of towing company in taking possession of plaintiff's car and towing it to storage garage pursuant to directions of a police officer was under color of law).

Price v Baker, 693 F2d 952 (10th Cir 1982) (sheriff's wife who was fighting in back seat of patrol car was not de facto deputy where sheriff was out of car and gave no directions; she acted alone and unofficially).

Martin-Marietta Corp v Bendix Corp, 690 F2d 558 (6th Cir 1982) (private corporation acted under color of law in intervening in state proceeding on the side of the state as a party plaintiff; the corporation was cloaked with the authority of the state under state law and also joined with state officials).

Hernandez v Schwegmann Bros Giant Supermarkets, 673 F2d 771 (5th Cir 1982) (per curiam) (supermarket's conduct in detaining suspected shoplifter until police called to arrest and book her was not state action in the absence of a pre-existing agreement; also, officer made his own independent evaluation).

Harris v City of Roseburg, 664 F2d 1121 (9th Cir 1981) (police intervention and aid in creditor's repossession of car constituted state action; mere acquiescence is not enough).

El Fundi v Deroche, 625 F2d 195, 196 (8th Cir 1980) (per curiam) ("state action is present when private security guards act in concert with police officers or pursuant to customary procedures agreed to by police departments, particularly when a state statute authorizes merchants to detain suspected shoplifters").

Private Individuals or Entities Using State Procedures

Cobb v Georgia Power Co, 757 F2d 1248 (11th Cir 1985) (power company which obtained temporary restraining order did not thereby act under color of law).

Duncan v Peck, 752 F2d 1135 (6th Cir 1985) (private parties' use of Ohio procedures authorizing service by publication where other party is a nonresident whose property has been attached was action under color of law when constitutionality of such procedures was challenged; *Lugar* governed).

Winterland Concessions Co v Trela, 735 F2d 257 (7th Cir 1984) (private misuse of a statute or state procedure is not, standing alone, state action even though state officers participate in implementing the statutory processes; joint action or a challenge to the statutory processes themselves is required).

Dahlberg v Becker, 748 F2d 85 (2d Cir 1984) (private attorneys who obtained contempt order did not act under color of law; *Lugar* distinguished because, unlike *Lugar*, plaintiff alleged the private misuse of a state statute: also, here no state rule of conduct implicated).

Goldie's Bookstore Inc v Superior Court, 739 F2d 466 (9th Cir 1984) (private parties acted under color of law in seeking to enforce state court judgment; constitutionality of state statute making stays discretionary challenged).

Buller v Buechler, 700 F2d 844 (8th Cir 1983) (private creditors acted under color of law when they prepared garnishment papers and had them served by sheriff; *Lugar* governed even though creditors were not required to file papers with the state or to have them served by sheriff).

Miller v Hartwood Apartments Ltd, 698 F2d 1239 (5th Cir 1982) (private landlord's use of state court procedures to obtain evictions was not state action; no claim of unconstitutionality of those procedures).

Earnest v Lowentritt, 690 F2d 1198 (5th Cir 1982) (private defendants' use of state

becomes necessary to decide whether the conduct of state agencies in administering federally funded and supervised programs is state action or action under color of law. In this regard, the Ninth Circuit has stated that "the relevant inquiry focuses not on whose law is being implemented but rather on whether the authority of the state was exerted in enforcing the law."[125] Further, *Polk County's* independent professional judgment criterion, which was applied by the Supreme Court to a public defender representing a criminal defendant with the result that there was no color of law, has been addressed in other contexts as well.[126]

The nexus approach of the Supreme Court has become increasingly influential in the circuits.[127] However, unlike the state function test which now

---

mortgage foreclosure proceedings was not state action or action under color of law; *Lugar* distinguished as involving state officials).

Taylor v Gilmartin, 686 F2d 1346 (10th Cir 1982) (deprogrammer's use of a state court judge to obtain a temporary guardianship by order was not state action in the absence of a conspiracy; also, there was no claim that the guardianship statute was procedurally defective; *Lugar* was thus distinguishable).

Johnson v Miller, 680 F2d 39 (7th Cir 1982) (bank's filing of a criminal complaint which resulted in plaintiff's arrest was not state action but the act of a private citizen).

Luria Bros & Co v Allen, 672 F2d 347 (3d Cir 1982) (private landlord's posting notice of distraint under state law not state action; *Flagg Bros* indistinguishable).

Dahl v Akin, 630 F2d 277 (5th Cir 1980) (daughter's use of judicial process to strip father of control over property and to commit him was not action under color of law).

District 28, United Mine Workers of Am v Wellmore Coal Corp, 609 F2d 1083 (4th Cir 1979) (use by private coal companies and a railroad of state judicial processes to obtain ex parte injunctions did not, standing alone, constitute state action).

[125] Tongol v Uscry, 601 F2d 1091, 1097 (9th Cir 1979). *Cf* RJ Williams Co v Fort Belknap Hous Auth, 719 F2d 979 (9th Cir 1983) (housing authority created by Indian tribal law pursuant to federal statute did not act under color of state law) *and* Ellis v Blum, 643 F2d 68 (2d Cir 1981) (state officials charged with improper termination procedures for Social Security disability benefits did not act under color of law; here, state officials acted as agents of federal government). *See also* Schultz v Wellman, 717 F2d 301 (6th Cir 1983) *and* Rowe v Tennessee, 609 F2d 259 (6th Cir 1979) (both finding state action in connection with the discharge of National Guard personnel where there was overlapping state and federal authority).

[126] *E.g.*, Calvert v Sharp, 748 F2d 861 (4th Cir 1984) (private physician who allegedly did not treat inmate properly did not act under color of law; *Polk County* followed, with emphasis on defendant's being a privately employed specialist who treated private patients as well as inmates and who had no custodial or supervisory duties); Chapman v Musich, 726 F2d 405 (8th Cir 1984) (post-*Polk County* case leaving open the question, as did *Polk County*, whether public defenders acting in their administrative or investigative capacities act under color of law). See **§2.08** where it is argued that *Polk County's* approach should result in a finding of no state action or color of law only where the professional's sole duty is to plaintiff.

[127] *E.g.*, Roberts v Louisiana Downs, 742 F2d 221 (5th Cir 1984) (nexus between state and denial to plaintiff of stalling privileges at private race track); Crowder v Conlan, 740 F2d 447 (6th Cir 1984) (no nexus between county and private hospital's restriction of doctor's staff privileges); Lubin v Crittenden Hosp Assn, 713 F2d 414 (8th Cir 1983) (no nexus between county and disciplinary action by private hospital against doctor; *Burton* should be limited to racial discrimination cases); Adams v Bain, 697 F2d 1213

only rarely results in a state action finding in the circuits,[128] the symbiotic relationship test of *Burton* is still viable.[129] This is sound despite the questionable assertion by the Eighth Circuit that the nexus approach has undermined *Burton,* with the result that *Burton* should therefore be limited to racial discrimination cases.[130]

   Burton is still good law because state action can be found under one approach even though not found under another. The Supreme Court has never held that a finding of state action must satisfy each and every one of the three general approaches that have been used.[131] Also, insisting on a nexus may be sensible in dealing with a concededly private person or entity; if state action is to be found in connection with the challenged conduct, there must be some precisely relevant governmental involvement shown.[132] On the other hand, once a state instrumentality is shown, there is no question that state action has made the challenged conduct possible, even if it did not compel that particular conduct. Even in *Jackson* itself the Court not only spoke of a nexus test, but independently considered whether *Burton's* symbiotic test could be used to find state action.[133] Consequently, there is and should be no nexus test generally applicable to all state action cases. In determining whether challenged conduct is in fact the action of a state instrumentality, *Burton's* case-by-case approach is still viable.

(4th Cir 1982) (nexus between county and removal of plaintiffs as volunteer firefighters).

   [128] *E.g.,* Ancata v Prison Health Servs, 769 F2d 700 (11th Cir 1985) (private entity responsible, pursuant to agreement with county, for providing medical care to those housed in county jail, was state actor under state function approach; this function is traditionally the exclusive prerogative of the state). See **§2.07** where it is suggested that the Supreme Court has become increasingly unwilling to expand the state function approach.

   [129] *E.g.,* Krynicky v University of Pittsburgh, 742 F2d 94 (3d Cir 1984) (University of Pittsburgh and Temple University state actors because of symbiotic relationship; earlier case so holding, Braden v University of Pittsburgh, 552 F2d 948 (3d Cir 1977) (en banc) still good law; *Burton's* symbiotic relationship test appropriate even after *Lugar, Rendell-Baker,* and *Blum*); Halet v Wend Inv Co, 672 F2d 1305 (9th Cir 1982) (symbiotic relationship between private apartment complex and Los Angeles County properly alleged); Janusaitis v Middlebury Volunteer Fire Dept, 607 F2d 17 (2d Cir 1979) (volunteer fire department had symbiotic relationship with town where firemen dismissed). *But cf* Frazier v Board of Trustees of Nw Mississippi Regional Medical Center, 765 F2d 1278, 1287 (5th Cir 1985) (*Burton* still good law, although "now subject to the gloss of *Rendell-Baker* and *Blum*. The 'joint' of 1961 does not the 'symbiosis' of today make"; indispensability is the core of *Burton*).

   [130] Lubin v Crittenden Hosp Assn, 713 F2d 414 (8th Cir 1983).

   [131] *See* **§§2.04-2.07.**

   [132] For example, the Fifth Circuit properly looked for a state nexus, but found none, in connection with a private kennel club's refusal to renew the §1983 plaintiff's booking contract to race dogs. Fulton v Hecht, 545 F2d 540, 543 (5th Cir), *cert denied,* 430 US 984 (1977).

   [133] Note that the Court in *Jackson* concluded there was no state action in the utility's termination of service even under the *Burton* test.

§2.10   State Action and Conspiracy

A private person acts under color of law and may thus be liable under §1983 for participation in a conspiracy with a state or local government official to violate a plaintiff's Fourteenth Amendment rights.[134] The existence of this kind of joint liability was made clear by the Supreme Court in *Adickes v Kress & Co*,[135] a case involving a possible conspiracy between a private restaurant owner and local police to discriminate on racial grounds. However, a different but related question previously split the circuits: whether a private person who conspired with an absolutely immune defendant such as a legislator, judge, or prosecutor,[136] acted under color of law. Before the Court's decision in *Dennis v Sparks*,[137] most of the circuits addressing this question concluded without much analysis that a private person did not act under color of law in such cases.[138] As a panel of the Seventh Circuit noted: "[I]t has been frequently stated that allegations of conspiracy between private persons and public officials who are themselves immune from liability under the facts alleged are insufficient to establish liability of the private persons under color of law for purposes of the Civil Rights Act."[139]

This conclusion was always questionable.[140] The state action inquiry is essentially independent of the absolute immunity issue because the former

---

[134] In addition to proving such a conspiracy, the plaintiff must of course prove the other elements of the prima facie §1983 cause of action. *See generally* §§2.02-2.03 & ch 3.

Certain civil rights conspiracies are also actionable against private parties as well as state officials under 42 USC §1985. Thus, §1985(2) creates a federal cause of action for damages against conspiracies which deter by force, intimidation, or threat to a party or witness in federal court (first part of §1985(2)) and against conspiracies which obstruct the due course of justice with intent to deny equal protection (second part of §1985(2)). A showing of discrimination is not required under the first part of §1985(2). Kush v Rutledge, 460 US 719 (1983). Section 1985(3) creates a cause of action against conspiracies which deprive persons of equal protection or other federal rights, privileges, or immunities. Here, the conspiracy must be motivated by racial or other class-based animus. Griffin v Breckenridge, 403 US 88, 100-02 (1971). For a thorough discussion of §1985 in a case also involving §1983 claims, *see* Bell v City of Milwaukee, 746 F2d 1205 (7th Cir 1984) (conspiracy actions by decedent's estate, decedent's father's estate, and decedent's siblings arising out of fatal shooting of black decedent by police officer and subsequent racially motivated cover-up to conceal relevant facts of shooting).

[135] 398 US 144 (1970). *See* §2.06.

[136] *See generally* ch 7.

[137] 449 US 24 (1980) discussed later in this section.

[138] Briley v California, 564 F2d 849 (9th Cir 1977); Kurz v Michigan, 548 F2d 172 (6th Cir), *cert denied*, 434 US 972 (1977); Hansen v Ahlgrimm, 520 F2d 768 (7th Cir 1975); Waits v McGowan, 516 F2d 203 (3d Cir 1975); Newcomb v Brennan, 558 F2d 825 (7th Cir), *cert denied*, 434 US 968 (1977); Hill v McClellan, 490 F2d 859 (5th Cir 1974); Guedry v Ford, 431 F2d 660 (5th Cir 1970); Haldane v Chagnon, 345 F2d 601 (9th Cir 1965), a previously much cited case.

[139] Hansen v Ahlgrimm, 520 F2d 768, 770 (7th Cir 1975).

[140] As argued in the First Edition of this book before *Dennis* was decided.

emphasizes state involvement with the purportedly private party[141] while the latter aims to avoid the chilling effect of potential §1983 damages litigation upon certain classes of official defendants.[142] Also, absolute immunity of a defendant under §1983 in no way precludes action under color of law. Indeed, strictly speaking, the absolute immunity question need not even be reached until after state action is found. Moreover, this reasoning was strongly supported by analogy to the Supreme Court's discussion in *Adickes v Kress & Co*[143] of the possibility of joint liability of a private defendant and a police officer despite the latter's protection by qualified immunity.[144]

Consequently, there was no inconsistency in concluding that a defendant was absolutely immune and at the same time characterizing a private person's conspiratorial participation with the absolutely immune defendant as state action. Those circuits which perceived such an inconsistency were simply avoiding the merits of the plaintiff's claim by an improper use of the state action doctrine. A concern with frivolous §1983 suits and with the relative ease with which a conspiracy can be alleged is better addressed, as the First Circuit indicated before *Dennis*, by an insistence that more than conclusory allegations of the conspiracy be pleaded.[145]

Hence, it was not surprising that even before *Dennis* several circuits began to question this derivative immunity rule,[146] and the First Circuit expressly held the contrary.[147] In *Dennis v Sparks*,[148] finally, the Supreme Court unanimously

---

[141] *See* **§2.04.**

[142] *See generally* **ch 7.**

[143] 398 US 144 (1970).

[144] The same appears in Downs v Sawtelle, 574 F2d 1 (1st Cir 1978) and Fine v City of New York, 529 F2d 70 (2d Cir 1975). *See also* Alexanian v New York State Urban Dev Corp, 554 F2d 15 (2d Cir 1977) (per curiam), similarly involving a §1983 conspiracy between a private person and a police officer, and relying on *Adickes. See* **§2.04.**

[145] Slotnick v Staviskey, 560 F2d 31, 33-34 (1st Cir 1977), *cert denied,* 434 US 1077 (1978). *See also* Sooner Prods Co v McBride, 708 F2d 510 (10th Cir 1983) (conclusory allegations, to effect that state judges were involved in an elaborate conspiracy with private defendants, were not sufficient to withstand motion to dismiss; "the pleadings must specifically present facts tending to show agreement and concerted action . . . . [The] standard is even stricter where the state officials allegedly involved in the conspiracy are immune from suit, as are the state judges here"); Henzel v Gerstein, 608 F2d 654 (5th Cir 1979) (allegations of conspiracy between private individuals and prosecutors "wholly conclusory and unsupported, and cannot withstand a motion for summary judgment"); Francis-Sobel v University of Me, 597 F2d 15 (1st Cir 1979) (pleading "requires at least minimum factual support of the existence of a conspiracy"); Mosher v Saalfield, 589 F2d 438 (9th Cir 1978) (per curiam) (general allegations of conspiratorial conversations legally insufficient in the absence of allegations as to their substance); Grow v Fisher, 523 F2d 875, 878-79 (7th Cir 1975). *See also* **§2.11** for further discussion.

[146] Briley v California, 564 F2d 849, 858 n 10 (9th Cir 1977) (matter "not clear"); Fine v City of New York, 529 F2d 70 (2d Cir 1975) (by implication); Grow v Fisher, 523 F2d 875, 878 (7th Cir 1975) (expressly).

[147] Downs v Sawtelle, 574 F2d 1 (1st Cir 1978); Kermit Constr Corp v Banco Credito Y Ahorro Ponceno, 547 F2d 1 (1st Cir 1976).

[148] 449 US 24 (1980).

held that a private defendant who conspires with an absolutely immune state judge acts under color of law and is not derivatively protected by that judge's absolute immunity. In *Dennis*, plaintiffs sued various private parties and a county judge for damages, alleging that an injunction had been corruptly issued by the judge as the result of a conspiracy between him and the other defendants. This injunction, it was claimed, deprived plaintiffs of their property without due process of law. The Supreme Court agreed with the en banc decision of the Fifth Circuit which had held that "there was no good reason in law, logic or policy for conferring immunity on private persons who persuaded the immune judge to exercise his jurisdiction corruptly."[149]

The Court first noted that a person can act under color of state law even if not an officer of the state if he or she is a "willful participant in joint action with the state or its agents."[150] Next, it asserted that for state action purposes, immunity "will be seriously eroded" unless a private co-conspirator is derivatively protected by a judge's absolute immunity. In no sense were the private co-conspirators performing a judicial act or functioning as the judge's official aides.

Furthermore, according to the Court, even if a judge becomes significantly involved as a witness in the trial of such a §1983 action for damages against co-conspirators and is forced to testify about and defend judicial conduct, the absolute judicial immunity policy of not undermining a judge's independence and judicial performance is not significantly compromised thereby because the judge cannot be held liable for damages. With respect to such third-party litigation, the scope of absolute judicial immunity is somewhat narrower than the scope of absolute legislative immunity which, as based on the speech or debate clause, protects members of Congress from responding to questions about their legislative acts. However, this modest limitation on absolute judicial immunity is justified, the Court concluded, because "the potential harm to the public from denying immunity to private co-conspirators is outweighed by the benefits of providing a remedy against those private persons who participate in subverting the judicial process and in so doing inflict injury on other person."[151]

If a §1983 cause of action can in fact be stated against a private person who participates in a conspiracy with an absolutely immune defendant, the question of available defenses arises.[152] Clearly, absolute immunity should not attach.

---

[149] *Id* 27.

[150] *Id.*

[151] *Id* 31-32. The ruling in *Dennis v Sparks* was readily applied by the Court in Tower v Glover, 467 US 914 (1984), set out at **§7.15,** to public defenders accused of conspiring with other state officials, including judges. Such public defenders, according to the Court, act under color of law for §1983 purposes.

[152] Conspiracy in a §1983 joint liability setting requires only an understanding by the parties to harm or injure another and act on the part of at least one of them which causes a deprivation of plaintiff's constitutional or federal statutory rights. Adickes v Kress & Co, 398 US 144 (1970). The co-conspirator need no more specifically intend that plaintiff be deprived of his rights than an individual, nonconspirator defendant need intend it. Such a specific intent requirement for §1983 liability was expressly rejected

First, that would amount to repeating the argument that no cause of action is stated against the private party because the alleged conspiracy was with an absolutely immune defendant. More important, the major purpose of absolute immunity, the protection of state legislators, judges, and prosecutors from the chilling effect of potential §1983 damages litigation, is typically not applicable to private persons.[153]

A private party who conspires with an absolutely immune defendant should similarly not be entitled to assert a qualified immunity. Qualified immunity is designed to protect official defendants in the performance of their official duties from liability for damages unless they are found to have acted in violation of clearly settled law.[154] This function is not relevant to private persons, however. The First Circuit made this point in an analogous case in which it rejected the qualified immunity defense raised by a private person who allegedly conspired with a *qualifiedly* immune official defendant:

> Private parties simply are not confronted with the pressures of office, the often split-second decision-making or the constant threat of liability facing police officers, governors and other public officials. Whatever factors of policy and fairness mulitate in favor of extending some immunity to private parties acting in concert with state officials were resolved by Congress in favor of those who claim a deprivation of constitutional rights.[155]

Consequently, once the plaintiff makes out a §1983 cause of action at trial against a private person who has conspired with an absolutely or qualifiedly immune official defendant, the plaintiff should prevail against that private person.

However, there is a significant qualification to the argument, at least in nonconspiracy cases. In *Lugar v Edmundson Oil Co,*[156] the Court held in a *nonconspiracy* setting that a party to a private dispute, sued for using state attachment procedures whereby state officials attach property on ex parte application, acts under color of law. The Court then went on to suggest that

---

in Monroe v Pape, 365 US 167 (1961), where the Court said that §1983 was to be interpreted against a "background of tort liability." *See generally* ch 3 on the prima facie §1983 cause of action.

[153] However, in Grow v Fisher, 523 F2d 875, 878 (7th Cir 1975), the Seventh Circuit stated in dictum:

> We are not unmindful that a policy rationale could be advanced for extending quasi-immunity to persons who bring to the attention of immune prosecuting officials alleged criminal activity which is followed by prosecution. For example . . . a private person who is the victim of a crime or a witness to a crime should not be discouraged from reporting that crime to proper authorities or from following the advice of a prosecuting attorney as to whether or not to sign an affidavit against the perpetrator of a crime.

[154] *See generally* ch 8.

[155] Downs v Sawtelle, 574 F2d 1, 15-16 (1st Cir 1978).

[156] 457 US 922 (1982). *See* §2.06.

as a matter of policy this private party might be protected by a qualified immunity for his or her good faith reliance on the constitutionality of such state attachment procedures.[157] This suggestion was followed by the Fifth Circuit which explicitly held that "a §1983 defendant who has invoked an attachment statute is entitled to an immunity from monetary liability so long as he neither knew nor reasonably should have known that the statute was unconstitutional."[158] The policy reasons relied upon included permitting ordinary citizens to rely on apparently valid state laws and protecting them when they reasonably use a legal process later found unconstitutional, so long as their role in such unconstitutional conduct is "marginal."[159]

It should be noted that these policy reasons will not ordinarily be applicable in conspiracy cases. Furthermore, even if qualified immunity is applicable in some conspiracy cases, where a private person involved in an actionable conspiracy to deprive a plaintiff of constitutional rights thereby knowingly or otherwise violates clearly settled law, then the defendant will fail the qualified immunity test.[160]

While most §1983 conspiracy cases involve state officials,[161] several circuits have indicated that *federal* officials who conspire with state officials act under color of *state* law for §1983 purposes. For example, although ultimately ruling for defendants on the merits, the First Circuit so assumed in a case involving allegations of a conspiracy to discriminate between a regional director of the federal Equal Employment Opportunity Commission and the officials of a state university.[162] In a case involving an alleged conspiracy with state officials, the Seventh Circuit expressly held: "[W]hen federal officials are engaged in a conspiracy with state officials to deprive constitutional rights, the state officials provide the requisite state action to make the entire conspiracy actionable under section 1983."[163] Relying for its approach on a Second Circuit decision,[164] the Seventh Circuit stated that the state action test in a case dealing with the joint exercise of a state power and a nonstate power is whether the state or its officials *played a significant role* in bringing about the constitutional

---

[157] 457 US at 941 n 22.

[158] Folsom Inv Co v Moore, 681 F2d 1032, 1037 (5th Cir 1982).

[159] See §8.03 on the objective qualified immunity test.

[160] *See id.*

[161] §1983, of course, applies only to acts under color of state, not federal, law. *See, e.g.,* Hubbert v United States Parole Commn, 585 F2d 857 (7th Cir 1978) (per curiam); *see also* §1.09.

[162] Francis-Sobel v University of Me, 597 F2d 15 (1st Cir 1979).

[163] Hampton v Hanrahan, 600 F2d 600, 623 (7th Cir 1979), *cert denied,* 446 US 754 (1980) (per curiam). To the same effect is Knights of the KKK v East Baton Rouge Parish School Bd, 735 F2d 895 (5th Cir 1984).

[164] Kletschka v Driver, 411 F2d 436 (2d Cir 1969). *Compare* the Ninth Circuit's language in Tongol v Usery, 601 F2d 1091 (9th Cir 1979), noted at §2.09, which concerned compliance with a federal regulation by a state agency.

violation. However, according to the Ninth Circuit,[165] the furnishing of information by federal officials to state officials conducting an investigation of the plaintiff was, standing alone, not enough to show a conspiracy between those officials for color of law purposes. The federal officials acted pursuant to *federal,* not state, law.

§2.11 Conspiracy in General: Governing Principles

Even apart from the state action-color of law issue, an extensive body of §1983 conspiracy case law has developed in the circuits involving the elements of conspiracy, the sufficiency of conspiracy allegations, and the sufficiency of evidence of conspiracy. In an important §1983 conspiracy case against federal and state law enforcement officers and others arising out of a gun battle during a raid on an apartment, the Seventh Circuit[166] set out the following civil conspiracy guidelines:

1. A civil conspiracy is a combination of two or more persons acting in concert to commit an unlawful act, or to commit a lawful act by unlawful means, where those persons agree to inflict an injury upon another and where there is an overt act resulting in damage

2. Circumstantial evidence may be sufficient to prove an agreement between the conspirators; direct evidence is not necessary

3. A plaintiff need not prove that *every* conspirator knew the exact details of the plan or the identity of all participants, so long as the conspirators shared the same conspiratorial objectives

4. The question whether a conspiracy existed should not be taken from the jury where the jury can infer from the circumstances that the defendants had a meeting of the minds and thus reached an understanding to bring about the conspiracy's objectives

5. In a §1983 conspiracy case, plaintiff must allege and prove both a conspiracy and an actual deprivation of rights

It is necessary for a §1983 conspiracy claim that there be alleged and proved a constitutional deprivation. A conspiracy standing alone is insufficient.[167] Also, the conspirators need not know that their conduct is unconstitutional;

---

[165] Scott v Roseberg, 702 F2d 1263 (9th Cir 1983).

[166] Hampton v Hanrahan, 600 F2d 600, 620-23 (7th Cir 1979), *cert denied,* 446 US 754 (1980) (per curiam).

[167] Villaneuva v McInnis, 723 F2d 414 (5th Cir 1984) (conspiracy to commit murder not actionable where no harm of any kind done to plaintiff and no constitutional deprivation).

specific intent to cause a constitutional deprivation is not required.[168]
However, there must be an understanding, or some concerted effort or plan,
to cause harm or injury to the plaintiff.[169] This requirement was put somewhat
differently by the Tenth Circuit: "Has the plaintiff demonstrated the existence
of a significant nexus or entanglement between the absolutely immune state
official and the private party in relation to the steps taken by each to fulfill the
objects of their conspiracy?"[170]

The rule is clear that allegations of conspiracy must provide some factual
basis supporting the existence of the conspiracy, that is, the plaintiff must plead
conspiracy in some detail. Simply alleging, for example, that the defendants
acted "jointly in concert" and "under color of state law" is not sufficient.[171]
However, conspiracy allegations were held sufficient where plaintiffs alleged
that hospital employees turned over gunshot fragments, his clothing, and

---

[168] *See* **§2.10.** See generally **ch 3** on state of mind requirements.

[169] Moore v The Marketplace Restaurant, 754 F2d 1336 (7th Cir 1985). Simply
providing false information to an arresting officer is not enough for the §1983
conspiracy liability of a private person. *Id.*

[170] Norton v Liddel, 620 F2d 1375, 1380 (10th Cir 1980).

[171] McGillicuddy v Clements, 746 F2d 76 (1st Cir 1984) (conspiracy allegations against
private accounting firm insufficient in absence of "specific fact allegations"; "jointly in
concert" and "under color of state law" allegations inadequate).
The following decisions similarly found insufficient allegations:

Second Circuit

San Filippo v United States Trust Co, 737 F2d 246 (2d Cir 1984) (allegation that
private defendants met with prosecutor and police officer prior to testifying insufficient;
such meetings are routine).
Sommer v Dixon, 709 F2d 173 (2d Cir 1983) (per curiam) (inmate's conspiracy claim
against prison officials unsupported by description of particular overt acts).

Fourth Circuit

Scott v Greenville County, 716 F2d 1409 (4th Cir 1983) (allegations that private
landowners conspired with public officials regarding construction of low-cost housing
insufficient; private citizen attempts to influence public officials, even if in private
meetings, are not enough in the absence of a joint plan of action).

Seventh Circuit

Tarkowski v Robert Bartlett Realty, 644 F2d 1204 (7th Cir 1980) (allegations of
conspiracy regarding discriminatory enforcement of zoning ordinances insufficient; a
private party who merely invokes the authority of a state official does not thereby
conspire with him or her).

Tenth Circuit

Shaffer v Cook, 634 F2d 1259 (10th Cir 1980) (per curiam) (insufficient allegations
against private attorneys and trial judge where only fact alleged was that one of the
attorneys spoke to judge in the courthouse before each hearing).
However, special solicitude is often shown to pro se inmate complaints. *E.g.*, Smith
v Bacon, 699 F2d 434 (8th Cir 1983) (per curiam) ("barely sufficient" allegations);
Richardson v Fleming, 654 F2d 366 (5th Cir 1981) (complaint could be read as alleging
conspiracy); White v Bloom, 621 F2d 276 (8th Cir 1980) (conclusory but "possible"
violation alleged); *see also* **§1.16.**

personal effects to police at their request;[172] that private defendants conspired with and directed police officers to issue a felony warrant against plaintiff, with all the defendants knowing that the information supplied was false;[173] that private defendants conspired with a sheriff and his deputies to put him out of business, with the officers causing the serving of a knowingly invalid summons, complaint, and garnishment;[174] and that private defendants arranged to have a police officer arrest and imprison plaintiff in order to force her to meet with a bank employee so as to pay her bank debt.[175]

As noted earlier,[176] circumstantial evidence may be used to prove a conspiracy, and such evidence must at least demonstrate that the defendants shared the same conspiratorial objectives. For example, in affirming the district court's grant of summary judgment in favor of the defendants who were accused of conspiring against the plaintiff by denying him a license to operate a discotheque because he was black, the First Circuit refused to infer the existence of a conspiracy from the fact that a license to operate a skating rink was granted instead to a white applicant.[177] There was affidavit evidence of general racial hostility in the community, but nothing specific tending to show that race was a motivating factor in the denial of his application. Also, plaintiff's promise that circumstantial evidence showing the conspiracy would emerge at trial was not enough in the absence of factual support.

Similarly, where a liquor license applicant sued various city officials alleging a conspiracy to prevent him from obtaining a license, the Fifth Circuit[178] reversed the district court's judgment against certain individual city council

---

[172] Fris v Barnes, 618 F2d 988 (2d Cir 1980).

[173] Mark v Furay, 769 F2d 1266 (7th Cir 1985).

[174] A&A Concrete Inc v White Mountain Apache Tribe, 678 F2d 1330 (9th Cir 1982).

[175] Lessman v McCormick, 591 F2d 605 (10th Cir 1979). The Tenth Circuit used what it called a "liberal construction test" against all the defendants, who included persons in addition to the police officer and the bank employee. It reasoned: "In many cases of conspiracy essential information can only be produced through discovery, and the parties should not be thrown out of court before being given an opportunity through that process to ascertain whether the linkage they think may exist actually does." *Id* 611.
Cf Dykes v Hosemann, 743 F2d 1488 (11th Cir 1984), *revd in part on other grounds,* 776 F2d 942 (11th Cir 1985) (en banc) where, according to the Eleventh Circuit, plaintiff stated a §1983 due process claim against the private attorney defendant who allegedly conspired with state officials to utilize an illegal child custody order to obtain permanent custody of plaintiff's child where it was also alleged that defendant knew or should have known that the order was illegal and improper. These allegations were enough for both color of law and the claim of conspiracy to violate due process. Judge Hill dissented as to the latter, arguing that there were alleged "absolutely no acts of conspiracy or active cooperation between [defendant] and the other defendants in this case, outside of actions within the normal attorney-client relationship." *Id* 1504. More than mere advocacy of a client's rights was required for an actionable conspiracy against an attorney.

[176] See discussion at the beginning of this section.

[177] Manego v Cape Cod Five Cents Savs Bank, 692 F2d 174 (1st Cir 1982).

[178] Bennett v City of Slidell, 697 F2d 657, 660 (5th Cir 1983), *revd on other grounds,* 728 F2d 762 (5th Cir 1984) (en banc).

members. Even though they had voted against the plaintiff's application and had failed to conduct an inquiry into the matter, "[t]he record contains no credible evidence that the council members voted for any reason other than those patently apparent [which were legitimate]." Thus, they had not participated in a conspiracy with the mayor, the city attorney, and the city building inspector.

In a Seventh Circuit case,[179] decedent was shot and killed in a struggle with a police officer in the course of his arrest after a high-speed automobile chase in which various police officers participated. Among other issues, the Seventh Circuit affirmed the district court's directed verdict in favor of the nonshooting police officers despite the plaintiff's allegation of a conspiracy. According to the court, "there was no evidence of any communication between the officers which might give rise to any inference of agreement to commit any acts, wrongful or otherwise."

And in a Ninth Circuit case, where plaintiff alleged that the defendant banks conspired with the FBI with the effect of violating her First and Fourteenth Amendment rights, the court affirmed the district court's grant of summary judgment in favor of defendants. It stated:

> The mere acquiescence of the [defendants'] bank employees to the investigation request of the FBI to view Fonda's bank records is, without more, insufficient to prove a conspiracy. While it is not necessary to prove that each participant in the conspiracy knew the exact parameters of the plan, they must at least share the general conspiratorial objective.[180]

Here, the banks dispelled the inference of any improper motive by asserting their ignorance of any plan to harm plaintiff. In short, there was no evidence of any "meeting of the minds" between the banks and the FBI.

In contrast, sufficient evidence of conspiracy was found in a Fifth Circuit case[181] where plaintiff, a discharged police officer, sued the city of New Orleans and various officials, alleging a conspiracy to create a code of silence protecting those who abided by this "blue curtain" and punishing those who violated it, as he did when he complained about police misconduct. Affirming the jury's verdict in favor of the plaintiff, the court noted that the record demonstrated the defendants participated in private meetings during which plaintiff's charges were discussed. There was also expert testimony that such a "blue curtain" existed in the New Orleans police department. Inasmuch as circumstantial evidence is often necessary to prove a conspiracy, there was sufficient evidence in this case to show a conspiracy directed against the plaintiff.

In another Fifth Circuit case,[182] in affirming a jury verdict against various city officials for conspiring to violate plaintiff's constitutional rights, the court

---

[179] Richardson v City of Indianapolis, 658 F2d 494, 500 (7th Cir 1981).

[180] Fonda v Gray, 707 F2d 435, 438 (9th Cir 1983). Judge Pregerson dissented, saying that the case should not be disposed of on summary judgment.

[181] Thomas v City of New Orleans, 687 F2d 80 (5th Cir 1980).

[182] Crowe v Lucas, 595 F2d 985 (5th Cir 1979).

observed that such plaintiffs must show that defendants agreed to commit an illegal act. This showing is typically met by circumstantial evidence because "conspirators rarely formulate their plans in ways susceptible of proof by direct evidence." In this case, defendants had participated in private meetings at which plaintiff was discussed, and they had engaged in illegal conduct, including several arrests, directed at plaintiff.

Similarly, in a Seventh Circuit[183] case where the plaintiff nursing home sued various officers and employees of a state's health and human services department alleging a conspiracy to deprive it of First and Fourteenth Amendment rights, the court held that there was sufficient evidence of a conspiracy to warrant submission of the conspiracy claim to the jury. Most of the defendants' notices of violation directed against the plaintiff were meritless but they were pursued nevertheless. Also, even though plaintiff timely appealed from defendants' decision to place plaintiff on an SOR (suspension of referrals) list, defendants went ahead regardless and placed plaintiff on this list which was sent to over 600 social service agencies and departments.

And in a Ninth Circuit case,[184] a son's §1983 suit against his parents, a judge, and others, alleging a conspiracy to "deprogram" him from the Unification Church, was improperly dismissed against the private defendants and the judge. Stating that there were material issues of fact in dispute, the Ninth Circuit noted that it was insufficient for conspiracy purposes that the private defendants carried out a judicial order. Plaintiff should have the opportunity to prove further that the private defendants reached an understanding with the judge to violate plaintiff's constitutional rights by fraudulently alleging plaintiff's residence to create jurisdiction and through the judge's abandoning his impartiality.

Where a plaintiff alleges and proves a §1983 conspiracy and the individual defendants are not protected by either absolute or qualified immunity, then the plaintiff will ordinarily be entitled to both compensatory and punitive damages.[185]

§2.12   Section 1983 and Federal Statutory Violations

Section 1983 makes actionable violations not only of "rights, privileges, or immunities secured by the Constitution" in the Fourteenth Amendment,[186] but also of those rights secured by the "laws." The question that divided the circuits, at least before the Supreme Court's recent pronouncements on the

---

[183] Cameo Convalescent Center Inc v Senn, 738 F2d 836 (7th Cir 1984).

[184] Rankin v Howard, 633 F2d 844 (9th Cir 1980).

[185] See generally ch 4 on damages. Local government defendants are absolutely immune from punitive damages liability, but not from compensatory damages liability. *See generally* ch 6.

[186] *See* §§2.02-2.03.

matter,[187] was which federal statutory violations gave rise to §1983 actions, especially where the particular federal statutes did not provide for causes of action in their own right.

The narrowest possible interpretation of "laws" would limit §1983 actions to those federal statutes which, like §1983 itself, were enacted pursuant to section 5 of the Fourteenth Amendment. The broadest possible interpretation would include all federal statutory violations, even those totally unrelated to civil rights or Fourteenth Amendment concerns.[188] This was more than an academic matter, especially before 1980 when the $10,000 jurisdictional amount requirement of 28 USC §1331 was eliminated.[189] If §1983 and its jurisdictional counterpart[190] could be used in connection with certain federal statutory violations, then the §1983 plaintiff did not have to worry either about satisfying the previous jurisdictional amount requirement of 28 USC §1331[191] or about using the device of pendent jurisdiction in order to obtain a federal forum.[192]

This "laws" question could not be avoided by characterizing it as involving rights under the Supremacy Clause, thereby converting every federal statutory right issue into a constitutional issue.[193] As was observed by the Second and

---

[187] Pennhurst State School & Hosp v Halderman, 451 US 1 (1981); Middlesex County Sewerage Authority v National Sea Clammers, 453 US 1 (1981); Maine v Thiboutot, 448 US 1 (1980); all of which are discussed later in this section.

[188] Each of these extreme interpretations was rejected by the Eight Circuit in Chase v McMasters, 573 F2d 1011, 1017 (8th Cir 1978) which held that an American Indian plaintiff stated a §1983 cause of action in connection with an alleged violation of 25 USC §465, a federal statute protecting tribal Indians.

[189] See §1.10 and discussion later.

[190] 28 USC §1343, discussed later, provides in relevant part that federal district courts have original jurisdiction of civil actions

> authorized by law to be commenced by any person: . . .(3) To redress the deprivation, under color of any State law, statute, ordinance, regulation, custom or usage, or any right, privilege or immunity secured by the Constitution of the United States or by any Act of Congress providing for equal rights of citizens . . .(4) To recover damages or to secure equitable or other relief under any Act of Congress providing for the protection of civil rights, including the right to vote.

Section 1343(3) is commonly considered to be §1983's jurisdictional counterpart. See Lynch v Household Fin Corp, 405 US 538, 543-44 n 7 (1972).

[191] 28 USC §1331 previously provided in relevant part that federal district courts had original jurisdiction over matters in controversy arising under the Constitution, laws, or treaties of the United States and exceeding "the sum or value of $10,000." This was general federal question jurisdiction. It is obvious why most §1983 welfare plaintiffs sought to avoid §1331; the $10,000 jurisdictional amount figure was typically unattainable.

[192] By using the device of pendent jurisdiction, a §1983 plaintiff with a substantial constitutional claim could join a federal statutory claim without having to satisfy 28 USC §1331's previous $10,000 jurisdictional amount requirement for the latter. See §§1.08-1.10.

[193] If a federal statue is valid, then it overrides inconsistent state law by virtue of the Supremacy Clause, art VI, cl 2 of the US Constitution which provides in relevant part

Third Circuits,[194] this would turn every federal statutory case into a constitutional case. Also, the "rights, privileges, or immunities" in fact arise not from the Supremacy Clause, but rather, where they exist, from the federal statute itself. Furthermore, the words "and laws" would be redundant in §1983.[195]

Closely related questions of interpretation similarly arose in connection with the language of §1983's jurisdictional counterpart. Section 1343(3) gives federal courts original jurisdiction without regard to jurisdictional amount over cases involving deprivations of rights, privileges, or immunities secured by the Constitution "or by any Act of Congress *providing for equal rights of citizens* or of all persons within the jurisdiction of the United States."[196] Section 1343(4) does the same for actions "[t]o recover damages or to secure equitable or other relief under any Act of Congress *providing for the protection of civil rights*, including the right to vote."[197] If "equal rights" and "civil rights" were read restrictively so as to exclude, for example, Social Security Act rights, the result would be that even if §1983 were read broadly as creating causes of action for many or all federal statutory violations, federal courts would have §1343 jurisdiction only in some of those cases.[198]

Before its recent "laws" decisions, the Supreme Court had said, in dictum, that §1983 covered not only "violations of rights conferred by federal civil rights laws, but. . . violations of other federal constitutional and statutory rights as well."[199] But it expressly left these troublesome §§1983, 1343(3), and 1343(4) questions open in *Hagans v Lavine*,[200] and the circuits were split in resolving them. The Second Circuit held that a federal court did not have jurisdiction to deal with an action based on the Social Security Act brought under §1983 by welfare recipients to compel state reimbursement for certain expenses incurred traveling to district offices.[201] The court rejected the contention that 28 USC §1343(3) or 1343(4) conferred jurisdiction. It stated

that "[t]his Constitution and the Laws of the United States which shall be made in Pursuance thereof . . . shall be the supreme Law of the Land; and the Judges in every State shall be bound thereby, any Thing in the Constitution or laws of any State to the Contrary notwithstanding."

[194] Gonzalez v Young, 560 F2d 160, 165-66 (3d Cir 1977); Andrews v Maher, 525 F2d 113, 118-19 (2d Cir 1975).

[195] Similarly redundant would be 28 USC §1343(3)'s reference to "any Act of Congress providing for equal rights of citizens. . . ." *See* **§1.02** for full text of §1343(3).

[196] (Emphasis added.)

[197] (Emphasis added).

[198] The possibility of using either federal question jurisdiction under 28 USC §1331 or pendent jurisdiction, see **§§1.10-1.12,** would then have to be pursued. If neither possibility existed, then filing in state court would have to be considered. *See* **§1.13.** This apparently anomalous result is precisely what the Court later arrived at in Chapman v Houston Welfare Rights Org, 441 US 600 (1979), discussed later.

[199] Greenwood v Peacock, 384 US 808, 829-30 (1966). *See also* United States v Price, 383 US 787, 797 (1966) where the Court made a similar observation about the scope of comparable language in 18 USC §242, the criminal counterpart of §1983.

[200] 415 US 528, 533-34 n 5 (1974).

[201] Andrews v Maher, 525 F2d 113 (2d Cir 1975).

that the Social Security Act was neither an act "providing for equal rights" nor one "providing for the protection of civil rights." It also did not accept the argument that §1983 itself was the relevant statute "providing for the protection of civil rights." It found instead that this language of §1343(4) was enacted as part of the Civil Rights Act of 1957 in order to ensure jurisdiction over claims based on that statute.[202] The Third Circuit reached the same result in a §1983 claim based on the Social Security Act seeking emergency assistance in the amount of $163.[203]

On the other hand, the Fourth Circuit took the contrary position in still another §1983, Social Security Act case.[204] It first broadly read the "laws" language of §1983 to include such cases. Turning to the jurisdictional statutes, it construed §1343(3) to be as broad and extensive as the cause of action granted by §1983.[205] It interpreted the term "equal rights" to include such statutory claims. Additionally, the Fourth Circuit construed §1343(4) as covering all §1983 actions, including those based on federal statute.[206] Finally, the court mentioned the possible use of the Supremacy Clause to convert the §1983 action into one based on "the Constitution."[207]

In a non–Social Security Act case the Fifth Circuit found federal jurisdiction under §1343(4) where a §1983 action was brought by migrant workers asserting rights under the Wagner-Peyser Act of 1933.[208] Similarly, the Eighth

---

[202] *Id* 119-20. That the Supreme Court has used §1343(4)'s "protection of rights" language for jurisdictional purposes in cases other than those involving the Civil Rights Act of 1957, Pub L No 85-315, 71 Stat 634, *e.g.,* Allen v Board of Educ, 393 US 544, 554 (1969) (Voting Rights Act of 1965) and Jones v Alfred H Mayer Co, 392 US 409, 412 n 1 (1968) (Civil Rights Act of 1866), was conceded by the First, Second, and Third Circuits. Gonzalez v Young, 560 F2d 160 (3d Cir 1977); Andrews v Maher, 525 F2d 113 (2d Cir 1975); Randall v Goldmark, 495 F2d 356 (1st Cir), *cert denied,* 419 US 879 (1974); As to why §1343(4) should not similarly be used for §1983 jurisdictional purposes, these courts simply noted that §1983 differed from the other federal civil rights statutes because it was much broader in scope and engendered considerably more litigation.

[203] Gonzalez v Young, 560 F2d 160 (3d Cir 1977). The First Circuit used this absence of §1343 jurisdiction approach in still another §1983 Social Security Act welfare case as an alternative ground for dismissing the plaintiff's complaint. Randall v Goldmark, 495 F2d 356 (1st Cir), *cert denied,* 419 US 879 (1974). The court also rejected the claim made on the merits. However, in Construction Aggregates Corp v Rivera de Vicenty, 573 F2d 86, 94 n 6 (1st Cir 1978) the §1343 jurisdictional issue was characterized as an open question.

[204] Blue v Craig, 505 F2d 830 (4th Cir 1974). See, approving this decision, Note, 43 Geo Wash L Rev 1343 (1975); see, on the use of "laws" by §1983 welfare plaintiffs, Note, 72 Colum L Rev 1404 (1972). The Seventh Circuit by implication accepted the use of §1983 in connection with Social Security claims. Bond v Stanton, 555 F2d 172 (7th Cir 1977), *cert denied,* 438 US 916 (1978).

[205] 505 F2d at 836-39.

[206] *Id* 842.

[207] *Id* 842-44. As noted earlier, this is not a persuasive argument. *See* **§2.10.**

[208] Gomez v Florida State Employment Serv, 417 F2d 569 (5th Cir 1969). The Wagner-Peyser Act appears at 29 USC §49 *et seq* (1970). However, 28 USC §1337, providing for federal jurisdiction over causes of action arising out of statutes regulating interstate commerce, was mentioned by the court as an alternative jurisdictional basis.

Circuit upheld a §1983 action brought by an Indian who asserted that certain statutory rights unique to Indians had been violated.[209] It rejected an argument that the "laws" language of §1983 was limited to those federal statutes enacted pursuant to section 5 of the Fourteenth Amendment, but did not discuss jurisdiction at all. Finally, a Tenth Circuit case could be read as holding that a §1983 action may be based on an alleged violation of federal extradition law.[210] Here, too, however, there was no discussion of jurisdiction.

The Supreme Court gradually began to address these difficult laws and jurisdictional questions. Before the effective date of the congressional amendment to 28 USC §1331 which eliminated the previous $10,000 jurisdictional amount requirement for federal question jurisdiction,[211] the Supreme Court held in *Chapman v Houston Welfare Rights Organization*[212] that federal courts do not have jurisdiction under 28 USC §1343(3) or (4) over §1983 laws claims based on violations of the Social Security Act. In an opinion by Justice Stevens, the Court concluded on the basis of the legislative history of §§1983 and 1343 that §1983 and the Social Security Act are statutes neither "providing for equal rights" under §1343(3) nor "providing for the protection of civil rights" under §1343(4). To this extent, the Court resolved several of the jurisdictional questions associated with §1983 laws claims which had split the circuits and been unresolved in *Hagans v Lavine*.[213] These jurisdictional questions, however, are now irrelevant after the Jurisdictional Amendment Act.[214] More to the present point, significant laws questions relating to the prima facie §1983 cause of action were once again sidestepped in *Chapman*. While such questions were addressed in the concurring and dissenting opinions, the majority opinion focused solely on the jurisdictional issues and did not deal with the important question of whether §1983 causes of action could be based on violations of the Social Security Act or other federal statutes.

However, in *Maine v Thiboutot*,[215] the Court resolved certain §1983 laws issues as well. In an opinion by Justice Brennan, the Court broadly held that §1983's laws language encompasses *all* statutory violations of federal law, including the Social Security Act violation in *Thiboutot* itself. Conceding that

---

[209] Chase v McMasters, 573 F2d 1011 (8th Cir 1978). The relevant federal statute appears at 25 USC §465. However, the court observed: "[T]he constitutional dimension of the claim is particularly evident. Congress has the plenary and exclusive power to deal with Indian tribes [citation omitted], a power derived from federal responsibility for treaty making, US Const. art. II, §2, cl. 2, and from the commerce clause, US Const art. I, §8, cl.3." 573 F2d at 1017.

[210] Sanders v Conine, 506 F2d 530 (10th Cir 1974). The relevant federal statute appears at 18 USC §3182. This reading of *Sanders* was given it by the Eighth Circuit in Chase v McMasters, 573 F2d 1011, 1017 (8th Cir 1978).

[211] Federal Question Jurisdictional Amendment Act of 1980, Pub L No 96-486, effective Dec 1, 1980.

[212] 441 US 600 (1979).

[213] 415 US 528, 533-34 n 5 (1974).

[214] *See also* §1.10.

[215] 448 US 1 (1980) also discussed at §1.20 in connection with attorney's fees awards.

legislative history provided no definite guide, the Court reached its conclusion based on the plain language of §1983 and the fact that the Court's prior decisions not only regularly suggested that §1983 broadly covers violations of federal statutory law, but also allowed §1983 federal statutory claims to go forward where pendent jursidiction was available. In these latter cases, "§1983 was necessarily the exclusive statutory cause of action because . . . the Social Security Act . . . affords no private right of action against a State."[216]

According to the Court, therefore, the scope of §1983's laws language, as interpreted in *Thiboutot,* is substantially broader than §1343(3)'s "equal rights" language, as interpreted in *Chapman.* However, there was "no inherent illogic" in this result because the §1983 laws plaintiff who could not use §1343(3) could either obtain jurisdiction under 28 USC §1331 (with its then-required $10,000 jurisdictional amount), use the device of pendent jurisdiction, or file the §1983 claim in state court.

Justic Powell, joined by Chief Justice Burger and Justice Rehnquist, sharply dissented.[217] They argued that the plain meaning and legislative history demonstrated that §1983's "laws" and §1343(3)'s "equal rights" must be given the same scope. Noting the existence of "literally hundreds of cooperative regulatory and social welfare enactments," they were also concerned with the practical impact of *Thiboutot's* landmark holding that a §1983 laws cause of action may exist whenever a state official violates federal law. In their view, "the Court's decision . . . significantly expands the concept of 'civil rights' and creates a major new intrusion into state sovereignty under our federal system."

These objections of the dissenters in *Thiboutot* had an impact one year later when the Court, in an opinion by Justice Powell, limited the apparently broad holding of *Thiboutot.* In *Middlesex County Sewerage Authority v National Sea Clammers Association,*[218] the Court was confronted with damages actions brought against various defendants, including local governments and sewerage boards, for their alleged discharges and ocean dumping of sewage and other waste which damaged fishing grounds. The Court first held that there is no implied right of action under the Federal Water Pollution Control Act (FWPCA) and the Marine Protection, Research, and Sanctuaries Act of 1972 (MPRSA). Then, reaching out to address a §1983 laws issue not raised by the parties, the Court went on to hold that the FWPCA and the MPRSA could not serve as the basis for a §1983 laws cause of action.

The Court reasoned that the existence of "quite comprehensive enforcement mechanisms" in these statutes demonstrated congressional intent to preclude the remedy of suits under §1983. By relying on this exception to the application of §1983 to statutory violations, it did not have to reach a second possible exception: whether the FWPCA and the MPRSA created "rights, privileges, or immunities" with in the meaning of §1983. These two exceptions to §1983 laws actions had previously been advanced by the Court in *Pennhurst State School &*

---

[216] 448 US at 6.

[217] *Id* 11.

[218] 453 US 1 (1981).

Hospital v Halderman,[219] where it had remanded for a determination of whether the Developmentally Disabled Assistance and Bill of Rights Act could serve as the basis for a §1983 laws cause of action.

Justices Stevens and Blackmun dissented in part, arguing that the language and legislative history of the FWPCA and the MPRSA "reveal . . . a clear congressional mandate to preserve all existing remedies, including a private right of action under §1983."[220] They maintained that the majority impermissibly placed on §1983 *plaintiffs* the burden of showing an explicit or implicit congressional intention that violations of federal statutes may be redressed in §1983 actions.

These conclusions follow from the Jurisdictional Amendment Act, *Chapman, Thiboutot,* and *National Sea Clammers:*

1. Where a plaintiff asserts a §1983 laws claim based on the Social Security Act, as now permitted after *Thiboutot:*

    (a) *Chapman* precludes jurisdiction under §1343(3) and (4). However, there is jurisdiction under §1331

    (b) A state forum may be used

2. Where a plaintiff asserts a §1983 laws claim based on any other federal statute:

    (a) A laws cause of action exists only where the federal statute relied on both demonstrates congressional intent not to foreclose §1983 actions *and* creates "rights, privileges, or immunities"[221]

    (b) Jurisdiction exists under §1343(3) or (4) only if the particular statute is one providing for either equal rights or civil rights as those terms are commonly understood[222]

    (c) Even if federal jurisdiction under §1343(3) or (4) is not present under the *Chapman* approach, §1331 federal question jurisdiction is currently available without a jurisdictional amount requirement

    (d) A state forum may be used

As a general matter, the §1983 laws issue was more important to potential §1983 litigants even before the Jurisdictional Amendment Act than the §1343 jurisdiction issue because, even in the absence of the §1343 jurisdictional basis, another federal jurisdictional basis could frequently be found. If necessary, a state court could be used. However, if there were no §1983 laws cause of action, then the plaintiff would lose regardless of forum. Consequently, *Thiboutot,* even

---

[219] 451 US 1 (1981).

[220] 453 at 31.

[221] In Pennhurst State School and Hospital, the Court distinguished between an individual's interest in "assurances" and a "right secured" by the laws of the United States within the meaning of §1983, *See* Justice Blackmun's concurring opinion questioning the Court's approach. 451 US at 32.

[222] *See* **§1.10.**

as limited by *National Sea Clammers,* represents a significant victory for §1983 plaintiffs, especially when coupled with the availability of §1331 federal question jurisdiction without a jurisdictional amount requirement, and of attorney's fees under §1988.[223]

It must be remembered, though, that every §1983 plaintiff, even a §1983 laws plaintiff, must allege and prove color of law, causation in fact, proximate cause, and an entitlement to damages or declaratory and injunctive relief.[224] In addition, where absolute immunity is not available to a §1983 laws defendant,[225] the qualified immunity test will be relevant, although the focus in a laws case will be on violations of clearly settled federal law, and not on Fourteenth Amendment violations.[226]

This discussion deals with the use of federal statutory violations as a basis for §1983 laws actions. It is important to distinguish such §1983 laws issues from the possible use of a federal statute to preclude a §1983 *constitutionally* based claim. The latter issue may now arise with some frequency after the Court's decision in *Smith v Robinson.*[227] *Smith* held that Congress, in enacting the Education of the Handicapped Act,[228] intended to exclude from the coverage of §1983 independent equal protection claims identical to claims covered by the Act, that is, the Act was the exclusive avenue for such claims. This statutory interpretation approach could also be used with other federal civil rights statutes to preclude §1983 constitutional claims.[229] However, before this is done, the legislative history should unequivocally demonstrate that this was indeed the intent of Congress.

§2.13 —In the Circuits

As the Supreme Court made clear, before a federal statutory violation may be made the basis of a §1983 laws action, two hurdles must be overcome in addition to color of law. First, the federal statute must be examined in order to determine whether Congress intended that it be the exclusive avenue for recourse. If Congress so states explicitly, then that is the end of the matter. Typically, though, Congress is silent. In such a case, the existence of a comprehensive regulatory scheme which Congress presumably did not want evaded through §1983 will ordinarily result in a ruling that §1983 should not be used.

But even where this first hurdle is overcome, there is a second: the existence

---

[223] *See* **§1.20** on the latter issue.

[224] *See* **chs 2-5.**

[225] *See* **ch 7.**

[226] *See* **ch 8.** Qualified immunity does not protect local governments.

[227] 104 S Ct 3457 (1984) also noted in an attorney's fees context at **§1.20.**

[228] 20 USC §1401 *et seq.*

[229] But see Trigg v Fort Wayne Community Schools, 766 F2d 299 (7th Cir 1985), and Day v Wayne County Bd of Auditors, 749 F2d 1199 (6th Cir 1984) (both holding that §1983 equal protection claims are not precluded by Title VII).

of a right, privilege, or immunity under the federal statute. While this question is similar to the question whether a federal statute gives rise to an implied cause of action under the guidelines of *Cort v Ash*,[230] the two questions are not identical: the conclusion that a federal statute does not give rise to an implied cause of action is not necessarily inconsistent with the conclusion that it creates a right, privilege, or immunity whose deprivation can be redressed in a §1983 laws action.[231] Otherwise, the availability of §1983 laws actions would in large measure be rendered meaningless except for the possibility of attorney's fees under §1988.[232]

The circuits have addressed §1983 laws issues arising out of the particular federal statutes set out later.[233] However, other laws related issues have arisen. Thus, where the plaintiff who was seeking attorney's fees under §1988[234] had prevailed on its contention that a state statute restricting the use by plaintiff of certain truck-trailers violated the commerce clause, the issue was whether the right to engage in commerce was a right secured by the Constitution and laws within the meaning of §1983. If so, plaintiff would be entitled to such fees. Ruling against plaintiff, the Eighth Circuit[235] held that just as the supremacy clause does not secure rights within the meaning of §1983, neither does the commerce clause. Unlike the Fourteenth Amendment, which deals with the protection of individual rights, the commerce clause deals with the relationship between national and state interests. Even the dormant or negative implication of commerce clause doctrine is designated "to further the national interest in an efficient economy" and not to protect individual rights. Also, the legislative

---

[230] 422 US 66 (1975). Under *Cort*, four questions must be addressed: (1) does the plaintiff belong to the class for whose *special* benefit the statute was enacted? (2) is there any indication of explicit or implicit legislative intent on the issue? (3) is the implication of a remedy for plaintiff consistent with the legislative scheme? (4) is the cause of action traditionally relegated to state law?

[231] *But see* Home Health Servs Inc v Currie 706 F2d 497, 498 (4th Cir 1983) ("[T]he conclusion that [plaintiff] has no right of action . . . under 42 USC §1395a [Medicare Act] compels the conclusion that [plaintiff] likewise has no cause of action under §1983 . . . . ").

[232] *Cf* Boatowners & Tenants Assoc v Port of Seattle, 716 F2d 669 (9th Cir 1983) (refusing to imply action under River and Harbor Improvements Act, 33 USC §§3540-3633 and to allow statute to serve as basis for §1983 laws action because Congress created no federal rights; the court stated that even though it used the *Cort v Ash* approach in the case before it, there might still be federal rights enforceable under §1983 which would not be enforceable through a directly implied cause of action).

[233] Note that a laws action can be based on the violation of valid *federal regulations. See, e.g.,* Alexander v Polk, 750 F2d 250 (3d Cir 1984) (regulations enacted under the Child Nutrition Act).

[234] *See §§1.18-1.26.*

[235] Consolidated Freightways Corp v Kassel, 730 F2d 1139 (8th Cir 1984). To the same effect is Gould Inc v Wisconsin Dept of Indus, Labor & Human Relations, 750 F2d 608 (7th Cir 1984) (successful claim that National Labor Relations Act preempted a state statute could not be brought as §1983 laws action; the claim was based on the commerce and supremacy clauses both of which "limited the power of a state to interfere with areas of national concern," not a §1983 concern; *Kassel* followed).

history of §1983 indicates that Congress did not have the commerce clause in mind but rather Fourteenth Amendment rights. Furthermore, §1983 laws actions protect only personal rights "akin" to those protected by the Fourteenth Amendment. For all these reasons, the court held that §1983 does "not provide a remedy for a dormant commerce clause claim." Thus, plaintiff was not entitled to attorney's fees under §1988.

In the wake of the Supreme Court's decision in *Smith v Robinson*,[236] which held that Congress intended to exclude from §1983's coverage equal protection claims identical to claims covered by the Education of the Handicapped Act (EHA),[237] the circuits are beginning to deal with such issues. Those that have done so in connection with the EHA—the Fifth, Eighth, and Eleventh, as of this writing—were careful to limit *Smith's* approach and held that only §1983 equal protection claims are precluded; §1983 procedural due process claims, and even substantive due process claims, are permitted.[238] As to other federal statutes, both the Sixth and Seventh Circuits[239] have ruled that §1983 equal protection claims are not precluded by Title VII.[240]

Particular Federal Statutes and §1983 "Laws" Actions

Anti-Peonage Act

The Fifth Circuit assumed that violations of the Anti-Peonage Act[241] are actionable under §1983[242]

---

[236] 104 S Ct 3457 (1984), noted in **§2.12.**

[237] 20 USC §1401 *et seq*, sometimes called the Education for All Handicapped Children Act (EAHCA)

[238] Manecke v School Bd of Pinellas County, 762 F2d 912 (11th Cir 1985) (§1983 procedural due process claim not precluded; important distinction in *Smith* between equal protection and procedural due process); Rose v Nebraska, 748 F2d 1258 (8th Cir 1984) (preclusion of §1983 equal protection claim but not of §1983 procedural due process claim); Teresa Diane P v Alief Indep School Dist, 744 F2d 484 (5th Cir 1984) (preclusion of §1983 equal protection claim but not of §1983 procedural and substantive due process claims; Judge Higginbotham dissented on the substantive due process claim). *Cf* Bonar v Ambach, 771 F2d 14 (2d Cir 1985) ("plaintiffs failed to allege or prove any entitlement to procedural due process independent of the procedures contained in the EHA"; as a result, there was no successful §1983 due process claim but only a successful EHA claim for which attorney's fees could not be awarded). *See also* Department of Educ v Katherine D, 727 F2d 809, 820 n 5 (9th Cir 1984) (pre-*Smith* case holding that EAHCA precludes §1983 equal protection claim identical to EAHCA claim).

[239] Trigg v Fort Wayne Community Schools, 766 F2d 299 (7th Cir 1985); Day v Wayne County Bd of Auditors, 749 F2d 1199 (6th Cir 1984).

[240] 42 USC §2000e *et seq*.

[241] *Id* §1994.

[242] Crain v Alexander, 756 F2d 1070 (5th Cir 1980).

Child Nutrition Act

The Third Circuit ruled that violations of the Child Nutrition Act[243] and its regulations are actionable under §1983[244]

Civil Rights Acts

Violations of Title VII[245] have been held not to be actionable under §1983 by the Fifth and Sixth Circuits[246]

Comprehensive Employment and Training Act

The Second Circuit held that violations of the Comprehensive Employment and Training Act of 1973[247] are not actionable under §1983[248]

Education of the Handicapped Act; Education for All Handicapped Children Act

The Second and Fourth Circuits held that certain violations of these Acts[249] may be actionable under §1983,[250] while the Fifth, Sixth, Seventh, Ninth, and Eleventh Circuits ruled that as a general matter violations of these Acts are not actionable under §1983[251]

Extradition

Violations of extradition statutes[252] have been held actionable under §1983 by the Fifth, Seventh, Eighth, and Ninth Circuits[253]

Federal Rules of Procedure

The Fifth Circuit rejected a laws claim based on an alleged violation of that portion of the Federal Rules of Civil Procedure dealing with an attorney's work product immunity[254]

---

[243] 42 USC §1786.

[244] Alexander v Polk, 750 F2d 250 (3d Cir 1984).

[245] 42 USC §2000e *et seq.*

[246] Irby v Sullivan, 737 F2d 1418 (5th Cir 1984); Teresa Diane P v Alief Indep School Dist, 744 F2d 484 (5th Cir 1984); Day v Wayne County Board of Auditors, 749 F2d 1199 (6th Cir 1984).

[247] 29 USC §801 *et seq.*

[248] Uniformed Firefighters Assn v City of New York, 676 F2d 20 (2d Cir 1982).

[249] 20 USC §1401 *et seq.*

[250] Quackenbush v Johnson City School Dist, 716 F2d 141 (2d Cir 1983); Hymes v Harnett County Bd of Educ, 664 F2d 410 (4th Cir 1981).

[251] Teresa Diane P v Alief Indep School Dist, 744 F2d 484 (5th Cir 1984); Dept of Educ v Katherine D, 727 F2d 809 (9th Cir 1984); Doe v Koger, 710 F2d 1209 (7th Cir 1983); Powell v Defore, 699 F2d 1078 (11th Cir 1983). *See also* McGovern v Sullins, 676 F2d 98 (4th Cir 1982).

[252] 18 USC §3182. *See also* US Const art IV, §2, cl 2, the extradition clause.

[253] Ricks v Sumner, 647 F2d 76 (9th Cir 1981) (per curiam); Crumley v Snead, 620 F2d 481 (5th Cir 1980); Brown v Nutsch, 619 F2d 758 (8th Cir 1980); McBride v Soos, 594 F2d 610 (7th Cir 1979) *and* 679 F2d 1223 (7th Cir 1982). *See also* Cuyler v Adams, 449 US 433 (1981).

[254] Bradt v Smith, 634 F2d 796 (5th Cir 1981).

Food Stamp Act

According to the Fifth Circuit, the Food Stamp Act of 1964[255] cannot be used in a §1983 laws action[256]

Hawaii Admission Act

Violations of the Hawaiian Admission Act[257] can be used in §1983 laws actions, according to the Ninth Circuit[258]

Housing Acts

According to the District of Columbia, Second, and Third Circuits, violations of certain United States Housing Acts[259] are actionable under §1983.[260] However, the Fourth Circuit ruled that tenants cannot use §1983 for violations in connection with a housing project[261]

Insecticide, Fungicide and Rodenticide Act

The Ninth Circuit held that violations of the Insecticide, Fungicide and Rodenticide Act[262] are not actionable under §1983[263]

Justice System Improvement Act

Violations of the Justice System Improvement Act[264] are not actionable under §1983, according to the Seventh Circuit[265]

Low-Income Home Energy Assistance Act

The Eighth Circuit ruled that violations of the Low-Income Home Energy Assistance Act[266] can be used in §1983 laws actions[267]

---

[255] 7 USC §2011 *et seq.*

[256] Tyler v Mimes Pasqua & Toloso, 748 F2d 283 (5th Cir 1984).

[257] Pub L No 86-3, 73 Stat 4, 5 (1959).

[258] Keaukaha-Panaewa Community v Hawaiian Homes Commn, 739 F2d 1467 (9th Cir 1984).

[259] 42 USC §1437 *et seq,* §4625.

[260] Samuels v District of Columbia, 770 F2d 184 (DC Cir 1985); Pietroniro v Borough of Oceanport, 764 F2d 976 (3rd Cir 1985) Beckham v New York Hous Auth, 755 F2d 1074 (2d Cir 1985).

[261] Perry v Housing Auth, 664 F2d 1210 (4th Cir 1981). *See also* Phelps v Housing Auth, 742 F2d 816 (4th Cir 1984) (tenants have no §1983-enforceable right to preferential admission or to receive notice of expected occupancy date).

[262] 7 USC §136 *et seq.*

[263] Almond Hill School v United States Dept of Agriculture, 768 F2d 1030 (9th Cir 1985).

[264] 42 USC §3789 g(a) & (b).

[265] Polchowski v Gorris, 714 F2d 749 (7th Cir 1983).

[266] 42 USC §§8621-8629.

[267] Crawford v Janklow, 710 F2d 1321 (8th Cir 1983).

Medicare Act

Violations of the Medicare Act[268] are not actionable under §1983, according to the Fourth Circuit[269]

Model Cities Act

The Second Circuit held that employment-related provisions of the Model Cities Act[270] can be enforced under §1983[271]

National Bank Act

The Eighth Circuit held that §1983 cannot be used where the National Bank Act[272] renders invalid a state law[273]

Rehabilitation Act

Rehabilitation Act[274] violations cannot be used as the basis for §1983 laws actions, according to the Ninth and Eleventh Circuits[275]

Resource Conservation and Recovery Act

According to the Fifth Circuit, violations of the Resource Conservation and Recovery Act of 1976[276] are not actionable under §1983[277]

River and Harbor Improvements Act

The Ninth Circuit ruled that violations of the River and Harbor Improvements Act[278] are not actionable under §1983[279]

Social Security Act

Violations of Title IV-E of the Social Security Act[280] are redressable under §1983, according to the First Circuit[281]

Wagner-Peyser Act

The Ninth Circuit avoided passing on the question of whether violations of the Wagner-Peyser Act[282] are actionable under §1983[283]

---

[268] 42 USC §1395(a).

[269] Home Health Servs Inc v Currie, 706 F2d 497 (4th Cir 1983) (per curiam).

[270] 42 USC §3301 *et seq.*

[271] Members of Bridgeport Hous Auth Police Force v City of Bridgeport, 646 F2d 55 (2d Cir 1981).

[272] 12 USC §85.

[273] First Natl Bank v Marquette Natl Bank, 636 F2d 195 (8th Cir 1980).

[274] 29 USC §§793-794.

[275] Manecke v School Bd of Pinellas County, 762 F2d 912 (11th Cir 1985) (§794); Meyerson v Nebraska, 709 F2d 1235 (9th Cir 1983) (§793).

[276] 42 USC §§6901-6987.

[277] Garcia v Cecos Intern Inc, 761 F2d 76 (1st Cir 1985).

[278] 33 USC §§540-633.

[279] Boatowners & Tenants Assn v Port of Seattle, 716 F2d 609 (9th Cir 1983).

[280] 42 USC §§670-676.

[281] Lynch v Dukakis, 719 F2d 504 (1st Cir 1983).

[282] 29 USC §49 *et seq.*

[283] Hawaiian Tel Co v State Dept of Labor, 691 F2d 905 (9th Cir 1982) (laws issue avoided on Tax Injunction Act grounds — see §5.03).

"[S]ubjects or causes to be subjected . . . to the deprivation"

3

§3.01 Summary

42 USC §1983 on its face says nothing about its basis of liability, that is, the state of mind of a defendant which the plaintiff must allege and prove in order to make out a prima facie cause of action. It simply requires that a defendant's conduct be a cause in fact of plaintiff's constitutional deprivation. In *Monroe*

v Pape,[1] however, the Court made three statements which are significant in dealing with this issue. First, specific intent is not required under §1983. Second, §1983 is to be interpreted against a "background of tort liability."[2] And third, one of the reasons this statute was enacted, according to the Court, was the lack of enforcement in the states of Fourteenth Amendment rights "by reason of prejudice, passion, *neglect*, intolerance, or otherwise."[3]

Relying on this language in *Monroe*, some circuits held that negligence could be a basis of liability under §1983 where it resulted in a constitutional deprivation. Others did not go this far, and held that either intent or gross negligence or its equivalent was necessary for a §1983 cause of action. Whether negligence is actionable under §1983 was before the Supreme Court in *Procunier v Navarette*[4] and *Baker v McCollan*,[5] but the Court sidestepped the issue in both of these cases.

However, stating the issue as whether negligence gives rise to a §1983 cause of action is misleading. The correct approach under §1983 is to ask, first, whether the defendant owed a Fourteenth Amendment duty to the plaintiff and, second, whether it was breached. The defendant's state of mind is relevant only to the existence of the claimed Fourteenth Amendment violation.[6] Although for the most part the Supreme Court has not explained why, different Fourteenth Amendment violations (and hence Bill of Rights violations)[7] apparently require different states of mind. The Supreme Court finally made this clear in *Parratt v Taylor*[8] when it held that, as a matter of statutory interpretation, §1983 imposes no independent state of mind requirement for the prima facie case. It also turns out, however, that negligent conduct is insufficient, for due process purposes, to constitute a deprivation of life, liberty, or property.[9]

The general rule, as stated in many early circuit court decisions and declared by the Supreme Court in *Monell v Department of Social Services*[10] is that respondeat superior does not operate in §1983 cases to make a supervisor or other superior liable for Fourteenth Amendment violations of subordinates. The only way to hold a superior liable under §1983 is to show involvement in or encouragement of the wrongful conduct, which includes a causal relationship of some kind

---

[1] 365 US 167 (1961), *overruled on the local government immunity issue alone* Monell v Department of Social Servs, 436 US 658 (1978).

[2] 365 US at 187.

[3] *Id* 180 (emphasis added).

[4] 434 US 555 (1978).

[5] 443 US 137 (1979).

[6] This position was taken in the First Edition.

[7] *See* **ch 2** on the relationship between the Fourteenth Amendment and various provisions of the Bill of Rights as well as on the "laws" aspect of §1983.

[8] 101 S Ct 1908 (1981), *overruled in part* Daniels v Williams, 106 S Ct 662 (1986). *See* **§§3.02 & 3.08-3.10.**

[9] Daniels v Williams, 106 S Ct 662 (1986) and Davidson v Cannon, 106 S Ct 668 (1986), both discussed at **§§3.02 & 3.08-3.10.**

[10] 436 US 658 (1978).

between the superior's conduct[11] and the plaintiff's constitutional deprivation. As discussed later, what is additionally required to show this involvement and thus in effect to impose a Fourteenth Amendment duty upon the superior and to show its breach should depend on the requirements of the particular constitutional provision at issue.

Tort concepts may be helpful occasionally by analogy in determining the scope of liability under §1983, but they should not be determinative. Rather, as the Supreme Court has several times indicated in connection with the relationship of tort law to §1983, federal law is ultimately what is being interpreted, federal purposes and interests are at stake, and these are often very different from tort law purposes and interests.[12] Nevertheless, perhaps because courts and litigants are familiar with tort concepts, and therefore comfortable with them, these are frequently used in §1983 cases. For example, in addition to the basis of liability issue, that law school favorite, proximate cause, occasionally appears to divert attention from the *real* issue, the existence of §1983 liability.

Cause in fact is expressly required by the language of §1983. The plaintiff must allege and prove that defendant's conduct actually caused the constitutional deprivation. Until the Supreme Court's decision in *Monell v Department of Social Services*,[13] this was more often a plaintiff's problem in showing damages[14] than it was in establishing accountability for the constitutional violation itself. Now, however, especially where a local government body or a superior is sued under §1983, proving the cause in fact relation between the defendant's conduct and the constitutional violation will frequently pose some difficulty.[15] Moreover, in emphasizing cause in fact as it did, *Monell* reflected some confusion over the differences between cause in fact and duty. Indeed, this confusion obscures difficult constitutional duty problems.[16] The local government liability aspect of this emphasis, as well as local government liability in general, is discussed in Chapter 6.

As with other civil litigation, the plaintiff has the burden of proving all of the elements of a §1983 cause of action by a preponderance of the evidence. In contrast with the elements of the prima facie §1983 cause of action where state tort law may be helpful but is not determinative, the general rule is that 42 USC §1988 requires that matters relating to the existence and scope of survival and

---

[11] As discussed later, *see* §3.18, such "conduct" can include both affirmative acts and failures to act.

[12] *E.g.*, Scheuer v Rhodes, 416 US 232 (1974) involving executive immunity. *See generally* ch 8.

[13] 436 US 658 (1978).

[14] The cause in fact relationship between defendant's conduct and plaintiff's damages is discussed at §4.02.

[15] The easiest case for plaintiff on this cause in fact issue is one in which the governmental employee acts pursuant to an official policy or custom. The hardest case for plaintiff is one in which the governmental entity or superior fails to act.

[16] *See* §3.18.

wrongful death actions brought under §1983 be governed by state law unless state law is inconsistent with §1983's policies.[17]

§3.02   Basis of Liability—General Principles

In *Monroe v Pape*,[18] a seminal §1983 damages case decided by the Supreme Court, the police allegedly entered plaintiff's home without warning, forced him and his family to stand naked in the living room, ransacked the entire house, arrested him, and later released him without bringing any charges. After explaining that the plaintiff did not need to allege and prove specific intent to violate his Fourteenth Amendment rights, the Court held that he stated a §1983 cause of action. It reasoned that §1983 "should be read against the background of tort liability that makes a man responsible for the natural consequences of his actions."[19]

If basis of liability concepts from tort law are applied in *Monroe*, the defendants probably committed the intentional torts of assault, battery, false imprisonment, intentional infliction of emotional distress, and invasion of privacy. *Monroe* implied that the tort concept of intent, defined as the purpose to bring about a certain *result* or knowledge with substantial certainty that this *result* will occur,[20] applied by analogy to the Fourteenth Amendment violations in *Monroe*. Yet *Monroe* does not demonstrate that intent is always necessary for a §1983 cause of action. In that case, the plaintiff's Fourteenth Amendment interests (or more precisely, his Fourth Amendment interests) coincided with his common law interests. It was, therefore, natural for the Court to apply the tort concept of intent to the facts in *Monroe*.[21]

Thus, it was unclear after *Monroe* whether §1983 had an independent state of mind requirement for the prima facie case and, if so, what it was. There were, however, hints, even though the Supreme Court for a time avoided this §1983 basis of liability question.[22] For it had cautioned that tort law, while sometimes helpful by analogy, was determinative neither of the scope of executive immunity under §1983[23] nor of the application of §1983 damages rules.[24] Section 1983 is, after all, a federal statute which gives a cause of action for damages for Fourteenth Amendment violations. Moreover, as the Court observed in *Bivens v Six Unknown Named Agents of the Federal Bureau of Narcotics:*

---

[17] *See* §§**3.19 & 3.20.**

[18] 365 US 167 (1961).

[19] *Id* 187.

[20] Restatement (Second) of Torts §8A (1965) reads as follows: "The word 'intent' is used throughout the Restatement of this Subject to denote that the actor desires to cause the consequences of his act, or that he believes that the consequences are substantially certain to result from it."

[21] See Carey v Piphus, 435 US 247 (1978) where the Court similarly applied damages concepts from tort law.

[22] Baker v McCollan, 443 US 137 (1979); Procunier v Navarette, 434 US 555 (1978).

[23] Scheuer v Rhodes, 416 US 232 (1974).

[24] Carey v Piphus, 435 US 247 (1978).

"The interest protected by state laws regulating trespass and the invasion of privacy, and those protected by the Fourth Amendment's guarantee against unreasonable searches and seizures, may be inconsistent or even hostile."[25] The District of Columbia Circuit had made the same point: "The common law . . . may create immunities that do not apply to an action under §1983. Conversely, the developing law of torts may extend potential liability to some defendants beyond the reach of the federal statute."[26]

Consequently, even before the Court's decision in *Parratt v Taylor*,[27] discussed later, the argument was made[28] that in §1983 cases the threshold question is whether a Fourteenth Amendment violation has occurred and additionally that §1983 has no independent state of mind requirement for the prima facie case. The relevance of a defendant's state of mind depends on the nature of the constitutional violation. For example, the Supreme Court held that at least "deliberate indifference" is necessary to make out an Eighth Amendment violation.[29] It also held that intentional interception of lawyer-client conversations by an informer or intentional use of the conversations must occur to make out a Sixth Amendment violation.[30] It further turns out that negligent conduct is insufficient, for due process purposes, to constitute a deprivation of life, liberty, or property.[31] In these §1983 cases, the Court properly focused on the constitutional question and for this sole purpose inquired into the defendants' state of mind. Similarly, in *Paul v Davis*,[32] a due process case, the Court held that no §1983 cause of action was stated even though the defendants published allegedly defamatory material about the plaintiff either intentionally or negligently; there was, according to the Court, no constitutionally protected interest invaded.

Those earlier cases which focused initially on negligence or unreasonable conduct as a §1983 requirement,[33] instead of on the existence of the Fourteenth Amendment violation or duty, confused the elements of the §1983 prima facie cause of action with the defendant's qualified immunity of

---

[25] 403 US 388, 394 (1971).

[26] Carter v Carlson, 447 F2d 358, 361 (DC Cir 1971), *revd on other grounds*, 409 US 418 (1972).

[27] 451 US 527 (1981).

[28] In the First Edition and in Nahmod, *Section 1983 and the "Background" of Tort Liability* 50 Ind LJ 5 (1974).

[29] Estelle v Gamble, 429 US 97 (1976).

[30] Weatherford v Bursey, 429 US 545 (1977).

[31] Daniels v Williams, 106 S Ct 662 (1986) discussed later and at §§3.08-3.11.

[32] 424 US 693 (1976).

[33] Whether conduct is unreasonable is determined by the fact finder using the factors of gravity of harm ("L"), probability of harm ("P"), and the cost or burden of avoiding the harm ("B"). If B is less than P L, defendant is negligent; if B is greater than P L, defendant is not negligent. This is Learned Hand's famous negligence "formula" in United States v Carroll Towing Co, 159 F2d 169 (2d Cir 1947). It is clear, however, that quantifying these factors is difficult if not impossible; hence the formula serves simply as a rough guide. *See further* Posner, *A Theory of Negligence* 1 J Legal Stud 29, 33 (1972); and Calabresi, The Costs of Accidents 26 (1970).

reasonable grounds for belief in the legal validity of the challenged conduct.[34] If negligence was part of the prima facie cause of action, then the burdens of pleading and proof were on the plaintiff. However, the Supreme Court's decisions on qualified immunity demonstrate that the defendant has the burdens of pleading and proving reasonable conduct.[35] In short, the argument went, it is only where the defendant's state of mind is relevant to the constitutional violation that it should be examined to determine whether plaintiff made out a prima facie §1983 claim.

Thus, under this approach, not every common law tort committed by an individual under color of law is actionable under §1983.[36] The existence and scope of the Fourteenth Amendment (or incorporated provision of the Bill of Rights) duty must be faced by the trial court, with the fact-finder passing on the other issues: breach of that duty, cause in fact, and any resulting damages. To put it another way by using terms from the negligence litigation process, the trial court determines the existence of the constitutional duty and the standard of care required, and the fact-finder decides whether the standard of care has been met.

This position was in effect adopted by the Supreme Court in *Parratt v Taylor*,[37] which held that there is no "express requirement of a particular state of mind" for the §1983 prima facie case, although a defendant's state of mind may be relevant to the existence of a Fourteenth Amendment violation. The Court put it this way:

> Accordingly, in any §1983 action the initial inquiry must focus on whether the two essential elements to a §1983 action are present: (1) whether the conduct complained of was committed by a person acting under color of state law; and (2) whether this conduct deprived a person of rights, privileges, or immunities secured by the Constitution or laws of the United States.[38]

Parratt involved a §1983 suit for damages of $23.50 brought by an inmate against two prison officials for their alleged negligence in causing the loss of hobby materials ordered by plaintiff through the mail. Plaintiff's complaint was couched in terms of the deprivation of property without due process. The district court entered summary judgment in favor of plaintiff, holding that negligence is actionable under §1983, that defendants' deprivation of plain-

---

[34] *See generally* **ch 8.** This "qualified immunity" is better characterized as an affirmative defense. *Id.*

[35] **§8.16.**

[36] Paul v Davis, 424 US 693 (1976); Wells v Ward, 470 F2d 1185 (10th Cir 1972); Howell v Cataldi, 464 F2d 272 (3d Cir 1972).

[37] 451 US 527 (1981), *overruled in part and on other grounds* Daniels v Williams, 106 S Ct 662 (1986).

[38] *Id* 535. Thus, *Parratt* did *not* rule that negligence was *always* actionable under §1983, but only that it was actionable where negligent conduct was sufficient for the underlying constitutional violation. *E.g.,* Crawford v Edmondson, 764 F2d 479 (7th Cir 1985).

tiff's property violated due process, and that defendants were not protected by qualified immunity. The Eighth Circuit Court of Appeals affirmed in an unpublished opinion.

Reversing in an opinion by Justice Rehnquist, the Court first addressed the question of whether negligence is actionable under §1983. It answered, as noted earlier, that negligence may indeed be actionable under §1983; a defendant's state of mind is not relevant to §1983 as such. However, it may be relevant to the constitutional violation asserted. Next—in a holding thereafter overruled by the Court in *Daniels v Williams*[39]—the Court held that plaintiff's loss, even though only negligently caused, constituted a deprivation of property and thereby implicated the due process clause.

Nevertheless, the Court ultimately concluded that the due process clause was not violated by the defendants' conduct. For one thing, there was an apparently adequate tort remedy under state law—a *post*deprivation hearing, in effect—which plaintiff could use to seek redress. For another, a *pre*deprivation hearing was not practicable for the state because the plaintiff's loss was caused not by a formal and established state procedure but rather by "random and unauthorized" acts of state employees. The Court emphasized that this due process result was sensible. Otherwise, every injury caused by a state official under color of law—for example, an injury arising out of an automobile accident—would constitute a due process violation and thus be actionable under §1983. This would improperly render §1983 a "font of tort law."

Justice Stewart concurred,[40] doubting whether a negligently caused loss is a deprivation of property for due process purposes. Justices White and Blackmun also concurred,[41] stressing, among other things, that they did not read the Court's due process discussion of negligent deprivation as applicable to deprivations of *life* or *liberty*. They also asserted that a state's providing a postdeprivation hearing might not satisfy due process where state employees act intentionally to deprive one of property.

Justice Powell concurred only in the result,[42] and argued at length that due process was not implicated in *Parratt* because a negligently caused loss of property does not constitute a deprivation of property under the due process clause. Rather, an intentional act is required for such a deprivation. He also criticized the Court's opinion for focusing solely on procedural due process and ignoring substantive due process. Finally, he suggested that the Court's opinion created the risk that both the due process clause and §1983 would become trivialized, giving as an example the $23.50 *Parratt* case itself. Justice Marshall concurred in part and dissented in part,[43] contending that it was not at all clear that there was an adequate state law remedy available to plaintiff.

---

[39] 106 S Ct 662 (1986) discussed later and at §§3.08-3.11.
[40] 451 US at 544.
[41] *Id* 545.
[42] *Id* 546.
[43] *Id* 544.

In *Daniels v Williams*,[44] the Court overruled only that portion of *Parratt* which held that negligence is enough for a deprivation of property. *Daniels* involved an inmate's claim that the negligent conduct of the defendants in leaving a pillow on a staircase, thereby causing him to injure himself, was a deprivation of liberty. Rejecting the argument, the Court held that more than negligence is required for a deprivation of life, liberty, or property because due process violations were abuses of governmental power. The implications of *Daniels* for the scope of due process are discussed elsewhere.[45] However, it is clear that *Daniels* left undisturbed the *Parratt* holding that § 1983 has no independent state of mind requirement.[46]

---

[44] 106 S Ct 662 (1986).

[45] *See* §§ 3.08-3.11.

[46] Several years before the *Parratt* decision, the Supreme Court had made several interesting observations in dicta about the relationship between basis of liability and § 1983. In Baker v McCollan, 443 US 137 (1979), the Court dealt with a § 1983 complaint against a county sheriff in connection with the detention for several days of plaintiff (arrested pursuant to a valid warrant) who protested repeatedly—and correctly, as it turned out—that he was the victim of mistaken identity. Reversing the Fifth Circuit, the Court held that no prima facie § 1983 cause of action was stated because the plaintiff's deprivation of liberty was not inconsistent with due process. The Court concluded that "a sheriff executing an arrest warrant is [not] required by the Constitution to independently investigate every claim of innocence . . . . Nor is the official charged with maintaining custody of the accused named in the warrant required . . . to perform an error-free investigation of such a claim." *Id* 145-46.

Prior to addressing this constitutional issue, the Court commented briefly in dicta on the relation between basis of liability and § 1983 without, however, resolving the matter. It first noted that the question of whether negligence can give rise to a § 1983 claim "is more elusive than it appears at first blush. It may well not be susceptible of a uniform answer across the entire spectrum of conceivable constitutional violations which might be the subject of a § 1983 action." *Id* 139-40. The Court also observed that even before this question is considered, "it is necessary to isolate the precise constitutional violation with which [defendant] is charged . . . . If there has been no such [violation], the state of mind of the defendant is wholly immaterial." *Id* 140. The Court next went on to point out that a defendant's state of mind may be relevant to the very existence of a constitutional violation; but it then distinguished this inquiry from the question of whether "§ 1983 contains some additional qualification of that nature before a defendant may be held to respond in damages under its provisions." *Id* 140 fn 1.

As stated earlier, to the extent that the Court's dicta in *Baker* emphasized that the threshold question in § 1983 cases is whether a Fourteenth Amendment violation exists, the approach was sound. Similarly sound was the statement that a defendant's state of mind may be relevant in determining whether the Fourteenth Amendment is violated. However, once such a violation is found, there should be no need, contrary to *Baker's* suggestion and as borne out later in *Parratt,* to inquire further into the defendant's state of mind for the § 1983 prima facie claim. To do so would have added an unwarranted state of mind gloss to § 1983's "subjects, or causes to be subjected" language which focuses essentially on cause in fact. Further, the Court's suggestion in *Baker* was inconsistent with its oft-repeated assertion that § 1983 creates no new substantive rights but simply aids in the enforcement of the Fourteenth Amendment. The corollary of this assertion is that § 1983 *similarly does not limit* the scope of Fourteenth Amendment substantive rights and § 1983 therefore does not impose additional state of mind requirements upon the prima facie § 1983 claim. In this connection it is also significant that the Court held that § 1983's color of law requirement *does not limit* the scope of § 1983

For these reasons, it is crucial in §1983 cases to study other cases dealing with particular constitutional violations. The cases in the following sections are representative only and are designed as a guide. Although the Supreme Court has increasingly focused on state of mind requirements for certain constitutional violations, all too often courts do not expressly deal with basis of liability, perhaps because intent in the tort sense is so frequently present. Lawyers confronted with particular constitutional provisions should research those provisions carefully, with special attention to Supreme Court decisions, in order to satisfy themselves as to the state of mind necessary for the specific Fourteenth Amendment violation. They should also be alert to the possibility that violation of the same constitutional provision may in different situations require different states of mind.[47]

§3.03   —First Amendment

Section 1983 cases involving the First Amendment typically arise in situations where government officials either intend the result of their challenged conduct, that is, the plaintiff's denial or lack of opportunity to speak or write or receive information, or where they knowingly punish a plaintiff for the exercise of First Amendment rights. Thus, for example, the Ninth Circuit held actionable an allegation that prison authorities intentionally interfered with the First Amendment right of an inmate to send mail.[48]

There are, however, several cases holding that negligent interference with First Amendment rights is also actionable. In an unusual District of Columbia case,[49] the district court held that corporation counsel could be liable for negligently supervising his subordinates. This negligence led to unreasonable delay in issuing a legal opinion about the validity of a permit requirement, and because of this delay, plaintiff was arrested under the invalid requirement. The court analyzed the issue in First Amendment duty terms, finding that the defendant was personally involved in the delay. Similarly, the Ninth Circuit held that prison authorities could be liable for negligently interfering with a prisoner's First Amendment right to send mail.[50] Granting certiorari to consider whether negligence was actionable under §1983, the Supreme Court

---

Fourteenth Amendment actions. *See* **§2.04.**

[47] For example, even after Daniels v Williams, 106 S Ct 662 (1986), it is possible that substantive due process violations may ultimately be held to require at least intent while procedural due process violations may ultimately be held to require at least gross negligence.

[48] Navarette v Enomoto, 536 F2d 277 (9th Cir 1976), *revd on other grounds sub nom* Procunier v Navarette, 434 US 555 (1978).

[49] Shifrin v Wilson, 412 F Supp 1282 (DDC 1976). This is not a §1983 case, but its First Amendment approach is helpful by analogy.

[50] Navarette v Enomoto, 536 F2d 277 (9th Cir 1976).

avoided the issue in *Procunier v Navarette*.[51] It assumed arguendo that negligence was actionable, but found for defendants on the ground of qualified immunity.

In a Third Circuit case[52] where faculty members sued university officials for allegedly violating their First Amendment rights, an interesting issue was whether the university's good faith belief that faculty picketing would be over matters subject to the exclusive grievance procedures of the collective bargaining agreement justified its sending a telegram to the effect that faculty picketing would constitute "a cause for discipline up to dismissal." The Third Circuit reversed the district court which had held, among other things, that such good faith was a "defense" to a First Amendment claim. The Third Circuit reasoned that good faith is only relevant to liability for damages and qualified immunity. It concluded:

> Good faith has never been accepted as a justification for a constitutional violation, and there is even less reason to accept it where the violation alleged is restraint of free speech, one of the most fundamental of all constitutional rights . . . [T]he conduct which gave rise to the cause of action is not [through good faith] therefore legitimized or exculpated . . . . "[53]

On the other hand, where the plaintiffs claimed that the school board defendants had brought a declaratory judgment action against them and others in order to deter them from speaking out in opposition to a new neighborhood school plan, the Fourth Circuit,[54] affirming the dismissal of their complaint, noted that there was no proof of "evil motive" designed to chill First Amendment rights. And where plaintiffs were unsuccessful in challenging the defendant sheriff's failure to reappoint them for alleged political patronage reasons, the Fifth Circuit[55] stated that plaintiffs had not proved that political discrimination was a substantial or motivating factor in defendant's employment decision. In the course of its discussion, the court asserted that the same burden of proof as to a defendant's impermissible motive which is imposed on a plaintiff in an equal protection case is applicable to a First Amendment case involving political discrimination in employment.

§3.04   —Fourth Amendment

Intent is typically present where a police officer, for example, is sued under §1983 for an allegedly wrongful arrest, search, or seizure in violation of the Fourth Amendment. The defendant invariably intends that the plaintiff be

---

[51] 434 US 555 (1978), extensively discussed at **§8.09.**

[52] Trotman v Board of Trustees, 635 F2d 216 (3d Cir 1980).

[53] *Id* 227.

[54] Bell v School Board, 734 F2d 155 (4th Cir 1984). Judge Rosenn concurred, noting there was not even an allegation that the board's lawsuit was intended to have that effect.

[55] Tanner v McCall, 625 F2d 1183 (5th Cir 1980).

constrained or confined, or that certain premises be searched.[56] But the fact that intent is present does not mean that such conduct is always sufficient to state a §1983 cause of action for a Fourth Amendment violation.[57] For example, a Minnesota district court[58] held that a police officer who shoved the legally arrested plaintiff had not committed a Fourth Amendment violation, although he may have committed a technical battery at common law. On the other hand, it was error, according to the District of Columbia Circuit,[59] for a district court to hold that proving a police violation of the Fourth Amendment for a wrongful search always requires evidence of assault or battery.

---

[56] *E.g.*, Pierson v Ray, 386 US 547 (1967); Joseph v Rowlen, 402 F2d 367 (7th Cir 1968); Cohen v Norris, 300 F2d 24 (9th Cir 1962). *See also* Gillard v Schmidt, 579 F2d 825 (3d Cir 1978) where the search by a school board member of a guidance counselor's office during the evening was found to constitute a Fourth Amendment violation.

[57] The importance in §1983 Fourth Amendment cases of focusing on the state of mind required by the Fourth Amendment is further demonstrated by a questionable Seventh Circuit case where plaintiff sued two police officers for wrongful arrests arising out of the use by another woman of plaintiff's name and savings account to defraud a bank. The first officer had arrested her under a valid search warrant which contained plaintiff's name, but an obviously incorrect description, including the wrong race. The second officer had later arrested her using substantially the same arrest warrant which was somehow erroneously reissued. In affirming the district court, the Seventh Circuit handed down a confused opinion which described §1983 as a "tort statute," mixed due process analysis with Fourth Amendment analysis, and seemed to suggest that the availability of state tort remedies precluded §1983 remedies. In any event, the court held that the plaintiff had not made out a prima facie Fourth Amendment-based §1983 claim against either officer.

As to the first arrest, there was no Fourth Amendment violation, despite the discrepancy in description, because the arrest warrant had the correct name—the "main thing" for the officer—and the plaintiff herself so acknowledged to the officer. Also, there was no allegation that this officer either intentionally or negligently deprived plaintiff of her liberty or property. As to the second arrest—a "more difficult issue"—the court read the complaint as alleging that the second officer "had reason to know that the warrant had been issued mistakenly and that he therefore was negligent in executing it without first checking back with his superiors." Still, there was no violation of the Fourth Amendment. Asserting that such an allegation "is not the stuff out of which a proper federal case is made," the Seventh Circuit, with minimal constitutional analysis, simply relied on the existence of state tort remedies. It did, however, suggest that the case would have been different had plaintiff alleged that defendants knowingly procured an arrest warrant based on mistaken identity in an effort to deprive plaintiff of her liberty or property. Johnson v Miller, 680 F2d 39 (7th Cir 1982). *Cf* Powe v City of Chicago, 664 F2d 639 (7th Cir 1981).

[58] Daly v Pedersen, 278 F Supp 88 (D Minn 1967). Similarly, the First Circuit rejected the plaintiff's §1983 false arrest argument that, regardless of the existence of probable cause, the arresting officers were liable for their "ulterior motive" in carrying out his arrest. This motive was alleged to be minimizing his resistance to their unconstitutional seizure of certain drugs. First, the charges against plaintiff were colorable. Second, there was "no precedent even suggesting that an arrest made with probable cause violates section 1983 because induced by such a motive." Mann v Cannon, 731 F2d 54, 63 (1st Cir 1984).

[59] Tarpley v Greene, 684 F2d 1 (DC Cir 1982).

A Fourth Circuit case, *Jenkins v Averett*,[60] described gross negligence as sometimes sufficient for a Fourth Amendment violation. In *Averett*, plaintiff, who was unarmed and had surrendered, was accidentally shot by a policeman. The court held that individuals have a Fourth Amendment right to the security of their persons against injuries arbitrarily inflicted by police officers. It characterized the defendant's conduct as an arbitrary abuse of police power: plaintiff's injuries were "the direct consequence of defendant's wanton conduct in the course of his attempt to apprehend the plaintiff."[61] However, it limited the scope of its decision to cases of "raw abuse of power by a police officer" and added that it was simply following state law in equating "gross or culpable" negligence with arbitrariness.[62]

Tennessee v Garner,[63] a recent Supreme Court decision dealing with the Fourth Amendment, will have a considerable impact in §1983 cases involving claims of police use of excessive force.[64] In *Garner*, the Court first observed that "[w]henever an officer restrains the freedom of a person to walk away, he has seized that person"[65] within the meaning of the Fourth Amendment. Such a seizure must be "reasonable" in the manner in which it is brought about; this determination involves balancing "the nature and quality of the intrusion on the individual's Fourth Amendment interests against the importance of the governmental interests alleged to justify the intrusion."[66] Applying this standard, the Court held violative of the Fourth Amendment the use of deadly force against an unarmed fleeing suspect where the only justification for its use was prevention of escape, despite the presence of probable cause to believe a burglary had been committed.

The *Garner* rule—that the Fourth Amendment requires the level of force used to seize a person to be reasonable—was applied in a Fifth Circuit case[67] in favor of a plaintiff who was found to have stated a Fourth Amendment claim where she alleged that she was "seized" when police officers deliberately placed a roadblock in front of the car in which they knew she was a passenger. The court commented that the ultimate result in the case would depend on evaluating "the magnitude of the need for the roadblock, the relationship of the level of force to that need, the severity of [plaintiff's] injuries, or the motives that drove [defendants]."[68]

---

[60] 424 F2d 1228 (4th Cir 1970).

[61] *Id* 1232.

[62] *Id.* Such conduct may also violate due process. *See* §§3.08-3.11.

[63] 105 S Ct 1694 (1985).

[64] Among other things, *Garner* may eliminate the need to rely on substantive due process in such cases. *See* §§3.08-3.11.

[65] 105 S Ct at 1699.

[66] *Id.*

[67] Jamieson v Shaw, 772 F2d 1205 (5th Cir 1985). *See also* Kidd v O'Neil, 774 F2d 1252 (4th Cir 1985) (police use of excessive force may implicate Fourth Amendment after *Garner:* specific intent not required; violation depends on factual circumstances).

[68] 772 F2d at 1211.

Garner was similarly applied by the Eleventh Circuit[69] in a case where plaintiff's decedent was beaten by police officers and, in the ensuing scuffle, was shot and killed. Following *Garner's* balancing approach, the court had "little difficulty" in concluding that decedent's beating and shooting were sufficiently serious to violate the Fourth Amendment. It was significant in this connection that there was no apparent threat from decedent to the safety of the police officers; also, decedent had done little to provoke the officers to beat him.[70]

§3.05 —Fifth Amendment

Fifth Amendment violation cases usually deal with defendants who acted intentionally with regard to the confession obtained or sought to be obtained through their challenged conduct. Thus, for example, a §1983 cause of action was stated in an early Seventh Circuit decision[71] in which police officers allegedly beat plaintiff in an attempt to force him to incriminate himself. While the court did not expressly rely on any particular constitutional provision, it would appear that there was a violation of the Fifth Amendment. Even clearer examples of Fifth Amendment violations for §1983 purposes are circumstances in which a confession is in fact improperly obtained through coercion and then used.[72]

Whether interrogations conducted in violation of *Miranda*[73] guidelines, standing alone and without use in subsequent criminal proceedings, amount to Fifth Amendment violations made actionable by §1983 is a question of Fifth Amendment interpretation. A Maryland district court[74] concluded that no §1983 cause of action is stated by alleging such facts, explaining: "Unlike an illegal arrest, or an illegal search or seizure, an improper interrogation is not itself a tort. Nor does an interrogation, in and of itself, constitute a denial of the constitutional rights of the person being interrogated."[75] A preferable statement of this conclusion would be that in the absence of the use of information so obtained, *Miranda* violations are not in themselves Fifth

---

[69] Gilmere v City of Atlanta, 774 F2d 1495 (11th Cir 1985) (en banc). The major concern of the court was the effect, under Parratt v Taylor, 451 US 527 (1981), on plaintiff's due process and Fourth Amendment claims of the existence of state tort remedies against the police officers. A majority of the court correctly concluded that postdeprivation remedies are irrelevant to substantive due process and Fourth Amendment violations. *See* §§3.08-3.11 for further discussion.

[70] Judge Tjoflat dissented on this issue, arguing that neither the beating nor the shooting was unreasonable under the circumstances. Gilmere v City of Atlanta, 774 F2d 1495, 1505 (11th Cir 1985).

[71] Hardwick v Hurley, 289 F2d 529 (7th Cir 1961).

[72] *E.g.*, Duncan v Nelson, 466 F2d 939 (7th Cir), *cert denied*, 93 S Ct 116 (1972); Kerr v City of Chicago, 424 F2d 1134 (7th Cir), *cert denied*, 400 US 833 (1970).

[73] Miranda v Arizona, 384 US 436 (1966).

[74] Allen v Eicher, 295 F Supp 1184 (D Md 1969).

[75] *Id* 1186. To the same effect is Thornton v Buchmann, 392 F2d 870 (7th Cir 1968).

Amendment violations. The reference to tort law is both unnecessary and confusing.

§3.06 —Sixth Amendment

A leading case, *Weatherford v Bursey*,[76] is a Supreme Court decision in which a plaintiff convicted of vandalizing draft board property brought a §1983 action against an informer-agent and his superior for a Sixth Amendment violation. The informer had maintained his cover until the day before trial and was present at several conferences between plaintiff and his lawyers pursuant to his superior's orders. Reversing the Fourth Circuit, the Supreme Court held that, in order to find liability, either the intent to intercept lawyer-client conversations, or their subsequent intentional use, had to be shown where plaintiff's claim was based on the Sixth Amendment. A per se rule was inappropriate and, since neither intent to intercept nor intentional use was present, no §1983 cause of action was stated. It is consistent with the duty analysis set out earlier that the Court focused on the Sixth Amendment duty and its scope, and not on §1983 basis of liability as such.

In an early Sixth Circuit decision,[77] plaintiff sued a sheriff who advised plaintiff to plead guilty without counsel in order to get off easier. Plaintiff did so, and was given a light sentence which he walked out on. He was later arrested and resentenced to serve the statutory penalty, but was subsequently released by means of federal habeas corpus proceedings based on the earlier absence of counsel. The court affirmed a directed verdict for the sheriff on various grounds,[78] one of which was that §1983 was aimed at "reprehensible" conduct whereas the sheriff neither tricked nor threatened plaintiff. It is unclear whether "reprehensible" means intent, bad faith, or both.

§3.07 —Eighth Amendment

There has been a great deal of §1983 litigation involving the Eighth Amendment, primarily because §1983 is a favorite of prisoners. Early circuit court decisions generally required at least gross negligence before finding liability for Eighth Amendment violations.[79] This requirement apparently was in part a response to considerable judicial fear of the potential for expansion

---

[76] 429 US 545 (1977). *Cf* Maine v Moulton, 106 S Ct 477 (1985) (defendant's postindictment statements, elicited by informer, violate Sixth Amendment and may not be used at trial on pending charge, where police knew or should have known such statements would result).

[77] Striker v Pancher, 317 F2d 780 (6th Cir 1963).

[78] Including the following: no state action, the advice was good, there were no damages, there was no negligence, and the sheriff was qualifiedly immune because the law regarding the right to counsel was not clear at the time the advice was given.

[79] *E.g.*, Parker v McKeithen, 488 F2d 553 (5th Cir), *cert denied*, 419 US 838 (1974).

of §1983-Eighth Amendment liability. This is reflected in *Roberts v Williams*,[80] a Fifth Circuit decision in which a panel first held that the superintendent of a prison farm was grossly negligent in giving a shotgun to an incompetent and dangerous trusty without instructions. The result of this negligence was plaintiff's being shot by the trusty without justification. This, the panel said, constituted an Eighth Amendment violation. However, it later modified its opinion so that the defendant's liability was based not on §1983 but on the pendent negligence claim under state law.

Many prisoner suits allege Eighth Amendment violations stemming from inadequate medical care. The circuits have long held that mere negligent provision of medical care does not constitute an actionable Eighth Amendment violation,[81] although willful denial of care might.[82] Currently, as the Supreme Court clarified in *Estelle v Gamble*,[83] Eighth Amendment violations in the area of medical care require at least "deliberate indifference" on the part of prison authorities; inadvertence and ordinary negligence are insufficient.[84]

The circuits have applied the standard of *Estelle v Gamble* to prison beatings and attacks by other inmates, as well as to conditions of confinement,[85] and

---

[80] 456 F2d 819 (5th Cir), *addendum*, 456 F2d 834 (5th Cir), *cert denied*, 404 US 866 (1971).

[81] *E.g.*, United States *ex rel* Gittlemacker v County of Philadelphia, 413 F2d 84 (3d Cir 1969), *cert denied*, 396 US 1046 (1970); Mitchell v Hendricks, 431 F Supp 1295 (ED Pa 1977).

[82] *E.g.*, Vinnedge v Gibbs, 550 F2d 926 (4th Cir 1977).

[83] 429 US 97 (1976). As discussed in **ch 4,** a plaintiff who proves an Eighth Amendment violation will ordinarily be entitled to a punitive damages instruction where the defendant is not protected either by absolute or qualified immunity—see **chs 7 & 8,** respectively.

[84] For example, in a First Circuit case, prison officials were sued for allegedly violating an inmate's Eighth Amendment rights through their "deliberate indifference to a serious medical need." In upholding the jury verdict against one official and overturning the verdict against the other, the First Circuit initially said that negligent failure to provide medical care is not violative of the Eighth Amendment. It then noted:

> [A] case involving nonconduct may, and this one does, present far more difficult questions than the case of an easily recognizable, affirmative act . . . . [T]he ultimate question is the state of mind of the defendant. When a supervisory official is placed on actual notice of a prisoner's need for physical protection or medical care, "administrative negligence can rise to the level of deliberate indifference to or reckless disregard for that prisoner's safety." Layne v Vinzant, 657 F2d 468, 471 (1st Cir 1981).

In contrast, in affirming the district court's dismissal of that portion of the plaintiff inmate's complaint alleging an Eighth Amendment violation by virtue of the inattention of prison doctors to his medical needs, the First Circuit concluded that plaintiff's pleadings only amounted to a disagreement over the quality and source of the medical treatment received. This was far different from the "deliberate indifference" required for an Eighth Amendment violation, according to the court. Ferranti v Moran, 618 F2d 888 (1st Cir 1980).

[85] As where, for example, a warden knows of the inhumane conditions of solitary confinement. Wright v McMann, 460 F2d 126 (2d Cir), *cert denied*, 409 US 885 (1972) (pre-*Estelle*). More recently, in reversing the district court's dismissal of the plaintiff inmate's complaint, the Fifth Circuit held that plaintiff had stated a §1983 Eighth

even to detention beyond the termination of a sentence.[86] Ordinarily, the negligent failure to protect an inmate from attack by another inmate does not give rise to an Eighth Amendment violation.[87] However, prison officials who know of such attacks and are deliberately indifferent to them or are grossly negligent may be liable under §1983.[88] Going even further, the Fourth Circuit[89] held that where there is a pervasive risk of harm to all prisoners, or to an identifiable group of them, prison officials have an Eighth Amendment duty to use reasonable care to protect prisoners from aggressive sexual assaults. It said: "Given the pervasive and unreasonable risk of harm, negligence by prison officials in their performance of their duty of care is a violation of the constitutional right and actionable under §1983."[90] Cause in fact, though, must still be shown as demonstrated by a Seventh Circuit decision[91] in which the court found that prison assaults resulted not from defendants' breach of their Eighth Amendment duty, but rather from the construction of, and overcrowding in, the jail.

Amendment cause of action in alleging that the defendant jail "partly intentionally subjected him to a cold, rainy, roach-infested facility and furnished him with inoperative, scum-encrusted washing and toilet facilities." Bienvenu v Beauregard & Parish Police Jury, 705 F2d 1457 (5th Cir 1983) (per curiam).

[86] Haygood v Younger, 769 F2d 1350 (9th Cir 1985) (en banc) (Eighth Amendment liability where deliberate indifference to prisoner's liberty interest).

[87] Williams v Field, 416 F2d 483 (9th Cir 1969), *cert denied,* 397 US 1016 (1970); Estate of Davis v Johnson, 745 F2d 1066 (7th Cir 1984).

In Clappier v Flynn, 605 F2d 519 (10th Cir 1979), the plaintiff inmate sued the sheriff for violating Eighth Amendment rights in connection with beatings inflicted upon plaintiff by other inmates. Noting that the sheriff was not shown to have had knowledge of these beatings, the Tenth Circuit vacated the district court judgment on various grounds and remanded. It stated:

> [T]he area of concern in terms of a Sec. 1983 liability involving an allegation of cruel and unusual punishment *relating to a claimed omission* requires proof of exceptional circumstances and conduct so grossly incompetent, inadequate or excessive as to shock the conscience or to be intolerable to basic fairness.

Id 533 (emphasis in original).

[88] Little v Walker, 552 F2d 193 (7th Cir 1977), *cert denied,* 435 US 932 (1978); Parker v McKeithen, 488 F2d 553 (5th Cir), *cert denied,* 419 US 838 (1974); Holt v Sarver, 442 F2d 304 (8th Cir 1971) (all pre-*Estelle* cases).

[89] Withers v Levine, 615 F2d 158 (4th Cir 1980).

[90] *Id* 162. In contrast to *Withers,* where an inmate sued prison officials alleging that they failed to protect him from homosexual rapes by other inmates, the Eighth Circuit affirmed as not clearly erroneous the district court's finding that defendants were not "deliberately indifferent" to plaintiff's exposure to such rapes. The warden never knew of plaintiff, the director of security was not shown to have been personally involved, and the assistant director of security experienced most of his personal contact and knowledge of plaintiff after the rapes, not before. It was not enough for deliberate indifference that the assistant director had failed previously to read the "alarming" file of one of the inmate-rapists who worked alongside plaintiff. The institutional failure to review files before assigning a "pretty boy" to a job alongside a rapist did not demonstrate a reckless or callous attitude toward plaintiff by any of the defendants. Branchcomb v Brewer, 683 F2d 251 (8th Cir 1982). But cf Martin v White, 742 F2d 469 (8th Cir 1984).

[91] Kish v County of Milwaukee, 441 F2d 901 (7th Cir 1971).

Estelle's deliberate indifference standard has been applied to beatings of inmates by prison guards. Thus, for example, the Fourth Circuit[92] "specifically" held that unjustified striking, beating, or infliction of bodily harm upon a prisoner gives rise to liability where there is no just cause for such conduct by a prison official. It emphasized that "unjustified striking, etc." and "without just cause" were standards of Eighth and Fourteenth Amendment interpretation, and not tort law standards. Similarly, according to the Fifth Circuit,[93] a prison guard's use of force against an inmate violates the Eighth Amendment: when it is "wanton," that is, when the guard intended harm; when it is "unnecessary" for the maintenance of discipline; and when it causes "pain," that is, more than momentary discomfort, but severe pain or lasting injury. In contrast, in affirming the district court's refusal to submit to a jury the plaintiff inmate's proposed instruction on the Eighth Amendment, the Fifth Circuit[94] asserted that an individual guard's isolated assault on an inmate is not punishment for Eighth Amendment purposes. Rather, punishment is that which is "applied to an inmate for a penal or disciplinary purpose and authorized by high prison officials."

The Eighth Amendment's deliberate indifference standard has even been found relevant in cases where prisoners have committed suicide. Thus, where police officers were sued for their conduct in arresting and incarcerating the plaintiff's decedent who committed suicide in jail, the Seventh Circuit[95] affirmed the district court's grant of summary judgment in defendants' favor. As to plaintiff's Eighth Amendment claim, the court observed that the defendants neither knew nor had reason to know that decedent had suicidal tendencies. They had removed decedent's belt and shoelaces, and even if they did not follow their own established cell-checking procedures, this was not "deliberate disregard for the possibility that [decedent] would take his own life."

However, a Fifth Circuit case,[96] holding explicitly that "deliberate indifference to a prisoner's suicidal behavior constitutes a violation of the Eighth Amendment under *Estelle*,"[97] found in the case before it that plaintiffs might be able to prove that the jail officials were deliberately indifferent to the "strong likelihood" that the plaintiffs' decedent could commit suicide. Defendants allegedly had notice of decedent's suicidal tendencies because of his aberrant behavior during arrest and transport to the station, because of a warning in decedent's wallet that he was under psychiatric care, because decedent's father had told the arresting officer of decedent's nervous breakdown, and because the jail's records showed that decedent had attempted suicide several months earlier during a prior detention.

---

[92] King v Blankenship, 636 F2d 70 (4th Cir 1980).
[93] Sampley v Ruettgers, 704 F2d 491 (10th Cir 1983).
[94] George v Evans, 620 F2d 495, 497 (5th Cir 1980) (per curiam).
[95] State Bank v Camic, 712 F2d 1140 (7th Cir 1980).
[96] Partridge v Two Unknown Police Officers, 751 F2d 1448 (5th Cir 1985).
[97] *Id* 1453. Judge Jolly dissented.

The Third Circuit[98] some time ago held that intentional conduct generally was sufficient for an action based on an Eighth Amendment violation where police officers allegedly beat plaintiff. It specified that *intent to punish* was not necessary. However, this approach was criticized by the Second Circuit[99] in dealing with a similar case, which held that an unprovoked attack by police officers constituted not an Eighth but a Fourteenth Amendment violation. It is now clear that the Eighth Amendment does not apply outside of the prison setting.[100]

Inasmuch as Eighth Amendment violations turn on the existence of at least deliberate indifference, the meaning of this standard will increasingly occupy the circuits.[101] For example, the Eighth Circuit[102] asserted that in an Eighth Amendment setting, deliberate indifference "denotes both recklessness and actual intent." More comprehensively, the Seventh Circuit[103] stated that deliberate indifference may be

> evidenced by either actual intent or reckless disregard . . . . Although the term "actual intent" is self-explanatory, reckless disregard is not. A defendant acts recklessly when he disregards a substantial risk of danger that either is known to him or would be apparent to a reasonable person in his position. Recklessness is characterized by highly unreasonable conduct or a gross departure from ordinary care in a situation where a high degree of danger is apparent . . . . The standard is an objective one . . . . Although subjective unawareness of the risk is no defense, the risk must be foreseeable. Indeed, risk is defined as a recognizable danger of injury . . . . The risk also must be substantial.

Despite the prevalence of *Estelle's* deliberate indifference standard in the circuits, the Supreme Court recently recast this standard in a prison security setting. In *Whitley v Albers*,[104] an inmate, shot by a prison guard during the

---

[98] Howell v Cataldi, 464 F2d 272 (3d Cir 1972).

[99] Johnson v Glick, 481 F2d 1028 (2d Cir), *cert denied,* 414 US 1033 (1973).

[100] Ingraham v Wright, 430 US 651 (1977).

[101] Similarly, it is to be expected that, after Daniels v Williams, 106 S Ct 662 (1986) and Davidson v Cannon, 106 S Ct 668 (1986), which held in a prison setting as well as more broadly that negligence is insufficient for due process violations, judicial attention will center on gross negligence, recklessness, and deliberate indifference, as well as the differences among them.

[102] Miller v Solom, 728 F2d 1020, 1024 (8th Cir 1984).

[103] Benson v Cady, 761 F2d 335, 339-40 (7th Cir 1985) (citations omitted). In an opinion dissenting on the application of this standard to the case before the Seventh Circuit, Judge Swygert noted that deliberate indifference can also be evidenced by "repeated examples of negligent acts which disclose a pattern of conduct" by prison medical staff and other prison officials. *Id* 344-45.

[104] Whitley v Albers, 106 S Ct 1078 (1986). Justices Marshall, Brennan, Blackmun, and Stevens dissented, arguing that the majority improperly imposed an "express intent to harm" requirement and that under the facts the jury should make the decision whether the necessary level of wantonness was reached.

course of a prison riot in which another prison guard was taken hostage, claimed that deadly force had been used against him in violation of the Eighth and Fourteenth Amendments. The Court first indicated that the Eighth Amendment's general prohibition against the unnecessary infliction of pain must, when applied, take account of the context in which the issue arises. The Court next observed that prison officials when confronted with prison disturbances must consider the "very real threats" to inmates and officers alike. Then, in ruling that the plaintiff's case should not go to a jury, the Court applied the following Eighth Amendment standard: whether force was applied in a good faith attempt to maintain or restore discipline or "maliciously and sadistically" in order to cause harm. The Court also went on to hold that the Fourteenth Amendment's due process clause provides inmates with no greater protection than the Eighth Amendment, at least in the prison security setting.

The Court's articulation in *Whitley* of an Eighth Amendment standard in effect amounting to "knowing willingness" that harm occur may be the first step in a movement to modify *Estelle's* deliberate indifference standard and, as thus modified, to apply it in *all* Eighth Amendment cases. Or, *Whitley* could be limited to prison security cases where the Court believes that considerable deference should be given to prison officials. If the latter turns out to be the case, then the Court has created a "variable" Eighth Amendment whose very standards depend on the context in which they are used.

§3.08 —Due Process Before *Parratt v Taylor* and *Daniels v Williams*

Due process standing alone, without incorporation of the Bill of Rights,[105] has both a procedural and a substantive aspect. Before due process can become an applicable concept, a life, liberty, or property interest must be identified. For example, in *Paul v Davis*,[106] the Supreme Court held that an interest solely in reputation is not protected by the due process clause. Once a protected interest is deprived, though, the next procedural due process question is the kind of notice and hearing required to permit the deprivation of such interest. This inquiry is addressed through the use of a cost-benefit analysis.[107] The substantive due process question is more general: is what the government did to the life, liberty, or property interest permissible? Often, substantive due process is another way of talking about a substantive right which is not based on any other particular constitutional provision. An example is the right to be free of bodily harm.

When denial of procedural due process is the focus, intent in the tort sense (not specific intent) is usually present because the life, liberty, or property interest which is allegedly taken without proper procedures is taken intention-

---

[105] *See generally* **ch 2.**
[106] 424 US 693 (1976).
[107] Mathews v Eldridge, 424 US 319 (1976).

ally. Thus, in *Wood v Strickland*,[108] for example, a Supreme Court qualified immunity decision, the students' 10-day suspensions meant that 10 days' schooling, amounting to a property interest, was taken intentionally by the school board. Similarly, in a Second Circuit[109] case, the complaint of a woman who sued welfare officials alleging that they had deprived her of her children without a court hearing was held to state a cause of action under §1983 for a procedural due process violation. She had a liberty interest in freedom of personal choice in family matters, and this was clearly intentionally interfered with or taken by the defendants.

At least before the Court's recent decision in *Daniels v Williams*,[110] discussed later, basis of liability was often a troublesome issue for courts in substantive due process cases because in these cases defendants conceivably could act intentionally, negligently, or even reasonably in bringing about the constitutional deprivation.[111] The easiest cases were those in which persons were physically beaten, either by governmental officials or as a result of the officials' knowing failure to protect them. Most of these rather numerous cases were handled on substantive due process grounds, with frequent references to Justice Frankfurter's phrase from *Rochin v California*[112] setting out one substantive due process test: "conduct which shocks the conscience." An early and leading Second Circuit case, *Johnson v Glick*,[113] involved unprovoked beatings by prison guards. Holding that a §1983 cause of action was stated against the guards,[114] the Court set out the following factors to be used in determining whether substantive due process was violated:

> [T]he need for the application of force, the relationship between the need and the amount of force that was used, the extent of injury inflicted, and whether force was applied in a good faith effort to maintain or restore discipline or maliciously and sadistically for the very purpose of causing harm.[115]

---

[108] 420 US 308 (1975). See **ch 8** on qualified immunity.

[109] Duchesne v Sugarman, 566 F2d 817 (2d Cir 1977).

[110] 106 S Ct 662 (1986).

[111] As suggested earlier, it is preferable to focus on the duty which these cases set out rather than on the basis of liability as such. *See* **§3.02.**

[112] 342 US 165, 172 (1952). It should, however, be noted that this test was vigorously attacked by Justice Black, dissenting in *Rochin. See also* Schmerber v California, 384 US 757 (1966); Breithaupt v Abram, 352 US 432 (1957); Irvine v California, 347 US 128 (1954).
Many such cases involving the use of excessive force by police officers can now be addressed in Fourth Amendment terms. *See* **§3.04.**

[113] 481 F2d 1028 (2d Cir), *cert denied*, 414 US 1033 (1973).

[114] To the same effect in the Ninth Circuit were Wiltsie v California Dept of Corrections, 406 F2d 515 (9th Cir 1968) and Brown v Brown, 368 F2d 992 (9th Cir), *cert denied*, 385 US 868 (1966).

[115] 481 F2d at 1033. Interestingly, the Supreme Court recently characterized *Johnson's* substantive due process standard as the appropriate *Eighth Amendment* standard in excessive use of force cases involving prison security. Whitley v Albers, 106 S Ct 1078 (1986). *See* **§3.07.**

Like *Johnson,* pre-*Daniels* cases from other circuits arising out of beatings and the like frequently dealt with intentional conduct that "shocks the conscience." For example, the Fifth Circuit[116] held that a warden who subjected arrested demonstrators to degrading treatment in jail violated due process. Similarly, the Seventh Circuit[117] held that a police officer has a Fourteenth Amendment duty to stop fellow officers from beating arrested persons in his presence.

However, it was generally held, even before *Daniels,* that substantive due process could also be denied through gross negligence or deliberate indifference. The Third Circuit[118] held that prison authorities must disarm and otherwise restrain an inmate who is known to be planning to attack plaintiff. The Seventh Circuit[119] reached a similar result in a case where a hospital was sued, holding that hospital authorities are required by due process to protect patients from unprovoked attacks. Even the knowing failure to provide medical care where it is clearly needed by a prisoner can amount to a due process violation, according to the Sixth Circuit.[120] Gross negligence resulting in a due process denial was specifically relied on by a California district court[121] in holding that a cause of action was stated against a sheriff and deputy sheriff based on the shooting of plaintiffs during a campus riot. The deputy sheriff allegedly was not properly trained by the sheriff, personnel generally were not properly selected, and there was inadequate planning and an absence of leadership.

These cases could readily be put in duty terms. Thus, police officers and prison guards had a due process duty not to cause bodily harm to those in their custody, either intentionally or with gross negligence; more generally, they had a duty not to engage in conduct which "shocks the conscience." Police superiors and prison authorities also had a due process duty to protect those within their custody, without gross negligence, from attacks by others. This latter duty, which required some personal involvement on the part of the superior, was carefully distinguished from liability based on respondeat superior which would not require any such personal involvement. Respondeat superior liability is not available in §1983 cases.[122]

Whirl v Kern[123] was at one time a leading Fifth Circuit decision that was often incorrectly referred to as a negligence case. In *Whirl,* the defendant sheriff was not told that charges against plaintiff, who was in custody, were dismissed. As a result, plaintiff remained in jail for almost nine months. Analogizing the case

---

[116] Anderson v Nosser, 456 F2d 835 (5th Cir) (en banc), *cert denied sub nom* Nosser v Bradley, 409 US 848 (1972).

[117] Byrd v Brishke, 466 F2d 6 (7th Cir 1972).

[118] Curtis v Everette, 489 F2d 516 (3d Cir 1973), *cert denied,* 416 US 995 (1974).

[119] Spence v Staras, 507 F2d 554 (7th Cir 1974).

[120] Fitzke v Shappell, 468 F2d 1072 (6th Cir 1972).

[121] Rundle v Madigan, 356 F Supp 1048 (ND Cal 1972). Cf Jenkins v Averett, 424 F2d 1228 (4th Cir 1970) where gross negligence was used as the basis of liability for a Fourth Amendment violation. *See* §3.04.

[122] *See* the discussion at §3.15.

[123] 407 F2d 781 (5th Cir 1969).

to a situation involving false imprisonment, the Fifth Circuit held that plaintiff stated a claim for a due process violation, even though defendant was found by the jury to have acted reasonably. While this seems to constitute §1983 strict liability, the case did in fact contain an element of intent in the sense that defendant intended to confine plaintiff even though he did not know it was wrongful to do so. Indeed, under tort law, defendant would similarly be liable for false imprisonment.[124] The Fifth Circuit later retreated somewhat from *Whirl* in allowing a qualified immunity defense to a defendant in such cases.[125] Yet *Whirl* still stood for the proposition that a sheriff (or warden) had a prima facie due process duty not to confine another illegally, regardless of any knowledge of whether the confinement is wrongful.

However, in *Baker v McCollan*,[126] the Supreme Court rejected the Fifth Circuit's conclusion that a sheriff or warden generally has a due process duty to prevent wrongful confinement. *Baker* involved a plaintiff whose brother was the true subject of an arrest warrant issued against plaintiff as a result of the brother's use of a duplicate of plaintiff's driver's license. Plaintiff was thereafter arrested and detained for several days, despite repeated protests of a mistake, until the error was discovered through comparison of a file photo of the wanted brother with plaintiff. In plaintiff's §1983 suit against the sheriff, the Fifth Circuit held, reversing the district court's directed verdict for the sheriff, that a §1983 prima facie case was made out because the plaintiff showed intent to confine, acts resulting in confinement, and the victim's consciousness of confinement. Section 1983's cause in fact requirement was satisfied, according to the Fifth Circuit, either by the acts of the sheriff's deputies in confining plaintiff or, if those acts were assumed to be unauthorized, by the failure of the sheriff "to transmit the identifying material," thereby causing plaintiff's continued detention.

Turning to the qualified immunity issue, the Fifth Circuit then held that it was a jury question whether the sheriff acted unreasonably in failing to institute a policy which would have prevented arresting and detaining the wrong person. It stated: "[T]he sheriff or arresting officer has a duty to exercise due diligence in making sure that the person arrested and detained is actually the person sought under the warrant and not merely someone of the same or a similar name."

The Supreme Court reversed. In an opinion by Justice Rehnquist, the Court

---

[124] Restatement (Second) of Torts §45 (1965) reads as follows:

> If the actor is under a duty to release the other from confinement, or to aid in such release by providing a means of escape, his refusal to do so with the intention of confining the other is a sufficient act of confinement to make him subject to liability for false imprisonment.

Weigel v McCloskey, 113 Ark 1, 166 SW 944 (1914) relied on by the Restatement for illustration 1, indicates that defendant need not know of a legal duty to release the plaintiff; intentional confinement after the duty arises is sufficient.

[125] Bryan v Jones, 530 F2d 1210 (5th Cir) (en banc), *cert denied*, 429 US 865 (1976).
[126] 443 US 137 (1979).

first touched briefly on the §1983-negligence issue, leaving it open,[127] and then flatly held that confinement of the plaintiff did not violate due process. Rejecting the Fifth Circuit's analysis of plaintiff's §1983 claims "exclusively in terms of traditional tort-law concepts," the Court focused instead on the alleged deprivation of liberty without due process of law. It found that, given a valid arrest warrant and no violation of the right to a speedy trial, "a detention of three days over a New Year's weekend does not and could not amount to such a deprivation" despite repeated protests of innocence. In effect putting the question in Fourteenth Amendment duty terms, the Court concluded:

> [W]e do not think a sheriff executing an arrest warrant is required by the Constitution to independently investigate every claim of innocence . . . . Nor is the official charged with maintaining custody of the accused named in the warrant required by the Constitution to perform an error-free investigation of such a claim.[128]

After *Baker*, those §1983 cases in which courts solely applied false imprisonment concepts to determine the existence of a due process violation are no longer good law, if they ever were. Just as the Court held in *Paul v Davis*[129] that a defamatory statement published by state officials is not for that reason alone a Fourteenth Amendment violation, and in *Estelle v Gamble*[130] that medical malpractice does not become a Fourteenth Amendment violation because the victim is a prisoner, *Baker* similarly emphasized that false imprisonment does not become a violation of the Fourteenth Amendment merely because the defendant is a state official. *Baker* consequently indicated that the intent to confine (without knowledge that the confinement is wrongful) is, standing alone, not sufficient to constitute a due process violation where that intent is accompanied by a relatively short confinement and a facially valid arrest warrant. On the other hand, the result in *Baker* would probably have been different had the defendant indeed known, or acted recklessly with regard to the fact, that plaintiff was the wrong person and nevertheless was confined. If this inference is correct, *Baker* stands for the proposition that a sheriff must

---

[127]See §3.02.

[128] 443 US at 145-46. Justice Blackmun concurred, adding that the conduct of the sheriff was not "conscience-shocking" and therefore passed the due process test of Rochin v California, 342 US 165 (1952) as well as the relevant Bill of Rights provisions incorporated by the Fourteenth Amendment. Justices Stevens, Brennan, and Marshall dissented. Justice Marshall argued separately that plaintiff's arrest and confinement constituted intentional, not negligent, action because defendant sheriff and the sheriff's deputies "made absolutely no effort for eight days to determine whether they were holding an innocent man" despite plaintiff's repeated protests and the ready availability of information in the sheriff's possession suggesting plaintiff was improperly arrested. All three dissenting justices argued jointly that the due process clause requires setting up procedures "reasonably calculated to establish that a person being detained for the alleged commission of a crime [is] in fact the person believed to be guilty of the offense" and that the absence of such procedures had caused plaintiff's liberty deprivation.

[129] 424 US 693 (1976).

[130] 429 US 97 (1978).

both intend to confine and know, or act recklessly regarding the fact, that the resulting confinement is wrongful before a Fourteenth Amendment violation and §1983 claim can exist. As will be seen, this reading of *Baker* is entirely consistent with the Court's recent due process decision in *Daniels v Williams.*[131]

§3.09 —The "New" Due Process

Parratt v Taylor

The Court's decision in *Parratt v Taylor*[132] was designed, as discussed earlier,[133] to clear up the confusion regarding §1983 basis of liability by holding that there is no independent state of mind requirement for the §1983 prima facie case; only that state of mind required for the underlying constitutional violation is relevant. But it will be recalled that *Parratt* had an important due process dimension as well. In *Parratt,* the Court held that the due process clause is implicated where a state official negligently causes a property loss under color of law. The plaintiff inmate had sued prison officials under §1983 for negligently causing the loss of hobby materials ordered through the mail in violation of due process. According to the Court, which treated the case as raising a *procedural* due process claim, this constituted a deprivation of property. Justices Stewart and Powell disagreed with this aspect of the Court's opinion and argued that negligence was not enough, while Justices White and Blackmun read the Court's opinion as limited to deprivations of property, and as not encompassing deprivations of life or liberty. The inmate nevertheless lost on the merits when the Court concluded that due process was not violated because, inasmuch as a predeprivation hearing was not feasible for negligent conduct, there was an apparently adequate state postdeprivation remedy available.

Read narrowly, *Parratt's* due process holding applied only to negligent deprivations of property and procedural due process. Read more broadly, however, the holding could apply to all procedural due process cases involving intentional deprivations of property as well as negligent and intentional deprivations of liberty. Read even more broadly, *Parratt* could also apply to substantive due process cases involving deprivations of liberty.[134] Thus, a state official's intentional deprivation of a plaintiff's liberty interest would not give rise to a violation of the Fourteenth Amendment if *Parratt's* due process holding were so interpreted, because a postdeprivation procedure might provide all the process due.

Thus, the broader the reading of *Parratt's* due process holding, the narrower the scope of procedural and substantive due process and, consequently, the

---

[131] 106 S Ct 662 (1986), discussed at **§3.09.**

[132] 451 US 527 (1981).

[133] *See* **§3.02.**

[134] For example, the use of excessive force cases described at **§3.08.**

narrower the scope of §1983. The concurring opinions of Justices Blackmun and Powell, however, indicated that the narrower reading of *Parratt's* due process was what the Court intended. Further support for the narrow reading of *Parratt's* due process holding was provided by *Logan v Zimmerman Brush Co,*[135] Here, the Court held that *Parratt* was inapplicable to a case where a state system, by operation of law, destroyed a property interest through failure to convene a timely conference to consider a person's claim of an unfair employment practice. The Court emphasized that it did not matter whether the state's failure to convene the timely conference was negligent, malicious, or otherwise. "*Parratt* was not designed to reach such a situation."

Nevertheless, the Court, partially resolving a split in the circuits, held in *Hudson v Palmer*[136] that *Parratt's* rationale, that predeprivation hearings are not practicable where a random, unauthorized *negligent* act of a state employee causes the loss of property, similarly applies to *intentional* deprivations of property. In *Hudson,* the plaintiff inmate alleged, in addition to a Fourth Amendment claim which the Court decided against him as well, that the defendant prison guard intentionally destroyed certain of his personal property during a shakedown search of his cell. Applying *Parratt,* and agreeing with the Fourth Circuit in this respect, the Court could find no "logical distinction" between negligent and intentional deprivations of property respecting the practicability of providing predeprivation process: "The State can no more anticipate and control in advance the random and unauthorized intentional conduct of its employees than it can anticipate similar negligent conduct."[137] Further, *Logan v Zimmerman Brush Co* was distinguished because there, unlike *Hudson,* the property deprivation was effected pursuant to an established state procedure. Hence, because a meaningful postdeprivation state remedy was available to the plaintiff under Virginia law, there was no violation of procedural due process.

Justices Stevens, Brennan, Marshall, and Blackmun concurred on the due process issue while dissenting at length on the Fourth Amendment issue. They simply added their "understanding" that the Court's due process holding did not apply to conduct violating a substantive constitutional right or to "cases in which it is contended that the established prison procedures themselves create an unreasonable risk that prisoners will be unjustifiably deprived of their property."[138]

Even though *Parratt* and *Hudson* were deprivation of property cases, the trend in the circuits, as will be seen, has been to extend the approach of these cases to procedural due process cases involving deprivations of liberty. This is sound—indeed it follows from the Court's pre-*Parratt* decision in *Ingraham v*

---

[135] 455 US 422, 435-36 (1982).
[136] 104 S Ct 3194 (1984).
[137] *Id* 3203.
[138] *Id* 3208 n 4.

Wright[139]—so long as courts first ask the question of whether a predeprivation hearing was feasible or possible. Only if the answer is negative should the postdeprivation state remedy be resorted to. It is also crucial to distinguish for this purpose between *procedural* due process cases involving liberty deprivations and *substantive* due process cases involving liberty deprivations. In substantive due process situations, it is inappropriate to apply *Parratt* and *Hudson* because the challenge is to the conduct itself, *not* to the absence of some kind of hearing.[140] The same is, of course, true for violations of incorporated provisions of the Bill of Rights. Here, too, the challenge is to the conduct itself, and asking whether a postdeprivation remedy is available is clearly improper.

Daniels v Williams

The Supreme Court in *Daniels v Williams*[141] recently reexamined the due process holding of *Parratt* and modified it to the extent of ruling that negligent conduct is insufficient for a procedural due process violation involving a claimed deprivation of property. Indeed, the Court went even further in *Daniels* and held that more than negligence is required for *all* due process violations, whether they involve substantive or procedural due process, and whether they involve claimed deprivations of liberty or property. In so doing, the Court cut back on the scope of due process, minimized the number of situations in which state governmental tort immunity schemes will be subjected to constitutional scrutiny, and possibly also reduced the §1983 caseload.

Daniels involved an inmate's claim that his due process rights were violated by prison authorities because they negligently left pillows on prison stairs on which plaintiff fell and injured himself. This, according to the plaintiff, amounted to an actionable negligent deprivation of liberty, i.e., his physical integrity. Initially, a panel of the Fourth Circuit[142] ruled that, even if there was a negligent deprivation of liberty, there was an adequate state remedy under Virginia law. The panel reached this result even though it conceded that Virginia law provided absolute tort immunity for the defendants. Upon en banc reconsideration,[143] the Fourth Circuit found that the federal plaintiff in reality had a tort action under Virginia law which was adequate; thus, there was no

---

[139] 430 US 651 (1977) (state tort remedies provide procedural due process for students intentionally deprived of their "liberty" interests through corporal punishment).

[140] Only if one reads *Parratt* broadly enough to hold that claimed substantive due process violation cases belong in state court where there are adequate postdeprivation remedies, and only if substantive due process is somehow different in kind from incorporated provisions of the Bill of Rights for *Parratt* purposes, can *Parratt* possibly be applied to substantive due process cases involving, for example, the excessive use of force by police officers. However, this reading of *Parratt* has generally been rejected in the circuits, and correctly so. *See* Nahmod, *Due Process, State Remedies and Section 1983* 34 Kan L Rev 217 (1985).

[141] 106 S Ct 662 (1986).

[142] 720 F2d 792 (4th Cir 1983).

[143] 748 F2d 229 (4th Cir 1984) (en banc).

due process violation and the question ruled on initially by the panel was not, strictly speaking, reached.

Granting certiorari in *Daniels* and in *Davidson v Cannon* [144] a Third Circuit case discussed next which raised related due process issues, the Court in an opinion by Justice Rehnquist affirmed *Daniels* on a different ground: that negligence is not enough for deprivations of liberty, whether in procedural due process cases or in substantive due process cases. The Court reasoned that the due process clause requires for its violation some abuse of governmental power and negligent conduct does not constitute such an abuse of power. In short, as a matter of due process interpretation, negligent conduct cannot bring about a deprivation of liberty. Also, in this respect overruling one of the *Parratt* holdings, the Court went on to hold that the same is true for deprivations of property: more than negligent conduct is required to bring about a deprivation of property.

Davidson involved an inmate's claim that prison authorities violated due process in negligently failing to prevent another inmate from harming him, despite plaintiff's warning to the defendants of such threats. Plaintiff contended that, because the defendants were protected by absolute immunity under state tort law, he was entitled to recover under the rationale of *Parratt*. The Third Circuit en banc had ruled against the plaintiff, holding that regardless of whether the plaintiff's claim was based on procedural due process or substantive due process, negligent conduct was insufficient to bring about a deprivation of liberty. Thus, the possible inadequacy of a state tort remedy was irrelevant. Upon review, the Supreme Court in *Davidson* relied on *Daniels* and affirmed the Third Circuit on this ground.

Justice Blackmun dissented in *Davidson*. [145] While he did not dispute the soundness of the *Daniels* standard, he argued that the fact pattern in *Davidson* indicated that the defendants were more than negligent. It was relevant to him that the plaintiff and his assailant were in the custody of the defendants and that, moreover, the plaintiff was powerless to help himself. Under these circumstances, in his view, more than negligent conduct was charged against the defendants. He therefore reached the inadequacy of state remedy issue and determined that a state tort remedy is inadequate where the potential state tort defendants are protected by absolute immunity. [146]

It is important to note carefully what *Daniels* (and *Davidson*) did *not* do. First, the Court did not expressly hold that due process can be violated by gross negligence, deliberate indifference, or recklessness. The Court held only that negligence is not enough, thereby leaving open the possibility that ultimately intentional conduct will be required for deprivations of liberty and property. The Court in this regard left open another possibility: that substantive due

---

[144] O'Lone v Cannon, 752 F2d 817 (3d Cir 1984) (en banc), *affd sub nom* Davidson v Cannon, 106 S Ct 668 (1986) discussed later.

[145] 106 S Ct at 671 (1986).

[146] As discussed at **§3.11,** it seems clear, as Justice Blackmun stated, that the existence of absolute immunity for all potential state tort defendants should preclude a finding of adequacy of state tort remedies.

process violations may require more culpable conduct than procedural due process violations.

Second, the Court did not deal with deprivations of life. However, it appears likely that the same minimum states of mind required for deprivations of liberty and property will be held applicable to deprivations of life. The Court's reasoning in *Daniels* regarding abuses of governmental power is applicable to deprivations of life as well. Supporting this assessment is the Court's partial overruling of *Parratt,* thereby subjecting deprivations of property and liberty to the "more than negligence" standard. And third, the Court did not have to reach the adequacy of state tort remedy issue in the two cases because in both it found no deprivations of liberty which would trigger *Parratt's* inquiry into the adequacy issue.

Nevertheless, the Court's new approach to due process as demonstrated by *Daniels* and *Davidson* is for many reasons quite significant for §1983 litigation based on the due process clause. The scope of due process has been cut back so that negligent conduct no longer triggers a due process analysis. It thus follows that possible federal judicial interference with state governmental tort remedial schemes will be significantly minimized, especially since immunity is often provided for negligent conduct by governmental employees. However, *Parratt* and its postdeprivation remedy approach are still very much alive in procedural (but *not* substantive[147]) due process cases where more than negligent conduct is alleged to have brought about a deprivation of life, liberty, or property. In such cases, the initial question remains whether a predeprivation hearing was feasible.[148] If not, then the availability of an adequate postdeprivation remedy must be looked into. If one does not exist, then an actionable due process violation has been established.

Daniels may, moreover, be expected to have a significant impact on those substantive due process cases raising difficult affirmative duty issues in the circuits. While such cases are more fully discussed later in this chapter[149] and in Chapter 6,[150] it should be noted that these cases typically deal with the assertion that a local government or its officials negligently breached a substantive due process affirmative duty to protect or rescue the plaintiff, thereby causing a deprivation of life or liberty. After *Daniels,* such cases will be

---

[147] As argued earlier, *Parratt* only applies in procedural due process cases where the plaintiff challenges the absence of a hearing; it does not and should not apply where the plaintiff challenges the defendant's conduct irrespective of a hearing. That is, *Parratt* does not apply either to substantive due process or to incorporated provisions of the Bill of Rights. *Daniels* and *Davidson* did not affect *Parratt's* applicability to procedural due process alone. *See also* §3.10.

[148] Cleveland Bd of Educ v Loudermill, 105 S Ct 1487 (1985) implicitly makes clear that a *Parratt* inquiry into adequate state postdeprivation remedies is only undertaken when a predeprivation hearing is impractical or not feasible. That is, this *Parratt* inquiry is not automatic whenever there has been a deprivation of life, liberty, or property in a procedural due process setting.

[149] *See* §3.16.

[150] *See* §6.07.

disposed of not on duty grounds but instead as a result of the absence of more than negligence.

Daniels may accomplish some other goals that the Court surely had in mind originally in *Parratt*. By reducing the scope of due process through a requirement of more than negligent conduct, the Court obviously hopes to promote federalism by reducing federal judicial intervention in what it considers to be state concerns. In this way, §1983 is less likely to become a "font of tort law" and the §1983 caseload in the federal courts may be reduced. Also, Justice Powell's concern (as expressed in *Parratt*) with trivializing the Constitution may be alleviated.

These goals suggest that the Court may eventually require intentional conduct for due process violations. Whether or not this occurs in the future, for the time being one can expect that, as a result of *Daniels,* many §1983 due process cases will be pleaded in gross negligence, deliberate indifference, and recklessness terms so as to avoid dismissal for failure to state a claim. In response, defendants will in all likelihood move in many such cases for summary judgment, claiming that no more than negligent conduct is present. The results in many cases will depend in large measure on the willingness of courts to grant summary judgment where state of mind issues are raised.

This focus on due process basis of liability will force courts in §1983 due process cases to begin to make subtle distinctions among different due process states of mind. Thus, the Court has now given state of mind—originally a tort concept—as prominent a role in due process as it has in equal protection and Eighth Amendment cases.

§3.10   —The "New" Due Process in the Circuits

Because *Daniels*[151] was so recently decided, it is too soon to consider its effect on due process cases. All that can be said with confidence is that, after *Daniels,* more than negligence is required for all procedural due process violations and for all substantive due process violations (excluding, of course, violations of incorporated provisions of the Bill of Rights). Any circuit court decisions to the contrary are no longer good law. It is also to be expected, as mentioned earlier, that as a result of *Daniels* the circuits will soon be confronted with numerous due process cases raising claims of gross negligence, recklessness, and deliberate indifference. Even before *Daniels,* though, *Parratt*'s[152] due process holding had a substantial impact in the circuits. This impact will be set out briefly, with the caveat that the purpose of this Text is not to discuss all of due process doctrine comprehensively.[153]

---

[151] Daniels v Williams, 106 S Ct 662 (1986).

[152] Parratt v Taylor, 451 US 527 (1981).

[153] Thus, for example, the standards for determining whether a liberty or property interest exists are well beyond the scope of this treatise. *See* Board of Regents v Roth, 408 US 564 (1972), the seminal case on this question. For recent and important cases holding that there are liberty interests in certain intimate family relationships, *see*

Procedural Due Process: The Proper Scope of *Parratt*

The circuits generally agree that a *Parratt* inquiry into the existence of an adequate postdeprivation remedy is only to be made in procedural due process cases and should not be made in cases involving either substantive due process or incorporated provisions of the Bill of Rights.[154] It is also the rule that, even in procedural due process cases (which now, after *Daniels*, require more than negligence), a postdeprivation remedy inquiry is not automatically undertaken. Only where the challenged conduct is random and unauthorized, and is not engaged in pursuant to an established state procedure, will a *Parratt* postdeprivation remedy inquiry be made.[155] In such cases, there will be a procedural due process violation where the state postdeprivation remedy is found inadequate under the standards discussed later.[156]

The Fifth Circuit correctly described the scope of *Parratt* when it said:

> *Parratt v Taylor* is not a magic wand that can make any section 1983 action resembling a tort suit disappear into thin air. *Parratt* applies only when the plaintiff alleges a deprivation of procedural due process; it is irrelevant when the plaintiff has alleged a violation of some substantive constitutional proscription. Further, in the context of procedural due process, *Parratt* applies only when the nature of the challenged conduct is such that the provision of predeprivation procedural safeguards is impracticable or infeasible.[157]

Trujillo v Board of City Commrs, 768 F2d 1186 (10th Cir 1985)(siblings) and Bell v City of Milwaukee, 746 F2d 1205 (7th Cir 1984) (parent-child).

[154] *E.g.,* Gilmere v City of Atlanta, 774 F2d 1495 (11th Cir 1985) (en banc) (incorporated provisions of Bill of Rights and substantive due process); Wilson v Beebe, 770 F2d 578 (6th Cir 1985) (en banc) (substantive due process); O'Quinn v Manuel, 767 F2d 174 (5th Cir 1985) (incorporated provisions of Bill of Rights); Guenther v Holmgreen, 738 F2d 879 (7th Cir 1984) (incorporated provisions of Bill of Rights); Sampley v Ruettgers, 704 F2d 491, 495 n 6 (10th Cir 1983) (incorporated provisions of Bill of Rights; "not settled" regarding substantive due process).

[155] *E.g.,* Stana v School Dist, 775 F2d 122 (3d Cir 1985); Wolfenbarger v Williams, 774 F2d 358 (10th Cir 1985); Haygood v Younger, 769 F2d 1350 (9th Cir 1985) (en banc); Rittenhouse v DeKalb County, 764 F2d 1451 (11th Cir 1985); Patterson v Coughlin, 761 F2d 886 (2d Cir 1985); Augustine v Doe, 740 F2d 322 (5th Cir 1984); Scott v Greenville County, 716 F2d 1409 (4th Cir 1983); Vail v Board of Educ, 706 F2d 1435 (7th Cir 1983), *affd by an equally divided court,* 465 US 1091 (1984); Keniston v Roberts, 717 F2d 1295 (9th Cir 1983); McKee v Heggy, 703 F2d 479 (10th Cir 1983); Evans v City of Chicago, 689 F2d 1286 (7th Cir 1982). *But cf* Oberlander v Perales, 740 F2d 116 (2d Cir 1984) (just because a deprivation is the result of an established state procedure, it does not necessarily follow that a prior hearing is always required); Campbell v Shearer, 732 F2d 531 (6th Cir 1984) (dissent argues that the seizure of plaintiff's property by state taxing officials was done pursuant to established state procedure); Brown v Brienen, 722 F2d 360 (7th Cir 1983) (predeprivation hearing would be burdensome and of little use).

[156] *See* §3.11.

[157] Augustine v Doe, 740 F2d 322, 329 (5th Cir 1984).

Substantive Due Process: Excessive Use of Force

In contrast with procedural due process challenges which are directed at the absence and inadequacy of hearings, substantive due process challenges are directed at the propriety of the conduct itself, irrespective of a hearing. Even after *Parratt* with its now overruled holding that there may be negligent procedural due process violations, the circuits correctly refused to permit negligence as a basis of liability for substantive due process violations. Instead, they continued to ask, as they did before *Parratt*—and as they will now surely do after *Daniels*—whether a defendant's conduct "shocks the conscience" within the meaning of *Rochin v California*.[158] This is especially apparent in excessive use of force cases where the Second Circuit's *Johnson v Glick*[159] multifactor version of the *Rochin* test is typically used in one form or another.[160] However, it is an open question whether the Supreme Court's decision in *Tennessee v Garner*,[161] in which a Fourth Amendment approach to the use of excessive (and deadly) force by police was applied, will eventually preempt the application of substantive due process standards in all use of excessive force cases.[162]

Substantive Due Process: Wrongful Confinement and Danger Creation

As it turns out in light of *Daniels*, the circuits are also correct in their insistence on more than negligence in other kinds of substantive due process cases. The circuits regularly distinguish the Court's substantive due process wrongful confinement decision in *Baker v McCollan*,[163] discussed earlier,[164] on the ground that *Baker* involved only negligence and no real abuse of governmental power. Where more than mere negligence is shown, a substantive due process violation for wrongful confinement may be found.[165] Similarly, in cases where

---

[158] 342 US 165 (1952).

[159] 481 F2d 1028 (2d Cir), *cert denied,* 414 US 1033 (1973), discussed at **§3.08.**

[160] *E.g.,* Young v City of Killeen, 775 F2d 1349 (5th Cir 1985) (police officers; abuse of governmental power); Wilson v Beebe, 770 F2d 578 (6th Cir 1985) (en banc) (police officers; *Rochin* and *Johnson* require intentional conduct); Davis v Forrest, 768 F2d 257 (8th Cir 1985) (police officers; *Rochin* and *Johnson* applied); Hewitt v City of Truth or Consequences, 758 F2d 1375 (10th Cir 1985) (police officers; abuse of state power required); Norris v District of Columbia, 737 F2d 1148 (DC Cir 1984) (correctional officers; *Johnson* factors applied); Freeman v Franzen, 695 F2d 485 (7th Cir 1982) (prison guards; *Johnson* applied); Shillingford v Holmes, 634 F2d 263 (5th Cir 1981) (police attack transcended "bounds of ordinary tort law"); Hall v Tawney, 621 F2d 607 (4th Cir 1980) (school officials; "brutal and inhumane").

[161] 105 S Ct 1694 (1985), discussed at **§3.04.**

[162] As argued by Judge Easterbrook, concurring in Gumz v Morrissette, 772 F2d 1395, 1404 (7th Cir 1985) (police officers; majority used *Rochin* and *Johnson*). *See* **§3.04.**

[163] 443 US 137 (1979).

[164] *See* **§3.09.**

[165] Circuit court decisions so distinguishing *Baker* include the following:
Coleman v Frantz, 754 F2d 719 (7th Cir 1985) (plaintiff incarcerated for almost three

it is claimed that police officers, for example, placed helpless persons in situations of serious danger in a grossly negligent manner and thereby caused them harm, it has been held that a substantive due process violation is made out.[166]

Substantive Due Process: Affirmative Duties

Other more difficult substantive due process issues are arising with increasing frequency in the circuits. These cases involve the possible imposition of affirmative duties upon local governments and their employees to prevent harm[167] and even to rescue.[168] The flavor of many such cases is captured by the Seventh Circuit's opinion in *Bowers v De Vito*.[169] In *Bowers*, where the plaintiff's decedent was killed by a mentally ill person, plaintiff sued various

---

weeks without an appearance before a judge or magistrate despite protests of innocence and requests for a court appearance); Gay v Wall, 761 F2d 175 (4th Cir 1985) (claim that defendants knew he was innocent but still detained him); McKay v Hammock, 730 F2d 1367 (10th Cir 1984) (defendants allegedly arrested plaintiff despite knowing that he had valid bond); Powe v City of Chicago, 664 F2d 639 (7th Cir 1981) (plaintiff, whose identification robber took, was repeatedly arrested under warrant directed against the robber; warrant failed to describe robber despite defendant's uncertainty about his true name); Douthit v Jones, 619 F2d 527 (5th Cir 1980), *petitions for rehg denied*, 641 F2d 345 (5th Cir 1981) (per curiam) (claim of deliberate imprisonment for 30 days beyond sentence imposed without valid commitment order and over plaintiff's objections); Reeves v City of Jackson, 608 F2d 644 (5th Cir 1979) (confinement for 19-1/2 hours after arrest for public intoxication without warrant or probable cause where defendants may have known that plaintiff was not in fact intoxicated).

[166] A leading case is White v Rochford, 592 F2d 381 (7th Cir 1979) (grossly negligent conduct by police officers in leaving three children without adult protection in an abandoned car on the side of a road on a cold evening). *But cf* Rankin v City of Wichita Falls, 762 F2d 444 (5th Cir 1985) (gross negligence of city and its employees in connection with employee's death in waste treatment plant not an abuse of governmental power, even if abuse of an employer's power); Hull v City of Duncanville, 678 F2d 582 (5th Cir 1982) ("intentional or negligent failure" of city to enforce its own speed limit against train traffic and to maintain crossing and traffic signals properly not violative of due process where plaintiff injured by train; at most, state tort law might be applicable); York v City of Cedartown, 648 F2d 231 (5th Cir 1982) (per curiam) (city's allegedly negligent design and construction of street and drainage system which caused property damage not violative of due process; this was not abuse of governmental power). *Also see* the following discussion in text of substantive due process affirmative duties.

[167] *E.g.*, Wright v City of Ozark, 715 F2d 1513 (11th Cir 1983) (rejecting claim of rape victim that due process clause imposed duty to warn public of prior rapes in high crime area; no special relationship); Dollar v Haralson County, 704 F2d 1540 (11th Cir 1983) (rejecting claim that due process clause imposed duty to construct a bridge over a pond in which plaintiffs' children had drowned).

[168] *E.g.*, Jackson v Byrne, 738 F2d 1443 (7th Cir 1984) (no due process duty on state to rescue children in fire; no positive entitlement to fire protection and no special relationship); Jackson v City of Joliet, 715 F2d 1200 (7th Cir 1983) (no due process duty on police and fire department personnel, despite claim of gross negligence, to rescue decedents who died as a result of being in a burning car; no special relationship). *See* §§6.05-6.19 on local government liability.

[169] 686 F2d 616 (7th Cir 1982).

defendants for violating due process by allegedly failing to keep the killer incarcerated, knowing that he was dangerous when they released him and acting recklessly in doing so. Affirming the district court's grant of summary judgment in favor of defendants, the Seventh Circuit stated:

> There is a constitutional right not to be murdered by a state officer, for the state violates the Fourteenth Amendment when its officer, acting under color of state law, deprives a person of life without due process of law. But there is no constitutional right to be protected by the state against being murdered by criminals or madmen. It is monstrous if the state fails to protect its residents against such predators but it does not violate the due process clause of the Fourteenth Amendment or, we suppose, any other provision of the Constitution. The Constitution is a charter of negative liberties; it tells the state to let people alone; it does not require the federal government or the state to provide services, even so elementary a service as maintaining law and order. Discrimination in providing protection against private violence could of course violate the equal protection clause of the Fourteenth Amendment. But that is not alleged here. All that is alleged is a failure to protect [decedent] and others like her from a dangerous madman, and as the State of Illinois has no federal constitutional duty to provide such protection, its failure to do so is not actionable under section 1983.[170]

Although analysis of the soundness of the *Bowers* no duty rule is beyond the scope of this Text—the rule reflects a restrained view of the nature of the state-citizen relationship under the Fourteenth Amendment—it is important to note that this rule prevails in the circuits.[171] There is, however, a significant qualification. The circuits make clear that the no duty rule does not apply where a *special relationship* between the plaintiff and the state exists. Such a *special relationship*, a concept borrowed from tort law,[172] can arise where the plaintiff is in the custody of the state or where the state has otherwise placed the plaintiff in a helpless or dependent position.[173]

---

[170] *Id* 618 (citations omitted).

[171] *See* Jackson v Byrne, 738 F2d 1443 (7th Cir 1984); Jackson v City of Joliet, 715 F2d 1200 (7th Cir 1983); Wright v City of Ozark, 715 F2d 1513 (11th Cir 1983). *See also* Jones v Phyfer, 761 F2d 642 (11th Cir 1985) (no duty to warn plaintiff about released criminal who raped her; no special relationship); Fox v Custis, 712 F2d 84 (4th Cir 1983) (*Bowers* followed where defendants did not supervise parolee who raped and otherwise harmed plaintiffs; no special relationship).

[172] *See* Restatement (Second) of Torts §§3.14A (1965) ("Special Relations Giving Rise to Duty to Aid or Protect") and 315 ("General Principle" regarding "Duty to Control Third Persons").

[173] *E.g.,* Stokes v Delcambre, 712 F2d 1120 (5th Cir 1983) (jailors owe constitutional duty to protect prisoners against harm from other prisoners); Doe v New York City Dept of Social Servs, 649 F2d 134 (2d Cir 1981) (due process duty to a foster child to supervise her placement in a foster home where she was abused). *But cf* Davidson v Cannon, 106 S Ct 668 (1986) (refusing to find affirmative duty to protect inmate where negligence alleged and both plaintiff inmate and his assailant were in government custody).

It is possible that after considerable intitial judicial reluctance to find such special relationships,[174] there will be increasing numbers of cases with egregious fact situations where such special relationships will be found.[175] However, the Supreme Court in *Davidson* refused to so do even though both the plaintiff inmate and his assailant were in government custody and, thus, under government control. Furthermore, it is clear from *Daniels* that negligence on the part of local governments and their employees is insufficient to give rise to an affirmative substantive duty to prevent harm or to rescue. Indeed, the results in most if not all of the pre-*Daniels* cases can be explained in *Daniels* terms. In some, only negligent deprivations of liberty or life were alleged.[176] In others—including *Bowers* itself—the circuits appear implicitly to hold that even recklessness is insufficient to give rise to affirmative substantive due process duties.[177] This rule is, of course, not inconsistent with *Daniels*.

Malicious Prosecution and Abuse of Process: The Relevance of Due Process

At common law the tort of malicious prosecution has four elements: (1) a criminal proceeding initiated or continued by the defendant against the plaintiff; (2) termination of the proceeding in plaintiff's favor; (3) absence of probable cause; and (4) a primary purpose in prosecuting plaintiff other than bringing him or her to justice.[178] The tort of abuse of process, in contrast, deals with "misusing, or misapplying process justified in itself for an end other than that which it was designed to accomplish."[179] The abuse of process defendant must have had an ulterior purpose and must have committed a willful and improper act in the use of the process.[180]

By now it is abundantly clear that not every common law tort committed by a local government or a government employee constitutes, for that reason alone, a Fourteenth Amendment violation actionable under §1983. Thus, strictly speaking, it is incorrect to talk about a §1983 malicious prosecution or abuse of process action premised solely on common law elements. Rather, what must be identified in every §1983 case, including these, is the constitutional provision allegedly violated. This is relatively easy to do where, for example,

---

[174] *E.g.*, Ellsworth v City of Racine, 774 F2d 182 (7th Cir 1985) (no duty to protect undercover narcotics officer's wife because no special relationship with her).

[175] *E.g.*, Estate of Bailey *ex rel* Oare v County of York, 768 F2d 503 (3d Cir 1985) (duty to provide protective custody for abused child who was killed by mother's boyfriend; gross negligence, deliberate indifference, and recklessness alleged; special relationship does not require a custodial relationship); Jensen v Conrad, 747 F2d 185 (4th Cir 1985) (suggesting, after extensive discussion of Supreme Court and circuit court case law, that a custodial relationship may not always be necessary for a special relationship).

[176] *E.g.*, Fox v Custis, 712 F2d 84 (4th Cir 1983); Dollar v Haralson County, 704 F2d 1540 (11th Cir 1983).

[177] *E.g.*, Jackson v City of Joliet, 715 F2d 1200 (7th Cir 1983).

[178] W. Prosser & W. Keeton, Law of Torts 871 (5th ed 1984).

[179] *Id* 897.

[180] *Id* 898.

a defendant without probable cause brings about the prosecution of the plaintiff, or misuses legal process against him or her, for a racially discriminatory motive or for a political motive. Here, the challenged conduct will probably violate equal protection or the First Amendment. It is where such motives do not appear that the possible applicability of due process to malicious prosecution or abuse of process arises.

In such cases, the first inquiry (assuming state action) must be into the existence of a liberty or property interest of the plaintiff. The second question, now requiring more than negligence for an affirmative answer, is whether there has been a deprivation of either of these interests. The third question is whether the plaintiff's so-called §1983 malicious prosecution or abuse of process claim is a substantive due process or procedural due process claim. This is crucial because even though more than negligence is required for both, different due process tests will apply depending on the answer. If the plaintiff's claim is based on procedural due process, then, if a predeprivation hearing was not feasible, an inquiry into the existence of an adequate state remedy must be made. In contrast, if the plaintiff's claim is based on substantive due process, then "conscience-shocking" conduct must be found, and state postdeprivation remedies are irrelevant.

Currently, there is some dispute in the circuits about the nature and scope of these §1983 malicious prosecution and abuse of process actions.[181] Nevertheless, the majority of the circuits acknowledge the possibility of such §1983 actions.[182] The Supreme Court has granted certiorari in *Cerbone v Conway*[183] and may shortly clarify some of the issues noted earlier. In *Cerbone* the plaintiff claimed that various public and private defendants had her prosecuted for issuing a bad check even though they knew that her check had

---

[181] *See, e.g.,* Cline v Brusett, 661 F2d 108 (9th Cir 1981) (general rule that malicious prosecution is not violative of due process and thus not actionable under §1983; exception where intent to deny a person equal protection or where person subjected to denial of constitutional rights) and Singleton v City of New York, 632 F2d 185 (2d Cir 1980) (applying state law to §1983 malicious prosecution claim, Judge Weinstein dissented, arguing that the majority had applied state tort law "with blinders" at expense of §1983 considerations).

[182] Bretz v Kelman, 773 F2d 1026 (9th Cir 1985) (en banc) (malicious prosecution); Anthony v Baker, 767 F2d 657 (10th Cir 1985) (malicious prosecution); Losch v Borough of Parkesburg, 736 F2d 903 (3d Cir 1984) (malicious prosecution); Wheeler v Cosden Oil & Chem Co, 734 F2d 254 (5th Cir 1984) and 744 F2d 1131 (5th Cir 1984) (malicious prosecution); Brown v Edwards, 721 F2d 1442 (5th Cir 1984) (abuse of process); Singleton v City of New York, 632 F2d 185 (2d Cir 1980) (malicious prosecution); Terket v Lund, 623 F2d 29 (7th Cir 1980) (malicious prosecution); Lucsik v Board of Educ, 621 F2d 841 (6th Cir 1980) (abuse of process); Hampton v Hanrahan, 600 F2d 600 (7th Cir 1979), *cert denied,* 446 US 754 (1980) (per curiam) (malicious prosecution); Lessman v McCormick, 591 F2d 605 (10th Cir 1979) (abuse of process); Welsh v Kinchla, 577 F2d 767 (1st Cir 1978) (malicious prosecution). *But cf* Cramer v Crutchfield, 648 F2d 943 (4th Cir 1981) (per curiam) (no §1983 malicious prosecution or abuse of process claim unless there is an act violating plaintiff's constitutional rights).

[183] 106 S Ct 878 (1986), *granting cert* in Conway v Village of Mount Kisco, 750 F2d 205 and 758 F2d 46 (2d Cir 1985).

been dishonored because she had ordered her bank to stop payment. In its first ruling the Second Circuit, reversing the dismissal of the §1983 malicious prosecution claim, looked solely to state tort law to determine the proper elements of that claim. In a subsequent second ruling, the Second Circuit found that plaintiff's malicious prosecution claim was actionable under §1983 because it alleged seven hours of detention and accompanying humiliation, ridicule, and mental anguish sufficient to constitute a deprivation of liberty.

While predicting Supreme Court cases is risky at best, it may at least be suggested that, if the Court does find a deprivation of liberty in *Cerbone*, it should conclude that the plaintiff's §1983 malicious prosecution claim is in reality a substantive due process claim. Here, as in many §1983 malicious prosecution cases,[184] there is no contention that the proceeding initiated against the plaintiff lacked the attributes of a fair hearing. Rather, the claim is that the proceeding should not have been initiated in the first place. Under these circumstances, a plaintiff is alleging a substantive due process violation based upon a deprivation of either liberty or property. Thus, *conscience-shocking conduct* will have to be proved, but *Parratt's* inquiry into the possible existence of an adequate postdeprivation remedy is inappropriate.

Whatever the outcome in *Cerbone*, it might be preferable in such cases to eliminate altogether tort-laden terminology which only serves to obscure meaningful constitutional analysis. In short, just as it is improper to speak of §1983 assault and battery cases and of §1983 false imprisonment cases, it is at best misleading to speak of §1983 malicious prosecution and abuse of process cases.

Substantive Due Process and "Taking" Law

The Fifth Amendment prohibits the taking of private property for a public purpose without just compensation, while the due process clause prohibits deprivations of property without due process of law. While taking law has its own standards[185] and is a subject well beyond the scope of this Text, a recent Supreme Court decision is instructive on the taking–due process relationship.

---

[184] *Compare* Vasquez v City of Hamtramck, 757 F2d 771 (6th Cir 1985) (petty harassment by police officer in issuing parking tickets to plaintiff not conscience-shocking) *with* Lusby v TG&Y Stores, Inc, 749 F2d 1423 (10th Cir 1984) (use of criminal complaints to coerce a release of civil liability is a malicious prosecution which is egregious and violates due process).

This is not to say that there can never be a viable §1983 procedural due process malicious prosecution or abuse of process claim. There could be situations where a plaintiff claims that the defendant's conduct precluded a fair trial, thereby amounting to a violation of procedural due process. *E.g.*, Bretz v Kelman, 773 F2d 1026 (9th Cir 1985) (en banc) (malicious prosecution conspiracy claim, apparently based on procedural due process, where plaintiff challenged direct abuse of the state process itself; no need therefore to resort to state postdeprivation remedy). The point is that it is the specific challenged conduct and the harm claimed by the plaintiff that are constitutionally determinative of the nature of the claim, not common law tort concepts.

[185] *See, e.g.*, Ruckelshaus v Monsanto Co, 467 US 986 (1984); Pennsylvania Coal Co v Mahon, 260 US 393, 415 (1922) (taking as regulation that "goes too far").

Williamson Co Regional Planning v Hamilton Bank[186] involved a claim that the defendants' application of various zoning laws and regulations to plaintiff's property amounted to a taking which should not only be enjoined but should also entitle the plaintiff to just compensation for past harm caused by such a *temporary* taking. The Court ultimately ruled that this claim, together with a related substantive due process claim, was premature for two reasons. The first was that plaintiff had not yet obtained a final decision regarding how it would be allowed to develop its property.

The second reason was more closely related to procedural due process. Reasoning by analogy to *Parratt*, the Court found that Tennessee had an apparently adequate state inverse condemnation remedy for damages which plaintiff had not used. The Court conceded that the analogy was not perfect because *Parratt* does not apply to deprivations effected through a state procedure, as was the case here. Nevertheless, unlike the due process clause which places value on predeprivation hearings, the Fifth Amendment did not. As to the related substantive due process claim, the Court curtly noted that it, too, was premature because there had been no final decision by defendants regarding the applicability of their regulations to plaintiff's property.

In *Williamson County*, the Court once again avoided the question whether so-called temporary takings may give rise to liability for compensatory damages.[187] However, its use of the *Parratt* analogy indicates its apparent preference for dealing initially with such claims in state proceedings. In any event, it is clear that after *Daniels*, any claim of a deprivation of property in violation of due process must be based on more than negligence. If the due process clause is ultimately held to have some application in temporary taking cases, then a distinction may have to be drawn between procedural due process claims and substantive due process claims. Such a distinction could be important because upon it may turn the relevance of state postdeprivation remedies as well as the requisite state of mind.[188]

---

[186] 105 S Ct 3108 (1985).

[187] Justice Brennan so argued in his dissent in San Diego Gas & Elec Co v San Diego, 450 US 621, 636 (1981). The Court granted certiorari in yet another temporary taking case, McDonald, Sommer & Frates v County of Yolo (No 84-2015) arising out of an unpublished California appellate decision, *see* 54 USLW 3263 (S Ct Oct 21, 1985), but again avoided a decision on the merits. 54 USLW — (S Ct June 25, 1986).

[188] The circuits have taken different approaches to due process claims in land use cases. *See, e.g.:*

Four Seasons Apartment v City of Mayfield Heights, 775 F2d 150 (6th Cir 1985) (taking and procedural due process damages claims based on rescission of apartment building permit decided against plaintiff; as to taking claim there was an adequate state inverse condemnation remedy for damages; as to procedural due process claim, state remedy should be used and, in any event, no procedural due process violation on the merits).

Rymer v Douglas County, 764 F2d 796 (11th Cir 1985) (even if defendants knew or should have known that plaintiffs' property was unsuitable for a septic tank system but issued a permit nonetheless and assisted in construction of system, this was not a substantive due process violation because it was not an abuse of governmental power beyond an ordinary tort; substantive due process "adds little or nothing that the taking

§3.11 —The "New" Due Process and the Adequacy of State Postdeprivation Remedies

Standards for determining the adequacy of state postdeprivation remedies are crucial after *Parratt*[189] and *Daniels*[190] for several reasons. First, an inadequate state remedy will not foreclose a procedural due process challenge even where *Parratt* and *Daniels* are otherwise applicable because a predeprivation hearing is not practicable or feasible. Second, whether a postdeprivation remedy is adequate should—given the procedural due process focus of *Parratt*—depend on whether that remedy provides to the plaintiff both a hearing consistent with procedural due process and the possibility of being made whole.

The adequacy inquiry requires courts to apply federal constitutional standards to state remedial schemes, a role which may result in substantial federal involvement in such matters. This outcome, which may not have been foreseen by the Court in *Parratt,* surely was one of the factors that led the Court in *Daniels* to require more than negligence for procedural due process violations. *Daniels* thereby reduced the possibility of such judicial intervention in these state remedial schemes. Indeed, in *Daniels* itself, the Court was able to avoid the adequacy of state remedy issue because the required procedural due process state of mind was not present.

Still, it is possible to make several useful observations about the adequacy issue. For example, in *Parratt* the Court made clear that a state remedy is not inadequate just because it does not provide relief coextensive with that of

---

clause does not encompass"; procedural due process claim foreclosed by adequate state remedy).

Raskiewicz v Town of New Boston, 754 F2d 38 (1st Cir 1985) (ordinary land use disputes should not be litigated under §1983, especially where state offers "panoply of administrative and judicial remedies").

Shelton v City of College Station, 754 F2d 1251 (5th Cir 1985) (damages remedy for arbitrary and discriminatory denial of zoning variance effected through established state procedure; no need to resort to state remedy).

Collier v City of Springdale, 733 F2d 1311 (8th Cir 1984) (no taking of plaintiff's property through sewage discharges; there was an adequate state remedy of inverse condemnation).

Albery v Reddig, 718 F2d 245 (7th Cir 1983) (negligent grant of building permit, followed by stop order, "not the stuff of a civil rights violation"; adequate state procedures for obtaining relief were available).

See also Littlefield v City of Afton, 54 USLW 2358 (8th Cir 1986) (substantive due process available to challenge arbitrary denial of building permit; such a claim is not governed by *Parratt* which applies to procedural due process; all circuits but the First agree that such arbitrary denials may constitute violations of substantive due process). Section 1983 may be useful to plaintiffs in such land use cases because it allows punitive damages awards against government officials, see **ch 4,** and entitles prevailing plaintiffs to attorney's fees under 42 USC §1988, see **ch 1.**

[189] Parratt v Taylor, 451 US 527 (1981).

[190] Daniels v Williams, 106 S Ct 662 (1986).

§1983.[191] Thus, the absence of a jury trial and the unavailability of punitive damages and attorney's fees did not render the state remedy inadequate in *Parratt*. This is sensible because a procedural due process challenge focuses on the presence and nature of a hearing and on the related meaningful opportunity to be made whole. However, procedural due process does not require more than this, and it surely does not guarantee that plaintiff will win on the merits.

The Court has said little about the adequacy issue since *Parratt*. As mentioned earlier,[192] in *Daniels* it avoided deciding whether the availability of absolute immunity to all potential tort defendants means that a state postdeprivation remedy is thus rendered inadequate. Only Justice Blackmun who, joined by Justice Marshall, dissented in *Davidson v Cannon*,[193] a Third Circuit case decided the same day as *Daniels*, argued that the answer must be yes. Justice Blackmun is correct; if procedural due process requires a meaningful opportunity to be made whole, it is hard to see how the answer could be otherwise.

However, this result creates some tension with the Court's apparent hands-off approach to state immunities in *Martinez v California*.[194] In *Martinez*, parole board officials were sued for their decision to parole a person who thereafter murdered plaintiffs' decedent. The Court rejected the argument that California's absolute tort immunity rule was an unconstitutional deprivation of plaintiffs' property interest in their tort claim against the parole board officials. The Court stated: "[T]he State's interest in fashioning its own rules of tort law is paramount to any discernible federal interest, except perhaps an interest in protecting the individual citizen from state action that is wholly arbitrary or irrational."[195] According to the Court, the state's decision to provide absolute immunity was reasonable in light of its interest in preventing inhibition of the exercise of parole board discretion.

The Court will ultimately have to reconcile the required inquiry into the adequacy of state postdeprivation remedies with *Martinez*. In the meantime, the circuits have already dealt with, and differed over, some aspects of the adequacy inquiry. Thus, it has been held that plaintiffs have the burdens of pleading and demonstrating inadequacy;[196] that a remedy was inadequate because it only provided for recovery for negligence while plaintiffs claimed that they had been intentionally denied a license;[197] that a remedy was inadequate because it did not provide for recovery of property where plaintiff sought the return of his seized property for its sentimental value and the state legislature had to

---

[191] Parratt v Taylor, 451 US at 544.

[192] *See* **§3.10.**

[193] 106 S Ct 668, 671, discussed at **§3.09.** *See also* Hudson v Palmer, 104 S Ct 3194, 3205 & n 15 (1984) (Court found state remedies adequate after determining that state law did not provide absolute immunity).

[194] 444 US 277 (1980).

[195] *Id* 282.

[196] Collins v King, 743 F2d 248 (5th Cir 1984); Marshall v Norwood, 741 F2d 761 (5th Cir 1984); Campbell v Shearer, 732 F2d 531 (6th Cir 1984).

[197] Wilkerson v Johnson, 699 F2d 325 (6th Cir 1983).

approve awards exceeding $2,000;[198] that a state grievance procedure which the discharged plaintiff had used was inadequate because it could neither protect his job by preventing the harm to him before it occurred nor award common law damages afterwards;[199] and that absolute immunity precluded a finding of adequacy where plaintiff had been intentionally deprived of a license.[200]

On the other hand, it has also been held that administrative procedures could, by compelling a full-scale evidentiary hearing, provide an adequate remedy where a nursing facility challenged a downward patient rate revision;[201] that a state remedy for an inmate's lost property was adequate because, while he could not sue the state, warden, or other supervisors, at least he could sue certain prison employees for their negligent ministerial conduct;[202] that a state tort claims remedy was adequate despite a $25,000 limit on damages, where a former inmate claimed that he was imprisoned seven days longer than he should have been;[203] that a remedy was adequate even though it did not provide for recovery of property taken from an inmate but only for its value;[204] and that a remedy was adequate despite the absolute immunity of all of the potential defendants.[205]

In addition, the question whether adequacy standards could be different for indigent plaintiffs was raised but not resolved in a Tenth Circuit case which remanded the matter to the district court for consideration.[206] The plaintiff inmate claimed he could not use an apparently adequate state postdeprivation procedure for the seizure of his property because he could not retain counsel, he would not be provided with counsel, and he would not be permitted to appear in court on his own behalf.

A thoughtful suggestion was made by several Fourth Circuit judges[207] for situations in which there is some doubt about the availability of absolute immunity under state law to all potential defendants. In such cases, they proposed, a plaintiff's §1983 procedural due process suit should only be dismissed on the condition that the plaintiff be given leave to reinstate if absolute immunity is ultimately held applicable in the state court proceeding.

---

[198] Bumgarner v Bloodworth, 738 F2d 966 (8th Cir 1984).

[199] Parrett v City of Connersville, 737 F2d 690 (7th Cir 1984).

[200] Roy v City of Augusta, 712 F2d 1517 (1st Cir 1983).

[201] Oberlander v Perales, 740 F2d 116 (2d Cir 1984).

[202] Williams v Morris, 697 F2d 1349 (10th Cir 1982) (per curiam).

[203] Wadhams v Procunier, 772 F2d 75 (4th Cir 1985). Cf Loftin v Thomas, 681 F2d 364 (5th Cir 1982) (state remedy adequate for negligent loss of inmate's property where $10,000 limitation of liability for each incident).

[204] Smith v Rose, 760 F2d 102 (6th Cir 1985) (no mention of sentimental value).

[205] Rittenhouse v DeKalb County, 764 F2d 1451 (11th Cir 1985) (reliance on Martinez v California, 444 US 277 (1980)).

[206] Coleman v Faulkner, 697 F2d 1347 (10th Cir 1982) (per curiam).

[207] Ausley v Mitchell, 748 F2d 224, 227 (4th Cir 1984) (en banc) (Judges Winter, Phillips, and Murnaghan concurring in part).

§3.12 —Right of Privacy

As a result of the Supreme Court's abortion and contraceptive ban decisions,[208] a constitutional right of privacy is now recognized. Protecting essentially, although not exclusively, procreation, marriage, and family matters, it is based on the due process clause. There is relatively little law on the §1983 basis of liability for privacy violations.[209] As in cases of other constitutional violations, a constitutionally protected interest must first be found. Thus, in *Paul v Davis*,[210] the Supreme Court held that the intentional or negligent publication of material disclosing the fact of plaintiff's arrest as a shoplifter does not give rise to an action for invasion of privacy.

A leading §1983 privacy decision in the circuits is *York v Story*,[211] an early Ninth Circuit case of first impression. In *York*, which clearly involved intentional conduct which "shocked the conscience,"[212] the plaintiff, a woman, complained to police about an assault. Officers took her picture in various nude poses over her protest and distributed copies to members of the force even though the photographs could not have aided in apprehending the responsible person. The court held that plaintiff stated a §1983 cause of action because of the arbitrary police intrusion upon a liberty interest, the security of privacy of the naked body. "Elementary self-respect and personal dignity" were implicated, according to the court.[213]

More recently, in a Tenth Circuit case[214] where plaintiff claimed that police officers violated his right to privacy by exhibiting improperly obtained "highly sensitive, personal, and private" photographs to a number of his acquaintances, the court distinguished *Paul v Davis* and ruled that plaintiff had stated a claim. There was more involved here than mere damage to reputation; the constitutional right to privacy included, in the words of *Whalen v Roe*,[215] the "interest in avoiding disclosure of personal matters." And in a Fifth Circuit case,[216] the court distinguished *Paul v Davis* and reversed the district court's dismissal of plaintiff's §1983 invasion of privacy conspiracy complaint against various defendants. Plaintiff alleged that he had revealed private information to a state attorney with assurances of confidentiality. However, the state attorney, without a legitimate state interest, had revealed the information to

---

[208] Roe v Wade, 410 US 113 (1973); Doe v Bolton 410 US 179 (1973) (abortion); Griswold v Connecticut, 318 US 479 (1965) (contraceptive ban). *But see* Bowers v Hardwick, 106 S Ct 2841 (1986) (state sodomy statute does not violate the constitutional right of homosexuals.

[209] The four kinds of common law invasion of privacy and their bases of liability are set out in Restatement (Second) of Torts §§652A-652E (1977).

[210] 424 US 693 (1976).

[211] 324 F2d 450 (9th Cir 1963).

[212] Rochin v California, 342 US 165 (1952).

[213] *Id* 455.

[214] Slayton v Willingham, 726 F2d 631 (10th Cir 1984).

[215] 429 US 589, 599 (1977).

[216] Fodjo v Coon, 633 F2d 1172 (5th Cir 1981).

a credit investigator who in turn had disclosed it to various life insurers. But in an Eleventh Circuit case,[217] it was held that distribution of an embarrassing photograph in which the plaintiff student's sexual organ was accidentally exposed during the course of a footrace was not an invasion of privacy. Nor was police questioning of a suspect about her gender and religious beliefs a violation of the right to privacy, according to the Fifth Circuit.[218]

§3.13   —Access to the Courts

The Fourth and Ninth Circuits expressly held some time ago that what might be termed a right of access to the courts, based on Supreme Court decisions interpreting the due process clause,[219] can be negligently infringed and thus made actionable under §1983.[220] An early Illinois district court decision, affirmed without opinion by the Seventh Circuit, held the contrary.[221]

The leading circuit court decision is *McCray v Maryland*,[222] in which plaintiff alleged that the defendant court clerk negligently impeded the filing of his petition for postconviction relief. Reversing the district court's dismissal, the Fourth Circuit held that a cause of action under §1983 was stated. It indicated without much discussion that the plaintiff's right of access was violated regardless of whether the defendant acted intentionally or negligently. As support for its conclusion, the court cited three cases from other circuits, only one of which, however, involved negligence.[223]

Considerably more analysis is set forth in *Navarette v Enomoto*,[224] in which the Ninth Circuit held that prison officials could be liable for negligently interfering with plaintiff's right of access to the courts. Relying on *Monroe v Pape's*[225] "background of tort liability" language, the court said, "[W]e believe that a deprivation of rights need not be purposeful to be actionable under

---

[217] Carroll v Parks, 755 F2d 1455 (11th Cir 1985).

[218] Ramie v City of Hedwig Village, 765 F2d 490 (5th Cir 1985).

[219] Boddie v Connecticut, 401 US 371 (1971), involving an indigent's right of access to divorce court. However, the Court rejected an indigent's claimed right of access to bankruptcy court and to appellate court review of agency reduction of welfare payments in United States v Kras, 409 US 434 (1973) and Ortwein v Schwab 410 US 656 (1973) (per curiam), respectively.

[220] McCray v Maryland, 456 F2d 1 (4th Cir 1972); Navarette v Enomoto, 536 F2d 277 (9th Cir 1976), *revd on other grounds sub nom* Procunier v Navarette, 434 US 555, (1978).

[221] Jenkins v Meyers, 338 F Supp 383 (ND Ill 1972), *affd without opinion*, 481 F2d 1406 (7th Cir 1973).

[222] 456 F2d 1 (4th Cir 1972).

[223] That case is Carter v Carlson, 447 F2d 358 (DC Cir 1971) *revd on other grounds*, 409 US 418 (1972). The other two cases, Jenkins v Averett, 424 F2d 1228 (4th Cir 1970) and Whirl v Kern, 407 F2d 781 (5th Cir), *cert denied*, 396 US 901 (1969), involved gross negligence and false imprisonment, respectively.

[224] 536 F2d 277 (9th Cir 1976), *revd on other grounds sub nom* Procunier v Navarette, 434 US 555 (1978).

[225] 365 US 167 (1961).

section 1983."[226] Cautioning that not all tortious conduct under color of law gives rise to a §1983 cause of action, the court observed that a §1983 plaintiff "must show that he has been deprived of a federally protected right by reason of that conduct."[227] It then found that plaintiff stated a cause of action by his allegations that his removal as prison law librarian, and the termination of a law student visitation program in which he participated, negligently deprived him of access to the courts.[228] Thus, the Ninth Circuit properly focused on the nature of the claimed constitutional violation and discussed state of mind only in this connection. In duty terms, *Navarette* and *McCray* held that prison authorities and court clerks have a Fourteenth Amendment duty to use reasonable care in connection with a prisoner's right of access to the courts.

In contrast, and especially instructive for present purposes, an early Illinois district court case, *Jenkins v Meyers*,[229] held that a §1983 cause of action was not stated against prison authorities alleged to have negligently, through inadvertence, failed to mail a trial transcript to plaintiff's attorney, and instead mailed it to another prisoner's mother. Conceding that improper motive is not necessary under §1983 and that the background of tort liability must be considered, the court stated that intent to bring about the result is required: "[A]lthough specific intent need not be present some intent must be involved."[230]

Explaining its reasoning, the court said that a §1983 cause of action would be stated if the defendants had intentionally mailed plaintiff's transcript to the wrong address thinking it was perfectly legal to do so. But here, when the defendants did not intend to mail the transcript to someone else, but only did so inadvertently, they "were not conscious of doing the act and did not intend the result."[231] Section 1983, according to the court, is to apply only to conscious intended acts. The court also acknowledged its concern that a different approach would "convert every minor mistake, especially in the milieu of the prison, into a violation of §1983. To hold prison officials to such a high standard of strict liability would impose such an impossible burden as to render prisons totally inoperable."[232]

The *Jenkins* court's concern was and still is misconceived. Even if prison authorities have a duty to use reasonable care to protect a prisoner's right of access to the courts, the §1983 plaintiff must still prove breach of that duty, or negligence. This is not the same as strict liability. Also, a constitutional violation must always be found and, as observed earlier,[233] some constitutional violations require intent or gross negligence while others, like the right of

---

[226] *Id* 281.

[227] *Id.*

[228] *Id* 280.

[229] 338 F Supp 383 (ND Ill 1972), *affd without opinion*, 481 F2d 1406 (7th Cir 1973).

[230] *Id* 389.

[231] *Id* 389, 390.

[232] *Id* 390.

[233] *See* **§3.02.**

access to the courts, may only require negligence. Finally, even if a plaintiff states a §1983 cause of action, the defendant may prove qualified immunity. All of this is a far cry from strict liability. In short, while the court's result may be correct in limiting availability of an action for denying the constitutional right of access to the courts, its reasoning is not persuasive.[234]

These cases, of course, were decided long before *Daniels v Williams*,[235] discussed earlier, which held that more than negligence is required for both procedural and substantive due process violations. If the right of access to the courts is based solely on due process and not, for example, on the First Amendment as well, and if *Daniels* is applied to it, then *McCray* and *Navarette* will no longer be good law.

The possibility that the right of access to the courts is not based solely on due process is raised in *Ryland v Shapiro*,[236] an important Fifth Circuit case. In this case, where plaintiffs, parents of the decedent, alleged that the defendant prosecutors concealed the fact that their daughter had been killed by another prosecutor and prevented a full investigation into the murder for 11 months, the court held that plaintiffs stated a cause of action under §1983 for wrongful and intentional interference with their access to the state courts to pursue a wrongful death action. Reviewing relevant case law, the court suggested that this right of access was a privilege and immunity of citizenship protected by Article IV of the Constitution, by the First Amendment's right to petition, and by the due process clause. In addition, the Fifth Circuit, reading state law as defining the right of parents to institute wrongful death claims[237] as a property right, determined that plaintiffs' complaint could also be properly read as alleging a deprivation of their right to procedural due process.

Earlier, in holding that the plaintiff inmate proved actionable interference by a prison official with his right of access to the courts, the Fifth Circuit[238] observed that neither intentional nor wanton conduct was required to show such interference. It stated:

> The right of access may be tortiously impinged by threats, in turn triggered by efforts at court access. . . . The mental processes of the state actor is [sic] immaterial to this analysis.
>
> The prisoner's reaction to the threats is likewise immaterial. It is not necessary to show that the prisoner succumbed to the threats as a predicate for securing §1983 relief.[239]

However, the Seventh and Ninth Circuits took a different approach to the

---

[234] A similar "floodgates" argument was made by Judge Bryan, dissenting in Jenkins v Averett, 424 F2d 1228, 1234 (4th Cir 1970).

[235] 106 S Ct 662 (1986).

[236] 708 F2d 967 (5th Cir 1983).

[237] *See* **§3.20** on §1983 wrongful death actions.

[238] Lamar v Steele, 693 F2d 559 (5th Cir 1982).

[239] *Id* 562.

need to find interference with access. According to the Seventh Circuit,[240] the plaintiff inmates' challenge to alleged denials of photocopying privileges could only be successful if there was a showing that these denials prevented plaintiffs from exercising their constitutional right of access to the courts. In short, "the reasonableness of a prison's photocopy policy becomes relevant only after the prisoner has shown that the policy is impeding that access. . . ."[241] And in a Ninth Circuit case,[242] plaintiffs alleged that the defendants, in a prior §1983 action brought and won by the same plaintiffs, conspired to commit perjury, to withhold evidence, and to obstruct justice. Ruling for defendants, the court asserted that had defendants been successful in their attempt to prevent access to the courts for plaintiffs' §1983 claim, the result might well have been different. Here, though, plaintiffs suffered no deprivation because they were not prevented from seeking and obtaining relief in the prior action.

§3.14 —Equal Protection

While there have been numerous significant §1983 equal protection equitable relief cases involving racial and other discrimination,[243] there have been relatively few §1983 equal protection damage cases. The general rule is that in both a nonracial and a racial context, negligence alone does not give rise to an equal protection violation actionable under §1983. Both the Sixth[244] and Ninth Circuits[245] long ago held that isolated instances of negligent failure by prison authorities to protect an inmate from attacks by others were not actionable under the equal protection clause.[246] The Ninth Circuit added: "In the factual surroundings of a prison it is thus necessary to show a bad faith oppressive motive in order to make a violation of the equal protection clause out of an isolated instance of failure to protect a prisoner from attack by a fellow inmate."[247]

The Supreme Court, going even further, established in *Washington v Davis*[248] that "the invidious quality of a law claimed to be racially discriminatory

---

[240] Jones v Franzen, 697 F2d 801 (7th Cir 1983).

[241] *Id* 803.

[242] Dooley v Reiss, 736 F2d 1392 (9th Cir 1984).

[243] Leading Supreme Court cases on racial discrimination in public education are collected in **app A.** These and similar §1983 cases do not ordinarily pose special problems unique to §1983 declaratory and injunctive relief litigation like exhaustion of state remedies and *Younger* abstention. Such matters are discussed extensively in **ch 5.** In contrast, questions relating to de jure and de facto segregation distinctions and the proper scope of judicial desegregation remedies are substantive equal protection issues beyond the scope of this text.

[244] Puckett v Cox, 456 F2d 233 (6th Cir 1972) (per curiam).

[245] Williams v Field, 416 F2d 483 (9th Cir 1969), *cert denied*, 397 US 1016 (1970).

[246] Neither are they actionable under the Eighth Amendment or the due process clause. *See* §§**3.07-3.08.**

[247] Williams v Field, 416 F2d 483, 486 (9th Cir 1969), *cert denied*, 397 US 1016 (1970).

[248] 426 US 229 (1976). *See also* Arlington Heights v Metropolitan Hous Dev Corp, 429 US 252 (1977).

must ultimately be traced to a racially discriminatory purpose."[249] Purpose or intent to discriminate must, therefore, according to the Court, be present before there is a violation of equal protection in a racial setting.[250] The Court's discussion indicates that discriminatory purpose or intent is generally required in all equal protection cases.

This is borne out by the Court's decision in *Massachusetts v Feeney*,[251] where it applied *Davis*'s discriminatory purpose or intent requirement in a §1983 case challenging a Massachusetts statutory veterans' preference for civil service appointments as discriminatory against women and hence violative of equal protection. In concluding that equal protection was not violated, the Court said:

> "Discriminatory purpose" . . . implies more than intent as volition or intent as awareness of consequences. It implies that the decision maker, in this case a state legislature, selected or reaffirmed a particular course of action at least in part "because of", not merely "in spite of", its adverse effects upon an identifiable group.[252]

§3.15 Respondeat Superior

The general rule in the circuits, even before *Monell v Department of Social Services*,[253] was and is that the doctrine of respondeat superior[254] is not applicable to render a supervisor or other superior liable under §1983 for the unconstitutional conduct of his subordinates.[255] The Ninth Circuit, in *Hessel-*

---

[249] 426 US at 240.

[250] *See also* Yick Wo v Hopkins, 118 US 356 (1886).

[251] 442 US 256 (1979).

[252] Id 279. The Seventh Circuit held the discriminatory purpose requirement of Washington v Davis and Massachusetts v Feeney applicable to §1983 claims based on violations of the equal protection clause. Plaintiffs' failure to allege purposeful discrimination in their §1983 equal protection count therefore justified the district court's dismissal of their §1983 claim. Mescall v Burris, 603 F2d 1266 (7th Cir 1979). And in a case involving a racially motivated campaign by a judge to discredit and damage the plaintiff, the Seventh Circuit characterized defendant's conduct as "an intentional tort inspired by racial animus," distinguished plaintiff's equal protection claim from common law defamation, and held that a §1983 cause of action was stated. Harris v Harvey, 605 F2d 330 (7th Cir 1979).

[253] 436 US 658 (1978).

[254] *See generally* on the liability of masters for the torts of their servants committed within the scope of employment, Restatement (Second) of Agency §§219-253 (1965).

[255] Duchesne v Sugarman, 566 F2d 817 (2d Cir 1977); Vinnedge v Gibbs, 550 F2d 926 (4th Cir 1977); Navarette v Enomoto, 536 F2d 277 (9th Cir 1976), *revd on other grounds sub nom* Procunier v Navarette, 434 US 555 (1978); Draeger v Grand Cent, Inc, 504 F2d 142 (10th Cir 1974); Jennings v Davis, 476 F2d 1271 (8th Cir 1973); Adams v Pate, 445 F2d 105 (7th Cir 1971).

gesser v Reilly,[256] a previously much cited but now rejected[257] decision, adopted the general rule but carved out an exception where a state statute made a superior liable for the conduct of his subordinates. In such a case, the court reasoned, it was not applying common law respondeat superior; rather, the sheriff in question had a *statutory* duty which made him liable under §1983 for his subordinates' Fourteenth Amendment violations. The District of Columbia Circuit, in *Carter v Carlson,*[258] contended that common law respondeat superior could never properly render a *superior* liable under §1983 since under common law rules both the superior and the subordinate are servants of the same master, the governmental entity. Thus, according to the District of Columbia Circuit, the doctrine of respondeat superior was only rejected in such §1983 cases because it was misunderstood. Interestingly, the District of Columbia Circuit then went on to apply the common law doctrine to render the District of Columbia liable as master under §1983 for the constitutional violations of its employees.

As it turns out, the Supreme Court's decision in *Monell v Department of Social Services,*[259] discussed extensively in connection with local government liability in Chapter 6,[260] demonstrates convincingly that respondeat superior cannot be applied *either* to superiors *or* to local government entities. *Monell* concluded specifically, in overruling the relevant holding of *Monroe v Pape,*[261] that local governmental entities are *persons* under §1983 and can be held liable for *their* unconstitutional policies, practices, and customs. However, respondeat superior, according to the Court, cannot be used against local governmental entities

---

[256] 440 F2d 901 (9th Cir 1971). *Hesselgesser's* approach was followed in Tuley v Heyd, 482 F2d 590 (5th Cir 1973), but was sidestepped in Kostka v Hogg, 560 F2d 37 (1st Cir 1977).

[257] In a suit for damages against a sheriff and sheriff's deputy for an alleged illegal search of plaintiffs' property, the Fifth Circuit reversed the district court's dismissal of the claim against the sheriff. Acknowledging that §1983 respondeat superior liability was clearly impermissible after *Monell,* the court stated that there was evidence on the record showing the sheriff's actual involvement in obtaining the warrant and in the resulting search. Baskin v Parker, 602 F2d 1205 (5th Cir 1979) (per curiam). Emphasizing *Monell's* reasoning, and withdrawing its earlier opinion at 588 F2d 965, the court also expressly disapproved its prior case law, which had permitted §1983 vicarious liability where *state law* would impose vicarious liability. 602 F2d at 1207-08. Judge Rubin dissented on this issue and argued at length that *Monell* does not and should not preclude vicarious liability as a theory of recovery where state law allows such liability. He also contended that §1983's *causes* language is not inconsistent with §1983 vicarious liability.

The court thereafter reaffirmed *Baskin v Parker,* in holding that "state law cannot, *ex proprio vigore,* impose [§1983] vicarious liability on a sheriff for the acts or omissions of his employees." Irby v Sullivan, 737 F2d 1418, 1425 (5th Cir 1984).

[258] 447 F2d 358, 370 (DC Cir 1971), *revd on other grounds,* 409 US 418 (1973). The same point was made in Santiago v City of Philadelphia, 435 F Supp 136, 148 (ED Pa 1977).

[259] 436 US 658 (1978).

[260] *See* §§6.05-6.07.

[261] 365 US 167 (1961).

because §1983's language requires a causal relation between the conduct of the *person* and the plaintiff's constitutional deprivation. This relation was held to be absent where a party seeks to impose liability solely on the basis of respondeat superior. More to the point, the Court also indicated rather clearly what an earlier §1983 decision, *Rizzo v Goode*,[262] had only hinted: this same personal involvement and causal relation are necessary where the *person* is an individual. It relied on the use of the word "cause" in §1983 to support this proposition.[263] Consequently, the circuits have been correct all along in refusing to apply respondeat superior to render a superior liable,[264] even though they have seldom articulated their reasons for so doing.[265]

There are also sound policy reasons for not applying respondeat superior to superior officers in §1983 cases. Respondeat superior in tort law is the functional equivalent of strict liability. Because strict liability focuses on risk allocation,[266] it has been characterized as inappropriate in a §1983 setting.[267] Also, in a tort context, the master usually bears some responsibility for choice of servants, while a superior defending a §1983 action frequently has not chosen his subordinates. Moreover, the master is thought to have the deeper pocket for loss spreading purposes in a tort situation; again, this is not necessarily true of superiors in §1983 cases. Consequently, in light of *Monell* and these policy reasons, the superior does not and should not invariably have a constitutional duty, solely by reason of position, to compensate a person whose constitutional rights have been violated by subordinates. What is required is that the superior personally act unconstitutionally as well. That is, the superior must possess the requisite state of mind for the constitutional violation and must have played a causal role in plaintiff's constitutional deprivation.

Circuit court cases following *Monell* have, therefore, been required to distinguish between barred §1983 respondeat superior claims and permissible §1983 claims. For example, in a Second Circuit case,[268] a corrections commissioner and the superintendent of a correctional center were properly

---

[262] 423 US 362 (1976). In *Rizzo* the Court rejected extensive equitable relief directed against those charged with operating the Philadelphia Police Department. Among the Court's concerns were the broad scope of the relief sought, the concomitant federal court supervision required, the federal-state relation, and the absence of any showing of personal involvement of supervisory personnel in unconstitutional conduct of various police officers. This last, of course, was the source of the "hint" referred to in the text.

[263] "[T]he fact that Congress did specifically provide that A's tort became B's liability if B 'used' A to subject another to a tort suggests that Congress did not intend §1983 liability to attach where such causation was absent." 436 US at 692.

[264] See the discussion at the beginning of this section.

[265] The Ninth Circuit's exception in Hesselgesser v Reilly, discussed earlier in this section, was rejected after *Monell*.

[266] According to Prosser, the true justification for respondeat superior is that it is "a rule of policy, a deliberate allocation of a risk. The losses are placed on that enterprise itself as a required cost of doing business." W. Prosser, Law of Torts 458 (4th ed 1971).

[267] *E.g.*, Jennings v Davis, 476 F2d 1271 (8th Cir 1973).

[268] McCann v Coughlin, 698 F2d 112 (2d Cir 1983).

found to have been personally involved in the plaintiff inmate's denial of procedural due process in connection with a prison disciplinary proceeding. The commissioner had either actual or constructive notice of the procedures used, while the superintendent had at least constructive notice of the procedures used. Thus, this was not respondeat superior. Rather, they were found liable not for their agents' actions, but for their own gross negligence and deliberate indifference to inmates' constitutional rights. They failed to act on the basis of available information.

Similarly, in reversing the district court's grant of summary judgment against the plaintiff inmate, the Fourth Circuit[269] remanded for trial plaintiff's claims against a prison guard and warden in connection with an assault on plaintiff by a fellow inmate while the guard watched, and the subsequent denial by that guard of prompt and adequate medical care. The court emphasized that the §1983 claim against the warden for failure to control the warden's subordinates which led to plaintiff's injuries was not based on respondeat superior: "By alleging and swearing that warden Zahradnick had neglected his duty to supervise and control the prison guards, Davis proceeded upon a proper theory of §1983 liability. . . ."[270]

In contrast, where plaintiff sued, among others, certain employees of the Georgia Department of Natural Resources as well as the commissioner for an allegedly illegal arrest, the First Circuit[271] upheld the grant of summary judgment in favor of the commissioner. Because the "arrest was not effected pursuant to either a direct order from [the commissioner] or a custom or policy instituted by [him]," his lack of personal involvement precluded §1983 liability.

In a similar Fifth Circuit case,[272] the court held that a §1983 suit against the defendant sheriff was properly dismissed because there was no personal involvement on the sheriff's part in the allegedly unconstitutional incarceration of one of the plaintiffs and her commitment to a state hospital. The sheriff could not be vicariously liable under §1983 for the acts of his deputies. Also, plaintiffs' allegations that the defendant sheriff "failed to supervise his deputies properly and to maintain adequate records of those imprisoned" were insufficient for §1983 purposes. First, they did not show his involvement in a pattern of activity designed to deny one of the plaintiffs her constitutional rights; and second, they were not relevant to the claims involved.

The Seventh Circuit determined that respondeat superior was implicated in

---

[269] Davis v Zahradnick, 600 F2d 458 (4th Cir 1979).

[270] *Id* 459 n 1.

[271] Howell v Tanner, 650 F2d 610, 615 (5th Cir 1981).

[272] Watson v Interstate Fire & Casualty Co, 611 F2d 120, 123 (5th Cir 1980). Similarly, in reversing a jury verdict and judgment against a sheriff and others accused of wrongfully committing plaintiff to a mental health center, the Eighth Circuit found insufficient evidence to show a causal connection between plaintiff's commitment and anything the sheriff did. Because the sheriff was not personally involved and his §1983 liability could not be based on respondeat superior, the sheriff could not be liable as a matter of law. Harris v Pirch, 677 F2d 681 (8th Cir 1982).

two cases before it. In one,[273] where plaintiff claimed he was fired without notice, those defendants who became aware of the problem only thereafter could not be held liable under §1983 for the constitutional deprivation itself. They could not have been personally responsible for it, since it was already complete at the time. In the other,[274] the court, reversing the district court's judgment against a department store whose detective allegedly detained the plaintiff for suspected shoplifting in violation of the Fourth Amendment, asserted that, like a municipal corporation, "a private corporation is not vicariously liable under §1983 for its employees' deprivations of others' civil rights."[275] A plaintiff in such a case has to show an unconstitutional policy of the department store. Plaintiff failed to do so here as a matter of law. All that was shown was the "entirely legitimate policy" of detaining shoplifting suspects and calling the police.

§3.16   Supervisory Liability and Duty

There are circumstances in which a supervisor or other superior may be liable under §1983 to third persons in connection with the conduct of subordinates even though respondeat superior is not applicable.[276] What is required, the Supreme Court has indicated, is personal involvement of the superior in the unconstitutional conduct of subordinates.[277] However, it has never been entirely clear what this means. The Court's decision in *Parratt v Taylor,*[278] which held that in certain circumstances negligent conduct could be violative of procedural due process and hence actionable under §1983, did not help matters. Instead, it led some circuits to state very broadly and incorrectly that supervisory liability could be based on negligent conduct regardless of the underlying constitutional violation asserted. Indeed, even though *Daniels v*

---

[273] Schultz v Baumgart, 738 F2d 231 (7th Cir 1984). *Cf* Wright v Collins, 766 F2d 841 (4th Cir 1985) (letter to warden telling him of alleged harm done by others at adjustment hearing in alleged violation of due process did not, standing alone, constitute personal involvement; the harm must continue over a period of time for liability; in contrast, letter regarding prison conditions could demonstrate personal involvement because those conditions were of a continuing nature).

[274] Iskander v Village of Forest Park, 690 F2d 126 (7th Cir 1982). Reaching a similar result, the Fourth Circuit held that just as a municipal corporation cannot be held liable under respondeat superior, so too, a private corporation cannot be held liable under respondeat superior for the allegedly unconstitutional conduct of its state-licensed security guard. The court relied on *Monell*'s discussion of §1983's causation language. State action—*see* ch 2—was not addressed. Powell v Shopco Laurel Co, 678 F2d 504 (4th Cir 1982).

[275] Iskander v Village of Forest Park, 690 F2d 126, 128 (7th Cir 1982).

[276] *See* **§3.15.**

[277] See **§§3.15** & **3.18** on respondeat superior and cause in fact, respectively. Note also that if the supervisor makes official policy or custom, the local government employer may be exposed to liability under §1983 as well. *See* **§§6.07-6.16.**

[278] 451 US 527 (1981), discussed extensively at **§§3.02** & **3.09.**

Williams[279] has now partially overruled *Parratt* and held that more than negligence is required for all due process violations, difficult supervisory liability issues will persist in the circuits.

What is at stake may be explained in the following manner. In any §1983 case involving a claimed Fourteenth Amendment violation, the threshold question is whether the defendant owed the plaintiff a Fourteenth Amendment duty and, if so, whether the defendant breached it and caused harm to the plaintiff. These duty issues can arise under the due process clause, as with the substantive due process affirmative duties addressed earlier.[280] Similarly, these duties can arise under any of the incorporated provisions of the Bill of Rights.[281] What must be emphasized is that this Fourteenth Amendment duty inquiry must be confronted whether the defendant is an individual who alone acted unconstitutionally, is a local government whose liability, as discussed in Chapter 6,[282] depends upon an official policy or custom, or is a supervisor whose subordinate brings about the plaintiff's constitutional deprivation.

Applying the constitutional duty approach in the supervisory liability situation may help explain what the Court could have meant (assuming it considered the matter at all) when it seemed to speak of a generally applicable personal involvement requirement for §1983 liability. This personal involvement requirement may be another way of saying that a supervisor may only be liable under §1983 for a Fourteenth Amendment violation when that supervisor himself or herself—as well as the subordinate—violated the applicable constitutional provision. To put it another way, the personal involvement requirement may well be a constitutional requirement whose precise content varies with the particular constitutional provision implicated, and may not as such be a §1983 requirement. Analogously, as discussed in Chapter 6,[283] the official policy or custom requirement for local government liability may be another way of saying that the official policy or custom must itself be unconstitutional. Hence, in both the supervisory context and the local government context, §1983 is under this approach being given a *Fourteenth Amendment interpretation.*[284]

If this is correct, then whether a supervisor may be liable for the constitutional violations of subordinates depends on whether the supervisor also violated the particular constitutional provision and thereby caused harm to the plaintiff through the subordinates. It should follow that the supervisor must personally possess the constitutionally required state of mind even though the subordinate already possesses it. Thus, as applied to due process cases, a supervisor cannot be held liable for negligent supervision. As applied

---

[279] 106 S Ct 662 (1986) discussed at **§3.09.**

[280] *See* **§3.09.**

[281] *See* **§2.03** on incorporation.

[282] *See* **§§6.05-6.19.**

[283] *See* **§6.13.**

[284] So characterized in Nahmod, *Constitutional Accountability in Section 1983 Litigation,* 68 Iowa Rev 1 (1982).

to equal protection cases, a supervisor cannot be held liable where in the course of supervising he or she has not engaged in purposeful discrimination.[285] And as applied to Eighth Amendment cases, a supervisor cannot be held liable in the absence of his or her reckless or deliberately indifferent supervision.[286] Of course, even where the supervisor possesses the requisite state of mind, the supervisor's conduct must have been a cause in fact of the plaintiff's constitutional deprivation.

However, another possible interpretation of §1983, called the *causation interpretation*, must also be mentioned.[287] Under this approach, a supervisor need not personally violate the plaintiff's constitutional rights. It is enough, where a subordinate does so, that the supervisor acted, say, negligently or recklessly with regard to preventing the subordinate from violating the plaintiff's constitutional rights. The supervisor would be liable because, under this interpretation, §1983 itself imposes such a duty on the supervisor to prevent harm, irrespective of the state of mind required for the particular constitutional violation.

The difference between the two interpretations may be subtle but the choice of interpretation makes a real difference in many cases. Suppose, for example, that a supervisor is grossly negligent with respect to preventing subordinates from engaging in purposeful racial discrimination in violation of equal protection. Under the *Fourteenth Amendment interpretation*, the supervisor would not be liable for an equal protection violation because he or she did not personally engage in purposeful racial discrimination even though the subordinates did. But under the *causation interpretation*, the supervisor may well be liable depending on the state of mind required for the §1983 duty.

The circuits do not as yet explicitly address supervisory liability in terms of either of these interpretations. They often speak of gross negligence, recklessness, and deliberate indifference as requirements for supervisory liability without making clear whether these requirements come from the particular constitutional provision or §1983.[288] The better interpretation as a matter of §1983's language, its legislative history, and its underlying policies is the *Fourteenth Amendment interpretation*.[289] This interpretation is more consistent than

---

[285] See **§3.14** on equal protection.

[286] See **§3.07** on the Eighth Amendment.

[287] *See* Nahmod, *supra* note 284, at 11.

[288] As in most of the cases set out later in this section.

[289] This is discussed at length in Nahmod, *supra* note 284. Arguing in favor of the Fourteenth Amendment interpretation are the following:
1. §1983's causation language is not inconsistent with it
2. §1983's legislative history indicates that §1983 is directed at those who themselves violate the Fourteenth Amendment
3. Even though negligence was the predominant basis of liability in 1871 when §1983 was enacted, §1983 liability does not depend on negligence at all. Indeed, Parratt v Taylor, 451 US 527 (1981), makes this clear
4. The Fourteenth Amendment interpretation directly furthers the primary purpose of §1983, the enforcement of the Fourteenth Amendment

the *causation interpretation* with *Parratt*'s holding that §1983 itself does not have an independent state of mind requirement apart from the underlying constitutional violation. Nevertheless, just as the analogous official policy or custom issue has not yet been resolved by the Supreme Court,[290] the supervisory liability question is similarly open in the Court[291] and in the circuits as well.

Consequently, all that can be done here is to describe briefly what the circuits have done in connection with supervisory liability. In many such cases, the courts focus on the personal involvement requirement without indicating whether its source is the constitutional provision or §1983. Moreover, state law duties imposed on supervisors often play a significant role in determining whether the requisite personal involvement is present. Clearly, though, state law duties and their breach should not, standing alone, determine the existence and breach of constitutional duties. The latter are issues of constitutional interpretation which are not dependent on state law.

The cases in which supervisors are found liable in connection with the unconstitutional conduct of subordinates range from situations in which there is, on the one hand, considerable personal involvement in the sense of actual knowledge, presence, and direction, to situations in which there is, on the other hand, relatively little such involvement. In all of these cases, it is important to be sensitive to the particular constitutional provisions involved since, as discussed earlier,[292] different states of mind are required for different constitutional violations. Not surprisingly, all of the circuits agree that, at a minimum, supervisory liability requires a cause in fact relationship between the supervisor's action or inaction and the plaintiff's constitutional deprivation.

---

5. This interpretation is supported by the Court's assertion that §1983 creates no new substantive rights. Chapman v Houston Welfare Rights Org, 441 US 600 (1979)

6. This interpretation explains the Court's §1983 decisions rejecting respondeat superior and requiring personal involvement

7. This interpretation retains the important differences between the prima facie §1983 cause of action and qualified immunity. *See* **ch 8** on the latter.

Arguing against the causation interpretation are the following:

1. While §1983's causation language is consistent with this interpretation, it tends to confuse the prima facie case with qualified immunity insofar as the latter deals with reasonableness

2. Too much reliance would be placed on common law negligence and state statutory duties, instead of federal law

3. There is no principled basis under this approach for stopping with negligence; cause in fact would appear sufficient. But this would raise very difficult line-drawing problems regarding the extent of liability

4. The personal involvement requirement would be reduced to cause in fact alone, which is inconsistent (by analogy) with the requirements for local government liability.

[290] *See* **§6.07.**

[291] Indeed, the Court has not even directly addressed the issue in the terms presented here.

[292] *See* **§3.02.**

That relationship need not be one of exclusive causation; joint causation is sufficient.

In cases involving the possible liability of prison supervisors for prison conditions, including beatings by prison guards and other inmates, most of the circuits insist on at least recklessness or deliberate indifference.[293] Several also emphasize the relevance of breach of state statutory duties to supervisory liability.[294] Notice of one or several incidents is typically not considered sufficient for supervisory liability, especially where the prison is a very large one.[295] On the other hand, several circuits indicate there are circumstances where negligence on the part of prison supervisors is sufficient.[296]

Where supervisory police officers are sued for the unconstitutional conduct of subordinates, the circuits typically require at least supervisory gross negligence or deliberate indifference.[297] Occasionally they speak of implicit authorization, approval, or knowing acquiescence as requirements for supervisory liability.[298] Isolated incidents of subordinate misconduct, in the absence of actual supervisory knowledge, are insufficient.[299] However, there was a suggestion by the Seventh Circuit[300] that negligent selection, supervision, or failure to discharge may be enough.

Similar requirements have been imposed for supervisory liability in other situations. Thus, the supervisory officials in a department of education were

---

[293] Miranda v Munoz, 770 F2d 255 (1st Cir 1985); Goodson v City of Atlanta, 763 F2d 1381 (11th Cir 1985); Martin v White, 742 F2d 469 (8th Cir 1984); Slakan v Porter, 737 F2d 368 (4th Cir 1984); Bellamy v Bradley, 729 F2d 416 (6th Cir 1984); Lozano v Smith, 718 F2d 756 (5th Cir 1983); Clark v Taylor, 710 F2d 4 (1st Cir 1983); Crowder v Lash, 687 F2d 996 (7th Cir 1982); Stringer v Rowe, 616 F2d 993 (7th Cir 1980) (per curiam).

[294] Miranda v Munoz, 770 F2d 255 (1st Cir 1985); Goodson v City of Atlanta, 763 F2d 1381 (11th Cir 1985); Clark v Taylor, 710 F2d 4 (1st Cir 1983); Messimer v Lockhart, 702 F2d 729 (8th Cir 1983); Barksdale v King, 699 F2d 744 (5th Cir 1983) (per curiam); Douthit v Jones, 641 F2d 345 (5th Cir 1982). See also Howard v Fortenberry, 723 F2d 1206 and 728 F2d 705 (5th Cir 1984).

[295] Bellamy v Bradley, 729 F2d 416 (6th Cir 1984); Crowder v Lash, 687 F2d 996 (7th Cir 1982); Layne v Vinzant, 657 F2d 468 (1st Cir 1981); Orpiano v Johnson, 632 F2d 1096 (4th Cir 1980).

[296] Matzker v Herr, 748 F2d 1142 (7th Cir 1984); Withers v Levine, 615 F2d 158 (4th Cir 1980).

[297] Voutour v Vitale, 761 F2d 812 (1st Cir 1985); Rogers v Rulo, 712 F2d 363 (8th Cir 1983); McLaughlin v City of LaGrange, 662 F2d 1385 (11th Cir 1981) (per curiam); Smith v Heath, 691 F2d 220 (6th Cir 1980).

[298] McKee v Heggy, 703 F2d 479 (10th Cir 1983); Hays v Jefferson County, 668 F2d 869 (6th Cir 1982).

[299] Merchant v City of Little Rock, 741 F2d 201 (8th Cir 1984).

[300] McKinnon v City of Berwyn, 750 F2d 1383 (7th Cir 1985). This was a substantive due process case which relied for its negligence holding on Parratt. Of course, in this due process respect, Parratt was overruled by Daniels v Williams, 106 S Ct 662 (1986), which required more than negligence for all due process violations. In any event, the statement about negligence may be dictum because there was a jury finding of recklessness. Also, the court at another point spoke of indifference to constitutional rights.

held liable for their gross negligence and deliberate indifference which led to the violation of plaintiffs' First Amendment rights.[301] Supervisory child placement personnel could be held liable for their deliberate indifference and breach of statutory duties which brought about constitutional deprivations.[302] On the other hand, a prosecuting attorney was held not liable for the unconstitutional conduct of police officers because under state law he had no authority to act with regard to such conduct.[303] A court clerk was found not liable for a deputy clerks' error in applying constitutionally valid office policy.[304]

It should be noted that on occasion even subordinates have a constitutional duty to protect persons against the conduct of their colleagues and others. In *Byrd v Brishke*,[305] the Seventh Circuit held that police officers have a due process duty to protect persons from the unwarranted brutality of their fellow officers which occurs in their presence. Noninvolvement will not do where intervention is possible. This case clearly involved intentional conduct by the defendants in the sense that absent an attempt to stop their fellow officers, the harm to plaintiff was substantially certain to follow. Consequently, even after *Daniels v Williams*,[306] *Byrd* is still good law because it is not a negligent due process case. However, in later circuit court decisions, *Byrd* has been distinguished on the grounds that there was no proof that the defendants were present and there was no time to intervene.[307] Still, *Byrd* was read broadly by the Eighth Circuit[308] to impose liability on a subordinate police officer for failure to intervene against his superior where the subordinate was present and knew what his superior was doing.

§3.17 Proximate Cause

Proximate cause,[309] analyzed either for tort or §1983 purposes, is ultimately a question of policy: should the defendant be held accountable for the results of his conduct? The §1983 proximate cause question of the extent of liability could conceivably be dealt with primarily as a question of the scope of the constitutional duty breached, thereby largely eliminating the terminology of

---

[301] Fernandez v Chardon, 681 F2d 42 (1st Cir 1982), *affd on other grounds sub nom* Chardon v Fumero Soto, 462 US 650 (1983).

[302] Doe v New York City Dept of Social Servs, 649 F2d 134 (2d Cir 1981). *See also* 709 F2d 782 (2d Cir 1983) (same case). In this case, the conduct of the supervisory personnel rendered their employing agency liable. *See* §6.07.

[303] Dommer v Crawford, 653 F2d 289 (7th Cir 1981) (per curiam).

[304] Thibodeaux v Arceneaux, 768 F2d 737 (5th Cir 1985).

[305] 466 F2d 6 (7th Cir 1972).

[306] 106 S Ct 662 (1986).

[307] Bruner v Dunaway, 684 F2d 422 (6th Cir 1982) (per curiam) (presence); Richardson v City of Indianapolis, 658 F2d 494 (7th Cir 1981) (time).

[308] Putnam v Gerloff, 639 F2d 415 (8th Cir 1981).

[309] See also the discussion of damages and proximate cause at §4.03.

proximate cause and the concomitant jury role.[310] Doing so could, however, result in "overloading" the constitutional inquiry by making it determinative not only of the constitutionally required standard of conduct, but also of ultimate liability, a remedial issue. Thus, it is probably better that courts in appropriate §1983 cases continue to use the language of proximate cause.[311]

Several points should be made about the applicability of proximate cause in a §1983 context. First, the question arises only after breach of constitutional duty and causation in fact are shown. Second, presenting the extent of §1983 liability in proximate cause terms may give the jury a meaningful role in this determination where reasonable persons can differ.[312] As a District of Columbia district court observed in a First Amendment case, the proximate cause question "whether the alleged deprivation of constitutional rights was a 'natural consequence' of the allegedly negligent actions of the defendant . . . is a question for the finders of fact."[313]

Just as basis of liability concepts of tort law do not determine §1983 basis of liability requirements,[314] proximate cause standards from tort law should not be dispositive of the §1983 extent of liability question. This is not to say, of course, that proximate cause standards from tort law are not useful. But tort law purposes and interests are often different from §1983 purposes and interests, and thus tort law concepts should not be blindly applied.[315]

For example, in *Duncan v Nelson*[316] the Seventh Circuit held that unconstitutional police questioning procedures which led to the petitioner's murder confession were not the proximate cause of the petitioner's conviction and imprisonment, and that the defendant police therefore could not be held liable for the petitioner's deprivation of liberty. The court so held even though the conduct complained of included solitary confinement for 18 days on another charge and 20 straight hours of questioning. Petitioner's confession had been admitted into evidence, but was held excludable by the Illinois Supreme Court after he had served eight years. He was acquitted at a second trial. The court used a foreseeability test for proximate cause, which might seem at first to make the defendants the proximate cause of the conviction and imprisonment, but then said: "Defendants were presumed to have known the then existing law concerning involuntary confession. . . . Therefore . . . the defendants knew or should have known that their actions in extracting this confession from the

---

[310] Professor Green would do this in the ordinary negligence case. Green, *Foreseeability in Negligence Law*, 61 Colum L Rev 1401 (1961).

[311] For a helpful discussion of proximate cause and the various tests used, see W. Prosser & W. Keeton, Law of Torts 272-321 (5th ed 1984).

[312] The jury similarly has an important proximate cause role in connection with the extent of tort liability.

[313] Shifrin v Wilson, 412 F Supp 1282, 1302 (DDC 1976).

[314] *See* §3.02.

[315] *See* §3.02.

[316] 466 F2d 939 (7th Cir), *cert denied*, 409 US 894 (1972).

plaintiff would render it involuntary and hence inadmissible."[317] In short, according to the court, defendants could not reasonably foresee that the trial court would erroneously admit the unlawful confession.

While the result of no liability for the conviction and imprisonment may be sound on the facts in *Duncan*, the court should have directly addressed the proximate cause issue in terms of §1983 policy. Not only did it not do so when it used a tort concept of proximate cause, but it even used the wrong tort law proximate cause standard, one derived from *negligence*, in a case involving defendants' *intentional* conduct leading to conviction and imprisonment. In such cases accountability may be more extensive than it is for negligence.[318] For intentional conduct resulting in unintended injury under both tort law and §1983, a panel of the Fifth Circuit[319] stated the correct proximate cause test as whether, "from the standpoint of the reasonable man, defendant's act has in some degree increased the risk of that harm."[320] The Fifth Circuit applied this standard to the question of the liability of a psychiatric administrator sued for allegedly confining the plaintiff illegally, resulting in an injury to the plaintiff's shoulder suffered when orderlies tried to give him medication. It characterized the question of whether defendant's confinement of plaintiff increased the "hazard of harm" as being for the fact finder.[321]

In another §1983 proximate cause case,[322] the Fifth Circuit en banc affirmed a jury verdict for defendants who arrested plaintiffs and had them detained at a state prison pending bond. The plaintiffs were not taken before a magistrate as required prior to detention, and while they were in detention the state prison superintendent subjected them to brutal treatment. The court held that the jury could have found that the brutal conduct of the prison superintendent was not foreseeable by the defendants when they had plaintiffs sent to the prison. It added: "Indeed, there is nothing in the record from which one might draw an inference that such unusual punishment was foreseeable."[323]

The Supreme Court addressed a §1983 proximate cause issue in *Martinez v California*.[324] Plaintiffs, decedent's survivors, sued state parole board officials for damages under §1983 in connection with their allegedly negligent and reckless decision to release one Thomas, who killed decedent five months later. In holding that no §1983 cause of action was stated, the Court, per Justice Stevens, found that Thomas, and not the state, had deprived decedent of her

---

[317] *Id* 942.

[318] W. Prosser & W. Keeton, Law of Torts 37 (5th ed 1984).

[319] Johnson v Greer, 477 F2d 101 (5th Cir 1973).

[320] *Id* 107 (*quoting* from Restatement (Second) of Torts §870 (1965)).

[321] 477 F2d at 108.

[322] Anderson v Nosser, 456 F2d 835 (5th Cir) (en banc), *cert denied sub nom* Nosser v Bradley, 409 US 848 (1972).

[323] 456 F2d at 841.

[324] 444 US 277 (1980).

life.[325] Second, and more important for present purposes, the Court concluded that decedent's death was "too remote a consequence of the parole officers' action to hold them responsible under the federal civil rights law."[326] This "remoteness" language rather clearly is another way of saying that the defendants' conduct was not the proximate cause of decedent's death.

The Court, however, did not use any particular proximate cause test. It first observed that it was irrelevant to the §1983 liability of the defendants whether under *state tort law* the parole board either had a duty to decedent to prevent harm to her or proximately caused her death. The Court then emphasized the following factors underlying its "remoteness" conclusion:

1.   Thomas killed decedent *five months* after his release
2.   Thomas was in no sense an agent of the parole board
3.   The parole board was not aware that decedent faced any special danger; whatever danger she faced was as a member of the public at large

The Court did not spell out *why* these factors led it to conclude that defendants' parole decision was not the proximate cause of decedent's death; the Court simply referred to the "particular circumstances of this parole decision." Several observations may nevertheless be made. First, plaintiffs had alleged that the defendants knew, or should have known, that Thomas's release "created a clear and present danger that such an incident would occur." Because the complaint was successfully demurred to at the trial level, these allegations must be taken as true on appeal and, therefore, what happened to decedent (although not her identity) was foreseeable to the defendants. Despite this, the Court found no proximate cause, thus indicating that foreseeability of some risk of harm to another is not always sufficient for §1983 proximate cause purposes.

Second, the Court may have given little guidance on the §1983 proximate cause issue in *Martinez* because its initial interest was whether parole board officials are entitled to absolute immunity or merely to qualified immunity.[327] From this perspective, the Court's rather conclusory finding of no proximate cause in *Martinez* to avoid this scope of immunity issue is another example of how proximate cause terminology, whether in tort or §1983 litigation, frequently will mask troublesome policy or duty issues. For example, one such issue in *Martinez* is whether and to what extent defendants, whose job it is to make parole decisions, should be subjected to potential liability resulting from the attendant second-guessing of such decisions, especially since there is typically a risk of some harm to society arising out of every parole decision. All that is clear from *Martinez* is that parole board officials are not liable under §1983 for making parole decisions in fact situations comparable to *Martinez*.

It is worth noting that the Court expressly said that it was *not* deciding that

---

[325] The state action aspect of *Martinez* is analyzed at **§2.04.**
[326] 444 US at 285.
[327] *See* **§8.18.**

parole board officials could never be liable under §1983 where a parole decision led to another's death. Perhaps if the parole board in *Martinez* had known of specific threats or danger to decedent from Thomas and if Thomas had killed decedent almost immediately upon parole, the proximate cause result would have been different. If remoteness had not been a problem, the Court would have had to address the question whether due process was violated—an issue treated *arguendo*,[328]—and then, assuming a due process violation, the scope of immunity of parole board officials.

Circuit court decisions following *Martinez* continue to use tort concepts of proximate cause, including foreseeable injury, superseding cause, and shifting responsibility. Thus, proximate cause was found where:

1. A warden was sued for causing the loss of plaintiff's job through improper interference with plaintiff's letter to an inmate in violation of the First Amendment and the subsequent disclosure of its contents; the harm to the plaintiff was the foreseeable or "likely outcome" of the warden's conduct[329]

2. Defendants' conduct in hiring and supervising their deputies led to

---

[328] 444 US at 284 n 9. See **§3.08** on due process. Relying on the Supreme Court's decision in *Martinez v California*, the Tenth Circuit affirmed the dismissal of a rape victim's suit against parole board officials. The rapist, who was a resident at a correctional facility where there was a "good deal of freedom and interaction in the community," had raped the plaintiff within two months of coming to the facility. According to the court, the actions of the parole board in placing the rapist at the facility were too remote in time from the crime. Also, the rapist was in no sense an agent of the state. Finally, the plaintiff had no special relationship with the rapist from which the defendants could have inferred a special danger to her. Humann v Wilson, 696 F2d 783 (10th Cir 1983) (per curiam). Cf Fox v Custis, 712 F2d 84 (4th Cir 1983) where the Fourth Circuit in a similar case analyzed the issue in duty terms.

[329] Trudeau v Wyrick, 713 F2d 1360 (8th Cir 1983). Cf Black v Stephens, 662 F2d 181 (3d Cir 1981) where a police chief, a detective, and a city were sued in connection with the claimed violation of plaintiffs' constitutional rights through, first, the use of excessive force by the detective and, second, the filing of unwarranted charges against them by that detective. Affirming the jury verdict of liability against the police chief, the court found there was sufficient evidence to show a causal connection between the police chief's actions and the detective's unconstitutional activity. The police chief's regulation, which delayed any disciplinary investigation of an officer's conduct until the underlying arrest was resolved, was found to have proximately caused the detective to file those charges because of their timing. In addition, the police chief had a policy of encouraging excessive force which was found to have proximately caused the detective's use of such force against plaintiffs. As support, there was the following:

1. A citizen's complaint about excessive force never went into an officer's permanent personnel file
2. The police chief had never initiated discipline against an officer solely because the officer used force
3. Promotion in the department, according to the police chief, was inappropriate for any officer who "backed down when force was involved"
4. The police chief had stated that very few arrests can be made without force

Judge Garth dissented, arguing that the evidence demonstrated no basis for finding causal links between the detective's conduct and the police chief.

plaintiffs' decedent's suicide; their conduct created a foreseeable risk that plaintiffs' decedent might hang himself in his jail cell[330]

3. A prison official offered cigarettes to inmates when he stated that plaintiff inmate's life was worth five or six packs; this conduct was the proximate cause of the later attack on plaintiff[331]

On the other hand, proximate cause was *not* found where:

1. Texas Rangers seized plaintiff's property without due process; the damage done to it by another claimant was not reasonably foreseeable[332]

2. Plaintiff was shot and killed in a struggle with a police officer after a high-speed car chase in which the defendant police officers participated; the chase had terminated without injury to decedent[333]

3. A polygraph operator and two sergeants were sued in connection with the arrest and incarceration of plaintiff; the filing of the criminal complaint by the district attorney insulated them from liability for damages suffered thereafter unless the district attorney could be shown not to have exercised independent judgment and so long as defendants did not act maliciously or recklessly[334]

4. A plaintiff was confined as a material witness for the duration of a proceeding; confinement resulted not from the defendants' conduct but because plaintiff could not make the bail set by a magistrate; the court order was the proximate cause of the confinement[335]

5. Plaintiff was arrested, searched, and indicted for alleged theft of IBM documents and trade secrets; no IBM employee or agent did anything that was the proximate cause of plaintiff's arrest and the search of his office; the "standard 'foreseeability' formulation of proximate cause" was used[336]

6. Plaintiff's decedent died at the mental hospital through the wrongful administration there of a drug after he had been transferred from the county jail when he was awaiting trial; the defendant sheriff could not have foreseen the turn of events at the mental hospital: "[T]here were

[330] Hirst v Gertzen, 676 F2d 1252 (9th Cir 1982).
[331] Glover v Alabama Dept of Corrections, 734 F2d 691 (11th Cir 1984).
[332] Reimer v Smith, 663 F2d 1316 (5th Cir 1981).
[333] Richardson v City of Indianapolis, 658 F2d 494 (7th Cir 1981).
[334] Smiddy v Varney, 665 F2d 261 (9th Cir 1981). *See also* McLaughlin v Alban, 775 F2d 389 (DC Cir 1985) (independent investigation by police a superseding cause). See §4.04 on damages in wrongful arrest and imprisonment cases.
[335] Houston v Bryan, 725 F2d 516 (9th Cir 1984).
[336] Arnold v IBM, 637 F2d 1350, 1355 (9th Cir 1981).

intervening acts subsequent to the time that [decedent] left the jail which render [the sheriff's actions] legally remote causes"[337]

7. Plaintiff inmate was sexually assaulted by other inmates; the defendants' conduct in framing him was not the proximate cause of this assault; the intentional and criminal acts of the other inmates were a superseding cause and absolved defendants of liability for the assault; furthermore, responsibility had shifted because custody of plaintiff had been transferred from the defendants to the state prison system which thereby assumed the duty to protect plaintiff[338]

The Supreme Court recently addressed in passing another proximate cause issue which arose where a police officer submitted an inadequate affidavit upon which a magistrate issued an arrest warrant against plaintiffs, causing their arrest and confinement. In *Malley v Briggs*,[339] the First Circuit held that "judicial approval of a warrant cannot serve as an absolute bar to the §1983 liability for false arrest of the officer who obtained the warrant." The court went on to emphasize that liability would attach "*only* where an officer is 'constitutionally negligent,' that is, where the officer should have known that the facts recited in the affidavit did not constitute probable cause."[340] In affirming, the Supreme Court dealt extensively with the qualified immunity aspect of *Malley*. For present proximate cause purposes it is significant that the Court clearly rejected the police officer's argument that there was no causal link between applying for the warrant and plaintiff's subsequent arrest after the warrant was issued. Section 1983's "background of tort liability" demonstrated that there is a causal link between the submission of a complaint by a police officer and an ensuing arrest.[341] And even before *Malley,* the Tenth Circuit had noted that most circuits took the position that "evidence of intentional or reckless misrepresentations made by police officer defendants in obtaining a warrant, if believed by the jury, would invalidate the warrant and expose the officers to liability."[342] Nevertheless, even though the proximate cause issue is now resolved in favor of the falsely arrested plaintiff in such cases, the police officer may still escape liability on the qualified immunity ground that clearly settled law was not violated.[343]

As a general matter, therefore, lawyers dealing with §1983 extent of liability issues should be prepared to address not only §1983 policy but tort law

---

[337] Daniels v Galbreath, 668 F2d 477, 479-80 (10th Cir 1982).

[338] Hibma v Odegaard, 769 F2d 1147 (7th Cir 1985) (relying extensively on Restatement (Second) of Torts §§320, 440, 441, 448 & 452 (1965)).

[339] 106 S Ct 1092 (1986), *affg* Briggs v Malley, 748 F2d 715 (1st Cir 1984) also discussed in connection with qualified immunity at **§8.11.**

[340] 748 F2d at 712 (emphasis in original).

[341] 106 S Ct at 1098 n 7.

[342] Easton v City of Boulder, 776 F2d 1441, 1448 (10th Cir 1985). The Fifth Circuit took a contrary position in Wheeler v Cosden Oil & Chem Co, 744 F2d 1131 (5th Cir 1984) but may have modified its view in Hindman v City of Paris, 746 F2d 1063 (5th Cir 1984).

[343] See **ch 8** on qualified immunity.

proximate cause issues as well.[344] *Monroe v Pape's*[345] "background of tort liability" made this inevitable.

§3.18   Cause in Fact

As the Supreme Court's decision in *Monell v Department of Social Services*[346] emphasized, the very language of §1983 requires a causal relation between defendant's conduct and plaintiff's constitutional deprivation.[347] Cause in fact is sharply distinguishable from proximate cause for both tort and §1983 purposes: the former concentrates on what happened *in fact* while the latter[348] focuses on whether the defendant *should be* liable for injury caused by the defendant. If cause in fact is not found, there is ordinarily no reason to reach the proximate cause question. Given this important distinction, lawyers should be sensitive to the possible confusion in §1983 cases between the two concepts.[349]

Cause in fact, which, like proximate cause, is often a question for the fact-finder,[350] calls for a common sense inquiry into physical causation. Two tests have emerged in tort law. One is the *but for* test, where the fact-finder asks hypothetically: would the plaintiff have been injured if the defendant had not acted wrongfully? If the answer is yes, then *but for* cause in fact is not present; if no, then it is. In a §1983 setting, a variation of the *but for* test has been used by the Supreme Court to determine the causal relation between plaintiff's *damages* and defendant's conduct, a subject discussed in Chapter 4.[351] The other test, which arose in large measure because of difficulties with the but for test in joint tortfeasor and failure to warn tort cases, is the *substantial factor* test.[352] This test was used by the Supreme Court in a §1983 case in considering whether defendant's conduct violated plaintiff's First Amendment rights. The

---

[344] *See* Bellamy v Bradley, 729 F2d 416 (6th Cir 1984); Crowder v Lash, 687 F2d 996 (7th Cir 1982); Layne v Vinzant, 657 F2d 468 (1st Cir 1981); Orpiano v Johnson, 632 F2d 1096 (4th Cir 1980).

[345] 365 US 167, 187 (1961).

[346] 436 US 658 (1978). *See* §§6.05-6.07.

[347] A cause in fact relation must also be shown between the defendant's conduct and plaintiff's damages. *See* §4.02.

[348] *See* §3.17.

[349] This confusion is comparable to that of many tort decisions as well.

[350] At least where reasonable persons can differ on the law application and fact-finding issues.

[351] At §4.02. The Court held that even where a defendant has violated a plaintiff's constitutional rights, the defendant may avoid liability for compensatory damages by showing that the plaintiff's damages would have occurred anyway. Mount Healthy City Bd of Educ v Doyle, 429 US 274 (1977).

[352] On cause in fact generally, *see* W. Prosser & W. Keeton, *Law of Torts* 263-71 (5th ed 1984). *See also* Thode, *The Indefensible Use of the Hypothetical Case to Determine Cause in Fact*, 46 Tex L Rev 423 (1968); Green, *The Causal Relation Issue in Negligence Law*, 60 Mich L Rev 543 (1962); Restatement (Second) of Torts §431 (1965).

Court, in *Mount Healthy City Board of Education v Doyle*,[353] put the constitutional violation question in terms of whether protected conduct by the plaintiff teacher played a "substantial part" in the defendant school board's decision not to renew his contract.

In most §1983 cases, showing a causal relation between defendant's conduct and the violation of plaintiff's constitutional rights poses no serious problem to the plaintiff. However, some rather difficult cause in fact questions may arise in those §1983 cases where it is alleged that the defendant acted or failed to act to prevent the violation of plaintiff's constitutional rights *by others*. Cause in fact is a crucial element where a local governmental body or a supervisor is sued for the constitutional violations of employees or subordinates because of the Supreme Court's emphasis in *Monell v Department of Social Services*.[354] *Monell* indicated that a local government body is a cause in fact of a plaintiff's constitutional deprivation, and may thereby be held liable for the deprivation, only "when execution of a government's policy or custom, whether made by its lawmakers or by those whose edicts or acts may fairly be said to represent official policy, inflicts the injury. . . ."[355] *Monell* also observed as to local government and supervisory or superior liability: "By our decision in *Rizzo v Goode* we would appear to have decided that the mere right to control without any control or direction having been exercised and without any failure to

---

[353] 429 US 274 (1977). *Mount Healthy* also dealt with cause in fact and damages. *See* **§4.02.**

In a case involving an inmate's challenge to his transfer to another prison on the ground that the transfer was motivated by a desire to punish him for filing suits against prison officials and rendering legal assistance to other inmates, the First Circuit misstated the *Mount Healthy* cause in fact test. While the court reversed the district court's dismissal of plaintiff's complaint, it erroneously declared, citing *Mount Healthy:* "Plaintiff must prove that he would not have been transferred 'but for' the alleged reason." McDonald v Hall, 610 F2d 16, 18 (1st Cir 1979). However, *Mount Healthy* in fact indicates that plaintiff has the burden of proving by a preponderance of the evidence that defendants' punitive purpose was a *substantial factor* in bringing about his transfer in order to make out a prima facie case. Once the plaintiff does so, the defendants thereafter may escape liability by proving by a preponderance of the evidence that plaintiff would have been transferred anyway. That is, defendants must prove the absence of *but for* causation.

On the other hand, the First Circuit correctly stated and applied the *Mount Healthy* cause in fact test in Brule v Southworth, 611 F2d 406 (1st Cir 1979), a case involving an action against prison officials for allegedly disciplining the plaintiff employees for the exercise of their First Amendment rights. The court affirmed the district court's findings in favor of plaintiffs. First, plaintiffs had proved that their critical comments were a substantial factor in defendants' disciplining of them. Second, defendants had not proved by a preponderance of the evidence that they would have made the same disciplinary decision even if the plaintiffs had not been unspoken critics of the prison administration.

[354] 436 US 658 (1978). *See generally* **ch 6.**

[355] 436 US at 694. Official policy or custom for purposes of §1983 local government liability is extensively discussed in **ch 6.**

supervise is not enough to support §1983 liability."[356]

Because local governments and supervisors are so often desirable defendants from the plaintiff's perspective,[357] this cause in fact question has become significant after *Monell*. As a result, lawyers in §1983 cases frequently find themselves researching not only constitutional law, but the tort concept of cause in fact.[358] Moreover, the role of the jury on the cause in fact issue should be assuming greater practical importance in §1983 cases than ever before. Plaintiffs' lawyers may find it difficult to get to the jury in certain extreme cases as, for example, where a mayor issues a "shoot to kill" order and both he and the policeman who shot the plaintiff are sued jointly under §1983.[359] In addition, it is likely that just as tort policy often affects a court's decision whether to send a cause in fact question to the jury,[360] so too will a court's perception of §1983 policy affect its decision whether to send a §1983 cause in fact question to the jury.

Most important of all, and as discussed in connection with local government liability in Chapter 6,[361] cause in fact after *Monell* masks a difficult duty issue. *Monell* seems to say that without a finding of cause in fact a defendant has no duty to the plaintiff who suffered the constitutional deprivation. The cause in fact relation, according to *Monell*, somehow gives rise to the defendant's duty. However, issues of cause in fact and duty must be treated separately because each is usually independent of the other. A duty to act affirmatively can exist even in situations where it is difficult or impossible for a plaintiff to show a cause in fact relation between breach of that duty and plaintiff's deprivation;[362] the converse is also true. Also, by emphasizing causation in fact, *Monell* created the risk of introducing into §1983 law the now discredited distinction between misfeasance and malfeasance on the one hand and nonfeasance on the other.[363]

---

[356] 436 US at 694 n 58 (citation omitted).

[357] Judgment proof subordinates, deeper pockets of these defendants (especially local governments), and greater deterrent effect frequently combine to make such defendants quite attractive.

[358] The same point was made earlier for basis of liability and proximate cause, **§§3.02 & 3.17** respectively.

[359] *See* Palmer v Hall, 517 F2d 705 (5th Cir 1975), where the district court's finding against the mayor was reversed by the Fifth Circuit on the cause in fact issue.

[360] *See* Malone, *Ruminations on Cause in Fact,* 9 Stan L Rev 60 (1956).

[361] *See* **§6.05.**

[362] For example, where the plaintiff claims the defendant should have trained or supervised another, or should otherwise have prevented the plaintiff's constitutional deprivation.

[363] This has caused a great deal of difficulty in the so-called Good Samaritan torts cases where the courts, confronted frequently with unconscionable defendant conduct, strain to find some sort of relation between defendant and plaintiff warranting the imposition of a duty to protect the plaintiff. Interestingly, especially in light of *Monell*, one such relation is cause in fact: where a defendant nonnegligently brings about plaintiff's perilous situation, this may give rise to a duty to use reasonable care thereafter for the protection of plaintiff. *See generally* Restatement (Second) of Torts §§321-324 (1965). On the cause in fact aspect, *see id* §322.

Therefore, the duty and cause in fact questions raised by *Monell* will continue to generate considerable litigation, as the limits of individual and governmental liability under §1983 are tested by plaintiffs' lawyers.[364]

In the circuits, a cause in fact relation between defendant's conduct and plaintiff's constitutional deprivation was *present* where:

1. One defendant personally ordered that plaintiffs be demoted, and another in a grossly negligent manner failed to interfere, all in violation of the First Amendment[365]

2. A police chief's regulation was found to have caused a detective to file unwarranted charges against plaintiff[366]

In contrast, a cause in fact relationship was *absent* where:

1. A plaintiff who claimed that the defendant prosecutors' alleged systematic leaks of information to the media deprived him of a fair trial could not prove that the publicity caused him to be found guilty[367]

2. A plaintiff claimed that defendant's false testimony before a grand jury caused his indictment; the grand jury had more than probable cause to indict without the misstatements[368]

3. Police officers who were not promoted alleged that city council members violated their First Amendment rights; one of the defendants whose vote against plaintiffs was based on constitutionally impermissible reasons was not liable because his vote was not decisive; "a single vote is not a cause when the same decision would have been reached without that vote"[369]

4. The alleged denial of due process to a father by the absence of a hearing was not a but for cause of the separation of the father from his children; at a later hearing the father was denied custody of his children[370]

5. Plaintiff claimed that a public defender should have removed an assistant public defender; the claimed denial of effective assistance of counsel at plaintiff's criminal trial was not caused by defendant; appointment of counsel was controlled by state court judges who had refused to remove plaintiff's appointed counsel[371]

---

[364] See §§**6.05-6.16** on local government liability under §1983 and cause in fact after *Monell.*

[365] Fernandez v Chardon, 681 F2d 42 (1st Cir 1982), *affd on other grounds sub nom* Chardon v Fumero Soto, 462 US 650 (1983).

[366] Black v Stephens, 662 F2d 181 (3d Cir 1981).

[367] Powers v McGuigan, 769 F2d 72 (2d Cir 1985). *See also* Powers v Coe, 728 F2d 97 (2d Cir 1984).

[368] Dale v Bartels, 732 F2d 278 (2d Cir 1984).

[369] Bowen v Watkins, 669 F2d 979, 985 (5th Cir 1982).

[370] Lossman v Pekarske, 707 F2d 288 (7th Cir 1983).

[371] Chapman v Musich, 726 F2d 405 (8th Cir 1984).

§3.19   Survival of §1983 Damage Actions

The general rule in the circuits is that §1983 actions survive the death of either the plaintiff or defendant if that would be the result under applicable state law.[372] Because §1983 is silent on the question of survival, 42 USC §1988 requires, in light of this "deficiency," that state law be used unless it is "inconsistent with the Constitution and laws of the United States."[373] The Supreme Court made this clear in *Moor v County of Alameda*[374] when it said: "Pursuant to §1988 state survivorship statutes which reverse the common-law rule may be used in the context of actions brought under §1983."[375]

In an important §1983 survival case, *Robertson v Wegmann*,[376] the Court dealt with the meaning of §1988's "inconsistent" language. Plaintiff Clay Shaw sued district attorney Jim Garrison and others under §1983 for their alleged bad faith prosecution attempts against him in connection with the assassination of President Kennedy. Shaw obtained an injunction but before a trial on damages could be held, he died. The executor of Shaw's estate was then substituted as plaintiff, prompting defendants' motion to dismiss on the ground that the §1983 action had abated. Under Louisiana law, Shaw's action only survived in

---

[372] The leading cases are Brazier v Cherry, 293 F2d 401 (5th Cir), *cert denied*, 368 US 921 (1961) (plaintiff's death) and Pritchard v Smith, 289 F2d 153 (8th Cir 1961) (defendant's death) both cited with apparent approval by the Supreme Court in Moor v County of Alameda, 411 US 692, 702-03 n 14 (1973).
See also White v Walsh, 649 F2d 560, 562 n 4 (8th Cir 1981) (applying Missouri survival law to a suit against the deceased defendant accused with others of conspiring to violate the plaintiff's right to a fair trial); Cunningham v Ray, 648 F2d 1185 (8th Cir 1981) (per curiam) (applying Iowa survival law to bar the plaintiff inmate's suit in his individual capacity seeking redress for his deceased brother's alleged constitutional deprivations; court spoke in terms of both survival and standing).
Cf Blake v Katter, 693 F2d 677 (7th Cir 1982), where the Seventh Circuit held that the plaintiff's death from natural causes while incarcerated did not cause his §1983 claim against police officers to abate. The court rejected defendants' attempt to characterize plaintiff's claim as a personal injury claim which would not have survived under Indiana law. However, the court did not otherwise explain the basis for its holding, except to note in passing that the question of whether plaintiff's widow was the real party in interest would be decided by the district court on remand.

[373] 42 USC §1988 provides in relevant part that jurisdiction of the district courts for the protection of civil rights

> shall be exercised and enforced in conformity with the laws of the United States, so far as such laws are suitable to carry the same into effect: but in all cases where they are not adapted to the object, or are deficient in the provisions necessary to furnish suitable remedies and punish offenses against law, the common law, as modified and changed by the Constitution and statutes of the State wherein the court . . . is held, so far as the same is not inconsistent with the Constitution and laws of the United States, shall be extended to and govern the said courts in the trial and disposition of the cause . . . .

Note the applicability of §1988 to state statutes of limitations at §4.14.

[374] 411 US 692 (1973). *Moor* dealt primarily with the status of counties as "persons" under §1983 as to which see generally **ch 6**.

[375] 411 US at 702-03 n 14.

[376] 436 US 584 (1978).

favor of certain close relatives, none of whom was alive when Shaw died. The district court refused to apply state law because it was thought to be inconsistent with federal law. Instead the court created "a federal common law of survival in civil rights actions in favor of the personal representative of the deceased."[377] The Fifth Circuit affirmed, emphasizing the inconsistency between Louisiana law and the broad remedial policies of §1983, as well as the need for uniformity in civil rights actions.

However, the Supreme Court reversed. Applying §1988, it found that Louisiana survival law generally was both reasonable and not inconsistent with the compensation and deterrent purposes of §1983, although the §1983 action abated in this unusual case. It said:

> A state statute cannot be considered "inconsistent" with federal law merely because the statute causes the plaintiff to lose the litiga tion. . . . §1988 quite clearly instructs us to refer to state statutes; it does not say that state law is to be accepted or rejected based solely on which side is advantaged thereby.[378]

The Court added that its decision was to be read narrowly because Louisiana law generally was not "inhospitable" to survival of §1983 actions and the particular result here had "no independent adverse effect on the policies underlying §1983."[379] It also observed that the case before it was far different from one in which the unconstitutional conduct actually causes the death.[380]

Robertson indicates that state survival law will almost always govern the survival of §1983 actions except in extreme situations as where, for example, state law significantly discriminates against those types of actions, including §1983 actions, that do not survive.[381]

In the circuits, §1988's *inconsistency* language was applied in favor of plaintiffs in two survival cases. In one, a Second Circuit case,[382] the court held with respect to the shooting death by police officers of plaintiff's decedent that a provision of New York law preventing the survival of a decedent's claim for punitive damages was inconsistent with federal law within the meaning of 42 USC §1988. It distinguished the case before it from cases involving death *not* resulting from constitutional violations such as the Supreme Court's decision in *Robertson v Wegmann.*

In the other, a Sixth Circuit case,[383] plaintiff sued various defendants for the

---

[377] *Id* 587, quoting from the district court's opinion.

[378] *Id* 593. Justices Blackmun, Brennan, and White dissented.

[379] *Id* 594.

[380] *Id.*

[381] Quoting from the district court, the Supreme Court in *Robertson* gave the example of a situation in which state law does not provide for tort actions' survival at all. *Id.*

[382] McFadden v Sanchez, 710 F2d 907 (2d Cir 1983). See also **§4.09** on damages in such cases.

[383] Jaco v Bloechle, 739 F2d 239 (6th Cir 1984). Cf Brazier v Cherry, 293 F2d 401 (5th Cir), *cert denied,* 368 US 921 (1961), a leading case discussed at **§3.20** which combined survival and wrongful death in reaching a similar result.

allegedly unjustified shooting death of her son by police officers. She claimed under §1983 that her son's constitutional rights were violated. The Sixth Circuit found that Ohio survival law did not save decedent's claim, since he had been killed instantly. Also, Ohio's wrongful death statute was irrelevant because decedent's claim was personal and not brought for any injury to the heirs. However, the court went on to hold that this result under Ohio's survival law was inconsistent with the federal policies underlying §1983. Distinguishing *Robertson v Wegmann*, the court said: "[T]o suggest that the Congress had intended that a civil rights infringement be cognizable only when the victim encounters pain and suffering before his demise, is absurd."[384] Thus, decedent's cause of action survived and the plaintiff, as decedent's legal representative, had standing to pursue her son's cause of action.

Nevertheless, §1983 actions that are to survive under state law must ordinarily seek to vindicate the constitutional deprivations of the decedent while he or she was alive. Thus, in a case involving an alleged cover-up by police of the wrongful shooting death of plaintiff's decedent, the Fifth Circuit[385] held that §1983 survival law was irrelevant to the cover-up claim because there could be no deprivation of plaintiff's decedent's constitutional rights occurring *after* decedent's death. Similarly, where the decedent's administratrix sued police officers alleging, among other things, that they had covered up the wrongful shooting and killing of the decedent, the Ninth Circuit held that there can be no §1983 action "on behalf of a deceased for acts occurring after the death of that person."[386] The court reasoned that a deceased is not a *person* protected by §1983. But the court sharply distinguished the case before it from one in which a plaintiff, representing a deceased, challenges actions committed *before* the decedent's death. The latter situation, according to the court, raises a survival issue.

§3.20 Section 1983 Wrongful Death Damage Actions

While both survival statutes and wrongful death statutes reverse contrary

---

[384] Jaco v Bloechle, 739 F2d 239, 244 (6th Cir 1984). To the same effect is Bass *ex rel* Lewis v Wallenstein, 769 F2d 1173 (7th Cir 1985) (Illinois survival law only provided for predeath injuries while Illinois wrongful death statute did not cover loss of decedent's life but was designed to provide certain survivors with pecuniary losses alone; thus, as applied to the §1983 suit brought for decedent's death in prison in violation of the Eighth Amendment, Illinois survival law was inconsistent with the purposes of §1983 and decedent's legal representative could recover for loss of life, pain, and suffering experienced just before death as well as punitive damages). *See also* **§3.20** on wrongful death and Bell v City of Milwaukee, 746 F2d 1205 (7th Cir 1984), discussed in **§3.17.**

[385] Whitehurst v Wright, 592 F2d 834 (5th Cir 1979) (*Brazier* distinguished).

[386] Guyton v Phillips, 606 F2d 248, 250 (9th Cir 1979).

common law rules, their purposes are different.[387] Survival statutes allow the cause of action to survive regardless of the death of the plaintiff or defendant. Wrongful death statutes, by contrast, provide for causes of action to arise in and for the benefit of certain designated persons in order to compensate them for pecuniary losses resulting from a decedent's death. Furthermore, unlike survival cases, for wrongful death the defendant's conduct must necessarily be the cause of death.

In a leading decision on survival and wrongful death, the Fifth Circuit in *Brazier v Cherry*[388] drew no distinction for §1983 and §1988 purposes between the applicability of Georgia's survival statute and its wrongful death statute. The case concerned allegations that police brutality had caused decedent's beating and death. In arguing that §1988 required the application of Georgia law in favor of the plaintiff, who was both the surviving widow and the administratrix of the decedent's estate, the court treated survival and wrongful death concepts alike.[389] Focusing on the "suitable remedies" language of §1988, after dealing earlier with the "party injured" language of §1983, the Fifth Circuit stated:

> The term "suitable remedies" . . . comprehends those facilities available in local state law but unavailable in federal legislation, which will permit the full effectual enforcement of the policy sought to be achieved by the statutes. And in a very real sense the utilization of local death and survival statutes does not do more than create an effective remedy. . . . To make the policy of the Civil Rights Statutes fully effectual, regard has to be taken of both classes of victims.[390]

The Supreme Court has not yet addressed the issue of wrongful death and §1983, although it suggested in *Robertson v Wegmann*,[391] albeit in terms of a survival statute, that abatement of a §1983 cause of action where defendant's conduct caused the plaintiff's death was a very different issue from that in the case before it where death was not so caused. As a matter of §1983 policy,

---

[387] On survival and wrongful death generally *see* D. Dobbs, Law of Remedies 551-68 (1973). It should be noted that some states have hybrid statutes combining features of survival and wrongful death actions. *Id* 555-56.

[388] 293 F2d 401 (5th Cir), *cert denied,* 368 US 921 (1961). In Williams v Kelley, 624 F2d 695 (5th Cir 1980) and Gullatte v Potts, 630 F2d 322 (5th Cir 1980), the Fifth Circuit approved without discussion the application of the wrongful death statutes of Georgia and Alabama, respectively, to §1983 actions for damages brought by mothers of deceased prisoners against various prison officials.

[389] Strictly speaking, *Brazier's* similar treatment of survival and wrongful death for §1983 purposes was unnecessary. Inasmuch as the plaintiff was, as noted in the text, both the surviving widow and the administratrix, once survival was found to be appropriate the court did not have to address the question whether a wrongful death claim *standing alone* is appropriate in §1983 cases. Further, there is no indication in *Brazier* that it made any practical difference to the plaintiff's recovery whether a wrongful death action could be asserted.

[390] 293 F2d at 408-09.

[391] 436 US 584 (1978).

however, *Brazier*'s approach to the use of wrongful death statutes seems sound. If wrongful death statutes could not be used for §1983 actions, then, where a defendant's unconstitutional conduct *immediately* caused the death of the decedent, the typical survival statute would also not be applicable.[392] There would thus be no vindication at all of the §1983 claim.

Thus, the Fifth Circuit appropriately observed in *Brazier:* "[I]t defies history to conclude that Congress purposely meant to assure to the living freedom from such unconstitutional deprivations, but that, with like precision, it meant to withdraw the protection of civil rights statutes against the peril of death."[393] However, *Brazier*'s reasoning applies to the use of state survival law as well. Indeed, because the claim in such cases is for the decedent's loss of his or her life, the "fit" between survival law and §1983 may even be better than that between wrongful death law and §1983. That may be why recent circuit court decisions tend in fact to use state survival law in §1983 cases and confront the inconsistency issue regarding damages limitations head on.[394]

Where a §1983 wrongful death action existed, it was held by the Colorado Supreme Court in *Jones v Hildebrant*[395] that state limitations on kind and amount of damages recoverable were applicable. The United States Supreme Court granted certiorari in *Jones* to deal with this very issue, but certiorari was dismissed as improvidently granted,[396] with Justices White, Brennan, and

---

[392] D. Dobbs, Law of Remedies 554 (1973).

[393] 293 F2d at 404. In a somewhat confusing opinion, the Tenth Circuit appears to have held, pursuant to 42 USC §1988, that where the defendant unconstitutionally shot and killed decedent, the personal representative of decedent could bring a §1983 wrongful death action under Wyoming law to redress the violations of decedent's constitutional rights. Rosa v Cantrell, 705 F2d 1208, 1221-24 (10th Cir 1982).

[394] *See* **§3.19.** As the Seventh Circuit put it, the "proper approach at this point under state law [where an estate cannot recover for loss of life] is not to transform the section 1983 action on behalf of [decedent] into a wrongful death action on behalf of those who survived him, but to determine whether state law is inconsistent with the . . . policies . . . [of] section 1983." Bass *ex rel* Lewis v Wallenstein, 769 F2d 1173, 1189-90 (7th Cir 1985).

[395] Jones v Hildebrant, 191 Colo 1, 550 P2d 339 (1976), dealing with the shooting and killing by the defendant policeman of the plaintiff's son. Two justices of the Colorado Supreme Court dissented on this measure of damages point, arguing that "Colorado's judicial limitation of net pecuniary loss as a measure of damages for wrongful death [did not apply] to actions founded on 42 U.S.C. §1983. . . ." 550 P2d at 345-46.

[396] 432 US 183 (1977). The reason for the dismissal was that the claim of the petitioner, decedent's mother, was not one of pecuniary loss resulting from her son's wrongful death, but was based on her own constitutional interests. Thus, the petitioner's claim was unrelated to the Colorado wrongful death statute. As the Court's per curiam decision stated:

> The question of whether a limitation on recovery of damages imposed by a state wrongful-death statute may be applied where death is said to have resulted from a violation of 42 U.S.C. §1983 would appear to make sense only where the §1983 damages claim is based on the same injuries. *Id* 187.

The dissenting justices argued that the measure of damages issue for §1983 wrongful death actions was in fact raised, and they intimated, *id* 190, that a §1983 wrongful death action should not be governed by state law.

Marshall dissenting. However, a comparable issue arose in *Bell v City of Milwaukee*[397] an important, lengthy, and complicated case where the Seventh Circuit dealt with, among many other issues, the relationship among §1983, §1988, and Wisconsin's survival and wrongful death statutes. The decedent's siblings brought an action for themselves, decedent's estate, and the estate of decedent's father for the wrongful and fatal shooting of decedent and a subsequent cover-up by the various defendants. Dealing first with the jury's $100,000 verdict in favor of decedent's estate for the loss of his life, the court determined that "the Wisconsin statutory scheme creates a survival action in favor of the estate for pre-death injuries and a wrongful death action in favor of the victim's survivors, and neither type of action traditionally allows recovery of damages for loss of life itself."[398] The court then went on to hold, distinguishing *Robertson v Wegmann*, that in this case Wisconsin's restrictive damages limitation was inconsistent with the policies underlying §1983, especially its deterrence function. The killing itself was the unconstitutional act, an act that should be deterred. Thus, decedent's estate could not be precluded from recovering damages for the loss of his life.

For similar reasons, the Seventh Circuit held that the jury's $25,000 punitive damages verdict for the estate should be upheld, even though Wisconsin law did not allow a decedent's estate to recover punitive damages.[399] As to the jury verdict of $75,000 to the *father's* estate for loss of his son's society and companionship, the Wisconsin limitation of $25,000 for this kind of loss was also inconsistent with §1983 policy. There was no real concern in this case with overcompensation in light of the testimony at trial of the close father-son relationship. Thus, $75,000 was not unreasonable and was affirmed.[400]

---

[397] 746 F2d 1205 (7th Cir 1984).
[398] *Id* 1236.
[399] *Id* 1241.
[400] *Id* 1250-53. *See also* **§3.19.**

"[S]hall be liable to the party injured in an action at law": Damages

4

§4.01   Summary

A plaintiff who has made out a prima facie 42 USC §1983 cause of action for damages against an individual or governmental defendant and overcomes the hurdles of absolute and qualified immunity, which are applicable to individual defendants,[1] must then somehow prove up those damages. Although §1983 on

---

[1] For discussion of the prima facie cause of action see chs **2 & 3;** for local government liability see **ch 6;** for absolute immunity, see **ch 7;** and for qualified immunity see **ch 8.**

its face says nothing about damage rules, damages under the section, like tort damages, can be nominal, compensatory, or punitive. In this connection the Second Circuit stated, " [T]here is no logical reason why general principles of damages should not apply to a civil rights action."[2] And indeed they do.

The Supreme Court held in a §1983 procedural due process case that compensatory damages cannot simply be *presumed*, but must be pleaded and proved; where they are not proved, only nominal damages of $1 may be awarded.[3] It appears that this ruling has since been extended to actions arising out of other Bill of Rights violations. Consequently, plaintiff's lawyers in §1983 cases should always introduce specific evidence of the two kinds of actual damage:[4] (1) *special* damages consisting of medical expenses, lost income, and the like, which are proximately caused by a defendant's conduct and (2) *general* damages consisting of pain, suffering, humiliation, embarrassment, emotional distress, and perhaps even damage to reputation.[5]

Evidence of these two kinds of actual damage will usually be easier to come by in cases of personal injury and confinement, such as many Fourth and Eighth Amendment violation cases, as well as in cases involving racial discrimination in housing and employment. Evidence will sometimes be harder to produce in cases dealing with violations of procedural due process and the First Amendment. An important consideration in showing damages in §1983 cases is the cause-in-fact issue: a defendant may show that even had a plaintiff's constitutional rights not been violated, the same damages would still have resulted. For example, a defendant may show that a plaintiff would have been dismissed even had he or she received a proper hearing. In such a case, a plaintiff cannot recover damages for back pay even though his or her procedural due process rights were violated.[6] Furthermore, a plaintiff's recovery for actual damages, particularly special damages, may be reduced to the extent damages suffered were reasonably avoidable. This *avoidable consequences* rule, or the duty to minimize damages, is applicable in §1983 cases just as it is in damage actions generally.[7]

The Supreme Court held that punitive damages may be awarded against *individuals* in appropriate circumstances for §1983 violations.[8] This has long

---

[2] Zarcone v Perry, 572 F2d 52, 55 (2d Cir 1978).

[3] Carey v Piphus, 435 US 247 (1978). *See also* Memphis Community School Dist v Stachura, 106 S Ct 2537 (1986), so indicating in a First Amendment setting.

[4] *See* §§4.03-4.07 on compensatory damages. Prejudgment interest on compensatory damages may be available. Heritage Homes v Seekonk Water Dist, 648 F2d 761 (1st Cir 1981) (prejudgment interest discretionary with district court; should be required where injuries suffered are not *intangible*); Furtado v Bishop, 604 F2d 80 (1st Cir 1979) (federal law, not state law, governs prejudgment interest).

[5] The special problem of damage to reputation is considered at §4.05.

[6] Mount Healthy City Bd of Educ v Doyle, 429 US 274, 285-87, (1977) (First Amendment); Carey v Piphus, 435 US 247 (1978) (procedural due process).

[7] *See* §4.03.

[8] Smith v Wade, 461 US 30 (1983). Actual malice is not required; recklessness or callous indifference is sufficient. See §§4.08-4.13 on punitive damages.

been the general rule in the circuits, and applies even where no actual damages are proved and where a contrary rule obtains under state law.[9] Whether punitive damages will be awarded depends on the fact-finder's evaluation of the defendant's conduct and on the award's likely deterrent effect on that defendant and others similarly situated. However, the Court has held that punitive damages may not be awarded against local governments.[10]

Both parties have a right to jury trial on the issue of liability for compensatory and punitive damages.[11] Generally speaking, jury awards of compensatory and punitive damages are upheld on review unless there have been erroneous instructions or unless the reviewing court concludes that the awards shock the conscience and are unjust. Attorney's fees may be awarded in certain circumstances to the prevailing party under the Civil Rights Attorney's Fees Awards Act of 1976.[12] Where a state claim is joined with a §1983 claim through pendent jurisdiction, courts have been careful to avoid a double recovery for the same actual damage, whether special or general.[13] And, where another federal civil rights claim with specific damage limitations has been joined with a §1983 claim, it has been held that the §1983 claim is not subject to such limitations.[14]

Section 1983 has no statute of limitations and, accordingly, damage actions must be governed by the analogous state statute of limitations pursuant to 42 USC §1988.[15] The Court has ruled that for this purpose, §1983 actions are analogous to personal injury actions.[16] Federal law determines the time of accrual of a §1983 damage action, but the Supreme Court has held that the tolling issue is to be determined by state law.[17] Despite the general use of state law, an otherwise applicable state statute of limitations will not be used by courts where it is either *inconsistent* with §1983's underlying policies within the meaning of §1988 or discriminatory against federal civil rights actions.

§4.02   *Carey v Piphus, Memphis Community Schools v Stachura,* and Presumed Damages: Analysis

The seminal Supreme Court decision discussing compensatory damages under

---

[9] *See* §4.08.

[10] City of Newport v Fact Concerts, 453 US 247 (1981), discussed at §§6.17-6.19. In contrast, local governments may be liable for *compensatory* damages. *See* §§6.05-6.19.

[11] *See* §1.17.

[12] Amending 42 USC §1988 (Supp 1977). *See* §§1.18-1.26.

[13] *See* §4.03.

[14] Bradshaw v Zoological Socy, 569 F2d 1066 (9th Cir 1978).

[15] *See* §4.14.

[16] Wilson v Garcia, 105 S Ct 1938 (1985), discussed at §4.14.

[17] Delaware State College v Ricks, 449 US 250 (1980) (accrual); Board of Regents v Tomanio, 446 US 478 (1980) (tolling).

§1983 is *Carey v Piphus*,[18] a case involving two consolidated suits by students seeking damages and other relief against school board members who violated their procedural due process rights. One student had been suspended for 20 days after the principal saw him smoking what was apparently a marijuana cigarette on school premises. The other had been suspended for 20 days for violating a school rule prohibiting the wearing of earrings by male students on the ground that this practice showed membership in certain violent street gangs which terrorized other students. The District Court declined to award damages because the plaintiffs "put no evidence in the record to quantify their damages and the record is completely devoid of any evidence which could even form the basis of a speculative inference measuring the extent of their injuries."[19] The Seventh Circuit reversed and remanded on this issue, holding that even if the suspensions were ultimately justified, the plaintiffs would be entitled to recover substantial *nonpunitive* damages simply for denial of procedural due process, despite the lack of proof of actual injury.

In an opinion by Justice Powell, the Supreme Court reversed, holding that a plaintiff seeking to recover compensatory damages for procedural due process violations must show actual injury caused in fact by the violations; damages are not to be presumed. Lacking such evidence of actual injury, a plaintiff can only recover nominal damages.[20] The Court, relying on the traditional concept of damages and on §1983's legislative history, agreed with the defendants that the basic purpose of §1983 damages liability is "to compensate persons for injuries caused by the deprivation of constitutional rights . . . Rights, constitutional and otherwise, do not exist in a vacuum. Their purpose is to protect persons from injuries to particular interests, and their contours are shaped by the interests they protect."[21]

In applying this *compensation principle,* the Court observed that damages concepts from tort law will often be helpful in §1983 cases, especially where the tort interests "parallel closely the interests protected by a particular constitutional right." Where this parallel does not exist, though, "the task will be the more difficult one of adapting common-law rules of damages to provide fair compensation for injuries caused by the deprivation of a constitutional

---

[18] 435 US 247, (1978).

[19] *Id* 251-52.

[20] The Court's language indicates that nominal damages of $1 *must* be awarded where a procedural due process violation has been found but no actual damages have been proved. Nevertheless, in Ganey v Edwards, 759 F2d 337 (4th Cir 1985), the Fourth Circuit held that even though the plaintiff's right of access to the prison law library was violated, he was not entitled to nominal damages (he had not proved actual damages). It emphasized that the legal consequences to the plaintiff were not affected by the absence of a nominal damages award. Judge Winter dissented on this issue, arguing that the absence of even a nominal damages award could affect the plaintiff's status as a prevailing party and his or her entitlement to attorney's fees. See §§1.19-1.22 on the latter.

[21] 435 US at 254. The Court, however, did not exclude the possibility of punitive damages. *Id* 257 n 11. *See* §§4.08-4.09.

right."[22] The Court regarded procedural due process violations as without parallel in the common law, and therefore rejected the plaintiffs' argument that the denial of a *feeling of just treatment* inherently gives rise to mental and emotional distress and thus, by analogy to presumed damages in defamation per se cases, that plaintiffs should not have to show actual damages in procedural due process cases.

The Court also noted that plaintiffs will usually have no particular difficulty in showing emotional and mental distress resulting from the denial of procedural due process itself: "Distress is a personal injury familiar to the law, customarily proved by showing the nature and circumstances of the wrong and its effect on the plaintiff."[23] Finally, the Court distinguished cases awarding damages for racial discrimination, the denial of voting rights, and the denial of Fourth Amendment rights as having involved either proof of actual injury or constitutional interests of a different order from the interest in procedural due process.

The Court's reasoning in *Carey,* insofar as it recognized the helpfulness of tort principles but did not find them invariably determinative, is sound.[24] Furthermore, as the Court observed, plaintiffs in procedural due process cases still have ample opportunity to show actual injury resulting from the procedural due process violation where it exists in fact. Often, all that is necessary is testimony about the circumstances of the violation and the effect of the violation on a plaintiff's emotional well-being, both of which can readily be provided by the plaintiff. In many due process cases, therefore, *Carey* may not make much practical difference.

The Court was apparently concerned that a holding that presumed damages could be recovered for all procedural due process violations would mean that juries, necessarily without much judicial guidance or control, could award such damages for numerous technical due process violations. This would not only affect potential defendants, but would use up scarce judicial resources as well. It is worth emphasizing, however, that the result in *Carey* does not appear to eliminate the deterrent function of § 1983. A plaintiff in a particularly egregious case who is unable to show actual damages may still, as the Court suggested, recover substantial punitive damages.[25]

The Court in *Carey* explicitly limited its decision to cases involving procedural due process. Thus, cases raising other constitutional interests could theoretically apply a different rule as to presumed damages.[26] For example, like procedural due process, the First Amendment does not appear to have a common law analogue from which damages rules could readily be borrowed. The question is, therefore, whether damages should be presumed from First Amendment violations. In *Carey,* the plaintiffs argued that a due process

---

[22] 435 US at 258.

[23] *Id* 263-64.

[24] For a general discussion of the background of tort liability in § 1983 cases see **§3.02.**

[25] Carey v Piphus, 435 US at 257 n 11 (1978). *See* **§§4.08-4.09.**

[26] 435 US at 264.

violation results in a feeling of denial of just treatment, and that this feeling results in mental and emotional distress. The Court rejected this contention, observing that distress is a familiar injury which can readily be proved. If a comparable argument were made to the effect that a First Amendment violation results, for example, in a denial of feelings of dignity and self-worth, then the Court might respond as it did in *Carey* by suggesting that a plaintiff can readily prove such feelings.

On the other hand, a First Amendment violation may be more closely tied to rights of representative government and of a person's self-expression and could thereby be analogized to the right to vote, the denial of which is likely to give rise to presumed damages.[27] In both cases, a plaintiff would have a hard time showing actual damages. It can, moreover, be suggested that unlike procedural due process rights which can frequently be violated technically without denying a feeling of just treatment, First Amendment violations generally make a difference to the person affected. Once the individual's First Amendment rights are violated, it is often difficult to restore the same opportunity for self-expression that was denied earlier. Even if the plaintiff is alleging unconstitutional punishment for past conduct, future chilling effect upon the plaintiff is hard to measure. Furthermore, like the insult of racial discrimination, the frustration resulting from a denial of one's right of self-expression is intuitively grasped. For these reasons, the better view would appear to be that damages should be presumed from First Amendment violations even absent proof of actual damages.[28] In this connection, it is possible, although not entirely certain, that the District of Columbia Circuit, the Third Circuit, and the Seventh Circuit took this position in several pre-*Carey* decisions.[29]

In post-*Carey* decisions, though, the Fifth and Seventh Circuits expressly stated that proof of actual damages is required even in First Amendment cases.[30] The Tenth Circuit,[31] rejecting a procedural-substantive distinction,

---

[27] See the Court's discussion of the voting denial cases *id* 264 n 22.

[28] This argument was also made in the First Edition.

[29] Dellums v Powell, 566 F2d 167 (DC Cir 1977); Paton v La Prade, 524 F2d 862 (3d Cir 1975); Slate v McFetridge, 484 F2d 1169 (7th Cir 1973). These cases are discussed at §4.06.

[30] Crawford v Garnier, 719 F2d 1317 (7th Cir 1983); Basiardanes v City of Galveston, 682 F2d 1203 (5th Cir 1982). *Cf* Owen v Lash, 682 F2d 648, 657 (7th Cir 1982) (noting split in the circuits and leaving question open). The Seventh Circuit also held that actual damages must be proved in civil rights *conspiracy* cases in order to recover more than nominal damages. Lenard v Argento, 699 F2d 874, 888-90 (7th Cir 1983). *See* §2.10 on conspiracy.

[31] Lancaster v Rodriguez, 701 F2d 864 (10th Cir 1983) (per curiam) (Eighth Amendment case in which court allowed an award of nominal damages only; *Carey* analyzed). *Cf* Ganey v Edwards, 759 F2d 337 (4th Cir 1985) (right of access to prison law library; whether presumed damages may be awarded not reached). *See also* Corriz v Naranjo, 667 F2d 892 (10th Cir 1981), *cert granted,* 50 USLW 3916 (S Ct May 17, 1982) (to deal in part with question whether substantive constitutional rights have intrinsic *great value* for the purpose of compensatory damages awards), *cert dismissed pursuant to Sup Ct R 53,* 51 USLW 3150 (S Ct Aug 19, 1982).

broadly asserted in an Eighth Amendment case that actual damages must be proved in all constitutional violation cases for an award of compensatory damages. On the other hand, the Eight Circuit broadly stated to the contrary that "violations of certain substantive constitutional rights are redressable by substantial compensatory damages awards independent of actual injury."[32] Of even greater significance is *Bell v Little Axe Independent School District*,[33] a recent decision of the Tenth Circuit which held, consistent with the argument above, that damages may be presumed and awarded for First Amendment violations in general and for Establishment Clause violations in particular even in the absence of proof of actual damages.

Even more recently, however, the Supreme Court in *Memphis Community Schools v Stachura*[34] may have rejected the argument that actual damages need not always be proved in First Amendment cases. In *Stachura*, a teacher was awarded $266,750 in compensatory damages and $36,000 in punitive damages by a jury for the violation of his procedural due process and First Amendment rights. The issue before the Court was the propriety of the following instruction which allowed the jury to award damages based on the value or importance of the constitutional rights violated:

> [Just] because these rights are not capable of precise evaluation does not mean that an appropriate monetary amount should not be awarded.
>
> The precise value you place upon any Constitutional right which you find was denied to Plaintiff is within your discretion. You may wish to consider the importance of the right in our system of government, the role which this right has played in the history of our republic, [and] the significance of the right in the context of the activities which the Plaintiff was engaged in at the time of the violation of the right.[35]

In an opinion by Justice Powell, the Court held the instruction erroneous in light of the rule of *Carey v Piphus* that the primary purpose of §1983 is to compensate for actual injuries suffered. Using broad language, it rejected the contention that *Carey* did not apply to substantive constitutional provisions like the First Amendment. There was no two-tier system of constitutional rights. Also, noncompensatory damages of the sort permitted by the instruction were not necessary for the vindication of constitutional rights and were, furthermore, too uncertain to be of much value. The Court finally refused to interpret the challenged instruction as authorizing presumed damages supposedly

---

[32] Villaneuva v George, 659 F2d 851, 855 (8th Cir 1981). *See also* Herrera v Valentine, 653 F2d 1220, 1227-31 (8th Cir 1981). *Cf* Brandon v Allen, 719 F2d 151, 155 (6th Cir 1983) (plaintiffs allowed recovery for dignitary harm resulting from police officer's unprovoked beating; *Carey* distinguished).

[33] 766 F2d 1391 (10th Cir 1985), also discussed at §4.06. See also Walje v City of Winchester, 773 F2d 729 (6th Cir 1985) (permitting an award of "general damages" for free speech violations because "very violation itself causes harm").

[34] Memphis Community Schools v Stachura, 106 S Ct 2537 (1986), *revg* Stachura v Truszkowski, 763 F2d 211 (6th Cir 1985).

[35] 106 S Ct at 2541.

compensatory in nature. This was not a case where such a compensatory purpose was intended; rather, the instruction was clearly designed to supplement an already provided compensatory damages award. The common law voting rights cases were distinguishable because there damages were awarded not for the value of the right itself; presumed damages were available in those cases for a nonmonetary harm not easily quantified.

Justices Marshall and Blackmun concurred in the judgment, while Justices Brennan and Stevens joined in the majority opinion as well as with Justices Marshall and Blackmun.[36] They argued that the majority had not foreclosed the possibility that in some circumstances the violation of a constitutional right, especially of the First Amendment, may itself constitute a compensable injury. For example, the loss of an opportunity to engage in a political demonstration was in their view compensable actual damage so long as the award was proportional to the actual loss incurred. However, they agreed that the instruction here was improper because the jury was not required to consider the loss actually sustained by the plaintiff.

These Justices are correct in contending that the majority opinion should be read narrowly and limited to the particular "intrinsic value" instruction involved in *Stachura*. For the reasons set out earlier, First Amendment violations should indeed give rise to presumed damages. However, it must be conceded that the majority's broad language, with its unfortunate emphasis on actual injury, may (except for Justices Brennan and Stevens) reflect its willingness to preclude presumed damages in *all* §1983 cases.

Even if, in light of *Stachura*, *Carey* is ultimately applied to all constitutional violations, including the First Amendment, the Court in *Carey* did suggest a difference between *presumed* damages and *inferred* damages.[37] The latter may still arise in situations such as racial discrimination and Fourth Amendment cases, where the particular circumstances imply actual damages like emotional and mental distress, without direct testimony of such damages. Some realistic flexibility is thus preserved by the *Carey* rule prohibiting presumed damages, although a plaintiff should not rely on recovering inferred damages and ought instead to introduce direct testimony as to actual damages.

It is important to distinguish between the existence of a constitutional violation and cause in fact for damages purposes. In *Carey*, the Court emphasized that a showing of cause in fact is crucial to the recovery of damages in §1983 procedural due process cases. If, after a plaintiff proves a procedural due process violation, the defendant can show that the plaintiff would have been dismissed even if there had been a proper hearing, then the defendant's due process violation is not considered to be a but-for cause in fact of the plaintiff's damages. This is a departure from the common law rule for damages. Unlike the common law rule which requires a *plaintiff* to show but-for causation

---

[36] *Id* 2546.
[37] Carey v Piphus, 435 US 264 n 22.

in fact,[38] the Supreme Court generally indicated in *Carey* and in the *Mount Healthy* decision, an earlier § 1983 case involving a First Amendment violation,[39] that once the plaintiff proves a constitutional violation, the burden of proof is on the defendant to show by a preponderence of the evidence that there was no but-for cause in fact relation between the constitutional violation and plaintiff's damages. If a defendant cannot do so, then the plaintiff recovers compensatory damages.

Where First Amendment and equal protection violations are implicated in employee discharge cases (in contrast to procedural due process), the *Mount Healthy* approach to cause in fact and damages should apply only to mixed motive cases where, for example, there is more than one motive for discharging an employee. If it turns out, however, that a plaintiff has proved by a preponderance of the evidence that an unconstitutional motivation was the *only* reason for the discharge, then there is no need to shift the burden of proof to the defendant.[40] Moreover, under *Mount Healthy* a defendant in any case should not be permitted to dredge up data to show that the employee would have been discharged anyway where the defendant did not know about the data at the time of discharge. This end run has been tried and rejected on the ground that the reasons on which a defendant may rely in order to avoid damages and

---

[38] D. Dobbs, Law of Remedies 149 (1973). This is often called the *but-for* test.

[39] Carey v Piphus, 435 US at 260-261. In Mount Healthy City Bd of Educ v Doyle, 429 US 274, 287 (1977), the Court said: "[T]he District Court should have gone on to determine whether the board had shown by a preponderance of the evidence that it would have reached the same decision as to plaintiff's reemployment even in the absence of the protected conduct."

For application of this test in the circuits, see, e.g., Barnes v Bosley, 745 F2d 501 (8th Cir 1984); Best v Boswell, 696 F2d 1282 (11th Cir 1983); White v South Park Indep School Dist, 693 F2d 1163 (5th Cir 1982) (plaintiff did not prove substantial motivating factor of an unconstitutional nature); Williams v City of Valdosta, 689 F2d 964, 969 (11th Cir 1982); Neal v Howell, 689 F2d 473, 476 (4th Cir 1982); Allen v Autauga County Bd of Educ, 685 F2d 1302 (11th Cir 1982) (application of "full" *Mount Healthy* test necessary only in mixed motive cases); Berry v Battey, 666 F2d 1183 (8th Cir 1981); Nekolny v Painter, 653 F2d 1164, 1166-68 (7th Cir 1981) (analysis of instructions); Correa v Nampa School Dist, 645 F2d 814, 817 (9th Cir 1981); Trotman v Board of Trustees, 635 F2d 216, 224-25, 231 (3d Cir 1980); Tanner v McCall, 625 F2d 1183, 1195-96 (5th Cir 1980); Ledford v Delancey, 612 F2d 883, 885-86 (4th Cir 1980); Fisher v Flynn, 598 F2d 663 (1st Cir 1979); Skehan v Board of Trustees, 590 F2d 470, 479-81 (3d Cir 1978), *cert denied*, 48 USLW 3211 (S Ct Oct 1, 1979); Goss v San Jacinto Junior College, 588 F2d 96, 99-100 (5th Cir 1979); Zoll v Eastern Allamakee Community School Dist, 588 F2d 246 (8th Cir 1978); Burt v Abel, 585 F2d 613 (4th Cir 1978).

These circuit court cases make explicit what is implicit in the cause in fact test of *Carey* and *Mount Healthy*: while the defendant has the burden of proving the *absence* of but-for causation in order to avoid liability for a plaintiff's damages, this burden is relevant at trial only after the plaintiff has first carried the cause in fact burden of proving the defendant's unconstitutional conduct was at least a *substantial factor* in bringing about the plaintiff's damages. *See also* §3.18.

[40] Allen v Autauga County Bd of Educ, 685 F2d 1302 (11th Cir 1982).

reinstatement must have been among the factors in the initial decision.[41] This result is sound. Otherwise, there is the potential for very serious abuse in employee discharge cases.

§4.03 Compensatory Damages—General Principles

Carey v Piphus[42] established the primacy of the *compensation principle* for damages under §1983. Accordingly, despite the remote possibility that constitutional violations other than procedural due process may allow recovery of *presumed* damages even in the absence of proof of actual damage,[43] the plaintiff's lawyer should introduce all relevant evidence on special and general damages at the outset. Once this is done, where the fact-finder has gone on to award compensatory damages based on its conclusion that the defendant's constitutional violation caused such damages[44] and the trial court has denied a motion to set aside the award as excessive, "the standard used for appellate review . . . is whether the award is so high as to shock the judicial conscience and constitute a denial of justice."[45]

While this standard appears extremely deferential to the fact-finder's judgment, cases will arise where courts find that compensatory damages awards are excessive. For example, in a Fifth Circuit case the plaintiff had obtained a jury verdict of $75,000 in compensatory damages against two deputy sheriffs after alleging an unconstitutional search and arrest, the use of excessive force, and the beating of the plaintiff after the arrest. The Fifth Circuit overturned the verdict as excessive and ordered a conditional remittitur. The factors that the Fifth Circuit used were the following: (1) there was no physical damage to the plaintiff's home; (2) what the defendant did to the plaintiff (arresting her unconstitutionally and imprisoning her) lasted "only two hours" and caused embarrassment and mental anguish; and (3) the excessive force used caused the plaintiff personal injuries, including a low-grade concussion, numbness, bruises, nightmares, and nervousness, but "the residual effect of the ill treatment apparently [did] not limit her activities."[46] A fourth factor, perhaps the most important of all, was that past medical expenses totaled only $329 and there was no evidence of future medical costs introduced. Of this $75,000 verdict, $74,000 was attributable to general damages—*speculative* items of recovery such as pain, suffering, mental anguish, and embarrassment—and that was just too much for the Fifth Circuit.

---

[41] Lee v Russell County Bd of Educ, 684 F2d 769 (11th Cir 1982).

[42] 435 US 247 (1978).

[43] *See* **§4.02.**

[44] *See* **§4.02.** *See also* **§3.18.**

[45] Zarcone v Perry, 572 F2d 52, 56 (2d Cir 1978).

[46] Keyes v Lauga, 635 F2d 330 (5th Cir 1981). *Cf* Whitley v Seibel, 676 F2d 245 (7th Cir 1982) where a $60,000 compensatory damages award was upheld despite the absence of medical or psychiatric testimony.

A Seventh Circuit case[47] involved three employees who were terminated because they had refused to get involved in political activities. There were compensatory damage awards of $5,000, $2,500 and $2,500, respectively, for each of these three plaintiffs for emotional and mental distress. There were also special damage awards of $40,000, $12,000, and $17,000, respectively. What is important is that the general damages awards of $5,000, $2,500, and $2,500 were overturned because of the evidence the court had before it. One plaintiff testified that he was "very depressed" on learning of his termination; another plaintiff testified that she became "a little despondent and lacked motivation"; and the third testified that he did not work for six weeks because he was completely humiliated and stayed close to home. The Seventh Circuit ruled that such testimony was not sufficient to sustain these compensatory awards.

In contrast, the Eighth Circuit[48] affirmed a jury's compensatory damages award of $300,000 because of what the defendant police officers had done to the plaintiff. She was an American Indian woman in late pregnancy who was kicked in a life-threatening manner and thrown to the ground; she was in extreme physical pain and lost her unborn child; her pain and suffering continued until the time of trial, three years later; the emotional trauma accompanying the stillbirth was devastating; the mental anguish she suffered by being driven away from a nearby hospital, combined with a police officer's threat at the time to kill her, added to her emotional injury; and finally, and almost in passing, she suffered "great indignity" by being denied her civil rights. In this case the court was obviously confronted with a tragically credible combination of special and general damages.

Similarly, the Seventh Circuit affirmed an $80,770 compensatory damages award to an inmate who was improperly placed in punitive segregation under inhumane conditions for over 22 months. In ruling that the award amounting to $119 per day of segregation was not excessive or shocking, the court also observed that the jury was properly instructed to consider "(1) the nature, extent and duration of the injury to the plaintiff; (2) general pain and suffering; (3) humiliation; (4) mental distress, and (5) the violation of constitutional rights".[49]

It is appropriate here to emphasize what should be obvious. A plaintiff's lawyer must seek damages initially. The failure to do so, the Third Circuit held,[50] barred the plaintiff from recovering compensatory damages even though the district court awarded damages on its own initiative. The Fourth Circuit ruled similarly regarding nominal damages.[51] A plaintiff's lawyer

---

[47] Nekolny v Painter, 653 F2d 1164 (7th Cir 1981).
[48] Herrera v Valentine, 653 F2d 1220 (8th Cir 1981).
[49] Smith v Rowe, 761 F2d 360 (7th Cir 1985).
[50] Lewis v Hyland, 554 F2d 93 (3d Cir 1977).
[51] Segarra v McDade, 706 F2d 1301 (4th Cir 1983) (emphasizing need for proper notice to defendants of possible exposure to damages and attorney's fees liability; right to jury trial also important).

should also be alert to jury instructions on damages. The Eighth Circuit[52] upheld a jury's rather low $10,000 award of compensatory damages in a police brutality case where the plaintiff's lawyer did not object to the district court's failure to instruct that loss of wages could be awarded as an element of damages, although the plaintiff was clearly entitled to such an instruction.

A plaintiff's proof of damages should, moreover, be as clear as possible. In this same Eighth Circuit case, the court rejected the plaintiff's claim that the jury's award of $10,000 as compensatory damages was inadequate. It stated:

> [T]he plaintiff's proof of her special damages at trial was exceedingly vague and confusing. Her own proof contained contradictory figures relating to her loss of wages, and the proof relating to her husband's loss of wages was equivocal. There also appears to be some discrepancy between the amount of damages claimed and proved with respect to babysitting and travel expenses.

> Because of the inadequacy of specific proof by the plaintiff, it is impossible to determine precisely what amount the jury awarded as special and general damages. . . .

> It would thus be exceedingly presumptuous of this court to overturn the jury verdict under these circumstances.[53]

The avoidable consequences doctrine, sometimes referred to as the plaintiff's duty to mitigate damages,[54] is applicable in §1983 cases. The standard is reasonableness. Thus, for example, a board of education employee who had been wrongfully discharged in violation of the First Amendment, because her children attended a private school, was refused an award of back pay by an Alabama district court.[55] The court observed that the plaintiff introduced no evidence to show that she ever attempted to find another job. Similarly, in a District of Columbia district court[56] case where the plaintiffs, wrongfully

---

[52] Taken Alive v Litzau, 551 F2d 196 (8th Cir 1977). Similarly, the Fifth Circuit rejected the plaintiff's contention that the district court erred in failing to instruct the jury on compensatory and punitive damages. The plaintiff had failed to object at the time and no showing was made of fundamental error leading to a miscarriage of justice. Whiting v Jackson State Univ, 616 F2d 116 (5th Cir 1980). *See also* Mann v Cannon, 731 F2d 54 (1st Cir 1984) (no objection made by the plaintiff to erroneous compensatory damages instruction).

[53] 551 F2d at 199.

[54] D. Dobbs, Law of Remedies 186-88 (1973).

[55] Berry v Macon County Bd of Educ, 380 F Supp 1244 (MD Ala 1971). *Cf* Miller v Marsh, 766 F2d 490 (11th Cir 1985) (Title VII case in which victim of sex discrimination held not entitled to back pay because she had enrolled as a full-time law student).

[56] Tatum v Morton, 386 F Supp 1308, 1311-12 (DDC 1974), *revd*, 562 F2d 1279 (DC Cir 1977). On this bond posting issue the District of Columbia Circuit criticized the district court's "per se approach—of imposing an absolute duty to mitigate" and said: "[T]here is no absolute rule that a defendant terminates his legal remedy by protesting the bail requirement, and yet the action has some bearing on the money value of the right involved. . . . The matter calls for more sensitive treatment on remand." *Id* 1283-84.

arrested and confined in jail, could have posted bond of $10 and been released pending trial, the court held that they could not recover for subsequent damages alleged to be $10,000 per plaintiff.

In contrast, in an important Seventh Circuit case[57] where the plaintiff inmate was wrongfully confined to punitive segregation for over 22 months, the court rejected the defendants' argument that the plaintiff failed to mitigate damages by her refusal to take another prison job, thereby increasing her time in segregation. The Seventh Circuit ruled that the district court had properly submitted the issue of mitigation to the jury as a question of reasonableness. This was an issue of fact for the jury[58] under the circumstances. Among other things, the plaintiff was convinced she was correct and that she was being deprived of her constitutional rights. In short, she acted on principle, or so the jury could reasonably have found.

In racial discrimination in employment cases, courts tend to be solicitous of plaintiffs on the issue of avoidable consequences. The Fourth Circuit[59] found that a black principal, wrongfully demoted to assistant principal, acted reasonably in refusing to accept an alternative position which involved teaching. The plaintiff had not taught for several years, the alternative employment was inferior, and his acceptance of it would have been seen as acquiescence in racial discrimination. The Eighth Circuit,[60] in another racial discrimination case, emphasized that the avoidable consequences burden of proof is on the defendant. Here, the defendant argued that the plaintiff, a black female schoolteacher, should not have quit a job obtained after wrongful discharge to join her husband who had moved elsewhere to obtain a job. Rejecting the argument, the court said:

> In determining the damages, the burden is on the school board to show what the teachers, through reasonable efforts, could have earned to mitigate them . . .
>
> We think that it is unreasonable to expect a married couple . . . to maintain separate residences for the sole purpose of reducing damages caused by the unlawful actions of the school board . . . [T]he burden is on the Board of Education to prove that she could have obtained employment as a teacher in or near the community where the family lived.[61]

The general bar against double recovery for the same injury is also applicable to §1983 cases. This poses no serious problem with respect to special damages which are usually shown by records, but courts are concerned about potential double recovery for general damages. This concern arose in a pendent

---

[57] Smith v Rowe, 761 F2d 360 (7th Cir 1985).

[58] Whether mitigation is a question of fact for the jury was an issue of first impression in the Seventh Circuit. The court, however, asserted that it was following the rule in the Third, Fourth, Fifth, Eighth, and District of Columbia Circuits. Id 366-67.

[59] Williams v Albemarle City Bd of Educ, 508 F2d 1242 (4th Cir 1974).

[60] Jackson v Wheatley School Dist, 464 F2d 411 (8th Cir 1972).

[61] Id 413-14.

jurisdiction context in an early Tenth Circuit decision[62] where the plaintiff sued a police officer under §1983 for various Fourth and Fourteenth Amendment violations, as well as for assault and battery. Because the jury awarded general damages on both counts, the court subtracted the compensatory damages award on the tort count from the award on the §1983 count in order to avoid a double recovery for bodily injuries.

The District of Columbia Circuit[63] vacated a jury's compensatory award of $500 per class member for Eighth Amendment violations arising out of the plaintiffs' arrest and incarceration. There was also a compensatory award for false arrest and imprisonment which the court held was duplicated by the Eighth Amendment award. Emphasizing the need to distinguish in jury damage instructions among different legally protected interests and related elements of damage, the court noted that the jury was told that false arrest and imprisonment damages could be awarded for insult, subsequent humiliation and mistreatment, and the duration of the loss of liberty. However, the jury was given no separate damage instruction as to the Eighth Amendment claim, except insofar as it was told that length and duration of confinement were relevant, factors that had already been taken into account for false arrest and imprisonment. In contrast, the jury was properly instructed as to the First Amendment violation in the case and how that claim differed from both false arrest and imprisonment and the Eighth Amendment.

Class actions may raise additional damages issues. The District of Columbia Circuit made an important practical point about damages for Eighth Amendment violations and, by analogy, for other violations, when it held that damages for mass Eighth Amendment violations could not be given "on a uniform basis to the class as a whole."[64] It relied on the verdict form itself which divided the class into four subclasses on the basis of length of incarceration, and on the nonuniform damages returned. Judge Leventhal, concurring, made the same point about the class damages of $7,500 per person awarded for the First Amendment violations. He questioned whether a uniform class award for such damages, especially general damages, could be fair because:

> [I]n the context of a large class action, there is simply too much room for variation on this item among members of the class. . . . The class award must focus on the injury sustained by all members of the class—the value

---

[62] Stringer v Dilger, 313 F2d 536 (10th Cir 1963). Another double recovery case, Clappier v Flynn, 605 F2d 519, 530 (10th Cir 1979), involved the "difficult problem of properly instructing the jury both on the comparative negligence claim and the non-comparative [1983] civil rights claim in a manner which would avoid duplicity, confusion and double recovery." The use of special interrogatories to the jury was suggested. *See also* Corriz v Naranjo, 667 F2d 892 (10th Cir 1981), *cert granted*, 456 US 971 (1982), *cert dismissed pursuant to Sup Ct R 53*, 458 US 1123 (1982) (waiver of double recovery contention).

[63] Dellums v Powell, 566 F2d 167 (DC Cir 1977).

[64] Dellums v Powell, 566 F2d 216, 227-28 (DC Cir 1977), *cert denied*, 438 US 916 (1978).

that each one of them would necessarily place on the rights of free expression and assembly in the circumstances of this case.[65]

In a class action based on racial discrimination in employment, the Fifth Circuit held that after class discrimination is shown, each person seeking back pay as damages has to show membership in the class which has suffered "deleterious economic consequences."[66] Thereafter the burden of proof shifts to the defendant to show that that person would not have been employed even in the absence of racial discrimination. If this burden is not carried, the person is entitled to back pay from what would have been the date of hiring.

As at common law,[67] there is a requirement that recoverable special damages be proximately caused by the defendant's conduct. For example, where an inmate alleged a procedural due process violation in connection with his placement in administrative segregation, a New Jersey district court[68] denied compensation for a subsequent beating without warning by another inmate. After first expressing doubt whether the procedural due process violation was a cause in fact of the beating, the court asserted that, all the same, "[t]he beating was an intentional intervening act by a third party"[69] and thus there was no proximate cause as a matter of law. Similarly, the Seventh Circuit[70] held that the conduct of defendant police officers in obtaining a confession illegally was not the proximate cause of a plaintiff's subsequent conviction and lengthy incarceration. The trial judge's admission of the confession into evidence was considered a superseding cause.[71]

Despite the common tort and damages language used in such cases, the Supreme Court early made clear, in reliance on 42 USC §1988, that neither the forum state's common law nor general common law is determinative for damage purposes. In *Sullivan v Little Hunting Park, Inc,*[72] the Court stated:

> Compensatory damages for deprivation of a federal right are governed by federal standards, as provided by Congress in 42 USC §1988. . . . This means, as we read §1988, that both federal and state rules on damages may be utilized, whichever better serves the policies expressed in the federal statutes. . . . The rule of damages, whether drawn from federal or state sources, is a federal rule responsive to the need whenever a federal right is impaired.[73]

---

[65] Dellums v Powell, 566 F2d at 205, 210 (DC Cir 1977) (concurring opinion).

[66] Mims v Wilson, 514 F2d 106 (5th Cir 1975).

[67] Dobbs, Law of Remedies 157-58 (1973).

[68] Urbano v McCorkle, 334 F Supp 161 (DNJ 1971), *affd,* 481 F2d 1400 (3d Cir 1973).

[69] *Id* 169.

[70] Duncan v Nelson, 466 F2d 939 (7th Cir), *cert denied,* 409 US 894 (1972).

[71] The general relationship between §1983 and proximate cause is discussed at **§3.17.** It also bears emphasizing that proximate cause is very different from cause in fact. *Id.*

[72] 396 US 229 (1969) (42 USC §1982 case).

[73] 396 US at 239-40. *See* Baskin v Parker, 602 F2d 1205, 1209-10 (5th Cir 1979) (per curiam) (following *Sullivan's* approach). *Cf* Smith v Wade, 461 US 30 (1983) (punitive damages), analyzed at **§4.08.**

Thus, in an important Seventh Circuit case[74] the court held that a parent could recover under §1983 for the loss of a son's society and companionship brought about by the wrongful shooting of the son by police officers. The Seventh Circuit reached this conclusion even though many states in 1871 (when §1983 was enacted) did not allow recovery for lost society and companionship in wrongful death actions.[75] It stated that its holding was "bolstered by the recognition that Section 1983 was enacted not simply to enforce existing wrongful death remedies but to give force to the newly-conceived constitutional amendments, which are remedial in purpose."[76]

The possible choice between state law and federal law is beginning to arise in a somewhat different but related damages setting. As a Fifth Circuit case put it, "what rule should apply in the case of liability of a defendant in a federal civil rights action after prior settlement with a joint tortfeasor":[77] a state rule or a federal rule? The plaintiff sued a police officer and a restaurant. The restaurant settled with the plaintiff for $30,000 while a jury awarded the plaintiff $25,000 against the police officer for the use of excessive force. The Fifth Circuit held that the settlement should not be credited to the police officer because he and the restaurant were not joint tortfeasors. The restaurant was charged with false arrest and malicious prosecution, but the jury award against the officer was for the use of excessive force. There was no joint liability here because the restaurant could not be held liable for the officer's use of excessive force. In short, the court did not have to reach the contribution and indemnification issues.

In contrast, in an Eighth Circuit case[78] the plaintiff sued a sheriff and a county for procedural due process violations in connection with the termination of his employment. He then settled with the county prior to trial for $7,500 and later received a $7,500 compensatory damages award against the sheriff (pursuant to an agreed upon remittitur reducing the $15,000 jury award). The Eighth Circuit held that the sheriff could not deduct from the judgment against him the amount of the earlier settlement. The court adopted as its federal rule of decision the Minnesota law as to the effect of a plaintiff's settlement with one defendant on an award of damages against a nonsettling defendant. There was no showing, according to the court, that the plaintiff had obtained a double recovery.

While there are too few circuit court decisions regarding this matter on which to base a definitive judgment at this time, it may be suggested that joint and several liability issues as such are issues of the scope of §1983 liability. These issues require uniform treatment and therefore raise questions of federal

---

[74] Bell v City of Milwaukee, 746 F2d 1205 (7th Cir 1984), also dealing with wrongful death, limitations, and preclusion. *See* §§**3.20, 4.14-4.17 & 5.17-5.20** respectively.

[75] *See* §**3.20.**

[76] Bell v City of Milwaukee, 746 F2d 1205, 1250 (7th Cir 1984).

[77] Dobson v Camden, 725 F2d 1003, 1004 (5th Cir 1984) (en banc).

[78] Johnson v Rogers, 621 F2d 300 (8th Cir 1980).

statutory interpretation which should not be determined by state law.[79] However, contribution and indemnification issues, typically involving relations among defendants alone, are issues which do not demand uniformity and regarding which §1983's language and legislative history appear to be deficient within the meaning of 42 USC §1988. Consequently, the forum state's law should be applied unless it is inconsistent with the federal policies of deterrence and compensation underlying §1983.[80]

§4.04 —Unlawful Searches, Seizures, Arrests, and Confinement

Fourth and Fourteenth Amendment violations are typically asserted against law enforcement officers in connection with arrests, imprisonment, searches and seizures, and the related use of force. Because these same circumstances also give rise to the common law torts of false arrest, false imprisonment, trespass, assault, and battery, courts generally do not have much difficulty in using the appropriate common law of damages.[81] There is evidence of special damages (medical expenses, lost income, and the like) in many such cases, but even where none is introduced, general damages for pain, suffering, humiliation, and emotional distress are recoverable.

Cases posing the least trouble to a plaintiff's lawyer on the damages question are those in which there are substantial special damages. The Sixth Circuit[82] affirmed a jury verdict of $800,000 in compensatory damages against a police officer who, while off duty, shot and paralyzed a plaintiff. The court found that the award was not excessive; it was supported by substantial evidence because there was extensive medical testimony regarding the paralysis, its scope and duration, and there was testimony as to past and future medical expenses as well as pain and suffering.

Similarly, the Fifth Circuit[83] affirmed a district court award of $35,000 compensatory damages against a police officer who wrongfully shot and seriously injured a plaintiff, and the Eighth Circuit[84] affirmed a jury verdict for

---

[79] However, in Hinshaw v Doffer, 785 F2d 1260 (5th Cir 1986), the court applied Texas law in holding a defendant liable for the full amount of a judgment even though the jury assessed that defendant and a co-defendant, exonerated on appeal, specific percentages of fault. The Fifth Circuit found no relevant federal law on the issue. It also determined that Texas law was not inconsistent with §1983's compensation policy. Why the jury was allowed to apportion fault in the first instance, though, is not clear. *See also* **§4.09** on joint and several liability for *punitive* damages.

[80] See **§§3.19, 3.20 & 4.14-4.17** for comparable deficiencies in §1983 law regarding survival, wrongful death, and limitations and for a discussion of *inconsistency*.

[81] The Court's reasoning in Carey v Piphus, 435 US 247 (1978), discussed at **§4.02,** indicates this is entirely appropriate.

[82] Stengel v Belcher, 522 F2d 438 (6th Cir 1975).

[83] Palmer v Hall, 517 F2d 705 (5th Cir 1975).

[84] Taken Alive v Litzau, 551 F2d 196 (8th Cir 1977).

$10,000 compensatory damages where the defendant police officer, in the course of his arrest of the plaintiff, fractured her arm in several places.

In a First Circuit case,[85] a jury's compensatory damages award of $75,000 against a police officer for the wrongful search and seizure of a plaintiff's property was upheld by the court. The plaintiff's business, which had netted $1,000 per week prior to the search, was destroyed as a business entity because of the search and the resulting publicity. Also, there was evidence of actual damage to the plaintiff's property. And, where the plaintiff was so badly beaten by police officers that he suffered a severe skull fracture which permanently diminished his intellectual capacity and later caused him to develop post-traumatic epilepsy requiring preventive medication, the Sixth Circuit[86] upheld a jury's $100,000 compensatory damages award.

However, extensive special damages need not be proved in order for a plaintiff to recover substantial compensatory damages. In a First Circuit case,[87] a prisoner successfully sued prison officials for administering a cancer-producing drug in violation of due process, the Fourth Amendment, and the plaintiff's right of privacy. Affirming the jury's compensatory damages award of $60,000, the First Circuit rejected the defendants' argument that the evidence was insufficient to show the plaintiff's "genuine fear of developing cancer" and that the plaintiff's future medical expenses were speculative. After noting the physical discomfort and resulting skin rashes from the drug, the court further observed that there was expert testimony demonstrating the real danger of developing cancer from the administration of the drug. Also, the jury was justified in believing that the plaintiff suffered pain and emotional distress upon discovering this greatly increased risk of cancer. Finally, the defendants had not asked the jury to make a specific award for future medical expenses. Consequently, the $60,000 award was not grossly excessive.

Similarly, in a Sixth Circuit case,[88] a district court awarded one plaintiff $5,450 and another plaintiff $10,000 in compensatory damages against the defendant police officer who had engaged in an unconstitutional search and seizure against the first and who had unconstitutionally arrested and detained the second. The defendant had "engaged in an unconstitutional orgy of unique proportions," including ransacking the plaintiff's apartment. Affirming these awards, the court found sufficient evidence of humiliation and emotional distress to warrant the district court's award, even though there was little quantifiable special damage shown. Among the "tangible factors" demonstrating humiliation and emotional distress were the arrest and detention and the search and seizure.

A much-cited Eighth Circuit case[89] also made the point that extensive special

---

[85] BCR Transp Co v Fontaine, 727 F2d 7 (1st Cir 1984).

[86] Bruner v Dunaway, 684 F2d 422 (6th Cir 1982) (per curiam).

[87] Clark v Taylor, 710 F2d 4 (1st Cir 1983).

[88] Smith v Heath, 691 F2d 220 (6th Cir 1982).

[89] Herrera v Valentine, 653 F2d 1220, 1233 (8th Cir 1981).
The *Herrera* case, especially its language at 653 F2d at 1227-31, was described in a later Eighth Circuit case as standing for the proposition that "violations of certain

damages are not necessary for a substantial compensatory damages award. In this case the court affirmed a jury's compensatory damages verdict of $300,000 against the defendants for mistreatment of the plaintiff by a police officer. The plaintiff, an American Indian in late pregnancy, was kicked in a life-threatening manner and thrown to the ground; she was in extreme physical pain afterward and lost her unborn child as a result; her pain and suffering continued to the time of trial, three years later; the emotional trauma accompanying the stillbirth was "devastating"; the mental anguish she suffered in being driven *away* from a nearby hospital, combined with the police officer's concurrent threat to kill her, added to her emotional injury; and she suffered "great indignity" by being denied her civil rights.

Finally, in a Seventh Circuit strip search case,[90] the plaintiffs successfully sued a city for its unconstitutional strip search policy directed against women arrested for misdemeanor offenses. Two of the plaintiffs each received $25,000 compensatory damages awards, a third received $30,000, and a fourth $60,000. Despite the discrepancy in these awards, the Seventh Circuit upheld them as supported by the evidence. The court emphasized the fact that each woman's testimony regarding emotional and mental distress resulting from the searches was "adequately corroborated" by persons who knew them. Results included shock, shame, rage, humiliation, and nightmares. As to the plaintiff with the $60,000 award, there were aggravating circumstances in her case apparently not present in the others. Two male officers were within view when she was searched and a group of prostitutes "jeered" at her while she was being searched. Even if this was not enough, standing alone, to justify the disparity in awards, still there was enough evidence in any event under the egregious circumstances to uphold the award as not grossly excessive. The court asserted that the jury was the community's conscience, even though the court itself might not have made a $60,000 award to the fourth plaintiff.

Nevertheless, there are limits in these search, seizure, arrest, and confinement cases with respect to substantial general damages awards. In a subsequent Seventh Circuit strip search case,[91] the court reduced a jury's award of $50,000

substantive constitutional rights are redressable by substantial compensatory awards independent of actual injury." Villaneuva v George, 659 F2d 851, 855 (8th Cir 1981). *See also* Grandstaff v City of Borger, 767 F2d 161 (5th Cir 1985) (affirming jury's award of $200,000 to father of son wrongfully killed by police for father's loss of society and companionship as well as mental anguish; close relationship and only son); Rock v McCoy, 763 F2d 394 (10th Cir 1985) (affirming jury's award of $100,000 against city arising out of excessive use of police force and failure to provide medical attention in jail; defendants' "focus on . . . minimal medical expenses ignores the humiliating effect that this incident had on him").; Bell v City of Milwaukee, 746 F2d 1205 (7th Cir 1984) (affirming jury's award of $75,000 to father of son wrongfully killed by police for father's loss of society and companionship; warm and close relationship).

[90] Mary Beth G v City of Chicago, 723 F2d 1263 (7th Cir 1983). *See* **Form 10, app B.**

[91] Levka v City of Chicago, 748 F2d 421 (7th Cir 1984). *See also* Taliferro v Angle, 757 F2d 157 (7th Cir 1985) (reducing jury's compensatory award of $47,000 to $25,000 for police officers' beating of plaintiff after they arrested him: there were minimal medical expenses and his destroyed personal belongings had only sentimental value;

to $25,000. There were no lost earnings and no aggravating circumstances, the plaintiff paid only one isolated visit to a psychiatrist, and the $50,000 award was out of line with other awards in similar cases. The jury in effect was improperly awarding punitive damages.

Similarly, in a Second Circuit case,[92] the court, using a shock the judicial conscience standard, reduced a jury's compensatory damages award to a plaintiff who had been subjected to excessive force by police from $55,000 to $25,000. Most of the plaintiff's injuries were temporary in nature: he had been struck with a blackjack, his bare feet were *stomped on,* and he was cuffed in the ears. His claims of permanent injury were related to a perforated left eardrum, a slight loss of hearing, and ear ringing. But the doctor who examined the plaintiff could not say that his perforated eardrum was "fresh"; also, the plaintiff did not mention his eardrum when he reported police brutality. Further, his hearing loss was minor. In short, his temporary discomfort did not last for long, and his permanent hearing impairment was "very minor."

A final example of judicial control is a Fifth Circuit case[93] where the plaintiff obtained a jury verdict totaling $75,000 in compensatory damages against two deputy sheriffs who unconstitutionally searched and arrested her, used excessive force in making the arrest, and beat her after making the arrest. Overturning the verdict as excessive and ordering a conditional remittitur, the Fifth Circuit emphasized the following:

1. There was no physical damage to the plaintiff's home

2. The unconstitutional arrest and imprisonment, lasting two hours, caused only embarrassment and mental anguish

3. The excessive force used caused plaintiff personal injuries, including a low-grade concussion, numbness in her left thumb, some bruises, continuing headaches, nightmares, and nervousness, but "the residual effect of the ill treatment apparently [did] not limit her activities"

4. Past medical expenses totaled $329 and no evidence of future medical costs was introduced

5. More than $74,000 of the verdict, an excessive amount under the circumstances, was thus attributable "to the more speculative items of recovery—pain and suffering, mental anguish, and embarrassment"

Wrongful confinement cases often pose troublesome valuation problems, especially where a plaintiff is already confined or where he or she is confined

---

"a routine if regrettable case of excessive force"; note the incorrect statement at 162 that "[g]eneral damages are not available in civil-rights tort cases . . . ": the court must have meant presumed damages); Young v City of New Orleans, 751 F2d 794 (5th Cir 1985) (jury's $5,500 award to plaintiff for excessive use of police force affirmed despite the plaintiff's claim that it reflected only out-of-pocket expenses and not pain and suffering or future expenses; there was conflicting testimony regarding the source of the plaintiff's injuries).

[92] Wheatley v Ford, 679 F2d 1037 (2nd Cir 1982).

[93] Keyes v Lauga, 635 F2d 330, 336 (5th Cir 1981).

for a very short time. In one such case, the First Circuit affirmed jury verdicts of $1,000 and $9,000 in compensatory damages, respectively, to two inmates who were wrongfully placed in segregated confinement. The court stated: "The measure of such damages is clearly the difference between the harsher and . . . deplorable conditions suffered in segregation and the conditions that prevailed in the general prison population."[94] In contrast, where a plaintiff was wrongfully arrested and confined for 90 minutes, the Seventh Circuit[95] affirmed a jury award of "$00.00" in actual damages. The court noted that the plaintiff received courteous treatment, no abusive language or force was ever directed at him, he was allowed to make phone calls, and bail was readily permitted.

In a Fifth Circuit case,[96] the court reversed and remanded for a new trial on damages where the jury awarded an improperly imprisoned plaintiff $40,000 in compensatory damages. The court acknowledged that the district court's instructions regarding physical and mental suffering were correct but held that the jury should have been permitted to hear about the plaintiff's prior imprisonment as relevant to determining the extent of mental suffering. In a District of Columbia Circuit decision,[97] the court affirmed jury verdicts for false arrest and imprisonment reached according to the following guidelines: 12 hours of detention were worth $120; 12 to 24 hours, $360; 24 to 48 hours, $960; and 48 to 72 hours, $1,800. Such an approach could also be used for Fourth Amendment violations.

However, awards for wrongful confinement can be high where there is objective evidence demonstrating substantial general damages. In a Seventh Circuit case,[98] a jury's compensatory damages award of $60,000 to a plaintiff who was wrongfully arrested and imprisoned for 113 days was not excessive. Describing its review function as narrow, the court noted the following: the plaintiff testified about nightmares, insomnia, and nausea after his release; his employer stated that the plaintiff was a "changed man, given to depression, vagueness and tears"; and his woman friend, who finally had to leave him, described his "nausea, cold sweats, outbursts of crying, and increased irascibility after his release." The absence of medical or psychiatric testimony was not fatal to plaintiff's damages award.

Wrongful searches and seizures, even unaccompanied by an arrest or imprisonment, can also give rise to general compensatory damages. A New Jersey district court awarded compensatory damages of $600 against police officers who were searching the cars and persons of "long-haired highway

---

[94] Furtado v Bishop, 604 F2d 80, 89 (1st Cir 1979).

[95] Joseph v Rowlen, 425 F2d 1010 (7th Cir 1970).

[96] Bryan v Jones, 519 F2d 44 (5th Cir 1975), *modified on other grounds*, 530 F2d 1210 (5th Cir) (en banc), *cert denied*, 429 US 865 (1976).

[97] Dellums v Powell, 566 F2d 167 (DC Cir 1977).

[98] Whitley v Seibel, 676 F2d 245 (7th Cir 1982).

travelers." The Third Circuit[99] reversed only because the plaintiffs did not originally seek damages.

There is occasionally judicial confusion about the difference between nominal damages on the one hand and special and general compensatory damages on the other. In a First Circuit case,[100] the district court awarded $500 in what it called *nominal* damages where the plaintiff sued police officers for an unreasonable search and an assault. The district court, obviously referring to the absence of special damages, noted that the plaintiff never consulted a physician, lost no work time, and suffered no physical harm at all. Reversing and remanding, the First Circuit stated correctly that if the district court in fact meant "nominal," then damages should be reduced to $1. However, the $500 award could stand if the court meant to award compensatory damages for "impalpable" injuries.

In a highly unusual Second Circuit case,[101] a jury awarded the plaintiff $80,000 in compensatory damages against a judge who, displeased with the plaintiff vendor's coffee, had the plaintiff brought handcuffed by the sheriff through the courtroom in full view of dozens of people, conducted a "pseudo-official inquisition" about the coffee, screamed at and threatened him and his livelihood for 20 minutes, and then later summoned the plaintiff to his chambers. The §1983 claim was apparently pleaded using the language of due process but was, as the district court noted, "basically a tort action for false arrest and imprisonment."[102] The compensatory award was not challenged on appeal, but in passing the Second Circuit noted the unpleasant consequences for the plaintiff: he was very upset, he could not sleep, he started to stutter and get headaches, he required hospital treatment, he could not work, and his wife asked him to leave their home.

Proximate cause[103] may also limit a defendant's liability for compensatory damages in such cases. In a Ninth Circuit case,[104] the court overturned a jury's compensatory damages verdict of $250,000 against two police sergeants and a polygraph examiner who caused a plaintiff's wrongful arrest and incarceration on a charge of murder. Four days after the plaintiff's arrest, the district attorney filed a criminal complaint against the plaintiff charging him with murder. According to the court which spoke in proximate cause terms, the filing of this criminal complaint insulated the defendants from liability for damages suffered subsequently unless the plaintiff could show that the district

---

[99] Lewis v Hyland, 554 F2d 93 (3d Cir 1977).

[100] Magnett v Pelletier, 488 F2d 33 (1st Cir 1973). *See also* Ganey v Edwards, 759 F2d 337 (4th Cir 1985) (although jury found constitutional violation, it was not required to award $1 in nominal damages in absence of any proof of actual damages; legal consequences to plaintiff the same whether $0 award or $1 award; Judge Winter dissented). *See* **§4.02.**

[101] Zarcone v Perry, 572 F2d 52 (2d Cir), *affd*, 581 F2d 1039 (2d Cir 1978).

[102] Zarcone v Perry, 438 F Supp 788, 790 (EDNY 1977), *affd*, 581 F2d 1039 (2d Cir 1978).

[103] See **§3.17** on proximate cause.

[104] Smiddy v Varney, 665 F2d 261 (9th Cir 1981).

attorney was pressured or caused by the defendants to act contrary to his independent judgment. The court also noted that the defendants had acted neither maliciously nor with reckless disregard of the plaintiff's rights. On remand, the fact-finder was to determine whether the plaintiff's arrest proximately caused the loss of a job opportunity, as well as the extent of any psychological damage.

§4.05   —Procedural Due Process

Carey v Piphus[105] made at least two points clearly. First, there can be no *presumed* damages for a procedural due process violation. A plaintiff must allege and prove actual damages, that is, special damages, general damages, or both. And second, a defendant may defeat a plaintiff's claim for actual damages by proving that the plaintiff would still have suffered those damages without any procedural due process violation. This *Mount Healthy* cause-in-fact rule differs from the common law rule; in a §1983 case, once the plaintiff proves a constitutional violation, the burden of proof is on the defendant to show the absence of but-for causation between that violation and damages.[106] The Court also disapproved of a line of cases arising in the Fourth and Fifth Circuits which dispensed with a but-for causation requirement.[107]

This rule, of course, requires someone, either the jury or the district court, to make the sometimes difficult judgment as to what would have occurred had procedural due process not been violated. As mentioned earlier,[108] a defendant who deprives a plaintiff of procedural due process in connection with, for example, a discharge, should not be permitted to carry the *Mount Healthy* burden by using information that was not relied on at the time the initial decision was made. Further, where the defendant does not carry this burden in a case involving the deprivation of a plaintiff's *property* interest in employment, the plaintiff should be entitled to compensatory damages, including back pay and other consequential damages. Where the defendant does not carry this burden in a case involving only a deprivation of the plaintiff's *liberty* interest in his or her name and future job opportunities, as, for example, through false charges of wrongdoing or incompetence, the plaintiff should similarly be entitled to compensatory damages, including back pay and other consequential damages stemming from the procedural due process violation. The false charges were the but-for cause of the loss of the plaintiff's job, even though

---

[105] 435 US 247 (1978).

[106] D. Dobbs, Law of Remedies 149 (1973). That the burden of proof is on the defendant appears from *Carey*, 435 US at 260-61, and Mount Healthy City Bd of Educ v Doyle, 429 US 274, 285-87 (1977). *See* **§4.02.**

[107] Disapproved were Thomas v Ward, 529 F2d 916 (4th Cir 1975); Burt v Board of Trustees, 521 F2d 1201, 1207-08 (4th Cir 1975) (opinion of Judge Winter); Zimmerer v Spencer, 485 F2d 176 (5th Cir 1973); Horton v Orange County Bd of Educ, 464 F2d 536 (4th Cir 1972). *See* Carey v Piphus, 435 US 247, 260 n 15 (1978).

[108] *See* **§4.02.** See also **§3.18** on cause in fact.

there was no deprivation of a property interest. This result is supported by analogy to a case in which an employee is discharged in violation of the First Amendment, and the defendant does not carry the *Mount Healthy* burden. Here, the plaintiff is surely entitled to compensatory damages that include back pay. For these reasons, the contrary position of the Fifth and Ninth Circuits[109] on the back pay issue in such deprivation of *liberty* cases (where the defendant does *not* carry the *Mount Healthy* burden) appears questionable.

A distinction for damages purposes between property and liberty deprivations may also be important where a defendant *does* in fact carry the *Mount Healthy* burden. In such cases, the plaintiff will be able to recover only those damages attributable to the procedural due process violation itself, and those damages may vary depending on whether a property or liberty interest was deprived. While the Fifth Circuit has expressed skepticism whether such damages can ever be shown,[110] the circuits overwhelmingly permit such a plaintiff the opportunity to do so. For example, in a Fourth Circuit case,[111] where a teacher discharged without procedural safeguards was subsequently determined to have been discharged for just cause, the Fourth Circuit directed the district court not to allow the plaintiff to allege lost pay or lost retirement fund contributions or damages attributable to the procedural deprivation. However, the plaintiff was permitted to attempt to prove "mental and emotional distress stemming from the denial of due process."

In a Fifth Circuit case[112] a doctor successfully sued a hospital for violating his procedural due process rights in connection with his discharge and received a $20,000 compensatory damages jury award for emotional distress, as well as $32,400 in lost salary. On appeal the difficulty of the damages issue stemmed from the fact that the plaintiff's discharge was substantively justified: the question then became whether the emotional distress suffered by the plaintiff was caused by the procedural due process violation—in which case it was compensable, or by the discharge itself—in which case it was not. Affirming the $20,000 award for emotional distress, the Fifth Circuit observed that the district court had properly instructed the jury in this respect. There was sufficient evidence of the plaintiff's severe anxiety and distress resulting from the summary discharge to support the award. Also, whether the hospital hearing at which the plaintiff appeared two years *after* his summary discharge effectively stopped the plaintiff's emotional distress was a question of fact for

---

[109] Graves v Duganne, 581 F2d 222 (9th Cir 1978); Dennis v S&S Consolidated Rural High School Dist, 577 F2d 338 (5th Cir 1978). *See also* Wells v Doland, 711 F2d 670 (5th Cir 1983) (where deprivation of liberty only, entitlement to name clearing hearing and to prove damages resulting from initial deprivation, not including back pay).

[110] Russell v Harrison, 736 F2d 283, 291 n 17 (5th Cir 1984); Wilson v Taylor, 658 F2d 1021 (5th Cir 1981). *Cf* Busche v Burkee, 649 F2d 509 (7th Cir 1981) (proximate cause approach, general damages proved) and Endicott v Huddleston, 644 F2d 1208 (7th Cir 1980) (general damages not proved).

[111] Burt v Abel, 585 F2d 613 (4th Cir 1978).

[112] Laje v Thomason Gen Hosp, 665 F2d 724 (5th Cir 1982). *But cf* Campbell v Pierce County, 741 F2d 1342 (11th Cir 1984) (no entitlement to damages in a deprivation of liberty case where name clearing hearing provided "only 14 days" after dismissal).

the jury. However, the Fifth Circuit ruled that the plaintiff was not entitled to the $32,400 back pay award because his discharge was ultimately found to be justified.

In a Ninth Circuit case,[113] the court overturned the district court's $9,000 compensatory damages award to the discharged plaintiff for her mental and emotional distress. The plaintiff had been validly discharged on the merits, so she was not entitled to reinstatement or back pay. Also, the record supported the finding that she had suffered emotional distress because she believed she was treated unfairly. However, reversal and remand were appropriate because the district court erroneously found that she had been deprived of both a liberty and a property interest, while in reality she had been deprived only of a property interest. Relying on *Vanelli v Reynolds School District*[114] the court observed that emotional distress damages might be different for a property interest deprivation alone.

Actual damages resulting from procedural due process violations include not only out-of-pocket losses or specials such as lost wages, but general compensatory damages as well. For example, in an Eighth Circuit decision[115] arising out of a wrongful attachment of the plaintiffs' mobile home and automobile, the court approved a jury award of over $9,000 in compensatory damages. It said: "Compensatory damages awardable . . . are not limited to the out-of-pocket pecuniary loss the plaintiffs suffered. They can be awarded for emotional and mental distress even though no actual damages are proven."[116]

However, here, as elsewhere, courts are sensitive to excessive awards for general damages. In an Eleventh Circuit case,[117] the court overturned a jury's compensatory damages award of $100,000 ($50,000 for each of two procedural due process violations) to a police officer improperly terminated. There was

---

[113] Jones v Los Angeles Community College Dist, 70 F2d 203 (9th Cir 1983). *See also* Miller v City of Mission, 705 F2d 368 (10th Cir 1983) (reversing jury's award of $70,895 for lost wages because the plaintiff did not prove property interest extending to retirement, but affirming jury's $20,000 award for deprivation of liberty interest in the plaintiff's reputation).

[114] 667 F2d 773 (9th Cir 1982). In *Vanelli* the Ninth Circuit reversed and remanded for a new finding on damages in a case where a teacher, who was dismissed without a pretermination hearing in violation of due process, was given a hearing one month later at which his discharge was found to be warranted. The district court had awarded $2,000 in emotional distress damages for the deprivation of the plaintiff's *property* interest alone. However, the Ninth Circuit held that the plaintiff's *liberty and property* interests had been deprived. A remand was thus necessary on the damages issue because the "intensity and degree of suffering" for the deprivation of both interests might be greater than for the property interest deprivation alone.

[115] Guzman v Western State Bank, 540 F2d 948 (8th Cir 1976). *See also* Chalmers v City of Los Angeles, 762 F2d 753 (9th Cir 1985) (street vendor awarded $12,500 for anguish, embarrassment, anxiety, and humiliation in addition to $15,723 for lost profits) and Simineo v School Dist No 16, 594 F2d 1353 (10th Cir 1979) (affirming $60,000 award for lost income and injury to reputation and physical and mental health).

[116] Guzman v Western State Bank, 540 F2d 948, 953 (8th Cir 1976).

[117] Wilson v Taylor, 733 F2d 1539 (11th Cir 1984). Judge Fay dissented, claiming that the initial award did not shock the conscience.

testimony that the plaintiff suffered emotional distress from each of the two violations. However, the awards were grossly excessive in light of the fact that the plaintiff was only angry or frustrated. There was no testimony of extreme emotional damage or injury stemming from the manner in which he was terminated. Thus, an award of $5,000 for each of the two violations was adequate to compensate the plaintiff; a remittitur was appropriate to that effect. In a Sixth Circuit case,[118] the court ruled excessive $2,500 awards for frustration and mental suffering to each of two plaintiffs wrongfully denied federal housing benefits. There was insufficient evidence of such frustration and mental suffering: the only relevant evidence was that one of the plaintiffs was "kind of angry."

Procedural due process violation claims frequently arise in a prison setting where it may sometimes be difficult to show actual damages of either a special or general nature. On the one hand, a Second Circuit decision[119] upheld a jury verdict of $1,000 as compensatory damages where an inmate was improperly disciplined in violation of procedural due process. The plaintiff was in solitary confinement for 12 days, 24 hours a day; he was subject to strip searches, was marched naked to his cell, not given exercise, and kept in solitary five days longer than permitted by prison regulations. In finding the jury award not excessive, the court explained that the plaintiff could be compensated for his anguish, anxiety, fear of indefinite confinement, and the psychological impact of his confinement.

Similarly, in a Seventh Circuit case[120] jury awards of $4,500 each were made to the two plaintiff inmates against members of a prison disciplinary committee who violated the plaintiffs' procedural due process rights. While the awards were "somewhat excessive," they were supported by the evidence. One plaintiff spent 35 days in segregation without access to the prison yard or other exercise facilities. He also lost other privileges. The other spent at least a week in extremely unsanitary and repulsive conditions. Both plaintiffs testified as to their anguish and frustration resulting from the unfairness of the hearings and the fear that this unfairness would continue in the future. The Seventh Circuit was unimpressed with the defendants' argument that the plaintiffs had simply been deprived of "creature comforts" and suffered only general anxiety.

On the other hand, where a plaintiff sued various prison officials for arbitrarily confining him to administrative segregation, the Third Circuit[121] reversed a district court award of $500 and instead awarded the plaintiff only nominal damages of $1. The court observed that conditions of administrative

---

[118] Davis v Mansfield Metropolitan Hous Auth, 751 F2d 180 (6th Cir 1984).

[119] United States *ex rel* Larkins v Oswald, 510 F2d 583 (2d Cir 1975).

[120] Saxner v Benson, 727 F2d 669 (7th Cir 1984), *affd on other grounds sub nom* Cleavinger v Saxner, 106 S Ct 496 (1985). *See also* King v Higgins, 702 F2d 18 (1st Cir 1983) (affirming $390 compensatory damages award to inmate sentenced to 15 days isolation in violation of due process; lost wages, pain, and suffering included).

[121] United States *ex rel* Tyrrell v Speaker, 535 F2d 823 (3d Cir 1976).

segregation were less restrictive than the plaintiff's earlier circumstances in prison and so there was no loss for which to compensate him.[122]

Although procedural due process violations in prison typically do not cause special damage, such damage has its functional equivalent in lost work and good time credits. Here, of course, the remedy is neither financial nor directed against the pocketbook of the defendant in an individual capacity, but is rather injunctive and directed against the defendant in an official capacity. For example, a New Jersey district court[123] found that a prisoner's procedural due process rights were violated in connection with his placement in administrative segregation. It directed the defendant correctional commissioner to restore lost work and good time credits, saying that these were the same as compensation in prison.

Occasionally, a plaintiff claims injury to reputation as a result of a procedural due process violation. In *Cox v Northern Virginia Transportation Commission*,[124] a questionable decision of the Fourth Circuit, a discharged transportation commission employee whose request for a hearing was denied, sued to recover for the injury to her reputation and her net loss of income. The commissioners of the transportation commission who fired her granted interviews to newspaper reporters attributing her discharge to the results of an investigation of a financial scandal at the commission. In fact, the plaintiff was not at all involved in any irregularities. The district court ruled that she was entitled to damages both for injury to her reputation and for her net loss of income. The jury gave her compensatory damages of $30,000.

The Fourth Circuit reversed and remanded for redetermination of damages to be measured only by the plaintiff's "loss of back pay and the value of fringe benefits with interest, after deducting interim earnings from other employment."[125] It ruled that damages for injury to her reputation were not recoverable, relying on *Paul v Davis*,[126] a Supreme Court decision which held that injury to reputation by a state officer does not give rise to a §1983 cause of action. The court reasoned as follows:

> [W]hen a government employee is dismissed without a hearing, having been publicly charged with dishonesty or other wrongdoing that will injure his or her liberty to obtain other work, the federal tort is not the defamation. The federal tort is the denial of a hearing at which the dismissed employee has an opportunity to refute the public charge. The

---

[122] *Cf* Thompson v Burke, 556 F2d 231 (3d Cir 1977) where a parolee sued a parole board member for alleged violations of procedural due process in revoking his parole thereby resulting in his incarceration. The court suggested that nominal damages would be appropriate because there was no evidence of actual damages.

[123] Urbano v McCorkle, 334 F Supp 161 (DNJ 1971), *affd,* 481 F2d 1400 (1973). *Cf* King v Wells, 760 F2d 89 (6th Cir 1985) (inmate entitled to $1,000 for emotional distress resulting from procedural due process violation but not to compensation for lost good time credits because defendant carried *Mount Healthy* burden).

[124] 551 F2d 555 (4th Cir 1976).

[125] *Id* 558.

[126] 424 US 693 (1976) discussed at **§§3.02 & 3.08.**

remedy, therefore, must be related solely to the employee's loss resulting from discharge without a hearing.[127]

However, the Fourth Circuit in fact misapplied *Paul v Davis.Paul* held only that injury to reputation, standing alone, was not a *liberty* interest protected by the due process clause. Thus, when a plaintiff seeks damages for injury to reputation only, a §1983 cause of action for damages is not stated. In *Cox,* however, the plaintiff's opportunity to get a new job was impaired;[128] hence, she stated a §1983 cause of action for damages. Once a §1983 cause of action is stated, actual damages, including damage to reputation, should be recoverable even after *Paul v Davis* so long as the plaintiff in a case like *Cox* can show a causal relation between the procedural violation and such actual damages. This is no different from a situation in which, for example, a plaintiff is wrongfully arrested and imprisoned. Because these facts of arrest and imprisonment also give rise to a §1983 cause of action, the plaintiff is entitled to allege and prove damage to his or her reputation as well as additional special and general damages. Subject to the *Carey v Piphus*[129] requirement that damages cannot be presumed, a plaintiff in either case should be permitted to show actual damages resulting from any injury to reputation caused by the defendant's conduct.[130]

In contrast to *Cox,* the Fifth Circuit properly distinguished the Supreme Court's decision in *Paul v Davis.* In the case before it, where the plaintiffs alleged that the defendants unconstitutionally injured their personal and business reputations, the Fifth Circuit emphasized the following:

1.   The plaintiffs alleged injury to their reputations not only as a result of certain statements made, but also as a result of an alleged unlawful search and seizure

2.   Florida law recognized business reputation, "to the extent it approximates good will," as a property interest

3.   Harm was caused to the plaintiffs' business and personal reputations *plus* to their protected property interest in good will, thereby satisfying the stigma-plus requirement of *Paul v Davis*

4.   The plaintiffs alleged harm to their reputations *plus* harm to their Fourth Amendment rights

---

[127] 551 F2d at 558.

[128] The court conceded this. *Id.*

[129] 435 US 247 (1978).

[130] It should be noted that even a subsequent hearing, with due process safeguards, at which a plaintiff prevails may not completely eliminate the actual damage to a plaintiff resulting from the injury to his or her reputation caused by the intitial improper hearing. For example, his or her later ability to obtain a job may be impaired even if his or her name is cleared at the subsequent proper hearing. This impairment, of course, must be traceable solely to the procedural due process violation, a difficult task for the plaintiff.

In response to the defendants' contention that the injury to the plaintiffs' personal and business reputations did not constitute a deprivation of liberty interests *because the defendants' defamatory statements did not cause the deprivation of plaintiffs' Fourth Amendment rights,* the court asserted: "[T]he defamation need not cause the deprivation of another interest in order for a liberty interest to be implicated."[131]

§4.06 —First Amendment

As with violations of the Fourth Amendment[132] and procedural due process,[133] a plaintiff whose First Amendment rights are violated can recover for actual damages caused, including special damages in the form of out-of-pocket losses and general damages such as emotional distress.[134] Whether or not it is ultimately held that there can be presumed damages for First Amendment violations, although not for procedural due process violations,[135] it is important for a plaintiff's lawyer to introduce evidence of actual damages. As a practical matter, this is usually relatively easy to do where a plaintiff's First Amendment rights are violated by discharge from employment.

The Second Circuit[136] upheld a district court award of $9,000 to a professor whose contract had not been renewed in violation of his First Amendment rights. The $9,000 represented special damages, the difference between what the plaintiff would have received and what he in fact received at the new position he immediately obtained. However, because the plaintiff introduced no medical evidence as to general damages—the only relevant testimony was the plaintiff's to the effect that he was "upset"—the Second Circuit affirmed the district court's refusal to award general damages for emotional distress. It also expressly refused to presume damages. In contrast, the Ninth Circuit[137] affirmed a district court award of $5,000 compensatory damages to a lifeguard

---

[131] Marrero v City of Hialeah, 625 F2d 499, 518 (5th Cir 1980). To the same effect in a First Amendment setting is Anderson v Central Point School Dist, 746 F2d 505 (9th Cir 1984) (per curiam).

[132] *See* §4.04.

[133] *See* §4.05.

[134] Judge Leventhal has stated: "I recognize that an individual plaintiff suing for violation of first amendment rights is not limited to out-of-pocket expenses but may, upon a proper showing, recover for emotional harm." Dellums v Powell, 566 F2d 167, 209-210 (concurring opinion).

[135] In Memphis Community Schools v Stachura, 106 S Ct 2537 (1986), the Court, relying on *Carey v Piphus,* held erroneous an instruction permitting the jury to award damages for the intrinsic value of First Amendment rights. *See generally* §4.02. *But cf* Walje v City of Winchester, 773 F2d 729 (6th Cir 1985) (permitting award of general damages for free speech violations; "the very violation itself causes harm").

[136] Stolberg v Members of Bd of Trustees, 474 F2d 485 (2d Cir 1973).

[137] Donovan v Reinbold, 433 F2d 738 (9th Cir 1970). Defendants were police officers who brought about the firing because of critical newspaper articles the plaintiff wrote about them. *See also* Trudeau v Wyrick, 713 F2d 1360 (8th Cir 1983) where the plaintiff, formerly a lay associate minister with the Catholic Church, successfully sued a warden

who had been fired in violation of his First Amendment rights. Acknowledging that special damages established were not extensive, the court held that damages could be awarded to compensate for emotional and mental distress. The court pointed out that the plaintiff was unusually dedicated to his job, that it meant a lot to him, and that he could not find similar employment in the same general area.

As with other constitutional violations, a plaintiff's compensatory damages award for emotional and mental distress in a First Amendment setting has a far better chance of surviving circuit court review where there is more than the plaintiff's own testimony. Thus, in a Fifth Circuit case, the court affirmed a jury's compensatory damages award of $16,000 against one defendant and $4,750 against another defendant, both of whom had discharged the plaintiff for engaging in political and other First Amendment protected activities. The Fifth Circuit mentioned the following factual support in the record: the publicity surrounding the plaintiff's discharge in the midst of his campaign had cast doubt upon his integrity; the firing had been done in an inflammatory manner; and while plaintiff eventually won the election, "the doubt and resulting mental anguish during the period of indecision would support the compensatory award."[138]

Contrast a Seventh Circuit case, where three plaintiffs, employees of a township, sued the township supervisor alleging that they had been terminated or forced to resign because of their campaign activity on behalf of the defendant's opponent. Each of the plaintiffs obtained a jury verdict for compensatory damages which included $5,000, $2,500, and $2,500, respectively, for emotional and mental distress, as well as larger amounts—$40,000, $12,000, and $17,000, respectively—representing lost earnings and fringe benefits for each plaintiff. Reversing the awards for emotional and mental distress, the Seventh Circuit found there was insufficient evidence of injury to support the awards. One plaintiff testified only that he was "very depressed" on learning of his termination; the second said only that she became "a little despondent and [lacked] motivation"; and the third testified that he didn't work

---

for interfering with his right to send a letter to an inmate, thereby ultimately causing the plaintiff to lose his job through the disclosure of the letter's contents to others. The jury returned a $1 nominal damages award and a $25,000 actual damages award against the warden. Upholding the verdict as not excessive, the Eighth Circuit mentioned the following: the plaintiff never finished his degree program; his later attempt to operate a retail business failed; he was often severely depressed and suffered "considerable emotional anguish, including alienation from his religious faith"; and the plaintiff was even now occasionally suffering emotional pain.

[138] Williams v Board of Regents, 629 F2d 993, 1005 (5th Cir 1980). Cf Brule v Southworth, 611 F2d 406 (1st Cir 1979), where the court affirmed the district court's compensatory damages award of $1,000 against prison officials who were found to have disciplined the plaintiff employees for their exercise of First Amendment rights in, among other things, publicly criticizing the defendant's lock-up policy. After stating that §1983 plaintiffs may recover compensatory damages for mental suffering, the First Circuit noted that the plaintiffs had testified "at some length to the emotional and mental distress which accompanied their suspensions, including such physical manifestations as sleeplessness, nervousness and irritability." 611 F2d at 411.

for six weeks, "was completely humiliated, and [he] stayed close to home." These statements by each plaintiff were not enough to establish injury because "the circumstances here do not approach . . . egregiousness. . . ."[139]

The relationship between the existence of a First Amendment violation in an employment setting and damages was addressed by the Seventh Circuit in an interesting case where a plaintiff, a city employee who had unsuccessfully run for mayor, sued the mayor and his subordinates for damages for allegedly violating her First Amendment rights. Specifically, she alleged that upon her return to work she was subjected to a campaign of petty harassment in retaliation for her running for public office. In reversing the district court's dismissal of the plaintiff's harassment claim, the Seventh Circuit stated:

> [E]ven in the field of constitutional torts *de minimis non curat lex*. Section 1983 is a tort statute. A tort to be actionable requires injury. It would trivialize the First Amendment to hold that harassment for exercising the right of free speech was always actionable no matter how unlikely to deter a person of ordinary firmness for that exercise—that if [defendant] had frowned at [plaintiff] for running for public office he would be liable for damages (unprovable, of course) under section 1983. . . , However, more is alleged here—an entire campaign of harassment which though trivial in detail may have been substantial in gross.[140]

Even where a plaintiff after wrongful discharge immediately obtains an equivalent job at the same or better pay and introduces no evidence of general damages, some special damages may still be recoverable. In a Tenth Circuit decision,[141] a teacher discharged in clear violation of his First Amendment rights was permitted to recover $4,100 in compensatory damages, an amount representing the costs of moving to his new teaching position. However, where no special or general damages of any kind are proved, then only nominal damages can be awarded.[142]

In prison situations it is often as difficult for an inmate to show special damages for First Amendment violations as it is in cases of procedural due process violations. However, as with procedural due process violations,[143] an inmate can recover compensatory general damages for emotional distress resulting from the violation of First Amendment rights. In a leading Second

---

[139] Nekolny v Painter, 653 F2d 1164, 1172-73 (7th Cir 1981). *See also* Knapp v Whitaker, 757 F2d 827 (7th Cir 1985) (reversing jury's $514,333 compensatory damages award to teacher discharged in violation of First Amendment: only $4,000 in financial loss proved; on remand, district court was to recalculate award to an amount between $200,000 and $400,000 to take account of emotional distress and the loss of the plaintiff's professional reputation).

[140] Bart v Telford, 677 F2d 622, 625 (7th Cir 1982).

[141] Smith v Losee, 485 F2d 334 (10th Cir 1973).

[142] *E.g.*, Berry v Macon County Bd of Educ, 380 F Supp 1244 (MD Ala 1971). This assumes presumed damages are not awardable for First Amendment violations. However, punitive damages may still be awarded. See §§4.08 & 4.12.

[143] *See* §4.05.

Circuit decision,[144] a plaintiff was placed in solitary confinement for over a year for his political beliefs and prison activities. He was in a 6-by-8 foot cell containing only a toilet and wash bowl with cold water, received about 3,000 calories a day, shaved and showered with hot water once a week, and was permitted limited access to reading materials. The district court awarded the plaintiff $25 a day compensatory damages for a total compensatory award of $9,300. The Second Circuit vacated only because the person primarily responsible for the plaintiff's solitary confinement had died shortly after the suit was commenced.

Similarly, in a Seventh Circuit case where an inmate charged that his wrongful transfer from a state farm to a state prison was in retaliation for the inmate's writ writing activity, the court reversed a district court determination that the plaintiff had proved no damages. Referring to "the less desirable circumstances" at the state prison, the court mentioned the plaintiff's relatively spacious room at the state farm, the better meals there, the fact that the plaintiff could move about more freely, and the less tense atmosphere. It concluded: "Admittedly it is difficult to move from these comparisons to a compensatory dollar amount. . . . Other courts have translated a series of conditions into a realistic dollar figure, and the district court should do so on remand."[145]

The harder First Amendment damages cases are those which involve neither the termination of an employment relationship nor confinement. In these other situations the courts in pre-*Carey* cases sometimes seemed to speak of presumed damages, although they did not expressly use that term. For example, a pre-*Carey* Seventh Circuit case[146] involved a wrongful delay in issuing a permit for a political rally, in violation of the plaintiffs' First Amendment rights. Without elaborating, the court simply remanded, saying that the defendants were liable for "damages for the delay in [defendant's] answer to plaintiffs, comprising, specifically, the period beginning with [defendant's] receipt of [plaintiff's] first letter and ending with [defendant's] call to [plaintiff] on July 29."[147] Perhaps the court had in mind special damages, including various out-of-pocket costs incurred by the plaintiffs which resulted from the delay, such as communication and transportation costs and possibly even lodging costs for those who came from elsewhere to participate in the political rally. The court may also have intended to include emotional distress, a kind of general damage, in its statement.

Similar ambiguity arose in an important pre-*Carey* District of Columbia Circuit case[148] in which the plaintiffs, class members, were awarded $7,500 each for the violation of their First Amendment rights by the United States Capitol police chief who wrongfully terminated a peaceful political protest on

---

[144] Sostre v McGinnis, 442 F2d 178 (2d Cir 1971), *cert denied*, 404 US 1049, 405 US 978 (1972).

[145] Buise v Hudkins, 584 F2d 223 (7th Cir 1978).

[146] Slate v McFetridge, 484 F2d 1169 (7th Cir 1973).

[147] *Id* 1177.

[148] Dellums v Powell, 566 F2d 167 (DC Cir 1977).

the steps of the Capitol. The District of Columbia Circuit ultimately vacated this award as "totally out of proportion to any harm that has been suffered," but its extensive discussion of damages for First Amendment violations is significant:

> Basically, what is at stake here is loss of an opportunity to express to Congress one's dissatisfaction with the laws and policies of the United States. Staged demonstrations—capable of attracting national or regional attention in the press and broadcast media—are for better or worse a major vehicle by which those who wish to express dissent can create a forum in which their views may be brought to the attention of a mass audience and, in turn, to the attention of a national legislature. It is facile to suggest that no damage is done when a demonstration is broken up by unlawful arrests simply because one could write an individual letter to a congressman or because the demonstration might be held at another day or time. Few letters to congressmen command a national or regional audience. And often it is the staging and theatrics—if you will, the time, place, and manner of the demonstration—which express the passion and emotion with which a point of view is held. The demonstration, the picket line, and the myriad other forms of protest which abound in our society each offer peculiarly important opportunities in which speakers may at once persuade, accuse, and seek sympathy or political support, all in a manner likely to be noticed. Loss of such an opportunity is surely not insignificant.[149]

It is difficult to know from this passage whether the court spoke of presumed damages—note that the term was never used—or whether, when it spoke later in the opinion of *intangible injuries,* it meant general compensatory damages of the familiar kind. The latter interpretation might derive some support from the concurring opinion of Judge Leventhal who observed that the $7,500 award "might have included damages for mental distress and suffering,"[150] a possibility he found disturbing in a class action.

The Third Circuit, in still another pre-*Carey* case,[151] also spoke of damages for a First Amendment violation without explaining what kind of damages it meant. In that case, an FBI agent obtained the name and address of a 16-year-old high school student who had written a letter to the Socialist Labor Party as part of a course assignment, and investigated her. The district court granted the defendant's motion for summary judgment on the ground that the plaintiff suffered no compensable injury. Reversing, the Third Circuit noted that word of the FBI investigation spread throughout the school, community, and country and that the plaintiff's standing might have been adversely affected. The court here clearly referred to general damages to the plaintiff's

---

[149] *Id* 195-96 (citations omitted).

[150] *Id* 209.

[151] Paton v La Prade, 524 F2d 862 (3d Cir 1975). This is not a §1983 case, but it is still relevant to the damages issue.

reputation. However, it also relied on the affidavits of social scientists as to the following possible kinds of future injury: stigmatization, invasion of privacy, interference with personality development, and interference with freedom of association through the decision of others to shun the plaintiff. Again, it is unclear from the opinion whether all of these must be proved as general compensatory damages or whether any one or more may be presumed.

The argument that compensatory damages for First Amendment violations might be presumed, even after *Carey*, has been set out earlier. However, as there noted, the Fifth and Seventh Circuits rejected this argument.[152] Nevertheless, the Tenth Circuit recently adopted it in *Bell v Little Axe Independent School District*,[153] an extensive and thoughtful opinion involving presumed damages for First Amendment violations in general and for Establishment Clause violations in particular. The court reasoned that First Amendment violations involve interests not directly analogous to dignitary torts, that voting rights with their presumed damages provide the appropriate analogy, and that a similar right of public participation is protected by the First Amendment, including the establishment clause. Hence, according to the Tenth Circuit, actual damages need not be proved in order to recover compensatory damages for First Amendment violations. More recently, however, the Supreme Court may have signaled its disapproval of this approach when it held in *Memphis Community Schools v Stachura*[154] that it was error to instruct a jury that it could award damages for the intrinsic value of First Amendment rights.

§4.07 —Racial Discrimination and Other Constitutional Violations

As with the constitutional violations previously discussed, compensatory damages for racial discrimination, whether §1983 or other civil rights statutes are involved, are not limited to out-of-pocket costs. They may also include emotional distress and humiliation. Where, for example, a district court awarded $100 in compensatory damages to plaintiffs who were refused rental of an available apartment because of their race, the Seventh Circuit remanded on the ground the award was inadequate to compensate the plaintiffs for general damages suffered.[155] Emphasizing such general damages, the Seventh Circuit in another case[156] upheld a district court award of $500 compensatory damages for racial discrimination in housing. The court said: "We conclude

---

152 *See* §4.02. This argument was also made in the First Edition. *But see* Crawford v Garnier, 719 F2d 1317 (7th Cir 1983); Basiardanes v City of Galveston, 682 F2d 1203 (5th Cir 1982).

153 766 F2d 1391 (10th Cir 1985). Judge Barrett dissented on this issue.

154 106 S Ct 2537 (1986), discussed at §4.02. *But cf* Walje v City of Winchester, 773 F2d 729 (6th Cir 1985) (permitting general damages awards for free speech violations; "the very violation itself causes harm").

155 Jeanty v McKey & Poague, Inc., 496 F2d 1119 (7th Cir 1974) (Title VII case).

156 Seaton v Sky Realty Co, 491 F2d 634 (7th Cir 1974) (42 USC §1982 case).

. . . that an award of compensatory damages . . . is appropriate for humiliation caused by the type of violations of rights established here. Humiliation can be inferred from the circumstances as well as established by the testimony. [Plaintiffs were] subjected to a racial indignity. . . ."[157]

Similarly, in a rather unusual case involving a county judge accused of conducting a racially motivated campaign both on and off the bench to discredit a former city police lieutenant, the Seventh Circuit affirmed a jury's compensatory damages award of $60,000. There was evidence showing that the plaintiff was injured "with respect to his reputation in the community, reputation and working ability within the police department, and opportunities for advancement within that department . . . [and that defendant's acts] caused the plaintiff humiliation, embarrassment and mental distress and interfered with his continued employment."[158]

Despite the willingness of courts to permit and even encourage general damages awards in cases involving racial discrimination, the plaintiff who can show special damages is obviously still better off. The Eighth Circuit,[159] for example, held that schoolteachers who were discharged for racially discriminatory reasons could be awarded damages for expenses incurred in seeking other employment and for lost earnings from and after the date of discharge. The court also indicated that the burden was "on the defendant school board to show what the teachers, through reasonable efforts, could have earned to mitigate their damages."[160] In a class action racial discrimination in employment case, the Fifth Circuit[161] held that members of the class discriminated against could recover back pay. The defendant had the burden of proving that a member of the class would not have been hired even in the absence of racial discrimination. If the defendant could not meet this burden, class members were entitled to back pay from the date they would have been hired either to the date they were offered employment or to the date they would have been terminated had they been hired.

The relationship between special damages and general damages in racial discrimination cases is demonstrated by two Ninth Circuit cases. In one,[162] involving a suit brought under 42 USC §1982 alleging racial discrimination in the defendant's refusal to rent office space to the black plaintiffs, the Ninth Circuit affirmed as not excessive a magistrate's compensatory damages award

---

[157] 491 F2d at 636.

[158] Harris v Harvey, 605 F2d 330, 336 (7th Cir 1979). *But cf* Bunn v Central Realty, 592 F2d 891 (5th Cir 1979) (per curiam) (affirming $500 compensatory damages award in housing discrimination case; rejecting plaintiff's argument for *inferring* damages).

[159] Jackson v Wheatley School Dist, 464 F2d 411 (8th Cir 1972).

[160] *Id* 413. Cf Williams v Albemarle City Bd of Educ, 508 F2d 1242 (4th Cir 1974) (en banc) which held that a black principal demoted to assistant principal on racial grounds was under no obligation to accept this alternative employment which was of an *inferior* kind. The court affirmed the district award of over $6,700 in compensatory damages.

[161] Mims v Wilson, 514 F2d 106 (5th Cir 1975).

[162] Phiffer v Proud Parratt Motor Hotel, 648 F2d 548 (9th Cir 1980).

of $7,500 to the plaintiff husband and $1,000 to the plaintiff wife. The husband, an insurance agent, had suffered a substantial wage loss as a result of locating his office elsewhere; he would have made more money at the defendant's location. Also, both plaintiffs had suffered emotional distress and humiliation through the racially motivated denial of the office space.

In the other case, in the course of affirming a jury's compensatory damages award of $48,500 against city officials who discriminated on the basis of race or national origin when they delayed the issuance of a liquor license to the two Mexican-American plaintiffs, the Ninth Circuit said:

> The evidence submitted showed that [plaintiffs] lost profits during the period they were without a liquor license, that the incurred additional attorney's fees because of the official protest, and that they suffered emotional distress from the selective protests and the denial of their application. These factors were entirely sufficient to sustain the damage award.[163]

Sometimes injunctive relief removes the basis for compensatory damages. In a Fifth Circuit case[164] involving racial discrimination in the sale of real estate, the court held that there was no loss to compensate the plaintiff for because the property now being sold to him at the original price pursuant to court-ordered specific performance had increased in value. The plaintiff was seeking only $100 in compensatory damages; the lot was worth $600 when the plaintiff made his offer and $1,000 when the case was tried.

In a rather unusual Pennsylvania district court racial discrimination case,[165] the plaintiff, an inmate, was awarded compensatory damages of $461.70 against the superintendent of a state correctional institution. The court computed the exact amount of money lost per day on his prison job—69¢—and multiplied it by the number of days worked. It also added an amount, apparently for general damages, reflecting his inability to buy eyeglasses, dental plates, and law books because of lost income. Finally, the court found that the plaintiff did not fail to mitigate damages by his refusal to accept a job paying only 5¢ more a day than the job on which he was then working.

Damages for racial discrimination may also be awarded to corporations. In a First Circuit case,[166] the plaintiff corporation, engaged in real estate development, sued the defendant water district for its racially discriminatory refusal to include a development within the district and thus to supply the development with water. Although the district court found for the plaintiff, it refused to award compensatory damages because the "plaintiff has effectively passed its losses on to the buyers of its homes." Reversing on that issue, the

---

163 Flores v Pierce, 617 F2d 1386, 1392 (9th Cir 1980).

164 Lee v Southern Home Sites Corp, 429 F2d 290 (5th Cir 1970) (42 USC §1982 case).

165 United States ex rel Motley v Rundle, 340 F Supp 807 (ED Pa 1972).

166 Heritage Homes v Seekonk Water Dist, 648 F2d 761 (1st Cir 1981), reaffd, 670 F2d 1 (1st Cir 1982).

First Circuit held that the plaintiff was entitled to an award of $43,690.44, an amount representing increased water supply costs minus the expense which the plaintiff would have incurred in connecting with the district's water supply. However, the court rejected the plaintiff's argument that compensatory damages should also include "the value attributed to the loss of use of the funds during the period when [plaintiff] was reasonably precluded from selling the property."[167] There was no evidence in the record showing either the appropriate interest rate or the fact that "the appreciation in value of the property over the entire period was less than what interest on the amount invested would have yielded."[168] The First Circuit did, though, allow prejudgment interest on the $43,690.44 award.

Compensatory damages for still other constitutional violations can be obtained in proper cases. Invasions of privacy may give rise to compensatory damages.[169] So, too, may violations of the right of access to the courts.[170] Also, in his concurring opinion in a Second Circuit case,[171] Judge Lumbard indicated that a prosecutor could be held liable for prejudicial pretrial statements to the press interfering with the plaintiff's Sixth Amendment right to a fair trial and could be required to compensate for additional expenses for counsel, travel, and delay in connection with a change of venue or grant of a continuance.

Further, a Pennsylvania district court[172] refused to dismiss the complaint of an inmate who asserted an Eighth Amendment claim against prison officials for their failure to provide medication for his epileptic condition. The plaintiff sought compensatory damages for "severe mental, emotional and physical anguish culminating in the violent epileptic seizure which required emergency medical treatment."[173]

Similarly, in a Fourth Circuit case,[174] the plaintiff inmate class was awarded a total of $210,000 in compensatory damages against the defendant county and various officials for their violation of the Eighth Amendment in connection with overcrowding and other jail conditions. Upholding the jury's verdict, the court noted that the jail was a terrible facility and that many actual and compensable injuries were presented by the plaintiffs at trial. And in a case where a deceased prisoner's parents claimed that jail officials violated the decedent's Eighth Amendment rights by displaying callous indifference to the prisoner's medical needs, thereby causing death, the Fifth Circuit upheld a jury's compensatory

---

[167] *Id* 763.

[168] *Id* 764.

[169] *E.g.,* Caperci v Huntoon, 397 F2d 799 (1st Cir), *cert denied,* 393 US 940 (1968).

[170] Ryland v Shapiro, 708 F2d 967 (5th Cir 1983).

[171] Martin v Merola, 532 F2d 191 (2d Cir 1976). See, however, the discussion of absolute prosecutorial immunity under §1983 at **§7.13.**

[172] Mitchell v Chester County Farms Prison, 426 F Supp 271 (ED Pa 1976).

[173] *Id* 273.

[174] McElveen v County of Prince William, 725 F2d 954 (4th Cir 1984). *See also* Maxwell v Mason, 668 F2d 361 (8th Cir 1981); Robinson v Moreland, 655 F2d 887 (8th Cir 1981); Mary & Crystal v Ramsden, 635 F2d 590 (7th Cir 1980); Chapman v Pickett, 586 F2d 22 (7th Cir 1978).

award of $70,000. It observed that the defendants introduced no expert medical evidence to support their contention that the decedent would not have lived long enough to earn much. The court also stated that "the jury instruction correctly did not limit the damages to compensation for lost wages. Plaintiffs presented evidence showing the personal loss to [decedent's] father, mother, and children. We cannot say $70,000 is too high."[175]

Putting the matter of compensatory damages for sex discrimination into proper perspective, the Tenth Circuit rejected the defendant's argument that a compensatory damages award of $2,117.40 was excessive with the following: "[I]n this day and age an award of compensatory damages in [this] amount in an employment sex discrimination case . . . is almost impervious to a charge of excessiveness."[176]

§4.08 Punitive Damages—*Smith v Wade*

Soon after §1983 actions for damages became more common, it was generally agreed in the circuits, even before *Smith v Wade*,[177] that punitive damages, as distinct from damages which compensate, could be awarded. In fact, a leading Third Circuit case, *Basista v Weir*,[178] held in reliance on 42 USC §1988 that punitive damages could even be awarded in the absence of actual damage. This, too, became the general rule.[179] Also, the Supreme Court in *Carey v Piphus* indicated that punitive damages could "be awarded in a proper case under section 1983 with the specific purpose of deterring or punishing violations of constitutional rights."[180] The Third Circuit in another pre-*Wade* decision suggested that "punitive damages as a deterrent may be more significant than ever today, in view of the apparent trend of [Supreme Court] decisions curtailing the power of federal courts to impose equitable remedies to

---

[175] Fielder v Bosshard, 590 F2d 105, 111 (5th Cir 1979).

[176] Wilson v Oklahoma, 726 F2d 636 (10th Cir 1984) (Title VII case).

[177] 461 US 30 (1983), discussed later in this section.

[178] 340 F2d 74 (3d Cir 1965).

[179] *E.g.*, Guzman v Western State Bank, 540 F2d 948 (8th Cir 1976); Silver v Cormier, 529 F2d 161 (10th Cir 1976); Spence v Staras, 507 F2d 554 (7th Cir 1974); Gill v Manuel, 488 F2d 799 (9th Cir 1973); Stolberg v Members of Bd of Trustees, 474 F2d 485 (2d Cir 1973); Caperci v Huntoon, 397 F2d 799 (1st Cir), *cert denied,* 393 US 940 (1968); Mansell v Saunders, 372 F2d 573 (5th Cir 1967).

This general rule was reaffirmed by the Fifth Circuit in McCulloch v Glasgow, 620 F2d 47, 51 (5th Cir 1980) which stated: "Punitive damages may also be awarded in a §1983 action even without actual loss, despite local law to the contrary." To the same effect is Stickney v Smith, 693 F2d 563, 564 (5th Cir 1982), where the court asserted "[T]he failure of proof of compensatory damages does not necessarily preclude an award of punitive damages. . . ." *See also* Glover v Alabama Dept of Corrections, 734 F2d 691, 694 (11th Cir 1984) (affirming jury verdict of $1 in compensatory damages and $25,000 in punitive damages where the defendant official was found responsible for having encouraged another inmate to stab the plaintiff inmate).

[180] 435 US 247, 257 n 11 (1978).

terminate such violations."[181] Finally, in *Smith v Wade*[182] the Court dealt with both entitlement to punitive damages against individuals and related state of mind requirements. Significantly, though, the Court held at the same time that punitive damages may not be awarded against local governments.[183]

In *Wade*, the Court held that punitive damages may be awarded by the factfinder against an individual in §1983 cases even where his or her conduct is not motivated by malice or evil intent; recklessness or callous indifference to a plaintiff's federally protected rights is sufficient. *Wade* involved an inmate who, after earlier placing himself in protective custody, was harassed, beaten, and sexually abused by his cellmates when they were put together in administrative segregation. He sued several prison guards, alleging that his Eighth Amendment rights were violated in that the defendants either knew or should have known that he was likely to be assaulted by these cellmates. The plaintiff received a $25,000 compensatory damages award and a $5,000 punitive damages award against one of the guards. The jury had been instructed that punitive damages can be awarded for conduct that shows "a reckless or callous disregard of, or indifference to, the rights or safety of others." The district court entered judgment on the verdict and the Eighth Circuit affirmed. Upon review by the Supreme Court, where the only issue was the award of punitive damages, the Court affirmed in an opinion by Justice Brennan.

The Court first asserted that punitive damages are appropriate in certain §1983 cases. Then, after extensively canvassing nineteenth and twentieth century standards for awarding punitive damages, it concluded that malicious intent is not the proper standard either for tort cases or for §1983 cases; reckless indifference, callous disregard, or even gross negligence is appropriate. Furthermore, a recklessness standard is not too vague in §1983 cases; even if there is some inevitable vagueness, it is ameliorated by the standard of liability for compensatory damages to which officials look in the first place.

Finally, the Court rejected the defendant's argument that, at least where an Eighth Amendment violation is proved with its requirement of deliberate indifference or callous disregard for liability for compensatary damages, the standard of liability for punitive damages should be higher. In response, the Court observed that unlike compensatory damages, punitive damages are not awarded as of right but only when a defendant's conduct merits such an award. Thus, there are in fact different standards for compensatory and punitive damages awards. In addition, there is no general common law rule that the standards for punitive damages must always be higher than those for compensatory damages.

Justice Rehnquist, joined by Chief Justice Burger and Justice Powell, dissented at length with an extensive historical discussion of punitive damages

---

[181] Cochetti v Desmond, 572 F2d 102, 105-06 (3d Cir 1978). On this trend, *see generally* **ch 5.**

[182] 461 US 30 (1983).

[183] City of Newport v Fact Concerts, 453 US 247 (1981), discussed at **§6.19.**

in general and §1983 in particular.[184] They disagreed with each of the majority's points. They not only argued that malicious intent is required for punitive damages in §1983 cases but even questioned whether Congress, in enacting §1983, intended that punitive damages be permitted at all. Justice O'Connor dissented separately on the ground that policy considerations, not ambiguous historical ones, dictate that malicious intent is necessary for an award of §1983 punitive damages.[185]

Wade's result is sound. It would have been anomalous had the rule for §1983 punitive damages been narrower than that for common law torts. Justice O'Connor was correct that §1983 policy ought to be determinative, but her conclusion on the merits is questionable. There is no persuasive policy reason for §1983 punitive damages to be more restrictive than the common law rule. To the contrary, the regulation of conduct function of §1983 might even cut in favor of a broader punitive damages rule.

After *Wade*, whenever a plaintiff makes out a prima facie case with regard to certain constitutional violations requiring at least recklessness or callous indifference, that plaintiff should (assuming the defendant fails the qualified immunity test) be entitled to a jury instruction on punitive damages. Examples include Eighth Amendment claims which by definition require deliberate indifference,[186] racial discrimination cases which require purposeful discrimination for equal protection violations,[187] and police excessive use of force cases.[188] However, there may be other situations where rather subtle definitional questions arise regarding the meaning of *Wade*'s *recklessness* terminology. In *Soderbeck v Burnett County*,[189] a recent Seventh Circuit case, the plaintiff claimed she was fired from her job in a sheriff's office in violation of the First Amendment. The district court entered judgment based on the jury's compensatory damages award against various individual and governmental defendants. However, the district court went on to hold that the punitive damages award against the defendant sheriff was improper because, although the punitive damages instruction properly spoke of *recklessness* (without, however, defining it), the evidence did not support the jury's apparent finding of recklessness. Affirming on this issue, the Seventh Circuit undertook an elaborate analysis of the term recklessness and concluded that *to be liable for punitive damages a defendant must at least have known that he or she was violating the plaintiff's legal rights.*

According to the Seventh Circuit, *deliberate* harm is the desire to hurt someone, while *reckless* harm is "knowing that hurting someone is the likely

---

[184] 461 US at 56.
[185] *Id* 92.
[186] Estelle v Gamble, 429 US 97, 104 (1976). *See* §3.07.
[187] Washington v Davis, 426 US 229 (1976). *See* §3.14.
[188] *See* §3.14.
[189] 752 F2d 285 (7th Cir 1985).

consequence of an act undertaken for a different end."[190] The latter requires knowledge of the danger that the defendant's act creates, "which in this case is a danger of depriving a public employee of her freedom of speech; and the knowledge of this danger presupposes some knowledge of the free speech rights of public employees."[191] The court found support for this interpretation by asserting that the deterrent effect of punitive damages will work only where a defendant knows "that the conduct which resulted in the injury to the plaintiff was forbidden."[192] In short, "a condition of awarding punitive damages [is] that the defendant almost certainly knew that what he was doing was wrongful and subject to punishment."[193] In the case before it, because the plaintiff did not show that the defendant knew he was violating her First Amendment rights, the defendant was not liable for punitive damages.

The Seventh Circuit's arcane discussion of recklessness is seriously questionable. First, despite the court's disclaimer, it seems to impose a specific intent requirement for punitive damages liability which depends on the defendant's actual knowledge that he or she was violating the plaintiff's constitutional rights. Second, where the defendant has such knowledge, it is inaccurate to call the conduct *reckless:* rather, such conduct is better characterized as intentional in the tort sense of knowledge with substantial certainty that a particular result—here, a plaintiff's constitutional deprivations—will occur.[194] Third, the court avoids discussing another possible kind of recklessness: where a defendant knows that he or she does *not* know the constitutionality of the proposed conduct, but proceeds to act regardless.[195] Indeed, this may well describe the defendant's conduct in the case before the Seventh Circuit. Fourth, imposing punitive damages liability even when the defendant did not know that he was acting unconstitutionally may still have a beneficial deterrent effect: the defendant and *others similarly situated* will have a considerable incentive to learn what the law is. Otherwise, *reckless* ignorance will not be discouraged.

Thus, the Seventh Circuit's actual knowledge requirement for recklessness is wrong both in the tort sense and, more important, for §1983 punitive damages purposes. Note, though, that the court at least hedged somewhat in suggesting that a plaintiff can show such knowledge by the circumstances surrounding the conduct. This apparently means that a defendant's mere statement that he or she did not know is not determinative for punitive damages purposes even in the Seventh Circuit. Also, the court stated that a defendant need not have known that his or her conduct violated federal rights. It is enough

---

[190] *Id* 290.

[191] *Id.*

[192] *Id.*

[193] *Id* 291.

[194] Restatement (Second) of Torts §8A(1965). The other sense is the purpose to bring about the particular result. Both states of mind can give rise to intentional tort liability.

[195] Derry v Peek 14 AC 337 (1889), a law school favorite. *See* W. Prosser & W. Keaton, Law of Torts 740-42 (5th ed 1984).

for punitive damages liability that the defendant knew that his or her conduct violated "some law" of any "sovereign."

A much-quoted portion of the pre-*Wade* Fifth Circuit decision in *Lee v Southern Home Sites Corp,*[196] which is still good law after *Wade,* sets out several factors which relate to §1983 punitive damages awards and judicial control of such awards:

> The general rule as to punitive damages, repeatedly found in the reported cases, is that they may be imposed if a defendant has acted wilfully and in gross disregard for the rights of the complaining party. Since such damages are punitory and are assessed as an example and warning to others, they are not a favorite in law and are to be allowed only with caution and within narrow limits.
>
> The allowance of such damages inherently involves an evaluation of the nature of the conduct in question, the wisdom of some form of pecuniary punishment, and the advisability of a deterrent. Therefore, the infliction of such damages, and the amount thereof when inflicted, are of necessity within the discretion of the trier of the fact.[197]

§4.09   —General Principles

A pattern or long-standing practice of constitutional violations is not ordinarily necessary for an award of punitive damages,[198] although in prison cases some courts have occasionally insisted on it because of a concern that otherwise no deterrent purpose would be served.[199] Even before *Wade,*[200] malice in the sense of "personal animosity or involvement between the parties"[201] was not required for punitive damages. As Justice Brennan indicated in a pre-*Wade* case,[202] punitive damages should be recoverable from a defendant who acted either with knowledge of violating a constitutional right or with reckless disregard of whether he or she was doing so. Moreover, that police officers acted like gentlemen in the course of violating a plaintiff's Fourth Amendment and privacy rights did not insulate them from punitive damages

---

[196] Lee v Southern Home Sites Corp, 429 F2d 290 (5th Cir 1970).

[197] *Id* 294 (citations omitted). *See also* Creamer v Porter, 754 F2d 1311 (5th Cir 1985) (following *Lee* and emphasizing the need to punish and to deter others in the future).

[198] Fountila v Carter, 571 F2d 487 (9th Cir 1978).

[199] Mitchell v Chester County Farms Prison, 426 F Supp 271 (ED Pa 1976); Sostre v McGinnis, 442 F2d 178 (2d Cir 1971), *cert denied,* 404 US 1049 *and* 405 US 978 (1972).

[200] Smith v Wade, 461 US 30 (1983).

[201] Gill v Manuel, 488 F2d 799 (9th Cir 1973).

[202] Adickes v Kress, 398 US 144 (1970) (concurring in part and dissenting in part). Note that Justice Brennan wrote the *Wade* majority opinion, taking the same position as he did in *Adickes* over a decade earlier.

in a First Circuit case.[203] Police officers who unnecessarily use deadly force and cause serious injury are particularly subject to assessment of punitive damages, especially where they shoot at close range or shoot a fleeing misdemeanant.[204] On the other hand, courts have occasionally expressed concern with the effect of punitive damages on the willingness of persons to be school board members. In a Second Circuit case[205] this was a relevant factor in the court's decision to affirm the district court's refusal to award punitive damages for a First Amendment violation.

The plaintiff has the burdens of pleading and proving an entitlement to punitive damages, and a claim for punitive damages must be timely.[206] A party must except to an instruction on punitive damages; otherwise any objection will be deemed waived.[207] An extensive instruction on punitive damages which did not contain any statement about their purposes was held to be erroneous, warranting a retrial on the issue of punitive damages.[208] It is even possible for erroneous instructions on punitive damages to affect the jury's verdict on the merits. In a Ninth Circuit case[209] where the jury rendered a verdict for the defendant police officers accused of various Fourth Amendment violations, the court remanded for a new trial, directing the district court to instruct the jury on punitive damages. The Ninth Circuit concluded that the district court's repeated emphasis to the jury that punitive damages could not be awarded prejudiced the plaintiff. Because these statements of the district court apparently reflected its view on liability, they could have affected the jury's finding on liability in the first place.

The circuits use different terms to describe the appropriate standard for appellate review of punitive damages awards. The Second Circuit described the applicable standard as the same used for appellate review of compensatory awards: "whether the award is so high as to shock the judicial conscience and constitute a denial of justice."[210] The Seventh Circuit used "aggravating circumstances."[211] The Ninth Circuit added "grossly excessive" and "mon-

---

[203] Caperci v Huntoon, 397 F2d 799 (1st Cir), *cert denied*, 393 US 940 (1968).

[204] Stengel v Belcher, 522 F2d 438 (6th Cir 1975); Palmer v Hall, 517 F2d 705 (5th Cir 1975).

[205] Stolberg v Members of Bd of Trustees, 474 F2d 485 (2d Cir 1973).

[206] Knapp v Whitaker, 757 F2d 827, 849 (7th Cir 1985) (affirming district court's refusal to allow the plaintiff to amend complaint to include punitive damages claim: "The inclusion of a punitive damage claim, well after entry of the final pretrial order, would have forced the parties to reopen discovery and obtain independent counsel to represent their individual interests on the issue of noninsured punitive damages").

[207] Basista v Weir, 340 F2d 74 (3d Cir 1965). *See also* Spanish Action Comm v City of Chicago, 766 F2d 315 (7th Cir 1975) (failure to object to instruction and to special verdict question at trial constituted waiver; plain error rule rejected in this case).

[208] Fountila v Carter, 571 F2d 487 (9th Cir 1978).

[209] Gill v Manuel, 488 F2d 799 (9th Cir 1973).

[210] Zarcone v Perry, 572 F2d 52, 56-57 (2d Cir 1978).

[211] Bell v City of Milwaukee, 746 F2d 1205, 1241 (7th Cir 1984).

strous."[212] Whatever characterization is used, it is clear that the standard is sufficiently flexible so that, particularly where substantial punitive damages are awarded, a reviewing court in effect can do what it wants. Thus, a plaintiff's lawyer should focus on those aspects of the case that tend to support a substantial punitive damages award. Conversely, a defendant's lawyer should emphasize, among other things, fairness to the defendant and the windfall to the plaintiff if the award is upheld.

Thus, for example, the Eighth Circuit[213] was confronted with a $25,000 punitive damages award against the bank responsible for an ex parte attachment of the plaintiffs' mobile home and car. After acknowledging that punitive damages were appropriate in light of the bank's conduct, it reduced the award to $10,000, saying only that $25,000 was "excessive."[214]

Similarly, the Ninth Circuit[215] was clearly troubled by a $5,000 punitive damages award for racial discrimination in housing. Saying that the award seemed excessive, the court noted:

> No pattern or practice of discrimination by [defendant], a woman well advanced in age, was demonstrated, but rather only a single, isolated incident. No evidence concerning [defendant's] wealth or lack thereof— an important factor for the jury to consider in awarding damages designed to punish—was introduced, save for the fact that she owned a single piece of real property worth approximately $59,000.[216]

The court went on to explain that it would ordinarily have felt constrained to uphold the award as not excessive, but was still able to vacate it on two grounds. First, there was a substantial disparity between the $1 award for actual damages and the $5,000 punitive damages award which was "consonant with our anxious concern that the verdict may have been reached in an improvident manner."[217] And second, the jury was not properly instructed about the purposes of punitive damages.

Where three law enforcement officers were successfully sued for a conspiracy to cover up the wrongful shooting death of a decedent, the Seventh Circuit[218] affirmed a $25,000 punitive damages award against one of them, but reduced a $350,000 punitive damages award against the second to $50,000 and

---

[212] Fountila v Carter, 571 F2d 487 (9th Cir 1978).

[213] Guzman v Western State Bank, 540 F2d 948 (8th Cir 1976).

[214] According to the court, the bank breached its duty to the plaintiffs; it gained their confidence and then conspired against them; it seized their mobile home in the dead of winter; it seized their car which was necessary for their jobs; its verified summons and complaint were false; and it refused to give the plaintiffs additional time to pay their overdue balance once the attachment was obtained.

[215] Fountila v Carter, 571 F2d 487 (9th Cir 1978).

[216] *Id* 492.

[217] *Id.*

[218] Bell v City of Milwaukee, 746 F2d 1205, 1266-68 (7th Cir 1984). *See also* Hollins v Powell, 773 F2d 191 (8th Cir 1985) (reducing $500,000 punitive damages award against mayor to $2,000; mayor had lost his job and was in financial difficulty).

eliminated entirely an $150,000 punitive damages award against the third. The first defendant acted deceitfully and egregiously. Even though the *Wade* standard was similarly met as to the second, punitive damages should not constitute a windfall, especially where the plaintiffs were also awarded substantial compensatory damages well in excess of $500,000 in total. Thus, a $50,000 award as to the second would fulfill the punitive damage policies of punishment and deterrence. However, the third defendant should not be liable for punitive damages at all. He was already liable for substantial compensatory damages. Also, his conduct did not merit punitive damages "retribution" in part because he was never advised fully of the course of the investigation into the decedent's death.

This is not to suggest, however, that substantial punitive damage awards always face an uphill struggle on review. Rejecting the contention that the "historic range of punitive damages awards in civil rights actions is only $500 - $2,500,"[219] the Second Circuit affirmed a jury's punitive damages award of $60,000 to a vendor after he was severely mistreated by a judge. In that case, the defendant judge, unhappy with the cup of coffee purchased from the vendor, ordered the plaintiff handcuffed, had him marched through the courthouse in full view of others, and finally conducted a "pseudo-official inquisition" in chambers. The plaintiff was screamed at, threatened, and thoroughly frightened. The Second Circuit justified the award as a deterrent for others even though the defendant judge himself was eventually removed from office because of this conduct. It also concluded that the award did not shock the judicial conscience and was therefore not excessive because of the judge's position and his responsibility and power in relation to the plaintiff. Finally, the court rejected the judge's contention that the award was improper because of lack of proof of his net worth. It pointed out that the defendant introduced no proof of his net worth, and characterized the burden to show modest means as a basis for minimizing punitive damages as placed on defendant.

The relationship between joint and several liability and punitive damages arose in an important Second Circuit case where a jury's punitive damages award of $200,000 against four police officers *jointly* was overturned by the Second Circuit on the ground that the jury should have assessed punitive damages *individually*. The officers had allegedly violated the plaintiff's decedent's constitutional rights in attempting an arrest which resulted in the decedent's death. Following what it called the Supreme Court's *analytical approach* in *Smith v Wade*, the court reasoned that as a matter of federal law the "function of punitive damages in section 1983 suits points forcefully toward assessing individually each defendant's liability for such damages and determining an appropriate amount."[220] It also relied on the common law majority rule favoring individual assessment of punitive damages. Alternatively, the

---

[219] Zarcone v Perry, 572 F2d 52, 54 (2d Cir 1978). See §§7.06-7.09 on absolute judicial immunity.

[220] McFadden v Sanchez, 710 F2d 907, 913 (2d Cir 1983). *See also* §4.03 on joint and several liability for compensatory damages.

Second Circuit noted that even if state law were to apply because of 42 USC §1988,[221] the applicable common law of New York similarly favored individual punitive damages assessment. The court also ruled that a New York statute preventing the survival of punitive damages claims was not applicable to this case where the defendants' conduct caused the decedent's death, because to apply such a state law here would be inconsistent with federal law within the meaning of §1988.

On this last point, the Seventh Circuit[222] reached a similar result regarding a suit by a decedent's estate against police officers and others for the wrongful use of deadly force against him, which killed him. Under Wisconsin law a victim's estate could not recover punitive damages. Ruling that the Wisconsin statute was inconsistent with federal policy, the court stated: "To disallow punitive damages in section 1983 actions solely on the basis of restrictive state tort law would seriously hamper the deterrence effect of section 1983."[223] Note, however, that this punitive damages limitation issue arises only where §1983 is deficient because it does not deal with the matter. Where §1983 is not deficient because there is in fact a §1983 rule (such as the punitive damages rule of *Smith v Wade*), inconsistent state law is irrelevant.

§4.10 —Unlawful Searches, Seizures, Arrests, and Confinement

Cases involving the unwarranted use of force, often by police officers, with resulting physical harm generally pose little problem for the plaintiff's lawyer seeking to get the punitive damages question to the jury. For example, the Fifth Circuit[224] upheld a district court award of $15,000 in punitive damages against a police officer who knowingly shot a juvenile in the back, although the juvenile was at most a fleeing misdemeanant. There is, however, no assurance that substantial punitive damages will be awarded by the fact-finder every time physical abuse occurs. Despite the fact that two plaintiffs were killed and the third paralyzed, a Sixth Circuit decision[225] upheld a jury's punitive damages award of only $1,000 for each of three plaintiffs shot at close range by the defendant police officer while he was off duty. Perhaps the jury was influenced by the very substantial $828,000 total compensatory damages award. Harder to explain is a jury award of no punitive damages in an Eighth Circuit case[226]

---

[221] *See* §§3.19-3.20 & 4.14. This statute requires federal courts to apply state law in civil rights cases where federal statutory law is *deficient* unless that state law is inconsistent with federal policy. Thus, in such cases the threshold question is whether federal statutory law is deficient.

[222] Bell v City of Milwaukee, 746 F2d 1205 (7th Cir 1984).

[223] *Id* 1241. See §§3.19-3.20 for further discussion.

[224] Palmer v Hall, 517 F2d 705 (5th Cir 1975). Compensatory damages of $35,000 were also awarded.

[225] Stengel v Belcher, 522 F2d 438 (6th Cir 1975).

[226] Taken Alive v Litzau, 551 F2d 196 (8th Cir 1977). Compensatory damages of

where the defendant police officer used excessive force in arresting an American Indian woman, and broke her arm.

A district court's refusal to instruct the jury on punitive damages, despite testimony that the defendant police officers beat the plaintiff when he was defenseless and caused serious injury, was found erroneous by the Ninth Circuit.[227] The district court had said that "a mere professional overreaction is not sufficient"[228] to warrant an instruction on punitive damages. The Ninth Circuit went on to state: "An instruction on punitive damages is appropriate when the facts are such that the jury could find the action and conduct of police officers to be wilful and malicious apart from any showing of personal animosity between the parties."[229]

In a more liberal statement from a plaintiff's point of view, the Third Circuit[230] indicated its approval of a jury award of $1,500 in punitive damages in a situation where there actually was personal animosity between the plaintiff and the defendant police officer. The jury could have found that "he vented his ill feeling toward [plaintiff] by subjecting him to a physical beating, to humiliation before his neighbors, and to incarceration, all under color of a policeman's badge."[231]

More recently, the Fifth Circuit[232] affirmed a jury's $15,000 punitive damages award, accompanied by a similar compensatory damages award, against the defendant police officer who used excessive force against the plaintiff while he was in custody. The defendant was six inches taller than the plaintiff and outweighed him by 60 pounds. Also, the defendant hit the plaintiff in the face and knocked him into a brick wall, breaking his tooth and injuring his mouth. There was thus a basis for the jury's punitive damages award; the defendant acted at least recklessly or callously with regard to the plaintiff's rights. In a comparable Sixth Circuit case[233] involving the severe beating and wrongful arrest of a plaintiff by the two defendant police officers, the court upheld a jury's punitive damages award of $25,000 against one defendant and $10,000 against the other. Compensatory damages awarded against both were only $520.

Finally, in a Tenth Circuit case the plaintiff in a police brutality suit tried before a jury obtained a $20,500 compensatory damages award against a police officer, a city, and a county, and also received a $70,000 punitive damages award against only the police officer. The Tenth Circuit affirmed the latter

---

$10,000 were awarded. There was apparently no contention on appeal that punitive damages should have been awarded.

[227] Gill v Manuel, 488 F2d 799 (9th Cir 1973).

[228] *Id* 801.

[229] *Id.*

[230] Basista v Weir, 340 F2d 74 (3d Cir 1965). Compensatory damages were not awarded.

[231] *Id* 80. A new trial was ordered on other grounds, however.

[232] Longoria v Wilson, 730 F2d 300 (5th Cir 1984).

[233] Vetters v Berry, 575 F2d 90 (6th Cir 1978).

award against various challenges. First, the district court had correctly instructed the jury that punitive damages are awarded to punish for extraordinary misconduct and to serve as an example or warning to others. Second, because federal standards govern damages in §1983 actions, whether the punitive damages awarded were excessive was not to be determined by state standards. Rather, the proper federal standard was whether the award was so excessive as to shock the judicial conscience. Applying this standard, the Tenth Circuit found that the shooting of the plaintiff was *oppressive;* it "resulted from an excessive and life-threatening use of force unwarranted by [defendant's] need to defend himself or his partner."[234] Thus, the punitive damages award was not excessive.

A wrongful arrest and confinement can result in an award of substantial punitive damages even where no physical harm results. In a Colorado district court case,[235] a plaintiff was arrested by defendant police officers and confined for 30 to 45 minutes even though he was not suspected of committing any crime. The jury's award of punitive damages was apparently in excess of $2,500, but the district court ordered the plaintiff to remit punitive damages above that amount. It said that $2,500 was still liberal under the circumstances, and indicated that the jury might have been influenced by the defendants' conduct toward two other persons who were arrested with the plaintiff.

In contrast, in a Sixth Circuit case[236] the court affirmed a district court's punitive damages awards for two plaintiffs of $5,000 and $2,500, respectively, against the defendant police officer who, instead of investigating a shooting, engaged in an unconstitutional search and seizure regarding the first plaintiff and wrongfully arrested and detained the second. This conduct was described by the district court as "an unconstitutional orgy of unique proportions." The Sixth Circuit found that the district court could have determined that the defendant's conduct was willful. Also, it was significant that the punitive damages awards were less than the compensatory damages awarded the plaintiffs, the first of whom had received $5,450, and the second, $10,000. According to the Sixth Circuit, the district court had used *considerable restraint* in awarding punitive damages.

However, in a case involving claims of wrongful search, seizure, and incarceration by two plaintiffs (husband and wife) against police officers, the

---

[234] Garrick v City & County of Denver, 652 F2d 969, 972 (10th Cir 1981). *See also* Taliferro v Augle, 757 F2d 157, 162 (7th Cir 1985) (affirming $25,000 punitive damages award against two police officers for wrongful arrest and use of excessive force; award was to be split between them; police brutality "is an exceedingly serious matter and $12,500 is not excessive punishment of a policeman who commits it.") and Clark v Beville, 730 F2d 739 (11th Cir 1984) (affirming jury's $10,000 punitive damages award against police officer for excessive force; $40,000 compensatory damages award also upheld).

[235] Rhoads v Horvat, 270 F Supp 307 (D Colo 1967).

[236] Smith v Heath, 691 F2d 220 (6th Cir 1982).

Seventh Circuit[237] affirmed a district court's judgment nov which struck a total of $23,500 in punitive damages awarded by the jury. While the court found that accompanying compensatory damage awards of $12,500 were supported by the evidence, it concluded as to punitive damages that there was no evidence of aggravating circumstances or malicious intent on the part of the defendants. The court also pointed out that the husband at the time of his arrest was allowed to cross the street, borrow a cigarette, and calm his wife. The wife was allowed to talk to her children through a window during detention. Further, there was no abusive conduct by the police officers.

Even where there is an unwarranted but nonviolent search of a person's premises, punitive damages can be awarded. In a First Circuit case,[238] a plaintiff's premises were searched three different times within a 24-hour period while the plaintiff's wife and daughter were present. The first search exceeded the bounds of the warrant obtained, and the last two were conducted without a warrant or probable cause. In addition, over 200 items were removed from the plaintiff's home. The First Circuit affirmed the jury award of punitive damages (no amount was indicated). It said: "The female plaintiff's concession that defendants 'acted like gentlemen' did not mean that their conduct was not an outrageous invasion of plaintiffs' privacy without color of right and for an improper motive."[239]

A distinction must be drawn for punitive damages purposes between police officers who conduct the unreasonable searches, seizures, and arrests and their superiors. According to the Third Circuit,[240] the latter are liable for punitive damages only where they "ordered or personally participated in the acts, or knew or should have known that the acts were taking place and acquiesced in them."[241] This rule holds, said the court, even where a superior officer might be liable for compensatory damages under the doctrine of respondeat superior.[242]

Such personal involvement was found in a Seventh Circuit case[243] where the court held that the district court erroneously set aside a jury's $1,000 punitive

---

[237] Konczak v Tyrrell, 603 F2d 13 (7th Cir 1979). Cf Creamer v Porter, 754 F2d 1311 (5th Cir 1985) (affirming district court's $1,000 punitive damages award against inadequacy challenge; deference paid to district court which acknowledged that $1,000 was not much money but it could persuade other police officers not to engage in unconstitutional searches; Judge Garwood dissented, arguing that the plaintiff was not entitled to punitive damages at all because the defendant honestly believed he was acting legally: *conscious indifference* standard thus not satisfied).

[238] Caperci v Huntoon, 397 F2d 799 (1st Cir), *cert denied,* 393 US 940 (1968).

[239] *Id* 801.

[240] Fisher v Volz, 496 F2d 333 (3d Cir 1974).

[241] *Id* 349.

[242] The court assumed arguendo that a supervisor's liability could be based on respondeat superior. However, the general rule in the circuits is to the contrary. Also, the Supreme Court's decision in Monell v Department of Social Servs, 436 US 658 (1978) supports the general rule that respondeat superior is *not* applicable in §1983 actions. *See generally* **§3.15.**

[243] Freeman v Franzen, 695 F2d 485 (7th Cir 1982).

damages award against a prison official who participated in the unwarranted beating of the plaintiff prisoner by prison guards. Although the evidence was close, it was adequate to support the award. The defendant had supervised the transfer of all prisoners during the search operation when the plaintiff was restrained; when the defendant arrived, he began to hit the plaintiff while the plaintiff was held by others; and the defendant thereafter allowed the plaintiff's assailants to continue escorting the plaintiff without the defendant's supervision. Also, the defendant's conduct was videotaped.

Punitive damages issues stemming from wrongful searches and seizures can also arise in a prison setting. For example, in a First Circuit case,[244] the court affirmed a jury's punitive damages award of $15,000 against prison officials accused of administering a cancer-producing drug to the plaintiff prisoner. In addition to evidence of actual damages of $60,000, there was sufficient evidence to show that the defendants acted with "reckless indifference" to the plaintiff's constitutional rights. And in a Seventh Circuit case, the plaintiff inmate was awarded $15,000 in punitive damages by a jury in connection with unconstitutional strip searches in prison. Compensatory damages were not awarded. The Seventh Circuit first noted that the jury could have found that the defendant prison guard "intentionally exceeded the permissible scope of the strip search by inserting his finger into [plaintiff's] anus."[245] This was conduct involving even more than reckless or callous indifference to the plaintiff's rights and the district court thus was wrong in ruling that there was no evidentiary basis for the jury's award. However, the award was excessive; in this case an upper limitation should be $6,000, an amount sufficient to deter and punish. The jury may improperly have desired to compensate the plaintiff "for his possible, though not proven, injuries."

§4.11 —Procedural Due Process

Procedural due process violations do not invariably provide a basis for punitive damages awards, perhaps because many such violations may be more technical than gross. Nevertheless, in a proper case substantial punitive damages can be awarded. An Eighth Circuit case[246] involved the wrongful attachment by the defendant bank of the plaintiffs' mobile home and car in violation of their procedural due process rights. The jury awarded the plaintiffs $25,000 in punitive damages against the bank, its president, and vice president. The Eighth Circuit first stated that punitive damages in civil rights actions can be awarded where the defendant "exhibits oppression, malice, gross negligence, wilful or wanton misconduct, or a reckless disregard for the civil rights of the

---

[244] Clark v Taylor, 710 F2d 4 (1st Cir 1983).

[245] McKinley v Trattles, 732 F2d 1320 (7th Cir 1984).

[246] Guzman v Western State Bank, 540 F2d 948 (8th Cir 1976). Compensatory damages awarded were $9,365.

plaintiff.''[247] It then found that an award of punitive damages was appropriate here because: the bank breached its duty to the plaintiffs; it gained their confidence, then conspired against them; their mobile home was seized in the dead of winter; the plaintiffs needed their car for work; the bank's verified summons and complaint were false; and the bank refused to give the plaintiffs additional time to pay the overdue balance after the attachment. Nevertheless, the court concluded, without giving reasons, that the $25,000 award was excessive and reduced it to $10,000.[248]

In a Tenth Circuit case,[249] the plaintiff was awarded $5,500 in punitive damages against an urban renewal official who threatened to withhold legally required payments if the plaintiff sought legal redress on another matter. Upholding the jury award, the court said:

> A jury may properly find that such conduct by a public official manifests a reckless indifference to the property rights of others, ill will, a desire to injure or malice . . . [These are] such aggravating circumstances . . . Recovery of punitive damages has been held to be permitted in actions under section 1983 even in the absence of actual loss.[250]

More recently, in a Third Circuit case,[251] the plaintiff obtained $2,000 punitive damages awards against each of five township commissioners for violating his procedural due process rights in connection with his firing as township director of roads and public property. Upholding the awards, the court first observed that the defendants had not properly preserved their challenge to these awards on appeal. But even if they had, there was sufficient evidence to uphold the awards. The plaintiff's firing occurred immediately without notice. Also, it was found by the jury that he was not fired for budgetary reasons, contrary to the defendants' contention. The jury thus could have found that the defendants acted with ill will and oppressiveness toward the plaintiff for his refusal to cooperate with their plan to reduce municipal services in wards represented by the minority faction.

In a Seventh Circuit case,[252] the court affirmed a district court's punitive damages award of $2,000 against a former mayor found to have ordered the plaintiff police officer's discharge in violation of procedural due process while he was mayor. The award was not clearly erroneous because the defendant had been repeatedly advised that he had no legal authority to order the discharge of the plaintiff. Also, even though the defendant might not be in a position in the future similarly to violate due process:

> [W]e think the district court could have reasonably concluded that an

[247] Id 953.
[248] Id 953, 954.
[249] Silver v Cormier, 529 F2d 161 (10th Cir 1976).
[250] Id 163.
[251] Abraham v Pakarski, 728 F2d 167 (3d Cir 1984).
[252] Busche v Burkee, 649 F2d 509, 520 (7th Cir 1981).

award of punitive damages in this case might deter executive officials in the future from willfully disregarding the legal rights of public employees in situations where such disregard might seem justified (and possibly politically compelled) in the heat of the moment.[253]

In a Tenth Circuit case, a jury's punitive damages awards of $20,000 for a plaintiff's property interest deprivation and $7,500 for the plaintiff's liberty interest deprivation were upheld. The jury could have found that the defendants acted maliciously, wantonly, or oppressively in discharging the plaintiff in violation of due process. Also, "[e]ven though defendants are no longer public officials themselves, the award of punitive damages against them will deter others in such positions of public authority from future disregard of the constitutional rights of others."[254]

On the other hand, in a Seventh Circuit case, the court affirmed the district court's setting aside of a $37,500 punitive damages award against the defendants who were accused by the plaintiff, a former county assessment supervisor, of not reappointing him in violation of the First Amendment and procedural due process. Ultimately finding only a procedural due process violation, the court held that compensatory damages could be awarded but *not* punitive damages. There was, according to the court, "simply no evidence of aggravating circumstances or malicious intent in the initial denial of due process from which a jury could award punitive damages."[255] The court observed that the defendants had consulted their legal advisor, also a defendant, to determine the proper procedures for the plaintiff's first hearing. Also, there was no evidence that the defendant legal advisor maliciously gave faulty legal advice. Further, the defendants adopted appropriate procedures for the plaintiff's second hearing.

§4.12 —First Amendment

As with other constitutional violations, and subject to the same general principles, First Amendment violations may give rise to punitive damages awards.[256] Thus, in an Eighth Circuit case,[257] a chief of police and his assistant

---

[253] *Id* 520.

[254] Miller v City of Mission, 705 F2d 368, 377 (10th Cir 1983). *See also* Simineo v School Dist No 16, 594 F2d 1353 (10th Cir 1979) (affirming jury's punitive damages award of $30,000 against school officials who discharged plaintiff teacher after a sham hearing; compensatory damages of $60,000 were also awarded).

[255] Endicott v Huddleston, 644 F2d 1208, 1217 (7th Cir 1980). *But cf* Merritt v De Los Santos, 721 F2d 598 (7th Cir 1983) (affirming $100 punitive damages award against prison guard's commanding officer; clear violation of administrative regulation and of right to impartial tribunal; deterrent effect on future willful violations).

[256] *See* §4.08. See also Soderbeck v Burnett County, 752 F2d 285 (7th Cir 1985) (affirming denial of punitive damages to plaintiff who was discharged by the defendant sheriff in violation of the First Amendment; court held that actual knowledge of illegality of conduct is necessary for a punitive damages award based on *recklessness*), analyzed critically at §4.08.

were held liable for punitive damages awards of $3,000 and $2,000 respective-ly, even though only nominal damages were otherwise awarded. Defendants in that case improperly evaluated and demoted the plaintiff for his exercise of First Amendment rights with regard to a supposed conversation the plaintiff had with a private attorney investigating civil rights violations directed at city prisoners.

More recent First Amendment punitive damages cases have involved rather substantial awards. Two Fifth Circuit cases provide examples. In one,[258] stating only that there was sufficient supporting evidence in the record, the Fifth Circuit affirmed a jury's $10,000 punitive damages award (together with a $20,000 compensatory damages award) to an officer at a city jail whose transfer and subsequent discharge were prompted by his criticism of his employers, in violation of his First Amendment rights. In the other,[259] the Fifth Circuit affirmed a jury's punitive damage awards of $50,000 against one defendant and $8,000 against another defendant, both of whom had wrongfully discharged the plaintiff from a university's police department in violation of the First Amendment. The court noted that the defendants committed malfeasance when they retaliated against the plaintiff for doing his duty; the plaintiff was subsequently maligned in the press, and defendants relied on a facially inapplicable policy to support their discharge decision. Sufficient evidence therefore existed to support the punitive damage awards.

Similarly, in a Seventh Circuit case, the court affirmed the jury's $23,500 punitive damages award against the defendant who discharged a plaintiff from city employment in violation of the First Amendment. The jury was properly instructed with respect to punitive damages, and the evidence supported the finding that the defendant "acted peremptorily and arbitrarily when he learned of plaintiff's magazine article" with "the purpose of oppressing or suppressing plaintiff's exercise of his first amendment rights."[260]

In contrast, two Fifth Circuit cases demonstrate that a court reviewing a jury's punitive damages award has considerable discretion to overturn it. In one,[261] where the plaintiffs prevailed on their First Amendment claims against the defendant board of education members for the unconstitutional nonrenewal

---

[257] Simpson v Weeks, 570 F2d 240 (8th Cir 1978).

[258] Cofield v City of Atlanta, 648 F2d 986 (5th Cir 1981).

[259] Williams v Board of Regents, 629 F2d 993 (5th Cir 1980).

[260] Crawford v Garnier, 719 F2d 1317, 1325 (7th Cir 1983). In Fact Concerts, Inc v City of Newport, 626 F2d 1060 (1st Cir 1980), revd in part, 453 US 247 (1981)—see §§4.01 & 6.19 on local government immunity from punitive damages liability—the defendant city, mayor, and council members violated the First Amendment right of the plaintiff to promote and produce two jazz concerts by interfering with the plaintiff's plans. The First Circuit affirmed a jury's punitive damage awards based on the First Amendment count and on a pendent state claim count: against the city for $75,000 (after reduction by remittitur); against the mayor for $20,000; against one council member for $20,000; against each of three council members for $10,000; and against each of two council members for $5,000. These awards were accompanied by a compensatory damages award against all defendants for $72,910.

[261] Wells v Hico Indep School Dist, 736 F2d 243 (5th Cir 1984).

of the plaintiffs' contracts, the jury's punitive damages awards against the defendants could not stand. There was absolutely no evidence that the board members acted with malice or callous or reckless disregard for the plaintiffs' rights. Indeed, they had visited one of the plaintiffs in her home to discuss a reading program and allowed her to present her views to them. Allowing punitive damages in this case would not serve the twin goals of deterrence and punishment.

In the other case,[262] where a nonrenewed teacher prevailed on his First Amendment claim, the Fifth Circuit affirmed the district court's grant of the defendant's motion for judgment nov on the issue of punitive damages. Despite the jury's finding that two of the defendants acted with malice, ill will or the specific purpose of violating the plaintiff's First Amendment rights and its consequent punitive damages award of $7,500, the Fifth Circuit asserted:

> Plaintiff's suit involves no class-wide wrong; there was no systematic oppression or a continuous course of harassment . . . [v]iewing the evidence . . . in the light most favorable to plaintiff, we conclude there is simply no evidence of the type of malevolent, outrageous or abusive conduct which justifies more than compensatory damages [here, $17,500].[263]

Other factors can enter into consideration of punitive damages. For example, the Second Circuit[264] affirmed the district court's refusal to award punitive damages to a professor whose contract was wrongfully not renewed by a board of trustees in violation of his First Amendment rights. The court first noted that punitive damages were not necessary to insure protection of the plaintiff's First Amendment rights because the defendants eventually offered the plaintiff a tenured position. It also expressed concern that punitive damages in such a case could discourage persons from serving on boards of trustees.

Punitive damages can also be awarded for First Amendment violations in prison, and there is no sound reason to insist that there must be a pattern or practice of constitutional violations. However, the Second Circuit,[265] in a questionable decision, reversed a $3,270 punitive damages award for this reason where the plaintiff had been placed in solitary confinement for over a year in violation of his First Amendment rights but no pattern of such treatment was shown.

---

[262] Brown v Bullard Indep School Dist, 640 F2d 651, 654 (5th Cir 1981) (per curiam).

[263] *Id* 654.

[264] Stolberg v Members of Bd of Trustees, 474 F2d 485 (2d Cir 1973).

[265] Sostre v McGinnis, 442 F2d 178 (2d Cir 1971), *cert denied,* 404 US 1049, 405 US 978 (1972). *See also* Mitchell v Chester County Farms Prison, 426 F Supp 271 (ED Pa 1976) where a motion to dismiss a claim for punitive damages was denied because the plaintiff alleged that the conduct complained of—the failure to provide medication for his epileptic condition—was part of a constant practice or pattern or behavior.

§4.13 —Racial Discrimination and Other Constitutional Violations

Punitive damage awards in racial discrimination cases were not uncommon, even before *Smith v Wade*,[266] largely because people have known that much racial discrimination is either prohibited by criminal law or made actionable civilly. For punitive damages purposes, the defendant need not have the specific intent to deprive the plaintiff of a federal right; all that is necessary is that the defendant act either with actual knowledge of, or reckless disregard for, the violation of the plaintiff's federal right.[267] It was stated by Justice Brennan well before *Wade* that for a defendant to discriminate on the basis of race in connection with service in a restaurant is to act with reckless disregard for a plaintiff's federal rights as a matter of law.[268]

An example of a substantial punitive damages award in a §1983 racial discrimination setting is a unique Seventh Circuit case[269] in which a county judge engaged in a campaign both on and off the bench to discredit and otherwise injure a black police lieutenant. The Seventh Circuit affirmed a jury's punitive damages award of $200,000; compensatory damages of $60,000 were also awarded. Surprisingly, neither amount was challenged on appeal. The court said:

> While this court might consider the punitive damages awarded to be unduly high, the district court explained in its post-trial opinion that the defendant had not shown that his financial circumstances required a lesser amount of punitive damages and that the court did not find the punitive damages award to be excessive or shocking to the judicial conscience since there had been "a serious abuse of judicial power. . . ." In view of the jury's finding that defendant had acted "maliciously, wantonly or oppressively," we may not disturb its award of punitive damages. However, the trial judge should consider reducing the $200,000 award if defendant can show financial hardship.

Many racial discrimination cases now arise either under recent civil rights acts or 42 USC §§1981 and 1982. Still, the cases are helpful in §1983 situations by analogy. Thus, in a Title VII racial discrimination case where the district court had refused to award punitive damages against a rental management

---

[266] 461 US 30 (1983), discussed at **§4.08,** which held that punitive damages may be awarded against a defendant who acts recklessly with respect to, or with callous disregard for, a plaintiff's constitutional rights.

[267] *Id. See also* Adickes v Kress, 398 US 144, 188, 233 (1970) (opinion by Brennan, J. concurring in part and dissenting in part).

[268] Adickes v Kress, 398 US at 188.

[269] Harris v Harvey, 605 F2d 330, 340-41 (7th Cir 1979). See **§§7.06-7.11** on judicial immunity.

business and the property owners, the Seventh Circuit[270] reversed and remanded for the district court to consider the motive and attitude of the defendants in refusing to rent an apartment to the plaintiff. In another Title VII case, the Ninth Circuit[271] agreed with the jury's verdict that punitive damages should be awarded against an elderly woman who refused to rent her home to the plaintiffs, but found that the award of $5,000 was excessive. It observed that this was a single isolated incident, there was no pattern or practice, the defendant was well advanced in age, and there was a *striking* disparity between the (so-called) actual damages award of $1 and the $5,000 punitive damages award.[272] Ultimately, however, the court relied essentially on erroneous instructions regarding punitive damages and reversed and remanded.

Similarly, in a §1982 case, the Seventh Circuit[273] affirmed a district court award of punitive damages of $1,000 against each of three defendants, real estate brokers, who discriminated on racial grounds. The court characterized as not clearly erroneous the district court's finding "that there was the degree of wilful and wanton disregard of plaintiffs' right not to suffer this sort of discrimination to warrant punitive damages."[274] Not only had the plaintiffs been greatly embarrassed, but they had made numerous trips between a home site and the defendants' offices.

In a Ninth Circuit case involving a racial discrimination suit brought under §1982, the court affirmed a magistrate's punitive damages award (adopted by the district court) of $1,000 for each of the two plaintiffs. Compensatory damages totaling $8,500 were also upheld. The court stated that actual malice is not necessary for punitive damages in racial discrimination cases; wanton conduct is enough. Here, the "defendants' repeated refusal to rent the available office space is sufficient to establish the wanton nature of their conduct when coupled with proof that the space was offered to a white applicant."[275]

Like racial discrimination, sex discrimination can be the basis for an award of punitive damages.[276] For example, the Eighth Circuit[277] upheld a jury's $1,000 punitive damages award against a county judge who had discriminated against the plaintiff because of her sex when he removed her from her position as a juvenile court hearing officer. The defendant's oft-repeated "sexist" comments reflected his bias against the plaintiff and could support a jury

---

[270] Jeanty v Mckey & Poague, Inc, 496 F2d 1119 (7th Cir 1974).

[271] Fountila v Carter, 571 F2d 487 (9th Cir 1978).

[272] *Id* 492.

[273] Seaton v Sky Realty Co, 491 F2d 634 (7th Cir 1974).

[274] *Id* 638.

[275] Phiffer v Proud Parrot Motor Hotel, 648 F2d 548, 553 (9th Cir 1980). *But cf* Bunn v Central Realty, 592 F2d 891 (5th Cir 1979) (per curiam) (refusing in a §1982 case to award punitive damages; no evidence showing that defendant acted either wilfully or in gross disregard of the plaintiff's rights).

[276] Bradshaw v Zoological Socy, 569 F2d 1066 (9th Cir 1978).

[277] Goodwin v Circuit Court, 729 F2d 541 (8th Cir 1984).

finding of intentional or reckless indifference to the plaintiff's right to be free from sex discrimination. The court also rejected the contention that punitive damages could not be awarded in light of the jury's $1 nominal damages award to the plaintiff. The amount of punitive damages did not necessarily depend on actual damages.

Generally speaking, various Bill of Rights violations can be a proper basis for a punitive damages award. The availability of punitive damages is not limited to situations involving violations of equal protection. Sometimes, as with Eighth Amendment violations,[278] the state of mind necessary to establish a prima facie cause of action is intimately related to the issue of punitive damages. That is, when proved, the same state of mind required for a finding of an Eighth Amendment violation[279] may entitle a plaintiff to have the fact-finder consider awarding punitive damages as well as compensatory damages.[280]

Prisoners may also receive punitive damages, even in substantial amounts, in non-Eighth Amendment cases. For example, in a Fifth Circuit case[281] the plaintiff, a misdemeanor arrestee who was brutally beaten and raped by fellow prisoners charged with serious felonies, sued various prison officials for their failure to prevent the occurrences. He obtained a jury's compensatory damages award of $70,000 and punitive damages awards totaling $310,000 ($205,000 in punitive damages against the sheriff and $105,000 in punitive damages against the deputy), all of which were affirmed by the Fifth Circuit. As to punitive damages, the court first noted that the district court's instruction regarding "malicious or wanton or oppressive acts" was consistent with the

---

[278] *E.g.*, Mitchell v Chester County Farms Prison, 426 F Supp 271 (ED Pa 1976). On the relationship between the prima facie §1983 cause of action and the defendant's state of mind, see **ch 3**. Smith v Wade, 461 US 30 (1983), the Court's seminal §1983 punitive damages case, is an Eighth Amendment case.

[279] *See* **§3.07.**

[280] Fielder v Bosshard, 590 F2d 105 (5th Cir 1979) ("no real difference between acting with 'deliberate' or 'callous' indifference and committing acts which are 'substantially certain' to harm a prisoner"). *But see* Layne v Vinzant, 657 F2d 468, 481 (1st Cir 1981), another pre-*Wade* case, where the plaintiff, an inmate, obtained punitive damages awards of $7,500, $7,500, and $15,000, respectively, against three correctional officers accused of "deliberate indifference to a serious medical need" in violation of the Eighth Amendment. Affirming the district court's setting aside of these punitive damages awards on various grounds, the First Circuit approved the district court's punitive damages instruction which distinguished conduct "intentionally malicious, or with reckless disregard [required for punitive damages] . . . from deliberate indifference [required for an Eighth Amendment violation]."
It then stated:

> We agree that the standard for awarding punitive damages is properly higher than the standard governing compensatory damages in this context. We need not specify at this time whether the additional component is properly termed willfulness, outrageousness, or maliciousness. . . . We do not accept the contrary view of the Fifth Circuit in *Fielder v Bosshard*. . . .

Id.

[281] Stokes v Delcambre, 710 F2d 1120, 1126-28 (5th Cir 1983).

Supreme Court's punitive damages standard in *Smith v Wade*. Also, the evidence showed that the defendant sheriff knew he was under a court order, which he did not obey, to separate prisoners according to the nature and type of crime involved; that he had no written rules for operating the jail; that he manned the jail with only one jailor, despite advice to the contrary; that jailors could not easily view the cell in which the plaintiff was beaten; and finally, that the sheriff did not tell the jailors about the rape for several weeks. Further, the evidence showed that the deputy sheriff, seeing the plaintiff bleeding badly, did not even question the assailant and left the plaintiff alone with the assailant after the beating. Moreover, the deputy knew that the plaintiff would be sexually assaulted. The total of $310,000, while "on the high side," was within the range of familiar treble damage schemes and was sustainable on the facts, and the individual awards of $205,000 and $105,000 were not necessarily the result of a quotient verdict.

The existence of a conspiracy which deprives a plaintiff of various constitutional rights may also, not surprisingly, give rise to a substantial punitive damages award. In a Fifth Circuit case,[282] a jury's punitive damages award of $50,000 (accompanied by a compensatory damages award of $17,399) was upheld by the court. The plaintiff police officer, after complaining about the illegal conduct of a fellow officer, proved that a conspiracy was directed against him resulting in his improper discharge in violation of the First Amendment, procedural due process, and equal protection. The Fifth Circuit stated that the punitive damages award, based on a general verdict, was supported by evidence that the defendants acted with deliberate indifference to the plaintiff's constitutional rights. The police department's internal investigative procedures were known to be ineffective in protecting a complaining police officer. Also, certain internal controls tending to assure impartiality were skirted. As to the amount of the award, the jury could reasonably have made the award based upon an evaluation of the defendants' conspiratorial conduct, the wisdom of some form of punishment, and the advisability of a deterrent.

§4.14 Statutes of Limitations—Choice

There is no federal statute of limitations applicable to §1983 causes of action. Consequently, 42 USC §1988[283] requires that because of this *deficiency*, state

---

[282] Thomas v City of New Orleans, 687 F2d 80 (5th Cir 1982).

[283] § 1988 provides in relevant part that jurisdiction of the district courts for the protection of civil rights

> shall be exercised and enforced in conformity with the laws of the United States, so far as such laws are suitable to carry the same into effect; but in all cases where they are not adapted to the object, or are deficient in the provisions necessary to furnish suitable remedies and punish offenses against law, the common law, as modified and changed by the constitution and statutes of the State wherein the court . . . is held, so far as the same is not inconsistent with the Constitution and laws of the United States, shall be extended to and govern the said courts in the trial and disposition of the cause. . . .

law must be applied where it is neither inconsistent with the policies underlying §1983[284] nor discriminatory against federal civil rights actions.[285] This has given rise to considerable complexity. At the outset, it is important to distinguish among choosing the appropriate limitations period, accrual, and tolling. As will be seen, the limitations period and tolling rules are based on the forum state's law, while accrual is governed by federal law.

Choosing the Analogous Limitations Period

Congress, as noted, did not provide a statute of limitations for §1983. As a result, the Supreme Court, interpreting 42 USC §1988, has asserted that *analogous* state limitations periods must be used.[286] The initial inquiry is what is the analogous state statute of limitations? However, the answer to this question until recently was not clear. Where, for example, an employee claims a discharge in violation of the First Amendment, what is the analogous state statute of limitations? Is it a contract statute of limitations,[287] a general tort statute of limitations,[288] or a particular one?[289] Is it the statute of limitations covering statutory causes of action?[290] Or is it a catchall statute of limitations?[291] Is the choice of an analogous limitations period to be governed by federal or state standards? That there were different answers to such questions in the circuits, depending upon the nature of the §1983 claim presented, was unfortunate. A plaintiff and a defendant should know in advance whether they are facing, for example, a two-year statute of limitations or a five-year statute of limitations. At the very least, uniformity and predictability within each state ought to be encouraged: one should *not* have to look at the fact pattern in each §1983 case and then ask what specific state cause of action the §1983 action is closest to *in that case.*

The Supreme Court provided some initial guidance on this question in *Burnett v Grattan.*[292] *Burnett* involved employment discrimination claims brought against officials of a state college in Maryland. Borrowing a six-month limitations period for the filing of employment discrimination complaints with the relevant state administrative body, the district court dismissed the plaintiffs'

---

[284] Occidental Life Ins Co v EEOC, 432 US 355, 370 (1977).

[285] Chambers v Omaha Pub School Dist, 536 F2d 222 (8th Cir 1976).

[286] *E.g.,* Board of Regents v Tomanio, 446 US 478 (1980).

[287] *But see, e.g.,* Movement for Opportunity & Equality v General Motors Corp, 622 F2d 1235 (7th Cir 1980) (rejecting contract limitations).

[288] *E.g.,* Walden III, Inc v Rhode Island, 576 F2d 945 (1st Cir 1978) (preference for general tort limitations).

[289] *E.g.,* Gashgai v Leibowitz, 703 F2d 10 (1st Cir 1983) (defamation limitations period).

[290] *E.g.,* Taylor v Mayone, 626 F2d 247 (2d Cir 1980) (statutory actions limitations period); Beard v Robinson, 563 F2d 331 (7th Cir 1977), *cert denied,* 438 US 907 (1978) (same).

[291] *E.g.,* Garmon v Faust, 668 F2d 400 (8th Cir 1982) (en banc) (state's general statute of limitations).

[292] 104 S Ct 2924 (1984).

claims as time-barred. Reversing, the Fourth Circuit found that the six-month period was inappropriate for civil rights suits because the Maryland law "governed the limitations of administrative proceedings which were informal, investigatory and conciliatory in nature."[293] Instead, the Fourth Circuit applied Maryland's three-year limitations period for all civil actions not otherwise provided for.

The Supreme Court affirmed in an opinion by Justice Marshall. It focused, as the Fourth Circuit had, on the functional differences between the civil rights claims and Maryland administrative law, as well as on the practicalities involved. Civil rights actions belonged in court and required considerable preparation—including obtaining counsel, investigating, and planning for the period beyond the initial filing. In contrast, under Maryland administrative law a complainant had little responsibility after the complaint was filed. Further, Maryland's concerns, as reflected in its six-month limitation period, were "inconsistent with, or of marginal relevance to, the policies informing the Civil Rights Acts" which include compensation and "prevention of the abuse of state power."[294] The Court went on to reject the defendant's argument that Maryland policy dictated that public employee disputes should be promptly asserted and resolved. The civil rights statutes, after all, made no distinctions based on classification of plaintiffs. In this regard, the Maryland policy of protecting state officials from suit was inconsistent with the broad remedial scheme of the civil rights statutes.

Thus, the Court in *Burnett* premised its decision on federal standards.[295] *Burnett* indicated that a state statute of limitations which is general in its remedies and nondiscriminatory as to federal plaintiffs is to be preferred over a limitations period directed at a particular claim or particular parties. To the extent that this approach promoted uniformity and predictability, it was sound. Of equal importance is the fact that *Burnett* sensibly directed that federal

---

[293] *Id* 2927 (quoting Grattan v Burnett, 710 F2d 160, 162 (1983)).

[294] *Id* 2931.

[295] *Id.* Justice Powell concurred in the judgment, stating simply and briefly that the defendants had not persuaded him that the Fourth Circuit erred in rejecting Maryland's six-month limitations period. *Id* 2933. Justice Rehnquist, with whom Chief Justice Burger and Justice O'Connor joined, also concurred in the judgment, but articulated an approach to choosing the appropriate state limitations period very different from that of the majority. *Id.* In their view, the majority was wrong in asking whether state law reflected the practicalities of civil rights litigation and whether it embodied policies analogous to those of the various civil rights statutes. Rather, if a state "legislature has indicated that a particular statute of limitations should apply to a claim, that statute is prima facie the most appropriate statute of limitations to apply to a federal civil rights action," *id* 2935, even if it applies only to a particular class of claims or involves a particular class of parties. In such a situation, the state limitations period must be applied unless it discriminated against the federal claim or did not afford a reasonable time in which to bring the claim. In this case, though, it was unlikely that Maryland intended its six-month limitations period to apply to civil rights actions. Hence, the three justices concurred in the Court's judgment. *But see* Wilson v Garcia, 105 S Ct 1938 (1985), discussed next in the text.

standards must be used in choosing the appropriate limitations period.[296] This means that even when a state legislature has expressly provided a nondiscriminatory limitations period for §1983 actions, its decision will be given deference, but will not be binding.

The result in *Burnett* was a promising step in the right direction. But, the Court's 1985 decision in *Wilson v Garcia*[297] is considerably more significant. Here, the plaintiff, two years and nine months after the events in question, sued a police officer and his supervisor in connection with the officer's alleged use of excessive force while arresting the plaintiff. The New Mexico Supreme Court had held that the two-year limitations period under the state's tort claims act governed §1983 actions.[298] Nevertheless, the district court and the Tenth Circuit, rejecting the state court's decision, ruled that the choice of an analogous limitations period was a matter of *federal law*. The Tenth Circuit went on to hold that every §1983 action was in essence "an action for injury to personal rights,"[299] to be so characterized for limitations purposes. Thus, the appropriate limitations period in New Mexico for §1983 actions was the three-year period applicable to personal injury actions.

The Supreme Court affirmed in an opinion by Justice Stevens, with only Justice O'Connor dissenting. It agreed with the Tenth Circuit's reasoning that such an approach would minimize "uncertainty and time-consuming litigation,"[300] especially since every §1983 claim could be "favorably analogized to more than one of the ancient common-law forms of action, each of which may be governed by a different statute of limitations."[301] Even though this approach would not bring about national uniformity, there would at least be uniformity within each state. This was a result not inconsistent with §1988. Moreover, an analogy to personal injury actions was the most appropriate alternative because §1983 was designed to create a remedy for tort-like misconduct. Using state personal injury limitations periods would also ensure "that the borrowed period of limitations not discriminate against the federal rights remedy."[302]

The Court's decision is to be commended in light of the excessive resources heretofore expended by lawyers, clients, and courts in playing the §1983 limitations guessing game. However, uncertainty remains. Some states may not clearly provide a particular limitations period for "the tort action for the recovery of damages for personal injuries."[303] In such cases there will still be a search, using federal standards, for the most appropriate limitations period.

For example, suppose a state has different limitations periods for intentional

---

[296] This is comparable to the use of federal standards in determining when a §1983 cause of action accrues. *See* the discussion at **§4.15.**

[297] 105 S Ct 1938 (1985), *affg* 731 F2d 640 (10th Cir 1984) (en banc).

[298] De Varges v State, 97 NM 563, 642 P2d 166 (1982).

[299] Garcia v Wilson, 731 F2d at 651.

[300] Wilson v Garcia, 105 S Ct at 1945.

[301] *Id.*

[302] *Id* 1947.

[303] *Id.*

torts and for negligence. The Eleventh Circuit, in a post-*Wilson* case, was confronted with a choice between Alabama's six-year limitations period for actions "for trespass to the person or liberty" and its one-year limitations period for actions for "injury to the person or the rights of another not arising from contract and not specifically enumerated in this section."[304] The court, characterizing the latter as dealing with trespass on the case, reviewed the legislative history of §1983 and, choosing the six-year trespass statute as applicable to a plaintiff's procedural due process claim, asserted: "[M]embers of the 42nd Congress considered direct acts of violence against Black citizens to be the paradigmatic wrong addressed by the new statute."[305] Similarly, the Fifth Circuit,[306] in a First Amendment employment termination case, chose Mississippi's one-year limitations period applicable to actions for assault, battery, and maiming and rejected its six-year residual statute for actions "for which no other period of limitation is prescribed," including negligence and strict liability. Like the Eleventh Circuit, the Fifth Circuit emphasized that the dominant purpose of §1983 was directed at acts of intentional and direct violence. Significantly, the Fifth Circuit rejected the argument that the six-year period was preferable because it was more general in applying to a broader class of actions.[307]

There is also the important question of the retroactive effect of *Wilson*. Clearly, *Wilson* should not be applied retroactively "to bar 'plaintiffs' right to their day in court when their action was timely under the law in effect at the time their suit was commenced.' "[308] However, more difficult retroactivity issues arise when the law was not clear when the suit was filed, or when a lawsuit was not yet filed on April 17, 1985, the day *Wilson* was handed down. The decision in such cases will depend on the three-factor nonretroactivity test set out in the important case of *Chevron Oil Co v Huson:*[309] "First, the decision to be applied nonretroactively must establish a new principle of law. . . . Second, . . . [will] retrospective operation further or retard [the new legal principle's] operation. . . . Finally, [will] retroactive application produce substantial inequitable results. . . ."[310]

Even when an analogous state limitations period is identified under the *Wilson* approach, however, it may still be inapplicable on the ground, noted

---

[304] Jones v Preuit & Mauldin, 763 F2d 1250 (11th Cir 1985).

[305] *Id* 1256.

[306] Gates v Spinks, 54 USLW 2178 (5th Cir Dec 26, 1985).

[307] A contrary approach was taken in Shorters v Chicago, 54 USLW 2178 (ND Ill Sept 6, 1985), where the district court chose an Illinois five-year residual statute instead of a two-year limitations period for direct physical injuries. *See also* §4.17.

[308] Wilson v Garcia, 105 S Ct at 1941-42, n 10 (quoting Jackson v City of Bloomfield, 731 F2d 652, 655 (10th Cir 1984)).

[309] 404 US 97 (1971). *Compare* Winston v Sanders, 53 USLW 2627 (ND Ill 1985) (prospective) *with* Wycoff v Menke, 773 F2d 983 (8th Cir 1985) (retroactive) *and* Rivera v Green, 775 F2d 1381 (9th Cir 1985) (retroactive) *and* Smith v City of Pittsburgh, 764 F2d 188 (3d Cir 1985) (retroactive). *See also* §4.17.

[310] 404 US at 106-07.

earlier, that it is *inconsistent* with federal law within the meaning of §1988. A limitations period is not inconsistent just because the plaintiff loses in a particular case.[311] On the other hand, if a state were to declare that all tort actions are governed by a two-year statute of limitations, but civil rights actions are governed by a six-or a three-month statute of limitations, this would amount to impermissible discrimination against a federal cause of action. The more difficult question is whether, in the absence of such overt discrimination, an unusually short limitations period for all personal injury actions—including §1983 claims—might for the reason of shortness alone be rejected as inconsistent with federal law.[312] If it is determined through the use of federal criteria—by analogy to *Burnett*—that an unusually short limitations period would unduly hamper the vindication of §1983 rights, then that limitations period should be deemed inconsistent with §1983 policy.

§4.15   —Accrual

The Supreme Court has held that accrual is determined by federal law, even though state statutes of limitations are being used. This makes sense because the question of when all of the elements of a §1983 cause of action are present ought to be a question of federal law.[313] The case so holding is *Delaware State College v Ricks*,[314] which involved a college professor who alleged discrimination because of his national origin in connection with his denial of tenure. In February 1973, the faculty tenure committee recommended that the plaintiff not receive tenure, and, upon reconsideration in February 1974, the committee reached the same conclusion. In March 1974, the faculty senate voted in support of this decision and the college board of trustees formally voted to deny tenure that same month. Thereafter, the plaintiff filed a grievance which was still pending when, in June 1974, the board of trustees formally notified the plaintiff that, pursuant to college policy, he would be offered a one-year *terminal* contract expiring in June 1975. The plaintiff signed the contract without objection or reservation in September 1974 and in that same month he was notified that the board of trustees had denied his grievance. The plaintiff ultimately filed his Title VII and §1981 actions in *September 1977* shortly after receiving an EEOC right to sue letter.

The district court dismissed both claims as time-barred under the applicable three-year Delaware statute of limitations. It found that the only unlawful

---

[311] *Cf* Robertson v Wegmann, 436 US 584, 593 (1978) (§1983 action abated by application of state survivorship law).

[312] *See, e.g.*, Knoll v Springfield Township School Dist, 699 F2d 137 (3d Cir 1983), *vacated*, 105 S Ct 1938 (1985) by holding in Wilson v Garcia. *See also* 763 F2d 584 (3d Cir 1985) (same case applying Pennsylvania's two-year limitations period to §1983 actions).

[313] *See* Rawlings v Ray, 312 US 96, 99 (1941) (non-§1983 case involving federal law: "when there [is] a complete and present [federal] cause of action . . . is a federal question and turns upon the applicable federal legislation").

[314] 449 US 250 (1980). Justices Stewart, Brennan, Marshall, and Stevens dissented.

employment discrimination practice alleged was the decision to deny tenure and that the plaintiff's causes of action accrued in June 1974 when the board of trustees formally notified the plaintiff that he would be offered the one-year terminal contract. The Third Circuit reversed. It concluded that the plaintiff's claims did not accrue until his terminal contract expired in June 1975. As a matter of policy, the Third Circuit reasoned, an employee in the plaintiff's position should not be required to consult a lawyer or file charges while still working. Also, employment termination decisions announced in advance are sometimes reversed. Finally, a rule focusing on the last day of employment would provide a bright line guide for courts and victims of discrimination.

The Supreme Court reversed the Third Circuit, rejecting its policy arguments. Instead, the Court emphasized that the sole discriminatory act alleged was the denial by the college of tenure to the plaintiff. The Third Circuit's approach, according to the Court, would improperly render a claim of discriminatory conduct a continuing violation where in fact none existed or was properly alleged in a plaintiff's complaint. In the case before it, the Court concluded, the college had established its official position and made that position apparent to the plaintiff no later than June 1974. Consequently, the plaintiff's causes of action accrued at that time as a matter of federal law, and his complaint filed in September 1977 was time-barred.

Furthermore, according to the Court in *United States v Kubrick*,[315] the appropriate federal accrual rule is the medical malpractice discovery accrual rule. *Kubrick*, a nonconstitutional case, involved the question of when a medical malpractice cause of action accrues under the Federal Tort Claims Act. The Court held that such a cause of action accrues when a patient is aware of an injury and its probable cause despite ignorance of the possibility of negligence. It reasoned:

> We are unconvinced that for statute of limitations purposes a plaintiff's ignorance of his legal rights and his ignorance of the fact of his injury or its cause should receive identical treatment. *That he has been injured in fact may be unknown or unknowable until the injury manifests itself; and the facts about causation may be in control of the putative defendant, unavailable to the plaintiff or at least very difficult to obtain.* The prospect is not so bleak for a plaintiff in possession of the critical facts that he has been hurt and who has inflicted the injury. *He is no longer at the mercy of the latter.* There are others who can tell him if he has been wronged, and he need only ask.[316]

This is also the rule in §1983 cases, and even applies to a plaintiff notified in advance of impending discharge or demotion.[317]

---

[315] 444 US 111 (1979).

[316] *Id* 122 (emphasis added).

[317] Chardon v Fernandez, 454 US 6 (1981); Delaware State College v Ricks, 449 US 250 (1980).

§4.16   —Tolling

Though accrual is governed by federal law, tolling is governed by state law, as set out by the Court in *Board of Regents v Tomanio*,[318] an opinion written by Justice Rehnquist. *Tomanio* dealt with a New York chiropractor whose request for a waiver of a chiropractor's examination was turned down by the board of regents without an evidentiary hearing on November 22, 1971. In January 1972, the plaintiff initiated state court proceedings challenging this waiver refusal as arbitrary and capricious; she did not, however, raise any constitutional challenge in the state proceedings. In November 1975, the New York Court of Appeals affirmed an order of an intermediate appellate court which had ruled against the plaintiff. Then, in June 1976, the plaintiff brought her §1983 action in federal court alleging that the board's refusal to grant the waiver request and give her a license violated due process.

Both the district court and Second Circuit ruled on the merits in the plaintiff's favor after rejecting the defendants' argument that res judicata and the applicable three-year New York statute of limitations barred the plaintiff's action. Res judicata was no bar because the plaintiff had not raised any constitutional challenge to the board's action in state court. Additionally, the three-year statute of limitations was not a bar. While the plaintiff's §1983 claim arose in November 1971 when the request for waiver was denied, the three-year limitations period was tolled during the state court litigation. Her §1983 action filed in June 1976 was not time-barred, because the tolling period ran from January 1972 to November 1975. In this regard both courts used a *federal tolling rule* which the Second Circuit considered justified in the interest of advancing the goals of federalism.

The Supreme Court reversed without reaching either the merits or the res judicata issue. In an opinion by Justice Rehnquist, the Court relied on the language of §1988 and its earlier decisions in *Robertson v Wegmann*[319] and *Johnson v Railway Express Agency*[320] for the principle that the *New York* rule for tolling the three-year statute of limitations—*not* a federal rule—must be applied. The New York rule as interpreted by the Court did not provide for tolling the three-year statute during the pendency of state court proceedings. The Court, applying §1988's *inconsistent* language, also determined that the New York tolling rule was not inconsistent with the §1983 policies of deterrence and compensation, and the general federal policy of uniformity. Furthermore, the Court rejected the related federalism argument that state remedies should be resorted to before the federal courts are utilized. While this approach may be "entirely sound and sensible" a state tolling rule that does not provide for prior resort to state court proceedings is not for that reason alone *inconsistent* with federal policy. After all, the Court observed, a §1983

---

[318] 446 US 478 (1980). That tolling is governed by state law was inferred in the First Edition from Johnson v Railway Express Agency, Inc, 421 US 454 (1975), a leading §1981 case.

[319] 436 US 584 (1978). *See* §3.19.

[320] 421 US 454 (1975).

action may be brought without prior resort to state judicial remedies. Consequently, the Court held that the plaintiff's §1983 action was time-barred by New York's three-year statute of limitations.

Justice Stevens concurred in the result. He argued that a litigant who decides to bring suit first in a state court should not be penalized because "such a decision . . . may obviate entirely any need to present the claim to a federal court."[321] He also suggested that it makes no sense in effect to require a plaintiff to sue in both the state and federal forums simultaneously. Thus, he concluded that the plaintiff's claim was not time-barred. On the merits of the plaintiff's claim, however, he found no due process violation.

Justices Brennan and Marshall dissented. Analogizing the matter to the abstention doctrine[322] and emphasizing §1988's language, they argued that where it is not clear a plaintiff has chosen to present both state and federal claims to a state court, "it [is] inconsistent with federal law and the Constitution to enforce state timing or res judicata rules that close the door of the federal courthouse."[323] They therefore reached the merits and concluded that while due process required some additional procedures, a full adjudicative hearing was not mandated.

Tomanio's reliance on state tolling law has been applied to §1983 class actions as well. In *Chardon v Fumero Soto*,[324] the plaintiffs filed a proposed federal class action against officials of the Puerto Rico Department of Education, alleging that they had been demoted or discharged from administrative positions because of their political affiliation. The proposed class action was filed in June 1978, some weeks before the expiration of the applicable one-year Puerto Rico limitations period. In August 1978, the proposed class action was denied class certification for lack of numerosity pursuant to Federal Rule of Civil Procedure 23. Thereafter, the plaintiffs filed individual §1983 suits in January 1978 and, in cases consolidated for jury trial, prevailed on the merits of their political discrimination charge.

On appeal to the First Circuit, the defendants argued that when the proposed class action was denied certification in August 1978, the Puerto Rico one-year limitation period, having only been *suspended* by the filing of the proposed class action, continued running. Consequently, the plaintiffs were time-barred since they had not filed their individual suits within the few weeks remaining after denial of class certification. The defendants relied for this suspension argument on *American Pipe & Construction Co v Utah*,[325] an antitrust class action case. In response, the plaintiffs argued that pursuant to 42 USC §1988, as interpreted in *Board of Regents v Tomanio*, state tolling law determines the tolling effect upon denial of class certification to a §1983 class suit. Under Puerto Rico's Spanish civil law-based tolling rules, the one-year statute of limitations

---

[321] 446 US at 493.
[322] *See* §5.16.
[323] 446 US at 497.
[324] 462 US 650 (1983), *affg* 681 F2d 42 (1st Cir 1982).
[325] 414 US 538, *rehg denied,* 415 US 952 (1974).

was not suspended but rather *began to run anew* when the class suit was denied certification. Thus, according to the plaintiffs, their individual suits were not time-barred.

The First Circuit agreed with the plaintiffs, holding that, pursuant to §1988, Puerto Rico tolling law governed the tolling effect of denial of class certification for §1983 federal class suits filed in Puerto Rico. Upon review, the Supreme Court affirmed in an opinion by Justice Stevens. He noted that the parties agreed that there was tolling during the pendency of the proposed class action, but disagreed as to the tolling effect of the subsequent class decertification. The Court then went on to read *American Pipe* as not establishing a generally applicable tolling rule of suspension for federal class actions denied certification. Rather, *American Pipe*'s tolling rule of suspension was based on the fact that the antitrust cause of action implicated in *American Pipe* itself provided a tolling rule of suspension. In contrast, because §1983 has no statute of limitations of its own, §1988—as interpreted in *Tomanio*—requires the applicability of the analogous state statute of limitations together with its tolling rules. Since Puerto Rico's tolling rule of renewal was applicable to the plaintiffs' individual §1983 suits, filed within one year after denial of class certification, those suits were timely under Puerto Rico's one-year limitations period.[326]

Justices Rehnquist, White, and Powell dissented. They read *American Pipe* more broadly as setting out a generally applicable tolling rule of suspension for all federal class actions denied certification. They also argued that such a rule would promote the federal interest in uniformity and would avoid litigation about what a state's tolling rule is. *Tomanio* was distinguishable, they suggested, because it did not involve Rule 23 federal class actions.

Fumero Soto indicates clearly that state tolling law applies to §1983 federal class actions just as *Tomanio* held that state tolling law applies to individual §1983 suits. Indeed, after *Tomanio*, a different result in *Fumero Soto* would have been anomalous. Consequently, state tolling law ordinarily governs *all* §1983 suits, whether brought in federal or state court. Thus, just as there is no national uniformity for limitations purposes, there is none for tolling either. On the other hand, while there was often uncertainty about the applicable limitations period within a particular state before *Wilson*, there will typically be far less uncertainty about a state's tolling rules. It is, moreover, not unfair to expect lawyers involved in §1983 litigation to know their own state's tolling rules.

§4.17 —In the Circuits

Choosing the Analogous Limitations Period

Because *Wilson v Garcia*[327] made clear that §1983 actions are to be treated

---

[326] It is worth noting that inasmuch as most common law jurisdictions have tolling rules using a suspension approach—unlike Puerto Rico's civil law-based renewal approach—the result in *Fumero Soto* is probably unique. However, Louisiana is also a civil law jurisdiction.

[327] 105 S Ct 1938 (1985), discussed at §4.14.

as personal injury actions for choice of limitations purposes, earlier circuit court decisions adopting a different approach are no longer good law. Nevertheless, such pre-*Wilson* case law may be relevant to the question whether *Wilson* should be applied retroactively[328] and is thus set out by circuit in the accompanying footnote.[329] As of this writing, with regard to post-*Wilson* case law, the Third Circuit[330] applied Pennsylvania's two-year limitations period for intentional and negligent conduct causing personal injuries to a §1983 sex discrimination claim. It also applied the same limitations period *retroactively* to a §1983 procedural due process claim.[331] The Fifth Circuit[332] applied Mississippi's one-year limitations period for the intentional torts of assault, battery, and maiming to a §1983 First Amendment employee discharge case. It rejected the Mississippi six-year residuary statute applicable to other actions, including negligence and strict liability. The Seventh Circuit[333] applied the Indiana two-year period for personal injury actions to the plaintiff inmate's §1983 suit claiming an unconstitutional confinement. And the Eleventh Court[334] applied Alabama's six-year limitations period for trespass actions to a plaintiff's §1983 procedural due process claim, rejecting Alabama's one-year period for other personal injury actions based on trespass on the case.

---

[328] *See* **§4.14.**

[329] Gashgai v Leibowitz, 702 F2d 10 (1st Cir 1983) (nature of underlying cause of action); Conway v Village of Mt Kisco, 750 F2d 205 (2d Cir 1984) (liability created by statute); Aitchison v Raffiani, 708 F2d 96 (3d Cir 1983) (nature of underlying cause of action); McCausland v Mason County Bd of Educ, 649 F2d 278 (4th Cir 1981) (analogous to personal injury action in absence of state limitations period applicable to civil rights violations); Suthoff v Yazoo County Indus Dev Corp, 722 F2d 133 (5th Cir 1983) (essential nature or *gravamen* of the plaintiff's complaint); Sevier v Turner, 742 F2d 262 (6th Cir 1984) (most analogous state limitations period); Blake v Catter, 693 F2d 677 (7th Cir 1982) (nature of claim unless state limitations period applies by its own terms); Garmon v Faust, 668 F2d 400 (8th Cir 1982) (en banc) (rejecting tort analogy as too cramped; §1983 a broad statutory remedy which requires use of either general or statutory liability limitations period); Lai v City & County of Honolulu, 749 F2d 588 (9th Cir 1984) (statutory liability limitations period: if none available, then residuary period); Garcia v Wilson, 731 F2d 640 (10th Cir 1984) (en banc) (use personal injury limitations period) *affd,* 105 S Ct 1938 (1985), discussed at **§4.14**; Solomon v Hardison, 746 F2d 699 (11th Cir 1984) (character of underlying claim).

[330] Knoll v Springfield Township School Dist, 763 F2d 584 (3d Cir 1985).

[331] Smith v City of Pittsburgh, 764 F2d 188 (3d Cir 1985). See **§4.14** on retroactivity.

[332] Gates v Spinks, 54 USLW 2178 (5th Cir Sept 26, 1985). See **§4.14** on choosing among different personal injury limitations periods.

[333] Bailey v Faulkner, 765 F2d 102 (7th Cir 1985). *See also* Rivera v Green, 775 F2d 1381 (9th Cir 1985) (post-*Wilson* case applying Arizona's two-year limitations period for personal injuries to §1983 claims apparently based on Fourth Amendment); Wycoff v Menke, 773 F2d 983 (8th Cir 1985) (post-*Wilson* case applying Iowa's two-year limitations period for personal injury actions to inmate's procedural due process claim regarding his segregation); Altair Corp v Pesquera De Busquets, 769 F2d 30 (1st Cir 1985) (post-*Wilson* case reaffirming applicability of Puerto Rico's one-year limitations period for fault or negligence to all §1983 claims).

[334] Jones v Preuit & Mauldin, 763 F2d 1250 (11th Cir 1985).

The Tenth Circuit, whose personal injury limitations approach was later adopted in *Wilson,* applied the Kansas two-year limitations period for actions "for injury to the rights of another" to a plaintiff's §1983 claim of wrongful termination.[335] Also, it twice held that its personal injury approach should not be applied retroactively.[336] Interestingly, in two other decisions, the Tenth Circuit found that neither Utah nor Colorado had a single limitations period applicable to injuries to the rights of another. Accordingly, it applied each state's respective residuary limitations period.[337] It thus took an approach very different from that of the Fifth and Eleventh Circuits.

Accrual

As mentioned earlier,[338] when a §1983 action accrues is a question of federal law, and the governing federal standard is the discovery rule derived from *United States v Kubrick,*[339] a Federal Tort Claims Act medical malpractice case. In a Second Circuit case,[340] the plaintiff, suing under both the Federal Tort Claims Act (FTCA) and §1983, alleged that in the early 1950s the defendants had caused the plaintiff's decedent's death through the injection of a drug while the decedent unknowingly served as a test subject in an Army chemical warfare experiment. The plaintiff also claimed that the defendants at the time conspired to cover up the facts surrounding the death. That the decedent had so died was revealed by the Army in August 1975, and the plaintiff filed her suit thereafter. Reversing the district court's dismissal of the complaint as time-barred, the Second Circuit applied the diligence-discovery standard of the Supreme Court's decision in *Kubrick.*

The court first observed that this standard was applicable outside the medical malpractice setting, "where plaintiffs face comparable problems in discerning the fact and cause of their injuries."[341] Next, it reasoned that even though the decedent's death was known in the 1950s, the defendants' conduct in covering up the wrongdoing of the United States warranted the use of the diligence-discovery rule. The "critical facts about causation and who inflicted [decedent's] injury were in the control of the Government and very difficult for his

---

[335] Pike v City of Mission, 731 F2d 655 (10th Cir 1984).

[336] Jackson v City of Bloomfield, 731 F2d 652 (10th Cir 1984) (action timely when filed; *Chevron Oil* test used); Abbitt v Franklin, 731 F2d 661 (10th Cir 1984) (new approach was clean break with established law; retroactive impact would have no beneficial impact, and substantial unfairness because of possible reliance on prior precedent; *Chevron Oil* test used).

[337] Mismash v Murray City, 730 F2d 1366 (10th Cir 1984) (Utah's four-year residuary period applied to claim of excessive force); McKay v Hammock, 730 F2d 1367 (10th Cir 1984) (different limitations periods applicable to intentional and negligent torts, a distinction having no place in §1983 cases; therefore, Colorado's three-year residency period applicable to claim of wrongful arrest and harassment).

[338] §4.15.

[339] 444 US 111 (1979), noted at §4.15.

[340] Barrett v United States, 689 F2d 324 (2d Cir 1982).

[341] *Id* 327.

estate to obtain."[342] Thus, both the *what* and *who* elements were missing, with the government blocking the unmasking of those who were responsible. In short, under the circumstances, the plaintiff and the decedent's family acted reasonably and with due diligence, and their FTCA and §1983 actions were not time-barred as a matter of law.

Similarly, in a Fifth Circuit case,[343] a plaintiff alleged, among other things, the medical malpractice of hospital personnel in performing a spinal tap upon him which caused permanent damage to his back. After discussing the possible meanings of the federal standard governing the accrual of a §1983 cause of action, the Fifth Circuit relied on *Kubrick* for the proposition that a §1983 cause of action accrues when the plaintiff is or should be aware of both the injury and its connection with the acts of the defendants. The court then reversed the district court's dismissal of the plaintiff's claim as time-barred under Louisiana's one-year statute of limitations and remanded.

Two important points should be noted. First, the court stated that it was proper to apply the *Kubrick* accrual standard to a §1983 action even though the standard was derived from a Federal Torts Claims Act setting. Second, the Fifth Circuit, in applying the *Kubrick* standard, focused more on *injury* than on its causal connection aspect when it said: "Until the plaintiff has reason to believe that the effects of a surgical procedure are different from those anticipated, it cannot be said that the plaintiff is aware of the injury which is the basis of his action."[344] Here, the plaintiff had long known of back pains, but had assumed they were the normal result of a spinal tap. Only later did he suspect the pains might be the result of the defendant's negligence. This original assumption of the plaintiff was what the Fifth Circuit strained to characterize as the plaintiff's ignorance of *injury*, thereby putting an interesting gloss on *Kubrick*.

Difficult accrual issues can also arise in connection with the continuing violation doctrine of *United Airlines v Evans*[345] and its relation to the Court's accrual decision in *Delaware State College v Ricks*.[346] A successful continuing violation claim can avoid dismissal of a plaintiff's complaint on limitations grounds. It is not sufficient, however, that the effects of a defendant's constitutional violation have continued during the limitations period; it is ordinarily necessary that the defendant have acted unconstitutionally during the limitations period. For example, according to the First Circuit, in order to make out a continuing violation claim of political discrimination in employment where a one-year limitations period was applicable, the plaintiffs had to show, but did not, that "a discriminatory act occurred or that a discriminatory policy existed in the year before they filed suit."[347] The plaintiffs offered only

---

[342] *Id* 329.

[343] Lavalee v Listi, 611 F2d 1129 (5th Cir 1980).

[344] *Id* 1132 n 7.

[345] 431 US 553.

[346] 449 US 250 (1980), discussed at §4.15.

[347] Velazquez v Chardon, 746 F2d 831 (1st Cir 1984). *See also* Ocean Acres Ltd Partnership v Dare County Bd of Health, 707 F2d 103 (4th Cir 1983) (due process claim challenging rejection of a development plan for septic tanks accrued at the time the

conclusory claims of political discrimination to support their continuing violation theory, which were not enough to create a disputed issue of material fact for the purpose of defeating the defendant's motion for summary judgment. The First Circuit thus did not have to reach the question of whether, if the continuing violation theory had been successful, acts of political discrimination occurring more than one year preceding the filing of the complaints would have been timely.

However, different constitutional claims may lead to different continuing violation results. Thus, in a Fifth Circuit case,[348] because the plaintiff teacher failed to file his claim for additional compensation within two years of the time it was first denied him, the claim, insofar as it was based on due process and First Amendment violations, was time-barred under Texas's two-year statute of limitations. There was no continuing violation because the plaintiff alleged only a single wrongful act. However, insofar as the plaintiff also asserted an equal protection violation to the effect that he was not paid on the same basis as other faculty members, he might make out a continuing violation. Since the evidentiary materials did not make this clear, and the defendants had the burden of showing no material fact in dispute, summary judgment should not be granted to the plaintiff.

Under *Ricks*, it is only necessary for the plaintiff in an employment situation to be effectively notified of a discharge for the cause of action to accrue at the time of notification. In a Sixth Circuit case,[349] where the plaintiff sued the defendants for their alleged violation of procedural due process in terminating her, it was agreed that Tennessee's one-year limitations period applied to civil rights cases. However, the plaintiff was time-barred because she filed her suit in August 1981, more than one year after the defendant board notified her by letter that her termination by the chancellor had been upheld. The board's letter was somewhat ambiguous in that it did not make clear whether the board

---

plaintiff knew or should have known of injury; no continuing violation despite later septic tank moratorium because the plaintiff challenged only the initial conduct); Ward v Caulk, 650 F2d 1144 (9th Cir 1981) (action challenging discriminatory failure to promote accured at time of alleged discrimination, even though several years later one of the defendants told the plaintiff that had he known of the plaintiff's attempt to obtain another county job he would have tried to prevent it); McCausland v Mason County Bd of Educ, 649 F2d 278 (4th Cir 1981) (no continuing violation where the plaintiff failed to allege any overt act of the defendants after their refusal to reinstate him to his position; action accrued on date of discharge); Dumas v Town of Mount Vernon, 612 F2d 974 (5th Cir 1980) (action for refusal to rehire on alleged racial grounds accrued at the time of refusal even though the plaintiff's name remained on list of eligibles; plaintiff at the outset viewed this refusal as discriminatory).

[348] Perez v Laredo Junior College, 706 F2d 731 (5th Cir 1983). In Domingo v New England Fish Co, 727 F2d 1428, 1443 (9th Cir 1984), a Title VII class action employment discrimination case, the Ninth Circuit, agreeing with the plaintiffs that a continuing violation was shown, nevertheless asserted that the plaintiffs could not recover for discriminatory acts which were not themselves timely, even though they were an early part of the continuing violation. However, evidence of such acts could be relevant as background in a proceeding where the current practice was at issue.

[349] Kessler v Board of Regents, 738 F2d 751 (6th Cir 1984).

intended to consider the matter further. Nevertheless, under the Supreme Court's *Ricks* decision the plaintiff's cause of action accrued at that time. The board's letter sufficiently apprised the plaintiff that her termination was upheld.

This applies as well to effective notification of a future discharge: the cause of action accrues at the time of notification, not when the discharge actually takes place later. Thus, attempting to distinguish *Ricks* from the case before it, the First Circuit[350] held that the 23 plaintiffs' §1983 causes of action for political discrimination in connection with their demotions and firings accrued only when they were actually demoted or fired, and not when they were notified in writing of their prospective demotions or firings. Reversing the district court's dismissal of the complaints, the First Circuit emphasized, among other things, that unlike *Ricks*, the case before it did not involve an adverse, formal tenure decision, and the plaintiffs had challenged their demotions or firings, and not the notices thereof. The court also reasoned that an accrual rule based on date of implementation furthered important policies of judicial administration and was in accordance with common understanding. However, the Supreme Court, holding *Ricks* indistinguishable, granted certiorari and summarily reversed.

The Eighth Circuit has held that "[i]n a conspiracy action, the statute of limitations begins to run from the occurrence of the last overt act resulting in damage to the plaintiff."[351] However, conspiracy claims involving allegations of coverup may pose unique questions which can be treated as either accrual or tolling matters. For example, in a Tenth Circuit case[352] the plaintiff was falsely charged with sodomy but did not know, until after the applicable Utah four-year catchall limitations period expired, that there had been a conspiracy against him. Applying Utah law, which was extensively canvassed, the court held that the limitations period may have been tolled, even though the plaintiff obviously knew of the injury to him when it occurred, because the defendants

---

[350] Fernandez v Chardon, 684 F2d 765 (1st Cir), *cert granted & summarily revd*, 102 S Ct 28 (1981). *See also* Sevier v Turner, 742 F2d 262 (6th Cir 1984) (action challenging coercion by judge in connection with support payments accrued at time the plaintiff's signature was first extracted from him, even though he only consulted a lawyer over four years later); Berry v Board of Supervisors, 715 F2d 971 (5th Cir 1983) (sex discrimination action accrued at time plaintiff became aware of discriminatory conduct directed against her, not when she discovered later that her replacement was male); Griffen v Big Spring Indep School Dist, 706 F2d 645 (5th Cir 1983) (racial discrimination in employment action accrued after initial nonrenewal decision was communicated to plaintiff); *Cf* Calhoun v Alabama Alcoholic Beverage Control Bd, 705 F2d 422 (11th Cir 1983) (per curiam) (racial discrimination action arising out of denial of the plaintiff's application for liquor license accrued when the plaintiffs discovered they had been discriminated against because white couple similarly situated was granted a liquor license, not earlier when their application was denied; applying *equitable modification*, the court asked when evidence of racial discrimination would have been apparent to a reasonable person).

[351] Buford v Tremayne, 747 F2d 445, 448 (8th Cir 1984).

[352] Vest v Bossard, 700 F2d 600 (10th Cir 1983) (pre-*Wilson*). Judges Logan and McKay concurred.

allegedly not only conspired to accuse the plaintiff falsely, but also conspired to cover up the matter thereafter. Thus, the plaintiff may have been kept by the defendants from discovering their identity as those who had brought about his injury. Accordingly, the district court should not have held on motion for summary judgment that the plaintiff was time-barred.

Similarly, in an important Seventh Circuit case,[353] the plaintiffs, siblings of the decedent, sued various police officials for their fatal shooting of the decedent and their subsequent racially motivated conspiracy to cover up their conduct. The plaintiffs sued on their own behalf, as well as for the estates of the decedent and decedent's father, alleging violations of §1981, §1982, §1983, §1985, and §1988. One of the many issues in this case revolved around the defendants' contention that the Wisconsin limitations period had run on the plaintiffs' claims. Rejecting this contention, the Seventh Circuit first observed that it did not matter whether it was Wisconsin's three-year period for wrongful death actions that applied or the six-year period for liability created by statute. While the decedent had been killed in 1958, the coverup was only revealed in 1978 and the plaintiffs filed their conspiracy claims in 1979, less than two years later. Thus, the coverup claim was independently timely.

Furthermore, the §1983 claims relating to a decedent's shooting death were similarly timely because, under Wisconsin tolling law, there was estoppel by fraudulent concealment. The jury found by special verdict that the defendants intentionally concealed many of the true facts surrounding the decedent's death. Also, there was no lost evidence or faded memory—primary concerns of limitations policy—that would be jeopardized by allowing tolling in this case. Many witnesses were still alive, relevant information about the shooting and investigation was available in police documents, one of the defendants admitted planting a knife in the decedent's hand after he was shot, and limitations had not been a bar to the prosecution for reckless homicide and perjury of the defendant who shot the decedent.

Tolling and Saving Statutes

When a state's limitations period is used in a §1983 action, the state's accompanying tolling rules are also used as mandated by *Board of Regents v Tomanio*,[354] even where there is a serious question as to the wisdom of the state's tolling rule.[355] Interestingly, circuit courts have occasionally gone beyond the state's statutory tolling law and considered what they call *equitable tolling*,[356] which typically involves either a claim that the defendant concealed relevant information from the plaintiff—sometimes also called equitable estoppel—or

---

[353] Bell v City of Milwaukee, 746 F2d 1205, 1228-31 (7th Cir 1984) (pre-*Wilson*).

[354] 446 US 478 (1980) discussed at §4.16.

[355] *E.g.*, Bailey v Faulkner, 765 F2d 102 (7th Cir 1985) (state tolling law for inmates applied even though "hopelessly archaic"); Miller v Smith, 625 F2d 43 (5th Cir 1980) (state tolling law for inmates applied even though inmates have access to the federal courts).

[356] *E.g.*, Hamilton v General Motors Corp, 606 F2d 576 (5th Cir 1979) (§1981 case).

an assertion that the plaintiff was for other reasons not at fault in missing the limitations deadline. To the extent that such equitable tolling is based on relevant state law, there is no inconsistency with *Tomanio*.[357] However, to the extent that such equitable tolling is based on federal law then there is an inconsistency with *Tomanio* which rejected the creation of federal tolling rules in §1983 cases.[358] However, it is possible to avoid this inconsistency by characterizing equitable tolling as an aspect of accrual, an inquiry which, as noted, is governed by federal standards, including the use of *Kubrick*'s discovery approach to accrual.

State saving statutes, which are a particular kind of tolling statute, are also applied in §1983 cases. These statutes typically toll the running of the applicable limitations period upon the filing of a timely suit, even though the suit is later dismissed for improper venue, for want of jurisdiction or for other reasons not going to the merits. For example, in a Sixth Circuit case,[359] it was held that the district court erred in finding time-barred the plaintiffs' refiled complaint which alleged that the defendants wrongfully arrested and assaulted them following a speeding infraction. Even if Ohio's one-year limitations period for intentional torts were applicable, as the district court found, it was incorrect not to apply Ohio's savings statute here. The initial filing was timely, the plaintiffs' first suit was not dismissed on the merits but only for want of prosectuion, the dismissal occurred after the limitations period (as measured uninterrupted from the date the action accrued) had expired, and the refiling took place within *one year* thereafter.

In an Eighth Circuit case, the plaintiff sued various officials, claiming a conspiracy against him through the misuse of a grand jury to indict him, the filing of libel suits against him, and his excommunication from the Mormon Church. His cause of action accrued on November 19, 1977 when he was indited; on October 22, 1980, he filed a request to proceed in forma pauperis to which was attached a copy of his complaint, but his request was denied. He thereafter paid the filing fee and refiled his complaint on May 15, 1981. While the district court dismissed the complaint as time-barred under the applicable Arkansas three-year limitations period, the Eighth Circuit reversed and remanded for determination of whether the plaintiff's in forma pauperis request tolled the limitations period under the Arkansas saving statute. This statute provided that "if an action is initiated within the statutory time limit and is dismissed without prejudice, the plaintiff may commence a new action within one year of the dismissal."[360] The court also asked the district court on remand

---

[357] *E.g.*, Bell v City of Milwaukee, 746 F2d 1205, 1228-31 (7th Cir 1984); Cross v Lucius, 713 F2d 153 (5th Cir 1983); Clulow v State of Oklahoma, 700 F2d 1291 (10th Cir 1983).

[358] *E.g.*, Pike v City of Mission, 731 F2d 655 (10th Cir 1984) (dictum).

[359] Harris v City of Canton, 725 F2d 371 (6th Cir 1984).

[360] Weston v Bachman, 682 F2d 202, 204 (8th Cir 1982). *See also* Griffen v Big Spring Indep School Dist, 700 F2d 645 (5th Cir 1983) (applying the Texas *wrong court* tolling statute where first suit dismissed for want of jurisdiction).

to decide whether equitable considerations required the paid filing to relate back to the initial in forma pauperis filing.

Relation Back

In certain circumstances pursuant to Rule 15(c) of the Federal Rules of Civil Procedure, where a suit is timely filed against various defendants and a defendant is thereafter added after the running of the limitations period, the addition of the defendant may relate back to the original filing and thus be timely. The claims against the new party must arise out of the same occurrence as the original claims, the added party must have received notice of the initial filing before the limitations period expired, and the added party must either have known, or should have known, that but for plaintiff's mistake, the action would have been brought against him or her.[361] In a Seventh Circuit case, however, relation back of a new party was not allowed. The plaintiff filed a §1983 action against certain named police officer defendants and others designated simply as "unknown and unidentified" two days before the statute of limitations would have barred it. Then, after the statute had run, the plaintiff moved to amend the complaint to add the names of the previously unknown police officers. The Seventh Circuit, applying Rule 15(c), refused to permit the amended complaint to relate back. It affirmed the district court's dismissal of the amended complaint as time-barred, finding there was nothing in the record to show that these defendants either knew or should have known within the limitations period that they would have been named as original defendants "but for mistake or even lack of knowledge of their identities."[362] The court added that the naming of a John Doe defendant in a complaint does not toll the statute of limitations until a name may be substituted.

In contrast, in a rather unique Fifth Circuit[363] relation back case, the plaintiff sued a city, its mayor, and its councilmen individually for damages arising from delays in obtaining a liquor license. The city was shortly thereafter dismissed because cities were then not suable persons—*Monell v Department of Social Services*[364] had not yet been decided—only to be reinstated several years later, when *Monell* held that cities *were* suable persons under §1983. The Fifth Circuit rejected the city's argument that the applicable Louisiana one-year limitations period had run during the interim between dismissal and reinstatement. It reasoned that the plaintiff's suit against the other defendants individually "tolled the running of the statute of limitations against the city, since they were potential obligors bound *in solido* with the city."[365] There was also no prejudice to the city.

Relation back can also cover situations where, after the limitations period has

---

[361] *See* Serrano v Torres, 764 F2d 47 (1st Cir 1985) (discussing relation back).

[362] Sassi v Breir, 584 F2d 234 (7th Cir 1978).

[363] Bennett v City of Slidell, 697 F2d 657, 660 (5th Cir 1983), *revd on other grounds*, 728 F2d 762 (5th Cir 1984) (en banc).

[364] 436 US 658 (1978) discussed in **ch 6.**

[365] 697 F2d at 660.

run, new claims are added to a timely complaint against an existing defendant.[366] Furthermore, where a relation back issue is raised in a §1983 case filed in federal court, federal law should govern, not inconsistent state law.[367]

Laches

While this section and §4.13 deal with damages actions, limitations issues may arise in connection with injunctive relief actions as well.[368] Strictly speaking, the doctrine of laches, which focuses on the plaintiff's delay and the possible resulting prejudice to the defendant, applies to determine whether injunctive relief actions are timely, while damages actions are governed by statutes of limitation. However, the relationship can be more complex. In an important Seventh Circuit case,[369] the court held that even though the limitations period had not expired, the defendants could raise the defense of laches against the plaintiff's §1983 equitable relief claim. According to the Seventh Circuit, the Supreme Court's limitations decisions in *Russell v Todd*[370] and *Cope v Anderson*[371] did not foreclose the argument that laches may shorten the applicable time limit. Further, the defendants showed that laches was applicable. The plaintiff had not exercised due diligence in bringing her equitable claim and there would be prejudice to the defendants regarding the conduct of their defense if the equitable claim were not barred by laches. Consequently, the plaintiff's §1983 equitable relief claim was time-barred.

Conversely, in a Tenth Circuit case, the plaintiff sued various state and bar association officers and others for conspiring to violate his due process rights by causing his involuntary commitments to mental institutions and his suspension from the practice of law. The Tenth Circuit held that Oklahoma's two-year limitations period for claims sounding in tort governed the plaintiff's claims because they corresponded to tort actions for interference with individual rights. Also, there were no continuing violations because each claimed due process violation was a discrete, unrelated event. Finally, the court rejected the plaintiff's argument that only laches, and not Oklahoma's statute of limitations, could bar his equitable claims. The Tenth Circuit determined that inasmuch as the plaintiff's claims were, or could have been, legal as well as equitable, the state limitations period applied: "[E]quitable relief should be withheld since the corresponding legal relief would be barred."[372]

In short, even though the applicable limitations period has not run, laches

---

[366] *E.g.*, Grattan v Burnett, 710 F2d 160 (4th Cir 1983) (finding actual nexus between the amendment and the original complaint), *affd on other grounds*, 468 US 42 (1984), discussed at §4.14.

[367] Hess v Eddy, 689 F2d 977, 981 (11th Cir 1982) ("This is a *federal* civil rights action, brought in a *federal* court, and it is the *Federal* Rules of Civil Procedure that must apply") (emphasis in original).

[368] *See generally* **ch 5** on injunctive relief.

[369] Cannon v University of Health Sciences, 710 F2d 351, 359 (7th Cir 1983).

[370] 309 US 280 (1940).

[371] 331 US 461 (1967).

[372] Clulow v Oklahoma, 700 F2d 1291, 1303 (10th Cir 1983).

can still bar a plaintiff's §1983 injunctive relief action. However, where the applicable limitations period has run, then irrespective of laches, the §1983 injunctive relief action will be time-barred.

"[S]uit in equity or other proper proceeding for redress": Equitable Relief and "Procedural" Defenses

5

§5.01 Summary

This chapter, which deals in part with obstacles to obtaining declaratory and injunctive relief against state officials, is a short course on the many ways federal courts can avoid granting such relief in 42 USC §1983 cases without a decision on the merits. While each of these obstacles could be the subject of a separate chapter or even a book, the major concern here is with doctrines which are especially tied to §1983 litigation. From a plaintiff's perspective, these complex doctrines have substantially undermined the utility of §1983. Covered in some detail, the doctrines are the Eleventh Amendment, exhaustion of state judicial and administrative remedies, the *Younger* rule, *Pullman* abstention, and res judicata and collateral estoppel. Many of these doctrines can serve as defenses to §1983 *damages* actions as well.[1] However, substantive constitutional law doctrines related to a §1983 plaintiff's entitlement to equitable relief and to the breadth of such relief are beyond the scope of this chapter.[2]

The Eleventh Amendment prohibits suits by private persons against states from being heard in federal court and applies to §1983 actions.[3] In contrast, the doctrine of exhaustion of state judicial and administrative remedies does not ordinarily bar §1983 relief.[4] The rule of *Younger v Harris*[5] requires outright dismissal of §1983 actions for declaratory or injunctive relief affecting pending state criminal proceedings against the federal plaintiff.[6] Using *Pullman* abstention, however, a federal court *defers* decision, though retaining jurisdiction, while the federal plaintiff seeks a state determination of an unclear state law issue which, when clarified, may render unnecessary a decision on the federal plaintiff's constitutional claim.[7] The Supreme Court has ruled that under 28 USC §1738, state preclusion law applies to determine the preclusive effect of a prior state court proceeding upon a later federal §1983 proceeding.[8]

Also covered in this chapter, but more briefly, are formal requirements for declaratory and injunctive relief,[9] the various statutory bars to injunctive

---

[1] This is true, for example, of the Eleventh Amendment, *Pullman* abstention, and especially the preclusion doctrines of res judicata and collateral estoppel. See **ch 4** on damages. On the other hand, justiciability issues and the *Younger* rule typically arise in connection with prospective relief.

[2] Examples of such doctrines include the distinctions between de jure and de facto racial segregation and the proper judicial remedy once a finding of de jure segregation has been made. See **app A,** Table of Leading Constitutional Law Cases, for cases dealing with these and similar issues of substantive constitutional doctrine. It should also be noted that injunctions can be either prohibitory or mandatory, or both; far-reaching injunctive relief is typically sought by §1983 plaintiffs interested in institutional reform. See **app A** for relevant cases; *also see generally Developments in the Law—Section 1983 and Federalism,* 90 Harv L Rev 1133, 1227-50 (1977) and *The Remedial Process in Institutional Reform Litigation,* 78 Colum L Rev 784 (1978).

[3] *See* §**5.08.**

[4] *See* §§**5.09-5.11.**

[5] 401 US 37 (1971).

[6] *See* §§**5.12-5.15.**

[7] The doctrine gets its name from Railroad Commn v Pullman Co, 312 US 496 (1941). *See* §**5.16.**

[8] *See* §§**5.18-5.19.**

[9] *See* §**5.02.**

relief,[10] and the justiciability doctrines of standing, ripeness, and political questions.[11]

§5.02   Threshold Formal Requirements

The Declaratory Judgment Act, 28 USC §§2201-2202,[12] gives federal courts the power to "declare the rights and other legal relations of any interested party seeking such declaration." An "actual controversy" between the parties must exist,[13] although by the terms of the statute neither injunctive relief nor damages need be sought as a condition precedent to obtaining a declaratory judgment. Also, declaratory relief may be granted even though some other adequate remedy exists.[14] In contrast, before a federal court issues an injunction of any kind, it must determine that the legal remedy is inadequate even if available. Furthermore, the plaintiff must show substantial and immediate "irreparable injury."[15]

In *City of Los Angeles v Lyons,*[16] an important case discussed later in connection with standing,[17] the Court held that a plaintiff who had been subjected to a dangerous chokehold after being stopped by police for a traffic violation could not enjoin the use of the chokehold. First, any claim of future injury to him was speculative, and hence he could not show the likelihood of irreparable injury. Second, his accompanying damages claim against the city constituted an adequate remedy at law.

The Court also asserted in *Lyons* that when federal courts are asked to oversee state law enforcement authorities, "normal principles of equity, comity and

---

[10] *See* **§5.03.**

[11] *See* **§§5.04-5.07.**

[12] These provisions read in relevant part as follows:

    2201.   Creation of remedy

        In a case of actual controversy within its jurisdiction . . . any court of the United States, upon the filing of an appropriate pleading, may declare the rights and other legal relations of any interested party seeking such declaration, whether or not further relief is or could be sought. Any such declaration shall have the force and effect of a final judgment or decree and shall be reviewable as such.

    2202.   Further relief

        Further necessary or proper relief based on a declaratory judgment or decree may be granted, after reasonable notice and hearing, against any adverse party whose rights have been determined by such judgment.

[13] See **§5.05** on standing requirements.

[14] Rule 57, Fed R Civ P. Jury trial may also be available in declaratory judgment actions under this Rule. *See* **§1.16.**

[15] *See generally* D. Dobbs, Law of Remedies 108 *et seq* (1973).

[16] 461 US 95 (1983). Justices Marshall, Brennen, Blackmun, and Stevens dissented.

[17] **§5.05.**

federalism" should inform this judgment.[18] Such concerns were important in a Sixth Circuit case[19] where, even though the plaintiff inmates prevailed in their class action challenging conditions of confinement, the Sixth Circuit ruled that the district court had erred in disqualifying three prison officers from participating in any institutional function requiring them to act in a quasi-adjudicatory capacity. There was a pattern and practice of unconstitutional harassment of inmates involving these and other officers, but the district court "breached precepts of comity and federalism by restricting the responsibilities and duties" of the three officers to whom these responsibilities had been delegated by the state. Instead, the district court should have imposed "the least intrusive remedy available," possibly an order enjoining the continuation of the unconstitutional practices with a monitoring system to ensure compliance. This conclusion was supported by the history of cooperation and good faith exhibited by the defendants.

Preliminary injunctions, a type of temporary relief aimed at maintaining the status quo pending adjudication, are granted only if, in addition to the necessary showing of irreparable injury, the applicant demonstrates the likelihood of prevailing on the merits.[20] Furthermore, Rule 65(a) of the Federal Rules of Civil Procedure requires notice and some kind of a hearing.

Temporary restraining orders, another and more drastic kind of temporary relief, may be granted, pursuant to Rule 65(b) of the Federal Rules of Civil Procedure, without notice of any kind to the other party. The remedy is available under such conditions only if immediate and irreparable injury would result if a hearing were to be held and if the applicant certifies to the court the efforts made to give notice to the other party. Other formal requirements for temporary restraining orders set out in Rule 65(b) should be consulted. Rule 65(c) requires, in most cases, that the applicant for either kind of temporary relief give security.

The Supreme Court put a gloss on Rule 25(d) of the Federal Rules of Civil Procedure. This rule provides for automatic substitution of the successor to a public officer, sued in an official capacity, who ceases to hold office through death, resignation, or otherwise. In *Spomer v Littleton*[21] and *Mayor of Philadelphia*

---

[18] 461 US at 112. See **§§5.12-5.15** on the *Younger* rule and the concepts of federalism and comity.

[19] Kendrick v Bland, 740 F2d 432 (6th Cir 1984).

[20] *See, e.g.,* Lasco v Northern, 733 F2d 477 (7th Cir 1984), where, according to the Seventh Circuit, the district court correctly denied plaintiff's request for a preliminary injunction to prevent a state agency reorganization and his resulting layoff, claiming a conspiracy to remove him because of his political affiliation. Plaintiff failed to establish a reasonable likelihood of prevailing on the merits. He was a difficult employee who did not get along well with co-workers; this may well have been the reason for his layoff. Also, the defendants may have had fiscal reasons for their conduct. Further, plaintiff failed to show irreparable injury and absence of an adequate legal remedy. Plaintiff, moreover, had corrective relief available through the state's civil service commission.

[21] 414 US 514 (1974).

v Educational Equality League,[22] the Court held that, in order for a §1983 action for declaratory or injunctive relief to continue against a substituted public official, there must be a claim and proof that the successor defendant will engage in the same unconstitutional conduct as the predecessor. Supplemental findings of fact are required for this purpose. In contrast, §1983 damages actions are not governed by this requirement since they are retrospective and directed at the predecessor solely in an individual capacity.[23]

§5.03   Statutory Bars to §1983 Injunctive Relief Against State Officials

The Supreme Court expressly held in *Mitchum v Foster*[24] that the Anti-Injunction Act[25] prohibiting federal courts from enjoining pending state proceedings does not apply to §1983 because the section is an exception "expressly authorized by Act of Congress."[26] However, two other statutory bars to injunctive relief against state officials appear to apply to §1983 cases, although the Supreme Court has not yet expressly so held.[27] One, the Johnson Act of 1934, removes from the federal courts jurisdiction to enjoin any state agency's order regarding public utility rate making where

1.   Jurisdiction is based on diversity of citizenship or inconsistency with the federal Constitution
2.   The order does not interfere with interstate commerce
3.   The order was made after reasonable notice and hearing
4.   The state provides a "plain, speedy and efficient remedy"[28]

---

[22] 415 US 605 (1975).

[23] However, a §1983 survival issue is raised upon the death of a government official sued for damages in his individual capacity. *See* **§3.19.**

[24] 407 US 225 (1972). Following *Mitchum* and its holding that §1983 actions are not covered by the Anti-Injunction Act, the Ninth Circuit stated: "[D]istrict Courts have subject matter jurisdiction over suits brought under §1983 even when the state action allegedly violating plaintiff's federally protected rights takes the form of state court proceedings." *Miofsky v Superior Ct,* 703 F2d 332, 335 (9th Cir 1983). Plaintiff sought a federal injunction against allegedly unconstitutional discovery proceedings in state court litigation.

[25] 28 USC §2283 reads as follows: "A court of the United States may not grant an injunction to stay proceedings in a State court except as expressly authorized by Act of Congress, or where necessary in aid of its jurisdiction, or to protect or effectuate its judgments."

[26] The judge-made *Younger* rule does, however, apply to prevent declaratory and injunctive relief against pending state criminal proceedings. *See* **§§5.12-5.15.**

[27] C. Wright, Law of Federal Courts 302 n 21 (4th ed 1983).

[28] 28 USC §1342. Where these four conditions are met, the Johnson Act specifically provides that the "district courts shall not enjoin, suspend or restrain the operation of, or compliance with, any order affecting rates chargeable by a public utility and made

The other statutory bar, the Tax Injunction Act,[29] which now almost certainly applies to §1983 actions, prohibits an injunction against "the assessment, levy or collection of any tax under State law" where "a plain, speedy and efficient remedy may be had in the courts of such state." Reasoning from the policies underlying this act, although not applying the act itself, the Supreme Court held in *Fair Assessment in Real Estate Association v McNary*[30] that the principle of comity bars federal courts from granting damages relief in §1983 cases challenging the constitutionality of the administration of a state tax system. The plaintiffs had alleged equal protection and due process violations through unequal taxation of real property.

In an opinion by Justice Rehnquist, the Court emphasized federalism considerations: the need for federal court respect for state taxing schemes, the concern for federal noninterference with state taxation, and the disruptive effect on state taxing systems of §1983 damages actions even where state tax officials are sued in their individual capacities. Justices Brennan, Marshall, Stevens, and O'Connor concurred in the judgment. They refused, though, to put the matter in comity terms as the majority had. Instead, while arguing that federal courts have jurisdiction over §1983 damages actions challenging the allegedly unconstitutional administration of state taxing schemes, these concurring justices contended that plaintiff taxpayers must first exhaust their state administrative remedies—*see* **§§5.10-5.11**—as a condition precedent to suit in federal court. They believed such an exhaustion requirement was supported by the principal purposes of the Tax Injunction Act.

The Court's opinion expressly left open the question of a §1983 claim *"which requires no scrutiny whatever of state tax assessment practices,* such as a facial attack on tax laws colorably claimed to be discriminatory as to race."[31] Also, the Court's holding was qualified by the requirement that state remedies be plain, adequate, and complete. The Court explained:

> [P]laintiffs seeking protection of federal rights in federal courts should be remitted to their state remedies if their federal rights will not thereby be lost. Numerous federal decisions have treated the adequacy of state remedies, and it is to that body of law that federal courts should look in seeking to determine the occasions for the comity spoken of today.[32]

However, it may be enough to satisfy this requirement that taxpayers can assert

---

by a state administrative agency or a rate-making body of a state political subdivision. . . ."

[29] 28 USC §1341.

[30] 454 US 100 (1981). The pre-*Fair Assessment* decision in Fulton Mkt Cold Storage Co v Cullerton, 582 F2d 1071 (7th Cir 1978) is no longer good law.

[31] 454 US at 107 n 4 (emphasis added).

[32] *Id* 116 n 8.

their §1983 claims in *state* court[33] where the Tax Injunction Act does not apply.[34]

It should be noted that neither the Tax Injunction Act nor the Johnson Act on its face prohibits declaratory relief. That the Supreme Court would therefore interpret these statutes to permit §1983 declaratory relief was never very likely, however, given the possible applicability of judge-made doctrines such as abstention and exhaustion of state judicial and administrative remedies.[35] And indeed, in *California v Grace Brethren Church*,[36] the Court expressly ruled that the Tax Injunction Act prohibits federal declaratory judgments holding state tax laws unconstitutional.

The reasoning in *Fair Assessment* was applied in an Eleventh Circuit case[37] to preclude the federal plaintiffs' damages suit against a county and its officials challenging the levy and tax sale of their properties. According to the court, comity governed tax collection as well as tax assessment. Further, it was well settled that state law provided a plain, adequate, and complete remedy for the purpose of raising the federal rights of taxpayers. Even though damages might not be recoverable under state law from the county, they were recoverable from county officials. Also, equitable relief might be available against the county in a proper case. It was not required that the state remedy be the best available, or even the equal of a possible federal remedy.

In an important Ninth Circuit case,[38] the plaintiff telephone company sought declaratory and injunctive relief on various constitutional and federal statutory grounds against the Hawaii Department of Labor's investigation into whether a strike at the company had substantially curtailed its operations. If it did not, this would result in the company's obligation under state law to repay the state employment fund in an amount related to benefits paid to the striking workers. Affirming the district court's dismissal of the complaint, the Ninth Circuit extensively analyzed its own case law as well as more recent Supreme Court decisions interpreting the Tax Injunction Act, and concluded that the company's suit for both declaratory and injunctive relief was barred. In its view, *Rosewell v LaSalle National Bank*[39] and *Fair Assessment* demonstrated the Supreme Court's refusal to treat §1983 actions as exceptions to the Tax Injunction Act.

The Ninth Circuit also countered the plaintiff's argument that the Tax

---

[33] *Id.*

[34] *See,* however, the rather unusual case of Redd v Lambert, 674 F2d 1032 (5th Cir 1982) dealing in part with a Mississippi Supreme Court decision applying the Tax Injunction Act to a *state court* §1983 injunction action against a state tax commission.

[35] C. Wright, Law of Federal Courts 301 & nn 19, 20 (4th ed 1983). See **§5.16** on abstention and **§§5.09-5.11** on exhaustion of judicial and administrative remedies in §1983 cases. See also Great Lake Dredge & Dock Co v Huffman, 319 US 293 (1943), described in Fair Assessment, 454 US 100, 103 (1981) as "holding that federal courts, in exercising the discretion that attends requests for equitable relief, may not even render declaratory judgments as to the constitutionality of state laws."

[36] 457 US 393 (1982).

[37] Ayers v Polk County, 697 F2d 1375 (11th Cir 1983). *Cf* Werch v City of Berlin, 673 F2d 192 (7th Cir 1982) (plaintiff's §1983 suit frivolous after *Fair Assessment*).

[38] Hawaiian Tel Co v State Dept of Labor, 691 F2d 905 (9th Cir 1982).

[39] 450 US 503 (1980).

Injunction Act only applies to state taxation schemes, but should not apply to Hawaii's unemployment compensation program because it was a joint federal-state taxation scheme. A Supreme Court case[40] had rejected such a contention regarding another state's unemployment compensation program. Hawaii's remedial scheme provided a plain, speedy, and efficient remedy within the meaning of the Tax Injunction Act. Administrative and judicial remedies were available under state law whereby a party might raise both federal and nonfederal claims. Moreover, equitable remedies were available if legal remedies proved inadequate. Even if these state remedies were burdensome, they were still plain, speedy, and efficient.

Similarly, the Fourth Circuit[41] applied the Tax Injunction Act in a case where the plaintiff taxpayers sought declaratory relief in a challenge to a county's levy of a utility tax. Relying on §1341, the Fourth Circuit affirmed the district court's dismissal of the complaint. Plaintiffs had an adequate and speedy remedy under Virginia law: a bill in equity would lie to correct plaintiffs' complaint and, even if it did not, there was a remedy at law available. Virginia law thus provided a full hearing at which the plaintiffs could raise all of their constitutional arguments.

§5.04   Justiciability and Declaratory and Injunctive Relief—An Overview

The concept of *justiciability*, frequently used by federal courts to avoid decisions on the merits, arises mainly from the Article III requirement of a *case or controversy* for federal jurisdiction. Justiciability comprehends both constitutional minimum requirements and judge-made limitations. The following sections will sketch very briefly certain important aspects of justiciability, notably standing, ripeness, and political questions, as they have emerged from Supreme Court decisions. Far more extensive analyses, which are beyond the scope of this chapter, may be found elsewhere.[42] Justiciability problems will typically arise where declaratory or injunctive relief is sought. While such problems can arise in §1983 suits for damages as well, they usually do not.

In addition to standing, ripeness, and political questions, justiciability encompasses three other doctrines which should at least be mentioned here. The first, mootness, requires a federal court to dismiss for want of a case or controversy when there is no longer any live dispute between the parties.[43]

---

[40] California v Grace Brethern Church, 457 US 393 (1982).

[41] Hutcherson v Board of Supervisors, 742 F2d 142 (4th Cir 1984). *Cf* Ludwin v City of Cambridge, 592 F2d 606 (1st Cir 1979) (assuming that §1341 applies to declaratory relief).

[42] *See generally* C. Wright, Law of Federal Courts 53-84 (4th ed 1983); J. Nowak, R. Rotunda & J. Young, Constitutional Law 61-94, 109-20 (2d ed 1983); P. Bator, P. Mishkin, D. Shapiro & H. Wechsler, The Federal Courts and the Federal System 64-241 (2d ed 1973).

[43] *E.g.,* Hall v Beals, 396 US 45 (1969) (per curiam). *See also* Powers v Coe, 728 F2d 97 (2d Cir 1984) (plaintiff's guilty plea did not moot damages claim for prosecutorial misconduct).

Exceptions to this doctrine include cases in which a party has voluntarily ceased the allegedly unconstitutional conduct[44] and those cases which will recur but are otherwise difficult to review if ordinary mootness doctrine is applied.[45] The second, collusion, requires a federal court to dismiss where there is only a feigned dispute between the parties rather than a real one.[46] The third, the bar against advisory opinions, requires a concrete dispute between adversary parties.[47]

§5.05 —Standing

A §1983 plaintiff, whether a natural person, a group, or other entity, must have standing to sue; otherwise the suit will be dismissed. Functionally, standing is premised on assumptions that parties with a real interest will more effectively litigate a case, that judicial resources will be used more efficiently as a result, and that unnecessary constitutional adjudication will be minimized. The issue entails an inquiry both into the existence of actual or threatened injury which stems from defendant's conduct and affects plaintiff directly, and into the relation between the plaintiff and the legal claim asserted. This injury in fact or *personal stake* requirement appears to be a constitutional minimum[48] and includes, but is not limited to, physical, economic, aesthetic, and environmental harm.[49] The need to examine the relation between the plaintiff and the legal claim asserted is what the Supreme Court calls a *prudential* limitation because it is judge made.[50] An example of such a limitation is the requirement that plaintiffs ordinarily may assert only their own constitutional claims.[51]

---

[44] *E.g.,* United States v WT Grant Co, 345 US 629 (1963). *See also* Flittie v Erickson, 724 F2d 80 (8th Cir 1983) (inmate's due process injunctive relief claim mooted because prison officials thereafter complied with due process); Halet v Wend Inv Co, 672 F2d 1305 (9th Cir 1982) (injunctive relief action against adults-only housing policy not mooted despite defendant's promise; defendant could revert to prior policy at any time).

[45] *E.g.,* Roe v Wade, 410 US 113 (1973). *Cf* DeFunis v Odegaard, 416 US 312 (1974). *See also* Bishop v Committee on Professional Ethics, 686 F2d 1278 (8th Cir 1982) (exception not applied to lawyer's challenge to disciplinary rules limiting advertising); Doe v Colautti, 592 F2d 704 (3d Cir 1979) (exception applied to challenge of time limits for state medical assistance benefits).

[46] *E.g.,* United States v Johnson, 319 US 302 (1943) (per curiam).

[47] *E.g.,* the leading case of Muskrat v United States, 219 US 346 (1911).

[48] Baker v Carr, 369 US 186 (1962).

[49] Sierra Club v Morton, 405 US 727 (1972). The Court went very far in finding injury in fact in United States v Students Challenging Regulatory Agency Procedures, 412 US 669 (1973). *See also* Trafficante v Metropolitan Life Ins Co, 409 US 205 (1972).

[50] Warth v Seldin, 422 US 490, 498-502 (1975).

[51] Also known as the jus tertii rule. See Singleton v Wulff, 428 US 106, 114-16 (1976) (opinion of Justice Blackmun, joined by Justices Brennan, White, and Marshall, describing relevant exceptions to jus tertii):

> [T]he Court has looked primarily to two factual elements. . . . The first is the relationship of the litigant to the person whose right he seeks to assert. If the

Standing is not hard to find in most §1983 damages cases because not only is the injury to the plaintiff clear, but the causal relation between the defendant's allegedly unconstitutional conduct and the claimed harm to the plaintiff is usually apparent as well.[52] Where declaratory or injunctive relief is sought, however, and even in some damages actions, the Supreme Court has very rigorously insisted on the existence of both injury in fact and a causal relation. Thus, the Court requires that a litigant show that the requested declaratory or injunctive relief would make a practical difference if granted. This is a kind of *but for* cause in fact approach to standing.[53]

A leading §1983 case on standing is instructive not only because of its insistent use of this but for approach, but also because Justice Powell, writing for the Court, comprehensively analyzed standing in general. In *Warth v Seldin*,[54] various plaintiffs, individuals and groups, sought declaratory and

(*Text continued on page 280*)

---

enjoyment of the right is inextricably bound up with the activity the litigant wishes to pursue, the Court at least can be sure that its construction of the right is not unnecessary. . . . Furthermore . . . the litigant . . . may be . . . fully, or very nearly, as effective a proponent of the right as the [third party]. . . . The other factual element . . . is the ability of the third party to assert his own right.

See also §1.16 on class action requirements.

[52] See generally **ch 4** on damages in §1983 cases.

[53] Compare the common law rule for damages, D. Dobbs, Law of Remedies 149 (1973), and the §1983 rule for damages, discussed at the end of **§4.02.** See also **§3.18** on cause in fact generally in §1983 cases.

[54] 422 US 490 (1975). *See also* Valley Forge Christian College v Americans United for Separation of Church & State, 454 US 464, 472 (1982) (plaintiff must show that he suffered actual or threatened injury, that the injury "fairly can be traced to the challenged action," and "is likely to be redressed by a favorable decision.")

The standing criteria set out in *Warth* and related Supreme Court decisions have been applied in the circuits as follows:

First Circuit

Cutting v Muzzey, 724 F2d 259 (1st Cir 1984) (plaintiff real estate developer had standing to assert §1983 claim of racial animus by members of town planning board against Italians even though he was not Italian; all of plaintiff's purchasers had Italian surnames; also, the fact that one of those purchasers could bring his or her own suit was irrelevant to plaintiff's own standing).

Des Vergnes v Seekonk Water Dist, 601 F2d 9 (1st Cir 1979) (§1983 claim for damages and injunctive relief by a low-income housing developer corporation against a water district for refusing, with the intent to discriminate against low-income persons and blacks, to allow the developer's real estate to be included in the district; standing found).

Third Circuit

Howard v New Jersey Dept of Civil Servs, 667 F2d 1099 (3d Cir 1981) (§1983 plaintiffs alleging sex discrimination in denial of employment with police department had no standing, although they suffered injury; they were unable to show necessary causal connection between challenged conduct and loss of job opportunity because they had failed a written examination required for the job).

Frissel v Rizzo, 597 F2d 840 (3d Cir 1979), *cert denied,* 48 USLW 3219 (S Ct Oct 2, 1979) (§1983 claim for injunctive relief brought by a newspaper reader against a city's mayor for denying public advertising to the newspaper in violation of the newspaper's First Amendment rights; standing not found).

Fourth Circuit

Scott v Greenville County, 716 F2d 1409 (4th Cir 1983) (real estate developer who unsuccessfully sought permit to construct low-income housing had standing to assert discrimination claims; he had a personal stake stemming from claimed business injuries resulting from denial of the building permit, and he was, as a developer, a proper party to raise racial discrimination claims for others as well as for himself in connection with his willingness to rent to minorities; also, he did not have to show that minorities would in fact reside in the proposed development).

Ledford v Delancey, 612 F2d 883 (4th Cir 1980) (§1983 plaintiff challenged his employment termination on First Amendment grounds but was later discovered to have been ineligible for the job initially; standing not found).

Fifth Circuit

Church of Scientology v Cazares, 638 F2d 1272 (5th Cir 1981) (§1983 action brought by church alleging deprivation of First Amendment rights through prohibition against practicing religion; standing found because church members could sue in their own behalf, the interests sought to be protected by the church were germane to its religious purpose, and, since claim affected the entire membership, individual participation by members was not required).

Finch v Mississippi State Medical Assn, 585 F2d 765 (5th Cir 1978) (§1983 individual and class declaratory relief claims of various plaintiffs dissatisfied with the racial composition of a state's board of health; standing found for black doctors' class action and for one black doctor, among others; not found for citizen either individually or as representative of the class of poor people or all females).

Sixth Circuit

Smith v City of Cleveland Heights, 760 F2d 720 (6th Cir 1985) (black plaintiff who was not himself steered had standing to challenge defendants' racial steering practices; "stigmatic injury alleged; Allen v Wright, 468 US 737 (1984) distinguished; Judge Wellford dissented).

Seventh Circuit

People Organized for Welfare v Thompson, 727 F2d 167, 168 (7th Cir 1984) ("an association that is dedicated to increasing the political power of the poor and the unemployed, but that has no members who are not registered to vote, [does not have] standing to litigate the question whether the First Amendment requires a state to permit local election officials to register voters in the state's public aid and unemployment compensation offices"; Judge Swygert dissented).

Minority Police Officers Assoc v City of South Bend, 721 F2d 197 (7th Cir 1983) (minority police officers' association did not have standing to raise claim that defendants discriminated against blacks and Hispanics in hiring and promotions; none of association's members were unsuccessful applicants for employment and there was no contention that the association itself was financially harmed by the alleged discrimination; "[f]eelings of solidarity do not confer standing to sue").

Hope Inc v County of DuPage, 717 F2d 1061 (7th Cir 1983) (individual plaintiffs and not-for-profit fair housing organization had standing to claim racial discrimination in connection with alleged conspiracy to engage in exclusionary housing; individual plaintiffs fell within the categories of eligibility for low- and moderate-income housing; there was already a significant subsidized housing development in the county, indicating that developers were willing and able to build other such developments and money was available for such developments; the not-for-profit organization had standing to seek housing for both its directors and low and moderate-income persons in general; *Warth* distinguished and Havens Realty Corp v Coleman, 455 US 363 (1982) relied on).

Ninth Circuit

Graham v Deukmejian, 713 F2d 518 (9th Cir 1983) (Jehovah's Witnesses had standing to challenge state policy of singling out for disciplinary proceedings those physicians willing to perform "bloodless" surgery; plaintiffs alleged that the injury to their

injunctive relief and damages, claiming that a town's zoning ordinance had been unconstitutionally interpreted and applied to exclude poor and moderate-income residents from the town. After thoroughly discussing the constitutional and prudential aspects of standing, the Court held that none of the plaintiffs had it.

The individual plaintiffs who said they had previously unsuccessfully sought low or moderately priced housing in the town were not able to show, concluded the Court, "that, absent the respondents' restrictive zoning practices, there is a substantial probability that they would have been able to purchase or lease in Penfield and that, if the Court affords the relief requested, the asserted inability of petitioners will be removed."[55]

The taxpayer plaintiffs from an adjoining city were found not to have standing, partly because they were attempting to assert the constitutional rights of poor and moderate-income persons. The conclusion that an association which had some town residents as members did not have standing was similarly supported. Finally, an organization of homebuilders was found not to have standing because none of its members was connected with any proposed or existing project in the town allegedly affected by the ordinance.

---

religious beliefs was traceable to defendants' conduct and that a favorable decision would redress their own injuries).

Hawaiian Tel Co v State Dept of Labor, 691 F2d 905 (9th Cir 1982) (telephone company did not have standing to challenge federal expenditures to state unemployment fund because there was no allegation that such expenditures violated a specific constitutional limitation; however, there was standing to challenge the state's administration of the unemployment compensation-taxation program because there was a claimed direct financial injury to the telephone company through unemployment tax liability).

Halet v Wend Inv Co, 672 F2d 1305 (9th Cir 1982) (§1983 plaintiff, a white who was denied apartment rental, challenged adults-only rental policy as violative of his family rights and as racially discriminatory against blacks and Hispanics; although he suffered injury and had standing to raise his family rights claim, he did not have standing, as a prudential matter, to raise the racial discrimination claims of others).

Tagupa v Board of Directors, 633 F2d 1309 (9th Cir 1980) (§1983 employment discrimination action brought by individual who responded to advertisement of job opening but was subsequently rejected; standing found even though job application process never completed; this was not a standing issue but rather a substantive element of cause of action).

Tenth Circuit

Dohaish v Tooley, 670 F2d 934 (10th Cir 1982) (§1983 plaintiff had no standing to sue in attempt to compel district attorney to prosecute a man who allegedly killed plaintiff's son; plaintiff suffered no violation of his own civil rights and, moreover, there was no guarantee of the effectiveness of granting the requested relief, inasmuch as there might be no conviction in the subsequent criminal case).

Eleventh Circuit

Lynch v Baxley, 744 F2d 1452 (11th Cir 1984) (inmate who had earlier been detained in county jail pending involuntary commitment proceedings had standing as class representative to challenge this practice; there was a likelihood that the inmate would spend more time in jail awaiting commitment proceedings).

[55] 422 US at 504.

Consequently, the §1983 plaintiff (and all others seeking a federal forum) must show that the challenged governmental conduct has already had, or will have, an effect on plaintiff personally. The standing issue is thus whether the plaintiff is a proper party; it is the *who* question.

This question arose recently in an important §1983 case, *City of Los Angeles v Lyons*,[56] where a divided Court made several significant, and limiting, points about standing to seek §1983 equitable relief, and about §1983 equitable relief in general. *Lyons* involved a plaintiff who, after being stopped for a traffic violation and offering no resistance, was allegedly subjected by police officers to a chokehold which rendered him unconscious and injured him. In addition to seeking damages against the officers and the city, plaintiff sought injunctive relief against the defendants barring the use of the chokehold on the ground of its unconstitutionality. He alleged that the police, pursuant to city policy, routinely applied this chokehold in nonthreatening situations, that numerous persons had been injured as a result, that he and others similarly situated were thereby threatened with irreparable injury, and that he feared that any future contact he might have with the city's police officers could result in his injury or death.

Plaintiff ultimately obtained a preliminary injunction against the use of the chokehold under circumstances not threatening death or serious bodily harm to police officers. After the Ninth Circuit affirmed, the Supreme Court, in an opinion by Justice White, reversed. At the outset, the Court observed that the case was not moot even though the city had imposed a six-month moratorium on the use of the chokehold under certain circumstances; this moratorium was by its terms not permanent. Still, the Court held that plaintiff had not made out an Article III case or controversy sufficient to give federal courts jurisdiction.

In the Court's view, even though plaintiff may have suffered a past wrong, this was not enough to confer standing to seek injunctive relief. The latter depended on whether plaintiff was likely to suffer personal injury from chokeholds in the future. Under the facts as alleged, this was speculative; the chance that plaintiff would be stopped for a routine traffic offense and then be subjected to a chokehold without provocation was mere conjecture. Also, no finding had ever been made that plaintiff faced a real and immediate threat of again being illegally choked.

Moreover, even if plaintiff's damages suit somehow conferred standing to seek injunctive relief, such relief was unavailable to him here. First, the speculative nature of plaintiff's claim of future injury meant that he could not satisfy the equitable requirement of likelihood of substantial and immediate irreparable injury. Second, plaintiff's damages remedy constituted an adequate remedy at law. The Court concluded by emphasizing that when federal courts

---

[56] 461 US 95 (1983).

are asked to oversee state law enforcement authorities, "normal principles of equity, comity and federalism" should inform this judgment.[57]

Justices Marshall, Brennan, Blackmun, and Stevens dissented at some length.[58] They argued that plaintiff clearly had standing to seek injunctive relief because he had already been injured and was seeking damages in a challenge to the constitutionality of the chokehold policy. This constituted the necessary personal stake in the outcome. They objected to the majority's "requiring a separate showing for each form of relief." They further contended that principles of federalism did not preclude the preliminary injunction issued by the district court because it required no extensive federal supervision of the police department's activities. Finally, the dissenting justices argued that the traditional prerequisites for preliminary equitable relief were present. The more stringent requirements of the *Younger* rule[59] were only applicable to injunctions against state criminal proceedings and had little place in a case like *Lyons*.

At a general level, *Lyons* reflects the Court's continuing split as to the proper scope of §1983 liability. More specifically, the majority in *Lyons* required that a plaintiff seeking different kinds of relief must have standing for each kind of relief. Because the *Lyons* plaintiff clearly suffered an injury in fact in the Article III sense, it appears that the majority's refusal to find standing for plaintiff's equitable claim was premised on prudential considerations. This, together with the Court's related view that the *Lyons* plaintiff's future injury was speculative and that equity and federalism principles similarly precluded injunctive relief, demonstrates the Court's insistence that federal courts be especially sensitive to such matters in §1983 equitable relief cases.

Indeed, this sensitivity is apparent in two post-*Lyons* cases which withheld equitable relief. In one, finding *City of Los Angeles v Lyons* on point, the Second Circuit[60] reversed the district court's injunction against the defendant city preventing the use of mace during arrest. Even though the plaintiff's damage suit, based on the use of excessive force against him, including the use of mace, was successful, he would have had to allege for injunctive relief standing purposes "that all city police officers always assault people they encounter with mace, or that the City authorizes its police officers to act in such a manner." Neither was true in this case. Any future injury to plaintiff was thus speculative at best. The court also rejected the "ingenious" argument that the plaintiff represented "inhabitants of a community in which a hazardous substance is being randomly applied to innocent and uninvolved civilians." Plaintiff was unable to show that he was any different in this respect from other members of the community. Further, such an injunction would improperly inject the federal courts into the internal policies of the police department.

---

[57] *Id* 112.

[58] *Id* 113.

[59] *See* §§5.12-5.15.

[60] Curtis v City of New Haven, 726 F2d 65, 68 (2d Cir 1984).

In the other, a Fifth Circuit case[61] where plaintiff challenged the constitutionality of the Mississippi fee scheme for constables on various grounds, the court, relying on *City of Los Angeles v Lyons,* held that he did not have standing to seek injunctive relief, although he had standing to sue the defendant constable for damages. The statute did not prohibit or restrict any conduct nor did it "authorize either the making or manner of making arrests or criminal charges." Plaintiff was no more likely than any other citizen again to be arrested or charged by any constable.

§5.06 —Ripeness

An issue closely related to but different from standing is ripeness. Similarly derived from the *case or controversy* requirement of Article III, ripeness requires an actual, concrete dispute between the parties which can be resolved judicially and examines the related question of whether the challenged governmental conduct has had any practical impact upon the plaintiff.[62] The ripeness issue thus relates to the timing of litigation and can be characterized as the *when* question. It promotes efficient use of judicial resources, avoids unnecessary and premature constitutional adjudication, and assures that the dispute between the parties is real, not hypothetical, so that a federal court can deal effectively and meaningfully with it.

As with standing, the ripeness issue usually poses no serious problem where damages are sought because the dispute has obviously already ripened as much as it can. Again, like standing, ripeness is considerably more troublesome where declaratory or injunctive relief is sought because the plaintiff is necessarily concerned with future governmental conduct. In making the ripeness determination, a court clearly has a great deal of discretion. It will often use what amounts to a balancing test based on the nature of the issue presented as well as the hardship to the plaintiff in denying relief.[63]

The leading case of *United Public Workers v Mitchell*[64] is a good example. Certain federal employees sought injunctive and declaratory relief against the enforcement of a provision of the Hatch Act prohibiting their active involvement in political campaigns. Only one of the plaintiffs had violated the Act; the others asserted they wished to do so. Concluding that these others did not present a ripe issue, the Court said, "A hypothetical threat is not enough. We

---

[61] Brown v Edwards, 721 F2d 1442 (5th Cir 1984).

[62] *E.g.,* Laird v Tatum, 408 US 1, 13 (1972) where the Court found no ripeness because "[a]llegations of a subjective 'chill' are not an adequate substitute for a claim of specific present objective harm or a threat of specific future harm."

[63] See Abbott Labs v Gardner, 387 US 136 (1967), a nonconstitutional case involving the ripeness for review of an administrative regulation, where the Court articulated such a balancing test. In United States *ex rel* Ricketts v Lightcap, 567 F2d 1226, 1232 (3d Cir 1977), a §1983 case, the court, after citing *Abbott Labs* for the proposition that an issue must have a practical impact on litigants for it to be ripe, said: "The usual standard for ripeness should not differ because an action is brought under section 1983."

[64] 330 US 75 (1947).

can only speculate as to the kinds of political activity the appellants desire to engage in or as to the contents of their proposed public statements or the circumstances of their publication."[65]

In contrast, the Court in *Steffel v Thompson*[66] found that plaintiff's claim for declaratory relief regarding the validity of a criminal statute was ripe. It was conceded by the defendants that the prosecutor would initiate criminal proceedings against the plaintiff if plaintiff violated the statute. Also, a companion of the plaintiff had violated the statute and had accordingly been prosecuted.[67]

§5.07 —Political Questions

Even if a §1983 plaintiff overcomes the standing and ripeness hurdles, a reviewability issue—the *what* question—may arise. The prime example in a constitutional setting is the political question doctrine which is based on separation of powers and judicial self-restraint.[68] Largely applicable to coordinate branches of the federal government, the doctrine was previously also used to preclude constitutional challenges to state legislature reapportion-

---

[65] *Id* 90.

[66] 415 US 452 (1974).

[67] However, the Court remanded for the purpose of determining whether the claim was moot.

Representative §1983 ripeness cases in the circuits include the following:

The Fifth Circuit held that plaintiff's §1983 declaratory and injunctive relief challenge to a five-year-old judgment was not ripe for review. The judgment had been unsatisfied for five years but no attempt had ever been made to collect it, no execution was threatened, and plaintiff was judgment-proof. Carter v Heard, 593 F2d 10 (5th Cir 1979).

In Hope Inc v County of DuPage, 717 F2d 1061 (7th Cir 1983), in contrast, the Seventh Circuit found that racial discrimination claims leveled against a county and others in connection with exclusionary housing were ripe for review. Defendants had clearly conveyed their negative attitude toward low- and moderate-income housing, not a single one of the many developments previously allowed included such housing, and plaintiffs for a decade had unsuccessfully sought such housing for themselves or their constituents. The absence of a particular denial of a development did not prevent a finding of ripeness.

In Wilson v Robinson, 668 F2d 380 (8th Cir 1981), where deputies obtained an injunction from the district court on non-First Amendment grounds prohibiting a sheriff from discharging them until compliance with county administrative procedures, the Eighth Circuit, affirming the injunction, ruled that the plaintiff's *accompanying* First Amendment claims were not ripe for review. It was possible that no terminations of plaintiffs would in fact occur.

The Eighth Circuit similarly held that a former judge's suit for injunctive relief against a prosecuting attorney, which alleged that the defendant, through providing information to the press, deprived the plaintiff of his Sixth Amendment right to an impartial jury in the event of a criminal prosecution, was not ripe. Plaintiff had not been charged with any crime and thus any possible denial of his Sixth Amendment right was speculative. Kaylor v Fields, 661 F2d 1177 (8th Cir 1981).

[68] C. Wright, Law of Federal Courts 75 (4th ed 1983). *See generally id* 74-81.

ment and other matters involving state voting. However, since the Court's reapportionment decisions beginning with *Baker v Carr*[69] in 1962, the political questions doctrine is no longer troublesome in such cases. Consequently, the political question issue as such is of relatively little significance in §1983 litigation which is directed at state action.[70]

§5.08   The Eleventh Amendment

States and their "alter ego" agencies may not be sued in *federal court* directly in their own names either for damages or for declaratory and injunctive relief by virtue of the Eleventh Amendment.[71] Suits against their political subdivisions are not so barred.[72] In order to deal with unconstitutional state action, however, and thereby give effect to the Fourteenth Amendment, the Supreme Court in a significant case decided in 1908, *Ex parte Young*,[73] permitted prospective injunctive relief against state officials accused of violating the Fourteenth Amendment. This was accomplished by the fiction that the individual and not the state was being sued. That is,

> the use of the name of the State to enforce an unconstitutional act to the injury of complainants is a proceeding without the authority of and one which does not affect the State in its sovereign or governmental capacity. . . . The officer . . . is in that case stripped of his official or representative character and is subjected in his person to the consequences of his individual conduct.[74]

In contrast, where a government official is the nominal defendant in a suit for damages, but the action is really against the state because the demand is for state money or property, it is clear that such a suit is barred by the Eleventh

---

[69] 369 US 186 (1962).

[70] The doctrine may still retain some viability in connection with political party conventions at the state level. *Compare* Cousins v Wigoda, 419 US 477 (1975) *with* O'Brien v Brown, 409 US 1 (1972) (per curiam).

[71] The Eleventh Amendment reads as follows: "The Judicial power of the United States shall not be construed to extend to any suit in law or equity, commenced or prosecuted against one of the United States by Citizens of another State, or by Citizens or Subjects of any Foreign State." The Amendment has been interpreted by the Supreme Court to bar suits in federal court by citizens of the defendant state. Hans v Louisiana, 134 US 1 (1890).

[72] Moor v County of Alameda, 411 US 693, 717-21 (1973); County of Lincoln v Luning, 133 US 529, 530 (1890).

[73] 209 US 123 (1908).

[74] *Id* 159-60. Such unconstitutional conduct by state officers will still ordinarily constitute "state action" for Fourteenth Amendment purposes. Home Tel & Tel Co v Los Angeles, 227 US 278 (1913). *See* Monroe v Pape, 365 US 167 (1961) and **§§2.04-2.09** on state action generally.

Amendment.[75] Furthermore, even a claim for equitable relief may be barred as the equivalent of a damage claim against the state. For example, the Court held in *Edelman v Jordan*,[76] distinguishing *Ex parte Young*, that an order requiring state officials to pay retroactive benefits to persons wrongfully denied them under invalid (but not unconstitutional) state regulations would violate the Eleventh Amendment. The Court pointed out that the money would come from the state's general revenues and "thus the award resembles far more closely the monetary award against the State itself." The Court also observed that designating the award as "equitable restitution" was not determinative.[77]

That a §1983 cause of action (based on another federal statute)[78] was asserted in *Edelman* made no difference, according to the Court, because §1983, unlike other federal civil rights statutes enacted pursuant to the Fourteenth Amendment, was not intended by Congress to operate as a waiver of Eleventh Amendment immunity. Later, in *Fitzpatrick v Bitzer*,[79] the Court explained its result in *Edelman:* because §1983 excludes cities and other municipal corporations as persons, "it could not have been intended to include States as parties defendant." However, because the Supreme Court thereafter held in *Monell v Department of Social Services*,[80] a 1978 decision, that counties and municipalities are persons for §1983 purposes, it may be suggested that the reasoning underlying the Court's treatment of §1983 and the Eleventh Amendment was weakened. Section 1983 could be interpreted after *Monell* to reflect congressional intent that states are persons and that the Eleventh Amendment does not operate as a bar in such cases. Indeed, Justice Brennan made just this point when he concurred in *Hutto v Finney*.[81] Nevertheless, the Court, at least with respect to the Eleventh Amendment issue, has rejected Justice Brennan's argument.[82]

Consequently, whenever a government official is sued in federal court under

---

[75] *E.g.*, Governor of Ga v Madrazo, 26 US (1 Pet) 110 (1828). In Ford Motor Co v Department of Treasury, 323 US 459, 464 (1945), the Court said: "[W]hen the action is in essence one for the recovery of money from the state, the state is the real, substantial party in interest and is entitled to invoke its sovereign immunity from suit even though individual officials are nominal defendants."

[76] 415 US 651 (1974).

[77] *Id* 665-66.

[78] See **§2.12** regarding §1983 actions based on federal statutes.

[79] 427 US 445, 452 (1976). In marked contrast with the Court's reluctance in both *Edelman* and *Fitzpatrick* to treat §1983 as intended to waive the states' Eleventh Amendment immunity, the Court in *Fitzpatrick* held that comparable relief under Title VII was permissible because it found congressional intent to effect such a waiver. Waiver as to Fourteenth Amendment violations made actionable under §1983 had been left open in *Edelman, see* dissenting opinion of Justice Marshall, 415 US at 694 n 2, but was then, as noted, discussed in *Fitzpatrick*.

[80] 436 US 658 (1978).

[81] 437 US 678 (1978).

[82] Quern v Jordan, 440 US 332 (1979). See **§6.20** on states as persons, a question analytically different from the Eleventh Amendment issue, and one with important practical implications.

§1983 either for damages[83] or for declaratory and injunctive relief,[84] the court must inquire whether the suit is in fact against the state. According to the Supreme Court, after it is determined that a government body is the real defendant, the resolution of the Eleventh Amendment issue "turns on whether the [body] is to be treated as an arm of the State partaking of the State's Eleventh Amendment immunity, or is instead to be treated as a municipal corporation or political subdivision to which the Eleventh Amendment does not extend."[85]

Dealing with this question in connection with an Ohio school board, the Supreme Court emphasized the following factors:

1.   Ohio law characterized school boards as political subdivisions, and not as the state

2.   There were many school boards in Ohio

3.   While subject to some guidance from the state board and receiving a significant amount of money from the state, Ohio school boards had extensive powers to issue bonds and levy taxes

On balance, the Court considered an Ohio local school board to be more like a county or city than "an arm of the State" and, therefore, not entitled to Eleventh Amendment immunity.[86]

(*Text continued on page 289*)

---

[83] *E.g.*, Scheuer v Rhodes, 416 US 232, 238 (1974), where the Governor of Ohio and others were sued under §1983 for damages. The Court found the claim was not barred by the Eleventh Amendment because the plaintiffs were "seeking to impose individual and personal liability on the *named defendants.*" (emphasis in original).

[84] Edelman v Jordan, 415 US 651 (1974). In a *declaratory judgment* case where a state had violated federal law prior to congressional amendment of that law, the Court held in Green v Mansour, 54 USLW 4011 (S Ct Dec 3, 1985) that the Eleventh Amendment barred declaratory relief (as well as "notice" relief) respecting those past violations. The Court asserted that the Eleventh Amendment was applicable because otherwise the requested federal declaratory relief could serve as res judicata in state court on the issue of the state's liability for preamendment violations. The federal statute of concern involved eligibility for Aid to Families with Dependent Children.

[85] Mount Healthy City School Bd of Educ v Doyle, 429 US 274, 280 (1977). After *Monell,* a local government body is a suable §1983 person for damages and equitable relief purposes, but this, of course, raises no serious Eleventh Amendment problem.

[86] *Id. Mount Healthy's* approach was used by the circuits in the following Eleventh Amendment cases:

First Circuit

Fernandez v Chardon, 681 F2d 42 (1st Cir 1982), *affd on other grounds sub nom* Chardon v Fumero Soto, 462 US 650 (1983) (Commonwealth of Puerto Rico's Department of Education may not be subject to a back pay award where Secretary of Education successfully sued in his official capacity for injunctive relief; this result despite the intermingling of state and federal funds).

Second Circuit

Holley v Lavine, 605 F2d 638 (2d Cir 1979) (county social agency not arm of state for Eleventh Amendment purposes even though part of, and supervised by, state social services department).

Third Circuit

Helfrich v Pennsylvania Dept of Military Affairs, 660 F2d 88 (3d Cir 1981) (per curiam) (Pennsylvania's Department of Military Affairs and its Soldiers and Sailors House were arms of the state for Eleventh Amendment purposes).

Fifth Circuit

Emory v Texas State Bd of Medical Examiners, 748 F2d 1023 (5th Cir 1984) (Texas State Board of Medical Examiners protected by Eleventh Amendment).

Laje v RE Thomason Gen Hosp, 665 F2d 724 (5th Cir 1982) (county hospital district in Texas, and hospital as part thereof, are independent in relation to the state and thus not arms of the state protected by Eleventh Amendment).

United Carolina Bank v Board of Regents, 665 F2d 553 (5th Cir 1982) (Steven F. Austin State University an arm of the state of Texas; Eleventh Amendment applicable even where payment not directly made out of the state treasury).

Gay Student Serv v Texas A&M Univ, 612 F2d 160, 165 (5th Cir 1980) (Texas A&M University may be protected by Eleventh Amendment depending on whether it is an arm of the state or is an independent political body; issue discussed but not resolved because prospective relief against university's officials sought in addition to monetary relief).

Moore v Tangipahoa Parish School Bd, 594 F2d 489 (5th Cir 1979) (awards of back pay against school board not barred by Eleventh Amendment).

Goss v San Jacinto Junior College, 588 F2d 96 (5th Cir 1979) (junior college, as an independent political subdivision under state law, not immune by virtue of Eleventh Amendment).

Sixth Circuit

Lee v Western Reserve Psychiatric Habilation Center, 747 F2d 1062 (6th Cir 1984) (Western Reserve Psychiatric Habilation Center an Ohio state facility protected by Eleventh Amendment).

Foulks v Ohio Dept of Rehabilitation & Correction, 713 F2d 1229 (6th Cir 1983) (Adult Parole Authority, a division of the Ohio Department of Rehabilitation and Correction, protected by the Eleventh Amendment).

Seventh Circuit

Cannon v University of Health Sciences, 710 F2d 351 (7th Cir 1983) (Southern Illinois University and University of Illinois, as state universities which are the "alter ego" of the state, protected by the Eleventh Amendment even if damages award would be paid through insurance or federal funds).

Mackey v Stanton, 586 F2d 1126 (7th Cir 1978), *cert denied*, 48 USLW 3211 (S Ct Oct 2, 1979) (independent county welfare department not protected by Eleventh Amendment).

Ninth Circuit

Almond Hill School v United States Dept of Agriculture, 768 F2d 1030 (9th Cir 1985) (California Department of Food and Agriculture protected by Eleventh Amendment).

Demery v Kupperman, 735 F2d 1139 (9th Cir 1984) (§1983 damages action against officials of California's Board of Medical Quality Assurance in their *individual* capacities was not an action against the state itself, even though state law required the state to pay damages awards against state officials "for acts performed in the course of their official duties"; if this indemnification argument were accepted, "a state would then have the power effectively to prevent vindication of federal rights in federal court"; in addition, the federal court could not order a state to pay damages where a state official was held personally liable, but could only order the official himself to do so; in short, the nature of the claim here did not impose liability directly on the state treasury; the Supreme Court's *Pennhurst* case did not declare a contrary rule).

A similar approach was used by the Court in *Lake Country Estates v Tahoe Regional Planning Agency*,[87] in holding that the Eleventh Amendment does not bar suits in federal court against an interstate-compact planning agency. The Court also suggested that the agency was a suable *person* for §1983 purposes.[88] The agency, called Tahoe Regional Planning Agency (TRPA), was created by compact between California and Nevada, was consented to by Congress, and was intended to regulate development in the Lake Tahoe basin resort area and conserve its natural resources through regional land use and other planning. In finding that TRPA was not protected by the Eleventh Amendment, the Court relied on the intent of Nevada and California, the terms of the compact, and TRPA's actual operation. More specifically:

1. Both states filed briefs before the Court disclaiming any intent to confer immunity on TRPA
2. The compact described TRPA as a "political subdivision"
3. Counties and cities appointed six of TRPA's ten governing members; the two states appointed only four
4. Counties, not the states, provided funding for TRPA
5. Neither state was responsible for TRPA's obligations
6. Land use regulation is traditionally a function performed by local governments

---

Peters v Lieuallen, 693 F2d 966 (9th Cir 1982) (Oregon State Board of Higher Education protected by the Eleventh Amendment).

Rutledge v Arizona Bd of Regents, 660 F2d 1345 (9th Cir 1981), *affd on other grounds*, 460 US 719 (1983) (Arizona Board of Regents and Arizona State University are protected by Eleventh Amendment; their funds are state funds even though possibly derived from insurance proceeds).

Tenth Circuit

Maestas v Board of Educ of Mora Indep School Dist, 749 F2d 591 (10th Cir 1984) (local school boards and school districts are arms of New Mexico and protected by Eleventh Amendment).

Eleventh Circuit

East Central Health Dist v Brown, 752 F2d 615 (11th Cir 1985) (not clear on record whether East Central Health District an independent governmental body or an arm of the State of Georgia).

Tuveson v Florida Governor's Council on Indian Affairs, 734 F2d 730 (11th Cir 1984) (§1983 damages action against Florida Governor's Council on Indian Affairs was a suit against the state itself within the meaning of the Eleventh Amendment; while the council was a nonprofit organization, it was created by the governor for the purpose of carrying out a governmental function, not a proprietary one, and was thus an executive council; also, under state antidiscrimination laws it was considered a state agency; on balance, despite the fact that sometimes the council acted as an arm of the state and at other times it acted independently, and regardless of the little information on the record respecting the council's funding and its control by the state, the council was protected by Eleventh Amendment immunity; there was no waiver because, under Florida law, an explicit act of the legislature was required and there was none here).

[87] 440 US 391 (1979).

[88] *Id* 405 n 29.

7. TRPA's authority to make rules was not subject to state veto
8. California had sued "in an unsuccessful attempt to impose its will on TRPA"

The Eleventh Amendment now also bars federal *injunctive relief,* whether prospective or retrospective, against state officials sued in their official capacities pursuant to a *pendent state claim,* according to the Court in *Pennhurst State School v Halderman.*[89] Plaintiff, resident of a Pennsylvania facility for the mentally retarded, brought a federal class action against state and county officials alleging the violation of various federal constitutional and statutory provisions, as well as the violation of a Pennsylvania mental health statute. Eventually, the district court awarded injunctive relief under state law, which was affirmed by the court of appeals after rejecting the defendants' Eleventh Amendment contention. Reversing on this ground, the Supreme Court, in an opinion by Justice Powell, reasoned that the Eleventh Amendment's *Ex parte Young* exception for federal injunctive relief actions brought against state officials was limited to Fourteenth Amendment claims which would not otherwise be vindicated if prospective injunctive relief were unavailable. There was no corresponding federal interest in allowing federal courts to enjoin state officials for their violations of state law even where the injunction would be prospective only.

Furthermore, the Court continued, there was no reason, for Eleventh Amendment purposes, to treat pendent jurisdiction[90] as different from federal jurisdiction otherwise obtained. In all cases filed in federal court, the Eleventh Amendment question depends on whether the relief sought and ordered has a direct impact on the state itself. Even if the application of the Eleventh Amendment to pendent state claims might result in federal claims being brought in state court, or in the bifurcation of claims, such considerations of policy cannot override constitutional limitations on the authority of the federal judiciary.

The Court went on to hold that injunctive relief could not be upheld against the county officials as well as the state officials. Among other things, funding for county mental retardation programs came almost entirely from Pennsylvania. Also, state law contemplated extensive cooperation between county and state mental health officials. Thus, any relief granted against county officials "would be partial and incomplete at best." The Court intimated[91] that the

---

[89] 465 US 89 (1984). The Sixth Circuit made clear that *Pennhurst* has no effect on §1983 damages actions against state officials sued in their individual capacities. Spruytte v Walters, 753 F2d 498 (6th Cir 1985). And the Ninth Circuit held that the *Ex parte Young* exception applies to §1983 "laws," prospective relief actions against state officials sued in their official capacities. Almond Hill School v United States Dept of Agriculture, 768 F2d 1030 (9th Cir 1985). See **§2.12** on "laws" actions.

[90] *See* **§1.11.**

[91] 465 US 89. Justices Stevens, Brennan, Marshall, and Blackmun dissented at considerable length, arguing that prior case law clearly demonstrated that the Eleventh Amendment does not apply to pendent state claims for injunctive relief and that in any event the Eleventh Amendment should not apply where the conduct of state officials is prohibited by state law. In their view, the majority's holding was "unprecedented."

county officials might themselves be protected by the Eleventh Amendment in this case because, given the state funding, the relief obtained would in effect run against the state itself.

After *Pennhurst,* several points must be emphasized. *Pennhurst* does not apply to pendent *state damages* claims against state officials sued in their *individual capacities,* just as the Eleventh Amendment does not apply to *§1983 damages* claims against state officials in their *individual capacities.* Similarly, *Pennhurst* does not apply to local government officials sued for injunctive relief in their official capacities unless, as the Court noted, such relief would directly implicate the state treasury.[92] However, to the extent that *Pennhurst* results in the bifurcation of claims, with the federal claims brought in federal court and the state claims brought in state court, troublesome preclusion issues might arise.[93]

According to the Court, a state may raise the Eleventh Amendment bar for the first time on appeal; not having raised it at the district court stage does not, standing alone, constitute a waiver.[94] In this connection, the Supreme Court has also emphasized that any Eleventh Amendment waiver by a state must appear clearly and will not easily be implied.[95] There may nevertheless be situations in which a state is found to have waived the Eleventh Amendment bar as to certain defendants.[96]

---

[92] In Crane v Texas, 759 F2d 412 (5th Cir 1985) the court exhaustively canvassed Supreme Court and circuit court case law, all of which in its view clearly established that Eleventh Amendment immunity does not extend to counties, including those in Texas. However, it then went on to consider and reject the *Pennhurst*-related contention that the county was protected because state funds would be used to pay any award. Defendant claimed that this result would occur because under Texas law all county property belonged to the state. The court gave the following reasons for its rejection of this argument. First, other counties and their states had the same relationship. Second, the county did not so hold all its property. And third, the county position was inconsistent with its position elsewhere where it sought to protect its own treasury. The Fifth Circuit also countered the contention that Texas counties were unique; they were similar to California counties and to counties in general.

[93] *See* §§5.17-5.20.

[94] Edelman v Jordan, 415 US 651, 677-78 (1974). *See also* Atascadero State Hosp v Scanlon, 105 S Ct 3142 (1985) (state statute or constitutional provision "must specify the state's intention to subject itself to suit in *federal court*").

[95] Edelman v Jordan, 415 US 651, 673 (1974).

[96] *Compare* Soni v Board of Trustees, 513 F2d 347 (6th Cir 1975), *cert denied,* 426 US 919 (1976) (waiver found) *with* Jagnandan v Giles, 538 F2d 1166, 1176-78 (5th Cir 1976) (waiver not found), *cert denied,* 432 US 910 (1977).

See also the following circuit court decisions discussing waiver:

First Circuit

Grotta v Rhode Island, 54 USLW 2395 (1st Cir Jan 17, 1986) (state's legislative intent to waive its Eleventh Amendment immunity from suit in federal court can be derived from state supreme court's interpretation of state statute as intending to waive Eleventh Amendment immunity even though such waiver not explicit in state statute).

Litton Indus Inc v Colon, 587 F2d 70 (1st Cir 1978) (Commonwealth of Puerto Rico and its Department of Education protected by Eleventh Amendment even though Puerto Rico statute authorized actions against commonwealth in its courts; waiver not expressly discussed).

The relationship between the Eleventh Amendment and whether a state is

---

Second Circuit

New York State Assn for Retarded Children v Carey, 727 F2d 240 (2d Cir 1984) (charitable associations could not obtain reimbursement from the state for expenditures they made in excess of state reimbursement rates; state did not waive its Eleventh Amendment immunity "by agreeing in the consent judgment to provide full and timely financing for services to the plaintiff class, or by subsequently accepting the appointment of a special master to monitor future compliance with . . . the consent judgment"; the "most express language" was required for such waiver).

Third Circuit

Skehan v Board of Trustees, 590 F2d 470, 486-88 (3d Cir 1978), *cert denied*, 48 USLW 3211 (S Ct Oct 1, 1979) (waiver not found).

Fifth Circuit

Reimer v Smith, 663 F2d 1316 (5th Cir 1981) (Texas Department of Public Safety an arm of the state; state's possible waiver of Eleventh Amendment immunity under state law not applicable to present case).

Eighth Circuit

Miener v Missouri, 673 F2d 969 (8th Cir 1982) (state did not waive its Eleventh Amendment immunity by participating in program of federal assistance for education of handicapped children).

Ninth Circuit

Department of Educ v Katherine D, 727 F2d 809 (9th Cir 1984) (child's parents were entitled to reimbursement from state for violations of Education for All Handicapped Children Act of 1975, 20 USC §1401 *et seq;* state waived its Eleventh Amendment immunity by choosing to participate in federally funded and regulated educational program for handicapped children; Congress authorized federal suits against states for violating the Act and the state's right to receive funds was conditioned upon its amenability to federal court suit).

Windward Partners v Ariyoshi, 693 F2d 928 (9th Cir 1982) (state of Hawaii, sued for claimed deprivation of property—an option to purchase—through threat of condemnation, was protected by the Eleventh Amendment; state constitutional provision providing for just compensation for takings not sufficiently clear waiver of sovereign immunity; alternatively, even if it were, jurisdiction only conferred on Hawaii state courts, not federal courts).

Eleventh Circuit

Tuveson v Florida Governor's Council on Indian Affairs, 734 F2d 730 (11th Cir 1984) (governor's council was protected by the Eleventh Amendment; there was no waiver inasmuch as under Florida law, an express act of the legislature was required; in addition, the council was not estopped from arguing that it was protected by the Eleventh Amendment even though it had argued in a state court proceeding that it was not a state agency; the council had made that argument for state law purposes only and, in any event, it had lost that argument in state court).

Cate v Oldham, 707 F2d 1176 (11th Cir 1983) (state sued in its own name for injunctive relief protected by the Eleventh Amendment; waiver not found; Florida statute waiving sovereign immunity for certain actions in tort not automatically applicable to suits in federal court or to §1983 actions in any event; comprehensive discussion of different kinds of waiver).

Williams v Bennett, 689 F2d 1370 (11th Cir 1982) (Alabama Board of Corrections and its officials, sued for damages in their official capacities, protected by Eleventh Amendment; state statute providing for payment up to $100,000 by state for judgments against employees and officials of board not a waiver of Eleventh Amendment immunity; this conclusion supported by analysis of statutory language and Alabama's "traditional reluctance to waive its sovereign immunity").

a suable *person* under §1983 is discussed elsewhere.[97] This is relevant both to waiver[98] of Eleventh Amendment immunity in *federal* court and to whether a state can be sued under §1983 in *state* court where the Eleventh Amendment is not applicable.

§5.09 Exhaustion of Judicial Remedies; Habeas Corpus

A plaintiff who has a §1983 cause of action for damages or declaratory or injunctive relief need not exhaust or pursue state judicial remedies before filing in a federal forum. The Supreme Court made this abundantly clear long ago in *Monroe v Pape,*[99] dealing with an action for damages against police officers for claimed Fourth Amendment violations, when it rejected the argument that plaintiffs should proceed in state court: "It is no answer that the State has a law which if enforced would give relief. The federal remedy is supplementary to the state remedy, and the latter need not first be sought and refused before the federal one is invoked."[100] Furthermore, *Monroe's* choice of judicial forum rule applies irrespective of the adequacy of the state judicial remedy.

However, as discussed extensively later,[101] there is a significant qualification of this rule of no exhaustion of judicial remedies. When certain state judicial proceedings, especially criminal, are already pending, a federal plaintiff seeking declaratory or injunctive relief against their continuation will typically be barred from the federal forum by reason of the Supreme Court's decision

---

[97] *See* **§6.20.**

[98] *See* Cate v Oldham, 707 F2d 1176, 1181 n 3 (11th Cir 1983), where the court asserted that whether a state is a person suable under §1983 in federal court if Eleventh Amendment immunity has been waived by the state was an open question which it did not have to reach.

[99] 365 US 167 (1961).

[100] *Id* 183. However, in City of Columbus v Leonard, 565 F2d 957 (5th Cir 1977) (en banc), *cert denied,* 47 USLW 3824 (S Ct June 25, 1979), dismissed police officers filed suit under §1983 in federal court before a scheduled administrative hearing was held, challenging their dismissal on procedural due process grounds. Thereafter, the dismissals were upheld by the police hearing board but, instead of seeking review of the decision in state court as they could have done, the officers pursued their §1983 action in federal court. The district court dismissed the action on the ground that plaintiffs could not pursue state remedies half-way and then switch; once chosen, the state route must be exhausted. The Fifth Circuit reversed and remanded, and the Supreme Court denied certiorari. However, a lengthy dissent from this denial by Justice Rehnquist, with whom Chief Justice Burger and Justice Blackmun joined, argued that state remedies should have been exhausted by plaintiffs prior to pursuing their §1983 action in federal court because those remedies were already initiated by plaintiffs. They also contended more broadly that the Court should seriously reconsider the propriety of its no-exhaustion rule in those §1983 cases "where the State can demonstrate that there is an available and adequate state remedy." *But see* **§5.10.**

[101] *See* **§§5.12-5.15.**

in *Younger v Harris.*[102] Barring the federal plaintiff amounts to a de facto exhaustion of judicial remedies requirement. Furthermore, it is even possible that the *Younger* rule will one day be extended by the Supreme Court to include equitable relief against all state judicial proceedings, even those of a civil nature between private parties.[103]

A prisoner, like other §1983 plaintiffs, need not exhaust state judicial remedies as, for example, in challenging prison procedures or conditions, or the acts of prison authorities generally.[104] However, the Supreme Court held in *Preiser v Rodriguez*[105] that a prisoner's §1983 challenge to the *fact or duration of his confinement* is in substance a petition for habeas corpus and must be treated as such by the federal courts. Because the federal habeas corpus statute requires exhaustion of state judicial remedies,[106] the effect of treating the §1983 claim as federal habeas corpus is the dismissal of that claim from the federal forum altogether in situations where state judicial remedies have not yet been pursued. As a practical matter, if a prisoner challenges both the conditions of confinement and its length or fact, the latter challenge, being in the nature of habeas corpus, will be dismissed and the prisoner sent to the state courts. However, the former claim can still be pursued in federal court while state judicial proceedings are being conducted.[107]

In some cases a decision adverse to a plaintiff's due process challenge amounts to a de facto requirement that state judicial remedies be exclusively pursued. For example, in *Paul v Davis,*[108] the Supreme Court held that a §1983 claim based on the due process clause was not stated where the plaintiff sought relief from being listed as an active shoplifter by police authorities. The Court held that no *liberty* or *property* interest was implicated; plaintiff's sole legal remedy was an action for defamation in the state courts. Similarly, in *Ingraham v Wright*[109] the Court held that procedural due process was not violated when school authorities imposed corporal punishment on students because students against whom excessive force was used would have a tort cause of action in the state courts. And in *Hudson v Palmer,*[110] the Court held that in certain circumstances intentional deprivations of property do not violate procedural due process where adequate postdeprivation remedies are available. These cases go beyond a de facto exhaustion of judicial remedies requirement in

---

[102] 401 US 37 (1971).

[103] *See* §5.13.

[104] Wilwording v Swanson, 404 US 249 (1971).

[105] 411 US 475 (1973).

[106] 28 USC §2254 contains this exhaustion requirement.

[107] Preiser v Rodriquez, 411 US 475, 499 n 14 (1973).

[108] 424 US 693 (1976).

[109] 430 US 651 (1977). Cf Baker v McCollan, 443 US 137 (1979), discussed at §3.08, where the Court held that the several days detention of plaintiff, who was arrested pursuant to a valid warrant but protested repeatedly and correctly that he was the victim of mistaken identity, did not constitute a due process violation.

[110] 468 US 517 (1984) discussed at §§3.02 & 3.08.

holding that no §1983 cause of action is stated at all;[111] the federal forum is rendered totally unavailable at any time. This is broader than an exhaustion of judicial remedies requirement which would only *postpone* access to the federal forum.

§5.10   Exhaustion of Administrative Remedies

The federal doctrine of exhaustion of administrative remedies[112] is a judicial creation in response to needs for administrative competence and orderliness of procedure.[113] This doctrine compels a prospective plaintiff to pursue federal administrative remedies as a condition precedent to filing in federal court. In §1983 cases, however, the Supreme Court has repeatedly asserted, beginning with *McNeese v Board of Education*[114] in 1963, that state administrative remedies, like judicial remedies, need not be exhausted before maintaining an action in federal court.

In a case decided in 1973 the Court intimated that perhaps exhaustion of state administrative remedies would be required in some §1983 cases as where, for example, "a license revocation proceeding has been brought by the state and is pending before one of its own agencies and where the individual charged is to be deprived of nothing until the completion of that proceeding. . . ."[115] But two justices promptly disagreed with the Court's characterization of the matter as an open question.[116] Also, the following year the Court reiterated, without qualification, its long-standing no-exhaustion rule for state administrative remedies.[117] In this connection it was significant that the Court had never in fact required exhaustion of state administrative remedies in a §1983 case.

---

[111] See generally **chs 2 & 3** on the §1983 prima facie cause of action.

[112] Exhaustion of administrative remedies must be sharply distinguished from the requirement of ripeness or finality. The Third Circuit, in United States *ex rel* Ricketts v Lightcap, 567 F2d 1226, 1232 (3d Cir 1977), said in this regard: "The doctrines of ripeness for adjudication and of exhaustion of administrative remedies are distinct and not interchangeable. While exhaustion is sometimes a jurisdictional prerequisite to a civil suit in a district court, ripeness is a product of the concept of justiciability." See **§5.04** on ripeness and other justiciability doctrines.

[113] A leading Supreme Court decision on the federal doctrine of exhaustion of administrative remedies is Myers v Bethlehem Shipbuilding Corp, 303 US 41 (1938).

[114] 373 US 668 (1963). King v Smith, 392 US 309 (1968); Damico v California, 389 US 416 (1967). However, the Court has never specifically dealt with the applicability of this no-exhaustion rule to §1983 actions based on violations of federal statutory law ("laws"). For discussion of this question see Construction Aggregates Corp v Rivera de Vicenty, 573 F2d 86, 94 n 6 (1st Cir 1978) (characterized as an "open" question).

[115] Gibson v Berryhill, 411 US 564, 574-75 (1973). Also, in Moore v City of East Cleveland, 431 US 633 (1977), Chief Justice Burger in dissent made the same argument at length. *Id* 521.

[116] Gibson v Berryhill, 411 US 564, 581 (1973), Justices Marshall and Brennan, concurring.

[117] Steffel v Thompson, 415 US 452, 472-73 (1974).

Finally, in *Patsy v Florida Board of Regents*,[118] the Supreme Court reaffirmed its long-standing rule that exhaustion of administrative remedies is not a condition precedent to filing a §1983 action. The Fifth Circuit, after an extensive policy analysis and examination of relevant Supreme Court decisions, had rejected an automatic no-exhaustion of administrative remedies rule in §1983 cases and reversed a panel decision which had held the contrary. *Patsy* involved a §1983 race and sex discrimination action brought by a secretary against a state university. Taking what it called a "flexible" approach, the Fifth Circuit had emphasized that exhaustion of administrative remedies should only be required where:

1. An orderly system of review is provided
2. The agency is able to grant the relief requested
3. Relief is available promptly
4. Agency procedures are fair, not unduly burdensome, and not used to harass
5. Interim relief is available to preserve the litigant's §1983 rights until the administrative process is concluded[119]

The Supreme Court reversed in an opinion by Justice Marshall. At the outset the Court asserted that the no-exhaustion requirement was not an issue of first impression but rather had not been deviated from for 19 years. Next, the Court rejected the argument that an exhaustion requirement should be adopted. It emphasized the following:

1. Section 1983's legislative history shows "Congress assigned to the federal courts a paramount role in protecting constitutional rights"; the "1871 Congress would not have wanted to impose an exhaustion requirement"; and many legislators interpreted §1983 as "enabling the plaintiff to choose the forum in which to seek relief"
2. Recognizing that reliance on §1983's legislative history alone would be "somewhat precarious," the Court read §1997e of the Civil Rights of Institutionalized Persons Act[120] and its legislative history as demonstrat-

---

[118] 457 US 496 (1982), *revg* 634 F2d 900 (5th Cir 1981) (en banc).

[119] 634 F2d at 912-13. Six judges dissented at length.

[120] *See* discussion later in this section. Justices O'Connor and Rehnquist concurred "reluctantly" on the ground of stare decisis. Justice White concurred in all the Court's opinion except for that part relating to the Court's reliance on the Civil Rights of Institutionalized Persons Act. Justices Powell and Burger dissented on the exhaustion question, with Justice Powell also arguing that there was a serious Eleventh Amendment jurisdictional issue that the Court incorrectly treated.

In an earlier case where a majority of the Supreme Court had held that state taxpayers are barred by the principle of comity from bringing §1983 damages action challenging the validity of the administration of state tax systems in federal court, four justices— Brennan, Marshall, Stevens, and O'Connor—rejected the majority's approach. Instead, they asserted that such taxpayers must first exhaust their state administrative remedies

ing "that Congress understood that exhaustion is not generally required in §1983 actions, and that it decided to carve out only a narrow exception to this rule [for adult prisoners bringing §1983 actions]"

3. The Court rejected the defendants' contention that various policy considerations, including federal court burdens, comity, and improved federal-state relations, warranted an exhaustion requirement. The policy considerations respecting the existence of such a requirement, besides being complex, did not all cut in the same direction. Also, the design and scope of an exhaustion requirement were equally difficult, and included categories of §1983 claims, standards for evaluating administrative procedures, tolling and limitations problems, res judicata and collateral estoppel issues, and the like

The Court's decision in *Patsy* is sound. It would have been anomalous to hold that exhaustion of judicial remedies is not required, while at the same time ruling that exhaustion of administrative remedies is required. In terms of comity, a state administrative tribunal should be entitled to no more deference than that accorded a state judicial tribunal.

While a prisoner's §1983 claim is sometimes treated as federal habeas corpus and thereby becomes subject to an exhaustion of state judicial remedies requirement,[121] a §1983 claim attacking prison conditions and events unrelated to the fact and duration of confinement is not, as a matter of §1983 interpretation, subject to an exhaustion of administrative remedies requirement.[122] However, Congress has legislated an exhaustion of administrative remedies requirement in certain circumstances for persons institutionalized in state or local government correctional facilities. The statute, called the Civil Rights of Institutionalized Persons Act, is codified as 42 USC §1997e.[123] Among other things, the Act specifically provides that an inmate who sues under §1983 shall, if appropriate and the interests of justice warrant, have his or her case continued by the court for 90 days so that the inmate may exhaust "such plain, speedy, and effective administrative remedies as are available." Exhaustion may only be ordered, however, where the applicable administrative procedures are either certified by the Attorney General or are determined by the court to comply substantially with certain minimum acceptable standards. These standards, promulgated by the Attorney General and published in the Code of Federal Regulations,[124] include:

1. An advisory role for the inmates
2. Time limits for written replies to inmate grievances

as a condition precedent to filing in federal court. Fair Assessment in Real Estate Assn v McNary, 454 US 100 (1981), discussed at **§5.03.**
[121] Preiser v Rodriquez, 411 US 475 (1973). *See* **§5.09.**
[122] Houghton v Shafer, 392 US 639 (1968).
[123] Pub L No 96-247, 94 Stat 349 (1980).
[124] 28 CFR §§4.01-22 (pt 40).

3.   Priority processing of emergency grievances
4.   Safeguards to avoid reprisals
5.   Independent review of the disposition of grievances

The rule of *Younger v Harris*[125] must be mentioned here as it was earlier in connection with exhaustion of judicial proceedings.[126] It is possible that a state's pending administrative proceedings will ultimately be regarded by the Supreme Court as the functional equivalent, for federalism purposes, of state judicial proceedings of a quasi-criminal nature.[127] If this occurs, the *Younger* rule will then ordinarily apply to prohibit declaratory and injunctive relief against a pending state administrative proceeding. Such a holding will in effect create an exhaustion of administrative remedies requirement in these §1983 cases.

§5.11   Exhaustion in the Circuits

Following the Supreme Court's lead in *Monroe v Pape*,[128] the circuits all adhere to the no-exhaustion rule in connection with state judicial remedies. The only exception arises where a prisoner challenges the fact or duration of confinement by using §1983. In such a case, as discussed earlier,[129] the §1983 claim is treated as a petition for federal habeas corpus, which in turn requires exhaustion of state judicial remedies.

This federal habeas corpus approach was expanded by the Fifth Circuit in an important post-*Preiser* case when it dismissed a federal plaintiff's challenge to state criminal convictions which he had fully discharged and as to which he was seeking, among other things, declaratory relief.[130] He had never before collaterally attacked his convictions. Rejecting plaintiff's argument that he would otherwise be left without a federal remedy, the Fifth Circuit observed that he had already had the chance of a federal remedy and not used it, adding:

> Stripped to the bone, the plaintiff's action under §1983 is little more than a habeas corpus action without a custody requirement. We do not believe that §1983 was meant to be a substitute for habeas corpus when there is not custody. . . . Under his theory of §1983, the appellant would have us sit in perpetual review of all criminal decisions.[131]

---

[125] 401 US 37 (1971).

[126] *See* **§5.09.**

[127] See **§§5.12-5.15** on the scope of the *Younger* rule. See also Gibson v Berryhill, 411 US 564 (1973) where the Court apparently implied, but did not hold, that pending state administrative proceedings are subject to the *Younger* rule.

[128] 365 US 167, 183 (1961).

[129] *See* **§5.09.**

[130] Cavett v Ellis, 578 F2d 567 (5th Cir 1978).

[131] *Id* 569. *See also* Siano v Justices of Mass, 698 F2d 52 (1st Cir 1983) (favoring *Cavett* but avoiding decision on the issue); Hanson v Circuit Ct of First Judicial Dist, 591 F2d 407 (7th Cir 1979) (adopting *Cavett's* reasoning).

In general, custody, the kind of relief sought, and the existence of a challenge to the validity of a conviction or confinement play an important role in circuit court decisions dealing with the question whether the claims before them are challenges to the fact or duration of confinement and hence habeas corpus. Thus, in a Third Circuit case,[132] an inmate's due process challenge to the denial of admission to a home furlough program was incorrectly characterized by the district court as a habeas corpus challenge to duration of confinement which required exhaustion of state judicial remedies. According to the Third Circuit, the inmate instead was attacking the conditions under which he was confined and, therefore, could sue directly under §1983. The court reasoned:

> Although a prisoner's total number [of] days actually spent behind bars can technically be reduced by the number of days during which he is out of prison on furloughs, it cannot be said that occasional short furloughs such as these reduce the duration of confinement in the same way as did the good time credits at issue in *Preiser,* where the credits would have had the effect of terminating the prisoner's sentence at an earlier calendar date.[133]

In contrast, in a Fourth Circuit case[134] where an inmate claimed that the defendant sheriff had conspired to arrest him and procured his conviction using perjured testimony, the "difficult" question was

> whether a state prisoner may challenge the validity of his conviction in a district court without having exhausted available state remedies upon the expedient of confining himself to a §1983 claim for monetary damages, a declaratory judgment, and prospective injunctive relief, with a seemingly deliberate omission of a request for immediate release from his imprisonment.

After analyzing relevant Supreme Court decisions and canvassing decisions in the circuits, the Fourth Circuit held that the complaint was in the nature of a request for habeas corpus relief—even though plaintiff did not request such relief—because it directly challenged the validity of the state court conviction. Not only would habeas corpus relief be available and appropriate, but plaintiff's complaint "has all the earmarks of a deliberate attempt to subvert the [exhaustion of state judicial remedies] requirement" of federal habeas corpus.
    Similarly, in a Fifth Circuit[135] case, it was determined that a prisoner's §1983

---

[132] Wright v Cuyler, 624 F2d 455 (3d Cir 1980).

[133] *Id* 458.

[134] Hamlin v Warren, 664 F2d 29, 30 (4th Cir 1981). Judge Winter dissented. *Compare* Jackson v Torres, 720 F2d 877 (5th Cir 1983) (the nature of the remedy sought is not determinative; what is important is whether the claim goes to the constitutionality of a state conviction).

[135] Stevens v Heard, 674 F2d 320 (5th Cir 1982). *See also* Hadley v Werner, 753 F2d 514 (6th Cir 1985) (inmate's damages action challenging appointed counsel fee schedule on ground that it caused both denial of effective assistance of counsel and his

suit for injunctive relief, alleging among other things that (1) two detainers were improperly lodged against him because the sentences so represented should have already run; (2) he should be promoted to trusty status; and (3) he should be retroactively awarded overtime would, if successful, have the effect of shortening plaintiff's sentence. Thus, according to the Fifth Circuit, the claims should have been raised through habeas corpus. In addition, plaintiff's damages claim—that the detainers prevented him from receiving proper medical care and emergency reprieves—similarly would entail a determination of the detainers' validity. It, too, could only be brought after federal habeas corpus relief was sought.

However, in an Eleventh Circuit case,[136] an inmate was sentenced after a disciplinary hearing to confinement to segregation and denial of contact visits for 30 days for violating a prison rule. Claiming a due process violation, he sued for damages as well as for ancillary relief, seeking a return to his original job assignment and removal of any record of the disciplinary hearing from his file. Reversing the district court in this respect, the Eleventh Circuit ruled that the inmate's complaint was properly brought as a §1983 action, and was not a petition for federal habeas corpus for which exhaustion of state judicial remedies is required. Here, the plaintiff sued for damages and, further, was not challenging the fact or duration of his confinement. It was also significant that

---

plea of guilty was in nature of habeas corpus because it challenged the validity of inmate's conviction and confinement; Alexander v Johnson, 742 F2d 117 (4th Cir 1984) (challenge to conditioning parole upon repayment of attorney's fees was in nature of habeas corpus); Dixon v Alexandra, 741 F2d 121 (6th Cir 1984) (claim that plea bargain containing parole provision inconsistent with state law should be enforced was in nature of habeas corpus); Todd v Baskerville, 712 F2d 70 (4th Cir 1983) (claim that good conduct time was not credited was in nature of habeas corpus if plaintiff in custody, even for damages purposes); Mokone v Fenton, 710 F2d 998 (3d Cir 1983) (challenge made under Interstate Agreement on Detainers to an out-of-state conviction for which a sentence is to be served in the future is in nature of habeas corpus); Walker v Prisoner Review Bd, 694 F2d 499 (7th Cir 1982) (challenge to parole board's procedures in denying parole was §1983 action, but claim that sentences were concurrent and not consecutive was in nature of habeas corpus); Ellison v De La Rosas, 685 F2d 959 (5th Cir 1982) (effective assistance of counsel claim went to validity of conviction and thus was in nature of habeas corpus); Delaney v Giarrusso, 633 F2d 1126, 1128 (5th Cir 1981) (per curiam) (damages suit against police officers claiming illegal arrest was in nature of habeas corpus, but claim of excessive force was not); Keenan v Bennett, 613 F2d 127 (5th Cir 1980) (challenge to method for computing good time credits was in nature of habeas corpus even though inmate did not seek restoration of those credits).

[136] McKinnis v Mosely, 693 F2d 1054 (11th Cir 1982). *See also* Lambert v Finley, 735 F2d 239 (7th Cir 1984) (inmate's claim that court clerk refused to send him transcript so he could appeal conviction not habeas corpus); Battieste v City of Baton Rouge, 732 F2d 439 (5th Cir 1984) (no "absolute rule" that person not meeting custody requirement of habeas corpus cannot challenge constitutionality of state court conviction resulting in fine); Alexander v Ware, 714 F2d 416 (5th Cir 1983) (challenge to prison's use of summary disciplinary procedure not habeas corpus but rather attack on prison disciplinary system itself); Chancery Clerk v Wallace, 646 F2d 151 (5th Cir 1981) (challenge to procedures used in involuntarily committing persons to state mental institutions not habeas corpus).

good time credits were not involved. His request for ancillary equitable relief did not change the nature of his §1983 suit into federal habeas corpus.

As to administrative remedies, the rule in the circuits is clear after *Patsy v Florida Board of Regents*[137] that exhaustion is not required as a matter of §1983 interpretation. Only where there is congressional intent to require exhaustion of administrative remedies in a particular kind of case, as for example, in the Civil Rights of Institutionalized Persons Act,[138] will such a requirement be imposed. Even here, the Ninth Circuit ruled,[139] the inmate's federal action must be continued while administrative remedies are pursued and may not be dismissed. Where a federal statute is used as the basis for a §1983 *laws* action, after the appropriate inquiry into congressional intent and the existence of a right, privilege, or immunity has been made,[140] then it is likely that exhaustion of administrative remedies will not be required.[141]

Despite *Patsy*, there may still be some situations where exhaustion of administrative remedies is still in effect required on other grounds. In a Third Circuit case[142] where ongoing administrative proceedings in the United States Department of Education dealt in part with plaintiffs' claims of racial discrimination in higher education, the court conceded that exhaustion of such remedies was not required for plaintiffs' §1983 and related claims. Nevertheless, it affirmed as not an abuse of discretion the district court's order temporarily staying the federal litigation on the ground that the administrative proceeding might obviate some of the controversy. It was significant that the district court was to actively monitor the progress of those administrative proceedings.

---

[137] 457 US 496 (1982), discussed at **§5.10.**

[138] 42 USC §1997e, set out at **§5.10.** *See* Johnson v King, 696 F2d 370 (5th Cir 1983) (§1997e requirements substantially different from those the Fifth Circuit had set out prior to Supreme Court's *Patsy* decision); Owens v Kimmel, 693 F2d 711 (7th Cir 1982) (remanding to determine whether prison's grievance procedures for dealing with loss of personal property was consistent with §1997e).

[139] Francis v Marquez, 741 F2d 1127 (9th Cir 1984) (emphasizing "shall . . . continue" language of §1997e).

[140] *See* **§2.12.**

[141] Pushkin v Regents of University of Colo, 658 F2d 1372 (10th Cir 1981) (no exhaustion of administrative remedies requirement applicable either to §504 of Rehabilitation Act of 1973 independently or through §1983 laws action). *Cf* Members of Bridgeport Hous Auth Police Force v City of Bridgeport, 646 F2d 55 (2d Cir 1981) (leaving question open regarding exhaustion requirement as applied to claim under Comprehensive Employment and Training Act, 29 USC §3801 *et seq* (1976) as the basis for a §1983 laws action) *and* Swan v Stoneman, 635 F2d 97 (2d Cir 1980) (pre-*Patsy* case holding that administrative remedies need not be exhausted for §1983 laws claim based on Rehabilitation Act of 1973 because state and federal remedies inadequate).

[142] Cheyney State College Faculty v Hufstedler, 703 F2d 732 (3d Cir 1983).

§5.12 Declaratory and Injunctive Relief Against State Criminal Proceedings—The Rule of *Younger v Harris*

Section 1983 on its face speaks of the availability of equitable relief, with no apparent exception for declaratory or injunctive relief against state criminal proceedings. One possible obstacle to granting such relief, at least where state criminal proceedings are pending, is the Anti-Injunction Act.[143] This obstacle, though, was removed by the Supreme Court in *Mitchum v Foster*,[144] in a holding that the Anti-Injunction Act does not apply to §1983 at all. Despite this, in a series of important decisions beginning in 1971 with *Younger v Harris*,[145] the Court began to set out a series of rather technical rules[146] for determining whether and when a federal district court can give declaratory and injunctive relief relating to the validity of state statutes involved in state criminal proceedings. *Younger* and its progeny clearly reflect the current Supreme Court's preference for an enhanced state court role in cases raising the constitutionality of state statutes.

Younger itself involved a federal plaintiff who had been indicted in a California state court for violating the Criminal Syndicalism Act. Upon indictment, he filed a complaint in federal district court seeking to enjoin the district attorney from prosecuting him. He claimed that the prosecution and the Syndicalism Act itself inhibited his exercise of First Amendment rights. The Supreme Court, in an opinion by Justice Black, reversed the judgment of the district court which had granted the injunctive relief sought because the judgment was "a violation of the national policy forbidding federal courts to stay or enjoin pending state court proceedings except under special circumstances."[147]

The Court gave several related justifications for its decision. First, equity

---

[143] 28 USC §2283, discussed at **§5.03.**

[144] 407 US 225 (1972).

[145] 401 US 37 (1971). *See also* Middlesex County Ethics Comm v Garden State Bar Assn, 457 US 423 (1982); Moore v Sims, 442 US 415 (1979); Trainor v Hernandez, 431 US 434 (1977); Wooley v Maynard, 430 US 705 (1977); Juidice v Vail, 430 US 327 (1977); Doran v Salem Inn Inc, 422 US 922 (1975); Hicks v Miranda, 422 US 332 (1975); Huffman v Pursue Ltd, 420 US 592 (1975); Steffel v Thompson, 415 US 452 (1974); Samuels v Mackell, 401 US 66 (1971); Perez v Ledesma, 401 US 82 (1971).

[146] These rules together constitute what is here called the "*Younger* rule," occasionally also referred to in the cases and elsewhere as "*Younger* abstention" and "*Younger* equitable restraint." The literature on the *Younger* rule is extensive and includes the following articles:
Comment, *Post-Younger Excesses in the Doctrine of Equitable Restraint: A Critical Analysis,* 1976 Duke LJ 523; *Developments in the Law - Section 1983 and Federalism,* 90 Harv L Rev 1133 (1977); Laycock, *Federal Interference with State Prosecutions: The Need for Prospective Relief,* 1977 Sup Ct Rev 193; Theis, *Younger v Harris: Federalism in Context,* 33 Hastings LJ 103 (1981); Wells, *The Role of Comity in the Law of Federal Courts,* 60 NCL Rev 59 (1981); Whitten, *Federal Declaratory and Injunctive Interference with State Court Proceedings: The Supreme Court and the Limits of Judicial Discretion,* 53 NCL Rev 591 (1975); *See generally* Wright, Law of Federal Courts 320-30 (4th ed 1983).

[147] *Younger,* 401 US at 41.

should not restrain a criminal prosecution when the moving party has an adequate remedy at law and will not suffer irreparable injury if denied equitable relief. Further, the "cost, anxiety, and inconvenience of having to defend against a single criminal prosecution are not in themselves 'irreparable.' " This rule "prevent[s] erosion of the role of the jury and avoid[s] a duplication of legal proceedings and legal sanctions."[148] Second, the notion of *comity*, a "proper respect for state functions," is intimately related to the third justification, "Our Federalism",

> a system in which there is sensitivity to the legitimate interests of both State and National Governments, and in which the National Government, anxious though it may be to vindicate and protect federal rights and federal interests, always endeavors to do so in ways that will not unduly interfere with the legitimate activities of the States.[149]

Younger was in large measure a response to the interpretation given by some federal courts to the Supreme Court's 1965 *Dombrowski v Pfister*[150] decision. *Dombrowski* held that plaintiffs were entitled to injunctive relief against threatened state prosecutions where the statute involved was so overbroad and vague that it impermissibly chilled plaintiffs' First Amendment rights. Some federal courts thereafter used *Dombrowski* as a basis to enjoin pending criminal prosecutions where the federal plaintiffs simply alleged a chilling effect. However, *Younger* limited *Dombrowski* considerably, emphasizing that in the earlier case the plaintiff's allegations were of bad faith and harassment. *Younger* also clearly indicated that allegations of chilling effect and claims of over-breadth and vagueness were insufficient of themselves, absent bad faith or harassment, to justify equitable relief against pending prosecutions.[151]

The *Younger* rule primarily affects the availability of federal relief where the federal plaintiff has already engaged in conduct which is possibly criminal but is arguably constitutionally protected, and asserts he or she wishes to engage in such conduct again in the future. It differs from abstention[152] in mandating outright dismissal of the federal claim and sending both federal and state claims to the state court. *Younger* did suggest, though, that pending prosecutions might nevertheless be enjoined where, as in *Dombrowski,* they are brought in bad faith or to harass or in other "extraordinary circumstances." An example of this last might be where a statute is "flagrantly and patently" unconstitutional.[153] It also expressly left open the question of the availability of relief against *threatened* criminal proceedings.[154] Whether *Younger* would extend beyond state criminal proceedings was not addressed at all. These and other matters were, however,

---

[148] *Id.* 44.
[149] *Id.*
[150] 380 US 479 (1965).
[151] 401 US at 50, 51.
[152] See **§5.16** on abstention.
[153] 401 US at 53-54.
[154] *Id* 41.

discussed in later Supreme Court cases which, as discussed next, for the most part considerably broadened the scope and coverage of *Younger*.[155]

§5.13 —The Current *Younger* Rule

A discussion of the current *Younger* rule, as fleshed out by the Supreme Court's post-*Younger* cases, follows.

A federal court may not award either declaratory[156] or injunctive[157] relief dealing with the constitutionality of a state statute involved in a pending state criminal proceeding in the absence of "extraordinary circumstances." The *Younger* rule is to this extent a de facto requirement that state judicial remedies be exhausted.[158] "Extraordinary circumstances," discussed later,[159] include prosecutions undertaken in bad faith or to harass, situations which involve a flagrantly or patently unconstitutional statute, and cases where the state tribunal is biased and therefore incompetent.

A federal court may award *declaratory* relief invalidating a state statute which might be the basis of a *threatened* (but not pending) state criminal proceeding even in the absence of "extraordinary circumstances"; it makes no difference whether the state statute is challenged on its face or as applied.[160] A federal court may also grant *injunctive* relief against the enforcement of a state statute through *threatened* criminal proceedings where the federal plaintiff has been convicted several times for the same conduct as long as the federal plaintiff does not seek in any way to undo the results of those unappealed convictions.[161]

The *Younger* rule prohibits declaratory or injunctive relief in connection with the validity of a state statute involved in a *pending* state criminal proceeding. This is true even if the federal suit was filed first, so long as the state proceeding is initiated before "proceedings of substance on the merits" in the federal suit.[162] A state criminal proceeding becomes *pending* simply by being initiated formally; in contrast, a federal suit avoids *Younger* dismissal only where proceedings of substance have occurred. However, a plaintiff may sometimes avoid *Younger* dismissal of a declaratory judgment suit by seeking preliminary injunctive relief as well.[163] The traditional equity requirements for such relief, irreparable injury and likelihood of prevailing on the merits, must still be satisfied.

Once a criminal proceeding is initiated, the *Younger* rule bars *all* declaratory

---

[155] See cases at note 145; *see also* §§**5.13-5.14.**

[156] Samuels v Mackell, 401 US 66 (1971).

[157] Younger v Harris, 401 US 37 (1971).

[158] See §**5.09** on exhaustion of state judicial remedies.

[159] *See* §**5.14.**

[160] Steffel v Thompson, 415 US 452 (1974). Federal justiciability requirements must still be met. *See* §**5.04.**

[161] Wooley v Maynard, 430 US 705 (1977).

[162] Hicks v Miranda, 422 US 332 (1975).

[163] Doran v Salem Inn Inc, 422 US 922 (1975).

or injunctive relief, even if the relief is not requested as to the initiated criminal proceeding, but is instead entirely prospective in nature.[164] Furthermore, a criminal proceeding is still considered pending even where the federal plaintiff takes no appeal from a conviction; state appellate remedies must be exhausted in order to get out from under the *Younger* rule.[165] There is, too, the strong indication that the *Younger* rule is applicable to pending criminal proceedings in which the federal plaintiff is not a party, but is directly interested or involved, and over which plaintiff exercises practical control.[166]

The Supreme Court, emphasizing the state interests involved and analogizing them to the state interest in the criminal process, has applied the *Younger* rule in several cases of a civil nature even though federalism concerns seem attenuated: where the state as a party invoked a public nuisance statute "in aid of and closely related to criminal statutes";[167] where the federal plaintiff sought to enjoin judicial contempt proceedings initiated by private parties against him and others;[168] and where the state "in its sovereign capacity" brought a "civil enforcement action" alleging welfare fraud, and sought the return of money and the attachment of certain of the federal plaintiff's funds.[169] Furthermore, the Court applied *Younger* to preclude federal injunctive relief against pending state court litigation initiated by state authorities directed against suspected child abuse and involving temporary state custody of the federal plaintiff children.[170] The Court has so far stopped short of applying the *Younger* rule to pending administrative proceedings[171] or to *all* pending civil proceedings. However, it seems clearly to be moving in this direction.[172]

A recent example of this movement is the Court's decision in *Middlesex County*

---

[164] This aspect of *Younger* is effectively criticized in Laycock, *Federal Interference with State Prosecutions: The Need for Prospective Relief,* 1977 Sup Ct Rev 193, where the author argues that "in many cases the criminal defense cannot provide an adequate remedy, because the criminal court cannot grant interlocutory, prospective or class relief." *Id* 194.

[165] Huffman v Pursue Ltd, 420 US 592 (1975). Once state judicial remedies are exhausted, the problem of res judicata arises. *See* **§5.18.**

[166] Hicks v Miranda, 422 US 322, 348-49 (1975).

[167] Huffman v Pursue Ltd, 420 US 592 (1975).

[168] Juidice v Vail, 430 US 327 (1977).

[169] Trainor v Hernandez, 431 US 434 (1977).

[170] Moore v Sims, 442 US 415 (1979)(important state interests; 5-4 decision).

[171] The Court avoided passing on the applicability of the *Younger* rule to administrative proceedings in Gibson v Berryhill, 411 US 564 (1973), but that case may be read as implying that it does apply. To the extent that the state may be considered a party to administrative proceedings, the "sovereign capacity" rationale of Trainor v Hernandez, 431 US 434 (1977) could be used to justify such a result. On the other hand, *Younger* and its progeny appear to be premised upon respect for the ability of state *courts* to decide constitutional questions involving state law, a respect inapposite to state administrative agencies.

[172] Some circuits have applied *Younger* in cases involving administrative proceedings or judicial proceedings of a noncriminal nature. *See* **§5.15.**

Ethics Committee v Garden State Bar Association.[173] It held that the *Younger* rule applied to a federal court challenge to the constitutionality of lawyer disciplinary rules which were the subject of a pending state disciplinary proceeding under the jurisdiction of a state supreme court. In this case, the plaintiffs sued a county's ethics committee seeking to enjoin pending attorney disciplinary proceedings on the ground that the disciplinary rules under which a plaintiff attorney had been charged were unconstitutional. Reversing the district court which had dismissed on the basis of the *Younger* rule, the Third Circuit held that *Younger* abstention was inappropriate "because the proceeding before the Ethics Committee fails to guarantee to [the plaintiff attorney] an adequate opportunity to make his constitutional arguments."[174] Judge Weis dissented, arguing that *Younger* was applicable because the ethics committee proceeding was judicial in nature and the attorney would have the opportunity to present constitutional issues to the New Jersey Supreme Court and even to the ethics committee.

In turn reversing, the Supreme Court held that *Younger* was applicable. Speaking through Chief Justice Burger, the Court emphasized the following:

1. The pending state bar disciplinary hearings, which were within the constitutionally prescribed jurisdiction of the New Jersey Supreme Court, constituted an ongoing state judicial proceeding

2. Those proceedings implicated important state interests in maintaining and assuring lawyers' professional conduct

3. There was an adequate opportunity in the state proceedings to raise constitutional challenges

Four justices concurred in the judgment. Justice Brennan reasserted his view that the *Younger* rule is generally inapplicable to civil proceedings. Justice Marshall, joined by Justices Brennan, Blackmun, and Stevens, argued that the *Younger* rule was applicable only because there were ongoing judicial proceedings in the New Jersey Supreme Court where constitutional challenges could be raised.

There is even the possibility that *Younger* may one day be applied to §1983 damages actions. Several of the justices apparently would so extend *Younger,* as reflected in the following statement of the Court made in passing in connection with a §1983 damages action against a public defender:

> [Because plaintiff no longer has state-court opportunities to have his conviction set aside, we] therefore have no occasion to decide if a Federal District Court should abstain from deciding a §1983 suit for damages

---

[173] 457 US 423 (1982), *revg* 643 F2d 119 *and* 651 F2d 154 (3d Cir 1981).
[174] 643 F2d at 121.

stemming from an unlawful conviction pending the collateral exhaustion of state-court attacks on the conviction itself.[175]

Justices Brennan, Marshall, Blackmun, and Stevens immediately objected, though, complaining that because this issue was never raised, briefed, or argued by the parties before the Court, it was gratuitous even to mention the matter.

It should be emphasized that the *Younger* rule, as set out by the Supreme Court, currently applies only to judicial proceedings. Actions for declaratory and injunctive relief from other kinds of governmental conduct are, therefore, not affected by it. The suggestion by the Court in *Rizzo v Goode*[176] that the *Younger* rule should apply to actions to enjoin executive conduct is questionable. First, the hint was only an alternative ground for the holding that granting extensive equitable relief against city officials and various other officials of the Philadelphia Police Department was improper.[177] Second, to extend *Younger* in this way would generally read the Anti-Injunction Act back into §1983, contrary to *Mitchum v Foster*,[178] as well as undercut §1983's "suit in equity" language. Third, this suggestion does not follow from the primary "Our Federalism" justification for the *Younger* rule: the deference to the state judiciary based on the assumption that an adequate legal remedy will be provided.[179] A more modest reading of this suggestion in *Rizzo* is that, before ordering extensive and intrusive injunctive relief against a state or local government executive department, a federal court should take into account federalism concerns.

The *Younger* rule does not apply where the federal claim is not directly addressed in the pending state proceeding and is instead merely collateral to

---

[175] Tower v Glover, 467 US 914 (1984), a public defender immunity case set out at **§7.15**. *See also* McCurry v Allen, 606 F2d 795 (8th Cir 1979), *revd on other grounds,* 449 US 90 (1980), an apparent case of first impression, where the Eighth Circuit applied the *Younger* rule to bar a §1983 *damages* action against police officers for, among other things, an allegedly illegal search and seizure; state appellate proceedings to review plaintiff's conviction had not "run their course." Noting that the Supreme Court had left open the applicability of *Younger* to §1983 actions seeking only damages in Juidice v Vail, 430 US 327, 339 n 16 (1977), the Eighth Circuit simply stated without explanation: "In deference to the state courts, however, we believe it appropriate to abstain under the present circumstances as well." 606 F2d at 799. The ground on which the Supreme Court reversed in *McCurry*, collateral estoppel in §1983 cases, is addressed in **§5.18.**

[176] 423 US 362 (1976). In *Rizzo*, plaintiffs sought §1983 injunctive relief against Philadelphia, its mayor, and other higher-up city and police officials which would have required the defendants to set up certain training programs and disciplinary procedures in order to reduce allegedly pervasive police brutality.

[177] Another ground was the Court's conclusion that there was insufficient evidence of the defendants' involvement in the allegedly pervasive police brutality to justify an injunction against the defendants. *See* **§3.15** on the inapplicability of respondeat superior in §1983 cases. *See also* **§§6.05-6.19** in connection with local governmental liability.

[178] 407 US 225 (1972).

[179] Comment, *Post-Younger Excesses in the Doctrine of Equitable Restraint: A Critical Analysis,* 1976 Duke LJ 523, 568.

that proceeding. Thus, the Court held unconstitutional a prejudgment repossession statute even though the federal plaintiffs were defendants in replevin actions,[180] and in another case the Court required preliminary hearings where the federal plaintiffs were defendants in pending state criminal prosecutions.[181] Additionally, the state may waive the *Younger* rule in the federal proceeding.[182]

§5.14   —The *Younger* "Extraordinary Circumstances" Exceptions

Just as the scope and coverage of *Younger* have been gradually broadened by the Supreme Court, the "extraordinary circumstances" exceptions to *Younger* have been narrowly construed. The Court has said: "[S]uch circumstances must be 'extraordinary' in the sense of creating an extraordinarily pressing need for immediate federal equitable relief, not merely in the sense of presenting a highly unusual factual situation."[183] There are, according to the Court, currently three exceptions to the *Younger* rule, although others may be developed:

1. Bad faith or harassment
2. Flagrantly and patently unconstitutional statutes
3. Bias[184]

A fourth exception, futility, has been rejected by the Court.[185]

The bad faith or harassment exception was first mentioned in *Younger* itself. Focusing on those situations where prosecutions are undertaken without hope of obtaining a valid conviction,[186] this exception includes those rare cases in which the federal plaintiff can show that the prosecutor will continue to file charges even after the statute is declared unconstitutional in the state criminal proceeding.[187] However, in *Hicks v Miranda* [188] the Supreme Court reversed the district court's finding of a pattern of bad faith and harassment even though the police had seized four copies of an allegedly obscene film pursuant to four

---

[180] Fuentes v Shevin, 407 US 67 (1972).

[181] Gerstein v Pugh, 420 US 103 (1975).

[182] Ohio Bureau of Employment Serv v Hodory, 431 US 471 (1977).

[183] Kugler v Helfant, 421 US 117, 124-25 (1975). *See* Moore v Sims, 442 US 415 (1979), noted at **§5.13,** where the Supreme Court, in applying *Younger* to bar federal injunctive relief, found that the federal plaintiffs were able to pursue their constitutional claims in the state proceeding and that none of the exceptions to *Younger* was applicable.

[184] 421 US at 124-25.

[185] Hicks v Miranda, 422 US 332, 350 n 18 (1975); Huffman v Pursue Ltd, 420 US 592, 610 (1975).

[186] Perez v Ledesma, 401 US 82, 85 (1971).

[187] *Developments in the Law - Section 1983 and Federalism,* 90 Harv L Rev 1133, 1323 (1977).

[188] 422 US 332 (1975).

separate warrants obtained with the intent to stop the showing of the film. Emphasizing the existence of judicial authorization, the Court said, "Absent at least some effort by the District Court to impeach the entitlement of the prosecuting officials to rely on repeated judicial authorization for their conduct, we cannot agree that bad faith and harassment were made out."[189]

The exception for flagrantly and patently unconstitutional statutes, also mentioned in *Younger,* was similarly narrowed considerably by the Court in *Trainor v Hernandez,*[190] a case testing the constitutionality of the Illinois Attachment Act. It rejected the argument that the Attachment Act was clearly violative of procedural due process under prior Supreme Court decisions and was, therefore, as the district court had found, an exception to the *Younger* rule. Instead, the Court insisted that the exception was limited to those rare cases "where a state statute is flagrantly and patently violative of express constitutional prohibitions in every clause, sentence and paragraph, and in whatever manner and against whomever an effort might be made to apply it."[191]

The exception for bias was first suggested by the Court in *Gibson v Berryhill*[192] where the federal plaintiff sought to enjoin a pending license revocation proceeding. The plaintiff alleged, and the district court agreed, that the state agency, composed of self-employed optometrists with a pecuniary interest in a decision adverse to plaintiff, a salaried optometrist, was incompetent because of bias to decide the case before it. The Supreme Court refused to apply the *Younger* rule and affirmed the injunction against the revocation proceeding, reasoning that "the predicate for a *Younger v Harris* dismissal was lacking."[193]

The reach of *Gibson,* where the facts presented a clear case of bias, was somewhat limited in *Kugler v Helfant*[194] where the federal plaintiff sought to enjoin a pending criminal proceeding. He alleged that *Younger* was inapplicable because "the significant role played by the members of the New Jersey Supreme Court in coercing his testimony made it impossible for him to receive a fair trial in the state court system." However, the Court rejected this contention and applied the *Younger* rule. It observed that "[i]t is impossible to conclude from these considerations . . . that the objectivity of the entire New Jersey court system has been irretrievably impaired so far as Helfant is concerned."[195] The Court also emphasized such facts as the existence of various state procedures for curing judicial bias as well as the extensive change in personnel of the New Jersey Supreme Court.

It might be thought that the *Younger* rule should not be applied where it would

---

189 *Id* 351.

190 431 US 434 (1977).

191 *Id* 447 (quoting from *Younger,* 401 US 37, 53-54, quoting in turn from Watson v Buck, 313 US 387, 402 (1941)).

192 411 US 564 (1973).

193 *Id* 577. The Court sidestepped the issue of *Younger*'s applicability to state administrative proceedings but may have implied that it is applicable.

194 421 US 117 (1975).

195 *Id* 127.

be futile to remit the federal plaintiff to a state court. However, the Supreme Court in *Huffman v Pursue, Ltd*[196] rejected this contention in requiring exhaustion of state appellate remedies in order to avoid the *Younger* rule. It said:

> [T]he considerations of comity and federalism which underlie *Younger* permit no truncation of the exhaustion requirement merely because the losing party in the state court of general jurisdiction believes that his chances of success on appeal are not auspicious. Appellee obviously believes itself possessed of a viable federal claim. . . . Appellee is in truth urging us to base a rule on the assumption that state judges will not be faithful to their constitutional responsibilities. This we refuse to do.[197]

Similarly, in *Hicks v Miranda*[198] the Court rejected the federal plaintiff's futility argument as to an obscenity statute despite a recent adverse intermediate appellate decision on point. The Court mentioned that state courts "sometimes change their minds" and added that the highest appellate court could have been asked again to pass on the statute's constitutionality.[199]

Consequently, a federal plaintiff seeking to avoid *Younger* dismissal of an action for declaratory or injunctive relief against pending state criminal proceedings has what amounts to a very heavy burden. The plaintiff must show that going through the state court proceeding can in no way provide an adequate legal remedy. It will be an unusual case indeed where a federal plaintiff can satisfy this burden.[200]

§5.15   The *Younger* Rule in the Circuits

Unlike other aspects of §1983 as to which the Supreme Court has been content to decide relatively few cases and leave the rest to the circuits,[201] the Court has, since its 1971 *Younger v Harris*[202] opinion, decided numerous cases elaborating on the *Younger* rule.[203] This reflects the importance the Court gives the *Younger* rule and its related concern that federal courts properly apply the rule. That the Court has not been reluctant to overturn a district court's findings of fact regarding, for example, bad faith or harassment also reinforces

---

[196] 420 US 592 (1975).

[197] *Id* 610.

[198] 422 US 332 (1975).

[199] *Id* 350 n 18.

[200] To this burden must be added the requirements of justiciability. *See* **§5.04.**

[201] *E.g.*, damages and qualified immunity, **chs 4 & 8** respectively.

[202] 401 US 37 (1971).

[203] By one count, there had been, as of 1977, 16 major cases and at least that number of cases where the *Younger* rule was discussed. Laycock, *Federal Interference with State Prosecutions: The Need for Prospective Relief*, 1977 Sup Ct Rev 193, 207.

this sense that the *Younger* rule is of considerable significance.[204] Consequently, law on the *Younger* rule has been made primarily by the Supreme Court, although there is a fair amount of *Younger*-related litigation in the circuits. It is the Court which has broadened the scope and coverage of the *Younger* rule, and it is the Court which has narrowed the exceptional circumstances exceptions.

The Supreme Court's drift toward expanding the scope and coverage of the *Younger* rule is, as noted, readily apparent. Nevertheless, some circuits have refused to apply the *Younger* rule to pending state administrative proceedings;

---

[204] Hicks v Miranda, 422 US 332 (1975).

Representative cases in the circuits dealing with bad faith or harassment and the other exceptions include the following:

First Circuit

Fernandez v Trias Monge, 586 F2d 848 (1st Cir 1978)(*Younger* rule not a bar because federal plaintiff had no adequate remedy in state courts; also, federal declaratory or injunctive relief would not affect pending criminal trial on the merits).

Second Circuit

Heimbach v Village of Lyons, 597 F2d 344 (2d Cir 1979)(per curiam)(bad faith or harassment exception applicable).

Fourth Circuit

Timmerman v Brown, 528 F2d 811 (4th Cir 1975)(bad faith exception found applicable).

Fifth Circuit

Smith v Hightower, 693 F2d 359 (5th Cir 1982)(*Younger* rule barred sheriff's injunctive relief action against criminal prosecution and removal from office; bad faith exception not applicable where plaintiff does not prove that "retaliation was a major motivating factor and played a prominent role in the decision to prosecute"; "strength of the evidence and seriousness of the charges should be considered in determining if retaliation or bad faith exists"; extensive discussion of requirements and burden of proof for retaliatory prosecution).

Wilson v Thompson, 638 F2d 799 (5th Cir 1981)(*Younger* rule a bar in absence of any showing by plaintiffs of prosecutor's improper motive for their prosecution: bad faith exception therefore not applicable).

Wilson v Thompson, 593 F2d 1375 (5th Cir 1979)(bad faith or harassment exception may be applicable even though no threat of repeated or multiple prosecutions).

Slavin v Curry, 574 F2d 1256 (5th Cir 1978)(bad faith exception found applicable).

Sixth Circuit

Martin-Marietta Corp v Bendix Corp, 690 F2d 558 (6th Cir 1982)(*Younger* rule not applicable to bar federal injunctive relief directed at pending state court proceedings to enforce antifraud provisions of Michigan corporate and securities statutes which were brought by state officials; otherwise, "great and immediate irreparable injury" would occur; also, the challenged statutory provisions "may well be flagrantly and patently violative of express constitutional prohibitions").

Seventh Circuit

Grandco Corp v Rochford, 536 F2d 197 (7th Cir 1976) (bad faith exception found inapplicable where multiple prosecutions generally successful).

Ninth Circuit

Krahm v Graham, 461 F2d 703 (9th Cir 1972) (bad faith exception found applicable where multiple prosecutions generally unsuccessful).

the *Younger* rule has similarly been held by some circuits to be inapplicable to pending state civil proceedings of a private nature.[205] On the other hand,

---

[205] Cases from the circuits holding *Younger inapplicable* to pending state administrative proceedings or to pending state civil proceedings of a private nature include the following:

First Circuit

Puerto Rico Intl Airlines Inc v Silva Recio, 520 F2d 1342 (1st Cir 1975)(civil proceedings of a private nature).

Third Circuit

The Third Circuit, after asserting that in light of Moore v Sims, 442 US 415 (1979), discussed at §5.13, *Younger* applies to *ongoing* state parental rights termination proceedings, distinguished the case before it. The final judgment issued by the state court was no longer appealable in the state courts. Thus, *Younger* did not bar the plaintiff mother's suit for declaratory and injunctive relief claiming that the state's termination proceeding violated due process and equal protection. Rhoades v Penfold, 694 F2d 1043 (3d Cir 1983).

New Jersey-Philadelphia v New Jersey State Bd of Higher Educ, 654 F2d 868 (3d Cir 1981) (*Younger* rule does not bar injunctive relief against pending state proceeding brought by board of higher education against church-supported college; certain plaintiffs in federal action were not parties to the state proceeding; Judge Rosenn disagreed with this aspect of the majority's decision).

Johnson v Kelly, 583 F2d 1242 (3d Cir 1978)(civil proceedings of a private nature).

New Jersey Educ Assn v Burke, 579 F2d 764 (3d Cir 1978)(civil proceedings of a private nature).

Fifth Circuit

Foley v Alabama State Bar, 648 F2d 355, 360 (5th Cir 1981)(*Younger* rule not applicable to bar injunctive relief against state bar's disciplinary proceeding against federal plaintiff lawyers because "[t]here is no indication that [plaintiffs] may vindicate their constitutional rights in the state bar disciplinary proceedings).

Seventh Circuit

United Church v Medical Center Commn, 689 F2d 693, 697 n 3 (7th Cir 1982) (*Younger* inapplicable to pending administrative proceedings because there was no adequate opportunity for the federal plaintiff to raise his federal constitutional challenges in the state administrative proceedings; Middlesex County Ethics Comm v Garden State Bar Assn, 457 US 423 (1982), discussed at §5.13, was thus distinguishable).

Eighth Circuit

The Eighth Circuit rejected the applicability of the *Younger* rule to a pending state administrative proceeding on several grounds, one of which was the inability of the administrative proceeding to resolve the federal plaintiff's constitutional claims. Walker v Wegner, 624 F2d 60 (8th Cir 1980).

Ninth Circuit

Playtime Theaters Inc v City of Renton, 784 F2d 527 (9th Cir 1984), holding *Younger* inapplicable to a federal declaratory action against city where city thereafter filed state declaratory action against federal plaintiff. *Younger* is generally inapplicable to civil cases. Also, the federal plaintiff did not violate the challenged ordinance and thus there was no enforcement action pending. Further, the state declaratory action did not implicate state interests vital to the operation of state government.

In Goldie's Bookstore Inc v Superior Ct, 739 F2d 466 (9th Cir 1984), plaintiff sought an injunction against the enforcement of a state unlawful detainer judgment against it. The Ninth Circuit found *Younger* inapplicable on the ground that the case did not involve

several circuit courts have applied *Younger* to certain pending state administrative proceedings and even to pending state civil proceedings of a private nature.[206] Consequently, as a practical matter, a federal plaintiff seeking

---

important state interests. It was rather a dispute between private parties. The Ninth Circuit's *Miofsky* decision, set out below, was primarily relied on, and the Supreme Court's *Middlesex County Ethics Comm* case—see **§5.13**—was distinguished on this basis. The court also observed that the Supreme Court has refused thus far to make any general pronouncement on the applicability of *Younger* to all civil cases. Judge Wright dissented, contending that important state interests involving disputes over real property were indeed implicated; thus, *Younger* was applicable.

The Ninth Circuit ruled that the *Younger* rule was not applicable to bar the federal plaintiff's attempt to enjoin discovery against him as a defendant in pending private state tort litigation. The state was not involved in the state tort litigation and those proceedings, moreover, were not brought to vindicate a "vital state interest." Noting that the issue of the possible expansion of *Younger* to private civil litigation has not been resolved by the Supreme Court and was an issue of first impression in the Ninth Circuit, the court concluded that *Younger* should not extend to conventional civil litigation. Miofsky v Superior Ct, 703 F2d 332 (9th Cir 1983).

In Tovar v Billmeyer, 609 F2d 1291 (9th Cir 1980) the Ninth Circuit held that the district court erred in dismissing plaintiffs' §1983 prospective relief challenge to a city council's refusal to issue a permit to operate an adult bookstore. The district court, improperly relying in part on the *Younger* rule, had based its decision to dismiss on the pendency of plaintiffs' state court challenge to the city council's decision.

Eleventh Circuit

In Cate v Oldham, 707 F2d 1176 (11th Cir 1983), the Eleventh Circuit held *Younger* inapplicable to a federal injunctive relief action brought against a prior state court malicious prosecution suit which was directed against the plaintiff. That a state official and the state itself were parties plaintiff in the malicious prosecution suit did not render *Younger* applicable inasmuch as there were no vital state interests at stake in the litigation. Thus, the malicious prosecution suit was purely private in nature.

[206] Cases from the circuits holding *Younger applicable* to pending state administrative proceedings or to pending state civil proceedings of a private nature include the following:

Second Circuit

McCune v Frank, 521 F2d 1152 (2d Cir 1975) (suggesting that *Younger* is applicable to administrative proceedings generally).

Anonymous v Association of the Bar of NY, 515 F2d 427 (2d Cir), *cert denied*, 423 US 863 (1975)(attorney disciplinary proceedings before bar association grievance committee treated as quasi-judicial and as implicating a significant state interest; *Younger* applicable).

Third Circuit

Gipson v New Jersey Sup Ct, 558 F2d 701 (3d Cir 1977) (per curiam) involving an attorney's attempt to vacate a suspension order of the New Jersey Supreme Court and to challenge the constitutionality of New Jersey's attorney disciplinary rules. The Third Circuit, in affirming the district court's reliance on *Younger*, broadly stated: "In view of the special relationship between state courts and members of their bars, we hold that the doctrine of federal noninterference is appropriate in suits concerning pending state attorney disciplinary proceedings." *Id* 704.

See also Middlesex County Ethics Comm v Garden State Bar Assn, 457 US 423 (1982), *revg* 634 F2d 119 (3d Cir 1981) *and* 651 F2d 154 (3d Cir 1981), discussed at **§5.13**.

Fourth Circuit

Lynch v Snepp, 472 F2d 769 (4th Cir 1973), *cert denied*, 415 US 983 (1974), finding

declaratory or injunctive relief[207] based on the validity of a state statute being used against such plaintiff in *any* pending state proceeding will probably face the federal defendant's argument that *Younger* requires dismissal.

However, before *Younger* is applicable, there must ordinarily be a pending state proceeding. In a District of Columbia Circuit case[208] the plaintiff landlords sued the District of Columbia agency responsible for administering

---

Younger applicable to bar federal injunctive relief against the enforcement of a state court order controlling public access to a county's public school; also suggesting a balancing of interests approach in each case to determine whether *Younger* rule should be applied.

Fifth Circuit

In Gresham Park Community Org v Howell, 652 F2d 1227 (5th Cir 1981), the Fifth Circuit held the *Younger* rule applicable to bar injunctive relief against the enforcement of a state court injunction obtained by a private litigant. The state court injunction prohibited the federal plaintiffs from picketing the state plaintiff's newly opened liquor store. Conceding that it was thereby extending the *Younger* rule, the court emphasized the significant state interest involved in the state court proceeding because the state plaintiff's suit was in aid of state criminal law prohibiting certain picketing and boycotts.

Duke v Texas, 477 F2d 244 (5th Cir 1973), *cert denied*, 415 US 978 (1974), applying *Younger* rule to bar federal injunctive relief after university obtained temporary restraining order in state court against federal plaintiffs prohibiting them from speaking at a campus rally protesting the Viet Nam War.

Sixth Circuit

In a series of decisions the Sixth Circuit similarly applied *Younger* to bar federal declaratory and injunctive relief from pending private civil proceedings. *See* Lamb Enters Inc v Kiroff, 549 F2d 1052 (6th Cir), *cert denied*, 431 US 968 (1977); Louisville Area Inter-Faith Comm v Nottingham Liquors Ltd, 542 F2d 652 (6th Cir 1976); Littleton v Fisher, 530 F2d 691 (6th Cir 1976) (per curiam).

Eighth Circuit

Williams v Williams, 532 F2d 120 (8th Cir 1976), applying *Younger* rule to bar federal declaratory and injunctive relief against the enforcement of a state court's adoption decree.

Tenth Circuit

Relying on the Supreme Court's *Middlesex County Ethics Committee* case, set out at §5.13, the Tenth Circuit ruled that *Younger* was applicable to the plaintiff physician's attempt to enjoin disciplinary proceedings against him, especially insofar as he claimed that the defendant members of the state board of healing arts acted improperly in their offer to settle the dispute. The court asserted: "[T]his issue is but an attempt to seek federal intervention in the state disciplinary process. . . . There is simply no justification for this court to intervene in this matter." Vakas v Rodriguez, 728 F2d 1293, 1295 (10th Cir 1984).

[207] *See* Spiegel v School Dist No 1, 600 F2d 264 (10th Cir 1979), where the court found it unnecessary to decide the possible applicability of the *Younger* rule to a situation involving a federal plaintiff's §1983 suit for *damages* at the same time state civil litigation was pending. Cf McCurry v Allen, 606 F2d 795 (8th Cir 1979), *revd on other grounds*, 449 US 90 (1980), noted at the beginning of this section. However, in Giulini v Blessing, 654 F2d 189 (2d Cir 1981), the Second Circuit implied that the *Younger* rule does not apply to a §1983 *damages* action which raises issues identical to those in a pending state criminal proceeding. Nevertheless, the court instructed the district court on remand to hold the §1983 damages action in abeyance until final adjudication of the constitutional issues in the state courts. *See also* §5.13.

[208] District Properties Assocs v District of Columbia, 743 F2d 21, 28 n 4 (DC Cir 1984).

rent control laws alleging, under §1983, due process violations and apparently seeking declaratory and injunctive relief. Reversing the district court, the court held that *Younger,* even if applicable to civil proceedings of an enforcement nature, was not applicable here because there were "no ongoing proceedings in the local courts in which [plaintiffs] could raise their federal constitutional claims." Similarly, where the plaintiff, seeking reappointment as a magistrate, sued defendants, a court clerk and senior judge, for failure to do so in alleged violation of the First Amendment, the Fourth Circuit[209] held that *Younger* was not applicable to bar her suit. There were no ongoing judicial proceedings, only the ministerial decision not to reappoint the plaintiff. Further, the appointment decision was ex parte and unilateral, not an adversary proceeding.

The *Younger* rule was applied by the Eighth Circuit even though the requested injunctive relief would not have interfered directly with a pending state criminal proceeding.[210] Plaintiff, who had been prosecuted but whose trial ended in a mistrial, sued the defendant prosecuting attorney for injunctive relief to enjoin his allegedly giving information to the press in an attempt to deprive plaintiff and others of the right to an impartial jury. Affirming the district court's dismissal of this claim, the Eighth Circuit relied on broad readings of the *Younger* rule and *Moore v Sims*[211] and held:

> Although the enjoining of the activity complained of here would not interfere directly with the state criminal proceeding, the exercise of our equitable powers is still inappropriate under *Younger,* where the plaintiff [will have] an opportunity to assert her federal claim in the state proceeding [if the state tries her again].[212]

However, as to plaintiff's claim that the defendant threatened to prosecute her in order to punish her for her political beliefs, there was no *Younger* bar because plaintiff could not raise her free speech claim as a defense in a criminal proceeding. Also, the plaintiff had challenged the defendant's conduct, not the constitutionality of the state statute dealing with the crime of misappropriation of county property. Thus, there was no danger of unduly hampering law enforcement.

§5.16 *Pullman* Abstention

Even if a §1983 plaintiff surmounts the previously discussed hurdles of justiciability, the Eleventh Amendment, exhaustion of state judicial and administrative remedies, and the *Younger* rule, the federal court may still refuse

---

[209] Lewis v Blackburn, 734 F2d 1000 (4th Cir 1984).

[210] Kaylor v Fields, 661 F2d 1177 (8th Cir 1981).

[211] 442 US 415 (1979) (applying *Younger* rule to pending state court litigation initiated by state authorities and relating to suspected child abuse; rejecting argument that federal plaintiffs' claim challenging certain state procedures used was unrelated to the custody issue in the state proceeding).

[212] Kaylor v Fields, 661 F2d 1177, 1181 (8th Cir 1981).

to consider plaintiff's claim for damages or prospective relief. In *Railroad Commission v Pullman Co*,[213] the Supreme Court declined to exercise jurisdiction

(*Text continued on page 318*)

---

[213] 312 US 496 (1941). *See generally* C. Wright, Law of Federal Courts §52 (4th ed 1983); J. Nowak, R. Rotunda & J. Young, Constitutional Law 99-106 (2d ed 1983). §1983 cases in the circuits involving abstention include the following:

First Circuit

Urbanizadora Versalles Inc v Rios, 701 F2d 993 (1st Cir 1983)(*Pullman* abstention inappropriate where a property owner sued state officials claiming a deprivation of property in violation of due process; no Puerto Rico statute was at issue and relevant Puerto Rico cases were clearly decided under commonwealth's constitution; also, essence of plaintiff's complaint was delay which would be exacerbated by applying *Pullman* abstention; further, it was "almost certain" that Puerto Rico courts would find the 14-year "freezing" of plaintiff's property excessive).

Third Circuit

New Jersey-Philadelphia v New Jersey State Bd of Higher Educ, 654 F2d 868 (3d Cir 1981)(*Pullman* abstention did not bar federal court's grant of preliminary injunctive relief against enforcement of state law challenged on First Amendment grounds; defendant's construction of state law left no room for limiting interpretation; also, state appellate courts could still ultimately adopt a narrow construction, avoiding the constitutional issue, which federal court would then take into account at a final hearing for injunctive relief).

D'Iorio v County of Delaware, 592 F2d 681 (3d Cir 1978)(*Pullman* abstention appropriate; "special circumstances" present, including uncertainty of state law underlying constitutional issues).

McKnight v Southeastern Pennsylvania Transp Auth, 583 F2d 1229 (3d Cir 1978)(*Pullman* abstention inappropriate; even though state law underlying constitutional claim unclear, abstention would serve no important state or federal interest).

Fourth Circuit

Wilkins v Rogers, 581 F2d 399 (4th Cir 1978)(per curiam) (abstention appropriate because resolution of pending state litigation could eliminate constitutional issue; however, neither *Pullman* case nor uncertainty of state law explicitly mentioned).

Fifth Circuit

Brooks v Walker County Hosp Dist, 688 F2d 334 (5th Cir 1982)(*Pullman* abstention proper where medically needy indigent plaintiffs sued claiming a violation of due process in connection with free medical services allegedly guaranteed by Texas constitution; constitutional provision ambiguous on its face as to claimed entitlement and no authoritative construction of this provision available; also, constitutional provision part of an integrated scheme which called for clarifying interpretation by state courts; further, determining nature of entitlement, if it exists, may affect ultimate disposition of due process claims; despite hardship to plaintiffs, issue one of considerable local importance with potentially significant impact on state).

Chancery Clerk v Wallace, 646 F2d 151 (5th Cir 1981)(*Pullman* abstention not applicable to federal challenge to state procedures for involuntary commitment of adults to state mental institutions; no showing by defendants that state scheme susceptible to narrow interpretation; no real doubt as to how state scheme operated in practice; serious question of whether alternative state forum was available for resolution of complaint; the possibility that state courts might find all or part of state scheme violative of state constitution was insufficient to warrant abstention).

Ziegler v Ziegler, 632 F2d 535, 539 (5th Cir 1980)(per curiam)(*Pullman* abstention appropriate; the construction ultimately placed on a new state statute by state courts in a pending proceeding "could eliminate the need to render a constitutional decision in the sometimes unpredictable area of benign, gender-based discrimination. Moreover, domestic relations law is a subject peculiarly within the province of the states . . .").

Finch v Mississippi State Medical Assn, 585 F2d 765 (5th Cir 1978)(*Pullman* abstention appropriate because complex and unclear state law issues would soon be adjudicated in pending state court proceeding; "uneconomical and vexatious" for federal court to resolve same issues).

Johnson v American Credit, 581 F2d 526 (5th Cir 1978)(*Pullman* abstention inappropriate because state law both clear and authoritatively construed by state courts).

Sixth Circuit

Martin-Marietta Corp v Bendix Corp, 690 F2d 558 (6th Cir 1982)(*Pullman* abstention not proper where federal plaintiff sought injunctive relief against the enforcement by state officials of antifraud provisions of a state's corporate and securities statutes; no statutory construction was suggested by defendants which could remedy the alleged constitutional defects in the relevant statutes).

Seventh Circuit

Mazanec v North Judson-San Pierre School Corp, 763 F2d 845 (7th Cir 1985)(*Pullman* abstention inappropriate regarding challenge to state compulsory schooling law; provisions relating to equivalent education not vague under state law; also, case was three years old and had already been tried when abstention ordered by district court; further, state asked for abstention only at end of trial).

Ninth Circuit

Pearl Inv Co v City & County of San Francisco, 774 F2d 1460 (9th Cir 1985) (*Pullman* abstention applicable to suit challenging conduct in connection with plaintiff's application for building permit; despite court's reservations about district court's abstention, it reviewed only for abuse of discretion; court retained the criterion of "sensitive social issue" relevant to abstention determination).

Playtime Theaters Inc v City of Renton, 748 F2d 527 (9th Cir 1984)(*Pullman* abstention inapplicable to First Amendment-based facial challenge to constitutionality of zoning ordinance regulating adult motion picture theaters; abstention would not eliminate constitutional issues; also, First Amendment cases involve strong federal interests and abstention could result in suppression of free speech).

Richardson v Koshiba, 693 F2d 911 (9th Cir 1982)(*Pullman* abstention raised sua sponte and found applicable to the plaintiff judge's damages action against members of a state judicial selection commission; "delicate" questions were presented by the suit, state law issues were potentially dispositive of the case, and an uncertain question of state law was presented; it was also significant in this civil rights case that it was the *plaintiff* who sought abstention; Judge Schroeder dissented on abstention issue).

Tenth Circuit

Western Food Plan Inc v MacFarlane, 588 F2d 778 (10th Cir 1978)(*Pullman* abstention appropriate because pending state court proceeding raised issue under state constitution which could dispose of §1983 action in federal court; outright dismissal from federal court rejected, with *Younger* rule distinguished in this regard).

Eleventh Circuit

Casines v Murchek, 766 F2d 1494 (11th Cir 1985)(*Pullman* abstention applicable where a state court decision to effect that a defendant was not bound by an agency order would resolve all constitutional issues).

Cate v Oldham, 707 F2d 1176 (11th Cir 1983)(*Pullman* abstention not applied even though issues of state law were unsettled because "this is a First Amendment case alleging immediate and ongoing irreparable injury" and the costs of abstention are great; however, the unsettled state law issues should be certified to the Florida Supreme Court pursuant to its certification procedure).

over claims that a state agency's order was unauthorized by state law and violative of various constitutional provisions, including the equal protection clause. Characterizing its decision to abstain as based on equitable principles and as made in order to prevent "the waste of tentative decision as well as the friction of a premature constitutional adjudication,"[214] the Court emphasized that the nonconstitutional claim was unclear under state law. Accordingly, the Court directed the parties to seek a decision on the state claim in state court, instructing the federal court to retain jurisdiction pending such a state determination.

Pullman abstention, which the Court has occasionally described as applicable only in "narrowly limited special circumstances,"[215] does not apply where the state law issue is clear, where there is no conceivable saving interpretation of state law, or where the state and federal constitutional provisions are identical or substantially similar. It is premised upon a finding by a federal court that a Fourteenth Amendment claim or a pendent state claim, that is, one joined with the §1983 claim,[216] raises an unresolved issue of state law whose resolution may avoid the need to deal with the §1983 constitutional claim.[217] If such a finding is made, the §1983 plaintiff may return to the federal forum after the state courts resolve the state issue.[218] This right to return to the federal forum is best preserved by informing the state courts formally of the intent to return to the federal forum.[219] If the §1983 plaintiff chooses at that time not to so return, but "unreservedly" litigates any federal claims in the state courts, the state courts may determine the federal claims as well, and thereby bring the doctrines of res judicata and collateral estoppel into play.[220] In such a case the only possible federal review from an adverse state decision on the §1983 claim would be in the Supreme Court.

While *Pullman* abstention usually arises in the area of equitable relief, as in the *Pullman* case itself, the Supreme Court has also held it applicable to an action for damages.[221] Furthermore, the doctrine applies to civil rights actions

---

Nasser v City of Homewood, 671 F2d 432 (11th Cir 1982)(*Pullman* abstention improper respecting landowners' substantive due process challenge to rezoning of their property; no unsettled issue of state law identified).

[214] 312 US at 500.

[215] Zwickler v Koota, 389 US 241, 248 (1967); Lake Carriers' Assn v MacMullan, 406 US 498, 509 (1972).

[216] *See* §§1.10-1.12.

[217] However, a federal court need not abstain because of the mere possibility that a state statute might be held invalid under a broad state constitutional provision. Examining Bd of Engineers, Architects & Surveyors v Flores de Otero, 426 US 572, 598 (1976).

[218] England v Louisiana State Bd of Medical Examiners, 376 US 411 (1964).

[219] *Id* 421.

[220] *See* §§5.17-5.20.

[221] Clay v Sun Ins Office Ltd, 363 US 207 (1960).

as well.[222] Unlike the *Younger* rule, which the defendants may choose not to assert,[223] *Pullman* abstention is apparently not waivable. It may therefore be raised by a federal court on its own initiative or by a party at any time during the federal proceeding.[224] Another significant difference between the *Younger* rule and *Pullman* abstention, even though the former is frequently spoken of as "*Younger* abstention," is that the federal court retains jurisdiction over the federal claim in *Pullman* abstention,[225] while application of the *Younger* rule results in outright dismissal from the federal forum and unconditional return to the state forum.[226]

As has frequently been observed,[227] *Pullman* abstention greatly increases the cost of litigation for the parties, creates excessive delays because the parties must shunt back and forth between the federal and state systems, and is often unproductive because no determinative decision of the state law issue by the highest state court is or can be obtained. These results are especially likely to occur where the forum state has no special certification procedure for expeditious handling of such state law questions. Furthermore, the condition precedent for *Pullman* abstention, the uncertainty of state law, is frequently an ambiguous matter and can therefore readily be found by a federal court in an effort to delay or avoid hearing a meritorious constitutional claim.[228] When this occurs, *Pullman* abstention becomes the practical equivalent of a requirement of exhaustion of state judicial remedies.[229]

The Supreme Court has not yet decided whether *Pullman* abstention applies to §1983 claims based on federal statutory issues.[230] However, since the doctrine's purpose is to avoid deciding constitutional questions unnecessarily, it should not apply to statutory cases.[231]

Plaintiffs in §1983 cases who want to avoid the costs of *Pullman* abstention should therefore consider carefully whether their assertion of a particular Fourteenth Amendment claim or of an available pendent state claim might cause the effective loss of their federal forum. However, only uncertainty of

---

[222] Harrison v NAACP, 360 US 167 (1959).

[223] *See* **§5.13.**

[224] Ohio Bureau of Employment Serv v Hodory, 431 US 471 (1977).

[225] Abstention "does not, of course, involve the abdication of federal jurisdiction, but only the postponement of its exercise." Harrison v NAACP, 360 US 167, 177 (1959).

[226] *See* **§§5.12-5.13.**

[227] C. Wright, Law of Federal Courts §52 (4th ed 1983); J. Nowak, R. Rotunda & J. Young, Constitutional Law 102-03 (2d ed 1983); Field, *The Abstention Doctrine Today,* 125 U Pa L Rev 590 (1977).

[228] Field, *The Abstention Doctrine Today,* 125 U Pa L Rev 590, 602-04 (1977).

[229] *See* **§5.09.**

[230] *See* **§2.12.**

[231] In Propper v Clark, 337 US 472, 490 (1949), a nonconstitutional case involving federal law, the Court did not abstain, saying: "Where a case involves a nonconstitutional federal issue, however, the necessity for deciding which depends upon the decision on an underlying issue of state law, the practice in federal courts has been, when necessary, to decide both issues."

state law triggers *Pullman* abstention; the Supreme Court stated that the doctrine does not apply to a federal action simply because a proceeding covering the same matter is already pending in state court.[232] Furthermore, there are offshoots of *Pullman* abstention which do not focus on avoiding constitutional decision making but which nevertheless compel federal abstention for other reasons.[233] These offshoots, though, seem to be of limited relevance in §1983 cases.[234]

---

[232] Colorado River Water Conservation Dist v United States, 424 US 800, 817 (1976). *But cf* Will v Calvert Fire Ins, 437 US 655 (1978)(plurality opinion reversing grant of mandamus by circuit court ordering federal district court to consider federal antitrust action which had been stayed in deference to a state court contract action where federal antitrust issue was raised; dissent spoke of "an ominous potential for the abdication of federal court jurisdiction"). *See also* Moses H Cone Memorial Hosp v Mercury Constr, 460 US 1 (1983), elaborating on the abstention test set out in the *Colorado River Water Conservation District* case, with its focus on the danger of piecemeal litigation. Cf Tovar v Billmeyer, 609 F2d 1291 (9th Cir 1980), where the Ninth Circuit held, after discussing the *Colorado River Water Conservation District* case, that the district court improperly dismissed on the ground of abstention the plaintiff's §1983 prospective relief claim against a city council's refusal to grant a permit to operate an adult bookstore. The district court had relied on the pendency of a state court challenge.

Also see Forehand v First Ala Bank, 727 F2d 1033 (11th Cir 1984), where the plaintiff sued defendant bank for seizing her property pursuant to writ in alleged violation of due process. Reversing the district court, the Eleventh Circuit found abstention under *Colorado River Water Conservation District* inappropriate. First, the plaintiff was not seeking a determination of ownership rights of the property over which a state court had control. Second, there was no inconvenience to the defendant in the federal forum. Third, plaintiff filed her §1983 action before she was added as a party to the bank's state court proceeding. Finally, plaintiff raised federal issues respecting §1983 which were properly in a federal forum. Even though there was an interest in avoiding piecemeal litigation, nevertheless this interest alone was not sufficient to warrant abstention under *Colorado River's* "exceptional circumstances" test. Judge Roney dissented.

[233] 424 US at 813, 814. *See also* C. Wright, Law of Federal Courts §52 (4th ed 1983). Such reasons include a reluctance to interfere with complex state regulatory matters based on local factors, Alabama Pub Serv Comm v Southern Ry, 341 US 341 (1951); Burford v Sun Oil Co, 319 US 315 (1943); and a reluctance to review difficult and important issues of state law whose significance extends beyond the particular case, Louisiana Power & Light Co v City of Thibodaux, 360 US 25 (1959).

[234] As the following circuit court decisions demonstrate, it will be a rare §1983 case where a *Burford* abstention assertion succeeds.

In District Properties Assn v District of Columbia, 743 F2d 21, 28 n 5 (DC Cir 1984), the court found *Burford* abstention inappropriate where the plaintiff landlords sued an agency for administering rent control laws in alleged violation of due process. "To invoke *Burford* merely because of the 'sensitivity' of the local policies in this case or because the case involves a state bureaucracy would be contradicted by all of the examples of federal enforcement of federally-guaranteed civil rights in the great school desegregation and voting rights cases, among others."

The Seventh Circuit, in Evans v City of Chicago, 689 F2d 1286 (7th Cir 1982), found *Burford* abstention inapplicable where judgment creditor plaintiffs sued a city for its practices in connection with delaying payment of certain tort judgments. While the enforcement of state court judgments and the management of city budgets were important matters: (1) no statute required the city to engage in the challenged practices; (2) the statutes in question were not particularly complex; and (3) there was no

§5.17 Res Judicata and Collateral Estoppel

An extensive discussion of the highly technical preclusion doctrines of res judicata—claim preclusion—and collateral estoppel—issue preclusion—is beyond the scope of this chapter.[235] However, these doctrines are becoming increasingly important in civil rights cases in general and in §1983 cases involving both damages and prospective relief in particular. This is reflected by the Supreme Court's decisions in six preclusion cases in recent years.[236] Consequently, the topic deserves considerably more than passing attention here.

A preclusion issue may arise where a §1983 plaintiff has been dismissed from

---

indication that the matter required specialized expertise.

Similarly, the Eighth Circuit found *Burford* abstention inappropriate where there was a challenge to the conditions of confinement in, and to treatment at, state facilities for the retarded. Treatment of developmental disabilities was not a highly regulated area under state law; no interpretation of complex state law was required; the issues raised by defendants would not in any event be resolved by a specialized state court; the state's economy was not intertwined with the subject matter of the case; and, finally, defendants cited no *Burford* abstention case supporting their position here. Association for Retarded Citizens v Olson, 713 F2d 1384 (8th Cir 1983).

In Heritage Farms Inc v Solebury Township, 671 F2d 743 (3d Cir 1982), the Third Circuit found *Burford* abstention inappropriate for a suit by developers alleging a conspiracy to destroy plaintiffs' rights to conduct a legitimate business. There was no uniform state policy for land use and development in Pennsylvania, according to the court. Also, the case was not a simple land use case, but rather one in which the defendants were accused of using their government offices in a "malevolent" way to further an illegal conspiracy.

Cf Nasser v City of Homewood, 671 F2d 432 (11th Cir 1982), where landowners challenged the rezoning of their property on substantive due process grounds. The Eleventh Circuit followed the Ninth Circuit's decision in IBEW, Local 1245 v PSC, 614 F2d 206 (9th Cir 1980) and held that *Burford* abstention is inappropriate where zoning ordinances are challenged on constitutional grounds. The court in *Nasser* emphasized the following factors in the case before it. Alabama had not established "a single forum for resolution of zoning disputes." Thus, there was no important state interest in uniformity to be disrupted by federal review. Also, the federal issues were easily distinguishable from the state issues.

[235] The related doctrines of res judicata and collateral estoppel are both designed to promote the policy of terminating litigation. Also of importance in this regard are the full faith and credit clause of the US Const art IV, §1, and 28 USC §1738 which requires federal courts to give the same effect to prior state decisions as would the courts of the state in which the decisions are rendered. Res judicata, or claim preclusion, becomes relevant when a second suit for the same claim as a prior suit is instituted; it includes the concepts of merger and bar. Collateral estoppel, in contrast, becomes relevant when the relitigation of specific issues, factual or legal, is presented in a second suit based on a different claim. *See generally* Restatement (Second) of Judgments ch 3 (1982); *Developments in the Law—Section 1983 and Federalism*, 90 Harv L Rev 1133, 1330-60 (1977); *Developments in the Law—Res Judicata*, 65 Harv L Rev 818 (1952).

[236] University of Tenn v Elliott, 106 S Ct 3220 (1986); McDonald v City of West Branch, 466 US 284 (1984); Migra v Warren City School Dist, 465 US 75 (1984); Haring v Prosise, 462 US 306 (1983); Kremer v Chemical Constr Corp, 456 US 461 (1982); Allen v McCurry, 449 US 90 (1980), all of which are discussed later.

federal court and remitted to state court by virtue of *Pullman* abstention[237] or the *Younger* rule.[238] Or, a plaintiff may simply have filed in the first instance in a state court or have been a defendant in a prior state criminal proceeding. Upon losing in the prior state proceeding, the question is whether and to what extent it is possible to proceed anew in a federal forum with respect to any §1983 claims.[239]

The answer is clear for *Pullman* abstention. The Supreme Court has expressly held that the federal plaintiff has a right to return to the federal forum after a loss in state court upon reserving the right to do so in advance, as long as the plaintiff does not "unreservedly" litigate the federal claim in the state proceedings.[240] On the other hand, even before the Court's recent preclusion decisions, it was likely in cases not involving *Pullman* abstention that a party in a prior state proceeding who raised and lost federal claims could not proceed thereafter to raise those claims anew in §1983 litigation in federal court. This was especially likely where the federal plaintiff initiated the previous state judicial proceeding.[241] Nevertheless, until the Supreme Court definitively resolved this issue, there was uncertainty about the matter.[242] This uncertainty persisted even though in dictum the Court had asserted in an early case where a §1983 suit was brought after the state proceeding:

> We in no way intend to suggest that there is a right of access to a federal forum for the disposition of all federal issues, or that the normal rules of res judicata and collateral estoppel do not operate to bar relitigation in actions under 42 USC §1983 of federal issues arising in state court proceedings.[243]

The Court finally set out the applicable preclusion rules in a series of civil rights cases dealing with prior *state* proceedings. In this connection it is extremely important to be sensitive to the distinction between prior *state* proceedings and prior *federal* proceedings. The preclusive effect of a prior state proceeding is ordinarily determined by state law pursuant to the mandate of 28 USC §1738, as reflected in the Supreme Court preclusion cases discussed

---

[237] *See* **§5.16.**

[238] *See* **§§5.12-5.15.**

[239] In such a situation, the federal defendant attempts to use preclusion defensively, which is typical in §1983 cases. However, it is also possible to use preclusion offensively as, for example, where a federal plaintiff argues that a prior favorable state ruling on a certain issue collaterally estops the federal defendant in the federal proceeding. *See* Mahoney, *A Sword as Well as a Shield: The Offensive Use of Collateral Estoppel in Civil Rights Litigation,* 69 Iowa L Rev 469 (1984).

[240] England v Louisiana State Bd of Medical Examiners, 375 US 411 (1964).

[241] *See* cases collected in *Developments in the Law - Section 1983 and Federalism,* 90 Harv L Rev 1133, 1336 n 27 (1977).

[242] *Id. See also* Theis, *Res Judicata in Civil Rights Act Cases: An Introduction to the Problem,* 70 Nw UL Rev 859 (1976).

[243] Huffman v Pursue Ltd, 420 US 592, 606 n 18 (1975). *See also* Preiser v Rodriquez, 411 US 475, 497-98 (1973).

in the following sections. This means, of course, that there is no national uniformity on preclusion issues in such situations. In contrast, the preclusive effect of a prior federal proceeding is determined by federal law.[244] Also, §1738 and its mandate to use state law apply, strictly speaking, only to prior state *judicial* proceedings, but not to unreviewed state administrative proceedings of a quasi-judicial nature. As will be discussed, the Supreme Court nevertheless in §1983 cases has created a federal rule of preclusion applicable to such quasi-judicial proceedings whereby federal courts must give the agency's fact-finding the same preclusive effect it would be given in the forum state's courts.[245]

§5.18 —Prior State Criminal Proceedings

In *Allen v McCurry*[246] the Supreme Court dealt directly for the first time with the preclusive effect of prior state criminal proceedings on §1983 actions. In *Allen*, plaintiff was convicted in state court proceedings of illegal possession and assault with intent to kill. Plaintiff's motion to suppress had been denied as to evidence found in plain view but had been granted as to evidence found hidden in drawers and elsewhere. Thereafter, while state court review of plaintiff's conviction was continuing, plaintiff filed a §1983 damages action against various defendants, including police officers and the St. Louis Police Department, alleging, among other things, an illegal search and seizure.

Reversing the district court's grant of defendants' motion for summary judgment, the Eighth Circuit rejected the argument that, because the search and seizure claim had been decided adversely to plaintiff at the criminal trial, plaintiff was collaterally estopped from raising the same claim in the §1983 action. The court left open, after noting that most other circuits had answered it in the affirmative, the broader question of whether collateral estoppel should apply to *all* issues raised in a §1983 suit where those issues have been decided adversely in an underlying state criminal trial. Instead, the Eighth Circuit narrowed the collateral estoppel inquiry to plaintiff's search and seizure claim, emphasized that typically such claims can no longer be raised by state prisoners in federal habeas corpus petitions, observed that federal courts have a special role in protecting civil rights, and held that collateral estoppel should not apply to plaintiff's §1983 search and seizure claim. However, the court then applied the *Younger* rule to plaintiff's damages action, and went on to abstain pending state appellate court review of plaintiff's conviction.[247]

---

[244] For recent discussions by the Court of the federal standards governing the preclusive effect of prior federal proceedings on subsequent federal proceedings, *see generally* United States v Mendoza, 464 US 154 (1984)(nonmutual offensive collateral estoppel) and United States v Stauffer Chem Co, 464 US 165 (1984)(mutual defensive collateral estoppel). For circuit court cases *see* **§5.19.**

[245] University of Tenn v Elliott, 106 S Ct 3220 (1986), discussed at **§5.19.**

[246] 449 US 90 (1980), *revg* 606 F2d 795 (8th Cir 1979).

[247] See **§§5.13 & 5.15** on the *Younger* rule and its possible relevance to damages actions.

The Supreme Court in *Allen* reversed and remanded on the collateral estoppel issue. In an opinion by Justice Stewart, the Court held that the plaintiff's inability to obtain federal habeas corpus relief on his Fourth Amendment claim[248] did not render the doctrine of collateral estoppel inapplicable to his §1983 claim. The Court first generally discussed the doctrines of res judicata and collateral estoppel and observed that 28 USC §1738 requires all federal courts to give preclusive effect to state court judgments whenever the state courts themselves would do so, and to the same extent. It then emphasized the following:

1. Virtually all the circuits agreed that §1983 "presents no categorical bar to the application of res judicata and collateral estoppel concepts"[249]

2. Neither the language nor the legislative history of §1983 showed congressional intent to deny preclusive effect to a prior state court judgment where the state court has given the parties "a full and fair opportunity to litigate federal claims." State courts are both obligated to follow federal law and competent to do so, according to the Court. Further, judgments in state criminal proceedings are entitled to no less deference than judgments in state civil proceedings, even though the federal plaintiff was involuntarily placed in the state criminal proceedings

3. The Court's decision in *Stone v Powell*[250] concerned only the "prudent exercise of federal court jurisdiction" in habeas corpus matters, and was thus irrelevant to the preclusive effect of prior state court judgments

Justices Blackmun, Brennan, and Marshall dissented.[251] They read §1983's legislative history very differently and argued that at least a criminal defendant who is an involuntary litigant in a state court should have access thereafter to a federal forum to assert a Fourth Amendment claim.

The Court's majority opinion expressly left open the question of preclusive effect in what it called "one peculiar circumstance": "[w]here a §1983 plaintiff seeks to litigate in federal court a federal issue which he could have raised but did not raise in an earlier state court suit against the same adverse party."[252] Regardless of this reservation, however, *Allen* indicated that the forum state's rules of res judicata and collateral estoppel apply to §1983 suits in federal court which deal with issues arising in prior state court proceedings.

State law was similarly used, but with a different result, in *Haring v Prosise*,[253] a case involving the preclusive effect of a prior state court guilty plea. Here, the plaintiff sued police officers for allegedly using excessive force in arresting him and conducting an illegal search and seizure. The Fourth Circuit

---

[248] *See* Stone v Powell, 428 US 465 (1976).

[249] 449 US at 97.

[250] 428 US 465 (1976).

[251] 449 US at 105.

[252] *Id* 97 n 10.

[253] 462 US 306 (1983), *affg* 667 F2d 1133 (4th Cir 1981).

affirmed the district court's decision on the merits as to the excessive force claim in favor of defendants but reversed as to the search and seizure claim. It disagreed with the district court's ruling that plaintiff's search and seizure claim was precluded by his guilty plea and resulting state conviction for manufacturing a controlled substance in the related state criminal prosecution.

First, the Fourth Circuit rejected the argument—based on *Tollett v Henderson*[254]—that the guilty plea had the effect of waiving any antecedent constitutional objection related neither to plaintiff's factual guilt or innocence nor to the right of plaintiff not to be tried. *Tollett* was read as applicable only to subsequent federal habeas corpus proceedings challenging criminal convictions. Second, after analyzing the Supreme Court's decision in *Allen v McCurry*, the court held that plaintiff's guilty plea was not preclusive as to the search and seizure claim. This issue was not actually litigated in the state court and, moreover, could only have been litigated in relation to the exclusion of evidence. It was also significant that the search and seizure claim was unrelated to the elements of the offense to which plaintiff had pleaded guilty. In reaching its conclusion, the Fourth Circuit carefully examined both state law and "general principles of collateral estoppel." It also emphasized that persons in plaintiff's position have little incentive to litigate a search and seizure claim in a criminal proceeding because there is often sufficient "untainted" evidence to support a conviction.

In an unanimous opinion by Justice Marshall, the Court affirmed. Relying on 28 USC §1738 as interpreted in *Allen v McCurry*, the Court described the threshold question as whether, under Virginia's collateral estoppel rules, the judgment of conviction based on plaintiff's guilty plea would prevent him from bringing a later civil action challenging the legality of a search producing inculpatory evidence. The Court answered in the negative on three grounds under Virginia law: (1) the legality of the search was not actually litigated in the criminal proceeding; (2) the criminal proceeding did not actually decide any significant §1983 issue; and (3) none of the §1983 issues would have "necessarily" been determined in the criminal proceeding. In addition, the Court rejected the argument that it should create a special rule of preclusion which would bar plaintiff's claim. It found no policy justification for creating such a rule. It was not enough that the plaintiff simply had the opportunity to raise the legality of the search issue earlier. Also, one could not assume that plaintiff's plea of guilty was based on his determination that he would lose his motion to suppress.

The Court concluded that plaintiff did not waive his Fourth Amendment claim by pleading guilty. *Tollett's* rule that a Fourth Amendment claim ordinarily may not be raised in a habeas corpus proceeding following a plea of guilty was not based on waiver but "rests on the simple fact that the claim is irrelevant to the constitutional validity of the conviction.[255] To hold that a plaintiff waives a Fourth Amendment claim by pleading guilty in state court "would threaten

---

[254] 411 US 258 (1973).
[255] 462 US at 321.

important interests in preserving federal courts as an available forum for the vindication of constitutional rights."[256]

It is clear from *Allen* and *Haring* that because of §1738, state law plays a determinative role in §1983 cases involving prior state criminal proceedings. However, collateral estoppel, and not res judicata, will typically be at issue in such situations because identity of parties—a requirement of res judicata—is absent.

§5.19   —Prior State Civil Proceedings

After *Allen*, it was all but certain that state collateral estoppel law applies not only where a prior state *criminal* proceeding is involved but where the preclusive effect of a prior state court *civil* proceeding is at issue as well. However, two other important questions were not addressed by *Allen*. First, does state preclusion law similarly apply for res judicata purposes? Second, might §1738 apply to prior state proceedings of a quasi-judicial nature? The answer to the first question is that it does, while the answer to the second is technically no, but *effectively* yes.

Just as it had in *Allen*, the Supreme Court in *Migra v Warren City School District Board of Education*[257] applied 28 USC §1738 in holding that a prior state judicial proceeding was to be given the preclusive effect mandated by state law in a later §1983 federal judicial proceeding. *Migra* involved a prior state *civil* proceeding, federal issues that could have been but were *not* raised in that proceeding, and res judicata. The plaintiff in *Migra* had been refused renewal of her contract of employment by the defendant school board and its officials. She thereafter sued various parties for breach of contract and wrongful interference with her contract of employment in Ohio state court, where she received reinstatement and compensatory damages. The state court decision was affirmed by the Ohio appellate court. Plaintiff then brought a §1983 action for damages against the defendants for violation of her First Amendment and procedural due process rights. The district court granted summary judgment in favor of the defendants, who had raised the defense of res judicata.

Granting certiorari, the Supreme Court vacated the district court judgment. Relying on 28 USC §1738 as interpreted in *Allen*, the Court in *Migra* asserted that the preclusive effect in federal court of the plaintiff's state court judgment must be determined by Ohio law. This was so even though the federal issues could have been raised, but were not in fact raised, in the state court proceeding. The Court rejected the argument that the policies underlying §1983 warranted treating §1983 suits differently from other federal suits for

---

[256] *Id* 322.

[257] 465 US 75 (1984). *See also* Marrese v American Academy of Orthopaedic Surgeons, 105 S Ct 1327 (1985)(§1738 mandates that state preclusion law be applied to determine the effect of a prior state court proceeding, where only a state antitrust claim could be raised, on a subsequent federal proceeding where the federal plaintiff made a federal antitrust claim; *Migra* followed).

preclusion purposes. Instead of affirming the district court outright, though, the Court, after briefly discussing Ohio preclusion law, went on to vacate and remand because it was not clear to the Court whether the district court had applied what it thought was Ohio preclusion law.

Justice White, with whom Chief Justice Burger and Justice Powell joined, concurred in the opinion.[258] They suggested that it was "unfortunate" that the preclusive effect of state proceedings on federal court proceedings should be determined solely by state law, because this raised the possibility that under state standards the federal issues could be litigated in federal court, even though there would be preclusion under federal standards. Nevertheless, they characterized the Court's construction of 28 USC §1738 as "one of long standing" which Congress had not seen fit to disturb.

After *Allen, Migra* was not surprising. Read together, they clearly demonstrate that §1738 renders state preclusion law applicable for both collateral estoppel and res judicata purposes where the prior state proceeding is *judicial* in nature. Even more recently, the Court held in University of Tennessee v Elliott[259] discussed later, that irrespective of §1738, state preclusion law similarly applies to prior state administrative proceedings of a quasi-judicial nature. Two pre-*Elliot* Supreme Court decisions bore some relevance to this question. In *Kremer v Chemical Construction Corp*[260] the Court, relying in part on *Allen,* held that where a Title VII federal plaintiff has previously lost on the merits after state administrative *and* judicial review proceedings, collateral estoppel, as determined by state law pursuant to 28 USC §1738, bars him from litigating the same claim in a subsequent Title VII action in federal court. The Court rejected the plaintiff's argument that he had not had a full or fair opportunity to litigate in the state proceedings because the state procedures were "fundamentally flawed." It found that those procedures did not violate due process. If they had, then state preclusion law would not have been applied because "[a] state may not grant preclusive effects in its own courts to a constitutionally infirm

---

[258] 465 US at 88.

[259] 106 S Ct 3220 (1986), discussed later in this section. In a nonconstitutional case involving a federal agency and the federal courts, the Supreme Court said:

> Occasionally the courts have used language to the effect that res judicata principles do not apply to administrative proceedings, but such language is certainly too broad. When an administrative agency is acting in a judicial capacity and resolves disputed issues of fact properly before it which the parties have had an adequate opportunity to litigate, the courts have not hesitated to apply res judicata to enforce repose.

United States v Utah Constr & Mining Co, 384 US 394, 421-22 (1966). *See also* Prentis v Atlantic Coast Line, 211 US 210 (1908)(quasi-legislative proceedings of state agency not given res judicata effect in later federal proceeding even though agency at other times acted quasi-judicially; the character of the proceedings, not of the body, is determinative).

[260] 456 US 461 (1982). Four justices dissented.

judgment and the state and federal courts are not required to accord full faith and credit to such a judgment."[261]

Because *Kremer* involved a state judicial review proceeding as well as an administrative proceeding, and because it extensively discussed Title VII's unique statutory scheme, *Kremer* was not very helpful directly on the question of the possible preclusive effect of prior state agency proceedings on later federal civil rights proceedings. However, somewhat more guidance was provided by *McDonald v City of West Branch*[262] where the Court held that 28 USC §1738 did not apply to require a federal court to give preclusive effect to an unappealed arbitration award in a case brought under §1983. The plaintiff, a discharged police officer, had lost in an arbitration proceeding established by a collective bargaining agreement when it was found that there was just cause for his discharge. Not appealing that decision, plaintiff sued the defendant city and various officials under §1983, alleging violations of his First Amendment rights. A jury verdict against one of the defendants was overturned by the Sixth Circuit on the ground that plaintiff's First Amendment claims were collaterally estopped.

The Supreme Court reversed in a unanimous opinion by Justice Brennan. At the outset, the Court asserted that §1738 applied only to judicial proceedings and not to the arbitration proceedings involved here. Thus, state preclusion law was irrelevant. Further, the Sixth Circuit erred in fashioning a federal preclusion rule barring the plaintiff's claims in this case because, according to the Court, giving preclusive effect to an arbitration award in a subsequent §1983 action would undermine the efficacy of §1983 in protecting federal rights. Four reasons were given. First, an arbitrator may not have the necessary expertise to resolve complex §1983 issues. Second, an arbitrator may not have the authority under the collective bargaining agreement to enforce §1983. Third, the union's interest and that of the affected employee do not always coincide. Fourth, and finally, "arbitral factfinding is generally not equivalent to judicial factfinding."

The Court concluded: "We therefore hold that in a §1983 action, a federal court should not afford res judicata or collateral estoppel effect to an award in an arbitration proceeding brought pursuant to the terms of a collective-bargaining agreement."[263]

McDonald's result is sound and followed from analogous Supreme Court precedent.[264] Two matters are noteworthy, however. First, the Court observed[265] that an arbitration decision may be admitted as evidence in §1983 cases, especially where the sole issue is one of fact decided by the arbitrator after presentation by the parties and on the basis of an adequate record. Second, *McDonald* strongly indicated, if only implicitly, that 28 USC §1738 does

---

[261] *Id* 482.

[262] 466 US 284 (1984).

[263] *Id* 292.

[264] *E.g.*, Alexander v Gardner-Denver Co, 415 US 36 (1974) a Title VII action, and Barrentine v Arkansas-Best Freight Sys Inc, 450 US 728 (1981), a Fair Labor Standards Act action.

[265] 466 US at 292 n 13.

not in §1983 cases mandate the application of state preclusion rules to prior state agency proceedings. Like arbitration proceedings, such agency proceedings, standing alone, should not ordinarily be considered judicial proceedings for §1738 preclusive effect purposes.

Nevertheless, certain agency proceedings could be characterized as quasi-judicial in nature, as the Second Circuit has done.[266] If those agency proceedings are, moreover, consistent with procedural due process, then the potential exists for preclusive effect under two possible approaches. If §1738 is applicable, then state law would govern. Even if §1738 is not applicable, a federal preclusion rule of some kind could be fashioned. The Supreme Court recently dealt with this very question in *University of Tennessee v Elliott*.[267] This case involved the preclusive effect on subsequent federal civil rights litigation under Title VII and §1983 of a prior, *unreviewed* state administrative judgment. A state administrative law judge had earlier found that the federal plaintiff's proposed discharge was not racially motivated.

In an opinion by Justice White, the Court ruled that §1738 does not by its terms apply to unreviewed state administrative proceedings. The Court next went on to hold that plaintiff's Title VII claim was not precluded because Congress did not intend preclusion to apply to Title VII actions filed after unreviewed state administrative proceedings. However, as to the §1983 racial discrimination claim, the Court, after noting that Congress had not intended when it enacted §1983 to dispense with normal preclusion rules, including those subsequently developed for administrative agencies, created a federal preclusion rule requiring federal courts to give the same preclusive effect to an unreviewed state agency's quasi-judicial factfinding that the forum state's courts would do. In effect, then, the Court applied the §1738 rule to §1983 actions even though §1738 was technically found inapplicable; it called this rule one of "administrative" preclusion supported by the policies of repose and federalism.

Elliott was not surprising. It demonstrates the Court's continuing insistence that the usual rules of preclusion apply to §1983 actions. It also reflects the Court's use of a functional approach, applying federal standards, to determine

---

[266] Zanghi v Incorporated Village of Old Brookville, 752 F2d 42 (2d Cir 1985)(quasi-judicial state administrative proceeding resulting in probable cause finding given collateral estoppel effect in subsequent §1983 action; New York law and §1738 interpreted and applied to case). *But see* Moore v Bonner, 695 F2d 799 (4th Cir 1982)(no preclusive effect given unappealed county administrative decision even though South Carolina law would do so; such decisions not entitled to full faith and credit). *Cf* Buckhalter v Pepsi-Cola Gen Bottlers, Inc, 768 F2d 842 (7th Cir 1985)("administrative res judicata" applied to give preclusive effect to unappealed quasi-judicial agency decision in later Title VII and §1981 federal court proceeding; §1738 found inapplicable). *But see* University of Tenn v Elliott, 106 S Ct 3220 (1986) on the Title VII issue.

[267] 106 S Ct 3220 (1986), *affg in part & revg in part*, 766 F2d 982 (6th Cir 1985). Justices Stevens, Brennan, and Blackmun dissented on this preclusion issue. 106 S Ct at 3227. The question presented in the certiorari petition referred to "issues fully and fairly litigated before [a] state administrative agency acting in judicial capacity."

whether an agency's decision should be treated as quasi-judicial for preclusion purposes. However, the Court in *Elliott* dealt only with administrative *fact-finding;* determinations of federal constitutional and statutory law should not be given similar preclusive effect because state agencies do not have sufficient competence on such issues to warrant federal judicial deference. Furthermore, collateral estoppel, and not res judicata, was implicated in *Elliott.* This will typically be the case inasmuch as state agencies cannot decide federal constitutional claims authoritatively. On the other hand, as Justices Stevens, Brennan, and Blackmun suggested in dissenting on the §1983 preclusion issue, one result of *Elliott* may be to discourage potential litigants from pursuing their state administrative remedies.

In response to this recent Supreme Court case law on preclusion, there has been a good deal of §1983 preclusion litigation in the circuits. Because such litigation usually involves §1738 and the application of state preclusion rules which vary from state to state, circuit court decisions dealing with these matters are set out in the accompanying footnote.[268] Just as lawyers dealing with §1983

(*Text continued on page 334*)

---

[268] Representative §1983 preclusion cases in the circuits dealing with prior *state* proceedings include the following:

District of Columbia Circuit

District Properties Assocs v District of Columbia, 743 F2d 21 (DC Cir 1984)(remanding landlords' suit against defendant agency to determine whether preclusive effect should be given to prior District of Columbia Court of Appeals decisions involving same issues).

First Circuit

BCR Transp Co v Fontaine, 727 F2d 7 (1st Cir 1984)(under Massachusetts law, no collateral estoppel effect of prior state criminal court determination of probable cause on plaintiff's §1983 action against police officer for illegal arrest, search, and seizure; it was questionable whether the issue was even litigated at plaintiff's suppression hearing but, even if it was, the prior determination was not "in litigation between the same parties"—i.e., there was no mutuality of estoppel—as required by state law).

Roy v City of Augusta, 712 F2d 1517 (1st Cir 1983)(res judicata under Maine law barred federal plaintiff's §1983 damages suit against the city, but was not a bar to §1983 damages suit against city officials, sued in their individual capacities, who were not parties in the prior state court civil action).

Second Circuit

Zanghi v Incorporated Village of Old Brookville, 752 F2d 42 (2d Cir 1985)(under New York law, administrative finding of probable cause given collateral estoppel effect on subsequent federal proceeding; administrative hearing used procedures like those used in courts and there was full and fair opportunity to litigate the issue).

Warren v Byrne, 699 F2d 95 (2d Cir 1983)(prior dismissal of state criminal charges against federal plaintiffs had no collateral estoppel effect under New York law on federal plaintiffs' §1983 suit; defendants were not parties or privies of parties in prior criminal proceedings, and burdens of proof are different in criminal and civil proceedings).

Third Circuit

Wade v City of Pittsburgh, 765 F2d 405 (3d Cir 1985)(under Pennsylvania law, no claim preclusion effect of state court summary judgment in favor of defendant on state law immunity ground; this was not a judgment on the merits and, indeed, the merits were never developed in the state proceeding; claim preclusion should be applied only where clearly appropriate).

New Jersey-Philadelphia Presbytery v New Jersey State Bd of Higher Educ, 654 F2d 868 (3d Cir 1981)(prior state court litigation in which private college had its state license revoked had no preclusive effect on subsequent §1983 federal litigation: res judicata was not applicable because no identity of parties and issues as required by New Jersey law; collateral estoppel was not applicable because issues not "distinctly put in issue" and "directly determined" adversely to party, and also because not clear what the grounds were for the state court decisions; prior agency proceedings similarly had no preclusive effect because no res judicata deference need be paid to administrative proceedings).

Fourth Circuit

Mears v Town of Oxford, 762 F2d 368 (4th Cir 1985)(under Maryland law, res judicata effect given to prior state court decision; there was a decision on the merits, the claim was substantially the same and the parties were the same or in privity; also, collateral estoppel effect given to state court decision on particular issue because issues were identical, there was a final judgment on the merits, and the party estopped was a party to the state court proceeding).

Lee v Winston, 717 F2d 888 (4th Cir 1983)(even if it were assumed arguendo under Virginia law that a state court order or a motion to compel evidence in a criminal case would have collateral estoppel effect on a subsequent §1983 proceeding, here there should be no such preclusive effect because the federal plaintiff was denied procedural fairness in the prior state proceeding with respect to raising his constitutional claims).

Moore v Bonner, 695 F2d 799 (4th Cir 1982)(no preclusive effect of prior adverse unappealed county administrative decision on federal plaintiff's §1983 suit, even though South Carolina courts would give total preclusive effect to such a decision; such unappealed county administrative decisions not entitled to the same full faith and credit given state judicial decisions; choice of judicial forum belongs to a plaintiff; *Allen* and *Kremer* distinguished).

Cramer v Crutchfield, 648 F2d 943 (4th Cir 1981)(per curiam)(failure to object to the admission of illegally obtained evidence at federal plaintiff's state criminal trial was a *waiver* of Fourth Amendment rights; this precluded his §1983 federal court claims of malicious prosecution and abuse of process arising out of the use of such evidence; collateral estoppel not addressed).

Fifth Circuit

Brown v Edwards, 721 F2d 1442 (5th Cir 1984) (federal plaintiff's guilty plea in state court to charges of public profanity and resisting arrest did not, under Mississippi law and in light of Supreme Court's *Haring* decision, have preclusive effect on claims of unlawful arrest and prosecution; the arrest's validity was not actually litigated in the criminal proceeding and the conviction could well be proper while the arrest was improper; although the unlawful prosecution claim was a "closer question" because the guilty plea could logically be related to the propriety of the charges, there might nevertheless be no preclusive effect under state law, because the unlawful prosecution claim was not actually litigated in the state proceeding; however, it was not necessary to reach this last issue because on the merits the plaintiff did not demonstrate any violation of his constitutional rights).

Brantley v Surles, 718 F2d 1354 (5th Cir 1983)(federal plaintiff's prior adverse state court decision rejecting her challenge to her discharge from public employment did not have res judicata effect upon her later §1983 suit also challenging her discharge; §1983 action involved "the determination of facts and issues which are distinct from those posed in the state court litigation"; Judge Garwood concurred, correctly pointing out in this pre-*Migra* decision that Mississippi law was applicable and that, since the various state court decisions were primarily based on jurisdictional grounds, the state would not give preclusive effect "to alternative determinations on the merits").

Watts v Graves, 720 F2d 1416 (5th Cir 1983)(federal plaintiff's guilty plea in state court proceeding to distributing a controlled substance did not, after *Haring,* preclude his §1983 action against various defendants alleging Fourth and Fourteenth Amendment violations; while Louisiana law did not recognize collateral estoppel as such, nevertheless, its "limited version of res judicata" applied only where the relevant matters were submitted for decision by the parties and actually decided by the court; furthermore, Louisiana did not have any clear rule giving convictions preclusive effect on later damages actions).

Griffen v Big Spring Indep School Dist, 706 F2d 645 (5th Cir 1983) (no collateral estoppel effect of prior state administrative decision on federal §1983 suit where administrative procedures unfair to federal plaintiff; court did not reach broader question of whether preclusive effect should ever be given to administrative decisions in federal civil rights actions).

Hernandez v City of Lafayette, 699 F2d 734 (5th Cir 1983)(per curiam)(res judicata under Louisiana law barred federal plaintiff's claim where prior state court proceedings adversely decided same constitutional claims).

Miller v Hartwood Apartments Ltd, 689 F2d 1239 (5th Cir 1982)(adverse decision in Mississippi detainer case had no collateral estoppel effect on subsequent federal §1983 suit where the constitutional issues could not have been litigated in the state court detainer action).

Folsom Inv Co v Moore, 681 F2d 1032 (5th Cir 1982)(federal plaintiffs not precluded by res judicata from litigating claim as to unconstitutional attachment of their property even though their claim of illegal attachment had been asserted in prior state court proceedings and rejected; *Kremer* mandated that state law—here, Louisiana's generally nonpreclusive civil law—must be applied).

Sixth Circuit

Duncan v Peck, 752 F2d 1135 (6th Cir 1985)(under Ohio law, no res judicata effect given to prior state court judgment because it was not based on same claim as that presented in later §1983 federal suit; this determination made after consideration of the facts necessary to sustain the two claims).

Loudermill v Cleveland Bd of Educ, 721 F2d 550 (6th Cir 1983), *affd on other grounds,* 105 S Ct 1487 (1985)(extensive discussion of Ohio preclusion law which indicated that res judicata effect was not to be given to prior state court decision dismissing plaintiff's state lawsuit on ground that it was too late to appeal from adverse commission ruling; this state court decision was not on the merits under Ohio preclusion law; thus, this case was distinguishable from *Kremer* because here the court ruling did not approve or affirm the commission decision on the merits; further, the Ohio commission's decision was not that of a judicial forum, because the commission "clearly lacked the power to grant the procedural due process claim").

Foulks v Ohio Dept of Rehabilitation & Correction, 713 F2d 1229 (6th Cir 1983)(prior Ohio court decision favorable to plaintiff had no preclusive effect on subsequent federal §1983 action where federal defendants were not and could not have been parties to the state proceeding; thus, federal defendants could not invoke res judicata in their favor and federal plaintiff could not invoke collateral estoppel in his favor).

Seventh Circuit

Buckhalter v Pepsi-Cola Bottlers, Inc, 768 F2d 842 (7th Cir 1985)(§1738 inapplicable to unappealed quasi-judicial agency decision; however, "administrative res judicata" applied to give that decision preclusive effect on later Title VII and §1981 federal court proceeding).

Vandenplas v City of Muskego, 753 F2d 555 (7th Cir 1985)(claim preclusion effect given to prior state court judgment even though constitutional claims were not raised; under Wisconsin law, they could have been, and that was sufficient).

Bell v City of Milwaukee, 746 F2d 1205, 1226-28 (7th Cir 1984)(under Wisconsin law, no res judicata effect of prior state court oral settlement and dismissal with prejudice of state court case on §1983 action brought by federal plaintiff for himself and his deceased son; in the first action, plaintiff was unable to present important evidence of wrongful conduct because of defendants' fraud and concealment).

Guenther v Holmgreen, 738 F2d 879 (7th Cir 1984)(under Wisconsin law, prior state court preliminary hearing determination of probable cause to arrest federal plaintiff had collateral estoppel effect upon later §1983 damages claim of Fourth Amendment violation; the probable cause issue—including both the sufficiency and integrity of the supporting evidence—was raised, litigated, and resolved against plaintiff; also, the plaintiff was given a full and fair opportunity to litigate his probable cause challenge at the preliminary hearing, even though he asserted that he did not testify at the preliminary hearing for fear he might incriminate himself; moreover, the probable cause standards of the Fourth Amendment were the same for both criminal and civil purposes; finally, plaintiff's due process claims would also be collaterally estopped to the extent that they depended upon the absence of probable cause).

Eighth Circuit

Smith v Updegraff, 744 F2d 1354 (8th Cir 1984)(no preclusive effect given under Iowa law to decision by civil service commission, which was upheld by state court, that plaintiff's discharge was proper; no claim preclusion because the parties were different and the plaintiff did not have an opportunity to raise his §1983 claim; no issue preclusion because no constitutional issues were raised or actually litigated).

Baker v McCoy, 739 F2d 381 (8th Cir 1984)(prior state ruling in criminal case that federal plaintiff's confession was voluntary and not the result of beatings by police officers had collateral estoppel effect under Missouri law on §1983 damages action against police officers; the issues were identical, there was a decision on the merits, the plaintiff was a party to the prior litigation, and he had a full and fair opportunity to litigate the issues in the prior proceeding).

Brown v St Louis Police Dept, 691 F2d 393 (8th Cir 1982)(under Missouri law, res judicata barred federal plaintiff's §1983 claim that he had been unconstitutionally discharged where he had lost in a prior Missouri court proceeding on state law grounds; his constitutional claims could have been raised in state court but were not).

Ninth Circuit

Piatt v MacDougall, 723 F2d 721 (9th Cir 1984)(under Arizona law, prior adverse state court determination had res judicata effect on inmate's federal constitutional claim for compensation for "porter/teacher" work but not on his federal constitutional claim of compensation for "outside" work; his state action for "porter/teacher" work, which was based on an Arizona statute, involved essentially the same facts as his constitutional claim; also, the fact that he could not afford the $20 filing fee for appeal did not change this result because this filing fee was not violative of the Constitution; however, the facts necessary for the "outside" work claim were very different from those presented for the "porter/teacher" claim because different times, places, and employers were involved; also, because the state court decision on the "outside" work claim was jurisdictional in nature and did not go to the merits, res judicata effect did not attach under Arizona law; the state court decision on the "porter/teacher" claim did not collaterally estop plaintiff's "outside" work claim because issues related to the latter claim were not actually decided as required by Arizona law).

Tenth Circuit

Lavicky v Burnett, 758 F2d 468 (10th Cir 1985)(under Oklahoma law, no collateral estoppel effect given to state court's initial decision denying plaintiff's pretrial suppression motion; because state court later excluded evidence resulting from challenged search, it was not convinced that Fourth Amendment standards had been complied with; thus, the illegality question was not "distinctly put in issue and directly determined" in the suppression decision).

litigation should be familiar with their forum state's limitations and tolling law,[269] so too should they know their forum state's preclusion law. Separately noted are the relatively few §1983 circuit court decisions dealing with the preclusive effect of prior federal proceedings, an issue of *federal* law.[270]

Slayton v Willingham, 726 F2d 631 (10th Cir 1984)(per curiam)(under Oklahoma law, the federal plaintiff's nolo contendere plea to a criminal charge in a prior state proceeding did not collaterally estop his suit against police officers for illegal arrests, searches, and beatings; these issues were "neither necessary to nor actually decided by the state court's judgment based on the guilty plea").

Eleventh Circuit

Casines v Murchek, 766 F2d 1494 (11th Cir 1985)(no res judicata effect under Florida law of state court's affirmance of civil service commission decision; there was no identity of parties, no identity of claims, and no identity of "the thing sued for"; Gorin v Osborne, 756 F2d 834 (11th Cir 1985) distinguished on ground that there the constitutional issue was actually litigated in the prior state proceeding).

Dykes v Hosemann, 743 F2d 1488 (11th Cir 1984)(remand to determine possible preclusive effect of prior state court proceeding on federal §1983 action; under Florida law, no res judicata effect unless the causes of action—together with necessary evidence—in both suits are the same; no collateral estoppel effect where causes of action are different except as to those issues actually litigated and decided).

Burney v Polk Community College, 728 F2d 1374 (11th Cir 1984)(*Kremer*'s reasoning applied to plaintiff's Title VII employment discrimination action; under Florida law, collateral estoppel effect would be given to prior state court affirmance of college board's decision, after hearing, to dismiss plaintiff despite his claim of discrimination; it was not significant that the college board was not the state agency statutorily authorized to enforce Florida's employment discrimination laws, inasmuch as it was the state court's decision which was, pursuant to §1738, to be given preclusive effect here, just as it was in *Kremer*).

Deweese v Town of Palm Beach, 688 F2d 731 (11th Cir 1982)(offensive collateral estoppel did not apply against the defendant city sued in federal court under §1983 even though it had lost on motion in a prior state criminal proceeding in which the federal plaintiff was a criminal defendant; the existence of alternative grounds for the state court's dismissal of the charges against the federal plaintiff made the application of offensive collateral estoppel "problematic" and unfair to the city; Florida law apparently not applied even though *Allen* previously decided).

[269] *See* §§4.14-4.16. 42 USC §1988 does for limitations and tolling what §1738 does for preclusion: both require the application of relevant state law.

[270] Representative §1983 preclusion cases in the circuits dealing with prior *federal* proceedings include the following:

First Circuit

Krohn v United States, 742 F2d 24 (1st Cir 1984)(prior unappealed federal district court decision purportedly ruling in criminal case that there was probable cause for the plaintiff's arrest not given preclusive effect on federal plaintiff's later action; prior district court determination was a ruling on a motion for speedy trial and the relevant factors for this kind of decision were unrelated to the issue of probable cause for the arrest; also, the district court may not even have made a probable cause ruling).

Fourth Circuit

Wright v Collins, 766 F2d 841 (4th Cir 1985)(no res judicata effect on inmate's damage claim from prior successful class action challenging conditions of confinement and seeking prospective relief and damages; inmate was not notified that his participation in the class action would preclude a subsequent individual damages action; Bogard v Cook, 586 F2d 399 (5th Cir 1978) and Crowder v Lash, 687 F2d 996 (7th Cir 1982) previously reached a similar conclusion).

§5.20   —Subsequent State Judicial Proceedings

The reverse of the prior state judgment preclusion problem arises where the federal forum has already declared a state statute unconstitutional on its face or as applied. The question is what effect should be given this declaratory judgment, or any other federal court determinations as to fact or law, in a subsequent state proceeding against the federal plaintiff.[271] The Supreme Court expressly left the matter open in *Steffel v Thompson*[272] where, writing for the Court, Justice Brennan said: "[T]he federal court judgment may have some res judicata effect, though this point is not free from difficulty and the governing rules remain to be developed with a view to the proper workings of a federal system."[273]

Justice White, concurring, stated that some res judicata effect surely ought to be given a federal declaratory judgment that a federal plaintiff's conduct is constitutionally immune from prosecution.[274] Justice Rehnquist, joined by Chief Justice Burger, announced that he expressed no opinion on the subject, but nevertheless observed:

Fifth Circuit

Nilsen v City of Moss Point, 701 F2d 556 (5th Cir 1983)(en banc)(federal res judicata principles applied to bar subsequent federal suit where prior federal suit raising different claims was dismissed on limitations grounds and where plaintiff in that prior suit unsuccessfuly moved for leave to add new claims; six judges dissented).

Seventh Circuit

Crowder v Lash, 687 F2d 996 (7th Cir 1982)(prior federal class action for equitable relief did not bar inmate's later federal §1983 damages suit against same defendants; defendants did not timely raise defense and in any event inmate was not notified that he was somehow required to adjudicate his damages claim as part of the prior class action suit for injunctive relief; also, federal plaintiff in later §1983 suit was not one of the original plaintiffs in the prior suit; however, prior federal class action proceeding had collateral estoppel effect on later and closely related federal suit for damages as to the constitutionality of the conditions of plaintiff's confinement, but not as to individual defendants' personal responsibility and qualified immunity defense).

Eleventh Circuit

Herron v Beck, 693 F2d 125 (11th Cir 1982)(res judicata did not bar inmate's §1983 damages suit where prior federal class action suit involving conditions of confinement sought only declaratory and injunctive relief and where later §1983 suit raised new issue).

Williams v Bennett, 689 F2d 1370 (11th Cir 1982)(prior federal class action litigation seeking declaratory and injunctive relief regarding conditions of confinement in prison had collateral estoppel effect on later §1983 suit brought by inmate as to issue of conditions of confinement, but not as to culpability of individual defendants).

[271] This question would not ordinarily arise as a practical matter where the prior federal proceeding led to injunctive relief which prohibited the institution of subsequent state judicial proceedings.

[272] 415 US 452 (1974).

[273] *Id* 470-71, (quoting from Justice Brennan's opinion in Perez v Ledesma, 401 US 82, 125 (1971)).

[274] *Id* 477-78.

However, I do note that the federal decision would not be accorded the stare decisis effect in state court that it would have in a subsequent proceeding within the same federal jurisdiction. Although the state court would not be compelled to follow the federal holding, the opinion might, of course, be viewed as highly persuasive.[275]

Practically speaking, there should be no serious res judicata concern where the Supreme Court has affirmed federal declaratory relief simply because any subsequent state conviction inconsistent in fact with the declaratory relief would be overturned by the Court on review.[276] But even where the Supreme Court has not affirmed the federal declaratory relief because the state has not appealed, the general rule is now clear that state courts must use *federal law* to determine what legal effect to give to federal judgments.[277]

---

[275] *Id* 482 n 3.

[276] Perez v Ledesma, 401 US 93, 124-25 (1971)(opinion of Justice Brennan, concurring in part and dissenting in part, joined by Justices White & Marshall).

[277] Degnan, *Federalized Res Judicata,* 85 Yale LJ 741, 744 (1976)(put in terms of the "federal common law" rule); *Developments in the Law—Section 1983 and Federalism,* 90 Harv L Rev 1133, 1357 n 129 (1977); Restatement (Second) of Judgments §87 (1982); C. Wright, Law of Federal Courts §100A (4th ed 1983).

"Every Person":
Governmental Liability

6

§6.01   Summary

Until the Supreme Court's 1978 decision in *Monell v Department of Social Services*,[1] cities and counties were consistently considered not to be *persons* within the meaning of 42 USC §1983 and hence were immune from liability for damages.[2] Because a bifurcated meaning of *person* was thought improper, the same rule was applied where cities and counties were sued for equitable relief only.[3] Furthermore, the Court similarly held that cities and counties were not persons for §1983 purposes even where a state's laws expressly permitted suits for damages against such entities[4] and went so far as to preclude suing cities and counties in federal court for violations of state law through the device of pendent jurisdiction.[5]

Monell changed much of this. Overruling this aspect of *Monroe v Pape*,[6] the leading case, the Court held that cities and counties are §1983 persons and thus suable in their own names for compensatory damages as well as for declaratory and injunctive relief. It is also clear from *Monell* that local government officials may be sued in their *official* capacities for both damages and injunctive relief even if this means that public funds are used to pay reparations for past wrongs.

As *Monell* points out, however, there is a significant condition of §1983 local government liability: *there must be a local government official policy or custom which is a cause in fact of the plaintiff's constitutional deprivation.* Respondeat superior is not a basis for rendering a local government liable for constitutional violations committed by its employees. Properly understood, this amounts to a duty approach to local government liability under §1983. This approach will be examined in greater detail in a later section.[7]

Monell's holding of local government liability applies only to compensatory damages; local governments are absolutely immune from punitive damages

---

[1] 436 US 658 (1978). While this chapter deals with constitutional violations, its discussion of local government liability applies to federal statutory ("laws") violations as well. *See* **§2.12.**

[2] The leading case was Monroe v Pape, 365 US 167 (1961) which held that the city of Chicago and municipalities in general were not persons suable for damages under §1983.

[3] City of Kenosha v Bruno, 412 US 507 (1973).

[4] Moor v County of Alameda, 411 US 693 (1972).

[5] Aldinger v Howard, 427 US 1 (1976). See **§§1.11-1.12** on pendent jurisdiction.

[6] 365 US 167 (1961). Having held in 1974—relying on *Monroe v Pape*—that the city of Jackson was not a suable person under §1983 in connection with an alleged riot at Jackson State University, the Fifth Circuit refused to allow the plaintiffs who had lost their §1983 jury trial against various individual defendants to pursue a new §1983 claim against the city on the basis of *Monell*. The court observed that *Monroe v Pape* had made no difference in the presentation of plaintiffs' case at trial and, in any event, the city would have not been found liable even if it had been a defendant at the time. Burton v Mississippi, 650 F2d 91 (5th Cir 1981) (per curiam).

[7] *See* **§6.06.**

liability.[8] As to compensatory damages, though, local governments, unlike individuals, are not protected by the affirmative defense of qualified immunity.[9]

The Eleventh Amendment currently bars federal court suits for damages and equitable relief (including §1983 suits) brought directly against states and their agencies.[10] Justice Brennan has argued unsuccessfully that in light of *Monell,* states might be persons for §1983 purposes, suable even in federal court despite the Eleventh Amendment.[11] Even apart from the Eleventh Amendment, it has, until recently, been generally held that states and their agencies are not §1983 persons; if this is correct, then states may not be sued under §1983 even in state courts.[12]

Before *Monell* was decided, some litigants successfully avoided the local government person problem by an implied Fourteenth Amendment action for damages approach against cities and counties based on a Supreme Court decision which implied a Fourth Amendment action for damages against *federal* officials.[13] Indeed, before *Monell* a majority of the circuits apparently approved of this approach.[14] After *Monell,* however, the validity of the approach is questionable.[15] In any event, the Supreme Court indicated that the implied

---

[8] City of Newport v Fact Concerts, Inc, 453 US 247 (1981). *See* **§6.18.**

[9] Owen v City of Independence, 445 US 622 (1980). See generally **ch 8** on qualified immunity.

[10] See **§5.08** on the Eleventh Amendment and its relevance to §1983.

[11] In Hutto v Finney, 437 US 678 (1978), involving the Civil Rights Attorney's Fees Awards Act of 1976. This suggestion was rejected by the Court in Quern v Jordan, 440 US 332 (1979). *See* **§6.20.**

[12] *See* **§6.20.**

[13] The Supreme Court decision is Bivens v Six Unknown Named Agents, 403 US 388 (1971). On several occasions the Court expressly left open the Fourteenth Amendment action for damages issue. Aldinger v Howard, 427 US 1, 4 n 3 (1976); City of Charlotte v Firefighters Local 660, 426 US 283, 284 n 1 (1976); Mount Healthy City School Dist Bd of Educ v Doyle, 429 US 274, 275-78 (1977).

[14] Turpin v Mailet, 579 F2d 152 (2d Cir 1978) (en banc), *vacated and remanded in light of Monell sub nom* City of West Haven v Turpin, 47 USLW 3234 (US Sept 1, 1978); Jamison v McCurrie, 565 F2d 483 (7th Cir 1977); Owens v City of Independence, 560 F2d 925 (8th Cir 1977), *vacated & remanded in light of Monell,* 98 S Ct 3118 (1978); Stapp v Avoyelles Parish School Bd, 545 F2d 527 (5th Cir 1977); Amen v City of Dearborn, 532 F2d 554 (6th Cir 1976); Cox v Stanton, 529 F2d 47 (4th Cir 1975); Hostrop v Board of Junior College Dist No 515, 523 F2d 569 (7th Cir 1975), *cert denied,* 425 US 963 (1976); Gray v Union County Intermediate Educ Dist, 520 F2d 803 (9th Cir 1975); Hanna v Drobnick, 514 F2d 393 (6th Cir 1975). Most of these cases, however, did not thoroughly address the *Bivens* issue, but instead confused it with the §1331 jurisdiction question.

[15] Implying a Fourteenth Amendment cause of action for damages from *Bivens* is not without considerable difficulty despite some very broad language in *Bivens. Bivens* provided a remedy against federal officials, not against a governmental entity, and the opinion also observed that existing state remedies were inadequate. Further, the Court in *Bivens* emphasized, first, that "[t]he present case involves no special factors counseling hesitation in the absence of affirmative action by Congress," 403 US at 396, and, second, the absence of an "explicit congressional declaration" barring a Fourth Amendment damage action, *id* 397. In contrast, a Fourteenth Amendment action for damages against a municipality must get around the existence of §1983, its post-*Monell*

Fourteenth Amendment action approach should no longer be taken.[16]

Local government liability after *Monell*—the major subject of this chapter—should be sharply differentiated from *individual* §1983 damages liability, discussed in Chapter 3,[17] and §1983 declaratory and injunctive relief directed nominally against governmental officials as individuals, discussed in Chapter 5.[18] Similarly, the related but distinguishable question of the implications of *Monell* for the possible liability of supervisory officials based on the unconstitutional conduct of their subordinates is discussed extensively in Chapter 3.[19]

§6.02   The Law Prior to *Monell*—The Origin of §1983 Governmental Immunity in *Monroe v Pape*

Prior to the Supreme Court's 1978 decision in *Monell v Department of Social Services*[20] holding that local governmental bodies are persons for §1983 defendant purposes, *Monroe v Pape*[21] was the leading case characterizing governmental entities as nonpersons. In *Monroe* the plaintiffs, alleging Fourteenth Amendment violations, sought damages under §1983 against individual police officers and, under a respondeat superior theory, against the officers' employer, the city of Chicago. Writing for the Court, Justice Douglas concluded that the city was not a person and, therefore, the district court had properly dismissed plaintiffs' cause of action against it.

Justice Douglas rejected plaintiffs' policy arguments—indeed, he did not discuss them—as to the desirability of municipal liability for damages for the purposes of compensating injured plaintiffs, encouraging official compliance with the Fourteenth Amendment, and assuring a federal forum for such claims.[22] Relying solely on particular legislative debates, Justice Douglas said simply: "[W]e are of the opinion that Congress did not undertake to bring municipal corporations within the ambit of [section 1983]."[23]

The Court's reading of the legislative history to exclude municipalities as

---

application to local governments, and §5 of the Fourteenth Amendment which would appear to give Congress the primary role in enforcing Fourteenth Amendment rights through legislation creating damage actions. In addition, a Fourteenth Amendment action for damages might not easily be limited to local governments but could eventually be extended to all state and local government officials. This result would render §1983 useless except for attorney's fees under 42 USC §1988.

[16] *See* **§6.16.**
[17] *See* **§§3.02-3.14.**
[18] *See* **§5.08.**
[19] *See* **§§3.15-3.16.**
[20] 436 US 658 (1978).
[21] 365 US 167 (1961).
[22] *Id* 191.
[23] *Id* 187.

persons was much criticized by commentators,[24] as follows: it was observed that the debates did not discuss the meaning of the word *person;* that the first version of the so-called Sherman Amendment on which the Court relied went well beyond the concerns of §1983 by imposing strict liability on all inhabitants; that the debates primarily reflected the fear that it would be unjust, unfair, and probably unconstitutional to impose liability on municipalities under either version when most municipalities did not have police forces 100 years ago; and that the debates said nothing about municipal liability for torts of employees. Still another argument criticized the Court's refusal in *Monroe* to analyze the purposes of §1983 in connection with its discussion of the word *person.*

While the Court's approach to the definition of *person* in *Monroe* may have been questionable, the result was clear. A municipality was not liable in damages under §1983 for the Fourteenth Amendment violations of its employees. A later case not unexpectedly added counties to the list of nonpersons.[25] After *Monroe,* the Court also rejected various imaginative end runs around the *Monroe* holding. In one case the Court held that local governmental bodies could not be sued directly under §1983 solely for *equitable relief,*[26] and in another that local governmental entities were not persons suable under §1983 even where a state's laws permitted damage suits against them.[27] Furthermore, the Court concluded that local governmental bodies which were not persons could not be sued in federal court for violations of state law through the device of pendent jurisdiction.[28]

§6.03   The Law in the Circuits Prior to *Monell* —Local Government Bodies and Their Agencies

Some federal courts held that a township[29] and a utilities district[30] were not persons simply because they were characterized as *municipal corporations* by state law. Interestingly, one such case, while using state law as its basis for determining that the utilities district was formally a municipal corporation, nevertheless ignored state law in rejecting the argument that the district was a person because it was not immune from liability under state law, and said: "We perceive no basis to import the often nebulous distinction between

---

[24] *E.g.,* Levin, *The Section 1983 Municipal Immunity Doctrine,* 65 Geo LJ 1483 (1977); Kates & Kouba, *Liability of Public Entities Under Section 1983 of the Civil Rights Act,* 45 S Cal L Rev 131 (1972); *Developments in the Law—Section 1983 and Federalism,* 90 Harv L Rev 1133 (1977).

[25] Moor v County of Alameda, 411 US 693 (1972).

[26] City of Kenosha v Bruno, 412 US 507 (1973).

[27] Moor v County of Alameda, 411 US 693 (1972).

[28] Aldinger v Howard, 427 US 1 (1976).

[29] Pressman v Chester Township, 307 F Supp 1084 (ED Pa 1969).

[30] Jorden v Metropolitan Utils Dist, 498 F2d 514 (8th Cir 1974).

proprietary and governmental functions of a municipal corporation into the federal law question of its civil liability under §1983."[31]

When a court could not use this formal approach,[32] the next question usually asked was whether the governmental entity was simply a part of *arm* of the municipality. Under this approach, a city hospital,[33] city planning commission,[34] city police department,[35] city civil service commission,[36] and a county planning board[37] and county hospital[38] were held to be nonpersons. The few courts that explained their reasoning emphasized that the particular agency was city or county owned, was operated as a part of city or county government and, if it were successfully sued, "it is the city [or county] which will pay."[39]

The circuits had considerably more difficulty dealing with those local bodies which were not themselves municipal corporations, were seemingly not dependent on municipal corporations, and possessed governmental powers which were exercised only for *special* purposes. In fact, it was correct as a general matter that the further the local governmental body was from being a city or county with general governmental powers (like those in *Monroe*[40] and its progeny), the more the confusion among the cases. The Supreme Court's lack of guidance on the person issue proved very troublesome in connection with such bodies. As the Second Circuit stated: "We know of no rule of thumb that may be deemed controlling on the question whether independent agencies are to be considered 'persons' for the purposes of §1983."[41]

Boards of education typically caused the most concern. The Seventh Circuit simply concluded without discussion that a board of education was not a municipal corporation, was thereby not covered by *Monroe,* and was thus a person.[42] The Eighth Circuit, without even stating this much, also apparently held that a school district was a person.[43] The Fourth Circuit reached the

---

[31] *Id* 516.

[32] Because the agency was not formally a municipal corporation.

[33] Hathaway v Worcester City Hosp, 475 F2d 701 (1st Cir 1973); United States *ex rel* Gittlemacker v County of Philadelphia, 413 F2d 84 (3d Cir 1969), *cert denied,* 396 US 1046 (1970).

[34] Garrett v City of Hamtramck, 503 F2d 1236 (6th Cir 1974).

[35] Henschel v Worcester Police Dept, 445 F2d 624 (1st Cir 1971); United States *ex rel* Lee v Illinois, 343 F2d 120 (7th Cir 1965).

[36] Lehman v City of Pittsburgh, 474 F2d 21 (3d Cir 1973).

[37] United Farmworkers Hous Project, Inc v City of Delray Beach, 493 F2d 799 (5th Cir 1974).

[38] Robinson v McCorkle, 462 F2d 111 (3d Cir), *cert denied,* 409 US 1042 (1972).

[39] Henschel v Worcester Police Dept, 445 F2d 624 (1st Cir 1971).

[40] Monroe v Pape, 365 US 167 (1961).

[41] Monell v Dept of Social Servs, 532 F2d 259, 263 (2d Cir 1976), *revd,* 436 US 658 (1978).

[42] Aurora Educ Assn East v Board of Educ, 490 F2d 431 (7th Cir 1973), *cert denied,* 416 US 985 (1974).

[43] Keckeisen v Independent School Dist 612, 509 F2d 1062 (8th Cir), *cert denied,* 423 US 833 (1975); Brenden v Independent School Dist 742, 477 F2d 1292 (8th Cir 1973).

contrary result as to a school board's person status with no reasoning whatever but over a dissenting opinion suggesting that the status of a board of education for §1983 purposes was an open question.[44] Only the Second and Fifth Circuits attempted to develop standards for handling the person status of independent local bodies under §1983.[45]

§6.04 —Suing Individual Officers Who Are Persons

Monroe[46] and its progeny stood for the proposition that cities and counties were not persons for purposes of either damages or equitable relief. One conceivable way around this was to sue government officials, who *are* persons, for damages or injunctive relief in their *official* capacity so that the judgment entered was in reality against the treasury of the municipality. However, the circuits were cautious in scrutinizing §1983 claims which might have appeared to be directed against government officials but which were in reality "subterfuges that contravene the exemption from §1983 announced in *Monroe*" for municipalities.[47] Generally speaking, as discussed next, the circuits could relatively easily distinguish between permitted actions for damages against government officials in their *individual* capacity, and prohibited actions for damages against such officials in their *official* capacity, on the basis that these were thought to be directed against the municipality itself. They had a more difficult time, however, distinguishing between permitted *equitable* relief directed against government officials in their official capacity[48] and prohibited equitable relief which was thought to involve *retrospective* relief equivalent to damages.

Two often cited pre-*Monell*[49] district court decisions had to do with claims for damages against government officials in their official capacity.[50] In both cases the courts viewed the complaints as attempts to obtain judgments

---

[44] Singleton v Vance County Bd of Educ, 501 F2d 429 (4th Cir 1974).

[45] Monell v Department of Social Servs, 532 F2d 259, 264 (2d Cir 1976), *revd*, 436 US 658 (1978), which, after weighing various factors, concluded that "the affairs of the New York City Board of Education are intimately connected with the city itself"; Muzquiz v City of San Antonio, 520 F2d 993 (5th Cir 1975), *affd*, 528 F2d 499 (5th Cir 1976) (en banc), which used a similar approach in concluding that a city's Police and Pension Fund Board of Trustees was not a "person".

[46] Monroe v Pape, 365 US 167 (1961).

[47] Judge Godbold, dissenting in Muzquiz v City of San Antonio, 520 F2d 993, 1009 (5th Cir 1975), *affd*, 528 F2d 499 (5th Cir 1976) (en banc).

[48] If directed against officials in their individual capacity, injunctions would be useless (even assuming plaintiffs overcame the *state action* hurdle) because the purpose of such relief is to change unconstitutional official acts or practices. *See* **app A** for important institutional reform cases.

[49] Monell v Department of Social Servs, 436 US 658 (1978).

[50] Bennett v Gravelle, 323 F Supp 203 (D Md), *affd on other grounds*, 451 F2d 1101 (4th Cir 1971), *cert dismissed*, 407 US 917 (1972); Westberry v Fisher, 309 F Supp 12 (D Me 1970).

establishing a municipality's liability payable out of public funds. This reasoning was followed by other district courts in traditional damage actions.[51] The Second Circuit used this same approach in an action for back pay and other damages against officials of the New York City Board of Education (not a person).[52] Characterizing "the nature of the relief sought—back pay—[a]s an award [which] must come out of the public treasury of the Board of Education" and therefore holding that the suit could not be maintained under §1983, the court stated:

> Just as the Congress which enacted the Eleventh Amendment . . . meant to protect the treasuries of the states, so the Reconstruction Congress which enacted the Civil Rights Act sought to protect municipal treasuries. The mere substitution of the name of the official for the name of the city in the complaint cannot be used as a subterfuge to circumvent the intent of Congress.[53]

It was settled, therefore, that damage suits against officials in their *official* capacity which amounted in effect to claims against a municipality's treasury would not be permitted. In contrast, suits for damages against officials in their *individual* capacity were always permitted, subject only to the availability to those officials of a qualified immunity.[54]

However, considerable difficulty arose in the matter of equitable relief directed against governmental officials in their official capacity. On the one hand, strictly prospective equitable relief was generally allowed even though the financial impact upon a municipality was significant. This rule derived from the Supreme Court's emphasis on the distinction between prospective and retrospective equitable relief in an analogous Eleventh Amendment context in *Edelman v Jordan*[55] and was applied as well to §1983 equitable actions. Indeed, to have held otherwise would have made §1983's express provision for equitable relief against government officials meaningless. On the other hand *Edelman* also indicated that characterizing as an equitable remedy what in fact amounted to an order to a state official "to use state funds to make reparation

---

[51] Patton v Conrad Area School Dist, 388 F Supp 410 (D Del 1975); Needleman v Bohlen, 386 F Supp 741 (D Mass 1974); Hines v D'Artois, 383 F Supp 184 (WD La 1974); Veres v County of Monroe, 364 F Supp 1327 (ED Mich 1973), *affd*, 542 F2d 1177 (1976), *cert denied*, 431 US 969 (1977); Hayes v Henlopen School Dist, 341 F Supp 823 (D Del 1972).

[52] Monell v Department of Social Servs, 532 F2d 259 (2d Cir 1976), *revd*, 436 US 658 (1978).

[53] *Id* 266.

[54] *See generally* **ch 8.**

[55] 415 US 651 (1974). The Court said:

> It is one thing to tell the Commissioner of Social Services that he must comply with the federal standards for the future if the state is to have the benefit of federal funds in the program head ministers. It is quite another thing to order the Commissioner to use state funds to make reparation for the past.

Id 665.

for the past"[56] would not avoid the Eleventh Amendment bar. The question then became the extent to which this reasoning prevented §1983 equitable relief against a government official in an official capacity where there was a retrospective monetary impact.

Several district court decisions[57] intimated that there was no difference for §1983 purposes between actions against officials in an official capacity for compensatory damages and for a back pay award pursuant to equitable reinstatement. Thus, neither action was permissible. The Fourth and Sixth Circuits took a contrary position. In *Burt v Board of Trustees*,[58] the Fourth Circuit apparently approved equitable relief including back pay and contributions to a retirement fund but did not seriously discuss the person issue. However, shortly thereafter the Fourth Circuit expressly read *Burt* as meaning that "[s]uch an award [of back pay] is an integral part of the equitable remedy of reinstatement" and that officials of a school district could be sued in their official capacity as persons for such equitable relief.[59] And in *Incarcerated Men of Allen County Jail v Fair*,[60] the Sixth Circuit stated that a "federal court may, however, award equitable relief against local officials, even though it will have a severe impact on local governmental funds, without infringing the policies behind §1983."

Far more analysis was given this troublesome issue by the Fifth Circuit. In a 1973 decision the Fifth Circuit initially indicated that school board officials were persons for equitable relief purposes even though back pay was a part of the reinstatement request.[61] The court held that "the prayer for back pay is not a claim for damages, but is an integral part of the equitable remedy of injunctive reinstatement."[62] Thereafter, although still prior to *Monell*, the Fifth Circuit took a different position on this issue. In *Muzquiz v City of San Antonio*,[63] a 1976 case, plaintiffs who had already abandoned their claim for compensatory damages sought an accounting, restitution, and refunds in connection with pension fund payments which they had made and which they now claimed were wrongfully withheld pursuant to an unconstitutional statute. Affirming an

---

[56] *Id.*

[57] Patton v Conrad Area School Dist, 388 F Supp 410 (D Del 1975); Needleman v Bohlen, 386 F Supp 741 (D Mass 1974); Hines v D'Artois, 383 F Supp 184 (WD La 1974), *revd on other grounds*, 531 F2d 726 (5th Cir 1976). The Third Circuit left this question open in Rochester v White, 503 F2d 263, 268 n 14 (3d Cir 1974). So did the Eighth Circuit. Owens v City of Independence, 560 F2d 325, 931-32 (8th Cir 1977), *vacated & remanded in light of Monell*, 438 US 902 (1978).

[58] 521 F2d 1201 (4th Cir 1975).

[59] Thomas v Ward, 529 F2d 916, 920 (4th Cir 1975). *See also* Reynolds v Abbeville County School Dist No 60, 554 F2d 638, 644 (4th Cir 1977).

[60] 507 F2d 281, 288 (6th Cir 1974).

[61] Harkless v Sweeny Indep School Dist, 427 F2d 319 (5th Cir 1970), *cert denied*, 400 US 991 (1971).

[62] *Id* 324.

[63] 528 F2d 499 (5th Cir 1976) (en banc).

earlier panel decision,[64] the court held that plaintiffs' claims would amount to restitution against the fund itself; therefore, pension fund refunds were precluded. Moreover, the majority held that declaratory and injunctive relief was prohibited as well.[65]

As will be discussed next, the Supreme Court's 1978 decision in *Monell v Department of Social Services*,[66] which overruled *Monroe v Pape*[67] on the local governmental immunity issue, changed much of this complicated prior law. Since *Monell*, local government bodies, general or special purpose, independent or dependent, are directly suable as *persons* for both damages and equitable relief. Also, after *Monell*, local government officials may be sued in their official capacity for damages and retrospective equitable relief even though the practical effect is that the local government body itself pays.[68] However, while still technically an open question, *Monell* may not have changed that prior law which consistently treated states and their agencies as nonpersons (like municipalities) and thus not suable directly under §1983 either in federal or state court for any type of relief.[69] Furthermore, the distinctions between, and confusion about, individual and official capacity suits have ironically reemerged, as reflected in post-*Monell* Supreme Court and circuit court decisions.[70]

§6.05   *Monell v Department of Social Services* —Local Government Bodies Are Now Persons

Monell v Department of Social Services[71] held that local governmental bodies are persons under §1983 and hence directly suable for compensatory[72] damages and declaratory and injunctive relief. With this holding, the Supreme Court overruled its earlier contrary holdings in *Monroe v Pape*[73] and *City of Kenosha v Bruno*.[74] The Court also concluded in *Monell* that local governmental officials may be sued in their official capacity for damages and retrospective declaratory

---

[64] 520 F2d 993, 1002 (5th Cir 1975). This panel decision, however, had ruled for the defendants *on the merits*.

[65] The majority reasoned that such injunctive and declaratory relief as to the statute's invalidity would mean that the plaintiffs were entitled to restitution, a result which was barred.

[66] 436 US 658 (1978).

[67] 365 US 167 (1961).

[68] *See* §§6.05–6.16.

[69] *See* §6.20.

[70] *See* §6.14.

[71] 436 US 658 (1978).

[72] But not punitive damages. *See* §6.19. Also, local governments are not protected by qualified immunity from compensatory damages liability. *See* §6.18.

[73] 365 US 167 (1961).

[74] 412 US 507 (1973).

and injunctive relief even though the local governmental body itself pays. While *Monell* may not have changed the settled prior law that states and their agencies are not persons for §1983 purposes,[75] the Court has since held that an interstate compact agency, created by California and Nevada, and for which federal approval was required and given, was a suable person for §1983 purposes.[76]

According to *Monell*, local governmental liability under §1983 (indeed, even *individual* liability, as discussed in Chapter 3) may not be based upon the theory of respondeat superior.[77] Respondeat superior would render the local governmental body liable for the unconstitutional conduct of its employees solely because of an employment relationship. Rather, what is required by *Monell* for local governmental liability is that the *"execution of a government's policy or custom,* whether made by its law makers or by those whose edicts or acts may fairly be said to represent official policy, *inflicts the injury. . . ."*[78] On the defense side, *Monell* expressly left open the possibility of a qualified local governmental immunity from §1983 liability,[79] a possibility that was thereafter rejected by the Court.[80]

In *Monell*, female employees of the Department of Social Services and the Board of Education of the City of New York brought a §1983 class action against the department, the board and its chancellor, and the City of New York and its mayor. Plaintiffs alleged that the defendants unconstitutionally and as a matter of official policy forced pregnant employees to take unpaid leaves of absence even though such employees were not required to do so for medical reasons.[81] The individual defendants were sued solely in their official capacities, with the plaintiffs seeking declaratory and injunctive relief against all defendants and back pay for the periods of the allegedly unlawful forced leave.

The district court held the claims for declaratory and injunctive relief moot because the City of New York and the Board of Education changed their maternity leave policies after the suit was filed. It then found the prior policy unconstitutional but denied back pay because such back pay would ultimately come from the City of New York and, if awarded, would circumvent the

---

[75] *See* **§6.20.**

[76] Lake Country Estates, Inc v Tahoe Regional Planning Agency, 440 US 391, 405 n 29 (1979), discussed in another context at **§7.05.**

[77] See **§3.15** on respondeat superior.

[78] 436 US at 694 (emphasis added). What constitutes an "official policy or custom" and the related cause in fact issue are discussed in this section and in **§§6.06-6.07.**

[79] *See* **§6.17.**

[80] Owen v City of Independence, 455 US 622 (1980). *See* **§6.18.**

[81] This practice was held unconstitutional in Cleveland Bd of Educ v LaFleur, 414 US 632 (1974) on "irrebuttable presumption" grounds. Cf General Elec Co v Gilbert, 429 US 125 (1976) a Title VII case involving exclusion of pregnancy from private disability plans, where the Court found no statutory violation.

absolute immunity of local governmental bodies.[82] The Second Circuit Court of Appeals affirmed. It first held that the Board of Education was not a §1983 *person* because "it performs a vital governmental function . . ., and, significantly, while it has the right to determine how the funds appropriated to it shall be spent . . ., it has no final say in deciding what its appropriations shall be."[83] However, while the officials were persons even though sued in their official capacity, the back pay claim against them was then held improper on the basis of *Monroe v Pape*.[84] The Second Circuit reasoned that if back pay were awarded, it would have to be paid by the city, a nonperson.

The Supreme Court, in an opinion by Justice Brennan, reversed.[85] Reviewing its earlier reading of the legislative history surrounding the so-called Sherman Amendment relied on in *Monroe v Pape*, the Court confessed error and acknowledged that its reading had been forced and wrong. It next considered other legislative history touching more directly on §1983 and then asserted: "Our analysis of the legislative history of the Civil Rights Act of 1871 compels the conclusion that Congress *did* intend municipalities and other local government units to be included among those persons to whom §1983 applies."[86]

The Court also analyzed §1983's cause in fact language—"*Every person who . . . subjects, or causes to be subjected,* any citizen . . . to the deprivation of any rights, privileges, or immunities . . ."—and stated that this language precluded the applicability of respondeat superior to §1983 liability.[87] In addition, the Court's consideration of the two policy justifications for respondeat superior persuaded it that both had in fact been rejected in the legislative debates on §1983.[88] Consequently, according to the Court, respondeat superior liability may not be imposed on local governmental entities under §1983.

This rule applies, according to *Monell*, even if *state law* imposes respondeat superior liability upon a local governmental body.[89] Rather, §1983 local governmental liability requires that "the action that is alleged to be unconstitutional implements or executes a policy statement, ordinance, regulation, or decision officially adopted and promulgated by that body's officers."[90] The Court noted that the facts in *Monell* did not present problems in this regard because it was undisputed that the governmental defendants' *official policy* for maternity leave was "the moving force" of the constitutional violation. Thus

---

[82] See §§**6.02-6.04** on pre-*Monell* law.

[83] 532 F2d 259, 263 (2d Cir 1976), *revd*, 436 US 658 (1978).

[84] 365 US 167 (1961). *See* §**6.02.**

[85] Justice Powell concurred, Justice Stevens concurred in part, and Justice Rehnquist and Chief Justice Burger dissented.

[86] 436 US at 690.

[87] *Id* 681-82. (emphasis in Court's opinion). Cause in fact and respondeat superior are discussed in an *individual* §1983 liability context at §§**3.18 & 3.15,** respectively.

[88] 436 US at 693-94. The two justifications discussed by the Court were accident reduction and loss-spreading under an insurance approach.

[89] *Id* 701 n 66.

[90] *Id* 690.

the requisite cause in fact relationship between governmental policy and plaintiffs' constitutional deprivation was present.

The Court in *Monell* expressly left open the question of any local governmental immunity from §1983 liability.[91] After holding that immunity is not, and should not be, absolute "lest our decision that such bodies are subject to suit under §1983 'be drained of meaning,'" it noted simply that the immunity question was not presented to it, was not briefed by the parties, and was not addressed by the district court or the Second Circuit. However, in *Owen v City of Independence*,[92] discussed later,[93] the Court ruled that local governments are *not* protected by qualified immunity.

§6.06 *Monell's* Official Policy or Custom Requirement for Local Government Liability—A Duty Analysis

Monell[94] emphasized that respondeat superior is not a permissible theory for holding a local governmental body liable for the constitutional violations of its employees.[95] Instead, a local governmental body is liable under §1983 when "a policy statement, ordinance, regulation, or decision officially adopted and promulgated by that body's officers" can be causally related to the allegedly unconstitutional conduct of the employee.[96] Significantly, though, *Monell* also pointed out that local governments "may be sued for constitutional deprivations visited pursuant to governmental 'custom' even though such a custom has not received formal approval through the body's official decisionmaking channels."[97] In this sense, according to the Court, custom includes well-settled practices of government officials which are not "authorized by written law."[98]

Monell spoke of the relationship between the local government's official policy or custom and the plaintiff's constitutional deprivation using cause in fact terms. Apparently the Court was concerned that local governments not be held liable under §1983 simply for their failure to act. This is borne out by a footnote in *Monell* in which the Court, citing *Rizzo v Goode*,[99] said: "[W]e would appear to have decided that the mere right to control without any control or

---

[91] *Id* 701.

[92] 445 US 622 (1980).

[93] *See* §6.18.

[94] Monell v Department of Social Servs, 436 US 658 (1978).

[95] This conclusion is extensively criticized in Blum, *From Monroe to Monell: Defining the Scope of Municipal Liability in Federal Courts,* 51 Temp LQ 409 (1978).

[96] 436 US at 690.

[97] *Id.*

[98] (Quoting from Adickes v Kress & Co, 398 US 144, 167-68 (1970), discussed at §2.05.)

[99] 423 US 362 (1976).

direction having been exercised and without any failure to supervise is not enough to support §1983 liability."[100]

However, as discussed in Chapter 3 in connection with §1983 liability of supervisors and other superiors for the unconstitutional conduct of their subordinates,[101] putting this requirement solely in cause in fact terms is at least confusing and perhaps even erroneous. *Monell* held in reality that a *local government has no duty* in certain circumstances to compensate a plaintiff who has been deprived of constitutional rights by that local government's employees. One example of such a no-duty case, according to *Monell*, is where all that can be shown of local governmental involvement in plaintiff's constitutional deprivation is "the mere right to control."[102] In short, *Monell* is essentially a §1983 duty case, not a cause in fact case.[103]

This distinction between duty and cause in fact can be made clear by a simple example from tort law. Suppose P is drowning at a public beach; D, readily able to save him, does nothing and P drowns. A cause in fact relationship between D's failure to act and P's drowning exists. However, D is not liable because in the absence of statute or some other basis for imposing a legal obligation, there is no duty to rescue. Now, suppose that D is a hired lifeguard. Again, the necessary cause in fact relationship exists between P's drowning and D's failure to act. This time, though, D will probably be liable because lifeguard status gives rise to a duty to rescue. In short, tort liability requires both duty and a cause in fact relationship between its breach and the plaintiff's injury.

In this light, therefore, while *Monell* spoke of cause in fact in a §1983 context, what it apparently meant is that regardless of the existence of a cause in fact relationship between a local government's failure to control an employee and that employee's unconstitutional conduct leading to plaintiff's injury, the local government will ordinarily have no duty to control. Hence there will be no §1983 liability. Similarly the rejection in *Monell* of respondeat superior indicates that there is no constitutional duty running from the local government to the deprived plaintiff unless there is something more than an employment relationship between the local government and the employee whose conduct caused the plaintiff's constitutional deprivation. As with tort liability, §1983 local government liability (and all other §1983 liability as well)[104] requires the existence of a duty to the plaintiff and a causal relationship between defendant's breach of that duty and plaintiff's constitutional deprivation.

Consequently, the significance of *Monell*'s official policy or custom requirement for local government liability is that, first, it is a condition precedent to the imposition of a constitutional and §1983 duty upon a local government to

---

[100] 436 US at 694 n 58.

[101] *See* §§**3.15-3.16.**

[102] 436 US at 694 n 58.

[103] There must, however, still be a cause in fact relation between the challenged official policy or custom and the plaintiff's constitutional deprivation.

[104] *See generally* **ch 3.**

protect the plaintiff. Second, that official policy or custom must be a cause in fact of plaintiff's constitutional deprivation. It should be emphasized in this connection, as discussed in Chapter 3,[105] that this analysis also applies to the possible §1983 liability of a supervisory official for the unconstitutional conduct of subordinates. Here, too, *Monell* rejected §1983 respondeat superior liability. Instead, some *personal involvement* of the supervisory official in the subordinate's unconstitutional conduct—analogous to *Monell's* official policy or custom requirement for local government liability—must be shown for §1983 liability.

The distinction in §1983 local governmental liability cases between duty and cause in fact has considerable practical significance. Plaintiffs may be expected to try to fit local government failure to act cases into *Monell's* category of official policy or custom. If duty and cause in fact are not kept distinct, the parties and the court will in all likelihood address the wrong issues and resolve those issues improperly. Thus, for example, an official policy may give rise to a duty to plaintiff in a situation where a cause in fact relation cannot be shown. Conversely, a local government's failure to act may cause plaintiff injury, but if the failure to act is not an expression of official policy or custom, there is no duty.

In short, a §1983 plaintiff suing a local government (or, indeed, any defendant) has to show both duty and a cause in fact relationship between breach of duty and plaintiff's constitutional deprivation. If only one of these is shown, plaintiff loses and defendant wins because no prima facie §1983 cause of action has been stated.[106]

§6.07 Application of the Official Policy or Custom Requirement: An Overview

Since *Monell*,[107] there has been, not surprisingly, an overwhelming amount of §1983 litigation involving local government liability. Before an analysis of the post-*Monell* Supreme Court and important circuit court decisions is undertaken, it is important to make the following comments.

The easiest cases in which to find an official policy are those cases, like *Monell* itself, where the local government formally and as a body makes a decision which, when executed by the body itself or by its employees, gives rise to a constitutional violation. Examples include policy statements, ordinances, regulations, and similar decisions. As will be seen,[108] it does not matter whether the policy or decision is general and in the form of an ordinance or regulation or whether it is specific and particularized, affecting only one or a few individuals.

More difficult issues of local government liability arise in cases where the

---

[105] *See* §§3.15-3.16.

[106] *See generally* ch 3.

[107] Monell v Department of Social Servs, 436 US 658 (1978).

[108] *See* §§6.08-6.12.

local government itself has not acted, but certain of its high ranking officials have. In this regard, *Monell* asserted that official policy or custom may be "made by . . . lawmakers or by those whose edicts or acts may fairly be said to represent official policy . . . ."[109] This suggests that where a high-ranking official of a local government body or a similar official in one of its departments declares or otherwise establishes a policy which, when executed by the official personally or by a subordinate, leads to a constitutional violation, then the local government (as well as the official) may be liable under §1983 even in the absence of a formally declared policy by the local government itself.

However, the troublesome question involves the standards to be used in determining which high-ranking officials make policy and under what circumstances. As discussed later,[110] state law is relevant to this determination. However, there is a split in the circuits on the matter. The Fifth Circuit[111] held that only the conduct of a high-ranking official to whom the local government has delegated policymaking authority may render that local government liable. Others take the position that the conduct of a high-ranking official who is the final repository of local government power may be attributed to the local government for §1983 liability purposes. This conflict has not as yet been definitively resolved despite the Supreme Court's recent holding in *Pembaur v City of Cincinnati*[112] that the decision by a county prosecutor and sheriff to force entry into a doctor's office on a single occasion constituted an official policy or custom.

Monell speaks not only of actionable official policy but of actionable custom as well. Thus, as set out later,[113] even where the local government and its high-ranking officials have not explicitly set out any policy which could render the local government liable, the §1983 plaintiff might be able to show that the local government as a body, or more likely its high-ranking officials, have a custom which brought about the constitutional violation either by the high-ranking officials themselves or by their subordinates. According to *Monell*, the custom must be persistent and well settled, and the plaintiff has the substantial burden of proving it. This burden is especially onerous in cases involving claims of local government failures to act.[114]

Custom thus seems to mean a de facto official policy. Custom differs from official policy primarily in that there is no formal evidence of its establishment. It is not sufficient for local government liability for a plaintiff to establish a custom which only lower-level employees are aware of and practice. Some awareness or approval of the custom on the part of the local government or its high-ranking officials is necessary to make the custom *official*. The particular

---

[109] 436 US at 695-96.

[110] *See* §6.09.

[111] Bennett v City of Slidell, 728 F2d 762 (5th Cir 1984) (en banc), discussed at §6.09.

[112] 106 S Ct 1292 (1986), *revg* 746 F2d 337 (6th Cir 1984). *See* §6.10.

[113] *See* §6.11.

[114] *See* §6.12. See also §§3.08, 3.16 & 6.15 on affirmative duties under the due process clause and other constitutional provisions.

state of mind of the local government or its high-ranking officials required for this purpose depends primarily on the constitutional violation alleged.[115] In such cases the circuits typically require more than negligence, insisting at a minimum on gross negligence or recklessness.[116]

Where a lower-level employee acts in an unauthorized or ultra vires manner unsupported by any official policy or custom, then the local government is clearly not liable under §1983. To impose liability here would amount to respondeat superior, an impermissible basis of liability after *Monell.* More must be shown to impose local government liability than the employment relation between the employee whose conduct is unconstitutional and the local government.

However, how much more must be shown before an actionable official policy or custom will be found is not clear. *Monell* stated that "the mere right to control without any control or direction having been exercised and without any failure to supervise is not enough to support §1983 liability."[117] The implication is that if the local government or its high-ranking officials in fact either exercise some direction or control over, or fail to supervise, lower-level employees engaging in unconstitutional conduct, then the local government may be liable. In other words, there are circumstances where a local government might be liable under §1983 even for its failure to act, so long as such failure amounts to an official policy or custom which causes the constitutional deprivation.

For example, there may be liability where a local government or its high-ranking officials inadequately train or supervise police officers, thereby resulting in the unconstitutional use of excessive force.[118] However, the Supreme Court has warned that a single incident of police officer use of excessive force cannot serve as the sole evidentiary basis for finding an official policy or custom of inadequate training or supervision.[119]

There are other significant local government liability issues beyond those arising in the foregoing kinds of cases. Thus, once an official policy or custom is identified, it is obvious that there must be a causal relation between that policy or custom and the plaintiff's constitutional deprivation.[120] However,

---

[115] *See* **§6.13.** See also **§3.02** on the relation between state of mind requirements and §1983 liability.

[116] *See* **§§6.12-6.13.**

[117] 436 US at 694 n 58.

[118] *See* **§6.12.**

[119] City of Oklahoma City v Tuttle, 105 S Ct 2427 (1985), discussed at **§6.12.**

[120] *E.g.,* Kranson v Valley Crest Nursing Home, 755 F2d 46 (3d Cir 1985)(carelessness of an employee in failing to follow a policy does not "fasten liability on the governmental agency . . . [t]he injury must occur as a result of the implementation of the [policy]"); Losch v Borough of Parkesburg, 736 F2d 903 (3d Cir 1984)(a plaintiff must "show a causal link between execution of the [city's] policy and the injury suffered"); Black v Stephens, 662 F2d 181 (3d Cir 1981) (police chief's official policy which delayed any investigation of an officer's conduct until underlying arrest was resolved was properly found by jury to have proximately caused detective to file unwarranted charges against plaintiffs; Judge Garth dissented); Rheuark v Shaw, 628 F2d 297 (5th Cir 1980)(county's official policy of attempting to curtail court reporter budget was not a cause in fact of

what is not so clear is whether the official policy or custom must itself be unconstitutional. While the better answer, as discussed later,[121] is that it must be, the Supreme Court seems to be divided on the issue.[122]

After *Monell*, it is also important to be sensitive to the sometimes confusing differences between official capacity and individual capacity suits. According to the Court, a §1983 damages suit against a local government official in his or her official capacity is a suit against the local government itself so long as notice and an opportunity to respond are provided and the case is treated by the court and parties as a suit against the local government.[123] However, the Court has also ruled that where a *state* official is sued in federal court for damages in both an individual and official capacity, that suit is—because of the Eleventh Amendment protection of the state[124] —necessarily one against the official in an individual capacity alone.[125] Hence, attorney's fees may not be awarded against the state.[126]

Another issue which should be mentioned in connection with local government liability relates to pleading requirements. The federal system is, of course, one of notice pleading.[127] Nevertheless, some federal courts, concerned with what they consider to be improper attempts by §1983 plaintiffs to sue local governments without a real basis for so doing, are increasingly tempted to impose pleading requirements closer to fact pleading. For example, the Seventh Circuit[128] was confronted with a case in which a plaintiff, allegedly arrested without probable cause and beaten by a police officer, claimed that policies of the city proximately caused this unlawful police conduct. However, apart from alleging the facts involving his own arrest, his complaint did not allege any others.

In affirming the district court's dismissal of the complaint for failure to state a claim, the Seventh Circuit stated that a "complaint that tracks *Monell's* requirement of official policy with bare allegations cannot stand when the policy identified is nothing more than acquiescence in prior misconduct."[129] It rejected the argument that a §1983 plaintiff cannot be expected to allege with specificity, prior to discovery, acts to which the plaintiff may not have been personally exposed but which might prove such an official policy or custom. Otherwise it would be too easy for a creative plaintiff's lawyer to allege a

---

the delay in preparing plaintiffs' statements of fact for appeal; rather, it was the district judge who caused the delay because he did not appoint additional court reporters to eliminate the backlog as he could have).

[121] *See* §6.13.
[122] City of Oklahoma City v Tuttle, 105 S Ct 2427 (1985).
[123] Brandon v Holt, 105 S Ct 873 (1985), discussed at §6.14
[124] See §5.08 on the Eleventh Amendment.
[125] Kentucky v Graham, 105 S Ct 3099 (1985), discussed at §§1.24 & 6.14.
[126] See §§1.18-1.20 on attorney's fees.
[127] *See* §1.16.
[128] Strauss v City of Chicago, 760 F2d 765 (7th Cir 1985).
[129] *Id* 767.

particular official policy or custom "and the doors of the federal courtroom would swing open." In short:

> We do not mean to imply that a plaintiff must plead in greater detail, but merely that the plaintiff must plead some facts tending to support his allegation that a municipal policy exists that could have caused his injury. Identifying such facts is of course more difficult when the policy through which plaintiff is aggrieved is one of acquiescence by the City in prior misconduct, thus encouraging the misconduct to continue, than when the policy is an affirmative one through which the City has acted to harm the plaintiff.[130]

Interestingly, *Monell* has also created potential conflicts of interest for lawyers representing local governments. For example, in *Dunton v County of Suffolk*,[131] a county and police officer were sued by the plaintiff for violating his constitutional rights in connection with his beating by the police officer. There was a jury verdict on the pendent state claim which was reversed by the Second Circuit on the ground that the county attorney represented the police officer despite a conflict of interest between the county and the police officer. It was to the county's advantage to characterize the police officer's conduct as that of an "irate husband"—the beating took place when the police officer suspected plaintiff of making advances to defendant's wife—while it was to the police officer's advantage to describe his conduct as having been taken in good faith and pursuant to the county's official policy or custom, thereby possibly rendering the county liable. The court stated: "Because of the imminent threat of a serious conflict, disqualification would have been appropriate here even before any proceedings began."[132] Thus, the entire case was remanded for trial against both the defendants.

§6.08 —Formal Acts of Local Government Bodies

Where a local government, or a department thereof, formally and as a body makes a decision, then that decision constitutes an official, but not necessarily an unconstitutional or actionable, policy. Thus, a county's "chain of command policy" regarding employees was an official policy,[133] as were: a school district's request, through the vote of its board of trustees, to a county judge to implement a state statute,[134] a school district's personnel decisions,[135] the declaration of a public road by a county's governing body and its later

---

[130] *Id* 769. See §1.16 for other situations where circuit courts insist on more than notice pleading because of a similar concern with nonmeritorious suits.

[131] 729 F2d 903 (2d Cir 1984).

[132] *Id* 907.

[133] Czurlanis v Albanese, 721 F2d 98 (3d Cir 1983).

[134] Familias Unidas v Briscoe, 619 F2d 391 (5th Cir 1980).

[135] Moore v Tangipahoa Parish School Bd, 594 F2d 489 (5th Cir 1979).

instigation of a criminal action,[136] the refusal of a school district's board of trustees to renew a teacher's contract,[137] and the rules of a city's police department regarding the use of deadly force in making arrests.[138]

§6.09 —Acts of High-Ranking Officials and Their Attribution to Local Governments

After *Monell*,[139] considerable litigation has centered around the question of the standards to be used in determining which high-ranking officials make policy and under what circumstances. Recall that *Monell* simply referred to those "whose edicts or acts may fairly be said to represent official policy . . . ."[140] In the circuit court cases that follow, state law often plays an important role, although the ultimate question is one of federal law. Once it is determined that the act of a high-ranking official constitutes an official policy of the local government, then an analytically distinct question arises regarding the constitutionality of that policy.[141]

While, as will be seen, there is a conflict in the circuits regarding the soundness of its approach, the Fifth Circuit's decision in *Bennett v City of Slidell*[142] is the starting point for discussion. Because this case is so important, it is set out at some length. In *Bennett,* the plaintiff sued a city for delays experienced in obtaining a liquor license and occupancy permit. A panel of the Fifth Circuit initially affirmed a jury verdict against the city. According to the panel, the city building inspector who had enforced the zoning ordinance in a discriminatory manner was vested with official power to pass on occupancy

---

[136] Evers v County of Custer, 745 F2d 1196, 1203 (9th Cir 1984)("It is difficult to imagine a case in which the act complained of more clearly [implemented an official policy] . . .").

[137] Stoddard v School Dist No 1, 590 F2d 829, 835 (10th Cir 1979)("The only way the School District can act is by and through its Board of Trustees").

[138] Acoff v Abston, 762 F2d 1543 (11th Cir 1985).

[139] Monell v Department of Social Servs, 436 US 658 (1978).

[140] *Id* 694.

[141] *See* **§6.13.** The important distinction between an official policy or custom and its unconstitutionality was crucial in Dominguez v Beame, 603 F2d 337 (2d Cir 1979) where plaintiff sued the New York City Police Department, the mayor and assistant mayor, the police commissioner, and two arresting officers, alleging an unconstitutional official policy to arrest suspected prostitutes for that reason alone, without probable cause (a Fourth Amendment violation), and with the knowledge that plaintiff and others similarly arrested would never be prosecuted ("summary punishment" violative of due process). The Second Circuit agreed with the district court that, while there was an official policy of arresting women suspected of being prostitutes on the charge of disorderly conduct, the policy—found to be constitutional—was in fact to arrest only those women engaged in activity which the police reasonably believed to constitute disorderly conduct. Thus, there was no unconstitutional official policy to arrest suspected prostitutes without probable cause, even though the plaintiff herself was arrested without probable cause. The latter went only to the personal liability of the arresting officers.

[142] 728 F2d 762 (5th Cir 1984)(en banc).

certificate applications. Also, he and the city attorney had together secured the disconnecting of plaintiff's electric power without notice or a hearing. However, upon rehearing en banc, the Fifth Circuit reversed in an opinion elaborating its view of *Monell*'s official policy or custom requirement.[143] Where a local government is to be held liable through its policymaking officials,

> the delegation of policymaking authority requires more than a showing of mere discretion or decisionmaking authority on the part of the delegee . . . [Rather, t]he governing body must expressly or impliedly acknowledge that the agent or board acts in lieu of the governing body to set goals and to structure and design the area of the delegated responsibility, subject only to the power of the governing body to control finances and to discharge or curtail the authority of the agent or board.[144]

In this case, according to the Fifth Circuit, the city attorney was only employed to give legal advice and the building inspector's job was only to execute the city's building code policy. Neither had any policymaking authority, even though the building inspector was chief of the city's office of permits and inspections. Further, there was no evidence showing a persistent practice by the city by which some builders were favored over others. Consequently, whether one looked at the conduct of the city attorney and building inspector or at the conduct of the city itself, there was no actionable official policy or custom.

Judge Garwood concurred, observing that the case did not present the question of whether a local government could be liable for a highly unusual and unforeseeable action by a "truly" policymaking official who acted within the scope of delegated authority.[145] Judge Politz, with whom Judges Garza, Tate, Johnson, and Williams joined, dissented.[146] They argued that the acts of the building inspector in the case before them could fairly be said to represent official policy. His decisions were effectively final, and represented the city's official zoning policy regarding occupancy permits. In their view, the "majority permits municipalities effectively to immunize themselves from §1983 damage liability for the unconstitutional actions of their appointed officials merely by articulating facially constitutional policies in the substantive areas in which the officials perform their delegated duties."[147] Moreover, according to the dissent, the majority would only allow local government liability for the aberrant conduct of its employees where that conduct was so notorious that it could be assumed that the local government approved the conduct. Such a proposition "emasculates *Monell.*" What was important, in short, was that the building inspector was empowered with de facto final authority to select goals

---

[143] 697 F2d 657 (5th Cir 1983), *revd on this ground,* 728 F2d 762 (5th Cir 1984)(en banc).

[144] 728 F2d at 769.

[145] *Id* 770.

[146] *Id.*

[147] *Id* 771.

and to devise the means of achieving those goals, even if theoretically he was not the ultimate authority.

Thereafter, in denying a petition for rehearing, the Fifth Circuit reaffirmed its en banc ruling and announced:

> A municipality is liable under §1983 for a deprivation of rights protected by the Constitution or federal laws that is inflicted pursuant to official policy. Official policy is:
>
> 1. A policy statement, ordinance, regulation, or decision that is officially adopted and promulgated by the municipality's lawmaking officers or by an official to whom the lawmakers have delegated policy-making authority; or
>
> 2. A persistent, widespread practice of city officials or employees, which, although not authorized by officially adopted and promulgated policy, is so common and well settled as to constitute a custom that fairly represents municipal policy. Actual or constructive notice of such custom must be attributable to the governing body of the municipality or to an official to whom that body has delegated policy-making authority.
>
> Actions of officers or employees of a municipality do not render a municipality liable under §1983 unless they execute official policy as above defined.[148]

The Fifth Circuit then went on explicitly to reject that line of authority

> which would permit policy or custom to be attributed to the city itself by attribution to any and all city officers endowed with final or supervisory power or authority. Only those policymakers . . . may, by their declaration of formal policy or accession to custom, subject the city to liability in the absence of such declaration or accession by the governing body itself.[149]

In rejecting the *final repository of power* approach to local government liability, the Fifth Circuit nevertheless expressly left open the possibility that a local government can impliedly acknowledge that the high-ranking official was delegated policymaking authority. Depending on the evidence necessary to show this implied acknowledgment, the difference between the *Bennett* formulation and the final repository approach may be very subtle.[150] If this is

---

[148] Bennett v City of Slidell, 735 F2d 861, 862 (5th Cir 1984)(per curiam).

[149] *Id.*

[150] To some extent this is demonstrated by the post-*Bennett* Fifth Circuit case of Thomas v Sams, 734 F2d 185 (5th Cir), *rehg denied with opinion*, 741 F2d 783 (5th Cir 1984), also discussed at §7.10 in connection with judicial immunity. In *Thomas*, a city mayor, who was also ex officio its magistrate and municipal judge, signed a criminal complaint against the plaintiff university president in connection with a sewer line dispute. Thereafter, in his capacity as magistrate, the mayor issued a warrant for plaintiff's arrest, resulting in detention. The plaintiff sued the mayor and the city, alleging, among other things, that the arrest was without probable cause. Reversing the district court in this regard, the Fifth Circuit, applying the *Bennett* rule, held that the

so, then despite the Fifth Circuit's obvious concern that local governments not be improperly held liable for the unconstitutional acts of lower level employees who are not policymakers because they do not set goals or structure and design the area of the delegated responsibility, the *Bennett* approach may not be worth the confusion created. The final repository of power approach, insofar as it focuses not only on the specific act challenged but on the kind of act as well, may be just as effective for this purpose. It also has the advantage of asking a simpler and more realistic question: did the official whose allegedly unconstitutional act is sought to be attributed to the local government have final decisionmaking authority regarding that kind of act as either a legal or practical matter?

A panel of the Eighth Circuit in *Williams v Butler*[151] criticized the *Bennett* approach in a case involving a §1983 damages suit by a former court clerk against a city judge and a city for the judge's firing of the plaintiff in violation of the First Amendment. Affirming the jury's verdict against the city in favor of the clerk, the court observed that, even though the clerk was processed through the city's personnel office when she was hired, was paid by the city, was given a city parking place, and worked in a city building, the judge "hired his own employees, and controlled and supervised their work. In other words, [defendant] was making employment decisions for the city." The court went on to point out that the city thereby "had established a policy of giving municipal judges *carte blanche* authority to make their personnel decisions."[152] Hence, it was clear that the judge had acted pursuant to that policy in firing plaintiff.

The court next considered the Fifth Circuit's *Bennett* decision. It first noted that before *Bennett* the Fifth Circuit had adopted a final repository of power approach.[153] It next observed that the Second, Third, Fourth, Ninth, and Eleventh Circuits already followed the Fifth Circuit's pre-*Bennett* approach.[154] It then went on to criticize *Bennett* directly:

---

mayor's unconstitutional conduct could be attributed to the city. The city council entrusted the entire conduct of the sewer line installation, including the later dispute, to the mayor. He was given final authority to define the city's goals for the entire project and to choose the means for completing the project. Even though the city council did not by resolution authorize the mayor to arrest plaintiff, "the unlawful arrest was the execution of a decision made by an official to whom the City's lawmakers *impliedly delegated authority* to see that the sewer line was completed, including authority to eliminate interference with its completion by means that included arrest of persons who interfered with the project." 741 F2d at 743 (emphasis added).

[151] 746 F2d 431 (8th Cir 1984), *also granting rehg en banc but thereafter affg district court by an equally divided court at,* 762 F2d 73 (8th Cir 1985)(en banc), *vacated,* 54 USLW 3659 (S Ct April 7, 1986).

[152] *Id* 436.

[153] In Familias Unidas v Briscoe, 619 F2d 391 (5th Cir 1980).

[154] Wilson v Taylor, 733 F2d 1539 (11th Cir 1984)(police chief had the final authority to fire police officer and thus his decision bound the city even though there was an appellate process available; Wellington v Daniels, 717 F2d 932 (4th Cir 1983)(police chief could have, but did not, make unconstitutional policy regarding the improper use by police officers of their flashlights as weapons); Rookard v Health & Hosps Corp, 710

Under . . . *Bennett,* any acts taken by these officials [to whom is given final authority to make decisions]—regardless of their constitutionality, regardless of whether the act was taken or decision made on behalf of the City, and regardless of whether the officials had the final authority on an issue—could not be attributable to the governing body absent facially unconstitutional laws. If this were the case, §1983 and *Monell* would be meaningless.[155]

The Eighth Circuit panel concluded:

Accordingly, we hold that: (1) if, according to a policy or custom established by a governing body, an official is delegated the authority, either directly or indirectly, to act on behalf of a governing body; and (2) if a decision made within the scope of the official's authority ends the matter, then the acts of the official may fairly be said to be those of the local governing body. Our decision is a narrow one. We are dealing here with an intentional, unconstitutional act taken for the City by a City official who was given final authority, pursuant to a custom established by the City through its personnel director, to make the decision which led to the act.[156]

Had the court stopped there, it would have made its point effectively. Unfortunately, the Eighth Circuit panel went on in a footnote[157] to distinguish between administrative decisions—where "the focus should be on the act taken pursuant to the policy, not on the policy"—and discretionary decisions—where "the appropriate focus may center around whether any given act itself is a policy." This distinction has no place in §1983 jurisprudence and can only serve to obscure analysis. The court's errors are in its assumption that a single personnel decision cannot be an official policy[158] and in its failure to distinguish

---

F2d 41 (2d Cir 1983)(hospital officials had "final authority" over personnel matters); McKinley v Eloy, 705 F2d 1110 (9th Cir 1983) (city manager had ultimate responsibility for city employees and thus his discharge of plaintiff was attributable to the city); Black v Stephens, 662 F2d 181 (3d Cir 1981)(city's liability based on police chief's official police regulation governing disciplinary hearings).

[155] 746 F2d at 438.

[156] *Id.* Judge McMillian dissented, contending that under the *Bennett* approach, the judge was not delegated policy-making authority by the city.

[157] *Id* 438-39 n 10.

[158] That a single personnel decision can be an official policy was recently made clear in Pembaur v City of Cincinnati, 106 S Ct 1292 (1986), discussed next. However, in Rhode v Denson, 776 F2d 107 (5th Cir 1985) (pre-*Pembaur*), which involved the unconstitutional conduct of a county's elected constable, the Fifth Circuit wondered whether *every* act of a policy-making official—even a "discrete tort"—is an official policy. The issue was avoided because the Court concluded that the constable did not make official county policy under the *Bennett* approach. *See also* Van Ooteghem v Gray, 774 F2d 1332 (5th Cir 1985)(pre-*Pembaur;* firing of plaintiff by county treasurer, a policy-maker regarding personnel decisions, was not an "episodic event" but reflected a "policy choice").

between an official policy and its unconstitutionality. Thus, in *Williams* itself, the judge's decision to fire the clerk was an official policy of the city because he was the final repository of city authority regarding such decisions. Furthermore, that official policy—the judge's act—was unconstitutional. In any event, the precedential value of *Williams* is questionable because the Eighth Circuit thereafter granted en banc reconsideration, only to affirm the district court's decision by an equally divided court, and the Supreme Court thereafter vacated.

§6.10   —*Pembaur v City of Cincinnati*

The Supreme Court recently dealt with some of these issues in *Pembaur v City of Cincinnati*.[159] *Pembaur* involved the question of whether the decision by a county prosecutor and sheriff to force entry unconstitutionally into a doctor's office on a single occasion constituted an official policy or custom of the county. The Sixth Circuit ruled that it did not, even though it believed that the prosecutor and sheriff could, in a proper case, establish county policy. In the case before it, the Sixth Circuit, after looking at the nature and duties of the sheriff, found it obvious that the sheriff was a county official who could establish county policy in some areas. So, too, was the county prosecutor. However, there was no proof that the sheriff and prosecutor forced entry on more than this one occasion. In contrast, there was proof of a policy and past practice of the *city*'s police department—which had assisted the sheriff's deputies in forcing entry—to use whatever force was necessary, including forcible entry, to serve a capias. Because it was not clear whether plaintiff suffered an injury as a result of this city policy, a remand was necessary.

In an opinion by Justice Brennan, the Supreme Court reversed and held that the county could be liable for plaintiff's Fourth Amendment deprivation. At the outset the Court pointed out that an official policy "may be imposed for a single decision by municipal policymakers under appropriate circumstances." An official policy may be tailored to a particular situation and need not be "intended to control decisions in later situations." The Court went on to assert that an official policy may be determined by an official who is "responsible for establishing final government policy respecting such activity." According to the Court, local government liability "attaches where—and only where—a deliberate choice to follow a course of action is made from among various alternatives" by such responsible officials.[160] In applying this standard to the case before it, the Court found, relying on the Sixth Circuit's examination of state law, that the county prosecutor made official policy regarding the forcible entry into plaintiff's office. The county sheriff had referred the matter to the county prosecutor and had followed the latter's instructions based upon his understanding of the law. This was more than the rendering of legal advice.

---

[159] 106 S Ct 1292 (1986), *revg* 746 F2d 337 (6th Cir 1984). The city's liability was not before the Court.

[160] 106 S Ct at 1300.

Justice White concurred, emphasizing that it was significant to him that the forcible entry here was not illegal under federal, state, or local law. In his view, had the controlling law placed limits on the prosecutor's and sheriff's authority in this regard, they would not have had the authority to establish contrary policy. Deliberate or mistaken acts contrary to local law would not render a local government liable. Justice Stevens concurred in part and in the judgment, arguing that respondeat superior liability was proper under §1983. Justice O'Connor also concurred in part and in the judgment. She agreed with Justice White that the prosecutor and sheriff had acted as policymakers within the meaning of *Monell.* However, she was concerned that the majority's reasoning went too far in exposing local governments to liability, especially where local law is violated.

Justice Powell, joined by Chief Justice Burger and Justice Rehnquist, dissented. They argued first that the Fourth Amendment principle, which had been declared by the Court in another case only *after* the events in question in *Pembaur,* should not be applied retroactively.[161] More important for present purposes, they also contended that the majority improperly focused on the status of the decisionmaker rather than on the nature and meaning of "policy." In their view, the majority made too much of state law. Rather, whether official policy has been made depends on the nature of the decision or act and the process by which the decision or act was determined. In this case, there was no rule of general applicability but only an ad hoc decision which should not render the county liable.

In *Pembaur,* a majority of the Court correctly ruled that even a one-time decision by a policymaker could render a local government liable. It also defined *policymaking* as "a deliberate choice to follow a course of action . . . from among various alternatives."[162] However, Justice Brennan's opinion with its repeated emphasis on authority to make final policy could conceivably indicate a preference for the *final repository of decisionmaking authority* approach of a majority of the circuits and a rejection of the Fifth Circuit's *Bennett* approach. On the other hand, perhaps too much should not be made of this. In an important footnote,[163] Justice Brennan observed that a county sheriff "may have discretion to hire and fire employees without also being the county official responsible for establishing county employment policy." What counts is whether the board of county commissioners, which ordinarily sets county employment policy, "delegated its power to establish final employment policy to the Sheriff." Only in such a case would the sheriff's employment decisions represent county policy. This footnote may be read as adopting the *Bennett* approach. It is also possible that the Court is suggesting, as argued earlier, that there is in reality not all that much difference between the *final repository* and

---

[161] Based on the nonretroactivity guidelines of Chevron Oil Co v Huson, 404 US 97 (1971). However, the county in *Pembaur* apparently did not raise this issue. In effect, then, the dissenters were providing free legal advice to local governments.

[162] 106 S Ct at 1300.

[163] *Id* 1300 n 12.

Bennett approaches, especially since the latter encompasses cases involving implicit delegations of policymaking authority.

Note, moreover, that two of the six-person *Pembaur* majority, Justices White and O'Connor, parted company with Justice Brennan's reasoning insofar as it might apply to render a local government liable for the conduct of an official who violates local law. This must be characterized as an open question after *Pembaur* since only four justices joined in that portion of Justice Brennan's opinion. Nevertheless, there surely could be situations where local government liability results from the conduct of policymaking officials, even where that conduct violates local law. Policymaking authority, when delegated, is typically based on the local government's expectation that resulting official conduct will be legal under local law. But this, standing alone, should no more insulate the local government from §1983 liability than the expectation that resulting official conduct will be legal under constitutional law. In this respect, then, local law should be relevant to local government liability but it should not automatically result in a finding of no government liability.

In the circuits there have been numerous additional cases involving high-ranking officials of all kinds. Officials who have been found to make official policy in certain circumstances include the following: hospital officials,[164] mayors,[165] sheriffs,[166] police superintendents and police chiefs,[167]

---

[164] Rookard v Health & Hosps Corp, 710 F2d 41 (2d Cir 1983) (hospital officials with final authority in personnel matters had policy of punishing "whistleblowers").

[165] Hollins v Powell, 773 F2d 191 (8th Cir 1985)(under city's governmental structure, mayor had authority to order city authority's commissioners arrested and removed from city hall; thus, city could be liable); Thomas v Sams, 734 F2d 185 (5th Cir), *rehg denied with opinion,* 741 F2d 783 (5th Cir 1984)(mayor to whom policy making authority was delegated by the city council established policy regarding arrest arising out of sewer line dispute); Berdin v Dugan, 701 F2d 909 (11th Cir 1983)(city ordinance gave the mayor, who had in fact fired plaintiff, authority over city employees with authority to hire and fire; he thus made policy which bound the city); Quinn v Syracuse Model Neighborhood Corp, 613 F2d 438, 448 (2d Cir 1980)(mayor made policy for plaintiff's discharge; "Surely the Mayor is the one city official whose edicts and acts represent municipal policy . . .").

[166] Garcia v Salt Lake County, 768 F2d 303 (10th Cir 1985)(despite contrary written county jail policy, sheriff, one of chief elected county officials who was independent of board of county commissioners, established county policy that unconscious individuals suspected of being intoxicated were admitted to county jail). Marchese v Lucas, 758 F2d 181 (6th Cir 1985)(under state constitution, sheriff is law enforcement arm of the county and makes county policy in police matters; thus sheriff's failure to train and discipline his officers was county policy); McKay v Hammock, 730 F2d 1367 (10th Cir 1984)(sheriff was official responsible for policies and procedures of county sheriff's office; sheriff's knowing involvement in unconstitutional arrest and harassment could therefore be attributed to county). Logan v Shealy, 660 F2d 1007 (4th Cir 1981)(challenged strip search policy promulgated by sheriff and enforced by his department might be chargeable to county).

[167] Grandstaff v City of Borger, 767 F2d 161 (5th Cir 1985) (police chief was policy-maker who established unconstitutional city policy on the use of deadly force by officers through his acceptance of their "dangerous recklessness" as well as his failure to make any changes); Murray v City of Chicago, 634 F2d 365 (7th Cir 1980)(if police superintendents past and present knew that "unwarranted arrests [based on invalid warrants] have occurred frequently," that would establish city policy).

county attorneys,[168] city managers,[169] clerks of court,[170] county treasurers,[171] and jail supervisors.[172] Similarly, the following special purpose bodies have been found to make official policy: a zoning adjustment board,[173] a police jury,[174] and a county's law enforcement committee.[175]

In contrast, high-ranking officials who have been found *not* to make official policy in certain circumstances include the following: police chiefs,[176]

---

[168] Crane v Texas, 759 F2d 412 and 766 F2d 193 (5th Cir 1985) (county attorney who himself established procedures to be followed by county in issuing misdemeanor capias made county policy; state law demonstrated that he was a county, not a state, official).

[169] Neubauer v City of McAllen, 766 F2d 1567, 1573 (5th Cir 1985)(under *Bennett* approach and in light of the city's code and personnel manual which indicated that he acted in lieu of the city in such matters, city manager was "the only official who possessed policymaking power in termination proceedings sufficient to hold the City accountable under section 1983").

[170] Burkhart v Randles, 764 F2d 1196 (6th Cir 1985) (county clerk of courts established employment policy; she was highest ranking official in the clerk's office and "was solely responsible for executing the policies and operation of the office").

[171] Van Ooteghem v Gray, 628 F2d 488 (5th Cir 1980)(county treasurer given complete authority by state law for hiring and firing of treasury personnel; thus, his firing of his assistant constituted the county's official policy), *affd with modifications on other grounds*, 774 F2d 1332 (5th Cir 1985)(under *Bennett* approach, county treasurer a policy-maker regarding personnel decisions; also, his firing of his assistant was not episodic but was the product of county treasurer's announced policy).

[172] Goodson v City of Atlanta, 763 F2d 1381 (11th Cir 1985)(jail supervisor whom ordinance made responsible for all inmates established policy with respect to knowing failures to train and supervise guards and supervise facilities).

[173] Shelton v City of College Station, 754 F2d 1251 (5th Cir 1985)(city found through ordinance to have delegated exclusive policy-making authority to zoning adjustment board with regard to variances; under *Bennett* approach, board therefore made city variance policy).

[174] O'Quinn v Manuel, 767 F2d 174 (5th Cir 1985)(under state law police jury did not have responsibility for daily operation of jail but was responsible for funding and physical maintenance; thus, under *Bennett* approach police jury could make policy regarding failure to provide adequate facilities).

[175] Soderbeck v Burnett County, 752 F2d 285 (7th Cir 1985)(county's law enforcement committee was a policy-making body whose acts were those of the county inasmuch as it was created for this purpose by county's board of supervisors which governed the county; thus, committee could make policy with regard to plaintiff's firing).

[176] Losch v Borough of Parkesburg, 736 F2d 903 (3d Cir 1984)(even though police chief allegedly a de facto policy-making official, a single incident of malicious prosecution was not enough for attribution to the borough); Brewer v Blackwell, 692 F2d 307 (5th Cir 1982)(pre-*Bennett* Fifth Circuit decision holding that police chief who controlled city jail did not make policy for the city because he was accountable to the city's aldermen and mayor; he was not the final repository of town power)

judges,[177] school superintendents,[178] constables,[179] and city personnel directors.[180]

§6.11 —Custom

Local governments may be liable not only for the policies that they establish formally themselves or through high-ranking officials, but for certain customs as well. This possibility stems from the language of §1983 itself. As mentioned earlier,[181] an actionable custom must be persistent and well settled and amount to a de facto official policy. Proving an actionable custom frequently constitutes a difficult hurdle for plaintiffs, especially in cases where plaintiffs assert that a local government's failure to act constituted an actionable custom. It is also important to be sensitive to the distinction between the existence of a custom and its possible unconstitutionality.

There are several ways in which custom can be shown. First, the local government body itself may customarily act in a certain manner, even though it does not formally make a declaration of policy. For example, the Fifth Circuit[182] ruled that more than two isolated instances of action of a county board of supervisors regarding the prevention of abuse of prisoners were necessary to prove a custom of that board.

Second, a high-ranking official who establishes a local government's official policy—either because he or she has been delegated policymaking authority by the local government or because he or she is the final repository of authority in the matter[183]—may similarly customarily act in a certain manner without a

---

[177] Carbalan v Vaughn, 760 F2d 662 (5th Cir 1985)(city judge's allegedly unconstitutional denial of bail did not constitute city policy; city exercised no control over the judge and gave him no guidance or instruction regarding such matters); Familias Unidas v Briscoe, 619 F2d 391 (5th Cir 1980)(pre-*Bennett* Fifth Circuit decision holding that county judge's compliance with school district's request through his issuance of statutory disclosure demands did not represent official county policy; while county judge was final repository of county power with regard to other activities involving county governance, here the judge simply carried out state policy having nothing to do with administering county government); Careaga v James, 616 F2d 1062 (8th Cir 1980)(city judge's comments at plaintiff's sentencing were not attributable to city).

[178] Rowland v Mad River Local School Dist, 730 F2d 444 (6th Cir 1984)(school superintendent was not a decision-maker who made policy in the areas of transfer and suspension of guidance counselors).

[179] Rhode v Denson, 776 F2d 107 (5th Cir 1985)(elected constable of Texas county not a policy-maker under *Bennett* approach; comparable under state law to a police officer; Judge Goldberg dissented).

[180] Hearn v City of Gainesville, 688 F2d 1328 (11th Cir 1982)(city's personnel director did not exercise final delegated authority over decision to delete plaintiff's position; thus his giving misinformation to the city manager which led to plaintiff's layoff was not attributable to the city).

[181] See §6.11.

[182] Craine v Alexander, 756 F2d 1070 (5th Cir 1985).

[183] See §§6.09-6.10. In Bennett v City of Slidell, 735 F2d 861, 862 (5th Cir 1984) (en banc), the Fifth Circuit defined official policy to include "a persistent, widespread practice of city officials or employees, which, although not authorized by officially adopted and promulgated policy, is so common and well settled as to constitute a custom that fairly represents municipal policy. Actual or constructive notice of such

formal declaration of policy and thereby bind the local government. For example, in a Fourth Circuit case[184] the racially discriminatory custom of a city manager and other high-ranking officials rendered the city liable for plaintiff's discriminatory discharge even in the absence of formal city approval.

Third,[185] lower-level employees may engage in a custom which is so pervasive that either the local government body itself or, more likely, certain of its high-ranking officials actually know of this custom or are reckless with regard to its existence. For example, in a highly publicized case where plaintiffs, on behalf of a decedent shot and killed by police officers, sued the officers and the city of Houston for damages, the Fifth Circuit[186] affirmed a jury verdict against the defendants. As to the city, there was sufficient evidence to show that it was police department policy or custom to use a "throw-down" gun to be put near an unarmed suspect who had been shot by police officers, so as to justify the shooting. Among other things: the throw-down was almost universally used in the police department; recruits learned to protect themselves in this way while still in the police academy; 20 police officers stood around decedent after he was shot and debated the use of a throw-down; the use of throw-downs was widely known to high officials in the police department, but they never told officers to stop; and officers knew they could get away with using throw-downs. All of this encouraged police officers in their illegal activities, including the shooting of decedent and the subsequent attempt to cover up by all levels of the police department.

On rehearing en banc in light of the approach to official policy or custom in *Bennett v City of Slidell*,[187] set out earlier, the Fifth Circuit initially vacated the jury's verdict against the city, which was based on the finding that the city maintained a custom of using excessive police force. The court observed that the district court instructed the jury contrary to the *Bennett* standard for local government liability—announced thereafter—and there was no way to square those instructions with *Bennett*. For example, the jury should have been instructed "to find whether the city council had expressly or impliedly acknowledged that the mayor or the chief of police could act in their stead to set goals and to structure and design the activities of the Houston Police Department."[188]

Five judges dissented from this disposition, arguing that the facts clearly

---

custom must be attributable to the governing body of the municipality or to an official to whom that body has delegated policy-making authority."

This definition is consistent with that in the text except insofar as (1) it does not expressly cover the custom of a governing body itself, and (2) it is limited to those high-ranking officials who are policy-makers. The latter, of course, reflects the Fifth Circuit's *Bennett* approach to attributing the conduct of certain high-ranking officials to local government bodies.

[184] Abasiekong v City of Shelby, 744 F2d 1055 (4th Cir 1984).

[185] *See* **§6.12.**

[186] Webster v City of Houston, 689 F2d 1220 (5th Cir 1982).

[187] 728 F2d 762 (5th Cir 1984)(en banc). *See* **§6.09.**

[188] Webster v City of Houston, 735 F2d 838, 841 (5th Cir 1984)(en banc).

demonstrated the existence of an unconstitutional custom of the city.[189] Such a custom could be found under §1983 even though so-called "policymakers" were not themselves involved. It was enough that police officers at all levels, bottom to top, were well aware of the throw-down custom. Alternatively, the mayor and the city council in fact delegated policymaking authority regarding police work to the chief of police and the police department. This was another reason to affirm the jury's verdict of city liability.

Further, there was sufficient evidence, according to the five judges, to infer that the city, through its high-ranking officials, implicitly authorized or approved of such conduct. This last approach was used by the district court and was consistent with the subsequently announced *Bennett* rule. In short, in *Bennett* a policy was found not to exist. Here, in contrast, "a custom was found to exist under a careful and fully adequate jury charge." Thus, the case should not be tried again. Thereafter, on further rehearing, the Fifth Circuit en banc again changed its mind and, affirming the verdict of city liability, held that the plaintiffs, their lawyers, and the trial judge should not be penalized for failing to anticipate the *Bennett* en banc decision. It was enough that the jury could have properly found liability under the instructions given.[190]

§6.12   —Acts of Lower-Level Employees; Single Incidents

Monell,[191] by rejecting respondeat superior, made clear that local government liability does not follow simply from the unconstitutional conduct of lower-level employees. However, there may be situations where local governments are in fact held accountable for such conduct, especially in police misconduct cases where certain claims of failure to train and supervise adequately are proved. While the circuits often do not make clear why they do so—in reality, it is (or should be) a question of the constitutionally required states of mind for substantive due process and Fourth Amendment violations[192]—they typically insist on at least gross negligence, recklessness, or deliberate indifference on the part of the local government or accountable high-ranking officials as a condition precedent for local government liability for such failures to train and supervise.

Currently the leading Supreme Court case is *City of Oklahoma City v Tuttle,* [193] involving the shooting death of plaintiff's decedent by a police officer where

---

[189] *Id* 842.

[190] 739 F2d 993 (5th Cir 1984)(en banc).

[191] Monell v Department of Social Servs, 436 US 658 (1978).

[192] *See* **§§3.02-3.14.** After Daniels v Williams, 106 S Ct 662 (1986) and Davidson v Cannon, 106 S Ct 662 (1986), discussed at **§§3.02 & 3.08-3.11,** it is now clear that negligent conduct is insufficient to constitute a substantive due process (or a procedural due process) violation.

[193] 105 S Ct 2427 (1985), *revg* 728 F2d 456 (10th Cir 1984). *Tuttle* was distinguished by the Sixth Circuit in Rymer v Davis, 775 F2d 756 (6th Cir 1985) (affirming jury finding of city's inadequate training of police officers; no inference from a single incident was involved).

the decedent had no weapon and did not threaten the officer. Plaintiff sued both the police officer and the city, which resulted in a jury verdict in favor of the police officer on the basis of qualified immunity but against the city for failure to train. Affirming the verdict against the city, the Tenth Circuit found that the district court had properly charged the jury that the city could be liable for gross negligence in failing to train if it had "actual or imputed knowledge of the almost inevitable consequences that arise from completely inadequate training or supervision."[194]

Also, there was sufficient evidence to support a finding of an official policy or custom of gross negligence and deliberate indifference, even though this finding was largely, if not completely, based on the single incident in question. "The act here was so plainly and grossly negligent that it spoke out very positively on the issue of lack of training. . . ."[195] In this connection, the jury had been charged that "a single, unusually excessive use of force may be sufficiently out of the ordinary to warrant an inference that it was attributable to inadequate training or supervision amounting to 'deliberate indifference' or 'gross negligence' on the part of the officials in charge."[196]

In addition, there was "plenty of independent proof of lack of actual training": the officer had been on the force for a very short time, he admitted his lack of training to cope with robberies, and yet he was permitted to go to a suspected robbery by himself which resulted in his "gross failure" to handle the matter satisfactorily. In short, "the single incident rule is not to be considered as an absolute where the circumstances plainly show a complete lack of training."[197] Judge Barratt concurred, saying that he was "at a loss" to ascertain the basis for the jury's finding of grossly negligent and deliberately indifferent training beyond the incident itself.

The Supreme Court reversed. There was no opinion for the Court but only Justice Stevens dissented as to the judgment (Justice Powell did not participate). Justice Rehnquist, joined by Chief Justice Burger and Justices White and O'Connor, held that the instruction was reversible error because it allowed the jury, on the basis of a single incident, to find a policy of training and supervising police officers which resulted in inadequate training and the claimed constitutional violations. It was significant that there was no claim that the city had a policy of authorizing its police force to use excessive force in apprehending criminals. Justice Rehnquist concluded:

> Proof of a single incident of unconstitutional activity is not sufficient to impose liability under *Monell*, unless proof of the incident includes proof that it was caused by an existing, unconstitutional municipal policy, which policy can be attributed to a municipal policymaker. Otherwise the existence of the unconstitutional policy, and its origin, must be separately proved. But where the policy relied upon is not itself unconstitutional,

---

[194] 728 F2d at 459.
[195] Id 461.
[196] Quoted at 105 S Ct at 2431.
[197] 728 F2d at 461.

considerably more proof than the single incident will be necessary in every case to establish both the requisite fault on the part of the municipality, and the causal connection between the "policy" and the constitutional deprivation.[198]

However, Justice Rehnquist expressed "no opinion on whether a policy that itself is not unconstitutional, such as the general 'inadequate training' alleged here can ever meet the 'policy' requirement of *Monell.* "[199] Further, he insisted that there "must at least be an affirmative link between the training inadequacies alleged, and the particular constitutional violation alleged," a requirement not satisfied by the fact that "a municipal 'policy' might lead to 'police misconduct'."[200]

Justice Brennan, joined by Justices Marshall and Blackmun, concurred in the judgment. He agreed with Justice Rehnquist that the jury instruction was defective. In Justice Brennan's view, the single incident instruction could result in unpermitted respondeat superior liability under §1983. However, he disagreed with Justice Rehnquist's approach to official policy or custom in general. Putting the matter in causation terms in light of §1983's "subjects" language, he rejected the "metaphysical distinction between policies that are themselves unconstitutional and those that cause constitutional violations." Instead, he contended that there could be liability for "a policy or custom that would foreseeably and avoidably cause an individual to be subjected to deprivation of a constitutional right. . . ."[201] Justice Stevens dissented, arguing that as a matter of both statutory interpretation and policy the Court had been wrong in *Monell* when in "dicta" it rejected respondeat superior as a permissible basis for §1983 liability. In his view the policy issue should be removed from §1983 litigation altogether.

The important but subtle difference between the views of Justices Rehnquist and Brennan regarding the question of whether an official policy or custom must itself be unconstitutional is discussed later.[202] For present purposes, it is clear that a majority of the Court agreed that it will be a rare case indeed in which a single incident of police officer misconduct can serve as the sole evidentiary basis for a finding of local government liability for failure to train.

It is also noteworthy that the Court did not deal with the question whether there was a violation either of due process or of the Fourth Amendment.[203] Thus, it did not reach the question of the requisite states of mind for these constitutional violations. However, in light of the Court's later due process

---

[198] 105 S Ct at 2436.

[199] *Id* 2436 n 7.

[200] *Id* 2436-37 n 8.

[201] *Id* 2441.

[202] See §6.13.

[203] 105 S Ct at 2433 n 4.

decisions in *Daniels v Williams*[204] and *Davidson v Cannon*,[205] more than negligent conduct is now required for local government liability based on substantive due process violations. As discussed in Chapter 3,[206] whether the Court will ultimately rule that intentional conduct is required and that consequently even gross negligence, recklessness, and deliberate indifference are insufficient is an open question. Nevertheless, as demonstrated by the circuit court decisions dealing with the matter,[207] gross negligence, recklessness, and deliberate

---

[204] 106 S Ct 662 (1986), discussed at **§§3.02 & 3.08-3.11.**

[205] 106 S Ct 668 (1986), discussed at **§§3.02 & 3.08-3.11.**

[206] *See* **§§3.02 & 3.08-3.11.**

[207] Circuit court decisions holding that local governments may be liable for more than negligent failure to train or supervise police officers and other lower-level employees include the following:

Second Circuit

Doe v New York City Dept of Social Servs, 709 F2d 782 (2d Cir 1983) (local government liability for deliberate indifference in failing to supervise child's placement in foster home where she was sexually abused).

Owens v Haas, 601 F2d 1242 (2d Cir 1979)(local government liability for gross negligence or deliberate indifference in failing to train or supervise prison guards who beat plaintiff; however, court's reliance on single incident now improper after *Tuttle*).

Third Circuit

Estate of Bailey *ex rel* Oare v County of York, 768 F2d 503 (3d Cir 1985)(local government liability for gross negligence, recklessness, or deliberate indifference in failing to prevent killing of a child by mother's boyfriend where some "special relationship" alleged).

Fourth Circuit

Avery v County of Burke, 660 F2d 111 (4th Cir 1981) (local government could be liable if its "failure to promulgate policies and regulations rose to the level of deliberate indifference to [plaintiff's] right of procreation or constituted tacit authorization of her sterilization").

Fifth Circuit

Languirand v Hayden, 717 F2d 220 (5th Cir 1983)(for local government liability purposes, city's failure to train police officers must be at least grossly negligent amounting to deliberate indifference).

Sixth Circuit

Hays v Jefferson County, 668 F2d 869, 874 (6th Cir 1982)(in absence of pattern of police misconduct, what is required for local government liability for inadequate training and supervision of police officers is "essentially a complete failure to train a police force, or training that is so recklessly or grossly negligent that future police misconduct is almost inevitable . . . or would properly be characterized as substantially certain to result").

Seventh Circuit

Rodgers v Lincoln Towing Serv, Inc, 771 F2d 194 (7th Cir 1985)(local government liability for failure to train police officers only where there is either intentional conduct at the municipal level or massive neglect; problems must be systemic in nature).

Lenard v Argento, 699 F2d 874 (7th Cir 1983) (local government liability for failure to train or supervise police only where there is an extremely high degree of culpability).

Tenth Circuit

Rock v McCoy, 763 F2d 394 (10th Cir 1985)(local government liability for gross negligence in failure to train police officers in connection with the use of force).

indifference are currently sufficient for local government liability for failure to train or supervise police officers or other lower-level employees in connection with substantive due process and other constitutional violations.

However, it is often difficult for plaintiffs to prove such an official policy or custom because failures to act, in contrast with affirmative acts, are involved. *Tuttle*, of course, made the plaintiff's task even more difficult than it already was because now a single incident of police officer misconduct, no matter how egregious, cannot serve as the sole evidentiary basis for a finding of an official policy or custom of failure to train or supervise. But irrespective of *Tuttle*, plaintiffs have a substantial burden in this kind of case, a burden which includes not only proof of an official policy or custom but its causal relation to the plaintiff's constitutional deprivation. For example, the Second Circuit, after questioning whether an official policy of inadequate training could be inferred from the knowing hiring of a police officer who had not completed a required training program, went on to insist: "For a victim of police brutality to establish the requisite causal connection between his injuries and a municipal policy of inadequate training, he must make some showing that specific deficiencies in the training given police officers led the misbehaving officer to engage in the alleged misconduct."[208]

Similarly, in a Fourth Circuit case,[209] plaintiff, an auto accident victim, sued the defendant city for its alleged failure to train emergency medical technicians and police officers who, when they arrived at the scene of the accident, did not properly render medical attention to her. This, according to the plaintiff, was reckless and careless indifference to her due process rights. Affirming the district court's dismissal of her complaint, the Fourth Circuit first observed that in its view an actionable official policy or custom could not be inferred from inaction alone regarding isolated employee constitutional deprivations. Also, even where such inaction might represent official policy, "it must be of such

---

Eleventh Circuit

Gilmere v City of Atlanta, 737 F2d 894 (11th Cir 1984), *revd on other grounds,* 774 F2d 1495 (11th Cir 1985)(en banc)(local government's gross negligence or deliberate indifference in failing to train *individual* police officer properly insufficient for liability; what is required is the existence of a custom of improper selection and training in general).

[208] Vippolis v Village of Haverstraw, 768 F2d 40 (2d Cir 1985). In another Second Circuit case, where the court stated that a city's tacit approval of police harassment can constitute an official policy for §1983 purposes, the juvenile plaintiff failed to prove at trial that his second arrest by one officer—after he had successfully sued another for the excessive use of force against him during a prior arrest—reflected an official policy of harassment against him. The mere failure of the board of police commissioners to discipline the other officer involved in the prior arrest, a single incident of illegality, was not enough to show a pattern or practice of harassment. Also, there was no evidence showing that the board knew or should have known of police animus toward plaintiff. Because reasonable persons could thus not find an official policy of harassment, according to the Second Circuit, the jury's conclusion to the contrary was erroneous. Turpin v Mailet, 619 F2d 196 (2d Cir 1980).

[209] Milligan v City of Newport News, 743 F2d 227 (4th Cir 1984).

a character that municipal employees could reasonably infer from it tacit approval of the conduct in issue."[210] Here, the plaintiff's claims of grossly negligent training were conclusory at best, with no allegations of known, widespread misconduct by city employees. That the city might have reduced, but did not, the risk of harm to plaintiff from the well-intentioned acts of its employees was not enough for liability.

In an Eighth Circuit case,[211] the plaintiffs sued various defendants, including a county and a "tri-county" human services board, in connection with the alleged wrongful commitment of the plaintiffs on the complaint of two board employees. Reversing the district court's ruling for the plaintiffs against the county—the board settled with plaintiffs but had a suit pending against the county for reimbursement—the Eighth Circuit found no actionable official policy or custom. It was not enough that the board's employees treated the plaintiffs wrongfully, improperly relying on the unsubstantiated word of a 15-year-old girl in committing them. The board's policy was to allow its employees to use their own discretion in deciding whether to bring information to the county attorney. There was no policy of any kind referring to 15-year-olds and unsubstantiated allegations. Thus, the board did not give official sanction to such uncorroborated accusations of teenagers. In short, the court concluded that the board's policy or decision to rely on its employees was neither unconstitutional nor the "moving force" of any constitutional violation. Further, the board's liability could not be based on the failure of a supervisory employee to supervise the two employees who acted improperly. This was a first-time incident, and the fact that the supervisor may have given discretion to his employees was not an unconstitutional and reckless failure to train and supervise for which the board (and through it the county) could be liable.

The Supreme Court may soon elaborate on what it meant in *Tuttle*. It has granted certiorari in *City of Springfield v Kibbe*,[212] a First Circuit case involving the use of excessive force by *several* police officers in a single incident and its relevance to a finding of an official policy or custom of inadequate police training. The First Circuit distinguished *Tuttle* in affirming a jury verdict against the city.

§6.13   —Must the Official Policy or Custom Be Unconstitutional?

As mentioned earlier,[213] the plurality opinion of Justice Rehnquist in *Tuttle* suggested that in order to be actionable, an official policy or custom must be unconstitutional. In contrast, Justice Brennan in *Tuttle* argued that there could

---

[210] *Id* 230.

[211] Dick v Watonwan County, 738 F2d 939 (8th Cir 1984).

[212] Kibbe v City of Springfield, 777 F2d 801 (1st Cir 1985), *cert granted*, 54 USLW 3594 (S Ct March 10, 1986).

[213] *See* §6.12.

be local government liability for "a policy or custom that would foreseeably and avoidably cause an individual to be subjected to deprivation of a constitutional right. . . ."[214] The difference between the views of Justices Rehnquist and Brennan is subtle but crucial. The former, adopting what might be called a *Fourteenth Amendment* interpretation, correctly narrows the scope of §1983 local government liability, while the latter, adopting a *causation* interpretation, improperly broadens it.[215] Under the Fourteenth Amendment approach, the local government must possess the required state of mind for the particular constitutional violation either itself or through attribution from a high-ranking official. However, under the causation approach it would be enough for liability that the local government should (reasonably?) have foreseen that its valid official policy or custom would bring about plaintiff's constitutional deprivation.

The Supreme Court had previously suggested in *Polk County v Dodson*[216] that a local government's §1983 liability must be based on an *unconstitutional* official policy or custom. The opinion dealt primarily with the state action issue implicated in public defender representation of an indigent criminal defendant and held that "a public defender does not act under color of state law when performing a lawyer's traditional functions as counsel to a defendant in a criminal proceeding."[217] More important for present purposes, the Court also considered the §1983 plaintiff's claim against Polk County and the Polk County Board of Supervisors. It addressed the following allegations: (1) that the public defender "had injured [plaintiff] while acting pursuant to administrative 'rules and procedures for . . . handling criminal appeals' and that her employers were therefore responsible for her actions"; (2) that "the County 'retains and maintains, advocates out of law school' who have on numerous occasions moved to withdraw from appeals of criminal convictions."[218]

Holding that neither allegation made out a prima facie §1983 cause of action, the Court stated:

> In this case the respondent failed to allege *any policy that arguably violated his rights* under the Sixth, Eighth, or Fourteenth Amendments . . . [A] *policy* of withdrawal from frivolous cases *would not violate the Constitu-*

---

[214] 105 S Ct at 2441.

[215] *See* Nahmod, *Constitutional Accountability in Section 1983 Litigation,* 68 Iowa L Rev 1, 24-29 (1982) where it is argued at some length that the *Fourteenth Amendment* interpretation is the correct one as a matter of statutory interpretation, Supreme Court precedent, and §1983 policy. *See also* **§3.16** where the argument is summarized in a supervisory liability setting. Supervisory liability should depend on whether the supervisor personally violated a plaintiff's constitutional rights, even if through an intervening human cause, *ie,* a lower-level employee. That is, the supervisor must possess the constitutionally required state of mind. Similarly, under a Fourteenth Amendment approach, the local government must possess the constitutionally required state of mind for it to be liable.

[216] 454 US 312 (1981).

[217] *Id* 325. See **§§2.04-2.10** on state action and color of law.

[218] 454 US at 325-26.

tion. . . . [There was] *no impermissible policy* pursuant to which the withdrawals might have occurred. Respondent further asserted that he personally was deprived of a Sixth Amendment right to effective counsel. Again, however, he failed to allege that this deprivation was *caused by any constitutionally forbidden rule or procedure.*[219]

This language indicated that a cause in fact relation between a §1983 plaintiff's constitutional deprivation and local government's *valid* official policy or custom was insufficient for §1983 local government liability. However, the question is now open, given the differing opinions on this issue in *Tuttle.*

As of this writing, there has been relatively little discussion in the circuits of this issue. In pre-*Tuttle* decisions, the Fourth, Fifth, and Seventh Circuits apparently took the position that the official policy or custom must itself be unconstitutional[220] while the Ninth Circuit rejected it.[221]

§6.14 —The Increasingly Important Distinction Between Official Capacity and Individual Capacity Damages Actions

It is important to be sensitive to the distinction between a §1983 damages action against a local government official in his or her *official* capacity—which is an action against the local government itself to which qualified immunity is not applicable—and a §1983 damages action against that official in his or her *individual* capacity—which is an action against the official personally to which qualified immunity is applicable. This distinction, discussed earlier[222] in a pre-*Monell*[223] setting, was clarified by the Court in *Brandon v Holt,*[224] where a police director was sued for damages before *Monell* was handed down. Reversing the Court of Appeals, which had ruled that the suit was against the director personally who was protected by qualified immunity, the Court held that the suit was against the city. District court documents demonstrated that such was the case, the parties throughout the trial made that assumption, and the city had notice and the opportunity to respond to the suit. Thus, the compensatory damages award against the director ran against the city, and the pleadings were amended to conform to the proof and the district court's finding. Chief Justice Burger concurred, wondering why the city was not simply named as a

---

[219] *Id* 326 (emphasis added).

[220] Bennett v City of Slidell, 728 F2d 762 (5th Cir 1984)(en banc)(so characterized in Ramie v City of Hedwig Village, 765 F2d 490 (5th Cir 1985)); Wellington v Daniels, 717 F2d 932 (4th Cir 1983); Iskander v Village of Forest Park, 690 F2d 126 (7th Cir 1982).

[221] McKinley v City of Eloy, 705 F2d 1110 (9th Cir 1983)(dictum).

[222] *See* **§6.04.**

[223] Monell v Department of Social Servs, 436 US 658 (1978).

[224] 105 S Ct 873 (1985).

defendant. Justice Rehnquist dissented, arguing that the Court's approach was unfair to local government defendants.

The distinction between official capacity and individual capacity damages actions was also significant in the attorney's fees decision of *Kentucky v Graham*.[225] In this case, the Court, confronted with a successful damages action against state officials, held that the state could not be held responsible for attorney's fees because under the Eleventh Amendment[226] it could not be held liable on the merits. Consequently, the damages action must have been directed at the defendants solely in their individual or personal capacities, and only they—and not the state—could be responsible for attorney's fees.

Brandon and *Graham* indicate that the best way for lawyers to avoid unnecessary litigation revolving around this issue is for them clearly and explicitly to sue the relevant individuals and/or local government. That is, if the lawyer desires to sue defendants in their individual or personal capacities for damages, then he or she should say so in the complaint. Where that is done, for example, then the possible applicability of qualified immunity and liability for punitive damages arises and, where state officials are sued, the Eleventh Amendment is irrelevant. Conversely, if the lawyer wants to sue a local government body, then the complaint should identify the local government as a party defendant and properly allege an actionable official policy or custom. Where that is done, for example, then qualified immunity and liability for punitive damages are inapplicable. Further, it is important to emphasize with regard to local government liability that *Brandon* surely did not dispense with the official policy or custom requirement of *Monell*. A plaintiff's lawyer cannot avoid this requirement simply by suing local government officials for damages in their official capacities.

The need to make clear whether a damages action is directed against government employees in their individual capacities or against their local government employer, or both, is demonstrated by a pre-*Brandon* Eighth Circuit case[227] where the plaintiff sued "John R. Farmer [the defendant police officer] and the City of Omaha." Plaintiff thereafter filed an amended complaint to which only the city responded. The district court then granted a motion for directed verdict on the ground that plaintiff did not prove an official policy or custom of the city. Reversing, the Eighth Circuit held that the suit was against the police officer in both his individual and official capacities. This was clear from the pretrial conference as well as from the references by both parties to the disputed issue of qualified immunity, an issue of concern

---

[225] 105 S Ct 3099 (1985), also discussed at **§1.24**. See generally **§§1.18-1.26** on attorney's fees. In an Eleventh Circuit pre-*Graham* case, the court ruled that where a county sheriff and deputy sheriff were successfully sued for *injunctive relief* in their official capacities, then the county could be liable for attorney's fees because the county attorney never contended that defendants had not acted in their official capacities or that their acts or edicts did not fairly represent official county policy. Odum v Clark, 748 F2d 1538 (11th Cir 1984).

[226] *See* **§5.08.**

[227] Rollins *ex rel* Agosta v Farmer, 731 F2d 533 (8th Cir 1984).

only for personal liability. Thus, while the directed verdict might be appropriate for the city, it was not relevant for the police officer who would have to deal with the merits and his qualified immunity.

In a post-*Brandon* case, the Sixth Circuit[228] found a county liable for damages based upon a jury verdict against a county sheriff in his official capacity. Relying on *Brandon,* the court found that the county's liability rested upon the attribution of the sheriff's unconstitutional conduct—he made official policy for the county in police matters—to the county. The Sixth Circuit also asserted that in its view "a judgment against a public servant 'in his official capacity' imposes liability on the entity that he represents provided, of course, the public entity received notice and an opportunity to respond."[229]

Significantly, the Seventh Circuit in a pre-*Brandon* case warned:

> In order to avoid further confusion on this issue [of potential local government liability where an official is successfully sued for damages in his or her official capacity] in the future, where a complaint alleges that the conduct of a public official acting under color of state law gives rise to liability under Section 1983, we will ordinarily assume that he has been sued in his official capacity and only in that capacity. . . . If a plaintiff intends to sue public officials in their individual capacities or in both their official and individual capacities . . . he should expressly state so in the complaint.[230]

This warning appears to constitute notice of the nature of official capacity damages actions to both §1983 plaintiffs and local governments in the Seventh Circuit and is consistent with *Brandon.*

§6.15   —Affirmative Local Government Duties to Act

Many local government liability cases involve failures to act, which means that the plaintiff asserts that the local government had a duty to act affirmatively to prevent harm. Good examples are the cases discussed earlier[231] in connection with the failure to train and supervise police officers adequately. There are, though, other more difficult cases where the plaintiffs seek to impose affirmative duties of a somewhat different nature. For example, in a Fifth Circuit case,[232] plaintiff, a minor seriously injured by a train at a crossing, sued a city for damages allegedly arising out of its intentional or negligent failure to enforce its own speed limit against train traffic, as well as by the

---

[228] Marchese v Lucas, 758 F2d 181 (6th Cir 1985).

[229] *Id* 187.

[230] Kolar v County of Sangamon, 756 F2d 564, 568-69 (7th Cir 1985)(citations omitted).

[231] *See* §6.12.

[232] Hull v City of Duncanville, 678 F2d 582 (5th Cir 1982).

municipality's failure to maintain the crossing and traffic signals properly. Affirming the district court's dismissal of the complaint for failure to state a claim, the Fifth Circuit found that the city's conduct was not sufficiently egregious to constitute an abuse of governmental power, and thus there was no federal right implicated. The city's challenged conduct was at most tortious.

In a comparable Eleventh Circuit case,[233] plaintiffs sued a county for negligently failing to construct a bridge over a ford, which caused plaintiffs' daughters to drown when attempting to cross the rain-swollen ford. According to plaintiffs, this deprived the plaintiffs' decedents of their right to life in violation of due process. Rejecting the argument, the Eleventh Circuit did not speak specifically in Fourteenth Amendment constitutional duty terms, but only asserted that there was no general duty, under state law or otherwise, on the part of the defendant to construct the bridge. It also emphasized the difference between misfeasance and nonfeasance or discretionary inaction.

And in yet another Eleventh Circuit case,[234] where the plaintiff sued a city, alleging that its suppression of information regarding prior rapes had brought about her rape in a high-crime area, the court affirmed the district court's dismissal of the complaint. Even though plaintiff claimed that the city's policy reflected a high degree of recklessness or deliberate indifference amounting to intentional misconduct, the city had not singled her out and, therefore, had breached no constitutional duty owed her under the due process clause. After stating that the matter could similarly be put in proximate cause terms, the court declared:

> [G]enerally, the due process clause of the Constitution does not protect a member of the public at large from the criminal acts of a third person, even if the state was remiss in allowing the third person to be in a position in which he might cause harm to a member of the public, at least in the absence of a special relationship between the victim and the criminal or between the victim and the state.[235]

Such local government affirmative duty cases, like those involving claims that government officials in certain circumstances have affirmative duties to act for the protection of members of the public,[236] are in reality constitutional duty cases. That is, their resolution depends on one's interpretation of the particular constitutional provision implicated and a determination of whether that provision imposes the asserted affirmative duty to act on the local government

---

[233] Dollar v Haralson County, 704 F2d 1540 (11th Cir 1983).

[234] Wright v City of Ozark, 715 F2d 1513 (11th Cir 1983). *See also* Ellsworth v City of Racine, 774 F2d 182 (7th Cir 1985) (city had no continuing constitutional duty to protect underground narcotics officer's wife where she was beaten after police bodyguard had left; city only assumed "limited special relationship" with plaintiff's family during certain periods of the day).

[235] Wright v City of Ozark, 715 F2d 1513, 1515 (11th Cir 1983).

[236] *See, e.g.,* Jackson v City of Joliet, 715 F2d 1200 (7th Cir 1983)(rejecting affirmative duty of police and fire department personnel to rescue), discussed at §§**3.10 & 3.16.**

or the government official. All that can reliably be said at this time regarding due process is that the Supreme Court's decision in *Daniels v Williams*[237] makes clear that negligent conduct is insufficient to cause a deprivation of liberty for substantive and procedural due process purposes. Insofar as many affirmative duty cases, like the three mentioned earlier, raise substantive due process claims, then where only negligence on the part of the local government (or a government official) is alleged, the substantive due process claim will be dismissed on this ground. Only where more than negligent conduct is alleged—gross negligence, recklessness, or deliberate indifference might be sufficient—might a court have to reach the substantive due process affirmative duty issue. In such a case, a plaintiff must, of course, have first proved that there was an official policy or custom regarding such gross negligence, recklessness, or deliberate indifference. Only then must the due process affirmative duty issue be dealt with. A more extensive discussion of substantive due process affirmative duties appears in Chapter 3.[238]

§6.16   —Fourteenth Amendment Damages Actions

The previous accelerating development in the circuits of a Fourteenth Amendment cause of action for damages against local governments as a way of getting around the pre-*Monell*[239] rule of absolute local governmental immunity has now been arrested. While still technically an open question in the Supreme Court,[240] it is seriously questionable after *Monell* whether such a theory, patterned after the implication by the Supreme Court in *Bivens* of a Fourth Amendment action for damages against federal officials,[241] would be permitted. If this is correct, it means that local government damages liability for Fourteenth Amendment violations cannot be based solely on the Fourteenth Amendment using respondeat superior or any other theory of liability.[242]

Justice Powell made this point in his concurring opinion in *Monell*.[243] In his view, and he is probably not alone on the Court, there appears no longer to be any need to take a Fourteenth Amendment action for damages seriously because *Monell* overruled *Monroe v Pape's* absolute local government immunity. Also, shortly after *Monell*, several circuits, notably the Fourth, Sixth, and Ninth, held that there can be no Fourteenth Amendment action for damages based

---

[237] 106 S Ct 662 (1986), discussed at §§3.02 & 3.08-3.11.

[238] *See* §§3.10 & 3.16.

[239] Monell v Department of Social Servs, 436 US 658 (1978).

[240] *See* §6.01.

[241] Bivens v Six Unknown Named Agents of Federal Bureau of Narcotics, 403 US 388 (1971). *See* §6.01.

[242] *See, e.g.,* Turpin v Mailet, 47 USLW 2474 (2d Cir Jan 16, 1979) (en banc), *on remand from the Supreme Court after vacating in light of Monell,* 47 USLW 3234 (S Ct Sept 1, 1978).

[243] 436 US at 713-14.

on respondeat superior.[244] The Supreme Court apparently will not even permit a Fourteenth Amendment damages action approach to local government liability which is based on official policy or custom. Prior to *Monell,* the Second Circuit adopted such a rule of Fourteenth Amendment liability, but the Supreme Court granted certiorari, vacated, and remanded in light of *Monell.*[245] Thus, the Court's message seems clear: §1983 plaintiffs are to pursue only their §1983 damages remedies against local governments, and should *not* attempt to rely on Fourteenth Amendment damages remedies.[246]

§6.17 Local Government Immunity After *Monell*

Once a prima facie cause of action for damages against a local government is made out, the question of local governmental immunity arises. *Monell*[247] clearly rejected absolute immunity for local governments for the common sense reason that such an immunity would undermine its holding that local governments are suable *persons* under §1983. However, *Monell* expressly left open the possibility of a qualified immunity of some sort without even speculating about its scope.

Despite the suggestion in several pre-*Monell* circuit decisions that local

---

[244] Cale v City of Covington, No 77-1239 (4th Cir Nov 3, 1978); Jones v City of Memphis, No 77-1704 (6th Cir Sept 19, 1978); Molina v Richardson, 578 F2d 846 (9th Cir 1978).

[245] Turpin v Mailet, 579 F2d 152 (2d Cir 1978) (en banc), *vacated & remanded in light of Monell,* 47 USLW 3234 (S Ct Sept 1, 1978).

[246] However, in Gordon v City of Warren, 579 F2d 386 (6th Cir 1978), the court stated:

> Whatever may be the ultimate determination by the Supreme Court with respect to the existence of direct causes of action under the 14th Amendment to recover damages for torts of a more personal nature, we conclude that a direct cause of action does exist against municipalities to recover damages resulting from a taking of private property for public use without just compensation. *Id* 391.

It should be noted that *Gordon* clearly involved an official policy and hence a §1983 action could have been asserted against the city.

In Morris v Washington Metro Area Transit Auth, 702 F2d 1037, 1042 n 10 (DC Cir 1983), the District of Columbia Circuit commented that the "availability of a *Bivens*-type Fourteenth Amendment remedy against nonfederal defendants is subject to serious question." It also observed that every circuit court reaching the issue after *Monell* had rejected this remedy.

In Harris v City of Canton, 725 F2d 371, 374 n 3 (6th Cir 1984), the Sixth Circuit stated that it was unclear after *Monell* whether an implied Fourteenth Amendment cause of action for damages could be asserted against local officials.

The Ninth Circuit asserted that Fourteenth Amendment actions for damages against state defendants are precluded by the availability of §1983. Ward v Caulk, 650 F2d 1144, 1148 (9th Cir 1981). To the same effect is the express holding of the Eleventh Circuit in Williams v Bennett, 689 F2d 1370, 1390 (11th Cir 1982) that such a remedy is unavailable against state officials under the Eighth and Fourteenth Amendments.

[247] Monell v Department of Social Servs, 436 US 658 (1978).

governments should have little or no immunity at all from damages liability,[248] it was a fair guess after *Monell* that the Court would ultimately apply to local governments a qualified immunity very similar to the qualified immunity available to individuals which is extensively discussed in Chapter 8.

For one thing, Justice Rehnquist and Chief Justice Burger dissented in *Monell.* Having lost that battle of the prima facie cause of action against local governments, they almost certainly favored a qualified immunity. Indeed, they emphasized local government reliance on the prior rule of absolute immunity[249] and argued that local governments should not have to predict the latest constitutional developments.[250] Moreover, Justice Powell in his concurring opinion dealt with this latter point and intimated that he, too, was receptive to a qualified immunity for local governments.[251]

Further, the Court's reasoning in *Monell* rejecting respondeat superior liability suggested that some kind of qualified immunity would be found applicable. If there were no local government qualified immunity, a local government would be liable even if its officials acted reasonably and in good faith, thereby passing the qualified immunity test for individuals. To impose governmental liability nevertheless in such a case would indicate that a kind of strict liability theory was being applied, designed primarily to compensate constitutionally deprived plaintiffs by loss spreading. Yet *Monell* apparently rejected this loss-spreading function when it held respondeat superior liability inappropriate in §1983 cases. Thus, despite the argument that local governments are better cost bearers than individuals and hence should not benefit from individual qualified immunity,[252] the chances were good that the Supreme Court would ultimately give them this protection.[253]

Nevertheless, in an important decision almost as surprising as *Monell* itself, the Supreme Court narrowly held in *Owen v City of Independence*[254] that a local government sued under §1983 is not protected by any kind of official immunity even where the individual defendants have successfully asserted their qualified immunity. On the other hand, the Court thereafter held in *City of Newport v Fact Concerts, Inc*[255] that punitive damages may *not* be awarded against local governments in §1983 actions.

---

[248] Kostka v Hogg, 560 F2d 37, 41 (1st Cir 1977); Hander v San Jacinto Junior College, 519 F2d 273, 277 n 1 (5th Cir 1975); Hostrop v Board of Junior College Dist No 515, 523 F2d 569 (7th Cir 1975), *cert denied,* 425 US 963 (1976).

[249] Based on Monroe v Pape, 365 US 167 (1961).

[250] 436 US at 717-18.

[251] *Id* 2047.

[252] *The Supreme Court, 1977 Term,* 92 Harv L Rev 57, 322-23 (1978).

[253] Indeed, it must be admitted that this was the prediction in the First Edition.

[254] 445 US 622 (1980) (5-4 decision).

[255] 453 US 247 (1981).

§6.18 —No Immunity from Compensatory Damages

Owen v City of Independence[256] involved a chief of police who was discharged by the city manager of Independence, Missouri, with no reason given, immediately after the city council passed a councilman's motion to have reports of an investigation of the police department released to the media and turned over to the prosecutor for presentation to the grand jury. The motion, which had been preceded by the councilman's personal attack on plaintiff's honesty and competence, also directed the city manager to take "appropriate action" against persons involved in the improper activities brought out by the investigation. Plaintiff then sued the city of Independence, the city manager, and members of the city council in their official capacities under §1983 and the Fourteenth Amendment. Alleging violations of procedural and substantive due process, the plaintiff sought declaratory and injunctive relief, including a hearing and back pay from date of discharge.

The district court ruled against plaintiff on the merits, but the Eighth Circuit initially reversed, awarding plaintiff damages and holding that a local government is not entitled to assert a qualified immunity in §1983 cases. Certiorari was thereafter granted and the case was remanded in light of *Monell.*[257] This time, however, the Eighth Circuit, after reaffirming its earlier decision that plaintiff's Fourteenth Amendment rights had been violated, held that all the defendants, including the city, were entitled to qualified immunity. It observed that the relevant procedural due process decisions of the Supreme Court[258] were decided two months *after* plaintiff's discharge; thus, the defendants could not reasonably have known they were violating plaintiff's Fourteenth Amendment rights.

In an opinion by Justice Brennan, the Supreme Court reversed. Noting that the circuits were divided on the question of "whether local governmental units are entitled to a qualified immunity based on the good faith of their officials,"[259] the Court held that they were not. The Court first considered the language and legislative history of §1983 and characterized §1983's purposes as broadly remedial. Next, the Court found that, unlike the tradition of immunity at common law of legislators, judges, police officers, and other government officials, there was no such tradition of immunity for municipal corporations at the time §1983 was enacted. It stated: "In sum, we can discern no 'tradition so well grounded in history and reason' that would warrant the conclusion that in enacting §1983, the 42nd Congress *sub silentio* extended

---

[256] 445 US 622 (1980).

[257] Monell v Department of Social Servs, 436 US 658 (1978).

[258] Board of Regents v Roth, 408 US 564 (1972) and Perry v Sindermann, 408 US 593 (1972).

[259] 445 US at 635 n 15.

to municipalities a qualified immunity based on the good faith of their officers."[260]

Further, the Court referred again to the broadly remedial purposes of §1983 and emphasized the important deterrent function of a damages remedy for Fourteenth Amendment violations, especially "when the wrongdoer is the institution that has been established to protect the very rights it has transgressed."[261] It rejected as irrelevant the policy arguments based upon (1) the injustice to a defendant held liable despite the absence of bad faith and (2) the danger that the threat of liability will undercut a defendant's willingness to perform his government job effectively. These considerations, the Court said, were applicable to individuals, but not to local governments in light of the principle of equitable loss spreading.

The first consideration was inapplicable to government immunity because the award will come from the public treasury, not from an official's pocket. Similarly inapplicable was the second consideration. For one thing, because the official is not personally liable, there will be little inhibiting effect on the official's job. For another, according to the Court, "consideration of the *municipality's* liability for constitutional violations is quite properly the concern of its elected or appointed officials . . . [A] decision maker [should] consider whether his decision comports with constitutional mandates and . . . weigh the risk that a violation might result in an award of damages from the public treasury."[262]

Justice Powell, joined by Chief Justice Burger and Justices Stewart and Rehnquist, dissented on both the merits and the governmental immunity issue.[263] Characterizing what the majority had done on the latter issue as imposing strict liability on local governments for constitutional violations, they argued that this was inconsistent with the legislative history of §1983 as well as the Court's other immunity decisions. The dissenters also read the common law background of municipal immunity very differently, finding that "the common law of the 19th century . . . recognized substantial tort immunity for municipal actions."[264] Finally, they worried about the effect of *Owen* on local governments and their officials who "will face the unnerving prospect of crushing damage judgments whenever a policy valid under the current law is later found to be unconstitutional."[265]

After *Owen,* there is little doubt that §1983 has become an even more potent plaintiff's sword than before. A local government will be liable under §1983 for constitutional violations caused by an official policy or custom even where the governmental officials responsible for that policy or custom pass the qualified immunity test discussed in Chapter 8. Such liability covers even situations where a challenged act properly deemed constitutional at the time

---

[260] *Id* 650.

[261] *Id.*

[262] *Id* 656.

[263] *Id* 658.

[264] *Id* 676.

[265] *Id* 683.

it occurred turns out to be unconstitutional. Indeed, *Owen* itself is such a case. *Owen* thus gives potential §1983 plaintiffs an attractive local government defendant with a "deep pocket." Furthermore, after *Owen* it does not matter for immunity purposes whether an award which is in fact taken from the public treasury of a local government held liable under §1983 is deemed legal or equitable. In either case such an award—back pay is a good example—cannot be defeated by the local government's assertion of a qualified immunity.

Nevertheless, several other points must be emphasized. First, and very important, *Owen* does not prevent a local government from arguing that a newly declared constitutional rule should not be applied to it *retroactively*.[266] Second, a §1983 plaintiff seeking to hold a local government liable must still show an official policy or custom which brought about a Fourteenth Amendment violation, as well as prove the other elements of the §1983 prima facie case.[267]

§6.19 —Absolute Immunity from Punitive Damages

Despite *Owen v City of Independence*,[268] the Supreme Court has given a kind of immunity to local governments not given to individual defendants. In *City of Newport v Fact Concerts, Inc*,[269] the Court held that considerations of history and policy do not support exposing a municipality to punitive damages for the bad faith actions of its officials. In *Fact Concerts*, the First Circuit, affirming a jury's compensatory and punitive damages awards against the City of Newport, among other defendants, for violating plaintiff's First Amendment right to promote and produce two jazz concerts, had rejected the city's challenge to the district court's instruction allowing the jury to award punitive damages against it.[270]

The Supreme Court reversed in an opinion by Justice Blackmun and held that punitive damages may not be awarded against local governments in §1983 actions. Using a three-step approach, the Court first found that the settled common law background of local government liability precluded punitive damages. Next, the Court maintained that there was nothing in the legislative history of §1983 to suggest that Congress intended to abolish local government immunity from punitive damages. To the contrary, according to the Court, Congress was worried about punishing innocent taxpayers and bankrupting local government.

The Court examined the objectives of punitive damages, considerations of public policy, and the purposes of §1983 and made the following points:

---

[266] Retroactivity guidelines in civil cases are set out in the leading case of Chevron Oil Co v Huson, 404 US 97 (1971). *See also* **§4.14** on retroactivity in limitations cases.

[267] *See* **§§6.06-6.16.**

[268] 445 US 622 (1980).

[269] 453 US 247 (1981). See **ch 4** on punitive damages awards against individuals.

[270] 626 F2d 1060 (1st Cir 1980).

1.   Local governments cannot have malice; only their officials can

2.   Punishment is not as prominent a purpose of §1983 as compensation and deterrence

3.   The deterrence purpose of §1983 does not justify allowing punitive damages awards against local governments because compensatory damages awards against local governments provide adequate incentives for officials and the public, and punitive damages awards against officials individually are an effective means of deterrence

4.   The cost of punitive damages awards against local governments may be excessive; such awards would create serious risks to the financial integrity of local governments by raising the prospect of unpredictable, substantial windfall recoveries to plaintiffs through the exercise by juries of their broad discretion in awarding punitive damages

The Court concluded: "Because absolute immunity from [punitive] damages obtained at common law and was undisturbed by the 42nd Congress, and because that immunity is compatible with both the purposes of §1983 and general principles of public policy, we hold that a municipality is immune from punitive damages under 42 U.S.C. §1983."[271]

After *Owen*, in a Fifth Circuit case,[272] a city, sued for damages under §1983 by a landowner who claimed that the city, through its zoning ordinances and failure to rezone his land, had violated due process and taken his property without just compensation, unsuccessfully attempted to distinguish *Owen*. The city argued that *Owen* involved executive, administrative, and managerial officials while the present case involved legislative acts. Rejecting the argument and holding that the city was not qualifiedly immune, the Fifth Circuit observed that *Owen* in fact involved a city council's legitimate legislative function— conducting an investigation. The court also relied on the absence of any well-established tradition of municipal immunity from damages to compensate for uncompensated takings. The Fifth Circuit, therefore, reversed the district court's grant of summary judgment in favor of the city.

Similarly relying on *Owen*, the Third Circuit[273] reversed the district court's refusal to award "the equitable remedy of back pay" to a blind teacher discriminated against by an official policy of the Philadelphia School District. The district court had suggested that a back pay award computed from the date she would have been offered employment absent discrimination would not be fair because the school district may not have had notice that its conduct toward plaintiff was unconstitutional. Rejecting this suggestion, the Third Circuit asserted that *Owen* established that, regardless of whether back pay is

---

[271] 453 US at 271-72. Justices Brennan, Marshall, and Stevens dissented. Without reaching the merits, they argued that the majority should also not have reached the merits because the city had failed at trial to object to the challenged punitive damages instruction in a timely manner.

[272] Hernandez v City of Lafayette, 643 F2d 1188 (5th Cir 1981).

[273] Gurmankin v Costanzo, 626 F2d 1115 (3d Cir 1980).

considered to be a legal remedy or an equitable one, the good faith of a school district is irrelevant to its liability.

In another post-*Owen* case, the Fifth Circuit[274] carefully distinguished between (1) good faith's relevance to the existence of a county's alleged Eighth Amendment violation in connection with the decedent prisoner's alleged suicide while incarcerated by banging his head against the wall, and (2) good faith's relevance to a possible immunity for the county (not permitted after *Owen*). The court emphasized that it was dealing only with the former in the case before it. Affirming the district court's judgment in favor of the county, the Fifth Circuit stated that the jury's finding that all the defendants, including the county, had acted in good faith precluded the "deliberate indifference" state of mind necessary for a violation of the Eighth Amendment. Thus, the county was not liable because it had not been shown to have violated the decedent prisoner's Eighth Amendment rights in failing to have placed the prisoner in a padded cell.

After *Fact Concerts,* the circuits have regularly overturned punitive damages awards against local governments unless a local government has waived the issue.[275] *Fact Concerts* has also been applied retroactively. Thus, in a Tenth Circuit case,[276] a jury's pre-*Fact Concerts* $7,500 punitive damages award against a city in connection with the termination of plaintiff's employment in violation of his Fourteenth Amendment rights was overturned in reliance on *Fact Concerts.* The Tenth Circuit observed that retroactive application of *Fact Concerts* would not result in injustice or hardship to the plaintiff, especially given a similar punitive damages award recoverable against various individuals.

Even though there is the suggestion in *Fact Concerts* that there might be "an extreme situation where the taxpayers are directly responsible for perpetrating an outrageous abuse of constitutional rights,"[277] thereby rendering a local government liable for punitive damages, it is unlikely that this will occur. For example, in a First Circuit case,[278] the defendant water district "engaged in a deliberate and remarkably overt display of racial discrimination" against the plaintiff development corporation. Refusing to affirm the district court's punitive damages award, the First Circuit observed that only 80 to 85 of the thousands of members of the water district attended the meeting, with 66 of those voting to exclude. Thus, most taxpayers were blameless. Further, according to the Court, a punitive damages award would serve little deterrent function under the circumstances.

---

[274] Wright v Wagner, 641 F2d 239, 242 n 2 (5th Cir 1981).

[275] *E.g.,* Barnett v Housing Auth, 707 F2d 1571 (11th Cir 1983) (waiver by housing authority); Black v Stephens, 662 F2d 181, 184 n 1 (3d Cir 1981) ("procedural default" by city). *But cf* Williams v Butler, 746 F2d 431 (8th Cir 1984), *also granting rehg en banc on other grounds but thereafter affg district court by an equally divided court at,* 762 F2d 73 (8th Cir 1985) (en banc), *vacated,* 54 USLW 3659 (S Ct Apr 7, 1986) (no waiver despite failure to object to punitive damages instruction during conference).

[276] Miller v City of Mission, 705 F2d 368 (10th Cir 1983).

[277] City of Newport v Fact Concerts, Inc, 453 US 247, 267 n 29 (1981).

[278] Heritage Homes v Seekonk Water Dist, 670 F2d 1 (1st Cir 1982).

Similarly, despite a special concurring opinion by Judge Goldberg in which he went on at length to express his "grief" about the case before him and his misgivings about the Supreme Court's decision in *Fact Concerts* immunizing local governments from punitive damages liability, the Fifth Circuit[279] overturned a jury's $200,000 punitive damages award against a city in connection with plaintiffs' decedent's shooting death at the hands of city police officers. The jury had found that it was a universally known and accepted police department policy to use "throw-down" guns to be placed near unarmed suspects who had been shot by police officers so as to make the shootings appear justifiable. According to the court, this was not a case where the outrageous conduct of the taxpayers themselves would justify an award of punitive damages against a city.

§6.20   States and State Agencies as Nonpersons

Prior to *Monell v Department of Social Services,*[280] in which the Supreme Court held, in overruling one aspect of *Monroe v Pape,*[281] that local governments are now suable persons under §1983, §1983 suits against states and their alter ego agencies were clearly barred for two reasons. First, if suit against a state or state agency was brought in federal court, the Eleventh Amendment operated as a bar, as discussed in Chapter 5. There was thus no need to get to the *person* issue. Second, even if suit was brought in state court to avoid the Eleventh Amendment problem,[282] it was uniformly held by every circuit which considered the question prior to *Monell* that a state and its agencies were not persons for §1983 purposes.[283]

Williford v California,[284] an oft-cited Ninth Circuit decision, expressed the pre-*Monell* reasoning most relied on: "A municipal corporation is but a political subdivision of a state and if a state's political subdivisions are not 'persons' under the statute, then neither is the state."

Additionally, this reasoning was applied, typically with little or no discussion, to those state agencies which were regarded as arms or alter egos of a state such that recovery would in fact be against the state.[285] On this basis, state

---

[279] Webster v City of Houston, 689 F2d 1220 (5th Cir 1982), *vacated on other grounds,* 735 F2d 838 (5th Cir)(en banc), *reinstated,* 739 F2d 993 (5th Cir 1984) (per curiam), also set out at **§6.11.**

[280] 436 US 658 (1978).

[281] 365 US 167 (1961).

[282] See **§1.13** on concurrent state jurisdiction over §1983 claims.

[283] United States *ex rel* Gittlemacker v County of Philadelphia, 413 F2d 84 (3d Cir 1969), *cert denied,* 396 US 1046 (1970); Deane Hill County Club, Inc v City of Knoxville, 379 F2d 321 (6th Cir), *cert denied,* 389 US 975 (1967); Loux v Rhay, 375 F2d 55 (9th Cir 1967); Williford v California, 352 F2d 474 (9th Cir 1965); United States *ex rel* Lee v Illinois, 343 F2d 120 (7th Cir 1965).

[284] 352 F2d 474, 476 (9th Cir 1965).

[285] In Bennett v California, 406 F2d 36, 39 (9th Cir), *cert denied,* 394 US 966 (1969), the Ninth Circuit said: "[S]tate agencies such as California Adult Authority and the

agencies which were held, prior to *Monell,* to be nonpersons included: state departments and bureaus of highways,[286] pollution control,[287] motor vehicles,[288] public welfare,[289] social services,[290] and corrections;[291] state employment commissions;[292] universities;[293] boards of regents;[294] bar associations;[295] and judicial departments.[296]

There were, however, a few pre-*Monell* cases in which entities in a close relation to states were nevertheless found to be persons. The Second Circuit classified the New York Housing Finance Agency as a person sufficiently independent of the state so as not to be its alter ego.[297] It relied on the following factors:

1.   An express waiver of sovereign immunity
2.   Express authority to sue and be sued
3.   Its role as only a credit or financing entity
4.   No power to take property in its own name or in the name of the state
5.   The "most crucial determination": the state was not liable for the agency's debts[298]

Similarly, a federal district court held that three state-related universities in Pennsylvania were insufficiently connected to the state to be treated as dependent state agencies, even though these semiprivate universities received more than a third of their funds from the state.[299] Applying what it called a "control" test, the District Court noted that:

California Department of Corrections, which are but arms of the state government, are not 'persons' within the meaning of the Civil Rights Act."

[286] Cheramie v Tucker, 493 F2d 586 (5th Cir), *cert denied,* 419 US 868 (1974).

[287] United Farmworkers Hous Project, Inc v City of Delray Beach, 493 F2d 799 (5th Cir 1974).

[288] Sykes v California Dept of Motor Vehicles, 497 F2d 197 (9th Cir 1974).

[289] Burris v State Dept of Pub Welfare, 491 F2d 762 (4th Cir 1974).

[290] Rosado v Wyman, 414 F2d 170 (2d Cir 1969), *revd on other grounds,* 397 US 397 (1970), *affd,* 402 US 991 (1971).

[291] Curtis v Everette, 489 F2d 516 (3d Cir 1973), *cert denied,* 416 US 995 (1974).

[292] Vick v Texas Employment Commn, 514 F2d 734 (5th Cir 1975).

[293] Avins v Mangum, 450 F2d 932 (2d Cir 1971).

[294] Prostrollo v University of SD, 507 F2d 775 (8th Cir 1974), *cert denied,* 421 US 952 (1975).

[295] Coopersmith v Supreme Court, 465 F2d 993 (10th Cir 1972).

[296] Zuckerman v Appellate Div Second Dept, Sup Ct, 421 F2d 625 (2d Cir 1970).

[297] Forman v Community Servs, Inc, 500 F2d 1246 (2d Cir 1974), *revd on other grounds,* 421 US 837 (1975).

[298] That is, there was no "intimate connection" between the agency and the state; further, the agency did not perform government functions warranting its treatment as a nonperson.

[299] Samuel v University of Pittsburgh, 375 F Supp 1119 (WD Pa 1974), *modified on other grounds,* 538 F2d 991 (3d Cir 1976).

1. Private citizens made up a majority of the boards of trustees
2. The universities had an independent corporate existence
3. They maintained their own facilities
4. They had the power to issue bonds for which the state was not obligated
5. Less than half their revenue came from the state[300]

To the extent that the view of states and their agencies as nonpersons may be inferred from the treatment given local government bodies in *Monroe v Pape*,[301] then *Monell* reversed this inference. Justice Brennan made this point in his concurrence in *Hutto v Finney*,[302] a Civil Rights Attorney's Fees Awards Act case decided shortly after *Monell*. He also characterized as undermined the pre-*Monell* local government immunity premise of several important cases in which the Court had asserted that §1983 did not constitute a waiver by the states of their Eleventh Amendment immunity.[303] However, Justice Powell argued in *Hutto* that even after *Monell*, §1983 should not be construed either as making states and their agencies suable persons or as waiving Eleventh Amendment immunity. Later, in *Alabama v Pugh*,[304] the Court summarily held that the Eleventh Amendment barred a §1983 injunctive relief suit in federal court brought against Alabama and its board of corrections.

In *Quern v Jordan*,[305] the Court subsequently may have held generally that states are not suable persons under §1983. However, because *Quern* involved a *federal court* action, it is also possible to read *Quern* more narrowly as an Eleventh Amendment case. Under this reading, Congress intended when it enacted §1983 that states not be sued in federal court even under §1983, but that states be suable persons for all other §1983 purposes. If *Quern* is thus understood to be an Eleventh Amendment case only, and not a person case, then a §1983 action could be brought against a state in *state court* because the Eleventh Amendment does not apply to state court suits. For example, in a Michigan case,[306] the court, after noting contrary authority in other jurisdic-

---

[300] *Id* 1126-28.

[301] 365 US 167 (1961).

[302] 437 US 678 (1978).

[303] Fitzpatrick v Bitzer, 427 US 445 (1976); Edelman v Jordan, 415 US 651 (1974).

[304] 438 US 781 (1978). Justices Brennan and Marshall dissented without opinion. Justice Stevens argued that the Court should not have granted certiorari because the issue had no practical significance, and then exclaimed: "Surely the Court does not intend to resolve summarily the issue debated by my Brothers [Brennan and Powell] in their separate opinions in *Hutto v. Finney. . . .*" *Id* 783. However, this seemed indeed to be the majority's intent. *See also* §5.08 on the Eleventh Amendment.

[305] 440 US 332 (1979) Justice Brennan concurred in the judgment, arguing that the majority had reached out to decide the person issue with Justice Marshall concurring in the judgment.

[306] Smith v State, 122 Mich App 340, 333 NW2d 50 (1983). *Contrary state authority includes the following:* State v Green, 633 P2d 1381 (Alaska 1981); Merritt v State, 696 P2d 871 (Idaho 1985); Edgar v State, 92 Wash 2d 217, 595 P2d 534 (Wash 1979); Boldt v State, 101 Wis 2d 566, 305 NW2d 133 (1981); *But see* State v Brosseau, 470 A2d 869 (NH 1983) (*Quern* an Eleventh Amendment case).

tions, interpreted *Quern* as an Eleventh Amendment decision and held that a state was a person for purposes of §1983 state court actions.[307] Moreover, if *Quern* is an Eleventh Amendment case, a §1983 action may even be brought in federal court against a state which is found to have waived its Eleventh Amendment immunity. Indeed, the First Circuit recently so held.[308]

In contrast to this current uncertainty regarding states, the Supreme Court indicated in *Lake Country Estates, Inc v Tahoe Regional Planning Agency*[309] that an interstate-compact agency, created by California and Nevada and approved by Congress, was a suable person under §1983. Also, the Eleventh Amendment did not bar suits in federal court against the agency.

---

[307] In Aubuchon v Missouri, 631 F2d 581, 582 (8th Cir 1980) (per curiam) the Eighth Circuit asserted that the "State of Missouri is not a proper party to an action brought under §1983." However, this case involved a federal court suit. In Gay Students Servs v Texas A&M Univ, 612 F2d 160, 163 n 3 (5th Cir 1980), however, the question whether a state university could be sued directly for damages was characterized as an Eleventh Amendment issue, and not a person issue. The court said: "An entity may be a 'person' under §1983 yet still not be sued for monetary relief due to Eleventh Amendment immunity based upon the entity's close connection with the State and its treasury."

[308] Grotta v Rhode Island, 781 F2d 343 (1st Cir 1986)(finding waiver of state's Eleventh Amendment immunity through state court's interpretation of state law; thereafter ruling that a state that has waived its Eleventh Amendment immunity is a suable person under §1983; no principled reason to distinguish between states and local governments). *Cf* Toledo Peoria & Western RR v Illinois Dept of Transp, 744 F2d 1296 (7th Cir 1984)(ruling that a state agency may not be sued in federal court under §1983 and asserting that a state agency is not a person for §1983 purposes; decision put in federal jurisdiction terms)

Under the approach which would distinguish the Eleventh Amendment issue from the person issue, Congress intended to include states within the purview of §1983 but did not go so far as to abrogate Eleventh Amendment immunity. This would represent an intermediate position. An extreme approach would be to *exclude* states entirely from §1983 coverage, whether in federal or state court, by ruling that they are not persons. The other extreme would be to *include* states as suable persons under §1983 in both federal and state courts in the course of determining that §1983 was indeed intended to abrogate Eleventh Amendment immunity. The Court has rejected the last approach but, as noted, has yet to take a clear stand on the other two.

[309] 440 US 391, 405 n 29 (1979).

"Every person": The Absolute Individual Immunity of Legislators, Judges, Prosecutors, and Others

7

§7.01   Summary

Not only were most governmental entities not *persons* before the Supreme Court's decision in *Monell v Department of Social Services*,[1] but certain classes of individual defendants, who are clearly persons, are nevertheless absolutely

---

[1] 436 US 658 (1978). *See generally* **ch 6.**

immune and hence not proper defendants for *damages* purposes[2] under 42 USC §1983. These classes, as determined by the Supreme Court, are state and regional legislators,[3] judges,[4] and prosecutors.[5] When legislators act within a *traditional legislative capacity,* when judges act *judicially within or in excess of jurisdiction* but not in *clear absence of all jurisdiction,* and when prosecutors act as *advocates* in the criminal process, they are absolutely immune from liability for damages under §1983. Otherwise, they are protected only by the affirmative defense of qualified immunity.[6] A significant difference between the two kinds of immunity is that there may be no inquiry into the absolutely immune defendant's state of mind, while such an inquiry may be necessitated by a qualified immunity claim.[7] Typically, therefore, the action against an absolutely immune defendant will be dismissed on a motion setting out the defendant's status and an allegation of action within official capacity. The policy underlying absolute immunity is a concern with the chilling effect of potential §1983 damages litigation upon the exercise of decision-making authority by persons in these four classes.

Absolute damages immunity protection has been extended, under a functional approach, beyond these four classes to include others engaging in legislative, judicial, or prosecutorial acts. For example, the trend in the circuits is toward absolute local legislator immunity for legislative, as distinct from administrative, conduct. Also, witnesses in criminal trials are absolutely immune from damages liability.[8] However, public defenders are not absolutely immune from damages liability for their conspiratorial conduct[9] and the United States Attorney General is not absolutely immune for unconstitutional law enforcement surveillance in furtherance of national security.[10] Note that absolute immunity from *damages* liability must be distinguished from absolute

---

[2] The emphasis is intentional. See, e.g., the discussion at **§7.12.**

[3] Tenney v Brandhove, 341 US 367 (1951). Regional legislators are now also absolutely immune. Lake Country Estates, Inc v Tahoe Regional Planning Agency, 440 US 391 (1979) discussed at **§7.05.**

[4] Stump v Sparkman, 435 US 349 (1978) and Pierson v Ray, 386 US 547 (1967).

[5] Imbler v Pachtman, 424 US 409 (1976).

[6] *See generally* **ch 8.** Whether private persons who conspire with absolutely immune defendants are entitled to absolute, qualified, or no immunity is discussed at **§2.10.**

[7] This was surely true of qualified immunity before Harlow v Fitzgerald, 457 US 800 (1982), and may still be true even after *Harlow,* especially in connection with a defendant's duty to know clearly settled law. Yet it must be acknowledged that the *objective* qualified immunity test is now closer to absolute immunity than previously. *See generally* **ch 8.**

[8] Briscoe v LaHue, 460 US 325 (1983), discussed at **§7.10.**

[9] Tower v Glover, 467 US 914 (1984), discussed at **§7.15** However, a public defender accused of nonconspiratorial conduct in connection with the representation of a client does not act under color of law, thereby receiving the equivalent of §1983 damages immunity. Polk County v Dodson, 454 US 312 (1981). *See* **§§2.04-2.10 & 7.15.**

[10] Mitchell v Forsyth, 105 S Ct 2806 (1984), set out at **§8.05.**

immunity from *injunctive* relief. The latter extends to legislators, but does not apply to judges and prosecutors.[11]

Finally, the Court has ruled that denials of defense motions for absolute and/or qualified immunity may be immediately appealable.[12]

§7.02   Legislative Immunity from Liability for Damages—*Tenney v Brandhove*

The Supreme Court first mentioned absolute immunity for persons under §1983 in *Tenney v Brandhove*.[13] Plaintiff in that case sought damages under the section against various individuals, including the members of a committee of the California legislature called the Senate Fact-Finding Committee on Un-American Activities. He claimed they had intimidated him in the exercise of his constitutional rights by wrongfully interrogating him in their investigation and by prosecuting him for contempt. The Court, per Justice Frankfurter, held that state legislators are absolutely immune from liability for damages when they act "in a field where legislators traditionally have power to act. . . ."[14] Characterizing the committee's investigation as within those bounds, the Court found the committee's members absolutely immune despite a claim of "unworthy purpose."[15]

The Court's reasoning is worth noting. In contrast with its reasoning 10 years later in *Monroe v Pape*[16] as to governmental immunity and its focus on §1983's legislative history,[17] the Court interpreted §1983's *person* language against a common law background of absolute legislative immunity from tort liability derived from English law and early American history. It also emphasized the policy underlying the Speech or Debate clause, Art I, Section 6, of the United States Constitution, suggesting that it "was a reflection of political principles already firmly established in the States."[18] The Court then asked the following question:

> Did Congress by the general language of its 1871 statute mean to overturn the tradition of legislative freedom achieved in England by Civil

---

[11] *See* **§7.12.**

[12] Mitchell v Forsyth, 105 S Ct 2806 (1984).

[13] 341 US 367 (1951).

[14] *Id* 379.

[15] Investigations, whether by standing or special committees, are an established part of representative government. . . . To find that a committee's investigation has exceeded the bounds of legislative power it must be obvious that there was a usurpation of functions exclusively vested in the Judiciary or the Executive. The present case does not present such a situation.
Id 377-78.

[16] 365 US 167 (1961). *Monroe* was overruled on the issue of local government liability by Monell v Department of Social Servs, 436 US 658 (1978). *See* **ch 6.**

[17] That is, the Court's express reliance in *Monroe* on the debates and the two versions of the Sherman Amendment for its conclusion that municipalities are not *persons*.

[18] 341 US at 373.

War and carefully preserved in the formation of State and National Governments here? Did it mean to subject legislators to civil liability for acts done within the sphere of legislative activity?[19]

And it answered: "We cannot believe that Congress—itself a staunch advocate of legislative freedom—would impinge on a tradition so well grounded in history and reason by covert inclusion in the general language before us.[20]

Despite the broad *person* language of §1983 which seems to admit of no exceptions and despite Justice Douglas's dissent[21] in *Tenney*, the result is probably justified on the basis of a concern with the democratic process and the chilling effect of potential §1983 damages litigation on the independence of legislators. *Tenney* prevents any inquiry into legislative motive, no matter how corrupt, for purposes of §1983 damages liability, as long as the state legislator is acting in a traditional legislative area. Thus, the remedies for such corruption must be the political process and the criminal laws.[22]

Using the *Tenney* approach one must first look to that status of the defendant. Next, if the defendant is found to be a state legislator, one must look to the nature of the action in order to determine whether it is within a traditional legislative field. *Tenney* tells us that a legislative committee's investigation is within the field to which absolute immunity attaches.

§7.03 —State Legislators and Protected Legislative Conduct

Under the *Tenney* approach,[23] once the defendant is found to have state legislator status, the next question is whether the challenged act is legislative in nature. The extreme cases are easy to deal with. At one end, for example, the act of a state legislator in driving negligently and injuring another is not a legislative act, nor is it even an act under color of law.[24] At the other is the situation in which the state legislator is sued under §1983 for enacting certain state legislation. It is unquestioned that absolute immunity attaches to such an act. As the Court's approach demonstrates, *Tenney* is closer to the latter extreme

---

[19] *Id* 376.

[20] *Id.*

[21] He argued that "when a committee perverts its power, brings down on an individual the whole weight of government for an illegal or corrupt purpose, the reason for the immunity ends." *Id* 383. His argument appears in effect to be for a qualified immunity, although he never used that term.

[22] "[W]e have never held that the performance of the duties of judicial, legislative, or executive officers, requires or contemplates the immunization of otherwise criminal deprivations of constitutional rights." O'Shea v Littleton, 414 US 488, 503 (1974). *See also* Gravel v United States, 408 US 606, 627 (1972).

[23] *See* §7.02.

[24] Clearly these two inquiries are often factually related. An affirmative finding on state action will tend to lead to a similar finding on official capacity. However, this does not mean that the two inquiries are identical. See §§2.04-2.10 on state action.

than to the former. The Court first inquired whether investigative hearings were a traditionally legislative function. Then, as a way of determining whether there was a legislative act, it asked whether the specific investigation had exceeded the bounds of legislative power. The test for reaching such a conclusion was: "[I]t must be obvious that there was a usurpation of functions exclusively vested in the Judiciary or Executive."[25] On the merits the Court had little difficulty in answering these questions in defendant's favor.

Following *Tenney*, courts in §1983 cases readily applied its reasoning to state legislators who voted for particular legislation[26] or housekeeping resolutions.[27] Legislator participation in committee work[28] and on a statutory commission[29] has also been covered by the *Tenney* reasoning, as well as the conduct of a state senate president who compelled a state legislator to attend a joint session.[30] These activities are clearly legislative acts and are properly protected. Furthermore, since *Tenney*, the Supreme Court has elaborated on the attributes of legislative acts under the Speech or Debate clause upon which the Court in *Tenney* so heavily relied. It stated that for purposes of congressional immunity, activities protected under that clause "must be an integral part of the deliberative and communicative processes by which Members participate in committee and House proceedings with respect to the consideration and passage or rejection of proposed legislation or with respect to other matters which the Constitution places within the jurisdiction of either house."[31]

Applying this standard for determining legislative acts, the Court held that speech or debate clause absolute immunity does *not* extend to a senator's alleged private arrangement with a private publisher to publish the Pentagon Papers,[32] and in a later case indicated that a congressman who arranges for the *public* (as distinguished from internal) distribution of committee materials allegedly infringing upon the rights of individuals is similarly not absolutely

---

[25] Tenny v Brandhove, 341 US 367, 378 (1951).

[26] City of Safety Harbor v Birchfield, 529 F2d 1251 (5th Cir 1976); Johnson v Reagan, 524 F2d 1123 (9th Cir 1975).

[27] Eslinger v Thomas, 476 F2d 225 (4th Cir 1973).

[28] Berrios v Agosto, 716 F2d 85 (1st Cir 1983) (per curiam), where the First Circuit held that absolute legislative immunity protected members of the judiciary committee of the Puerto Rico legislature from injunctive relief in connection with plaintiffs' attempt to enjoin public hearings and the gathering of evidence respecting a shooting incident in which police officers were involved. Here the investigation was designed to probe alleged executive wrongdoing and was therefore within the sphere of legitimate legislative activity; Star Distrib, Ltd v Marino, 613 F2d 4 (2d Cir 1980), finding absolute immunity applicable to state legislators, members of a state legislative committee investigating child pornography, who issued subpoenas to plaintiffs; Green v De Camp, 612 F2d 368 (8th Cir 1980), ruling that the preparation and issuance of a legislative committee's report were protected by legislative immunity; Gambocz v Sub-Committee on Claims of Joint Legislative Comm, 423 F2d 674 (3d Cir 1970).

[29] Bergman v Stein, 404 F Supp 287 (SDNY 1975).

[30] Schultz v Sundberg, 759 F2d 714 (9th Cir 1985) (per curiam).

[31] Gravel v United States, 408 US 606, 625 (1972).

[32] Gravel v United States, 408 US 606 (1972).

immune.[33] The Court's reasoning was that, despite arguments for a legislative informing function, such acts go beyond the reasonable requirements of such function.

Circuit courts have also been sensitive to those situations in which legislators act officially but not legislatively and have accordingly, although only occasionally, held absolute immunity inapplicable. In a New Jersey district court decision,[34] the court concluded that absolute immunity did not shield state legislators who were accused of improperly excluding another legislator from a party caucus. While sufficient state involvement was found to constitute state action, the court determined that this was an area in which legislators traditionally did not act.

Similarly, after discussing relevant Supreme Court decisions, the Fifth Circuit[35] held that state legislators were protected by absolute legislative immunity in connection with a legislative committee's investigation of alleged wrongdoing in the Alabama Military Department. Plaintiff had alleged that two legislators, with others, conspired to deprive him of his good name, his right of free speech, and certain property rights. However, while the court found that defendants' actions taken during the legislative investigation were so protected, their actions and statements, including those made on radio, television, and privately, which occurred *after* the committee dissolved, were *not* protected by absolute immunity.

A well-reasoned and thoughtful opinion concerns the official immunity of a congressman sued for damages for sex discrimination against a staff employee. In this case, *Davis v Passman*,[36] a Fifth Circuit panel curtly rejected the

---

[33] Doe v McMillan, 412 US 306 (1973). The arrangement must go beyond merely voting for it. *Id* 312. For Supreme Court decisions setting forth the general rule under the speech or debate clause that evidence of legislative acts and the motives behind them is not admissible in prosecutions against a member of Congress, see United States v Heltoski, 442 US 477 (1979); United States v Brewster, 408 US 501 (1972); and United States v Johnson, 383 US 169 (1966).

However, no comparable privilege exists for *state* legislators in connection with federal criminal prosecutions against them because the strong federal interest in enforcing *federal criminal statutes* outweighs the state's interest in legislative independence. United States v Gillock, 445 US 360 (1980). The availability to state legislators and other absolutely immune defendants of this evidentiary privilege in *civil* cases was not addressed.

See Hutchinson v Proxmire, 443 US 111 (1979) on the difference, for Speech or Debate clause purposes, between a senator's voting and preparing committee reports on the one hand and issuing newsletters and press releases on the other. *See also* McSurely v McClellan, 753 F2d 88 (DC Cir 1985) (per curiam) for an extensive discussion of the scope of immunity of Senate subcommittee members accused of involvement in the unconstitutional seizure of private documents and their use in connection with a federal investigation.

[34] Ammond v McGahn, 390 F Supp 655 (DNJ 1975), *revd on other grounds*, 532 F2d 325 (3d Cir 1976).

[35] Cole v Gray, 638 F2d 804 (5th Cir 1981).

[36] 544 F2d 865 (5th Cir 1977), *revd on other grounds after rehg* 571 F2d 793 (5th Cir 1978) (en banc). In Davis v Passman, 442 US 228 (1979), the Supreme Court reversed the *en banc* decision of the Fifth Circuit and, relying on Bivens v Six Unknown Named Agents,

congressman's defense of absolute immunity. The court first observed that "the constitutional proscription of blatant sex discrimination does not impair [defendant's] legitimate control over his staff to any extent at all."[37] Next, after canvassing the speech or debate clause cases, the court concluded: "[L]egislators are not legislating when they dismiss staff members. For the same reasons that the speech or debate clause does not extend to staff dismissals, [defendant] cannot invoke absolute immunity."[38]

The Fifth Circuit panel's insistence that "the immunized act must be intimately cognate to the legislative process"[39] is similarly appropriate under §1983. As observed, the *Tenney* Court reasoned from both the historical purpose of the speech or debate clause and the concern, in the Fifth Circuit's words, "that the prospect of an unsuccessful but burdensome lawsuit might affect a legislator's performance of his or her legislative duties, thus distorting the democratic process."[40] There is thus a class of cases in which a state legislator acting within an official capacity may be denied an absolute immunity because the act is not legislative in nature. This result may even occur where the state legislator has acted in a reasonable good faith belief in the protection of absolute immunity. It is true that this is not discussed in *Davis*, in *Tenney*, and in the speech or debate clause cases, perhaps because it was not raised. Still, these cases appear to use an objective test for the *legislative act* inquiry, with no attention paid to the legislator's state of mind.[41] However, the state of mind of a legislator, once an absolute immunity has been denied, may be relevant to the applicability of qualified immunity.[42]

---

403 US 388 (1971), held that a Fifth Amendment cause of action was stated by the plaintiff who alleged sex discrimination against a United States congressman for firing her as his deputy administrative assistant. Because the Fifth Circuit had not reached the issue of speech or debate clause immunity, the Supreme Court similarly did not address it.

[37] 544 F2d at 870.

[38] *Id* 881. But cf Agromayor v Colberg, 738 F2d 55 (1st Cir 1984), where the First Circuit held that the Speaker of the Puerto Rico House of Representatives was protected by absolute immunity from damages and injunctive relief liability for the Speaker's refusal to hire the plaintiff, a journalist, as a House press officer in alleged violation of the First Amendment. While the Supreme Court had not yet decided whether the employment of legislative assistants was an absolutely protected legislative act, in this case the court reasoned the press officer job was of direct legislative importance because it dealt with deliberative and communicative processes. Also, the job was "both ill-defined and open-ended," and it was inappropriate for the court to inquire too deeply into the job's functions because this very kind of inquiry was inconsistent with the "principles that absolute immunity was intended to protect."

[39] 544 F2d at 879.

[40] *Id.*

[41] See the discussion at §7.07 regarding judicial acts.

[42] An issue of interest is the possibility of a Fourteenth Amendment action for damages against state legislators, judges, and prosecutors who have an absolute immunity under both the common law and §1983. Does this immunity survive a Fourteenth Amendment challenge? The answer is probably yes. Berrios v Agosto, 716 F2d 85 (1st Cir 1983) (per curiam). Compare §6.16, involving Fourteenth Amendment

It should finally be noted that legislative immunity is not limited to damages. As discussed more fully later,[43] the Supreme Court held in *Supreme Court v Consumers Union*[44] that state legislators, and judges exercising a state's entire legislative authority over a subject, are absolutely immune from both damages and injunctive relief liability for their legislative acts. The Court relied in part on its decision in *Eastland v United States Servicemen's Fund*,[45] which held that the speech or debate clause immunizes congressmen from suits for prospective relief as well as suits for damages. The Second Circuit[46] similarly ruled that absolute immunity from injunctive relief was applicable to state legislators, members of a state legislative committee investigating child pornography, who issued subpoenas to plaintiffs.

§7.04   —State Legislative Employees

There has been some confusion in the cases about the proper treatment of §1983 suits for damages against legislative employees. *Tenney*, standing alone, suggests that such employees may be held liable for damages under §1983. Citing *Kilbourn v Thompson*,[47] where a judgment was entered against the House's Sergeant-at-Arms for an illegal arrest, the Court said: "Legislative privilege in such a case [where the defendants are members of a legislature] deserves greater respect than where an official acting on behalf of the legislature is sued. . . ."[48] Courts have generally heeded this dictum and have held that legislative employees are protected only by a qualified immunity.[49] However, several have modified this stand by holding that certain legislative employees are absolutely immune. The Fifth Circuit, relying on *Tenney*, has said that employee-investigators of a statutory investigative committee are absolutely immune.[50] An Indiana district court has held the same for legislative employees.[51] These decisions seem questionable not only in light of *Tenney's* dictum but also because legislative employees differ from legislators in that they do not require the independence which is so necessary for the effective operation of representative government. A qualified immunity should ordinari-

---

actions against governmental bodies, with **§8.12,** dealing with the applicability of a qualified immunity to federal officers sued for violating Fourth Amendment rights.

[43] *See* **§7.12**.

[44] 446 US 719 (1980).

[45] 421 US 491 (1975).

[46] Star Distrib, Ltd v Marino, 613 F2d 4 (2d Cir 1980).

[47] 103 US 168 (1880).

[48] Tenney v Brandhove, 341 US 367, 378 (1951). This theme is reiterated in Dombrowski v Eastland, 387 US 82, 85 (1967).

[49] Eslinger v Thomas, 476 F2d 225 (4th Cir 1973).

[50] Martone v McKeithen, 413 F2d 1373 (5th Cir 1969).

[51] Porter v Bainbridge, 405 F Supp 83 (SD Ind 1975). There were no citations or reasoning. Also, while the court spoke of immunity, the case actually seemed to involve injunctive relief and federalism concerns.

ly be sufficient to ensure that employees are not unduly hampered by litigation and deterred from performing their jobs.[52]

However, the suggested general applicability of a qualified immunity to legislative employees must be limited in one significant respect. In several speech or debate clause cases, the Supreme Court put a gloss on its language in *Tenney* and extended absolute immunity to congressional aides, committee staff, and committee consultants who investigated and introduced material at committee hearings.[53] In determining whether these acts were legislative acts and thus absolutely immune, the Court was concerned with "freeing the legislator from executive and judicial oversight that *realistically threatens to control his conduct as a legislator.*"[54] It therefore asked whether the acts would have been protected had they been done by the legislator himself. To the extent that these speech or debate clause cases are relevant to the §1983 legislative immunity issue by analogy, the inquiry must focus on the nature of the act itself as well as the defendant's status. Viewed in this light, a legislative employee is only absolutely immune from liability under §1983 when the act is such that the legislator would have been immune for doing it.[55]

§7.05   —Local and Regional Legislators: The Functional Approach of *Lake Country Estates*

The prior general rule in the circuits was that local legislators were not given

---

[52] An interesting case with a twist is Saffioti v Wilson, 392 F Supp 1335, 1343-44 n 10 (SDNY 1975), in which a governor who was sued for injunctive relief for exercising a veto was likened to a legislator in dictum by the court which suggested that the governor should be protected by absolute immunity. On the one hand, this dictum seems inconsistent with Scheuer v Rhodes, 416 US 232 (1974), which held that executives are protected only by a qualified immunity and Wood v Strickland, 420 US 308 (1975), which held the same for school board members regardless of whether they exercise quasi-legislative or quasi-judicial functions. On the other hand, the dictum suggests a functional approach to absolute immunity. *See* **§7.10**. In any event, the court resolved the matter on the merits in favor of the governor.

[53] Doe v McMillan, 412 US 306 (1973); Gravel v United States, 408 US 606 (1972).

[54] Gravel v United States, 408 US at 618 (emphasis added).

[55] This approach to a legislative employee's immunity is similar to the approach used for determining the scope of immunity of a judicial employee who is following a judge's order or direction. *See* **§7.10**. An additional factor justifying these approaches is the unfairness in withholding an absolute immunity from a legislative or judicial employee while the person responsible for the challenged conduct—the person ordering it—gets its protection.

See Green v De Camp, 612 F2d 368 (8th Cir 1980), which held that counsel for a select state legislative committee was protected from liability by absolute legislative immunity where that counsel and certain state legislators, similarly protected, were sued under §1983 in connection with the preparation and issuance of a committee report made available to the public.

the *Tenney*[56] absolute immunity. In contrast, regional legislators acting under interstate compacts were and are given absolute immunity for their legislative acts. A leading Sixth Circuit case on local legislators, *Nelson v Knox*,[57] involved a suit for damages against a number of city commissioners, among others, for allegedly intentionally destroying plaintiff's garage business by the passage and enforcement of arbitrary and discriminatory ordinances. Judge, later Justice, Stewart, writing for the court, first correctly characterized the scope of the commissioners' immunity under §1983 as a question of federal, not state, law. Then, relying in part on the Supreme Court's decision in *Hague v CIO*,[58] Judge Stewart held that the commissioners "were not clothed with complete immunity but enjoyed instead a qualified privilege."[59] He acknowledged that *Hague* concerned injunctive relief, not damages, but contended that this made no difference. More to the point, Judge Stewart accepted the view of Judge Magruder in *Cobb v City of Malden*,[60] who had concluded that local legislators should not be absolutely immune under §1983 because they had only a qualified immunity at common law.

Until recently, circuit court cases applied *Nelson* and a narrow reading of *Tenney* to local legislators. For example, absolute immunity was denied to members of a county's fiscal court who were accused of violating procedural due process. This was not an ordinary judicial tribunal but rather had entirely legislative and administrative powers.[61] The same reasoning was also applied to a city's aldermen accused of racial discrimination against plaintiff's ambulance service,[62] to county supervisors allegedly discriminating against public employees who were members of a union,[63] and to the members of an aldermanic police committee accused of illegally revoking a cabdriver's license.[64] Federal district courts did the same,[65] although there were several which took a contrary view[66] based either on a broad reading of *Tenney* to

---

[56] Tenney v Brandhove, 341 US 367 (1951).

[57] 256 F2d 312 (6th Cir 1958).

[58] 307 US 496 (1939).

[59] 256 F2d at 315.

[60] 202 F2d 701, 707 (1st Cir 1953) (concurring opinion). Gaffney v Silk, 488 F2d 1248 (1st Cir 1973) also applied a qualified immunity to local legislators for legislative acts.

[61] Lynch v Johnson, 420 F2d 818 (6th Cir 1970).

[62] Curry v Gillette, 461 F2d 1003 (6th Cir), *cert denied*, 409 US 1042 (1972).

[63] Thomas v Younglove, 545 F2d 1171 (9th Cir 1976). *Tenney* is read here as applying to state legislators, "not necessarily to those other state or local officials whose duties can be characterized as partially 'legislative.'" *Id* 1173. *But cf* Gillibeau v City of Richmond, 417 F2d 426 (9th Cir 1969).

[64] Lane v Inman, 509 F2d 184 (5th Cir 1975).

[65] Kucinich v Forbes, 432 F Supp 1101 (ND Ohio 1977); Owen v City of Independence, 421 F Supp 1110 (WD Mo 1976), *affd in part revd in part on other grounds*, 560 F2d 925 (8th Cir 1977), *vacated & remanded*, 438 US 902 (1978); Smetanka v Borough of Ambridge, 378 F Supp 1366 (WD Pa 1974).

[66] Teamsters Local 822 v City of Portsmouth, 423 F Supp 954 (ED Va 1975), *affd*, 534 F2d 328 (1976); Shannon Fredericksburg Motor Inn, Inc v Hicks, 434 F Supp 803 (Ed Va 1977). The latter, after canvassing the relevant cases and arguments, concluded:

protect individuals who legislate at any governmental level or on an interpretation of the common law, which confers absolute immunity.

It was thus an open question what the Supreme Court would do if presented with the issue of the scope of immunity for local government legislators. On the one hand, and favoring a qualified immunity only, *Tenney* involved state legislators, and the Court there historically compared the functions of state legislators and congressmen. Also, according to Judge Magruder in *Cobb*, the common law rule for local legislators is that of qualified immunity. Whether or not Judge Magruder was correct, later Supreme Court decisions have made it clear that while common law immunity rules for governmental officials may be relevant, they are not dispositive of §1983 immunity.[67]

On the other hand, and favoring absolute immunity, *Tenney* may be read on a purely functional basis as emphasizing the need for absolute immunity for all legislators, regardless of governmental level. *Pierson v Ray*,[68] the Court's later decision on absolute judicial immunity, may also be relevant on this point because there the judge was a "municipal police justice." The Court in *Pierson* emphasized the judicial function and not the level of government at which the individual judged. Additionally, as mentioned above, the common law immunity rules may not in fact be what Judge Magruder in *Cobb* said they are. In this regard it was stated that only a "scant majority" of the states accord a qualified immunity for defamation, while a substantial number do not;[69] for other torts the general rule seems to be to extend the same absolute immunity to members of inferior legislative bodies as to state and national legislators.[70]

For these reasons, the issue has been a close one. However, *Lake Country Estates, Inc v Tahoe Regional Planning Agency*,[71] a 1979 Supreme Court decision dealing with officers legislating under the authority of an interstate compact, indicates that local legislators will ultimately be given absolute immunity for their legislative acts by the Supreme Court. This case involved a §1983 action against an interstate-compact planning agency and its officers. The basis of the suit was the agency's adoption of a land use ordinance and general plan that allegedly destroyed the value of the plaintiffs' property. The Court, per Justice Stevens, first found that the defendants' conduct had been undertaken *under color of state law* within the meaning of §1983, even though federal approval was required and had been given for the interstate compact.[72] Thus, a §1983 cause of action was stated. The Court next concluded that the Eleventh Amendment

---

"If indeed there is a rational basis for distinguishing the safeguards necessary to permit local legislators to carry out their legislative duties from those which have been clearly accorded the state legislators, same escapes the Court." *Id* 805.

[67] *E.g.*, Scheuer v Rhodes, 416 US 232 (1974).

[68] 386 US 547 (1967).

[69] W. Prosser, Law of Torts 782 (4th ed 1971).

[70] *Id* 988.

[71] 440 US 391 (1979).

[72] US Const art I, §10, cl 3.

did not bar suits in federal court against the planning agency[73] and also suggested that the agency was a suable person under its decision in *Monell v Department of Social Services*.[74]

Finally, the Court held that the individual officers of the interstate planning agency were absolutely immune from §1983 damages liability for actions taken in their legislative (as distinct from executive) capacities. Repeating *Tenney v Brandhove*'s assertion that "[o]ne must not expect uncommon courage even in legislators,"[75] the Court reasoned that it was for the public good that regional legislators, as well as federal and state legislators, be protected by an absolute immunity. It then remanded for determination of whether the defendants acted in a legislative capacity, that is, "in a capacity comparable to that of members of a state legislature."

Justices Brennan, Marshall, and Blackmun dissented on the immunity issue and argued that the individual defendants should not have *Tenney*'s absolute immunity protection. Justice Blackmun specifically questioned whether the defendants were even properly characterizable as "regional legislators":

> Their duties are not solely legislative; they possess some executive powers. They are not in equipoise with other branches of government, and the concept of separation of powers has no relevance to them. They are not subject to the responsibility and the brake of the electoral process. And there is no provision for discipline within the body, as the Houses of Congress and the state legislatures possess.[76]

As to the relevance of *Lake Country Estates* for the immunity of local legislators, the Court expressly left that question open. However, Justice Marshall in his dissent was probably correct in asserting that "the majority's reasoning in this case leaves little room to argue that municipal legislators stand on a different footing than their regional counterparts."[77] The Court applied a functional test for absolute immunity to the defendants in *Lake Country Estates*, a test which, if applied to the legislative acts of local legislators, would in all likelihood lead to the same result. Also, the Court paid minimal attention to §1983 policy and the fact that expansion of the category of absolutely immune defendants flies in the face of §1983's *person* language. This reading of *Lake Country Estates* thus suggests that the Court will eventually confer absolute immunity on legislators at all governmental levels for their legislative acts.[78]

---

[73] See **§5.08** on the Eleventh Amendment.

[74] 436 US 658 (1978). The Court's suggestion appears in *Lake Country Estates*, 440 US at 405 n 29.

[75] 341 US 367 (1951). *See* **§§7.02-7.04.**

[76] 440 US at 408-09.

[77] *Id.*

[78] See **§7.03** on protected legislative conduct. Note the functional approach used by the Court in Butz v Economou, 438 US 478 (1978) in connection with the quasi-judicial and quasi-prosecutorial acts of federal executives in federal agency adjudicatory proceedings. *See* **§7.10.**

Indeed, this is how the circuits have read and responded to *Lake Country Estates*. Where legislative acts are involved, such as the passing of an ordinance[79] or reducing the number of liquor licenses,[80] then absolute immunity has been conferred. Several circuits have even conferred absolute immunity of city executives when they act in a legislative capacity, for example, by vetoing an ordinance.[81] However, the circuits have been struggling to develop standards by which to distinguish between legislative acts entitled to absolute immunity and nonlegislative acts of local legislators protected only by qualified immunity. For example, the First Circuit[82] confronted a developer's suit against the defendant members of a town planning board for their alleged imposition, for ethnically discriminatory reasons, of "outrageous" conditions upon his subdivision. Ruling that the defendants were not protected by absolute immunity, the court emphasized that no general policy or overall plan was challenged—these would be legislative in nature—and plaintiff also did not challenge any sanction for violation of a plan, permit, or license—this would be adjudicatory in nature. Instead, the challenged conduct was administrative in nature and related to the defendants' insistence that a particular road be completed before they approved a proposed subdivision. This decision was administrative because, first, it was not based on legislative facts and, second, its impact was not general but instead particularized.

Similarly, where plaintiff, a real estate developer, sued various defendants, including members of a city council, for conspiracy in violating various constitutional rights, the Fourth Circuit[83] held that the city council members were not protected by absolute legislative immunity. Applying a functional test, the court observed that the council's actions in directing the withholding of plaintiff's building permit were considered under state law as "functionally in the nature of executive review of a special building permit application" and thus not within the range of "legitimate legislative duties." It said: "When local zoning officials do more than adopt prospective, legislative-type rules and take the next step into the area of enforcement, they can claim only the executive qualified immunity appropriate to that activity."

Another example is a Ninth Circuit decision[84] involving a damages suit against city council members for allegedly violating plaintiff's First Amendment rights by denying entertainers access to a public forum through rejection of six proposed rock concerts. After acknowledging that local legislators have absolute immunity from suits based on their legislative acts, the court nevertheless ruled that the defendants were not absolutely immune. It stated:

---

[79] Aitchison v Raffiani, 708 F2d 96 (3d Cir 1983); Hernandez v City of Lafayette, 643 F2d 1188 (5th Cir 1981); Bruce v Riddle, 631 F2d 272 (4th Cir 1980); Gorman Towers v Bogoslavsky, 626 F2d 607 (8th Cir 1980).

[80] Reed v Village of Shorewood, 704 F2d 943 (7th Cir 1983).

[81] Aitchison v Raffiani, 708 F2d 96 (3d Cir 1983); Hernandez v City of Lafayette, 643 F2d 1188, 1194 (5th Cir 1981).

[82] Cutting v Muzzey, 724 F2d 259 (1st Cir 1984).

[83] Scott v Greenville County, 716 F2d 1409, 1423 (4th Cir 1983).

[84] Cinevision Corp v City of Burbank, 745 F2d 560 (9th Cir 1984).

[T]he City Council was simply monitoring and administering the contract by voting on the various proposed concerts. Administration of a municipal contract—a contract between a private party and a municipality —would generally seem to be an executive function . . . . Administration of a contract does not involve the formulation of policy "as a defined and binding rule of conduct." Rather, it is more the type of ad hoc decisionmaking engaged in by an executive.[85]

Just as local legislators are given the same absolute immunity protection from damages liability as their state counterparts, they are, like their state counterparts,[86] probably similarly protected by absolute immunity from injunctive relief for their legislative conduct. They should not, though, be protected by such absolute immunity for their law enforcement acts[87] or their administrative acts.[88]

§7.06   Judicial Immunity from Liability for Damages—*Pierson v Ray*

Pierson v Ray[89] established absolute judicial immunity from liability for damages under §1983. In *Pierson*, plaintiffs had been arrested by the defendant police officers in 1961 and then convicted and given the maximum sentence by the defendant municipal police justice for violating a Mississippi breach of the peace statute. This statute was held unconstitutional by the Supreme Court as applied to similar facts four years later[90] but prior to the Court's decision in *Pierson*. After plaintiffs had been vindicated in a trial de novo, they sued the defendants for damages under §1983 as well as for false arrest and imprisonment at common law.

In holding that the police justice was absolutely immune from liability for damages under §1983,[91] the Court compared judicial immunity at common law to legislative immunity. Following *Tenney's*[92] approach, the Court stated:

The legislative record gives no clear indication that Congress meant to abolish wholesale all common-law immunities. . . . The immunity of judges for acts within the judicial role is equally well established [as absolute legislative immunity], and we presume that Congress would have

---

[85] *Id* 580.

[86] Supreme Court v Consumers Union, 446 US 719 (1980), discussed at **§7.12**. *See also* **§7.03**.

[87] Fernandes v Limmer, 663 F2d 619 (5th Cir 1981).

[88] *Cf* Stanley v Magrath, 719 F2d 279 (8th Cir 1983).

[89] 386 US 547 (1967).

[90] Thomas v Mississippi, 380 US 524 (1965).

[91] The police officers' qualified immunity is discussed in **ch 8**.

[92] Tenney v Brandhove, 341 US 367 (1951).

specifically so provided had it wished to abolish the doctrine.[93]

As to the scope and application of the doctrine, the Court observed that the only act of the police justice was to find plaintiffs guilty. It then went on to hold that judges are absolutely immune from liability for damages

> for acts committed within their judicial jurisdiction. . . . even when the judge is accused of acting maliciously and corruptly. . . . It is a judge's duty to decide all cases within his judicial jurisdiction that are brought before him, including controversial cases that arouse the most intense feelings in the litigants. His errors may be corrected on appeal, but he should not have to fear that unsatisfied litigants may hound him with litigation charging malice or corruption. *Imposing such a burden on judges would contribute not to principled and fearless decision-making but to intimidation.*

Reading §1983 as excluding judges[95] is more open to question than reading it to exclude state legislators in *Tenney*. As Justice Douglas pointed out in dissent, the legislative history of §1983 and its criminal law model, now 18 USC §242, indicates that it is to apply to judges and that, indeed, "[i]t was recognized that certain members of the judiciary were instruments of oppression and were partially responsible for the wrongs to be remedied."[96] It has also been suggested that judicial immunity at common law was not so well established as the Court thought in *Pierson*, when contrasted with the history of legislative immunity set out in *Tenney*.[97]

Nevertheless, the result in *Pierson* was probably inevitable given *Tenney's* approach in reading §1983 against a common law immunity background. It is worth noting on this point that with few exception,[98] federal courts, especially after *Tenney*, and even before *Pierson*, began consistently to apply the doctrine of absolute judicial immunity.[99] Consequently, after *Pierson*, the question is no longer the existence of absolute judicial immunity, but rather its *scope*. When, if ever, does a judge lose this absolute judicial immunity? *Pierson*, a relatively

---

[93] 386 US at 554-55.

[94] *Id* 555 (emphasis added).

[95] There is no serious question as to Congress's power to impose criminal sanctions upon state judges for constitutional violations. *Ex parte* Virginia, 100 US 339 (1879). The same is true for civil liability. In *Pierson*, the question was one of congressional *intent*, not power.

[96] 386 US at 558, 559-63. He argues in effect for a qualified immunity for judges. *See also* Kates, *Immunity of State Judges Under the Federal Civil Rights Act: Pierson v. Ray Reconsidered*, 65 Nw UL Rev 615 (1970).

[97] *See* Comment, *Liability of Judicial Officers Under Section 1983*, 79 Yale LJ 322, 325 (1969); Note, *Developments in the Law–Section 1983 and Federalism*, 90 Harv L Rev 1133, 1201 (1977).

[98] One early exception was Picking v Pennsylvania RR, 151 F2d 240 (3d Cir 1945), *overruled in*, Bauers v Heisel, 361 F2d 581 (3d Cir 1966), *cert denied*, 386 US 1021 (1967).

[99] So noted in *Pierson*, 386 US at 547 n 9.

easy case which involved a judge who acted in the most traditional judicial capacity, held, not surprisingly, that a judge acts within his or her judicial jurisdiction even in applying a statute unconstitutionally.

§7.07 —The Scope of Judicial Immunity: *Bradley v Fisher* and *Stump v Sparkman*

Bradley v Fisher

Pierson[100] was a relatively easy case in which to find that the police justice acted within his *judicial jurisdiction*. This term comes from *Bradley v Fisher*,[101] an 1871 Supreme Court decision cited with approval in *Pierson*, in which a criminal court judge of the District of Columbia was sued for damages by a lawyer whom he removed from practice before his court without notice and the opportunity to defend. The Court elaborately set out the general rules:

> [J]udges of courts of superior or general jurisdiction are not liable to civil actions for their judicial acts, even when such acts are in excess of their jurisdiction, and are alleged to have been done maliciously or corruptly. *A distinction must be here observed between excess of jurisdiction and the clear absence of all jurisdiction over the subject-matter. Where there is clearly no jurisdiction over the subject-matter any authority exercised is a usurped authority, and for the exercise of such authority, when the want of jurisdiction is known to the judge, no excuse is permissible. But where jurisdiction over the subject-matter is invested by law in the judge, or in the court which he holds, the manner and extent in which the jurisdiction shall be exercised are generally as much questions for his determination as any other questions involved in the case, although upon the correctness of his determination in these particulars the validity of his judgments may depend.* Thus, if a probate court, invested only with authority over wills and the settlement of estates of deceased persons, should proceed to try parties for public offences, jurisdiction over the subject of offences being entirely wanting in the court, and this being necessarily known to its judge, his commission would afford no protection to him in the exercise of the usurped authority. But if on the other hand a judge of a criminal court, invested with general criminal jurisdiction over offences committed within a certain district, should hold a particular act to be a public offence, which is not by the law made an offence, and proceed to the arrest and trial of a party charged with such act, or should sentence a party convicted to a greater punishment than that authorized by the law upon its proper construction, no personal liability to civil action for such acts would attach to the judge, although those acts would be in excess of his jurisdiction, or of the jurisdiction of the court held by him, for these *are particulars for his judicial consideration, whenever his general jurisdiction over the subject-matter is invoked.*

---

[100] Pierson v Ray, 386 US 547 (1967).
[101] 80 US 335 (1871). *Bradley* is, of course, not a §1983 case.

> Indeed some of the most difficult and embarrassing questions which a judicial officer is called upon to consider and determine relate to his jurisdiction, or that of the court held by him, or the manner in which the jurisdiction shall be exercised. And the same principle of exemption from liability which obtains for errors committed in the ordinary prosecution of a suit where there is *jurisdiction of both subject and person,* applies in cases of this kind, and for the same reasons.[102]

In applying these principles to the facts before it, the Supreme Court in *Bradley* observed that, while the defendant judge had the power to remove a lawyer from the bar, this should not ordinarily be done without notice and an opportunity to explain and defend. Nevertheless, even though the defendant judge erred in not giving plaintiff such notice, this action constituted at most an excess of jurisdiction but "did not make the act any less a judicial act. . . . It was not as though the court had proceeded without any jurisdiction whatever over its attorneys."[103] Thus, the defendant judge was absolutely immune from liability for damages for the allegedly wrongful disbarment.

Several points should be emphasized. Most striking is the Court's distinction between *excess of jurisdiction* and the *clear absence of all jurisdiction* over the subject matter. Second, the Court mentioned subject matter jurisdiction several times, but mentioned jurisdiction over the person only once. In *Bradley* itself, it would appear that while the defendant judge may not have given the plaintiff notice of the disbarment, the judge did have personal jurisdiction over the plaintiff. This was so even though the jury in the case in which plaintiff and defendant were involved had already been discharged. However, the relevance of personal jurisdiction, an issue that has recently emerged in the circuits,[104] is nowhere made clear.

The Court's two examples are intriguing. One is a probate judge who tries criminal offenses, acting, according to *Bradley,* in clear absence of all jurisdiction. The Court may have intimated that the probate judge's state of mind is relevant to a finding of clear absence of all jurisdiction, because at one point it described this clear absence as "necessarily known" to the probate judge, and at another similarly qualified its clear absence rule by adding "when the want of jurisdiction is known to the judge." The Court seemed to be setting up a test for judicial immunity containing both objective and subjective elements: the judge must know of a clear absence of subject matter jurisdiction which exists in fact before immunity is lost.

The Court's other example concerns a judge with general criminal jurisdiction who either convicts a person of an act which is not in fact criminal or who gives a person an unauthorized sentence. This judge, according to the Court, has only acted in excess of jurisdiction and has not lost judicial immunity. The

---

[102] *Id* 351-52 (emphasis added). Because of its importance to the analysis which follows and its continuing importance even after Stump v Sparkman, 435 US 349 (1978), also discussed in **§7.07,** the quote from *Bradley* is set out quite extensively.

[103] 80 US at 357.

[104] *See* the discussion at **§7.09.**

puzzling aspect is why the Court characterized this mistake as jurisdictional, when it appears to be an error of law going to the merits. Further, if it is somehow jurisdictional, suppose the judge actually knows that the act is not a crime or that the sentence is unauthorized. Is this an act in clear absence of jurisdiction?

Pierson retained the jurisdictional language of *Bradley* in holding that the police justice acted within his *judicial jurisdiction.* Indeed, as mentioned, applying the *Bradley* approach in *Pierson* poses no serious problems because the police justice clearly had both subject matter jurisdiction and personal jurisdiction. Using *Bradley*'s terms he acted at most only in excess of his jurisdiction when he convicted the plaintiffs under an unconstitutionally applied statute. However, the failure of the *Pierson* court even to inquire whether he knowingly did so suggests that a judge's state of mind is irrelevant at the time of making a legal error. The judge will not lose absolute immunity regardless of any alleged state of mind, and will still have acted only in excess of jurisdiction in *Bradley*'s terms.[105] Such a result seems consistent with the emphasis in both *Brandley* and *Pierson* on preventing litigants from challenging a judge's motivation and on encouraging resort instead to the appellate process to correct legal errors.

Following the *Bradley-Pierson* jurisdictional approach, circuit courts, in pre-*Stump v Sparkman*[106] decisions, held absolute judicial immunity applicable to the following §1983 allegations:

1. A judge who presided at a burglary trial conspired with others in order to suppress certain exonerating information in a police report[107]

2. A judge improperly imprisoned a traffic court defendant for contempt for refusing to answer a prosecutor's questions on the ground of self-incrimination[108]

3. A justice of the peace wrongfully entered a default order evicting plaintiff because the summons contained an erroneous return date[109]

---

[105] The Mississippi statute involved in *Pierson* was, it is true, held unconstitutional as applied to similar facts only after the police justice convicted the plaintiffs. However, the Supreme Court, in Boynton v Virginia, 364 US 454 (1960), had also *previously* held a similar statute unconstitutional as applied to "virtually identical" facts. *Boynton* was apparently brought to the timely attention of the police justice. *See* Kates, *Immunity of State Judges Under the Federal Civil Rights Acts: Pierson v. Ray Reconsidered,* 65 Nw UL Rev 615 (1970).

[106] 435 US 349 (1978), discussed later in this section.

[107] Barnes v Dorsey, 480 F2d 1057 (8th Cir 1973). The court stated that the judge acted withing the scope of his judicial authority.

[108] Berg v Cwiklinski, 416 F2d 929 (7th Cir 1969). The court first noted that the judge had subject matter jurisdiction and therefore a general power to hold a defendant in contempt. The judge, however, had no authority to do what he did. "But however erroneous [he] was in thinking that he had the power . . . he was nevertheless in performance of his judicial duties." *Id* 931.

[109] Mississippi *ex rel* Giles v Thomas, 464 F2d 156 (5th Cir 1972). The court simply asserted that the justices of the peace had absolute immunity.

4.   A judge ordered the plaintiff committed under a repealed statute[110]

5.   A judge, following a trial and the plaintiff's disparaging comments about him to a crowd outside the courtroom, had plaintiff, an attorney, brought back into the courtroom, threatened him with bodily harm and jail, and forced him to retract his earlier comments[111]

6.   A judge issued a warrant for the arrest of plaintiff for committing an act which was not a criminal offense[112]

7.   A judge indicted plaintiff on a baseless charge and participated in a settlement conference at a lawyer's office with the parties, all with the purpose of destroying plaintiff's business[113]

8.   A judge from one county who specially presided over plaintiff's criminal trial (resulting in his conviction) in another county improperly issued an order for his arrest and commitment under the seal of the first county and also improperly imprisoned him for a crime which carried no prison sentence[114]

9.   A probate judge caused emotional distress when he improperly denied plaintiff custody of her minor son[115]

10. A justice of the peace maliciously ordered the attachment and sale of plaintiff's entire stock of hogs on the pretext of satisfying a $55 misdemeanor fine[116]

11. A judge violated plaintiff's civil rights by convicting him for possession of narcotics paraphernalia[117]

---

[110] Robinson v McCorkle, 462 F2d 111 (3d Cir), *cert denied*, 409 US 1042 (1972). The court said that even if the statute were assumed to be repealed, this judicial error would not eliminate absolute immunity protection.

[111] Dean v Shirer, 547 F2d 227 (4th Cir 1976). The court found that the judge still retained subject matter jurisdiction over the case and that his acts were judicial acts because they were part of his exercise of the contempt power.

[112] Keeton v Guedry, 544 F2d 199 (5th Cir 1976) (per curiam). The plaintiff's act was stopping payment on a check after he discovered that a purchased truck had defects. The court emphasized that the judge "clearly believed that criminal conduct possibly had occurred."

[113] Smith v Martin, 542 F2d 688 (6th Cir 1976) (per curiam), *cert denied*, 97 S Ct 1697 (1977).

[114] Wiggins v Hess, 531 F2d 920 (8th Cir 1976) (per curiam). The court said without explanation that plaintiff's allegations were insufficient to state a claim that the judge acted in the clear absence of jurisdiction.

[115] Harley v Oliver, 539 F2d 1143 (8th Cir 1976). The court observed that the judge had statutory jurisdiction over guardianships.

[116] Duba v McIntyre, 501 F2d 590 (8th Cir 1974), *cert denied*, 424 US 975 (1976). The court, while conceding that the justice of the peace acted in excess of jurisdiction, still held that his acts were within the general power of judges to issue executions to recover fines imposed for violations of municipal ordinances.

[117] Connor v Pickett, 552 F2d 585 (5th Cir 1977) (per curiam). The court said the case before it was clearly controlled by *Pierson*.

12. A justice of the peace improperly denied bail to plaintiff[118]

13. A judge conspired with the prosecutor and defense counsel during plea bargaining to deny plaintiff effective assistance of counsel[119]

14. A judge conspired to confine plaintiff to a mental institution even though he was not convicted of any crime and was sane[120]

15. A judge improperly attached certain conditions to plaintiff's bail[121]

16. A judge improperly withheld information regarding plaintiff's illegal extradition from Canada, thereby resulting in his imprisonment[122]

The results in these cases are consistent with the *Bradley-Pierson* jurisdictional approach. In all of them the courts had both personal jurisdiction over the plaintiff and subject matter jurisdiction over the disputed issues (including contempt). At most, these cases involved errors of fact or law which constituted what *Bradley* would call an excess of jurisdiction. Thus, these cases tell us relatively little more about the scope of judicial immunity than could reasonably be inferred from *Bradley v Fisher*.[123]

Somewhat more helpful in evaluating the proper scope of judicial immunity are those few pre-*Stump v Sparkman*[124] cases in which courts held that judges did lose their absolute immunity. A Sixth Circuit decision, *Lucarell v McNair*,[125] held that a plaintiff alleging that a juvenile court referee illegally incarcerated him in connection with traffic court proceedings stated a cause of action; the referee acted *in absence of all jurisdiction* because, according to the complaint, he lacked power to incarcerate under state law.[126] A similar and

---

[118] Grundstrom v Darnell, 531 F2d 272 (5th Cir 1976) (per curiam). The court noted that the justice of the peace had subject matter jurisdiction and was to be treated like any other judge.

[119] Humble v Foreman, 563 F2d 780 (5th Cir 1977) (per curiam). The court simply cited *Pierson*.

[120] Franklin v Meredith, 386 F2d 958 (10th Cir 1967). The court held the judge absolutely immune after pointing out that he had continuing jurisdiction over the plaintiff under state law.

[121] Jacobson v Schaefer, 441 F2d 127 (7th Cir 1971). Although the judge did not in fact have the authority to do what he did, the court emphasized that he had general jurisdiction over the subject matter.

[122] Waits v McGowan, 516 F2d 203 (3d Cir 1975). The court summarily affirmed the judge's dismissal.

[123] See, however, the discussion later of the Supreme Court's most recent judicial immunity case, Stump v Sparkman, 435 US 1099 (1978).

[124] 435 US 349 (1978), discussed later in this section.

[125] 453 F2d 836 (6th Cir 1972).

[126] The court emphasized that it relied solely on the complaint and thus it did not have to reach the issue of the scope of the defendant's contempt power. The court also did not discuss the assault contention in connection with immunity. See, however, Gregory v Thompson, 500 F2d 59 (9th Cir 1974), cited with apparent approval in Stump v Sparkman, 435 US 349, 361 n 16 (1978) where the court characterized such an act as not of a judicial nature and denied absolute immunity to the defendant. In *Gregory* the court said:

once much cited Ohio district court case, *Wade v Bethesda Hospital*,[127] involved a §1983 claim against a probate judge who allegedly conspired with others to sterilize plaintiff. In considering whether the defendant acted outside the scope of his jurisdiction, the court set out the following three-pronged test:

> The cases are clear that the term jurisdiction means that the judge must have both [1] jurisdiction over the person and [2] subject matter if he is to be immune from suit for an act performed in his judicial capacity. . . . [3] A third element . . . [which] enters into the concept of jurisdiction . . . is the power of the Court to render the particular decision which was given . . . [that is] whether the defendant's action is authorized by any set of conditions or circumstances.[128]

After finding that no Ohio statute authorized a judge to order sterilization for any purpose and no judicial precedent for such an order existed absent a specific statute, the court concluded: "Because there was no set of circumstances or conditions under Ohio law which would permit defendant Gary to order plaintiff to submit to sterilization, the Court determines that defendant Gary acted wholly without jurisdiction in this matter. Consequently, defendant Gary is not protected by the doctrine of judicial immunity."[129]

Lucarell and *Wade* seem to go beyond the *Bradley-Pierson* approach in regarding the defendant judges as acting in clear absence of jurisdiction. First, the courts apparently considered these cases' fact situations to be substantially similar to *Bradley*'s example of a probate judge who tries criminal cases, and substantially different from the other *Bradley* example of a criminal court judge who either convicts a person of an act which is not a crime or imposes an unauthorized sentence upon a person. Why this is so is unclear, however, since the incarceration in *Lucarell* might be termed an unauthorized sentence and the sterilization in *Wade* might be termed an illegal order. Unlike the *Bradley* probate judge example, these judges had the power to do something with the plaintiffs in areas related to the reasons that brought the plaintiffs before the defendants.[130]

Thus, *Lucarell* and *Wade* appear in fact to be cases where the judges acted in excess of their jurisdiction and not in clear absence of it. To put it another way, the errors made by these judges as to their powers in the particular cases before them should not necessarily be seen as acts in clear absence of jurisdiction. As

---

> The decision to personally evict someone from a courtroom by the use of physical force is simply not an act of a judicial nature, and is not such as to require insulation in order that the decision be deliberately reached . . . [W]hen a judge exercises physical force in a courtroom, his decision is not amenable to appellate correction. 500 F2d at 64.

[127] 337 F Supp 671 (SD Ohio 1971), *reconsideration of motion to dismiss denied*, 356 F Supp 380 (SD Ohio 1973).

[128] 337 F Supp at 673.

[129] *Id* 674.

[130] In *Lucarell*, the defendant could have fined the plaintiff; in *Wade*, there was a statute giving the defendant general subject matter jurisdiction over mentally retarded persons.

Bradley itself recognized, "some of the most difficult and embarrassing questions" for a judge involve issues of jurisdiction and powers.[131] This was also acknowledged in a Second Circuit decision dealing with a claim based upon plaintiff's conviction of assault by a justice of the peace who did not have subject matter jurisdiction over this offense.[132] In holding that absolute immunity attached, the court said: "Where jurisdiction depends on the resolution of factual issues or involves debatable questions of law judges do not lose their immunity . . . [E]xceptions must be confined to situations in which it is perfectly clear that the court acted wholly without jurisdiction."[133]

Stump v Sparkman

That a judge with general subject matter jurisdiction loses absolute immunity in erring grossly and issuing an unauthorized order—the proposition associated with *Lucarell* and *Wade*—was thus questionable even before the Supreme Court's 1978 decision in *Stump v Sparkman*.[134] After *Stump,* which reversed a Seventh Circuit decision holding that the judge had lost his absolute immunity, it is clearly untenable. *Stump* involved the question, reminiscent of *Wade,* of the judicial immunity of a judge who ordered the sterilization of a 15-year-old girl, Linda, upon her mother's petition.[135] The facts in *Stump* apparently shocked the Seventh Circuit which noted that the order was issued "in an ex parte proceeding. No guardian ad litem was appointed to represent Linda's interests and no hearing was held. Linda received no notice of the petition and neither the petition nor the order was ever filed in the DeKalb County Circuit Court."[136]

Applying the *Bradley-Pierson* test, the Seventh Circuit reversed the district court and found that the defendant had acted in clear absence of subject matter jurisdiction. It made this finding even though the Circuit Court of DeKalb County was by statute a court having "original, exclusive jurisdiction in all cases at law and in equity." In order for the judge's act to come within the statute, the court said, "it must have a statutory or common law basis."[137] After examining Indiana law, the court found no such basis. Further, it presented two arguments in rejecting the defendant's stand that he was exercising his power to fashion new common law. First, judges "may not use the power to create new decisional law to order extreme and irreversible remedies such as sterilization in situations where the legislative branch of government has indicated that they are inappropriate . . . [Otherwise] we would be sanctioning

---

[131] Bradley v Fisher, 80 US 335, 352 (1871).

[132] Fanale v Sheehy, 385 F2d 866 (2d Cir 1967).

[133] *Id* 868.

[134] Stump v Sparkman, 435 US 349 (1978), *revg* Sparkman v McFarlin, 552 F2d 172 (7th Cir 1977).

[135] Plaintiff was not told the true reason for her hospitalization. Instead, a pretext was used.

[136] 552 F2d at 173.

[137] *Id* 174.

tyranny from the bench."[138] Alternatively, the Court described the defendant's exercise of his common law power as illegitimate "because of his failure to comply with elementary principles of procedural due process."[139]

The Supreme Court, in an opinion by Justice White, reversed. As it had in *Pierson*, the Court cited *Bradley* for its approach distinguishing between excess of jurisdiction and the clear absence of all jurisdiction. It then mentioned the difficult nature of jurisdictional questions and concluded: "[W]e cannot agree that there was a 'clear absence of all jurisdiction' in the DeKalb County Circuit Court to consider the petition presented by Mrs. McFarlin."[140] In reaching this conclusion, the Court mentioned the broad jurisdictional grant and, turning the Seventh Circuit's argument around, observed that "there was no Indiana statute and no case law in 1971 prohibiting a circuit court, a court of general jurisdiction, from considering a petition of the type presented to Judge Stump."[141] The Court, citing *Bradley* again, also rejected the Seventh Circuit's due process argument as "misconceiv[ing] the doctrine of judicial immunity. A judge is absolutely immune from liability for his judicial acts even if his exercise of authority is flawed by the commission of grave procedural errors."[142] In short, the Court broadly construed the scope of the judge's jurisdiction because "the issue is the immunity of the judge."[143]

The Court then considered and rejected an argument that the judge was nevertheless not entitled to immunity because the informality of his approval of the petition kept it from being a "judicial act."[144] Noting that this was the first time such an issue had ever been before it in connection with judicial immunity, the Court agreed that judicial immunity would only attach to a judicial act. Relying on one of its own decisions in a different type of case[145] and on several circuit court decisions,[146] the Court stated:

---

[138] *Id* 176.

[139] *Id.*

[140] 435 US 349 at 357.

[141] *Id* 358.

[142] *Id* 359.

[143] *Id* 356.

[144] "[T]he petition was not given a docket number, was not placed on file with the clerk's office, and was approved in an *ex parte* proceeding without notice to the minor, without a hearing, and without the appointment of a *guardian ad litem*." *Id* 360.

[145] *In re* Summers, 325 US 561 (1945), in which the Court held that the lack of formality involved in a state court's consideration of an application for admission to the bar did not prevent it from presenting a case or controversy reviewable by the Court.

[146] Gregory v Thompson, 500 F2d 59 (1974), where a judge's physical assault upon plaintiff was held not to be a judicial act; McAlester v Brown, 469 F2d 1280 (5th Cir 1972), where the judge was entitled to judicial immunity even though he had plaintiffs arrested (in the apparent exercise of his contempt power) when he was not in his robes, not in the courtroom, and in apparent violation of procedural requirements for contempt citations; Lynch v Johnson, 420 F2d 818 (6th Cir 1970), where a judge serving on a board with only legislative and administrative powers was not acting in a judicial capacity.

> [T]he factors determining whether an act by a judge is a "judicial" one
> relate to the nature of the act itself, i.e., whether it is a function usually
> performed by a judge, and to the expectations of the parties, i.e., whether
> they dealt with the judge in his judicial capacity.[147]

Applying these factors to the facts before it, the Court concluded that despite
the informality of the proceedings and their ex parte nature, the approval of
the petition was a judicial act and hence protected.

Justices Stewart, Marshall, and Powell dissented, arguing that what the judge
did "was beyond the pale of anything that could sensibly be called a judicial
act."[148] They criticized the factors used by the majority in determining what
constitutes a judicial act, and contended that the meaning of the term derives
from those considerations set out in *Pierson* supporting absolute immunity in
the first place. In this case,

> there was no "case," controversial or otherwise. There were no litigants.
> There was and could be no appeal. And there was not even the pretext
> of principled decisionmaking. [There was a] total absence of *any* of these
> normal attributes of a judicial proceeding. . . . [Thus] the conduct
> complained of . . . was not a judicial act.[149]

Justice Powell emphasized what he considered central: defendant's "preclusion
of any possibility for the vindication of [plaintiff's] rights elsewhere in the
judicial system." He added that the major reason for absolute immunity is the
existence of "alternative forums and methods for vindicating [private] rights,"
and that absent such forums, "the underlying asumption of the *Bradley* doctrine
is inoperative."[150]

Stump indicates clearly that the *Lucarell* and *Wade* cases were incorrectly
decided: in both those cases, there was general subject matter jurisdiction and
the defendants' acts were judicial in nature under the *Stump* majority's
reasoning. However, in continuing to use the *jurisdiction* approach of *Bradley* and
Pierson, the Court did little to clarify the factors which distinguish *excess of
jurisdiction* from *clear absence of all jurisdiction* and the confusing relation between
those two concepts and the merits. In any event, since the Court addressed the
judicial act question in *Stump,* the inquiry into judicial immunity has now
become roughly parallel to the inquiry into legislative immunity. The first
question is one of status: is defendant a legislator or a judge?[151] Next, did the
legislator or judge act with *jurisdiction*: did the legislator act in a traditional
legislative field or did the judge act with or in excess of jurisdiction? Finally,

---

[147] 435 US at 362.

[148] *Id* 365.

[149] *Id* 368-69.

[150] *Id* 369-70.

[151] Note, however, that under a functional approach, there are occasions where a
nonlegislator is protected by absolute legislative immunity—see §§7.03-7.05—and a
nonjudge is protected by absolute judicial immunity—see §7.10.

and closely related to the second inquiry: is what the legislator did a legislative act[152] or is what the judge did a judicial act? Thus, despite the *jurisdiction* jargon of the judicial immunity cases, the same general kinds of questions are being asked in determining both legislative and judicial immunity.

However, what is especially disturbing about *Stump* is the Court's failure[153] to answer Justice Powell's point about alternative forums becoming unavailable to plaintiff as a result of the judge's conduct. Where there is a physical assault by a judge upon a person, an act which the Court agreed is not a judicial act, there is no alternative forum available to the injured person to stop the judge; the damage has already been done. Thus, it makes sense to hold that there is no judicial immunity. In *Stump*, the sterilization of plaintiff was the equivalent of a physical assault for which there was also no recourse. In both cases the remedy could only be retrospective. For this reason, both acts were similarly not functions "normally performed by a judge," contrary to the majority's characterization of the judge's approval of the petition.

In this light, *Stump's* message is clear: it will be a rare case indeed in which a judge will lose absolute immunity. The Court may be saying about judges what it said long ago about the immunity under federal law of the Postmaster General:

> As in the case of a judicial officer, we recognize a distinction between action taken by the head of a Department in reference to matters which are manifestly or palpably beyond his authority, and *action having more or less connection with the general matters committed by law to his control or supervision.*[154]

§7.08 —The Scope of Judicial Immunity in the Circuits

In the circuits, there have been numerous judicial immunity cases applying *Stump*. Many of these cases involved relatively straightforward applications of *Stump's* pro-immunity jurisdiction and judicial act criteria. For example, absolute immunity has been conferred upon judges accused of improperly

---

[152] See §7.03 on protected legislative conduct.

[153] The Court, 435 US at 361 n 10 mentions the issuance of search warrants as an example of an ex parte proceeding without recourse to appeal. However, while the issuance cannot be undone by appeal, its adverse effect, if any, can be by a motion to suppress. This sharply distinguishes search warrants from the ex parte approval of the sterilization petition in *Stump*.

[154] Spalding v Vilas, 161 US 483, 498 (1896) (emphasis added). Consider, though, the Supreme Court's decision in *Dennis v Sparks*, 449 US 24 (1980), discussed at §2.10, where the Court held that a private person who conspires with an absolutely immune judge acts under color of law and is unprotected by the judge's absolute immunity from §1983 damages liability. In the course of its opinion, the Court noted that one result of its holding in *Dennis* is that judges will occasionally be called upon to testify in third-party civil proceedings in explanation and defense of their judicial conduct.

instructing a court reporter to alter the record of a criminal trial;[155] "maliciously" signing a criminal arrest warrant;[156] ordering the plaintiff arrested while he, the judge, was not in his courtroom;[157] conspiring to frame plaintiff, improperly setting bond and ordering court reporters to alter a trial transcript;[158] amending a criminal sentence while plaintiff's appeal was pending;[159] appointing an attorney to represent plaintiff at a criminal drunk driving trial, accepting the entry of a guilty plea, and assessing a fine;[160] singling out a juror at a murder trial in open court as having been the only juror to vote against the death penalty;[161] delaying for four years a ruling on a petition for postconviction relief;[162] and commenting from the bench and in chambers, suggesting that a party in a divorce proceeding before him obtain a vasectomy in order to get a favorable property settlement.[163]

On a related procedural issue, and reflecting its impatience with loosely drafted complaints, the Fifth Circuit[164] in a judicial immunity case insisted, after considerable discussion of relevant provisions of the Federal Rules of Civil Procedure:

> Once a complaint against a defendant state legislator, judge, or prosecutor (or similar officer) adequately raises the likely issue of [absolute] immunity the district court should on its own require of the plaintiff a detailed complaint alleging with particularity all material facts on which he contends he will establish his right to recovery, which will include detailed facts supporting the contention that the plea of immunity cannot be sustained.

Despite such obstacles for plaintiffs, there are important circuit court decisions which hold that absolute judicial immunity is inappropriate. For example, in a Fifth Circuit decision,[165] a judge sued for conducting contempt

---

[155] Green v Maraio, 722 F2d 1013 (2d Cir 1983).

[156] Heimbach v Village of Lyons, 597 F2d 344 (2d Cir 1979) (per curiam).

[157] Watson v Interstate Fire & Casualty Co, 611 F2d 120 (5th Cir 1980). *See also* Adams v McIlhany, 764 F2d 294 (5th Cir 1985).

[158] Slavin v Curry, 574 F2d 1256 (5th Cir 1978).

[159] Billingsley v Kyser, 691 F2d 388 (8th Cir 1982) (per curiam).

[160] Birch v Mazander, 678 F2d 754 (8th Cir 1982).

[161] Emory v Peeler, 756 F2d 1547 (11th Cir 1985).

[162] Lowe v Letsinger, 772 F2d 308 (7th Cir 1985).

[163] Scott v Hayes, 719 F2d 1562 (11th Cir 1983).

[164] Elliott v Perez, 751 F2d 1472, 1482 (5th Cir 1985). See §1.16 on notice pleading in federal court litigation.

[165] Harper v Merkle, 638 F2d 848, 859 (5th Cir 1981). Cf Ammons v Baldwin, 705 F2d 1445 (5th Cir 1983), applying, as did *Harper*, a four-part test:

1.   Was the offending conduct a normal judicial function?
2.   Did it occur in a court room or chambers?
3.   Did it involve a case pending before the judge?
4.   Did it arise out of a visit to the judge in his official capacity?

However, not all four factors need be present for judicial immunity to apply. Holloway v Walker, 756 F2d 517 (5th Cir 1985).

proceedings against plaintiff and ordering him incarcerated was not protected by absolute immunity because those were not judicial acts. The controversy leading to plaintiff's incarceration was not, in any way, pending before the defendant. Rather, plaintiff's domestic problems were brought to defendant's attention in a social, not judicial, forum. Also, plaintiff did not visit defendant in his official capacity, but was seeking only his former wife. Thus, even though the defendant's finding plaintiff in contempt was a normal judicial function which took place in the judge's chambers, defendant's actions were not judicial acts under the *Stump v Sparkman* test. However, after stating that it was not reaching the question of whether the defendant had acted in *complete absence of jurisdiction,* the Fifth Circuit emphasized the narrowness of its holding:

> [W]e hold only that when it is beyond reasonable dispute that a judge has acted out of personal motivation and has used his judicial office as an offensive weapon to vindicate personal objectives, and it further appears certain that no party has invoked the judicial machinery for any purpose at all, then the judge's actions do not amount to "judicial acts."

In another Fifth Circuit[166] case, the court reversed the district court's directed verdict for the defendant justice of the peace and remanded. While the defendant's issuance of an arrest warrant based on an officer's affidavit was a protected judicial act, the following alleged conduct was not:

1. Defendant's arrest of plaintiffs at a dump; justices of the peace had no arrest powers and, in any event, the plaintiffs were not arrested in the defendant's official quarters
2. Defendant's pursuit of plaintiffs in his private automobile
3. The "trial" of plaintiffs by defendant on criminal charges; justices of the peace had jurisdiction only over minor civil cases, and thus defendant's alleged conduct was in clear absence of jurisdiction

Two important Seventh Circuit decisions demonstrate the need to distinguish in the same case between those acts protected by absolute judicial immunity and those not so protected. The first[167] involved, in the words of the Seventh Circuit,

> the scope of judicial immunity to be afforded . . . to a judge who engaged in highly irregular conduct. On the night of October 16, 1975, defendant Vanderwater, then an Illinois judge, arrested plaintiff Flor Lopez, caused him to be charged with petty theft, convicted him on the basis of a guilty plea that is alleged to have been forged, and sentenced him to jail for 240 days. Vanderwater accomplished all this with minimal aid from a business

---

[166] Brewer v Blackwell, 692 F2d 387 (5th Cir 1982). *See also* Crowe v Lucas, 595 F2d 985 (5th Cir 1979) where a judge was found to have acted to maintain order at a meeting while in his other capacity as an alderman.

[167] Lopez v Vanderwater, 620 F2d 1229 (7th Cir 1980).

associate and several police officers; he proceeded without the assistance of a prosecutor, a defense attorney, a court reporter, or a court clerk. The conviction took place near midnight in a police station in Aurora, Illinois.[168]

After noting that the defendant had general jurisdiction except in felony cases, the Seventh Circuit rejected plaintiff's argument that defendant, in arraigning, convicting, and sentencing, acted in *clear absence of all jurisdiction* because he acted outside a courtroom and had not been assigned to sit in Aurora or to hear the case. First, judicial acts are frequently performed outside the courtroom. Second, even though it was unclear under state law whether the assignment requirement was jurisdictional, at the most the defendant acted in excess of jurisdiction, not in its clear absence. As to the latter point, the Seventh Circuit compared the defendant's conduct to the protected conduct of a criminal court judge "who invents a crime and convicts someone of it" and distinguished it from the unprotected conduct of a probate judge who conducts a criminal trial.[169]

Further, the court concluded that the irregular arraignment, conviction, and sentence were judicial acts under the *Stump v Sparkman* criterion of functions usually performed by a judge. A second criterion—whether the parties dealt with the judge in his judicial capacity—was found inapplicable. However, the defendant's prosecutorial acts—deciding to prosecute, determining the offense to be charged, preparing the written charge, the guilty plea, and the waiver of jury, and presenting the charge and plea form to himself—were not judicial acts and were therefore not protected by absolute judical immunity. Nor were those acts protected by absolute prosecutorial immunity because defendant made no such claim and was "obviously" not entitled to it because he was not a prosecutor.[170]

In the second case[171] involving a racially motivated campaign by a county judge to discredit and damage the plaintiff, a former police lieutenant, the Seventh Circuit affirmed the district court's judgment against the defendant judge and rejected his argument that absolute immunity was applicable to all his conduct. The challenged acts of defendant included repeated communications to the press and to city officials, over the period of a year, which were critical of plaintiff and demanded action against him. Also, many of these communications were made while plaintiff was awaiting trial on certain charges. Using the *Stump* test for judicial acts, the Seventh Circuit concluded that most of defendant's acts were undertaken in the *absence of all jurisdiction*: those acts were not functions normally performed by a judge, the parties did not deal with him in his judicial capacity as to those acts, and they occurred outside of his courtroom.

---

[168] *Id* 1231.

[169] *Id* 1234 n 8.

[170] *Id* 1237 n 17.

[171] Harris v Harvey, 605 F2d 330 (7th Cir 1979).

The court also held that while the defendant was indeed absolutely immune from liability in connection with his judicial conduct at a criminal hearing involving plaintiff—the jury had properly been so instructed—evidence of this conduct was admissible to show his state of mind and racial prejudice. It reasoned: "The doctrine of judicial immunity does not require the exclusion of judicial acts from evidence but merely protects a judge from liability for those acts. Under Rule 404(b) of the Federal Rules of Evidence, the defendant's judicial acts were clearly admissible as proof of his racially discriminatory motive."[172]

In a comparable Sixth Circuit decision,[173] plaintiff sued a juvenile court judge and his employee, among others, alleging that the judge performed the prosecutorial function of collecting overdue child support payments from fathers within the county under a contract with the county. This was done through use of threats to prosecute, extraction of consent orders from fathers, and threats of contempt, all of which were in alleged violation of due process and plaintiff's right to counsel. Reversing the district court, the Sixth Circuit held that the defendants' involvement in initiating both the criminal prosecution and the civil contempt proceeding against the plaintiff, if proven, would constitute nonjudicial acts exposing them to liability for resulting damages. Such conduct was not a function normally performed by a judicial officer and was to be sharply distinguished from the judge's conduct during the criminal and contempt proceedings themselves, which was protected by absolute immunity.

§7.09 —The Relevance of Prior Agreements and Personal Jurisdiction

Two important issues, both of which are implicated in the Ninth Circuit's

---

[172] Id 337. Compare on this point the general rule protecting members of Congress under the speech or debate clause: evidence of legislative acts and the motives behind them is not admissible in criminal prosecutions against those members. See, e.g., United States v Heltoski, 442 US 477 (1979). If an analogous rule were applied to judicial immunity in civil cases, then evidence of judicial acts and their motivation would similarly not be admissible in connection with liability for nonjudicial acts. On the other hand, the Supreme Court held in United States v Gillock, 445 US 360 (1980) that evidence of legislative acts is admissible in federal criminal prosecutions against *state* legislators charged with bribes or otherwise obtaining money unlawfully. It is worth noting, however, that the Court emphasized that it was the strong federal interest in enforcing federal criminal statutes which outweighed the state's interest in legislative independence. Thus, the availability to absolutely immune defendants of this evidentiary privilege in *civil* cases was not addressed. Still, in Dennis v Sparks, 449 US 24 (1980), where the Court held that a private person accused of conspiring with an absolutely immune judge acts under color of law and is unprotected by absolute immunity, the Court noted that as a result judges will occasionally be called upon to testify in third-party civil proceedings in explanation and defense of their judicial conduct.

[173] Sevier v Turner, 742 F2d 262 (6th Cir 1984).

decision in *Rankin v Howard*,[174] must be addressed. The first deals with the question whether a prior private agreement between a judge and another—involving a bribe, for example—is covered by absolute immunity. The second deals with the effect on the scope of immunity of the absence of *personal* jurisdiction, in contrast to *subject matter* jurisdiction. *Rankin* involved a Kansas judge who allegedly agreed in advance with other defendants to order the issuance ex parte of guardianship papers covering the plaintiff whose parents sought to have him "deprogrammed" from the Unification Church. The petition to order guardianship fraudulently alleged that plaintiff was a resident of a Kansas county when in reality he lived in Missouri. Also, the plaintiff claimed that the petition violated a Kansas jurisdictional requirement and the federal Constitution by failing to give him notice and the opportunity to be heard. Pursuant to the order of guardianship, plaintiff, after coming to Kansas for what he thought was a social visit, was taken into custody and confined to a motel room for "deprogramming." He escaped after nine days.

The Ninth Circuit first noted that because the judge was a probate judge, he had "at least a semblance of subject matter jurisdiction" under Kansas law. Next, applying one of the judicial act criteria of *Stump v Sparkman*—the expectations of the parties—the court held that "a judge's private, prior agreement to decide in favor of one party is not a judicial act" because judicial impartiality is one such expectation.[175] Thus, a judge could be liable upon proof of such an agreement even if absolutely immune for subsequent judicial acts.

Then, after analyzing the Supreme Court's statements on personal jurisdiction and judicial immunity, the Ninth Circuit reasoned that where a court lacks jurisdiction over a party, it lacks jurisdiction to adjudicate that party's rights, whether or not there is subject matter jurisdiction. For judicial immunity purposes, though, it is not enough that there was no personal jurisdiction in fact. To lose absolute immunity, the judge must know that he lacks personal jurisdiction, or act "in the face of clearly valid statutes or case law expressly depriving him of jurisdiction."[176] Accordingly, the Ninth Circuit reversed the district court's grant of summary judgment in favor of the judge, and remanded for determination of whether the judge knew the petition's jurisdictional allegations to be fraudulent or whether valid Kansas statutes precluded personal jurisdiction over a proposed ward in ex parte proceedings for temporary guardianship. Remand was also appropriate to determine whether the judge lost his absolute immunity by entering into a nonjudicial agreement.

The Ninth Circuit's approach to a private prior agreement between a judge and another is unsound in the light of the broad scope of judicial immunity reflected in Supreme Court case law. Even though the circuits have generally

---

[174] 633 F2d 844 (9th Cir 1980).

[175] *Id* 847.

[176] *Id* 849. *See also* Beard v Udall, 648 F2d 1264 (9th Cir 1981) (per curiam) (following *Rankin*) and Ashelman v Pope, 769 F2d 1360 (9th Cir 1985) (following *Rankin* and *Beard*).

insisted that allegations of conspiracy must not be conclusory,[177] it is nevertheless often not difficult to allege a prior agreement between a judge and another with enough specificity to avoid dismissal on that ground.[178] Thus, what may occur as a result is precisely what is not supposed to happen to judges: a full inquiry into the judge's decision-making process in a collateral proceeding. So long as the harm claimed by the plaintiff stems from the judge's judicial conduct, then that plaintiff should not be permitted to end-run absolute judicial immunity despite the resulting injustice. Otherwise, insurmountable line-drawing problems would develop. This reasoning is supported by the Supreme Court's decision in *Dennis v Sparks*,[179] where the Court suggested that judicial immunity covers a claim that a judge and a private party conspired as the result of a bribe.

For these reasons, the Fifth and Eleventh Circuits[180] have correctly rejected *Rankin*'s first holding. However, a panel of the Eleventh Circuit initially followed *Rankin*'s second holding, dealing with personal jurisdiction, in *Dykes v Hosemann*.[181] Here, the plaintiff sued a judge and others for damages for depriving her of the right to raise her child in alleged violation of due process. The judge allegedly awarded custody of plaintiff's child to her husband in an ex parte dependency proceeding which plaintiff knew nothing about—no summons was issued, as required by statute—and the grounds for the custody decision were the facts that plaintiff's husband was the son of a judge and that the petition, while not officially "sponsored" by the state social service agency, was presented by an official of that agency. The Eleventh Circuit, as noted earlier, rejected the plaintiff's argument based on the Ninth Circuit's *Rankin v Howard* decision that judicial immunity did not apply to advance agreements between a judge and other parties regarding the outcome of a judicial proceeding. The court then went on to reject the contention that the judge did not have subject matter jurisdiction; that he erred in concluding that the child was dependent did not deprive him of subject matter jurisdiction as a circuit court judge with exclusive jurisdiction over such matters under state law.

However, plaintiff's argument that the judge did not have *personal jurisdiction* over her to enter the custody order, thereby abrogating his judicial immunity, was an issue of first impression in the Eleventh Circuit. The panel adopted the *Rankin* approach to this issue and held that a judge acts in the clear absence of jurisdiction and thereby loses absolute immunity where he knows that he lacks personal jurisdiction or acts in the face of valid statutes expressly

---

[177] *See* §2.10.

[178] *E.g.*, Ashelman v Pope, 769 F2d 1360 (9th Cir 1985) (prisoner's allegations that judge and prosecutor contacted each other and agreed to shut off plaintiff's access to law library and deny him effective assistance of counsel were sufficient to state claim; absolute immunity not applicable in Ninth Circuit to such prior agreements).

[179] 449 US 24 (1980). See §2.10 where *Dennis* is set out in detail.

[180] Holloway v Walker, 765 F2d 517, 522 (5th Cir 1985); Krempp v Dobbs, 775 F2d 1319 (5th Cir 1985); Dykes v Hosemann, 743 F2d 1488 (11th Cir 1984), *revd in part*, 776 F2d 942 (11th Cir 1985) (en banc).

[181] 743 F2d 1488 (11th Cir 1984), *revd in part*, 776 F2d 942 (11th Cir 1985) (en banc).

depriving him of personal jurisdiction. It concluded: "When a court acts without personal jurisdiction, its authority is as much a usurped authority as when the court acts without subject matter jurisdiction."[182] Since the judge's state of mind was not considered by the district court, a remand was necessary.

Upon en banc reconsideration, the Eleventh Circuit reversed the panel decision on the personal jurisdiction issue.[183] Rejecting *Rankin,* the court contended that "[w]ithdrawing judicial immunity where a judge has subject matter jurisdiction over a party conflicts with all of [the] policies" underlying absolute judicial immunity.[184] These policies, set out in *Bradley v Fisher*[185] include: promoting independent decision making; the likelihood that a losing party will ascribe "malevolent motives" to the judge; avoiding wasteful judicial self-protection; the lack of a real need for a §1983 remedy, given the availability of appeal and impeachment; and the ease of alleging bad faith which would force judges to defend their motivations in court. In short, a "judge [should not] defend a charge that he knowingly entered an order adversely affecting a party over whom the court had not acquired personal jurisdiction. . . ."[186]

The Eleventh Circuit incorrectly rejected the *Rankin* court's approach to personal jurisdiction. Simply reiterating *Bradley*'s policy considerations is unpersuasive since they could cut in favor of absolute judicial immunity even when a judge acted in the clear absence of all subject matter jurisdiction. In a sense, personal jurisdiction, like subject matter jurisdiction, is related to the judicial act inquiry which focuses on the dealings between a judge and the parties. But it is analytically distinguishable from both because there can be acts which are clearly judicial even though they affect a person who is not a party and even though there is not subject matter jurisdiction. Nevertheless, it should be remembered that personal jurisdiction issues, like subject matter jurisdiction issues, are often difficult to resolve. Only where there is a clear absence of all personal jurisdiction should a judge lose his or her absolute immunity. Even an egregious error as to the existence of personal jurisdiction is not sufficient.

§7.10 —Who Is Protected: The Functional Approach of *Butz*

Judges at all levels, acting in a judicial capacity,[187] are protected by absolute

---

[182] Judge Hill dissented on this issue, arguing that the judge had only committed "grave procedural errors" regarding notice and hearing which should not deprive him of absolute immunity. The majority's approach, he asserted, was inconsistent with Stump v Sparkman, 435 US 1099 (1978).

[183] Dykes v Hosemann, 776 F2d 942 (11th Cir 1985) (en banc).

[184] *Id* 949.

[185] 80 US 335 (1872), discussed at §7.07.

[186] 776 F2d 950. Judge Hatchett dissented on this issue.

[187] *See generally* §§7.06-7.09.

immunity. This includes judges ranging from justices of the peace[188] and municipal referees[189] to those at the appellate level.[190] Occasionally it becomes necessary to decide whether an institution which is called a court in fact exercises a judicial function; if it does not, but is, for example, entirely legislative or administrative, then its members are not considered judges, whatever they are called, their acts are not judicial, and thus they are not protected by absolute immunity.[191] The absolute immunity of prosecutors, as declared by the Supreme Court in *Imbler v Pachtman*,[192] and its relation to the judicial process, are discussed later in this chapter.[193]

There is language in some of the cases suggesting broadly that acts of persons "in the performance of an integral part of the judicial process" are for that reason alone protected by absolute judicial immunity.[194] This reasoning has been applied to clerks of court,[195] sheriffs,[196] probation officers,[197] court reporters,[198] court-appointed medical examiners,[199] witnesses,[200] and others.[201] However, as the Fourth Circuit pointed out in *McCray v Maryland*,[202] this reasoning is flawed because the functions requiring absolute immunity for judges are not performed by these other officials who do not make judicial decisions. It makes considerably more sense to hold that clerks and

---

[188] Turner v Raynes, 611 F2d 92 (5th Cir 1980); Pennebaker v Chamber, 437 F2d 66 (3d Cir 1971).

[189] Lucarell v McNair, 453 F2d 836 (6th Cir 1972).

[190] Clark v Washington, 366 F2d 678 (9th Cir 1966) (assumed).

[191] Lynch v Johnson, 420 F2d 818 (6th Cir 1970), finding a fiscal court to be nonjudicial in nature.

[192] 424 US 409 (1976).

[193] *See* §§7.13-7.14.

[194] Burkes v Callion, 433 F2d 318, 319 (9th Cir 1970), *cert denied*, 403 US 908 (1971).

[195] Slotnick v Garfinkle, 632 F2d 163 (1st Cir 1980) (per curiam); Morrison v Jones, 607 F2d 1269 (9th Cir 1979) (per curiam); Denman v Leedy, 479 F2d 1097 (6th Cir 1973); Smith v Rosenbaum, 460 F2d 1019 (3d Cir 1972); Marcedes v Barrett, 453 F2d 391 (3d Cir 1971); Davis v McAteer, 431 F2d 81 (8th Cir 1970).

[196] Tymiak v Omodt, 676 F2d 306 (8th Cir 1982) (per curiam); Mississippi *ex rel* Giles v Thomas, 464 F2d 156 (5th Cir 1972).

[197] Douglas v Muncy, 570 F2d 499 (4th Cir 1978); Thompson v Burke, 556 F2d 231 (3d Cir 1977); Burkes v Callion, 433 F2d 318 (9th Cir 1970), *cert denied*, 403 US 908 (1971); *Cf* Galvan v Garmon, 710 F2d 214 (5th Cir 1983) (per curiam).

[198] Stewart v Minnick, 409 F2d 826 (9th Cir 1969).

[199] Burkes v Callion, 433 F2d 318 (9th Cir 1970), *cert denied*, 403 US 908 (1971).

[200] Burke v Miller, 580 F2d 108 (4th Cir 1978); Blevins v Ford, 572 F2d 1336 (9th Cir 1978); Brawer v Horowitz, 535 F2d 830 (3d Cir 1976). See Briscoe v LaHue, 460 US 325 (1983), discussed at §7.11.

[201] Pomerantz v County of Los Angeles, 674 F2d 1288 (9th Cir 1982) (county jury commisioner); Slavin v Curry, 574 F2d 1256 (5th Cir 1978) (members of a bar association's grievance committee).

[202] 456 F2d 1 (4th Cir 1972).

others,[203] insofar as they do not act as judges, are protected only by qualified immunity.[204] They should, however, be protected by an absolute judicial immunity when they act pursuant to court order or direction.[205] This exception to the qualified immunity rule, acknowledged by the Fourth Circuit in *McCray* and suggested by the Supreme Court in *O'Connor v Donaldson*,[206] both promotes fairness and prevents disruption of the judicial process.[207] Furthermore, it explains the results in many cases purporting to apply an absolute immunity rule.[208]

Nevertheless, as a result of the Supreme Court's 1978 decision in *Butz v Economou*,[209] which adopted a functional approach to absolute judicial immunity, increasing numbers of executives and other nonjudicial officials are being given absolute immunity protection. *Butz*, the seminal Supreme Court decision dealing with the scope of immunity in *Bivens*[210] actions, established several important principles. First, *Butz* made clear that even members of the President's cabinet are not absolutely immune from *Bivens* liability. Instead, they are only protected by the qualified immunity developed for state and local

---

[203] Rheuark v Shaw, 628 F2d 297 (5th Cir 1980) (court reporter).

[204] The Eighth Circuit followed *McCray* in Barnes v Dorsey, 480 F2d 1057 (8th Cir 1973), as did the Seventh Circuit in Lowe v Letsinger, 772 F2d 308 (7th Cir 1985) (concealing the entry of an order). *See also* LeGrand v Evan, 702 F2d 415 (2d Cir 1983); Henrikson v Bentley, 644 F2d 852 (10th Cir 1981). As to witnesses, see the concurring opinion of Judge Winter in Burke v Miller, 580 F2d 108, 110 (4th Cir 1978) and §7.11.

[205] In Lockhart v Hoenstine, 411 F2d 455, 460 (3d Cir), *cert denied*, 396 US 941 (1969), the court emphasized both the "manifest unfairness of subjecting one to suit as a consequence of action taken at the direction of officials over whom the individual actor has no power or control," and the likelihood of dismissal if the defendant refuses to comply. *See also* Property Management & Inv, Inc v Lewis, 752 F2d 599 (11th Cir 1985) (court-appointed receiver); McCaw v Winter, 745 F2d 533 (8th Cir 1984) (per curiam) (court clerk); Hughes v Chesser, 731 F2d 1489 (11th Cir 1984) (probation officer); Briscoe v LaHue, 663 F2d 713 (7th Cir 1981), *affd on other grounds*, 460 US 325 (1983) (court reporter); Tarter v Hury, 646 F2d 1010 (5th Cir 1981) (court clerk); Fayle v Stapley, 607 F2d 858 (9th Cir 1979) (hospital superintendant and county treasurer); Mosher v Saalfield, 589 F2d 438 (9th Cir 1978) (per curiam) (conservator of estate); T&W Inv Co v Kurtz, 588 F2d 801 (10th Cir 1978) (court-appointed receiver); Robinson v McCorkle, 462 F2d 111 (3d Cir), *cert denied*, 409 US 1042 (1972); Smith v Martin, 542 F2d 688 (6th Cir 1976); Sullivan v Kelleher, 405 F2d 486 (1st Cir 1968).

[206] 422 US 563, 577 (1975). The Court applied a qualified immunity to a state psychiatrist after it observed that he did not contend he acted pursuant to court order in keeping the plaintiff confined.

[207] Note, *The Doctrine of Official Immunity Under the Civil Rights Acts*, 68 Harv L Rev 1229, 1239 (1955). *See also* Hazo v Geltz, 537 F2d 747 (3d Cir 1976), where a deputy sheriff was sued under §1983 for allegedly causing an invalid levy against plaintiff's personal property pursuant to a default judgment. In remanding, the court held that only a qualified immunity would apply unless evidence of "direct judicial supervision," not simply administrative convenience, were shown. *Id* 751.

[208] *E.g.*, Mississippi *ex rel* Giles v Thomas, 464 F2d 156 (5th Cir 1972); Smith v Rosenbaum, 460 F2d 1019 (3d Cir 1972).

[209] 438 US 478 (1978).

[210] Bivens v Six Unknown Named Agents, 403 US 338 (1974).

government executives in §1983 actions.[211] Second, and more important for present purposes, *Butz* established that those executives who function as judges and prosecutors in connection with federal agency adjudicatory proceedings are protected by absolute immunity.[212]

Butz involved a damages action brought against various officials in the Department of Agriculture who had investigated plaintiff and his corporation and had initiated an adjudicatory proceeding against him. The defendants included the Secretary and Assistant Secretary of Agriculture, the Judicial Office and Chief Hearing Examiner, the agency attorney who presented the enforcement proceeding, and several auditors who investigated plaintiff, or who were witnesses against him. Several of plaintiff's claims were based on the First and Fifth Amendments.[213] The district court dismissed the action on the ground that the defendants were absolutely immune from liability for all discretionary actions within the scope of their authority.[214] The Second Circuit reversed and held that all the defendants were protected by only qualified immunity.[215] Vacating and remanding, the Supreme Court held that the defendant agency officials were protected by qualified immunity except insofar as their challenged conduct consisted of initiating, continuing, or prosecuting the adjudicatory proceeding or acting as judges in that proceeding.[216]

The Court rejected an across-the-board absolute immunity rule for federal executive officials. It distinguished its earlier plurality opinion in *Barr v Matteo,* [217] which applied absolute immunity to the discretionary conduct of the acting director of an agency who had been sued by former employees for malicious defamation. In *Barr,* the executive's conduct was within the outer perimeter of his line of duty, while here, because the challenged conduct was allegedly unconstitutional, it was unauthorized.[218] The Court similarly distinguished *Spaulding v Vilas,* [219] which held the Postmaster General to be absolutely immune from liability for defamation and interference with plaintiff's contractual relationships. According to the *Butz* Court, the defendant in *Spaulding* also had not acted beyond the scope of his official duties.

Further, while *Barr* and *Spaulding* did not address the executive immunity issue in connection with constitutionally derived *Bivens* actions, the analogous issue had already been considered by the Court in the §1983 case of *Scheuer*

---

[211] *E.g.,* Scheuer v Rhodes, 416 US 238 (1974). See generally **ch 8** on qualified immunity.

[212] 438 US at 508-17.

[213] *Id* 483 n 5.

[214] *Id* 483-84.

[215] *Id* 484-85.

[216] *Id* 486, 516.

[217] 360 US 564 (1959).

[218] Some question this distinction and consequently argue that *Barr* is no longer good law even for common law tort actions. *See, e.g.,* Note, *Government Immunity—Civil Rights—constitutional Law—Scope of Immunity Available to Federal Executive Officials* 1979 Wis L Rev 604.

[219] 161 US 483 (1896).

v Rhodes.[220] The Court reasoned that if, under *Scheuer,* a state's highest executive—its governor—and other executive officials are protected only by qualified immunity, then a similar standard also should apply to federal executives sued pursuant to *Bivens.* The Court stated: "[I]n the absence of congressional direction to the contrary, there is no basis for according to federal officials a higher degree of immunity from liability when sued for a constitutional infringement as authorized by *Bivens* than is accorded state officials when sued for the identical violation under section 1983."[221] Finally, granting absolute immunity to all executive officials exercising discretion would undercut the *Bivens* holding.[222]

Nevertheless, the Court went on to assert that there may be "exceptional situations where it is demonstrated that absolute [executive] immunity is essential for the conduct of the public business."[223] Canvassing decisions holding that judges and prosecutors are absolutely immune from common law and constitutional damages liability,[224] the Court ruled that despite their status as executives, executive officials exercising such special functions are entitled to absolute immunity in connection with those functions. Because adjudication within a federal administrative agency shares many important characteristics of the judicial process,[225] hearing examiners and administrative law judges are "functionally comparable" to judges and should be protected by absolute immunity. Similarly, agency executives performing functions comparable to those of a prosecutor are also entitled to absolute immunity.[226] This includes those who initiate or continue adjudicatory proceedings, as well as agency attorneys who conduct such proceedings.[227]

For the first time in a qualified immunity case, the Court in *Butz* took an expressly functional approach to the scope of immunity issue. While most executives are entitled to qualified immunity, executive status does not automatically confer only qualified immunity protection. The Court's sensitivity both to the need for executive flexibility[228] and to the nonexecutive functions

---

[220] 416 US 232 (1974). *See* **§8.13.**

[221] 438 US at 500.

[222] Analogously, it has been argued that the legislative history of §1983 demonstrates that higher-level executives should not be absolutely immune from §1983 liability. *See* Freed, *Executive Official Immunity for Constitutional Violations: An Analysis and a Critique,* 72 Nw UL Rev 526 (1977) (pre-*Butz*).

[223] 438 US at 507.

[224] Imbler v Pachtman, 424 US 409 (1976); Pierson v Ray, 386 US 547 (1967); Yaselli v Goff, 275 US 503 (1927), *summarily affg* 12 F2d 396 (2d Cir 1926); Bradley v Fisher, 80 US 335 (1871).

[225] According to the Court, these factors included the following: the similarity of the powers of hearing examiners and judges; the exercise by hearing examiners of independent judgment free from pressures; and the similarity of procedural safeguards in adjudicatory and judicial proceedings. 438 US at 513-14.

[226] *Id* 513.

[227] *Id* 515-17.

[228] This factor was surely critical to the Court's decision in Nixon v Fitzgerald, 457 US 731 (1982) that the President of the United States is absolutely immune from *Bivens* damages liability for official conduct within the outer perimeter of his duties.

of certain executive officials led it to decide that those executives acting as judges or prosecutors in adjudicatory proceedings should, like their judge and prosecutor counterparts, be absolutely immune.

The Court increasingly has applied the *Butz* functional approach to §1983 cases involving both qualified and absolute immunity. The Court held that when regional legislators function like state legislators they are absolutely immune from §1983 liability for their legislative acts.[229] Similarly, police officers, ordinarily protected by qualified immunity, are protected by absolute immunity from liability for their testimony as witnesses in state criminal trials.[230] The Court also ruled that state judges, who are delegated legislative powers over a particular subject, are protected by absolute immunity for their legislative acts.[231]

On the other hand, the Court recently held in *Cleavinger v Saxner*[232] that members of a federal prison's disciplinary committee who hear cases involving inmate rule infractions are protected by qualified immunity, not absolute immunity. Such persons are not functionally comparable to judges: they are not independent, they are not professional hearing officers, and they are under pressure to resolve disputes in favor of the institution. In addition, there often are few procedural safeguards available in the prison disciplinary context. Thus, according to the Court, such defendents should be treated the same way as school board members who adjudicate.[233]

A functional approach does not lead inevitably to more protection for an official ordinarily protected by absolute immunity. For example, the Court held that state judges are not protected by absolute immunity from injunctive relief liability for their prosecutorial role in initiating law enforcement.[234] It also intimated that a congressman is not absolutely immune from damages liability for a challenged administrative act constituting sex discrimination.[235] Thus, while a functional approach frequently will benefit those defendants ordinarily protected by qualified immunity, there will also be times when defendants such as legislators and judges who ordinarily are protected by absolute immunity for their legislative and judicial acts will not be so protected from liability for nonlegislative and nonjudicial acts.

The Court's functional approach to judicial immunity, with its focus on the judicial attributes of the decision-making process, has had a considerable

---

[229] Lake Country Estates, Inc v Tahoe Regional Planning Agency, 440 US 391 (1979), discussed at **§7.05.**

[230] Briscoe v LaHue, 460 US 325 (1983), discussed at **§7.11.**

[231] Supreme Court v Consumers Union, 446 US 719 (1980), discussed at **§7.12.**

[232] 106 S Ct 496 (1985). Chief Justice Burger and Justices Rehnquist and White dissented.

[233] Wood v Strickland, 420 US 308 (1975). *See* **§8.02.**

[234] Supreme Court v Consumers Union, 446 US 719 (1980). In Pulliam v Allen, 104 S Ct 1970 (1984), the Court held that judges are not absolutely immune from injunctive relief liability for their judicial conduct as well. *See* **§7.12.**

[235] Davis v Passman, 442 US 228 (1979).

impact on the circuits. Using this approach on a case-by-case basis, circuit courts have applied absolute immunity to the following:

1. Members of a prison disciplinary committee sued for violating due process[236]

2. A mayor, who was also a magistrate and judge, for issuing a warrant and setting bond[237]

3. A mayor, acting as liquor control commissioner, accused of violating due process[238]

4. Parole board officials reviewing parole applications and revoking parole[239]

5. A governor for his failure to appoint members of a state's personnel review board[240]

6. The members of a state's board of healing arts accused of violating procedural due process[241]

7. A court clerk who issued warrants based on his own determination of possible cause[242]

8. The director of a state's civil rights division for refusing to proceed against plaintiff's former employer for lack of probable cause[243]

On the other hand, circuit courts using the same functional approach have refused to extend absolute immunity protection to:

1. Members of a state's judicial selection committee sued for their denial of a former judge's petition for reappointment[244]

---

[236] Segarra v McDade, 706 F2d 1301 (4th Cir 1983); Ward v Johnson, 690 F2d 1098 (4th Cir 1982) (en banc). *But see* Cleavinger v Saxner, 106 S Ct 496 (1985), *affg* Saxner v Benson, 727 F2d 669 (7th Cir 1984), discussed earlier, which took a contrary position. In Stewart v Thigpen, 730 F2d 1002, 1006 n 1 (5th Cir 1984), the Fifth Circuit left the question open.

[237] Thomas v Sams, 734 F2d 185 (5th Cir 1984).

[238] Reed v Village of Shorewood, 704 F2d 943 (7th Cir 1983).

[239] Hilliard v Board of Pardons & Paroles, 759 F2d 1190 (5th Cir 1985) (per curiam) (application); Trotter v Klincar, 748 F2d 1177 (7th Cir 1984) (revocation); Walker v Prisoner Review Bd, 769 F2d 396 (7th Cir 1985) (denial); United States *ex rel* Powell v Irving, 684 F2d 494 (7th Cir 1982) (application). *See also* **§8.18.**

[240] Johnston v Herschler, 669 F2d 617 (10th Cir 1982).

[241] Vakas v Rodriquez, 728 F2d 1293 (10th Cir 1984).

[242] Scott v Dixon, 720 F2d 1542 (11th Cir 1983).

[243] Wilhelm v Continental Title Co, 720 F2d 1173 (10th Cir 1983) (analogy to judge and prosecutor).

[244] Richardson v Koshiba, 693 F2d 911 (9th Cir 1982).

2. Members of a state's board of medicine accused of violating procedural due process[245]

3. Members of a prison disciplinary committee accused of violating due process[246]

4. Members of a town planning board in connection with their imposing certain allegedly discriminatory conditions on a proposed development[247]

§7.11   —Witnesses

In *Briscoe v LaHue*,[248] a case closely related to the Supreme Court's judicial immunity decisions, the Court ruled that police officer witnesses accused of perjury at criminal trials are absolutely immune from damages liability. *Briscoe* involved consolidated cases in which the plaintiffs sued police officers and a private party for allegedly testifying falsely at their respective criminal trials and thereby violating plaintiffs' rights to due process and to trial by an impartial jury. The Seventh Circuit held that all these defendants were entitled to absolute immunity in connection with their testimony. It relied not only on the common law tradition of absolute witness immunity, but also on the potential §1983 liability of private parties charged with conspiring with public officials. Such liability could lead to the filing of "baseless" retaliatory suits by "angry former defendants." In addition, cross-examination and possible prosecution for perjury constituted adequate safeguards.

Upon review, the Supreme Court affirmed in an opinion by Justice Stevens. The Court observed that when §1983 was enacted, the common law background of absolute lay witness immunity was well established. The underlying policy was the prevention of witness self-censorship. Similarly, judges are absolutely immune under §1983 for the protection of the judicial process itself. Thus, whether a police officer witness is like a lay witness or like an official playing an important role in the judicial process, the police officer witness is entitled to absolute immunity. The Court also found nothing in §1983's legislative history to compel a different conclusion.

Finally, the Court rejected the contention that there should be an exception for police officer witness immunity on the ground that the policy reasons for lay witness immunity do not apply with the same force to police officers who testify as part of their official duties. The Court took a functional approach to absolute immunity, as opposed to a status approach. Justices Brennan,

---

[245] Marion v Michigan Bd of Medicine, 765 F2d 590 (6th Cir 1985).

[246] Saxner v Benson, 727 F2d 669 (7th Cir 1984), *affd sub nom* Cleavinger v Saxner, 106 S Ct 496 (1985), discussed earlier, and Redding v Fairman, 717 F2d 1105 (7th Cir 1983).

[247] Cutting v Muzzey, 724 F2d 259 (1st Cir 1984).

[248] 460 US 325 (1983), *affg* 663 F2d 713 (7th Cir 1981).

Marshall, and Blackmun dissented,[249] arguing that police officer witnesses accused of perjury are not entitled to absolute immunity.

The result in *Briscoe* is not surprising. However, two matters are noteworthy. First, the Court continued the expansion of its functional approach to immunities. Second, it expressly left open the question of whether police officer witnesses accused of perjury at pretrial proceedings such as probable cause hearings are entitled to absolute immunity.[250] As to the latter, however, the Seventh Circuit,[251] following *Briscoe*'s approach, held that absolute immunity similarly protects a witness at a grand jury proceeding. In addition, *Briscoe*'s absolute witness immunity rule has been applied in other circuit court decisions to testimony by private parties at grand jury proceedings, except insofar as an extrajudicial conspiracy is proved,[252] to testimony by a public defender at a criminal trial,[253] and to testimony by a police chief at a civil service commission hearing.[254] However, the First Circuit[255] refused to apply *Briscoe*'s absolute immunity rule to a police officer swearing out a warrant affidavit, and the Fifth Circuit[256] refused to apply *Briscoe*'s absolute immunity rule to a private party's testimony at a probable cause hearing.

In any possible *Briscoe* witness immunity situation, it is important—just as it is for *Butz*-type absolute judicial immunity—to focus on the challenged conduct for functional purposes. This was apparently not done, though, by the Sixth Circuit[257] in a case where plaintiffs sued various defendants for allegedly terminating their parental rights in violation of due process. In an extension of *Briscoe* which was questionable because it did not focus as it should have on the particular challenged conduct of the defendants, the Sixth Circuit held that they were all protected by absolute immunity analogous to that provided persons involved in trials. Those defendants who were agency officials responsible for the prosecution of child neglect and delinquency petitions should not have to worry about intimidation and harassment from dissatisfied parents. Those defendants who were psychologists and psychiatrists, who examined the plaintiffs' child and whose findings were thereafter relied upon,

---

[249] *Id* 346.

[250] *Id* 329 n 5.

[251] Kincaid v Eberle, 712 F2d 1023 (7th Cir 1983) (per curiam). This was questioned, though, in Wheeler v Cosden Oil & Chem Co, 734 F2d 254 (5th Cir), *modified on rehg*, 744 F2d 1131 (5th Cir 1984). *See also* Anthony v Baker, 767 F2d 657 (10th Cir 1985) (*Briscoe* not applicable to testimony before grand jury).

[252] Macko v Byron, 760 F2d 95 (6th Cir 1985) (not mentioning this possible exception); San Filippo v United States Trust Co, 737 F2d 246 (2d Cir 1984) (mentioning this possible exception).

[253] Conley v Office of Pub Defender, 653 F2d 1241 (8th Cir 1981) (per curiam).

[254] Lentsch v Marshall, 741 F2d 301 (10th Cir 1984).

[255] Krohn v United States, 742 F2d 24 (1st Cir 1984) (administrative in nature).

[256] Wheeler v Cosden Oil & Chem Co, 734 F2d 254 (5th Cir) (no such immunity at common law; few procedural safeguards), *modified on rehg on proximate cause ground*, 744 F2d 1131 (5th Cir 1984). See §3.17 on proximate cause.

[257] Kurzawa v Mueller, 732 F2d 1456 (6th Cir 1984).

performed a function analogous to that of witnesses. Even the attorney who functioned as guardian ad litem for the child was placed "squarely within the judicial process to accomplish . . . [the] goal" of acting in the child's best interests: "A failure to grant immunity would hamper the duties of a guardian ad litem in his role as advocate for the child in judicial proceedings."[258]

§7.12   Injunctive Relief: An Exception to Absolute Immunity

Even before the Supreme Court's recent decision in *Pulliam v Allen*[259] so held, it was generally accepted in the circuits, and had been implied by the Supreme Court,[260] that judicial immunity was limited to damages and did not extend to injunctive relief. *Littleton v Berbling,*[261] a leading case from the Seventh Circuit, so ruled where class discrimination based on race was alleged in the application of the criminal laws. It relied primarily on two decisions, also involving class discrimination based on race, which read *Pierson*[262] to apply only to judicial immunity from damages.[263] However, the pre-*Pulliam* injunctive relief exception apparently reached beyond class discrimination cases. The Second Circuit, in a case where plaintiff was attempting to enjoin disciplinary proceedings instituted against him by the judges of the Appellate Division of New York, stated: "[N]o sound reason exists for holding that federal courts should not have the power to issue injunctive relief against the commission of acts in violation of a plaintiff's civil rights by state judges acting in their official capacity."[264] The Fourth Circuit took a similar position.[265]

Despite this pre-*Pulliam* general acceptance of an injunctive relief exception,[266] concern was expressed about interfering with the exercise of judicial discretion. As stated by Judge Dillon, dissenting in *Littleton:*

---

[258] *Id* 1458.

[259] 466 US 522 (1984).

[260] O'Shea v Littleton, 414 US 488, 499 (1974).

[261] 468 F2d 389 (7th Cir 1972), *revd on other grounds sub nom* O'Shea v Littleton, 414 US 488 (1974).

[262] Pierson v Ray, 386 US 547 (1967).

[263] United States v McLeod, 385 F2d 734 (5th Cir 1967) and United States v Clark, 249 F Supp 720 (SD Ala 1965) (three-judge court).

[264] Erdmann v Stevens, 458 F2d 1205, 1208 (2d Cir), *cert denied,* 409 US 889 (1972). *See also* Law Students Civil Rights Research Council, Inc v Wadmond, 299 F Supp 117, 123 (SDNY 1969) (three-judge court), *affd,* 401 US 154 (1971).

[265] Timmerman v Brown, 528 F2d 811 (4th Cir 1975). *See also* Fowler v Alexander, 478 F2d 694 (4th Cir 1973) which relied on *Littleton. Fowler* did not involve class discrimination.

[266] *See* Shipp v Todd, 568 F2d 133 (9th Cir 1978), where the court stated that while a court clerk acting pursuant to judicial direction was absolutely immune from liability for damages, he was not immune from injunctive relief ordering him to expunge the plaintiff's state criminal conviction.

> [I]n the cases . . . in which this [exception] has been applied, the equitable relief granted has invariably been in the form of a prohibitory injunction, confining such officials to the limits of their legal authority. There is a great difference between ordering an official not to do a particular act, measurable by objective standards, and in ordering him to exercise his discretion in a certain general way, measurable only by subjective standards.[267]

The Fifth Circuit sounded a similar note of caution in a case where plaintiff in effect was asking the federal court to hold the decision of a state appellate court unconstitutional. While it eventually relied on collateral estoppel, the court did observe that plaintiff's "requested relief would directly and irrebuttably interfere with a discretionary judicial function."[268] However, the concern reflected in such cases is not so much with the threat to judicial independence which arises from giving an action to unhappy litigants, a threat presented where actions for damages are allowed. The concern is rather with the sensitive relationship between state and federal courts when the latter attempt to regulate state judicial conduct. Indeed, the Supreme Court made this very point in discussing injunctive relief directed against judges and prosecutors who were allegedly enforcing the criminal laws in a racially discriminatory way.[269] This concern is therefore part of the broader issue of comity discussed elsewhere.[270]

The Supreme Court, before rejecting absolute judicial immunity from injunctive relief in *Pulliam,* addressed several important questions relating to the scope of the absolute immunity of legislators, judges, and prosecutors in *Supreme Court v Consumers Union.*[271] The Court also passed on the propriety of attorney's fees awards against absolutely immune defendants. *Consumers Union* involved a §1983 suit against, among others, the Supreme Court of Virginia and its chief justice (in his official capacity) challenging on First Amendment grounds the Virginia Supreme Court's disciplinary rule for lawyer advertising. A three-judge district court held the challenged rule unconstitutional and enjoined the defendants from enforcing it. In addition, the district court awarded attorney's fees under §1988 against the Virginia Supreme Court and its chief justice in his official capacity. Defendants' argument that absolute immunity protected them both from declaratory or injunctive relief and from an award of attorney's fees was rejected.

In an opinion by Justice White, the Supreme Court vacated and remanded. It first found that the Virginia Supreme Court acted in a legislative capacity in promulgating lawyer disciplinary rules. In fact, "the Virginia Court is exercis-

---

[267] 468 F2d at 415.

[268] Cheramie v Tucker, 493 F2d 586, 588 (5th Cir), *cert denied,* 419 US 868 (1974).

[269] O'Shea v Littleton, 414 US 488, 499-502 (1974). This was the second ground for reversing the Seventh Circuit, *see* Littleton v Berbling, 468 F2d 389 (7th Cir 1972). The first ground was the absence of a case or controversy.

[270] See §§5.12-5.15 on the *Younger* rule.

[271] 446 US 719 (1980).

ing the State's *entire legislative power* with respect to regulating the Bar, and its members are the *State's legislators* for the purpose of issuing the Bar Code.''[272] The Court then discussed its decision in *Eastland v United States Servicemen's Fund* [273] which held that the speech or debate clause immunizes members of Congress from suits for both prospective relief and damages. The Court reasoned, citing *Tenney v Brandhove*,[274] that *Eastland*'s concern with interference with the federal legislative function through injunctive relief was equally applicable to state legislators sued under §1983 for prospective relief. Thus, because the Virginia Supreme Court had acted in a legislative capacity in promulgating the challenged rule, it and its members were absolutely immune from suit.

Nevertheless, the Court, after expressly leaving open the question of whether judicial immunity bars prospective relief, held that the Virginia Supreme Court and its chief justice could be sued for injunctive relief in their *enforcement* capacities (as distinguished from their legislative and judicial capacities) like other enforcement officers and agencies. The Court here referred to the Virginia Supreme Court's "independent authority of its own to initiate proceedings against attorneys," and affirmed that prosecutors, despite their absolute immunity from liability for damages,[275] could be sued for injunctive and declaratory relief.

Finally, the Court held that attorney's fees under the Civil Rights Attorney's Fees Awards Act of 1976, 42 USC §1988,[276] could not be awarded against the Virginia Supreme Court and its chief justice in his official capacity in connection with challenged acts protected by absolute legislative immunity. Relying on §1988's legislative history, the Court found that "there is no indication that Congress intended to permit an award of attorney's fees to be premised on acts that themselves would be insulated from even prospective relief." However, the Court commented that fees could be awarded against the Virginia Supreme Court for challenged acts in connection with its enforcement role.

Consumers Union indicated the following:

1. State legislators and judges who exercise a state's entire legislative authority over a subject are absolutely immune from §1983 actions for damages and prospective relief. Also, such challenged legislative activity cannot serve as the basis for an award of attorney's fees under 42 USC §1988

2. It was still an open question whether judges were absolutely immune from §1983 suits for prospective relief regarding judicial acts. However, while the Court stated that the circuits were "divided" on the issue, it

---

[272] *Id* 734 (emphasis added).
[273] 421 US 491 (1975).
[274] *See* §7.02.
[275] *See* §§7.13-7.14.
[276] See §§1.17-1.26 on attorney's fees.

is worth noting that the circuit decisions which it cited[277] suggested that judges are *not* absolutely immune from suits for declaratory and injunctive relief. Furthermore, the Court's footnote discussion of the legislative history of §1983 and the congressional concern with the use of state courts "to harass and injure citizens" reflected a possible willingness to deny to judges an absolute immunity from suits for prospective relief[278]

3. Prosecutors and judges who have an enforcement role are not absolutely immune from suits for prospective relief. Also, such challenged enforcement activity can serve as the basis for an award of attorney's fees under 42 USC §1988

In *Pulliam v Allen*[279] the Supreme Court, finally answering the question left open in *Consumers Union*, held that judges are not absolutely immune from injunctive relief. The Court also ruled that judges successfully sued for prospective relief for judicial acts could have attorney's fees awarded against them under 42 USC §1988. *Pulliam* involved a §1983 prospective relief action against a magistrate accused of unconstitutionally imposing bail on persons arrested for nonjailable offenses under Virginia law and of incarcerating those persons if they could not meet the bail. The district court found for the plaintiffs, enjoined the practice, and awarded attorney's fees against the defendant magistrate under §1988. The Fourth Circuit affirmed, as did the Supreme Court in a opinion by Justice Blackmun.

The Court first addressed the issue of judicial immunity from prospective relief liability. Acknowledging that there were no injunctions against common law judges, the Court nevertheless found a parallel in the collateral relief available against judges through the use of "the King's prerogative writs," especially prohibition and mandamus. It next observed that it had never declared an absolute judicial immunity rule for prospective relief, that the prevailing approach in the circuits was that there was no such immunity, and that the absence of such immunity had not had a "chilling effect" on judicial independence. Further, Article III limitations on injunctive relief against a judge, together with equitable requirements in general, both assured that injunctive relief against judges would be sparingly granted and provided sufficient safeguards of comity and federalism. Finally, there was no indication that Congress in enacting §1983 intended to provide absolute judicial immunity from prospective relief. Indeed, all indications in the legislative history were to the contrary.

As to attorney's fees under §1988, the Court tersely noted that it was for Congress, not the Court, to provide for judicial immunity from attorney's fees awards. Since §1988 was intended to provide fees in actions to enforce §1983, it applied as well to judges successfully sued for prospective relief.

---

[277] 466 US at 735 n 13.

[278] *Id* 735 n 14. As indeed the Court ruled in Pulliam v Allen, 466 US 522 (1984).

[279] 466 US 522 (1984).

Chief Justice Burger and Justices Rehnquist and O'Connor joined in a dissenting opinion by Justice Powell.[280] They contended that, under the common law, judges were absolutely immune from prospective relief liability as well as from damages liability. Both kinds of immunity were necessary to protect judicial independence from the burdens of litigation. Also, they rejected the majority's reliance on prerogative writs as misplaced: such writs were used "only to control the proper exercise of jurisdiction, they posed no threat to judicial independence and implicated none of the policies of judicial immunity." Finally, the dissenters argued that the effect on judicial independence of §1983 prospective relief suits would be aggravated by the possibility of attorney's fees awards under §1988.

After *Consumers Union* and *Pulliam,* therefore, judges and prosecutors are not absolutely immune from injunctive relief even for their judicial and prosecutorial conduct, so long as Article III requirements for standing and the like[281] are satisfied. In contrast, state and regional legislators (and probably local legislators as well) are absolutely immune from injunctive relief, but only regarding their legislative conduct.[282] Furthermore, since *Consumers Union* applies a functional approach in an injunctive relief setting, there will be situations where even nonlegislators are absolutely immune from injunctive relief for their legislative conduct.

Nevertheless, even after *Consumers Union* and *Pulliam,* some reluctance to enjoin state judges is to be expected. For example, in a First Circuit case,[283] the plaintiff lawyers sued various defendants, including the justices of the Puerto Rico Supreme Court, for declaratory and injunctive relief in a challenge to the constitutionality of statutes requiring members of the Puerto Rico bar to belong to and support the Puerto Rico Bar Association. They also challenged disciplinary proceedings which had suspended some of them from the practice of law. Holding that the defendant justices could not be sued in this case, the First Circuit expressed concern for the "special institutional harm" the justices would suffer "by being forced to remain parties. . . against their will." It first

---

[280] *Id* 544.

[281] *See* **ch 5.**

[282] *See* §§**7.02-7.05.** See also Star Distrib, Ltd v Marino, 613 F2d 4 (2d Cir 1980) which held that state legislators are absolutely immune from §1983 injunctive relief actions directed against legislative activity. Plaintiffs had sought to enjoin the enforcement of subpoenas issued by a state legislative committee investigating child pornography, claiming the subpoenas violated their First Amendment rights. The court relied upon the Supreme Court's decision in Eastland v United States Servicemen's Fund 421 US 491 (1975), a speech or debate clause case where the Court emphasized that injunctive relief actions, if permitted, could distract members of Congress and interfere with legislative functions. Rejecting a distinction between federal legislators and state legislators, while at the same time conceding that the deterrent effect of the threat of injunctive relief is less than that of damages liability, the Second Circuit concluded that state legislators required absolute immunity from §1983 injunctive relief actions in order not to be "chilled" in the performance of their duties as a result of the cost, inconvenience, and distractions of a trial.

[283] *In re* Justices of the Supreme Court, 695 F2d 17 (1st Cir 1982) (pre-*Pulliam*). The First Circuit's reasoning was followed in RWT v Dalton, 712 F2d 1225 (8th Cir 1983).

stated that judges are ordinarily "not proper party defendants in § 1983 actions challenging the constitutionality of state statutes." The Supreme Court's decision in *Consumers Union* was distinguishable from this case because there the requirements attacked had been promulgated by the judges themselves in the form of court rules. Next, there was no need here to enjoin the justices in order to ensure full relief to the plaintiffs. Moreover, even if plaintiffs were suing the justices for their enforcement role in the exercise of their inherent authority to discipline, there was no reason to believe that the justices would view noncompliance with the challenged statutes as misconduct warranting the imposition of discipline by them through exercise of this inherent authority. Thus, plaintiffs stated no claim against the justices either in their adjudicative capacity or in their enforcement capacity.

Similarly, the Sixth Circuit,[284] relying on an earlier decision,[285] ruled that a plaintiff was not entitled to declaratory and injunctive relief against a state court judge even after the Supreme Court's *Pulliam* decision. Abstention in such cases was appropriate in all but "extraordinary circumstances" because otherwise federal courts would have to intrude unduly upon and monitor the day-to-day conduct of state hearings and trials. The plaintiff did not show, as he was required to do, that the state courts were unwilling to enforce his constitutional rights.

The injunctive relief exception to judicial immunity seems to be the equivalent of a bifurcated approach to the meaning of *person* under § 1983. That is, a judge, because of absolute immunity, is considered not to be a person for damages purposes, but is treated as a person for injunctive relief purposes. On the surface, therefore, *City of Kenosha v Bruno*,[286] which rejected a similar approach for certain governmental entities, appears inconsistent with *Pulliam*. However, this is not so. One could rely on the *Ex parte Young*[287] fiction and consider the judge being sued for injunctive relief as an individual stripped of official functions and thus a person for § 1983 purposes. Furthermore, the judicial immunity of a judge does not mean that the judge is not a person, but rather a person who is absolutely immune from liability for damages and not from injunctive relief.

---

[284] Sevier v Turner, 742 F2d 262 (6th Cir 1984) (post-*Pulliam*). Judge Edwards dissented.

[285] Parker v Turner, 626 F2d 1 (6th Cir 1980). Cf Owens v Kelley, 681 F2d 1362 (11th Cir 1982), a pre-*Pulliam* case, where the Eleventh Circuit held that a judge sued for prospective relief in connection with a challenge to the constitutionality of certain conditions of plaintiff's probation was entitled to absolute immunity. After asserting that the granting of probation and the setting of probation conditions "are clearly judicial acts involving the exercise of discretion," the court reasoned that judicial immunity from prospective relief was necessary in such cases to prevent inhibiting the exercise of judicial discretion. 681 F2d at 1370.

[286] 412 US 507 (1973). Municipalities are now persons suable under § 1983 for damages and equitable relief. Monell v Department of Social Servs, 436 US 658 (1978). *See generally* ch 6.

[287] 209 US 123 (1908). See §5.08 on the Eleventh Amendment.

§7.13   Prosecutorial Immunity—*Imbler v Pachtman*

The Supreme Court's decision in *Imbler v Pachtman*[288] on prosecutorial immunity from liability for damages under §1983 relies on *Tenney v Brandhove,*[289] *Pierson v Ray,*[290] and later cases relating to the immunity of various governmental officials.[291] In *Imbler,* plaintiff sued a state prosecutor for the allegedly knowing use of perjured testimony and the suppression of material evidence at plaintiff's trial which resulted in his conviction for murder. The Court, speaking through Justice Powell, put the issue this way: "[W]hether a state prosecuting attorney who acted within the scope of his duties in initiating and pursuing a criminal prosecution is amenable to suit under 42 U.S.C. §1983 for alleged deprivations of the defendant's constitutional rights."[292] It then held the prosecutor absolutely immune.

The Court first canvassed its earlier decisions on immunities under §1983, saying that *Tenney* "established that Section 1983 is to be read in harmony with general principles of tort immunities and defenses rather than in derogation of them."[293] It then generalized by observing that "each [earlier decision on §1983 immunities] was predicated upon a considered inquiry into the immunity historically accorded the relevant official at common law and the interests behind it."[294] Using this approach, the Court next asserted that at common law prosecutors were absolutely immune from tort liability with respect to their decisions to initiate and conduct prosecutions[295] for at least two reasons:

1.   The danger of harassment by unfounded litigation which would divert attention from their duties

2.   The effect of litigation on their independence in making decisions

---

[288] 424 US 409 (1976).

[289] 341 US 367 (1951).

[290] 386 US 547 (1967).

[291] Wood v Strickland, 420 US 308 (1974) (school board officials exercising quasi-judicial functions) and Scheuer v Rhodes, 416 US 232 (1974) (executives).

[292] 424 US at 410.

[293] *Id* 418.

[294] *Id* 421.

[295] Judge Learned Hand wrote of prosecutorial immunity in the much-cited case of Gregoire v Biddle, 177 F2d 579, 581 (2d Cir 1949), *cert denied,* 339 US 949 (1950) as follows:

> As is so often the case, the answer must be found in a balance between the evils inevitable in either alternative. In this instance it has been thought in the end better to leave unredressed the wrongs done by dishonest officers than to subject those who try to do their duty to the constant dread of retaliation.

Finally, in concluding that for the same reasons the common law rule should be the §1983 immunity rule as well, the Court mentioned the following additional considerations:

3.   The danger to the honest prosecutor from those suits which would survive a pleadings challenge

4.   The virtual retrial of criminal offenses in a new forum, with the resolution of technical cases by the jury

5.   The adverse effect on the criminal justice system because often the finders of fact would be denied relevant evidence

6.   The availability to the convicted defendant of various posttrial procedures, and to the public of criminal prosecution and professional discipline[296]

Imbler is expressly limited to those activities of a prosecutor which are "intimately associated with the judicial phase of the criminal process, . . . functions to which the reasons for absolute immunity apply with full force."[297] The Court left open the question whether *Imbler*'s rationale would also protect "those aspects of the prosecutor's responsibility that cast him in the role of an administrator or investigative officer rather than that of advocate."[298] It did, however, note that a prosecutor in the role of advocate frequently acts outside the courtroom as well as in it,[299] thereby suggesting that this role is quite broad and is protected in its entirety by absolute immunity. Also, the Court rejected the distinction put forth by Justices White, Brennan, and Marshall between a prosecutor's knowing use of perjured testimony—to which immunity should attach—and knowing suppression of evidence—to which the three justices argued it should not.[300] Further, the Court hinted that a public defender and perhaps even court-appointed defense counsel likewise share in absolute immunity when it stated: "Attaining the system's goal of accurately determin-

---

[296] 424 US at 424-27.

[297] *Id* 430-31.

[298] *Id.*

[299] *Id* 431 n 41. Included in the prosecutor's role as advocate, according to the Court, are the following: deciding whether to present a case to a grand jury or to file an information, deciding whether and whom to prosecute, deciding what evidence and witnesses to present and obtaining, reviewing, and evaluating evidence in connection with all the above. Chief Justice Burger and Justices Rehnquist and O'Connor have intimated that absolute immunity should attach to the conduct of a prosecutor who is present during questioning of a suspect in order to advise on compliance with Miranda v Arizona, 384 US 436 (1966). *See* Johnson v Rex, No 84-1990, 54 USLW__ (S Ct Nov 5, 1985) (dissenting from denial of certiorari).

[300] The three justices reasoned that absolute immunity should not extend to claims of unconstitutional suppression of evidence because to do so would discourage the disclosure of evidence by prosecutors and thereby injure the judicial process as well as the defendant in a criminal case. However, the majority rejected this approach in part because it believed that a claim of using perjured testimony could easily be converted into a claim of suppressing evidence.

ing guilt or innocence requires that *both the prosecution and the defense* have wide discretion in the conduct of the trial and the presentation of evidence."[301] However, as discussed later,[302] the Court has since held that public defenders are not absolutely immune from damages liability for their conspiratorial misconduct.

Note, finally, that the Court has made clear that prosecutors are not absolutely immune from injunctive relief.[303]

§7.14   —In the Circuits

Since *Imbler*,[304] it is clear that prosecutorial immunity from liability for damages attaches to those acts of the prosecutor performed in the role of advocate. For example, immunity protects the prosecutor who allegedly conspires to bring false criminal charges against the plaintiff;[305] who allegedly withholds evidence favorable to plaintiff and instructs a witness to testify evasively, if not falsely;[306] and who allegedly improperly has the plaintiff indicted and, at the criminal trial, suborns perjury and files false affidavits.[307] Furthermore, *Imbler* has been applied to a prosecutor who acts in a civil enforcement proceeding to enjoin deceptive trade practices and obtain restitution for defrauded consumers[308] and to government attorneys involved in litigation in the collection of income taxes.[309] Not so clear, however, is where the prosecutor's role as advocate ends and other roles begin. This was a recurring issue in the circuits before *Imbler*. It remains so because *Imbler* expressly left open the question of the scope of prosecutorial immunity in nonadvocacy situations. In so doing, *Imbler* made inevitable the use of a functional approach to prosecutorial immunity.

The prosecutor as *investigator* has been the subject of considerable litigation. In a much-quoted pre-*Imbler* decision a prosecutor was accused of various attempts to intimidate plaintiff into confessing to a murder she did not commit, despite the lack of probable cause to hold her in custody during the period of

---

[301] 424 US 426 (emphasis added).

[302] *See* **§7.15.**

[303] Supreme Court v Consumers Union, 446 US 719 (1980). *See* **§7.12.**

[304] Imbler v Pachtman, 424 US 409 (1976).

[305] Siano v Justices of Mass, 698 F2d 52 (1st Cir 1983); Perez v Borchers, 567 F2d 285 (5th Cir 1978) (per curiam); Jennings v Shuman, 567 F2d 1213 (3d Cir 1977).

[306] Hilliard v Williams, 540 F2d 220 (6th Cir 1976) (per curiam).

[307] Bruce v Wade, 537 F2d 850 (5th Cir 1976).

[308] Ledwith v Douglas, 568 F2d 117 (8th Cir 1978). Even though *Imbler* dealt with criminal proceedings as such, this result is probably sound. The civil enforcement proceeding in *Ledwith* is comparable functionally to a criminal proceeding.

[309] Flood v Harrington, 532 F2d 1248 (9th Cir 1976). Although *Flood* is not a §1983 case, *Imbler*'s reasoning was found applicable.

alleged intimidation. The Ninth Circuit held[310] that the investigative activities of a prosecutor are protected only by a qualified immunity:

> We believe, however, that when a prosecuting attorney acts in some capacity other than his quasi-judicial capacity, then the reason for his immunity—integral relationship between his acts and the judicial process—ceases to exist. If he acts in the role of a policeman, then why should he not be liable, as is the policeman, if, in so acting, he has deprived the plaintiff of rights, privileges, or immunities secured by the Federal Constitution and laws? . . . To us, it seems neither appropriate nor justifiable that, for the same act, immunity should protect the one and not the other.[311]

The Seventh Circuit, in another leading pre-*Imbler* case, *Hampton v City of Chicago*,[312] explicitly used this approach to counter the prosecutors' claim of absolute immunity. In *Hampton*, plaintiffs' complaint could have been read as alleging that the prosecutors and others had conspired to plan and execute a raid in order to kill certain members of the Black Panther party. The court read the complaint more narrowly as alleging the planning and execution of the raid simply to obtain evidence. Still, the court rejected the contention that "evidence gathering is so closely related to the presentation of evidence at trial that it should also be clothed with immunity."[313]

A post-*Imbler* district court decision followed *Robichaud* and *Hampton* in holding that absolute immunity was not available to a prosecutor who allegedly used threats and coercion to force the plaintiff to become a police agent and informant.[314] The court simply characterized this activity as "of a police/investigative nature."[315] However, *Imbler* casts some doubt upon the propriety of a bright line test to sharply delineate roles which simply asks whether the activity is of the kind which police engage in. In a possibly significant footnote, the Supreme Court observed:

> We recognize that the duties of the prosecutor in his role as advocate for the State involve actions preliminary to the initiation of a prosecution and actions apart from the courtroom. . . . *Preparation, both for the initiation of the criminal process and for a trial, may require the obtaining, reviewing, and evaluating of evidence* . . . Drawing a proper line between these functions

---

[310] Robichaud v Ronan, 351 F2d 533 (9th Cir 1965).

[311] *Id* 536-37. *Robichaud* relied on the earlier similar case of Lewis v Brautigan, 227 F2d 124 (5th Cir 1955), in which the defendant prosecutor allegedly attempted to coerce a guilty plea to a criminal charge. The Fifth Circuit held that prosecutorial immunity does not extend to such investigative activity.

[312] 484 F2d 602 (7th Cir 1973), *cert denied*, 415 US 917 (1974).

[313] *Id* 609.

[314] Tomko v Lees, 416 F Supp 1137 (WD Pa 1976).

[315] *Id* 1139.

may present difficult questions, but this case does not require us to anticipate them.[316]

This language strongly suggests that the Court realizes both that prosecutorial functions may overlap and that the scope of the prosecutor's role as advocate is quite broad.

Despite this suggestion, the circuits almost always distinguish between police-like investigative conduct and conduct closely related to judicial proceedings. For example, in a Second Circuit[317] case, plaintiff, a former state commissioner of transportation, sued a state's attorney and his assistant in connection with their initiation and conduct of a grand jury investigation into the department of transportation and the plaintiff's subsequent prosecution. Plaintiff claimed, among other things, that defendants leaked grand jury information to the press maliciously, they fraudulently induced plaintiff to resign on the basis of an agreement not to prosecute which was later breached by defendants, they wiretapped his telephone calls, they entrapped him, and they misused the grand jury. The Second Circuit affirmed in part and reversed in part the district court's dismissal of plaintiff's complaint. The claimed press disclosures were protected only by qualified immunity because dealing with the press was administrative in nature and not closely related to the criminal process. The wiretaps also were protected only by qualified immunity because they were investigative in nature; their purpose was to catch plaintiff.

However, the alleged breach of promise was so similar to a plea bargain that, like it, the breach of promise should be protected by absolute immunity under the functional analysis used in a previous Second Circuit opinion.[318] The entrapment claim was also covered by absolute immunity because it amounted to "little more than the assertion" that defendants prosecuted plaintiff without cause. Finally, the claimed misuse of the grand jury was protected by absolute immunity even though one of a grand jury's functions, especially that of the Connecticut one-person grand jury, was investigative in nature. The court reasoned: "[T]he grand jury . . . as an institution plays a central role in that decision-making process by the prosecutor whether to prosecute . . . [A] prosecutor must be permitted to work with a grand jury totally free of the threat of civil suit."[319]

---

[316] 424 US at 431 n 33 (emphasis added).

[317] Powers v Coe, 728 F2d 97 (2d Cir 1984).

[318] Taylor v Kavanagh, 640 F2d 450 (2d Cir 1981), where the Second Circuit held that a prosecutor was absolutely immune from damages liability in connection with allegedly lying to plaintiff during plea bargaining and violating the terms of a negotiated plea agreement. The court first stated that while prosecutors are absolutely protected in connection with quasi-judicial activities, they are not so protected in connection with investigative or administrative activities. It then used what it called a *functional approach* to plea bargaining, emphasizing both that plea bargaining is an essential component of the criminal justice system which should not be chilled, and that the only harm alleged to have resulted from the prosecutor's challenged conduct was imprisonment, "an injury for which the *Imbler* doctrine of immunity protects the prosecutor." *Id* 453.

[319] Powers v Coe, 728 F2d 97, 104 (2d Cir 1984).

In another Second Circuit decision[320] which used a *type of harm* approach to distinguishing between prosecutorial and investigative conduct, the court held that prosecutors who allegedly engaged in certain misconduct, including the falsification of evidence and the coercion of perjured testimony from a number of witnesses, were absolutely immune from §1983 liability for damages. The Second Circuit adopted the district court's "useful and sensible" method of distinguishing between a prosecutor's *prosecutorial* conduct for which there is absolute immunity, and *investigatory* conduct, for which there is not, on the basis of the type of harm allegedly suffered. Where the §1983 suit is to recover for an injury arising out of the prosecution itself, e.g., standing trial or being imprisoned, there is absolute immunity. But where the alleged harm is inflicted independently of the prosecution, e.g., an illegal search violative of one's privacy, there is no absolute immunity. In this case the alleged harm to plaintiff included his deprivation of liberty, multiple trials, and resulting emotional and economic injury. Thus, defendants were absolutely immune. The Second Circuit went on to say, however, that "a prosecutor might not enjoy absolute immunity from suit by a *witness* who was allegedly threatened and imprisoned to obtain his perjured testimony."[321]

Finally, in an important case, the Seventh Circuit[322] confronted difficult questions regarding the proper scope of prosecutorial immunity in connection with the events surrounding a predawn raid on an apartment occupied by members of the Black Panthers, of whom two were killed and four injured. Plaintiffs alleged two conspiracies: one involved the defendants, among whom were several prosecutors who participated in the preraid preparations and planning and the raid itself; the other included many of the same defendants and their alleged cover-up of evidence relating to the preparation and execution of the raid and their postraid legal harassment of plaintiffs. Relying on *Imbler* and distinguishing between a prosecutor's advocacy functions and investigative functions, the Seventh Circuit held that the defendant's participation in the planning and execution of the raid was protected only by qualified immunity because it was a police-like investigation.

Next, the court addressed the postraid conspiracy and held that one defendant prosecutor's decision to file charges against the raid's survivors, his presentation of evidence to the grand jury, and his deal with a United States assistant attorney general to drop state charges were protected by absolute immunity. However, other postraid conduct, including the generation by the defendant prosecutors of postraid publicity through deceptive press releases, press conferences, and a television re-enactment of the raid, was only protected by qualified immunity. The Seventh Circuit reasoned that a prosecutor's

---

[320] Lee v Williams, 617 F2d 320 (2d Cir 1980).

[321] *Id* 322.

[322] Hampton v Hanrahan, 600 F2d 600 (7th Cir 1979), *cert denied,* 446 US 754 (1980) (per curiam). *Cf* Mancini v Lester, 630 F2d 990 (3d Cir 1980) (per curiam), distinguishing between an investigation carried out pursuant to preparing a prosecutor's case, as to which absolute immunity attaches, and an investigation which is police-like and administrative, as to which absolute immunity does not attach.

decision to publicize his actions or the actions of others—a public relations matter—is essentially unrelated to the *judicial phase* of a prosecutor's duties. There was, in the court's words, "no compelling justification for extending absolute immunity" to such decisions.

In addition to distinguishing advocacy from the investigatory role of prosecutors, courts have distinguished the advocacy role from still other prosecutorial activities.[323] The District of Columbia Circuit held, albeit in a non-§1983 situation, that the United States Attorney General's role in directing law enforcement activity was not absolutely protected from liability for damages for alleged Fourth and Fifth Amendment violations,[324] a rule subsequently declared by the Supreme Court in *Mitchell v Forsyth*.[325] The prosecutor's role as advocate has been distinguished, too, from a situation in which corporation counsel allegedly failed to issue an advisory opinion which would have permitted plaintiff to speak at a public gathering.[326] Also distinguished was a case in which a prosecutor sent a critical letter to a legislative investigating committee, with copies to the press, about the plaintiff against whom a murder charge had been dismissed with no further judicial proceedings pending or contemplated.[327] It was stated in these early post-*Imbler* cases that there was no judicial or quasi-judicial significance to the defendants' conduct. A pre-*Imbler* Ninth Circuit case reached a similar conclusion about an allegedly wrongul advisory opinion given by a city attorney which resulted in plaintiff's discharge from his job.[328] The court refused to extend absolute immunity

> to a lawyer in a public law office giving legal advice to a public entity in respect of matters that are not the subject of pending litigation. The purpose of according judicial immunity is to protect the integrity of the judicial process . . . not to shield lawyers . . . when the alleged invasion did not occur during the performance of acts that are an integral part of the judicial process.[329]

More recent circuit court decisions, using a functional approach, have applied prosecutorial immunity to the following:

---

[323] A commentator categorized the various roles as follows: executive, ministerial, investigatory, civil/advisory, public official, and individual. Note, *Delimiting the Scope of Prosecutorial Immunity from Section 1983 Damage Suits*, 52 NYUL Rev 173, 187-88 (1977). For an interesting case involving the prosecutor as witness, *see* Briggs v Goodwin, 569 F2d 10 (DC Cir 1977), *cert denied*, 437 US 904 (1978). *See also* §7.11.

[324] Apton v Wilson, 506 F2d 83 (DC Cir 1974).

[325] 105 S Ct 2806 (1985). The Court ruled that the Attorney General's use of surveillance in the name of national security was not protected by absolute immunity because it was not prosecutorial. *See* §8.03

[326] Shifrin v Wilson, 412 F Supp 1282 (DDC 1976).

[327] Walker v Cahalan, 542 F2d 681 (6th Cir 1976), *cert denied*, 430 US 966 (1977).

[328] Donovan v Reinbold, 433 F2d 738 (9th Cir 1970).

[329] *Id* 743.

1. Members of a bar association committee on the unauthorized practice of law who sent plaintiff a letter requesting him to discontinue his divorce mediation business[330]

2. A state's attorney who obtained a capias from a judge which was used to arrest plaintiff to secure her presence as the state's witness at a criminal trial[331]

3. A prosecutor's presentation of a case to a grand jury[332]

4. An attorney for a county department of social services who requested a child abuse arrest warrant from a judge[333]

5. A prosecutor's conduct in handling appeals[334]

6. A prosecutor who maliciously presented evidence to a grand jury to clear a suspect of wrongdoing[335]

7. A prosecutor's interviewing of witness before presenting their testimony to a grand jury[336]

8. Prosecutors who maliciously caused plaintiffs to be indicted and arrested for perjury[337]

9. A prosecutor, acting with a judge, who amended the plaintiff's criminal sentence even though they knew there was no jurisdiction to do so because an appeal of that conviction was pending[338]

10. An attorney general who first deprived plaintiff of his constitutional rights in connection with a quasi-judicial medical license revocation proceeding and thereafter deprived him of his right to appeal[339]

11. A prosecutor's decision, before plaintiff's trial but after investigation, to release certain of plaintiff's property[340]

---

[330] Werle v Rhode Island Bar Assn, 755 F2d 195 (1st Cir 1985) (alternate holding).

[331] Betts v Richard, 726 F2d 79 (2d Cir 1984).

[332] Maglione v Briggs, 748 F2d 116 (2d Cir 1984) (per curiam).

[333] Walden v Wishengrad, 745 F2d 149 (2d Cir 1984).

[334] Henzel v Gerstein, 608 F2d 654 (5th Cir 1979).

[335] Morrison v City of Baton Rouge, 761 F2d 242 (5th Cir 1985) (per curiam).

[336] Cook v Houston Post, 616 F2d 791 (5th Cir 1980).

[337] Macko v Bryon, 641 F2d 447 (6th Cir 1981) (per curiam).

[338] Billingsley v Kyser, 691 F2d 388 (8th Cir 1982) (per curiam) (excess of jurisdiction, not its complete absence).

[339] Demery v Kupperman, 735 F2d 1139 (9th Cir 1984).

[340] Ybarra v Reno Thunderbird Mobile Home Village, 723 F2d 675 (9th Cir 1984). *Cf* Coleman v Turpen, 697 F2d 1341 (10th Cir 1983) (distinguishing between the custody of plaintiff's property relating to plaintiff's criminal case and the custody of plaintiff's property unrelated to that criminal case: the latter was administrative in nature).

12.   A city attorney, with authority under local law to file charges based on *city* ordinances, who filed charges for violations of *state* law[341]

13.   Prosecutors who issued search warrants, interrogated plaintiff, signed the arrest warrant, withheld material exculpatory evidence, and offered perjured testimony[342]

14.   An attorney general who, in reviewing proposed contracts with the state for correct form and legality, was found to have acted in a quasi-judicial capacity[343]

In contrast, recent circuit court decisions have *refused* to apply prosecutorial immunity in the following circumstances:

1.   A prosecutor's knowing failure to stop the removal of exculpatory material from a police locker[344]

2.   A city attorney who advised city officials to delay issuing plaintiff's liquor license[345]

3.   Prosecutors who covered up the murder of plaintiff's daughter by another prosecutor through, among other things, falsifying the death certificate[346]

4.   Prosecutors who participated in an illegal search and seizure and thereafter slandered plaintiff[347]

5.   Prosecutors who assisted in the improper alteration of a trial transcript[348]

6.   A county attorney who hired a private person to work undercover against the plaintiff and to "get" the plaintiff, even if it meant framing him, and who threatened to prosecute plaintiff if he attacked the sheriff's office during his discharge hearing[349]

7.   A prosecutor who personally ordered that plaintiff be confined to a particular jail under offensive conditions[350]

8.   A prosecutor who knowingly caused a baseless criminal charge to be filed

---

[341] Lerwill v Joslin, 712 F2d 435 (10th Cir 1983) (excess of authority, not clear absence of authority; "honest" mistake). *But see* Beard v Udall, 648 F2d 1264 (9th Cir 1981) (per curiam).

[342] Fullman v Graddick, 739 F2d 553 (11th Cir 1984).

[343] Mother Goose Nursery Schools v Sendak, 770 F2d 668 (7th Cir 1985).

[344] Henderson v Fisher, 631 F2d 1115 (3d Cir 1980) (per curiam).

[345] Bennett v City of Slidell, 697 F2d 657 (5th Cir 1983), *revd on other grounds,* 728 F2d 762 (5th Cir 1984) (en banc).

[346] Ryland v Shapiro, 708 F2d 967 (5th Cir 1983) (conferring absolute immunity "would make a mockery of the judicial system").

[347] Marrero v City of Hialeah, 625 F2d 499 (5th Cir 1980).

[348] Slavin v Curry, 574 F2d 1256 (5th Cir 1978).

[349] Smith v Updegraff, 744 F2d 1354 (8th Cir 1984) (the conduct "exceeded the scope" of the county attorney's duties).

[350] Price v Moody, 677 F2d 676 (8th Cir 1982) (per curiam).

against plaintiff in order to further a civil suit the prosecutor had filed as a private attorney on behalf of his client[351]

9.   A prosecutor who advised police regarding the need to obtain a search warrant[352]

10. A deputy district attorney who coerced an involuntary confession[353]

11. A prosecutor's posttrial conduct in allowing third parties to claim plaintiff's property without a hearing[354]

12. A prosecutor who conspired with a judge in advance of plaintiff's criminal trial to deny plaintiff access to a law library and effective assistance of counsel[355]

The Third Circuit confronted what it called the "thorny issue" of prosecutorial immunity in connection with still another prosecutorial role: the defendant's firing of plaintiff, his first assistant, for publicly contradicting him about his role in a concluded criminal case.[356] The defendant argued "that prosecutorial immunity should be held to cloak administrative actions such as the discharge involved here. The hiring and firing of the subordinates through whom he acts . . . is the District Attorney's ultimate discretionary act in his service to the public. . . ."[357] But the court ruled against plaintiff on the merits and avoided the problem. It would appear, though, that the defendant's action was clearly administrative and not taken in his role as advocate. Just as a legislator's discharge of an employee was held not protected by the legislator's absolute immunity because it was not a legislative act,[358] so too it is likely that this defendant's conduct would not be protected by a prosecutor's absolute immunity because it was not an advocate's act.

There may even be situations in which the prosecutor is found to have acted outside any legitimate prosecutorial role. A Third Circuit decision indicated that a special prosecutor without authority to prosecute in the plaintiff's case would not be absolutely immune as to the claim that he conspired with others to bring false criminal charges against plaintiff.[359] In another Third Circuit decision, the plaintiff, a former congressman, sued a United States Attorney for allegedly attempting to destroy him politically by deliberately leaking false

---

[351] Beard v Udall, 648 F2d 1264 (9th Cir 1981) (per curiam) (actual conflict of interest and knowledge of baseless charges as narrowing factors).

[352] Benavidez v Gunnell, 722 F2d 615 (10th Cir 1983).

[353] Rex v Teeples, 753 F2d 840 (10th Cir 1985) ("police-related" work; Judge Barrett dissented on this issue).

[354] Lavicky v Burnett, 758 F2d 468 (10th Cir 1985).

[355] Ashelman v Pope, 769 F2d 1360 (9th Cir 1985). *See* Beard v Udall, 648 F2d 1264 (9th Cir 1981) (per curiam) which was followed in *Ashelman*. *See also* **§7.09** on the relevance of prior agreements to absolute judicial immunity.

[356] Sprague v Fitzpatrick, 546 F2d 560 (3d Cir 1976), *cert denied*, 431 US 937 (1977).

[357] *Id* 564.

[358] Davis v Passman, 544 F2d 865 (5th Cir 1977), *revd on other grounds after rehg*, 571 F2d 793 (5th Cir 1978) (en banc), *revd*, 442 US 228 (1979). *See* **§7.03.**

[359] Jennings v Shuman, 567 F2d 1213 (3d Cir 1977).

information about grand jury proceedings to the press.[360] In holding the defendant protected only by qualified immunity, the court left open the scope of prosecutorial immunity in a nonadvocacy context. Instead, it found that the allegations of deliberate leaks went beyond the roles of the prosecutor as investigator and administrator as well as advocate.

This concern with the various roles of the prosecutor is unique. Unlike legislators and judges whose exposure to potential liability will generally (but not invariably) arise in the course of either lawmaking or judging, the prosecutor not only prosecutes, but regularly investigates, administers, executes, and the like. A prosecutor's exposure to potential liability will arise in different situations which seem to admit of no straightforward, relatively easy to apply immunity approach. To the extent, therefore, that *Imbler*'s rationale is tied to the prosecutor's role as advocate, not matter how broadly construed, and is based on a concern with policies like independent decision making, retrying criminal offenses, and the adverse impact on the criminal justice system, distinctions will inevitably have to be drawn between this role and all the others.

Regardless of where the *Imbler* absolute immunity line is drawn, it is clear that one of the major purposes of such immunity is to avoid implicating the merits of the unlawful conduct allegations made against a prosecutor. Thus, reasoning in pre-*Imbler* cases finding liability for prosecutorial conduct which is "clearly beyond the proper exercise of his authority and exceed[ing] any possible construction of the power granted to this office."[361] is no longer to be followed, because it improperly focuses on the unauthorized or ultra vires nature of the conduct rather than on the role of the prosecutor. Such pre-*Imbler* reasoning led to a result in a Seventh Circuit decision which is also now clearly incorrect.[362] There, the refusal of a prosecutor to assist the plaintiff in regaining his property by prosecuting those unlawfully in possession was characterized as outside the scope of a prosecutor's duties and illegal and hence protected by qualified immunity only.

Surprisingly, the Ninth Circuit used this very approach in a post-*Imbler* case. *Briley v California*[363] was a §1983 action for damages brought against a trial judge, prosecuting attorneys, and others for alleged violations of plaintiff's constitutional rights in obtaining a bargained plea of guilty to a lesser offense than child molestation on condition that plaintiff consent to castration. Plaintiff consented to this surgery even though the plea bargain was never recorded and a court order was never entered approving it. On the immunity issue, plaintiff

---

[360] Helstoski v Goldstein, 552 F2d 564 (3d Cir 1977) (per curiam) (United States Attorney). *See also* Boyer, *Civil Liability for Prejudicial Pretrial Statements by Prosecutors* 15 Am Crim L Rev 231 (1978).

[361] Martin v Merola, 532 F2d 191, 195 (2d Cir 1976) (Lombard, J, concurring).

[362] Holton v Boman, 493 F2d 1176 (7th Cir 1974).

[363] 564 F2d 849 (9th Cir 1977). *See also* Beard v Udall, 648 F2d 1264 (9th Cir 1981) (per curiam) where, in a questionable decision, the existence of a conflict of interest was deemed relevant to the prosecutorial immunity issue in connection with a criminal case initiated by the prosecutor.

argued that absolute immunity was inappropriate since there was no legal authority whatever for district attorneys to require castration. Agreeing with this view of prosecutorial immunity, the Ninth Circuit remanded to determine whether the state trial judge "would have arguably had some common-law or statutory basis for ordering Briley to submit to castration had he been convicted for the child molestation charge. If such authority is found and, thus, judicial immunity attaches, the district attorneys . . . would be immune from Section 1983 liability for misrepresentations. . . ."[364] The court cited the Seventh Circuit in *Stump v Sparkman* (prior to reversal by the Supreme Court)[365] and the district court in *Wade v Bethesda Hospital*[366] as "persuasive authority that a court, at least when ordering the extreme remedy of sterilization, must have specific legislative or common-law authority for doing so,"[367] and then made the district attorneys' immunity depend on the judges's.

After *Imbler*, however, and even without the decision in *Stump*, it is clear that the district attorneys should be immune whenever they are acting as advocates in connection with a specific criminal case. To make their immunity dependent solely upon the judge's immunity misdirects the inquiry. It also, to the extent of its focus on statutory or common law authority, necessarily implicates the merits, and this is the very inquiry that *Imbler* was designed to preclude where a prosecutor acts as an advocate. Furthermore, the *Stump* decision now makes abundantly clear that the *legislative or common law authority* approach to judicial immunity is wrong. Consequently, *Briley*'s approach is similarly incorrect.

Several additional observations should be made regarding prosecutorial immunity. First, at least one circuit,[368] after extensive discussion, now insists that in a §1983 suit against a prosecutor (or any other potentially absolutely immune defendant) a plaintiff must allege "with particularity all material facts on which he contends he will establish his right to recovery, which will include detailed facts supporting the contention that the plea of immunity cannot be sustained." Second, because the functional approach is used in prosecutorial immunity cases, just as it is in legislative and judicial immunity cases, absolute prosecutorial immunity has been conferred on certain individuals who are not prosecutors but who nevertheless have been found to perform prosecutorial functions. Examples include a pathologist hired by a coroner to perform an autopsy,[369] the director of a state civil rights division who closed plaintiff's

---

[364] 564 F2d at 858.

[365] Sparkman v McFarlin, 552 F2d 172 (7th Cir 1977), *revd sub nom* Stump v Sparkman, 435 US 349 (1978).

[366] 337 F Supp 671 (SD Ohio 1971).

[367] Briley v California, 564 F2d 849, 857 (9th Cir 1977).

[368] Elliott v Perez, 751 F2d 1472 (5th Cir 1985). See also §1.16 on notice pleading in federal court litigation.

[369] Lawyer v Kernodle, 721 F2d 632 (8th Cir 1983) (analogy to immunity of prosecutor's investigators whose findings are used in prosecutor's decision whether to institute criminal charges).

employment discrimination file,[370] and bar officials charged with investigating, drawing up, and presenting attorney discipline cases.[371] And third, in contrast with prosecutorial immunity from liability for damages, *injunctive* relief is available against prosecutors in appropriate situations.[372]

§7.15　The Immunity of Public Defenders

Before the issue of absolute immunity for public defenders is reached in a given case, the state action question must be addressed[373] This is significant even where a government-funded public defender agency is involved because the agency will often be set up as a separate corporate entity. In *Polk County v Dodson*,[374] the Supreme Court held that a public defender does not act under color of state law when performing a lawyer's traditional functions as counsel to a defendant in a criminal proceeding. Accordingly, the Court did not have to reach the scope of immunity issue. Still, the result in *Polk County* in effect conferred absolute immunity from §1983 damages liability upon public defenders in connection with their representation of indigent criminal defendants.[375]

Nevertheless, the scope of immunity issue may arise even after *Polk County* in certain circumstances. For example, a public defender may be accused of conspiring with a defendant who acts under color of state law.[376] Or, a public defender may be sued under §1983 in connection with the performance of

---

[370] Wilhelm v Continental Title Co, 720 F2d 1173 (10th Cir 1983).

[371] Clulow v Oklahoma, 700 F2d 1291 (10th Cir 1983). *But see* Marion v Michigan Bd of Medicine, 765 F2d 590 (6th Cir 1985) (members of a state board of medicine protected only by qualified immunity; no showing of need for absolute immunity protection even though prosecutorial and adjudicatory functions performed). Cf Lopez v Vanderwater, 620 F2d 1229, 1237 n 17 (7th Cir 1980), asserting that the defendant judge was "obviously" not protected by prosecutorial immunity for his prosecutorial conduct because he was not a prosecutor, and Harris v Harvey, 605 F2d 330 (7th Cir 1979) suggesting that the defendant judge was protected by prosecutorial immunity for his conduct of a "John Doe proceeding" against plaintiff. See §§7.06-7.11 on judicial immunity and §§8.13-8.14 on the applicability of absolute prosecutorial immunity to quasi-prosecutorial conduct of state and local government executives.

[372] Supreme Court v Consumers Union, 446 US 719 (1980), discussed at §7.12. The Supreme Court has, however, expressed its reservations where injunctions appear either to interfere unnecessarily with a prosecutor's discretion, O'Shea v Littleton, 414 US 488 (1974), or to impinge upon comity concerns. See §§5.12-5.15 regarding the latter policy issue. Cf Dohaish v Tooley, 670 F2d 934 (10th Cir 1982) (reluctance to interfere with prosecutorial discretion in choosing not to prosecute).

[373]See §§2.04-2.10 on state action.

[374] 454 US 312 (1981).

[375] Thus, those circuits which held, pre-*Polk* County, that public defenders are absolutely immune must be read in light of *Polk County*. *E.g.*, Housand v Heimar, 594 F2d 923 (2d Cir 1979); Miller v Barilla, 549 F2d 648 (9th Cir 1977); Minns v Paul, 542 F2d 899 (4th Cir 1976); Brown v Joseph, 463 F2d 1046 (3d Cir 1972), *cert denied*, 412 US 950 (1973).

[376] *See* §2.10.

certain administrative or investigative functions.[377] In both cases, the public defender could be found to have acted under color of law, thereby compelling an inquiry into the scope of immunity.

Indeed, following *Polk County,* the Court in *Tower v Glover*[378] confronted just such a case, where public defenders were sued for damages by the plaintiff who alleged that they had conspired with various state officials, including judges, to secure his conviction. In an opinion by Justice O'Connor holding that the defendants were *not* absolutely immune for such conduct, the Court first noted that in light of *Dennis v Sparks,*[379] the plaintiff's conspiracy allegations against the public defenders satisfied §1983's color of law requirement. Next, it noted that at common law there was no immunity for public defenders because in 1871, when §1983 was enacted, no such position existed. Also, even English barristers—cousins to American public defenders—have never enjoyed immunity from liability for intentional misconduct. Further, current state laws did not provide public defenders with immunity from liability for intentional misconduct. Finally, even if as a matter of public policy public defenders should be absolutely immune, this argument was for Congress, not the Supreme Court.[380]

---

[377] Polk County v Dodson, 454 US at 324-25.

[378] 467 US 914 (1984). Thus, Black v Bayer, 672 F2d 309 (3d Cir 1982), holding the contrary, is no longer good law.

Compare Tower with Ferri v Ackerman, 444 US 193 (1979), a non-§1983 case, where the Court held as a matter of federal law that an attorney appointed by a federal judge for an indigent federal criminal defendant is not entitled to absolute immunity when sued by his former client in a state legal malpractice suit. The Court rejected the argument that just as other federal officers—the judge, prosecutor, and the grand jurors—are protected by absolute immunity from tort liability, court-appointed defense counsel likewise should be protected. It reasoned that the other federal officers represent the interest of society as a whole, while court-appointed defense counsel function like privately retained counsel. Thus, according to the Court, the primary rationale for absolute immunity for judges, prosecutors, and others does not apply to appointed counsel. Note that the Court expressly stated it did not have to reach the question of congressional power to create immunity for appointed defense counsel in federal criminal cases. 444 US at 205. Also observe that *Ferri* involved a nonconstitutional state claim asserted against the defendant attorney.

[379] 449 US 24 (1980). Set out at **§2.10.**

[380] The Court's decision holding that there is no public defender immunity for conspiratorial conduct was unanimous. However, four justices objected to the Court's statement, made in passing without briefing and argument, that there was no occasion in *Tower* to decide whether a federal court "should abstain from deciding a §1983 suit for damages stemming from an unlawful conviction pending the collateral exhaustion of state court attacks on the conviction itself." *See* **§§5.12-5.15.**

Qualified Immunity for "Persons": An Affirmative Defense

8

§8.01 Summary

Once the prima facie 42 USC §1983 violation is established, and it turns out that the individual defendant is not absolutely immune from liability for

450

damages,[1] the question becomes whether the defendant is nevertheless entitled to some kind of defense against or immunity from damages liability. Because §1983 on its face makes no provision for defenses or immunities, it might be thought that none would be available. However, in a series of decisions beginning in 1967, the Supreme Court, relying on the background of tort liability and on policy considerations, has extended a qualified immunity to police officers, executives, school board members, mental hospital administrators, and prison officials.[2] This qualified immunity test reflects a balance between the interest in preventing, and compensating for, constitutional violations and the interest in avoiding the overdeterrence of independent decision making by government officials. However, the Court's use of a functional approach to immunity in *Butz v Economou*[3] has led it to apply absolute witness immunity to police officers accused of testifying falsely at criminal trials.[4] Also, the functional approach has encouraged the circuits to apply absolute immunity to the quasi-judicial conduct of parole board officials[5] and other state and local government executives.[6]

The qualified immunity test had two parts before the Court's significant decision in *Harlow v Fitzgerald*,[7] an objective part and a subjective part, the latter now largely eliminated by *Harlow*. The objective part imposes liability only for violations of clearly settled law which a defendant, in the absence of extraordinary circumstances, has a duty to know. Where there was no clearly settled law at the time the defendant acted, the defendant escapes §1983 damages liability. Thus, a plaintiff's lawyer who, in seeking damages from a government official, asserts that the constitutional issue before the court is of first impression or is especially difficult, has probably lost his or her damages claim. Typically, the existence of clearly settled law is a question for the court. Also, violations of clearly settled *state* law do not necessarily result in §1983 liability.[8]

Harlow's objective qualified immunity test reflects the Court's increasing concern with the risk of overdeterring independent decision making by government officials and is intended to reduce the costs of defending against §1983 litigation. This concern has also led the Court to hold that denials of

---

[1] *See* **ch 7.**

[2] Procunier v Navarette, 434 US 555 (1978)(prison officials); O'Connor v Donaldson, 422 US 563 (1975) (mental hospital administrators); Wood v Strickland, 420 US 308 (1975) (school board members); Scheuer v Rhodes, 416 US 232 (1974) (executives); and Pierson v Ray, 386 US 547 (1967) (police officers).

[3] 438 US 478 (1978), set out at **§7.10.**

[4] Briscoe v LaHue, 460 US 325 (1983). *See* **§§7.11 & 8.11.**

[5] *See* **§8.18.**

[6] *See* **§§8.13-8.14.**

[7] 457 US 800 (1982) discussed at **§§8.03-8.04.**

[8] Davis v Scherer, 104 S Ct 3012 (1984).

defense motions for summary judgment based on clearly settled law grounds are immediately appealable.[9]

The defendant should have the burden of proving this qualified immunity by a preponderance of the evidence.[10] While the burden of going forward with evidence may shift to the plaintiff after the defendant has introduced some evidence, the ultimate burden of proof remains on the defendant. In this respect, qualified immunity is an affirmative defense.

Like the *reasonable person* standard for negligence in tort law, the best way to understand the §1983 qualified immunity is to see how courts apply it to certain kinds of defendants in concrete circumstances. Simply stating the general rules is insufficient, although these general rules are helpful because the Supreme Court has developed a unitary standard for qualified immunity.

§8.02   *Wood v Strickland:* The Leading Case Before *Harlow v Fitzgerald*

Two Supreme Court decisions on qualified immunity preceded the Court's 1975 decision in *Wood v Strickland.*[11] These two cases, *Pierson v Ray*[12] and *Scheuer v Rhodes,*[13] presented a qualified immunity test for police officers and governors composed of two parts: an objective part requiring reasonable grounds for the defendant's belief in the legality of the challenged conduct, and a subjective part requiring good faith in fact. In part because the facts in *Pierson* and *Scheuer* involved executives at various law enforcement levels, many questions were left open.[14] Since *Wood* addressed these questions and dealt with other important aspects of the scope of qualified immunity, it was, therefore, at least before

---

[9] Mitchell v Forsyth, 105 S Ct 2806 (1985).

[10] *See* **§8.16.**

[11] 420 US 308 (1975).

[12] 386 US 547 (1967).

[13] 416 US 232 (1974).

[14] *Pierson* and *Scheuer,* read together, held only that executives at various law enforcement levels are protected by a qualified immunity. Thus, important questions were unanswered. These two cases did not speak to the general availability of a similar qualified immunity to other government officials who make decisions, for example, of a quasi-judicial nature. It could be argued that such officials are absolutely immune for the same reasons that judges are absolutely immune under §1983. *See* **§7.06.** Further, *Pierson* and *Scheuer* did not thoroughly discuss the relevance of legal knowledge to the reasonable grounds, good faith belief standard. *Pierson* said only that police officers are not expected to predict the development of constitutional doctrine—a general proposition which appears unassailable. *Scheuer* did not discuss the issue of legal knowledge at all because there the challenged conduct related to the defendants' judgment as to factual information. Moreover, after *Scheuer,* there was confusion in the circuits concerning the factors relevant to the existence of qualified immunity, with some circuits employing subjective factors and others emphasizing objective factors. *Wood,* 420 US at 315-18 and n 7. *Pierson* and *Scheuer* are discussed in some detail at **§§8.11 & 8.13** respectively.

Harlow v Fitzgerald,[15] probably the most important of the qualified immunity cases.

Wood arose when the plaintiffs were expelled from school for violating a regulation prohibiting intoxicating beverages at school or school activities. In §1983 actions against school board members for damages and other relief, plaintiffs alleged that the expulsions violated procedural and substantive due process. The district court directed a verdict for defendants, after a mistrial, on the ground that they were immune as a matter of law because there was no "proof of malice in the sense of ill will" toward plaintiffs.[16] The jury had earlier been instructed that such ill will was necessary to a finding for plaintiffs. Disagreeing, the Eighth Circuit said: "It need only be established that the defendants did not, in the light of all the circumstances, act in good faith. The test is an objective, rather than a subjective, one."[17]

Writing for a five-person majority on the immunity issue,[18] Justice White first noted the confusion in the circuits regarding qualified immunity: "[T]he courts have either emphasized different factors as elements of good faith or have not given specific content to the good-faith standard."[19] After analyzing its earlier cases on qualified immunity, the Court observed that "state courts have generally recognized that [school board members] should be protected from tort liability under state law for all good-faith, nonmalicious action taken to fulfill these official duties."[20] The Court went on to acknowledge that school board members function variously as legislators and adjudicators, roles which involve the exercise of considerable discretion over both the long and short term.[21] Finally, the Court held that school board members are protected by a qualified immunity of the same general kind which protects executives, one which combines elements of both an objective and subjective nature.[22]

The key to understanding the significance of *Wood*'s approach lies in the following quotation from Justice White's majority opinion:

---

[15] 457 US 800 (1982) which, as discussed at **§§8.03-8.04,** largely eliminated the subjective part of the test.

[16] *Quoted* in *Wood,* 420 US at 310.

[17] *Id* 314.

[18] The Court unanimously agreed there was no substantive due process violation but remanded for consideration of a possible procedural due process violation.

[19] 420 US at 315.

[20] *Id* 318.

[21] In so doing, the Court appeared at the time to reject a functional approach which could have, for example, afforded absolute immunity protection for quasi-legislative and quasi-judicial conduct of school board members. However, the recent development of a functional approach to immunities, stemming in large measure from Butz v Economou, 438 US 478 (1978), could conceivably lead to a conflict with this aspect of *Wood. See generally* **§§7.05, 7.10 & 8.18.** However, the result in *Wood* was recently reaffirmed by the Court in Cleavinger v Saxner, 106 S Ct 496 (1985), discussed at **§§7.10 & 8.18.**

[22] It remanded to consider whether there was a due process violation and, if there was, to apply the *Wood* qualified immunity standard to the defendants.

The official himself must be acting sincerely and with a belief that he is doing right, but an act violating a student's constitutional rights can be no more justified by *ignorance or disregard of settled, indisputable law* on the part of one entrusted with supervision of students' daily lives than by the presence of actual malice. To be entitled to a special exemption from the categorical remedial language of §1983 in a case in which his action violated a student's constitutional rights, a school board member, who has voluntarily undertaken the task of supervising the operation of the school and the activities of the students, must be held to a standard of conduct based not only on permissible intentions, but also on *knowledge of the basic, unquestioned constitutional rights of his charges.* Such a standard imposes neither an unfair burden upon a person assuming a responsible public office requiring a high degree of intelligence and judgment for the proper fulfillment of its duties, nor an unwarranted burden in light of the value which civil rights have in our legal system. Any lesser standard would deny much of the promise of §1983. Therefore, *in the specific context of school discipline, we hold that a school board member is not immune from liability for damages under §1983 if he knew or reasonably should have known that the action he took within his sphere of official responsibility would violate the constitutional rights of the student affected, or if he took the action with the malicious intention to cause a deprivation of constitutional rights or other injury to the student.* That is not to say that school board members are "charged with predicting the future course of constitutional law." . . . A compensatory award will be appropriate only if the school board member has acted with such an impermissible motivation or with such disregard of the student's clearly established constitutional rights that his action cannot reasonably be characterized as being in good faith.[23]

In its emphasis upon settled rights as an element of the reasonableness test, the majority imposed upon school board officials a duty to know students' "basic, unquestioned constitutional rights" in the area of discipline. Put another way, after *Wood* the reasonable grounds part of the qualified immunity test requires a finding as to whether the defendant school board member should have known that the challenged conduct was violating constitutional rights; where the relevant rights are "settled," then a duty to know these rights arises. This duty to know constitutional law might have been hinted at by negative implication in *Pierson v Ray*,[24] but it was not mentioned at all in *Scheuer v Rhodes*.[25] Consequently, the majority in *Wood* added content to the objective part of the test of qualified immunity. Moreover, the Court explained more fully then it had in *Pierson* and *Scheuer* what the subjective part entailed: an inquiry into the school board member's state of mind in order to determine the existence of malicious intent to violate a student's constitutional rights

---

[23] 420 US at 321-22 (emphasis added).
[24] 386 US 547 (1967).
[25] 416 US 232 (1974).

or to cause other injury. As it turned out, though, the Court in *Harlow v Fitzgerald*[26] largely eliminated this inquiry from the qualified immunity test.

The four-person dissenting opinion, written by Justice Powell, attacked the majority's duty to know requirement as imposing "a higher standard of care upon public school officials sued under §1983, than that heretofore required of any other official."[27] The dissent characterized this second-guessing by a fact-finder of a school board member's decision making as a "harsh standard," because of the difficulty that even lawyers and legal scholars have in describing constitutional rights as "settled," "indisputable," and "unquestioned." It also questioned whether most school boards and officials have ready access to counsel in making many decisions for the operation of public schools and emphasized the effect of potential liability upon the willingness of the citizens to serve on school boards. Justice Powell expressed greater satisfaction with the test of *Scheuer,* arguably more flexible in not specifically mentioning a duty to know settled constitutional law. In short, the majority and dissenting opinions differed not as to the existence of an objective or reasonable grounds part of qualified immunity, but as to whether that part includes a duty to know settled rights.[28]

The dissenting justices improperly responded to the statement of the duty to know requirement of *Wood.* In *Wood* itself the duty was applied to school board members in the context of student discipline which, after *Goss v Lopez,*[29] is surely an area about which it is reasonable to expect school board members at least to seek legal advice. To say otherwise would mean there is little realistic incentive for school board members to comply with procedural due process. Moreover, the cost of such legal advice will properly be borne by the taxpayers, including many parents, who have an important interest in the efficient and legal operation of the school.

§8.03 The Qualified Immunity Test: The Objective Part and *Harlow v Fitzgerald*

The objective part of the qualified immunity test has been the subject of considerable litigation and confusion in the circuits. First, *Wood*'s[30] duty to know settled law might be read as *supplementing* the earlier and more general

---

[26] 457 US 800 (1982). *See §8.03.*

[27] 420 US at 327.

[28] Justice Powell, at 420 US at 331 n 4 said that under *Pierson,* "[N]ot even police officers were held liable for ignorance of 'settled, indisputable law.' " However, this was not at issue in *Pierson* where the unconstitutionality of the breach of the peace statute was rather clearly not settled or indisputable. Moreover, even if the issue was settled, a police officer might not have a duty to know this while, in contrast, a higher level executive or agency official might have such a duty. *See §§8.11 & 8.13.*

[29] 419 US 565 (1975) (procedural due process applicable to short-term student suspension).

[30] Wood v Strickland, 420 US 308 (1975).

objective part of the qualified immunity test. Under this reading the Court did not intend to substitute *Wood*'s duty to know for the reasonable grounds requirement of *Scheuer v Rhodes*.[31] Rather, *Wood* stands for the proposition that there are situations in which breach of the duty to know settled law in itself constitutes an absence of reasonable grounds for a defendant's belief that his or her conduct has legal validity. And conversely, even though a defendant may act in an area where there is little settled law, it is still possible that the action may not have been reasonable.[32] In short, *Wood* under this interpretation operates to make it easier to find unreasonableness in that category of cases involving violations of clearly settled rights.

The reasonable person test from tort law is helpful in thinking about the nature and scope of *Wood*'s objective part of the test for qualified immunity. In ordinary negligence cases, the reasonable person test establishes a vague standard of care for defendants. Because of this vagueness, it is realistic to describe the jury as in effect making law by establishing its own standard of care for each case. This happens despite the court's instructions to the jury on the elements of reasonable care. The jury then proceeds to decide whether the defendant has met that standard of care. The jury's role is not troublesome because the input of the community and its common sense are desirable elements in the negligence litigation system. Further, the jury is considered competent to define reasonableness, that is, the standard of care, and to decide whether it has been breached, although in some situations, such as medical malpractice cases, expert testimony is necessary.

The objective part of the qualified immunity test is similarly vague by definition. Accordingly, by analogy to ordinary negligence, the jury might have been expected to have the same broad discretion in establishing the qualified immunity standard of care and the fact of its breach. Thus, unless reasonable persons could not differ as to the defendant's breach of the qualified immunity standard of care, this question would be for the jury, just as the analogous law application question is similarly for the jury in ordinary negligence cases.

However, it is not that simple. The qualified immunity test requires an inquiry into what the defendant knew or should have known as to the legality of the conduct engaged in, including an evaluation of clearly settled rights and their possible violation. To the extent such legal issues are necessarily implicated in the objective part of the test, a district court would frequently find it easier to keep the whole issue away from the jury and decide the reasonableness question itself. Also, where the question should properly go to the jury, there may be a need for expert legal testimony as to the status of the rights allegedly violated at the time defendant originally acted.[33] In short, there

---

[31] 416 US 232 (1974), discussed at **§8.13.**

[32] *Developments in the Law - Section 1983 and Federalism*, 90 Harv L Rev 1133, 1214-17 (1977). *See also* Freed, *Executive Official Immunity for Constitutional Violations: An Analysis and A Critique*, 72 Nw UL Rev 526, 557 (1977); Yudof, *Liability for Constitutional Torts and the Risk-Averse Public School Official*, 49 S Cal L Rev 1322, 1336 (1976).

[33] *E.g.*, Laverne v Corning, 522 F2d 1144 (2d Cir 1975), a rather unusual case in which a law professor testified as to the state of the law regarding administrative searches in

was an appropriate judicial concern both with the jury's competence and with fairness in subjecting a defendant to second-guessing about the legal validity of past conduct. Indeed, many of the qualified immunity cases reflect this judicial concern.

The Court's decision in *Harlow v Fitzgerald*[34] substantially changed *Wood*'s qualified immunity test by largely eliminating the subjective part and by insisting that the objective part of the test—now the primary part—should be applied by courts in a prodefendant manner.[35] The Court's purpose was to permit the defeat of insubstantial claims without resort to trial. *Harlow* involved actions for damages against White House aides to former President Nixon based on certain federal statutes and the First Amendment. In ruling that these aides were protected only by qualified immunity, the Court went on to eliminate what it called the subjective part of the test as derived from *Wood v Strickland:* acting with malicious intention to cause a deprivation of constitutional rights or injury.

The Court observed that an official's subjective good faith typically has been considered a disputed question of fact which should not be decided on motion for summary judgment. As a result, "substantial costs attend the litigation of the subjective good faith of government officials," including extensive judicial inquiries into subjective motivation which can be "peculiarly disruptive of effective government." Thus,

> we conclude today that bare allegations of malice should not suffice to subject government officials either to the costs of trial or to the burdens of broad-reaching discovery. *We therefore hold that government officials performing discretionary functions generally are shielded from liability for civil damages insofar as their conduct does not violate clearly established statutory or constitutional rights of which a reasonable person would have known.*
>
> Reliance on the objective reasonableness of an official's conduct, as measured by reference to clearly established law, should avoid excessive disruption of government and permit the resolution of many insubstantial claims on summary judgment. *On summary judgment, the judge appropriately may determine, not only the currently applicable law, but whether that law was clearly established at the time an action occurred. If the law at that time was not clearly established, an official could not reasonably be expected to anticipate subsequent legal developments, nor could he fairly be said to "know" that the law forbade conduct not previously identified as unlawful. Until this threshold immunity question is resolved, discovery should not be allowed. If the law was clearly established, the*

1962. In concluding that "there was reasonable ground for belief that the entries were lawful at the time they took place in 1962," the professor relied for his opinion on the applicable ordinance, then-existing Supreme Court decisions, and the village attorney's advice to the defendants. *Id* 1151.

[34] 457 US 800 (1982).

[35] Also indicating that the objective part is to be applied in a prodefendant manner are Davis v Scherer, 104 S Ct 3012 (1984), discussed at **§8.01** and Procunier v Navarette, 434 US 555 (1978), discussed at **§8.09**.

immunity defense ordinarily should fail, since a reasonably competent public official should know the law governing his conduct. Nevertheless, if the official pleading the defense claims extraordinary circumstances and can prove that he neither knew nor should have known of the relevant legal standard, the defense should be sustained. But again, the defense would turn primarily on objective factors.

By defining the limits of qualified immunity essentially in objective terms, we provide no license to lawless conduct. The public interest in deterrence of unlawful conduct and in compensation of victims remains protected by a test that focuses on the objective legal reasonableness of an official's acts. Where an official could be expected to know that certain conduct would violate statutory or constitutional rights, he should be made to hesitate; and a person who suffers injury caused by such conduct may have a cause of action. But where an official's duties legitimately require action in which clearly established rights are not implicated, the public interest may be better served by action taken "with independence and without fear of consequences."[36]

There may still be situations where the defendant official's subjective state of mind—i.e., what he or she actually knew—will be relevant to the objective qualified immunity test. As Justices Brennan, Marshall, and Blackmun pointed out in their concurring opinion, the new standard "would not allow the official who *actually knows* that he was violating the law to escape liability for his actions, even if he could not 'reasonably have been expected' to know what he actually did know."[37] They agreed, however, that such a subjective inquiry would become relevant only where the state of the law was sufficiently unambiguous at the time of the alleged violation that it could have been known.[38]

§8.04   —Analysis

Harlow's[39] change in the qualified immunity test demonstrates the Court's increased sensitivity to the costs to *defendants* of defending against constitution-

---

[36] *Harlow*, 457 US at 818-819 (emphasis added, citations and footnotes omitted). The Court rather clearly indicated that its discussion of qualified immunity encompassed §1983 actions. *Id* n 30. This was made clear in Wolfel v Sanborn, 691 F2d 270 (6th Cir 1982), where the Sixth Circuit construed a Supreme Court remand order to mean that, after *Harlow*, state officials are protected by the same qualified immunity in §1983 actions as are federal officials in *Bivens* actions. *See* Wolfel v Sanborn, 666 F2d 1005 (6th Cir 1981), *vacated & remanded*, 102 S Ct 3476 (1982). The Sixth Circuit further indicated that *Harlow* should be applied retroactively to litigation pending at the time *Harlow* was decided. Note also that an official's state of mind may be relevant to the prima facie case. *See generally* **ch 3.**

[37] 457 US at 821 (emphasis in original).

[38] *Id.*

[39] Harlow v Fitzgerald, 457 US 800 (1982).

al tort litigation,[40] at the same time showing the Court's reduced concern for the financial and psychological costs to constitutional tort *plaintiffs* of conducting such litigation. It also reflects, in part, the Court's own continuing split over the proper scope of §1983 liability, a split ranging from local government liability through punitive damages to standing to seek injunctive relief.[41]

The Court's list of costs in *Harlow,* set out in order to justify eliminating the subjective part of the qualified immunity test, is particularly instructive and merits comment. The Court first spoke of what it called *general costs,* or the individual and social costs of exposure of innocent defendants to the risks of trial. These included the following: (1) the expenses of litigation; (2) the diversion of official energy from pressing public issues; (3) the deterrence of able citizens from accepting public office; and (4) the chilling effect on the discharge of official duties.[42]

As to these general costs, several features are noteworthy. First, the Court assumed that these are borne by the innocent. While this may be true, they are borne by the guilty as well. Second, these costs are virtually identical to the costs discussed in some of the Court's absolute immunity cases.[43] The Court never before spoke of these costs in a qualified immunity setting to justify a change in qualified immunity, but only to explain why absolute immunity should apply rather than qualified immunity.[44] In earlier cases, once qualified immunity was found to be appropriate, general costs, to the extent they were present, were considered unavoidable and to be borne by defendant officials, their government employers, and the public at large.

The Court next spoke of what it called the *special costs* of the subjective part

---

[40] As distinct from the costs of being sued and the costs of an adverse judgment. *See* P. Schuck, Suing Government: Citizen Remedies for Official Wrongs 60 (1983). The distinction is important. The modified qualified immunity test was not as such designed by the Court to reduce the costs of being sued, i.e., those costs stemming from the filing of the suit itself. In contrast, the availability of absolute immunity significantly reduces the filing of such suits against certain defendants. Similarly, the modified qualified immunity test was not viewed by the Court as reducing the likelihood of adverse judgments, in light of *Harlow*'s assertion that under the prior two-part test most defendants who had prevailed on the objective part through motion would win on the subjective part at trial. Rather, modifying the qualified immunity test was directed at reducing the costs of defending against constitutional tort litigation. This being true, however, it is clear that if the modified test works as planned by the Court, fewer constitutional tort cases will be filed, thereby reducing these two other costs.

[41] Smith v Wade, 461 US 30 (1983) (5-4 decision) (punitive damages liability for individuals even without actual malice); City of Los Angeles v Lyons, 461 US 95 (1983) (5-4 decision) (separate, independent standing inquiries for related §1983 damages and injunctive relief actions); Owen v City of Independence, 445 US 622 (1980) (5-4 decision) (no §1983 immunity for local governments). *See* **chs 4, 5 & 6** respectively.

[42] 457 US at 816.

[43] *E.g.,* Imbler v Pachtman, 424 US 409 (1976) (absolute prosecutorial immunity from damages liability).

[44] In Imbler v Pachtman, 424 US 409 (1976), the Court did not question general cost (3). The Court has, of course, referred to general costs (3) and (4) in cases holding that qualified immunity, and not absolute liability, is applicable. *E.g.,* Wood v Strickland, 420 US 308, 313-22 (1975); Pierson v Ray, 386 US 547, 553-55 (1967).

of the qualified immunity test. It noted that executive discretionary decisions are influenced by a decision maker's experiences, values, and emotions. It then observed that: (1) subjective intent can rarely be decided by summary judgment; (2) there is no clear end to relevant evidence; (3) discovery is often wide-ranging, including the deposing of professional colleagues as well as numerous other persons; and (4) such inquiries into state of mind can cause disruption of government.[45] This list of general and special costs led the Court to do away with the subjective part of the test, because, in its view, federal courts were not otherwise able to weed out frivolous claims prior to trial.[46] By so doing, the Court may have considerably increased the margin for error of defendants in §1983 cases.

There are, however, serious questions about the Court's list and its use of these costs. It is always easy for a court to list costs implicated in a course of conduct or activity—here, liability for constitutional torts—that it wishes to discourage.[47] Also, it is beyond dispute that, to some extent, these general and special costs do exist. Indeed, §1983 liability is supposed to have an effect on executive decision making. But the Court discussed no data showing that the costs to government officials of the two-part test in fact had a significant adverse effect on executive decision making. Additionally, the Court did not appear to consider all the costs of modifying the qualified immunity test. Because the two-part test had an additional hurdle, it would seem to follow that defendants were more often held liable under the two-part test than they will be under the modified objective test.[48] Consequently, there will be more situations under the modified test than there were under the prior two-part test in which defendants violate constitutional rights with no remedy for plaintiffs. These unremedied violations impose costs on society which have not been, and perhaps cannot be, measured satisfactorily. Such costs include disrespect for authority, disrespect for the Constitution and laws generally, the erosion of Fourteenth Amendment values, and the prospect that some executives might be undeterred in connection with Fourteenth Amendment compliance.[49] There are also, of course, costs to the individual, such as the actual harm caused and the feeling of being victimized.

A related criticism of the Court's approach may be made by considering the

---

[45] *Harlow*, 457 US at 816. Note that state of mind inquiries are frequently relevant to the prima facie case as well. *See generally* **ch 3.**

[46] 457 US at 816-19. A similar concern with possible harassment suits against executives and overdeterrence is addressed in Cass, *Damage Suits Against Public Officers*, 129 U Pa L Rev 1110, 1153-74 (1981).

[47] *Cf* United States v Leon, 104 S Ct 3405, 3430 (1984) (Justice Brennan's cost-benefit analysis observation).

[48] Circuit court decisions in which defendants failed the subjective part of the test include, *e.g.*, Wolfel v Sanborn, 666 F2d 1005 (6th Cir) *cert denied*, 452 US 916 (1982); Williams v Board of Regents, 629 F2d 993 (5th Cir 1980), *cert denied*, 452 US 926 (1981); Flores v Pierce, 617 F2d 1386 (9th Cir 1980); Crowe v Lucas, 595 F2d 985 (5th Cir 1979), *cert denied*, 455 US 907 (1982).

[49] These costs are also relevant to the argument made later that the objective test should not be rigidly applied in a prodefendant manner.

benefits of the prior two-part test. When the *Harlow* Court was deciding whether to change the prior test by calculating its costs, it should also have calculated its benefits, as well as the benefits of the modified test. Only in this way could the costs and benefits of the prior test and the modified test have been compared for the purpose of deciding which test was better over all, resulting in greater social benefit. This is not to suggest that such cost-benefit analysis is or should be determinative, or even that it is possible for it to be meaningful when dealing with constitutional compliance. After all, as the Court has asserted in other contexts, there are higher substantive values in our constitutional scheme than efficiency, even if calculable.[50] Indeed, it has been urged that even procedure has value independent of efficiency.[51] Nevertheless, if the Court is going to play the cost-benefit game, it should abide by the rules.

The *Harlow* opinion bears a striking resemblance to Justice White's opinion for the Court in *United States v Leon*[52] and his earlier separate opinion in *Illinois v Gates*,[53] setting out the argument that the exclusionary rule is a judicially created remedy for Fourth Amendment violations which is to be evaluated by a cost-benefit analysis. Unlike the exclusionary rule, though, §1983 is a congressional creation for the protection and vindication of Fourteenth Amendment rights. Congress has already made the decision that as a general matter the benefits of Fourteenth Amendment compliance outweigh the costs of such compliance. Thus, judicially overstating costs and understating benefits in order to limit this congressional remedy against individual defendants is indefensible. Nevertheless, *Harlow* reflects the Court's determination to run this risk of underprotecting Fourteenth Amendment rights, rather than overprotecting them at the possible expense of independent executive decision making.[54]

---

[50] Immigration & Naturalization Serv v Chadha, 462 US 919, 958-59 (1983) (holding unconstitutional the congressional legislative veto and stating: "[I]t is crystal clear from the records of the convention, contemporaneous writings and debates, that the Framers ranked other values higher than efficiency"). *See also* Stanley v Illinois, 405 US 645 (1972). The Court stated:

> Indeed, one might fairly say of the Bill of Rights in general, and the Due Process Clause in particular, that they were designed to protect the fragile values of a vulnerable citizenry from the overbearing concern for efficiency and efficacy that may characterize praiseworthy government officials no less, and perhaps more, than mediocre ones.

Id 656.

[51] *See* Laycock, *Due Process and Separation of Powers*, 60 Tex L Rev 875 (1982); Mashaw, *The Supreme Court's Due Process Calculus for Administrative Adjudication in Mathews v Eldridge: Three Factors in Search of a Theory of Value*, 44 U Chi L Rev 28 (1970). *See also* Schweiker v McClure, 456 US 188, 194 (1982) (fairness as value); McNabb v United States, 318 US 332, 347 (1943) ("The history of liberty has largely been the history of observance of procedural safeguards").

[52] 104 S Ct 3405 (1984).

[53] 462 US 213 (1983). *See also* Posner, *Rethinking the Fourth Amendment*, 1981 Sup Ct Rev 49 (exclusionary rule overdeters).

[54] Compare United States v Leon, 104 S Ct 3405 (1984), where the Court held that there should be a *good faith* exception to the Fourth Amendment's exclusionary rule when a search warrant is obtained from a "detached and neutral magistrate." If the

An analysis of the objective part of the qualified test reinforces this view. Whatever one thinks of the advisability of doing away with the subjective part of the test,[55] the clearly settled law part of the test has the independent potential for dramatically reducing the scope of liability for executives. This is so because many constitutional rules and their application turn out not to be clearly settled for liability purposes. Under *Harlow*, defendants on summary judgment motion frequently will be dismissed without a consideration of the merits. This being the case, the Court has, in a constitutional tort context, limited individual liability by converting qualified immunity into the equivalent of absolute immunity.

The settled law component is closely related to the costs of defending against constitutional tort litigation. As the margin for error of §1983 defendants is reduced, the general and special costs of litigation described by the *Harlow* Court will tend to increase. Conversely, when the margin for error is increased, then these costs of litigation will tend to decrease. Although, as mentioned earlier, *Wood*'s duty to know settled law initially might have suggested that the margin for error should be reduced for defendants, the Court in *Procunier v Navarette*,[56] a pre-*Harlow* case involving prison officials, quickly corrected that impression by turning *Wood* on its head and using it against plaintiffs. *Navarette* dealt with settled law in three related respects: (1) Was there a settled constitutional rule at the time of the challenged conduct? (2) If so, should defendants have known of this rule? (3) Finally, if they should have known of the rule, should they have known that their conduct violated this rule?

In *Navarette*, where plaintiff inmates sued prison officials for refusing to send outgoing mail in alleged violation of the First Amendment, the Court never got past the first hurdle for the defendants. Refusing to extrapolate from existing case law, the Court held that at the time of the challenged conduct there was no First Amendment right of inmates to send mail. The Court's message as to the meaning of settled law was clear: the margin for error of defendants should be significant. In addition, the *Harlow* Court found that even when clearly settled law exists "out there," there may be exceptional circumstances when

---

Court ultimately goes beyond *Leon* to adopt generally a *good faith* test for the exclusion of evidence obtained by police in violation of the Fourth Amendment, whether with or without a search warrant, then what the Court considers to be improper judicial interference with police officer decision making will be reduced even more. Also, the deterrent effect of both constitutional tort liability and the exclusionary rule will be significantly reduced as well. Thus, there will be no available remedy in most cases when a police officer violates a citizen's Fourth Amendment rights, unless that violation is egregious.

[55] If, however, one believes that every defendant who passes the objective part of the test will also pass the subjective part, and that every defendant who fails the subjective part will also fail the objective part, then the subjective part will be viewed as superfluous.

[56] 434 US 555 (1978), discussed at **§8.09.**

an official is under no obligation to know of its existence—a second hurdle.[57] The scope of this exception remains unclear, although it may refer to situations where a particular defendant may not have had meaningful access to legal advice.[58] Moreover, the law application condition—a third hurdle—requires that defendants know settled law as applied to their situation in order to be liable. This creates further play in the joints of the settled law requirement.[59] The Court may have intended that not only must there be a settled constitutional rule of general applicability, but there must also be a relevant prior case on point holding unconstitutional the same kind of conduct as that challenged.[60]

It would be preferable, despite this Supreme Court case law, to give settled law a more flexible application, as some courts have done,[61] and not automatically rule for defendants as a matter of law. Hence, in appropriate circumstances executives might be found to have breached duties to extrapolate from then existing law as to both the existence of general constitutional rules and their application. Indeed, the dissenters in *Wood* who argued against *Wood*'s duty to know settled law contended that there is and can be very little, if any, settled constitutional law.[62] Their point was a good one, even though their conclusion was not. Rather, their argument actually cuts in favor of such extrapolation when the situation warrants it.[63]

Consequently, an executive's margin for error should not be as wide as the Court in *Harlow* and *Navarette* may have wanted to make it. Now that the

---

[57] 457 US at 819. However, as Justice Brennan, joined by Justices Marshall and Blackmun, stated in his concurring opinion, the new standard "would not allow the official who *actually knows* that he was violating the law to escape liability for his actions, even if he could not reasonably have been expected to know what he actually did know." *Id* 821 (Brennan, J., concurring) (emphasis in original).

[58] *See, e.g.,* Barnett v Housing Auth, 707 F2d 1571 (11th Cir 1983); Treen v White, 693 F2d 45 (8th Cir 1982).

[59] This is demonstrated by cases ruling for defendants on such law application grounds. *E.g.,* Saldana v Garza, 684 F2d 1159, 1164-65 (5th Cir 1982), *cert denied,* 460 US 1012 (1983); Withers v Levine, 615 F2d 158 (4th Cir), *cert denied,* 449 US 849 (1980).

[60] Such a rigid approach appears to have been used in Knell v Bensinger, 522 F2d 720 (7th Cir 1975) and in Shirley v Chagrin Falls Exempted Village Schools Bd of Educ, 512 F2d 1329 (6th Cir 1975), *cert denied,* 424 US 913 (1976).

[61] *E.g.,* Blackburn v Snow, 771 F2d 556 (1st Cir 1985); King v Higgins, 702 F2d 18 (1st Cir 1983); Scott v Davis, 691 F2d 634 (3d Cir 1982); Maxwell v Mason, 668 F2d 361 (8th Cir 1981); Logan v Sheaiy, 660 F2d 1007 (4th Cir 1981), *cert denied,* 455 US 942 (1982); Seguin v Eide, 645 F2d 804 (9th Cir 1981); Johnson v Duffy, 588 F2d 740, 745 (9th Cir 1978); Buise v Hudkins, 584 F2d 223 (7th Cir 1978), *cert denied,* 440 US 916 (1979); Ware v Heyne, 575 F2d 593 (7th Cir 1978); Little v Walker, 552 F2d 193 (7th Cir 1977); *cert denied,* 435 US 932 (1978); Wagle v Murray, 546 F2d 1329 (9th Cir 1976), *vacated on other grounds & remanded,* 431 US 935 (1977); Slate v McFetridge, 484 F2d 1169 (7th Cir 1973).

[62] Wood v Strickland, 420 US 308, 329 (1975).

[63] Compare those negligence cases where defendants are treated as if they did know, or at least were under an obligation to find out, certain information. W. Prosser & W. Keeton, Law of Torts 182-85 (5th ed 1984).

subjective part of the qualified immunity test is gone,[64] it is more important than ever to be sensitive to the need to encourage compliance with the Fourteenth Amendment despite the risk of overdeterrence. The out-of-pocket costs of such compliance should be borne by the defendants or their employers, the relevant government bodies. These costs are as much legitimate costs of government as other employment costs, especially in the absence of any clear indication that government decision making is being seriously hampered. Otherwise, if individual constitutional tort liability is undercut by expansion of the scope of individual immunity, there will be even less incentive for constitutional compliance than there is now.

Nevertheless, the prodefendant intention of the Court was further confirmed in *Davis v Scherer*[65] and *Mitchell v Forsyth*,[66] which found no relevant clearly settled law. *Mitchell* even went so far as to rule, in reliance on the policy of *Harlow*, that denials of defense motions for absolute and/or qualified immunity may be immediately appealable.

§8.05 —*Davis, Mitchell,* the Relevance of State Law, and Interlocutory Appeals

In *Davis v Scherer*,[67] the Court demonstrated that it would apply the clearly settled law component in a prodefendant manner. The Court in *Davis* also held that a defendant who otherwise passes the *Harlow*[68] qualified immunity test regarding clearly settled *constitutional* law does not lose his or her qualified immunity for violating clearly settled *state* law.

Davis involved a §1983 suit brought by a former Florida highway patrol employee—discharged because of an employment conflict of interest—against officials of the highway patrol for damages for their alleged violation of his procedural due process rights in not providing him with a formal pretermination or prompt posttermination hearing. The district court found for plaintiff on the ground that defendants had violated clearly settled state law even though plaintiff's due process rights had not been clearly established at the time he was discharged in 1977. Hence, defendants' belief in the legality of their conduct was unreasonable. The Fifth Circuit affirmed, but the Supreme Court reversed in an opinion by Justice Powell. At the outset, the Court conceded that plaintiff's due process rights were violated, but it rejected plaintiff's argument that those rights were clearly established in 1977. The Court simply observed that the Fifth Circuit itself, in 1981, had held that "the State had violated no clearly established due process right when it discharged

---

[64] For the questionable argument that *Harlow* did not eliminate the subjective part of the qualified immunity test, see McElveen v County of Prince William, 725 F2d 954 (4th Cir 1984). *See* **§8.15.**

[65] 104 S Ct 3012 (1984), discussed at **§8.05.**

[66] 105 S Ct 2806 (1985), discussed at **§8.05.**

[67] 104 S Ct 3012 (1984).

[68] Harlow v Fitzgerald, 102 S Ct 2727 (1982).

a Civil Service employee without *any* pretermination hearing."[69] As to the Supreme Court's own prior due process precedents, which earlier established that some kind of hearing is required where a property interest may be at stake, Justice Powell asserted that those precedents did not deal with "minimally acceptable procedures for termination of employment." Here, plaintiff was informed several times of his employer's objections to his second job and had even presented his reasons to his employer. Also, the official who decided to discharge plaintiff had those reasons and other information before him. Thus, plaintiff's due process rights to a formal pretermination or prompt posttermination hearing were not clearly established in 1977.

The Court had somewhat more difficulty with plaintiff's second argument: that the defendants' violation of their own personnel regulations, which clearly required a complete investigation and an opportunity for the employee to respond in writing, undercut defendants' qualified immunity even though those regulations were not the basis of plaintiff's claim. While this contention had "some force," the Court expressed concern that such an approach would render government officials liable in "indeterminate amount for violation of any constitutional right . . . merely because their official conduct also violated some statute or regulation." Also, state law related matters could not always be resolved on summary judgment.

Justices Brennan, Marshall, Blackmun, and Stevens dissented on the qualified immunity issue. They focused on whether plaintiff's due process rights were clearly established in 1977 when he was discharged. To them the question was whether governing case or statutory law would have given a reasonable official cause to know, at the time of the relevant events, that those acts or omissions violated the plaintiff's rights. Here, plaintiff was never told prior to his discharge that his retention of a second job was grounds for termination. This violated the Court's own clearly established requirements of meaningful notice and a reasonable opportunity to be heard, regardless of the Fifth Circuit's "dubious and cursory" per curiam opinion to the contrary in 1981. Indeed, *other* prior Fifth Circuit precedent was consistent with the Supreme Court's clearly established due process requirements. Finally, and in passing, the dissenters suggested that "the presence of a clear-cut regulation obviously intended to safeguard public employees' constitutional rights certainly suggests that [defendants] had reason to believe they were depriving [plaintiff] of due process."[70] While the violation of such a regulation would not necessarily be determinative of the qualified immunity issue, it should be relevant to the *Harlow* analysis.

Davis warrants several observations. First, a majority of the Court intended that *Harlow*'s (and *Wood*'s) clearly settled law component be applied in a prodefendant manner. The Court seems unwisely to insist that there be little or no ambiguity in relevant case law as a condition to finding clearly settled law; a case on point appears to be required. Unlike the dissenters, they would

---

[69] 104 S Ct at 3018 (emphasis in original).
[70] *Id* __.

admit no duty to extrapolate from preexisting case law. Second, the Court will not consider the violation of a clearly established state law to be relevant to the *Harlow* analysis where constitutional rights are involved and where the state law is not related to the §1983 plaintiff's cause of action. In short, once there is no clearly settled constitutional law violated by a defendant, there is no liability for compensatory damages even if clearly settled *state* law was violated. Note, however, that violations of clearly settled *federal* law will be relevant in §1983 "laws" actions.[71]

This prodefendant application of the *Harlow* qualified immunity test is further demonstrated by *Mitchell v Forsyth*,[72] where a former United States attorney general was sued for damages for allegedly warrantless and thus unconstitutional electronic surveillance of the plaintiff. On interlocutory appeal from the district court's denial of his claims of absolute and qualified immunity, the Third Circuit held that the defendant was not entitled to absolute immunity because he did not engage in either adjudicative or prosecutorial functions within the meaning of *Butz v Economou*[73] and *Imbler v Pachtman*.[74] Further, the district court's rejection of the attorney general's *special functions* argument was correct even after *Harlow* because *Harlow* did not make new law in this respect.

The Third Circuit next went on to rule that the qualified immunity issue was not properly before it. Even though *Harlow* eliminated the subjective part of the qualified immunity test so as to encourage "the summary disposition of insubstantial claims brought against government officials," it did not "relax . . . the rule limiting interlocutory appeals."[75] Judge Weis dissented, arguing not only that the qualified immunity issue was properly before the court in light of prevalent authority in other circuits, but also that the defendant did not violate clearly established law. Only after the wiretap had been removed in this case did the Supreme Court hold that there was a right to be free from warrantless government surveillance in domestic security cases. He distinguished earlier Supreme Court decisions establishing the need for a warrant for electronic surveillance as not dealing with national security considerations. Also, the defendant's conduct did not violate clearly established federal statutory law at the time.

In an opinion by Justice White, the Supreme Court agreed with the Third Circuit that the defendant was not protected by absolute immunity. It rejected the argument that there should be absolute immunity protection for the attorney general when he or she engaged in a "national security function." First, there was no common law support for the argument. Second, unlike the judicial process, which is open, national security decisions are secret, without

---

[71] *See* §2.12.

[72] 105 S Ct 2806 (1985), *affg in part & revg in part sub nom* Forsyth v Kleindienst, 729 F2d 267 (3d Cir 1984).

[73] 438 US 478 (1978), set out at §7.10.

[74] 424 US 409 (1976), discussed at §7.13.

[75] 729 F2d at 273.

"overt winners and losers." Thus, there was less fear of unfounded and burdensome litigation. Finally, there were relatively few other restraints on the national security activities of the attorney general. Hence, absolute immunity was not appropriate.[76]

However, the Court disagreed with the Third Circuit on the qualified immunity–summary judgment appealability issue. The denial of a defense motion claiming absolute immunity was appealable before final judgment under the collateral order doctrine of *Cohen v Beneficial Industrial Loan Corp*[77] because the claimant might be entitled not to stand trial at all. Similarly, the defendant claiming qualified immunity on clearly settled law grounds after *Harlow* was also possibly entitled not to stand trial. Thus, under the collateral order doctrine, a defendant raising the question of the absence of clearly settled law in a qualified immunity–summary judgment motion could, where the motion was denied, appeal that denial.[78]

The Court, reaching the qualified immunity issue, ruled for the defendant on the ground that it was not clearly established in 1970, the time when the defendant approved the warrantless surveillance, that such surveillance was unconstitutional. It was only after the surveillance was concluded that the Court itself decided in *United States v United States District Court*[79] ("*Keith* ") that the Fourth Amendment does not permit the use of warrantless wiretaps in cases involving domestic threats to the national security. Before that time, the question was explicitly described as "open" by the Court. In addition, even though shortly after the surveillance in this case had terminated (but before *Keith*) several district court decisions had held that such surveillance *was* unconstitutional, other district courts had indicated, prior to the surveillance here (obviously before *Keith*), that such surveillance might indeed be constitutional. Consequently, the defendant's motion for summary judgment on qualified immunity grounds should have been granted inasmuch as the defendant did not violate clearly settled law.

Chief Justice Burger and Justice Stevens concurred, contending that the attorney general should be protected by absolute immunity for the exercise of a national security function delegated by the President of the United States. Justice O'Connor would not have reached this issue, while Justices Brennan and Marshall dissented on the qualified immunity–summary judgment appealability issue. In their view, there was no justification for distinguishing between denial of a defendant's claim of qualified immunity and numerous other pretrial motions that may be reviewed only on appeal of the final judgment in the case, especially in light of other recent collateral order doctrine decisions by the Court. They also argued that summary judgment was improper in any event

---

[76] *See* §§**7.10** & **7.14.**

[77] 347 US 541 (1949).

[78] Even before *Mitchell,* the First Circuit reached the same conclusion in Krohn v United States, 742 F2d 24 (1st Cir 1984). So did the Eighth Circuit in Tubbesing v Arnold, 742 F2d 401 (8th Cir 1984), even though the defendants were sued for injunctive relief as well as damages.

[79] 407 US 297 (1972).

because there was a disputed issue of material fact relating to the defendant's motive in approving the surveillance.

Mitchell, like *Davis v Scherer,* demonstrates that *Harlow* was not an aberration. The Court continues to be concerned with the possible overdeterrence of executive officials stemming from their need to defend against §1983 and other constitutional tort actions. This concern is so pervasive that it has led the Court to eliminate the subjective part of the qualified immunity test (*Harlow*), to treat as irrelevant violations of clearly settled state law (*Davis*), and to carve out an apparent exception to the normal procedural rules governing appealable orders (*Mitchell*). Thus, *Harlow* and its progeny are a powerful weapon for defendants, and the often troublesome question of the existence of clearly settled law will continue to be the focus of much §1983 litigation involving potential individual damages liability.

It is also worth noting that the Court in *Mitchell* "[did] not intend to suggest that an official is always immune from liability or suit for a warrantless search merely because the warrant requirement has never explicitly been held to apply to a search conducted in identical circumstances." However, if there is "a legitimate question whether an *exception* to the warrant requirement exists," then a warrantless search does not violate clearly settled law.[80]

§8.06 —In the Circuits

As noted previously, even before *Harlow*[81] the circuits struggled with the objective part of the *Wood*[82] qualified immunity test. Now, after *Harlow* and its progeny, the objective qualified immunity test has, not unexpectedly, been the subject of considerable debate in the circuits. The extensive qualified immunity case law regarding particular categories of individual defendants is set out later in this chapter. For present purposes the following should be noted. The question whether there was relevant clearly settled law at the time of the defendant's conduct will almost always be for the court. This is in contrast to any disputed issues of fact relevant to the prima facie case, which will be for the jury. The clearly settled law issue is for the court even where the elements of the prima facie case, for example, probable cause, appear similar to those of the qualified immunity test. The Seventh Circuit[83] put it aptly when it stated:

> The issue of immunity as redefined in *Harlow* is whether when the defendant violated the plaintiff's rights the law appeared to authorize the defendant's misconduct. This is an issue of law, for the judge to decide. What the defendant believed, an issue of fact, is neither here nor there. The good sense of *Harlow* in withdrawing the issue of immunity from the jury is particularly evident in a case such as this, where the police are

---

[80] *Mitchell,* 105 S Ct at 2820 n 12.
[81] Harlow v Fitzgerald, 457 US 800 (1982).
[82] Wood v Strickland, 420 US 308 (1975).
[83] Llaguno v Mingey, 763 F2d 1560 (7th Cir 1985).

charged with having acted without probable cause. The question whether they had probable cause depends on what they reasonably believed with reference to the facts that confronted them, as the judge instructed. . . . To go on and instruct the jury further that even if the police acted without probable cause they should be exonerated if they reasonably (though erroneously) believed that they were acting reasonably is to confuse the jury and give the defendant two bites at the apple.[84]

In addition, it is often not clear how a court should determine clearly settled law. Suppose that there are no decisions by the Supreme Court or the particular circuit on the issue in question, for example, the legality of student searches. In such a case, the Ninth Circuit,[85] after it had reviewed decisions of state courts, another circuit, and various district courts, found that the basic Fourth Amendment rights of students had been sufficiently clearly established at the time to preclude immunity for the defendants. Such inquiries require the expenditure of extensive judicial and lawyer resources. Perhaps this is not a serious problem where the result is a finding of clearly settled law. But where the result is a finding that clearly settled law did not then exist, a determination as to the constitutionality of the defendant's conduct at the time of decision has been avoided because the defendant will now prevail on qualified immunity grounds. Thus, even after considerable resources may have been expended, the status of the current law has not been clarified.

It is important to be sensitive to the distinction between the question whether a new judicial decision is to be applied retroactively under the test set out by the Supreme Court in *Chevron Oil Co v Huson*[86] and the question whether a defendant violated clearly settled law. For example, in an Eleventh Circuit case,[87] the court found that the Supreme Court's decision in *Tennessee v Garner*,[88] which limited the use by police officers of deadly force to stop a fleeing felon, "was not an entirely new and unanticipated principle of the law that would justify nonretroactivity." Nevertheless, in remanding on the issue of the defendant police officer's qualified immunity, the Eleventh Circuit asserted that the clearly settled law standard for immunity purposes required a higher "level of clarity" than the nonretroactivity standard of *Chevron Oil.*

§8.07 School Officials

Wood v Strickland[89] specifically applied the qualified immunity test to school

---

[84] *Id* 1569. See also Bates v Jean, 745 F2d 1146 (7th Cir 1984) where it was observed that leaving the qualified immunity issue with the court avoids the problem of inconsistent verdicts.

[85] Bilbrey v Brown, 738 F2d 1462 (9th Cir 1984), also noted at **§8.07.**

[86] 404 US 97 (1971).

[87] Acoff v Abston, 762 F2d 1543 (11th Cir 1985).

[88] 105 S Ct 1694 (1985).

[89] 420 US 308 (1975).

board members. Later decisions in the circuits, both before and after *Harlow*,[90] illustrate the factors used in determining when school officials pass the objective part of the qualified immunity test. In a suit against school board members for allegedly improperly denying sick leave benefits for normal pregnancy, the Ninth Circuit[91] affirmed injunctive relief but held as a matter of law that the defendants did not breach their duty to know in denying those benefits. Emphasizing the uncertainty of the legal issue, the court noted the split in the circuits as to whether pregnancy may be permissibly excluded from sick leave coverage. However, perhaps even more important was the court's observation that the defendants had specifically asked the State Director of Legal and Executive Services for a ruling on the issue and acted in reliance thereon. Similarly focusing on the uncertainty of the legal issue, the Tenth Circuit[92] held that school board members who dismissed a teacher for "immorality" in violation of certain procedural due process guidelines did not as a matter of law breach their duty to know, and affirmed the district court's directed verdict for defendants. The court found that, at the time the hearings took place, earlier judicial decisions "did not stake out the extent of the procedural rights which we now recognize in the circumstances of this case."[93]

The *settled rights* part of the qualified immunity test is sometimes applied

---

[90] Harlow v Fitzgerald, 457 US 800 (1982).

[91] Hutchison v Lake Oswego School Dist No 7, 519 F2d 961 (9th Cir 1975), *cert granted, judgment vacated on other grounds & remanded,* 429 US 1033 (1977). *Cf* Clanton v Orleans Parish School Bd, 649 F2d 1084 (5th Cir 1981) (right to be free from certain maternity leave regulations not clearly settled in 1972 when defendants acted but settled in 1974 when Supreme Court decided relevant case; no pre-1973 case on point).

[92] McGhee v Draper, 564 F2d 902 (10th Cir 1977). Compare Sullivan v Meade Indep School Dist No 101, 530 F2d 799 (8th Cir 1976), where a teacher was discharged in effect for living with a man to whom she was not married. The district court found for defendant school board members on the merits, concluding there was no constitutional violation. The Eighth Circuit affirmed on the ground of qualified immunity and avoided the constitutional issue. Applying *Wood* to a school board member's duties generally, it stated:

> While the right of a couple to live together without benefit of matrimony eventually may be held to fall within the penumbra of the constitutional right to privacy, it had not been so held at the time the Board dismissed the appellant plaintiff. Thus it cannot be said that the members of the School Board either knew or reasonably should have known that these actions would violate a "constitutional right" of [plaintiff].

Id 806.

For criticism of such judicial use of qualified immunity to avoid passing on the constitutionality of state statutes, see Kattan, *Knocking on Wood: Some Thoughts on the Immunities of State Officials to Civil Rights Damage Actions,* 30 Vand L Rev 941, 989-95 (1977).

Also compare with *McGhee,* Hostrop v Board of Jr College Dist No 515, 523 F2d 569 (7th Cir 1975) where the court held that defendants did not act unreasonably in terminating plaintiff without a hearing in 1970 because the relevant Supreme Court case on procedural due process in a teacher termination setting was not then decided.

[93] McGhee v Draper, 564 F2d 902, 915 (10th Cir 1977).

rather rigidly in a defendant's favor. In a Sixth Circuit case[94] a schoolteacher sued school board members for requiring her to take pregnancy leave prior to her fifth month of pregnancy. The district court had found against the defendants and characterized as unreasonable their reliance on another district court decision upholding an end of the semester rule on the grounds that the present case was distinguishable. Reversing as a matter of law, the Sixth Circuit emphasized that there was no Sixth Circuit decision on point and that a Supreme Court decision on sex discrimination was distinguishable. In short, "at the time the Board decision was made, there had in fact been no adjudication binding on the Board that its existing pregnancy policy was unconstitutional, let alone unquestionably so."[95] The Sixth Circuit seemed to require a case on point before the breach of duty to know issue could go to the jury.[96]

However, even where there is a case on point, it does not follow that it will be dispositive. The Fifth Circuit[97] inexplicably ignored such a case. There, the plaintiff sought damages arising out of the compulsory ROTC training program in his high school. The court held, without reaching the merits of the constitutional claim, that it was not settled that compulsory ROTC violated the Constitution at the time plaintiff was refused admittance to high school. But the court paid little attention to a Sixth Circuit case[98] holding compulsory ROTC unconstitutional, which was decided one month prior to the high school's refusal to admit plaintiff. Further, even if that opinion was not yet published or otherwise available, the Fifth Circuit did not even mention the district court opinion in that same case which also held compulsory ROTC unconstitutional 16 months prior to the conduct challenged here.

These school official cases indicate, not surprisingly, that courts have a great deal of discretion to find no breach of the duty to know as a matter of law, stemming in large measure from the peculiarly legal nature of this aspect of the qualified immunity test. Unless there is a case on all fours from the relevant circuit or the Supreme Court, most legal issues can be made to appear relatively uncertain. But this emphasis on the need for a case on point has been criticized. In a pre-*Harlow* non-school board case where the majority found no constitutional violation, Judge Oakes in dissent argued that the defendants had breached their duty to know and observed: "[T]he law in this area at the relevant time was about as 'settled' and 'unquestioned' as law can ever be in

---

[94] Shirley v Chagrin Falls Exempted Village Schools Bd of Educ, 521 F2d 1329 (6th Cir 1975), *cert denied,* 424 US 913 (1976).

[95] *Id* 1334.

[96] By its use of the word *binding,* the court may have suggested that the particular adjudication must have involved the Board. This, of course, would be even more stringent than a case on point requirement.

[97] Sapp v Renfroe, 511 F2d 172 (5th Cir 1975).

[98] Spence v Bailey, 465 F2d 797 (6th Cir 1972). The opinion was filed Aug 8, 1972.

our system of case-by-case development of the contours of constitutional rights."[99]

In effect, Judge Oakes recognized that a case on point need not necessarily be found. It may be appropriate in some situations to find a breach of the duty to know where the relevant constitutional doctrine is extrapolated or derived from cases which are relevant without being directly on point. This was done, for example, in a Ninth Circuit decision[100] involving a teacher whose contract was not renewed because of his exercise of First Amendment rights. Holding that the defendant school board members breached their duty to know as a matter of law, the court referred to several of its earlier decisions which indicated that terminating a teacher is unlawful even where only partially in retaliation for the exercise of constitutional rights.

In a post-*Harlow* decision, the Ninth Circuit[101] again extrapolated from existing case law where the plaintiff students sued a principal and teachers alleging an unconstitutional search of their persons (including a strip search of one plaintiff) for drugs. Reversing the jury verdict for the defendants, the Ninth Circuit held that defendants violated clearly settled Fourth Amendment law. Even though at the time there were no Supreme Court or Ninth Circuit decisions on point, "the basic Fourth Amendment rights of students had been sufficiently well-established that [defendants] were adequately on notice." That is, case law, including an Oregon Court of Appeals decision, generally established that there was a requirement of reasonable cause for student searches. Indeed, even the school board's own regulations imposed a probable cause requirement for student searches. Thus, defendants were on notice and should have been aware of these requirements.

Two circuit court decisions indicate that reliance on advice of counsel may insulate school officials even where they violated clearly settled law. In one,[102] the legal advisor to the school board, whose advice was relied on, had erroneously predicted, based on state court developments, that the challenged affirmative action plan would be held unconstitutional. In addition, the school board had rejected an earlier different opinion of another lawyer. Still, the

---

[99] Gilliard v Oswald, 552 F2d 456, 465 (2d Cir 1977). This case raised a procedural due process claim against prison officials in connection with the confinement of plaintiffs for one month in lock-up. Disagreeing with the majority, Judge Oakes referred to earlier decisions not on point as such and, reading them broadly, said: "Given these two decisions, no state prison official could reasonably have believed in February, 1973, that substantial deprivations could be visited upon inmates without granting them any form of due process." *Id.* 465.

[100] Wagle v Murray, 546 F2d 1329 (9th Cir 1976), *cert granted, vacated on other grounds & remanded,* 431 US 935 (1977). Extrapolation was also used in Slate v McFetridge, 484 F2d 1169, 1176 (7th Cir 1973), where a park superintendent and others were held liable for failing to give a park permit promptly to plaintiffs who wanted to organize a political rally. The Seventh Circuit first discussed a Supreme Court obscenity decision and then observed: "[D]efendants had notice by [the obscenity decision] that their prompt resolution of [plaintiffs'] permit request was a dictate of due process in the protection of First Amendment rights."

[101] Bilbrey v Brown, 738 F2d 1462 (9th Cir 1984) (Judge Kilkenny dissented).

[102] Schmidt v Oakland Unified School Dist, 662 F2d 550 (9th Cir 1981).

defendants passed the qualified immunity test as a matter of law. Similarly, in the other case where defendants passed the qualified immunity test,[103] the board attorney erroneously advised the board that no formal hearing was required before the plaintiff could be discharged. However, Judge McMillian argued in dissent[104] that the defendants were liable because they violated clearly settled procedural due process law. After *Harlow*, especially, this was the proper inquiry, not whether the defendants acted reasonably in relying on advice of counsel. Any other result, he argued, would reward ignorance and excuse them from their duty to know settled law.

Circuit courts have affirmed: a jury verdict for school officials accused of violating the plaintiffs' First Amendment rights in discharging them, where the relevant Supreme Court cases were not yet decided;[105] a district court finding for student plaintiffs against school officials who dismissed them from their school newspaper posts in violation of the First Amendment where defendants failed to seek legal advice and there was a two-month-old decision on point in the same circuit which did not dramatically change existing law;[106] a jury verdict against a superintendent accused of violating plaintiff's First Amendment rights where it was clearly established at the time by the Supreme Court that teachers cannot be disciplined for exercising their First Amendment rights;[107] and a district court finding for defendant school board members who allegedly had violated plaintiff employees' procedural due process rights in denying them a hearing before a layoff where relevant Supreme Court cases were not yet decided and a layoff was not so drastic an action as a termination.[108]

The qualified immunity test with its duty to know settled rights has been applied in the circuits to others besides local school board members, including principals, superintendents, presidents of colleges and universities, members of state boards of education, college trustees, and heads of university departments.[109]

---

[103] Okeson v Tolley School Dist, 766 F2d 378 (8th Cir 1985) (on pet for rehg).

[104] *Id* 379.

[105] Bertot v School Dist No 1, 522 F2d 1171 (10th Cir 1975).

[106] Schiff v Williams, 519 F2d 257 (5th Cir 1975).

[107] Anderson v Central Point School Dist, 746 F2d 505 (9th Cir 1984) (per curiam).

[108] Mims v Board of Educ, 523 F2d 711 (7th Cir 1975).

[109] Wagle v Murray, 546 F2d 1329 (9th Cir 1976), *cert granted, vacated on other grounds & remanded*, 431 US 935 (1977) (principal and superintendent); Skehan v Board of Trustees, 538 F2d 53 (3d Cir), *cert denied*, 429 US 979 (1976) (college trustees and university department head); Schiff v Williams, 519 F2d 257 (5th Cir 1975) (university president); Smith v Losee, 485 F2d 334 (10th Cir 1973) (en banc), *cert denied*, 417 US 908 (1974) (college president and members of a state board of education). For a thoughtful discussion of the liability of school officials see Yudof, *Liability for Constitutional Torts and the Risk-Averse Public School Official*, 49 S Cal L Rev 1322 (1976).

Note that in Cleavinger v Saxner, 106 S Ct 496 (1985), the Court reaffirmed its decision in *Wood v Strickland* that school board members are protected only by qualified immunity for their quasi-judicial conduct. *See* §§**7.10, 8.02, 8.10, & 8.18.**

§8.08   Mental Hospital Officials

The Supreme Court made clear in *O'Connor v Donaldson*[110] that mental hospital officials, like school officials, are protected by a qualified immunity.

O'Connor was an action against the superintendent of a mental hospital and others for allegedly confining plaintiff wrongfully for 15 years. The jury returned a verdict for plaintiff and the Fifth Circuit affirmed. The Supreme Court affirmed the jury verdict to the extent of its finding that the superintendent had knowingly violated plaintiff's right to freedom. In so doing, the Court held for the first time that "a State cannot constitutionally confine without more a nondangerous individual who is capable of surviving safely in freedom by himself or with the help of willing and responsible family members or friends."[111] However, the Court remanded to the Fifth Circuit to consider whether the trial court's instructions to the jury on the defendant's qualified immunity were correct in light of *Wood.*[112]

The trial court had instructed the jury that defendant was immune from damages if:

> He reasonably believed in good faith that the detention of plaintiff was proper for the length of time he was so confined. . . . However, mere good intentions which do not give rise to a reasonable belief that detention is lawfully required cannot justify plaintiff's confinement in the Florida State Hospital.

The trial court had also rejected defendant's requested instruction that "if defendants acted pursuant to a statute which was not declared unconstitutional at the time, they cannot be held accountable for such action."[113]

The Supreme Court, in remanding in light of *Wood,* directed the Fifth Circuit to consider whether the trial court's refusal "to instruct with regard to the effect of defendant's claimed reliance on state law rendered inadequate the instructions as to defendant's liability. . . ."[114] Chief Justice Burger, concurring, added that other factors should also be considered on remand in determining defendant's compliance with *Wood.* He mentioned the plaintiff's consistent refusals to accept treatment. He also contended that even more important were the repeated refusals by state courts to give plaintiff relief: defendant "would surely have been justified in considering each such judicial decision as an approval of continued confinement and an independent intervening reason for continuing plaintiff's custody" regardless of the reasons for the state courts' decisions and regardless of their soundness.[115]

O'Connor clearly indicates—if it was not clear before—that the duty to know

---

[110] 422 US 563 (1975).

[111] *Id* 576.

[112] Wood v Strickland, 420 US 308 (1975).

[113] These instructions are quoted in *O'Connor,* 422 US at 570 n 5, & 571-72.

[114] *Id* 577.

[115] *Id* 579.

clearly settled law aspect of *Wood* has general applicability beyond school board members who act in disciplinary situations.[116] The majority opinion seems questionable, however, to the extent it appears to equate the defendant's requested but refused instruction regarding reliance on a statute not held unconstitutional with an instruction on the existence of reasonable grounds for a defendant's belief that the challenged behavior was constitutional. That is, just because a court has not yet declared a specific state practice or statute unconstitutional, it does not follow that any particular defendant should not know that the statute or practice is indeed unconstitutional.[117] A better reading of this aspect of *O'Connor* is not that the requested instruction in particular should have been given but only that an instruction more fully complying with *Wood* should have been given.[118]

Chief Justice Burger, it will be recalled, dissented in *Wood*. His opinion in *O'Connor* is best seen as an attempt to dilute the duty to know aspect of *Wood*. Still, it is not entirely clear what he meant when he suggested that plaintiff's repeated refusals to accept treatment were relevant to the defendant's qualified immunity. Further, to the extent that *Wood* might require a hospital administrator like defendant to seek legal advice, Chief Justice Burger's assertion that state court decisions adverse to plaintiff were relevant to the existence of reasonable grounds for defendant's belief in the legal validity of his conduct, regardless of the state courts' reasons and the soundness of their decisions, seems inconsistent with *Wood*.

Since *O'Connor*, circuit court decisions have applied the qualified immunity test to mental health officials. In a pre-*Harlow* case[119] where suit was brought by former and present mental hospital patients against mental hospital staff members challenging certain forcible medication and seclusion practices as violative of due process, the First Circuit affirmed the district court's finding that the defendants had passed the objective part of the qualified immunity test. On the forced medication issue, the court asserted that the plaintiffs' right to refuse medication in an institution was not clearly established before 1975. On the seclusion issue, the plaintiffs could "not point to a single precedent holding that civilly committed mental health patients have a substantive constitutional

---

[116] *O'Connor* was applied in Goodman v Parwatikar, 570 F2d 801 (8th Cir 1978).

[117] See the discussions at §§8.04 and 8.07 on extrapolation from existing case law.

[118] What the Fifth Circuit did on remand bears out this interpretation. It found that the instructions actually given were inadequate to define the scope of official immunity after *Wood*. Donaldson v O'Connor, 519 F2d 59 (5th Cir 1975). See also Sebastion v United States, 531 F2d 900, 903-04 (8th Cir 1976) where the court affirmed the district court's grant of summary judgment in favor of deputy sheriffs and a doctor, among others, who played a role in plaintiff's wrongful commitment to a mental hospital. Relying on *O'Connor*, the court found that the deputy sheriffs "acted at all times in good faith reliance on Arkansas law, without reason to believe that the plaintiff had been committed without notice and hearing." It also found that the doctor who recommended that plaintiff be hospitalized "acted both reasonably and in good faith."

[119] Rogers v Okin, 634 F2d 650 (1st Cir 1980).

right not to be placed in seclusion except in emergencies. . . ."[120] The court rejected the plaintiffs' attempt to use a state statute to demonstrate that they had a clearly established state-created liberty interest in being free from nonemergency seclusion. Among other things, the state statute was not as clear as the plaintiffs contended.

In a post-*Harlow* Third Circuit decision,[121] plaintiff, originally charged with burglary, was found insane and placed in a state hospital for 35 years, during which time his status as a mental incompetent was never reviewed. Also, he was never treated for a psychiatric condition. After release, he sued various mental health officials for violating his due process rights by neither treating nor releasing him. Affirming the district court, the Third Circuit ruled that, even though various defendants had violated plaintiff's constitutional rights, they neither knew nor should have known that their failure to supervise therapeutic programs at the state hospital would violate plaintiff's rights. They thus passed *Harlow*'s objective qualified immunity test.

In contrast, in another post-*Harlow* Third Circuit decision,[122] defendant mental hospital officials were not entitled to have the plaintiff patient's due process claims dismissed on qualified immunity grounds pursuant to *Harlow*. Even though at the time they acted, the precise constitutional basis of plaintiff's claims—the rights to be free from unreasonable restraints and to adequate treatment—may not have been sufficiently defined, the right to be free from inhumane conditions had been long established.

In a Fifth Circuit case,[123] mental hospital officials sued by a former patient in connection with his confinement were, according to the court, protected by qualified immunity as a matter of law. Avoiding the constitutionality of the hospital's admission policies, the court held that the "defendants could not have known that their policy of temporarily placing new admittees into Ward 1 for observation would give rise to a constitutional violation" of plaintiff's right to be held in an environment least restrictive of his civil rights and liberties. While this right was generally established, its claimed violation in the case before the court was sufficiently close to allow the district court's directed verdict in favor of defendants to stand.

And in a post-*Harlow* Seventh Circuit case,[124] plaintiffs, criminal defendants found unfit to stand trial, were confined to a maximum security mental health facility in violation of due process. Under state law, they had a liberty interest in being confined to the least restrictive environment. Nevertheless, the defendant mental health officials were not liable for damages; when they acted, there was no prior case law determining the significance of the statute creating the liberty interest found here. In addition, the defendants' telephone policy,

---

[120] *Id* 662.

[121] Stuebig v Hammel, 714 F2d 292 (3d Cir 1983) (per curiam).

[122] Scott v Plante, 691 F2d 634 (3d Cir 1982). The court's additional reliance in its opinion on state law duties is now questionable after Davis v Scherer, 104 S Ct 3012 (1984), discussed at **§8.05.**

[123] Dilmore v Stubbs, 636 F2d 966 (5th Cir 1981).

[124] Johnson v Brelje, 701 F2d 1201, 1211 (7th Cir 1983).

which illegally restricted access to the courts, was not clearly unconstitutional at the time. While there was a clearly settled right of access to the courts, no prior case law had relied on this right to hold invalid a mental health regulation. Further, the violation of plaintiffs' rights to move freely around the mental health facility's grounds would not warrant a damages award because "the law controlling the substantive due process issue had been quite unsettled." The Seventh Circuit therefore affirmed the district court's findings on qualified immunity.

§8.09   Prison Officials—*Procunier v Navarette*

In *Procunier v Navarette,*[125] a 1978 decision, the Supreme Court held that qualified immunity protects prison officials at both the supervisory, high discretion level and the subordinate, ministerial, minimal discretion level.[126] In *Navarette,* plaintiff, a prison inmate, sued the director of the California Department of Corrections, the warden and assistant warden of a state prison (supervisory officials), two correctional counselors, and a member of the prison staff in charge of handling incoming and outgoing mail (subordinate officials) on various §1983 grounds, including negligent interference with his constitutional right to mail outgoing letters. The district court granted summary judgment for all defendants on this claim, but the Ninth Circuit reversed, holding that plaintiff had stated a §1983 cause of action and that summary judgment was improper given the affidavits presented by the parties. Although the Supreme Court had granted certiorari to deal with the existence under §1983 of a prima facie cause of action based on negligence,[127] it sidestepped this issue and decided instead that summary judgment for defendants was appropriate on a qualified immunity ground.

The reasoning used is particularly instructive because the Court showed how it applied the duty to know settled rights aspect of the qualified immunity inquiry. The opinion first characterized the qualified immunity available to executives, school board members, mental hospital superintendents, and police officers as a unitary standard, and quoted the *Scheuer v Rhodes*[128] reasonable grounds, good faith belief formulation. It then applied the pre-*Harlow*[129] two-part test elaborated in *Wood*[130] to the defendants in *Navarette.*

The first part related to (1) whether at the time in question, 1971 and 1972, defendants knew or should have known of the existence of the right asserted and (2) whether they knew or should have known that they were violating it.

---

[125] 434 US 555 (1978).

[126] There already had been, however, indications of the applicability of a qualified immunity to subordinates in the earlier decision of Scheuer v Rhodes, 416 US 232 (1974), discussed at **§8.13.**

[127] *See* **ch 3.**

[128] 416 US 232 (1974).

[129] Harlow v Fitzgerald, 457 US 800 (1982).

[130] Wood v Strickland, 420 US 308 (1975).

In answering that defendants both did not know and should not have known, the Court concluded that there was no such federal right at the time. It observed that the Ninth Circuit itself had only upheld such a right in 1973 and 1974, and a three-judge court opinion to the same effect from California was also decided in 1973.

Further, the Supreme Court's own 1974 opinion on a similar issue[131] dealt with it from the perspective of the constitutional right of the addressee, rather than the perspective of the prisoner, the specific issue involved in *Navarette*. Other more timely California federal district court decisions from 1970 through 1972, offered by the plaintiff to show that a prisoner's right to send mail was clearly established by 1971 and 1972, were described by the Court as distinguishable and inapposite to a showing of a clearly established right. Thus, because no decisions of the Supreme Court, the various circuit courts, and the local district court definitively set out a prisoner's right to send mail in 1971 and 1972, the Court held as a matter of law that defendants acted reasonably and without "disregard for the established law."[132]

The Court also added a new gloss to the second, subjective part of the qualified immunity test, the part since eliminated by *Harlow*, which had been described in *Wood* as acting with "the malicious intention to cause a deprivation of constitutional rights or other injury."[133] The Court in *Navarette* characterized the second part as speaking "of 'intentional injury,' contemplating that the actor intends the consequences of his conduct."[134] It also cited Restatement (Second) of Torts, Section 8A which defines *intent* as including a belief that "the consequences are substantially certain to result" from the act. Because the defendants were all charged either with negligent interference with plaintiff's mail or with negligent failure to provide proper training to mail handlers, depending on their positions, the Court held that defendants' intent to cause harm was clearly not involved.[135] Thus, the Court held, again as a matter of law, that the defendants also passed the second, subjective part of the qualified immunity test.[136]

Justice Stevens dissented.[137] He criticized the Court's assumption in both *O'Connor*[138] and *Navarette* that every government officer was protected by the same qualified immunity under §1983. More importantly, he contended that, if this were indeed to be the general rule, it was important "that the contours

---

[131] Procunier v Martinez, 416 US 396 (1974).

[132] Procunier v Navarette, 434 US 555, 565 (1975).

[133] *Wood* 420 US at 322.

[134] 434 US at 566.

[135] Even though before *Harlow*, intent was relevant to the qualified immunity test, there was no inconsistency with the rejection in Monroe v Pape, 365 US 167 (1961) of a specific intent requirement for the prima facie §1983 cause of action.

[136] 434 US 555, 556.

[137] Chief Justice Burger also dissented, but on the ground that the Court should have considered and rejected negligence as a basis of liability under §1983.

[138] O'Connor v Donaldson, 422 US 563 (1975).

of this affirmative defense be explained with care and precision."[139] The Court did not do this in *Navarette,* according to Justice Stevens, because no evidence was even heard and the available record suggested the possibility that plaintiff might have been able to rebut the factual basis for qualified immunity of the defendants. He maintained that this possibility seemed especially significant to the issue of the defendants' state of mind and plaintiff's claim that they acted maliciously toward him. Finally, Justice Stevens argued that in 1971 prisoners had a well-established right of access to the courts and to legal assistance and thus at least some of the defendants knew or should have know that plaintiff's right of access was interfered with.[140]

Despite Justice Steven's dissent, the relevant claim of plaintiff involved his right to send mail, not access to the courts as such. Furthermore, it is clear that plaintiff alleged negligence, thereby precluding him in effect from rebutting defendants' assertions in their affidavits that they did not act with the intention to harm him. The Court apparently utilized *Navarette* as a vehicle for further discussion of the duty to know settled rights, which was perhaps the most controversial aspect of *Wood,* and to show that this duty would not result in the equivalent of strict liability under §1983.

Navarette did not portend the abandonment of the duty to know aspect of the qualified immunity test. It indicated, rather, even before *Harlow,* that the Court favored a prodefendant application of the clearly settled law inquiry, perhaps even to the extent of requiring a case on point setting forth the existence of a constitutional right. Moreover, even where such a right is found clearly to exist, the next inquiry must be, according to *Navarette,* whether the defendant should have known that the conduct engaged in was violating the right. At this level, the duty to know test is more complicated because often there will not be a case which deals expressly with the kind of conduct charged against the defendant. This is where the duty to know will necessarily involve interpretation of and extrapolation from existing case law. If *Navarette* means that there must be a case on point as to the specific kind of conduct charged, then *Wood's* duty to know settled rights, which originally had a proplaintiff thrust, has been substantially undercut.[141] Indeed, as discussed earlier,[142] the Court's decisions in *Harlow, Davis,* and *Mitchell* bear out this interpretation.

§8.10   —In The Circuits

Even before *Navarette,*[143] it was generally accepted in the circuits that a qualified immunity was applicable to prison officials.[144] Just as the objective

---

[139] 434 US at 569.

[140] *Id* 569-70.

[141] See the criticism of such an approach at §§**8.04 & 8.07.**

[142] *See* §§**8.03-8.05.**

[143] Procunier v Navarette, 434 US 555 (1975).

[144] *E.g.,* Kellerman v Askew, 541 F2d 1089 (5th Cir 1976) involving an Eighth Amendment claim against prison officials for inadequate medical treatment. Reversing

part of the qualified immunity test posed problems in application to school officials and others, similar problems arose in cases of prison officials. To some extent the objective part of the test—including the duty to know settled rights—caused even more problems as applied to prison officials than to others because judicial involvement in, and supervision over, prisons have intensified dramatically in the last decade.

The Seventh Circuit[145] used an extrapolation approach in determining the duty to know of prison officials. The officials were sued for allegedly failing to prevent attacks by other inmates against plaintiff. The district court found for defendants on the ground that they did not fail to apply the law as it existed at the time. It cited a Fourth Circuit decision[146] in support of this conclusion as to the earlier status of the law. Reversing as a matter of law, the Seventh Circuit held that defendants "should have known that their actions within the sphere of their official responsibility would violate plaintiff's constitutional rights."[147] The court noted that the Fourth Circuit decision was clearly distinguishable on its facts and, in any event, a strong dissenting opinion in that case became the Fourth Circuit rule one year later. It also emphasized that prison officials must be "sensitive and alert" to the protections given inmates by "the developing judicial scrutiny of prison conditions and practices." To this end, a defendant "cannot hide behind a claim that the particular factual tableau in question has never appeared *in haec verba* in a reported opinion. If the application of settled principles to this factual tableau would inexorably lead to a conclusion of unconstitutionality, a prison official may not take solace in ostrichism."[148]

A similar extrapolation approach was used by the First Circuit[149] where the plaintiff inmate successfully sued a prison superintendent for denying due

---

the district court which had held that defendants could only be liable for actual knowledge of constitutional violations, the Fifth Circuit remanded in light of the objective part of the *Wood* qualified immunity test.

[145] Little v Walker, 552 F2d 193 (7th Cir 1977), *cert denied*, 435 US 932 (1978).

[146] Breeden v Jackson, 457 F2d 578 (4th Cir 1972).

[147] 552 F2d at 198.

[148] *Id* 197.

[149] King v Higgins, 702 F2d 18, 20-22 (1st Cir 1983). *See* Blackburn v Snow, 771 F2d 556 (1st Cir 1985) (Fourth Amendment law of prison visitor strip searches clearly settled in 1977 even though "exact parameters of official authority . . . not yet clear" in such cases at the time; defendant consulted no legal or professional authority); McCann v Coughlin, 698 F2d 112 (2d Cir 1983) (defendants not entitled to read prior circuit court case law narrowly so as to limit those cases to their facts). *But cf* Wilson v Schillinger, 761 F2d 921 (3d Cir 1985) (even if inmate was denied equal protection because a hair length regulation was enforced against him, a Rastafarian, but not against adherent to Indian religion, it was not clearly settled that plaintiff's religion was officially recognized as such); Security & Law Enforcement Employees v Carey, 737 F2d 187 (2d Cir 1984) (prison officials not expected to predict "future" constitutional law developments in connection with strip searches); Withers v Levine, 615 F2d 158 (4th Cir 1980) (prior circuit court decision only defined inmate's right to be free from sexual assaults "in broad outline" at time of defendants' conduct; the existence and application of this right then not clearly settled).

process at a prison disciplinary proceeding through a lack of prior notice, and by not being told of his rights to advice of counsel, to confront the complaining officer, and to present witnesses. Affirming the district court's award of compensatory damages to plaintiff, the First Circuit held that defendant had failed the objective qualified immunity test. Even though the precise bounds of due process in prison disciplinary proceedings were not entirely clear at the time, "it had long been clear that at a hearing which could result in such [substantial] punishment plaintiff was entitled at least to notice and the opportunity to present evidence in his own behalf." No specific judicial articulation was necessary to demonstrate that these procedural safeguards were assurances of elemental fairness. In addition, defendant had violated department regulations of which he knew or should have known. In short, in light of the information before him, defendant had a duty "to assure that the proceedings below were constitutionally sound" and at least to have conducted some investigation. That defendant did not do so constituted reckless disregard of plaintiff's constitutional rights.

The question of what case law a court is to look at in ascertaining the existence of clearly settled law has concerned the circuits in prison cases. For example, the Second Circuit[150] affirmed a district court judgment in favor of prison officials accused of violating the plaintiff inmate's procedural due process rights in connection with his nonpunitive transfer from the general prison population to administrative segregation. While the transfer had violated procedural due process, the defendants were properly found to have passed the qualified immunity test. The court found that, at the time plaintiff was transferred to administrative segregation, "the Supreme Court caselaw indicated that transfers did not necessarily require procedural due process even if they substantially deprived a prisoner of privileges, and the First Circuit caselaw indicated . . . that that rule applied to an intraprison transfer . . . ." Even though a federal district court in California reached a contrary result prior to plaintiff's transfer, the defendants could not be required "to stay abreast of district court case law from across the country."[151]

In another case[152] the plaintiff inmate sued the chairman of a prison disciplinary committee which had sentenced him to a loss of eight recreation periods in alleged violation of procedural due process. The right allegedly violated by defendant was the denial of plaintiff's right to call live witnesses at his hearing on the ground that their testimony would have been irrelevant or cumulative. Finding that this right was not "clearly established" in the Fourth Circuit at the time, the court relied on a Fourth Circuit decision affirming *without opinion* a *published* district court opinion holding that the choice

---

[150] Raffone v Robinson, 607 F2d 1058 (2d Cir 1979). *See also* Capoeman v Reed, 754 F2d 1512 (9th Cir 1985) ("look to whatever decisional law is available . . . ").

[151] 607 F2d at 1062.

[152] Ward v Johnson, 690 F2d 1098 (4th Cir 1982) (en banc). Judges Winter and Ervin dissented. After Cleavinger v Saxner, 106 S Ct 496 (1985), *Ward* is no longer good law as to its holding that prison disciplinary committee members are protected by absolute immunity. *See* §8.15.

of permitting an inmate to call live witnesses was discretionary. Knowledge of a contrary *unpublished* Fourth Circuit opinion could not reasonably be charged to the defendant. Even if the two rulings somehow cancelled each other out, the plaintiff's asserted right could still not be described as clearly established.

State law may even be relevant to the existence of clearly settled law, despite the insistence of the Supreme Court in *Davis v Scherer*[153] that clearly settled state law is not determinative of clearly settled constitutional or federal statutory law. For example, in a Sixth Circuit case,[154] an inmate challenged on procedural due process–deprivation of property grounds a rule of the defendant prison officials that prohibited him from receiving a book from his mother. Distinguishing *Davis* as involving a state regulation unrelated to the *Davis* plaintiff's underlying §1983 claim, the court ruled that the clearly settled state regulation here—which allowed inmates to receive any books not threatening order or security—created a property interest and defined the criteria for the defeat of that interest. Because defendants violated this clearly settled state regulation, they were as a matter of law not entitled to qualified immunity in connection with plaintiff's procedural due process claim.

In connection with the duty to know of prison officials, the Second Circuit[155] distinguished between Eighth Amendment rights and other rights. Plaintiff, an inmate, alleged First and Eighth Amendment violations resulting from his punishment for possession of certain "inflammatory" religious writings and his being placed in strip cell on various occasions. Reversing the district court's summary judgment for defendants, the court stated:

> The conception of what is meant by "cruel and unusual punishment" in the language of the Eighth Amendment has been evolving in the past two decades. . . . It reflects an evolving view of society as interpreted by the Supreme Court. . . . When we deal with violations of other constitutional rights of prisoners, however, there may be a sharper distinction between conduct that was allowable at the time and conduct that had already been declared beyond the limits of disciplinary prerogatives. . . .[156]

The Second Circuit immediately blurred its distinction, however, when it added:

> But the test of liability ought not ignore entirely the mores of the times or even the particular mores of prison guards, untrained in the lawyers' view of life. The growth of constitutional protection in recent years in the area of First, Fourth, and Fifth Amendment rights is illustrative of

---

[153] 104 S Ct 3012 (1984).

[154] Spruytte v Walters, 753 F2d 498 (6th Cir 1985).

[155] Mukmuk v Commissioners of Dept of Correctional Serv, 529 F2d 272 (2d Cir), *cert denied*, 96 S Ct 2238 (1976).

[156] 529 F2d at 277-78.

situations where retroactive application of newly declared doctrine may be unfair.[157]

In another case involving the use of strip cells, the Tenth Circuit[158] affirmed the district court's finding for defendant prison officials. Even though strip cells were now violative of the Eighth Amendment, the defendants had not acted unreasonably in using them earlier. The court emphasized the following factors:

1. No court had held the practice unconstitutional
2. It was a long-standing practice in the state
3. It was customary in other states
4. It was apparently authorized by statute
5. Eighth Amendment concepts are constantly changing[159]

Similarly, the Second Circuit[160] affirmed a judgment for defendant prison officials accused of procedural due process violations relating to punishment. The Commissioner of Corrections was not sufficiently involved in the violations to subject him to personal liability, while the defendants who were at the prison acted reasonably because the "cases indicated that at the time the courts were only beginning to fill in the details of procedural due process required in the context of prison discipline."[161]

The existence of a prisoner's right can be *settled* and yet the circumstances of its violation may be unclear, thereby resulting in a judgment for prison officials.[162] For example, in a Seventh Circuit decision,[163] the plaintiff claimed his right of access to the courts was violated when he was placed in disciplinary isolation for 15 days. Affirming the district court's judgment for defendants, the Seventh Circuit agreed with plaintiff that the asserted right was clearly in existence when he was placed in isolation. However, it pointed out that the deprivation was limited, not absolute, and concluded that the defendants might reasonably have believed that this denial of access to the courts for 15 days for

---

[157] *Id* 278.

[158] Poindexter v Woodson, 510 F2d 464 (10th Cir) (per curiam), *cert denied,* 423 US 846 (1975). *Cf* Wycoff v Brewer, 572 F2d 1260 (8th Cir 1978), a post-*Navarette* case in which prison officials who confined plaintiff in administrative segregation were found to be qualifiedly immune.

[159] 510 F2d at 465, 466.

[160] McKinnon v Patterson, 568 F2d 930 (2d Cir 1977), *cert denied,* 434 US 1087 (1978).

[161] 568 F2d at 935.

[162] See the discussion at the end of §8.04 on the difference between reasonableness in connection with knowing a right exists and knowing it is violated. The latter is a more factually oriented judgment because it requires the application of constitutional principles to particular facts.

[163] Knell v Bensinger, 522 F2d 720 (7th Cir 1975).

disciplinary purposes "was *de minimis* and justified by the exigencies and considerations of prison discipline."[164]

There may even be situations where, despite the existence of clearly settled law, a prison official can show *Harlow*'s "exceptional circumstances" exception to the duty to know. For example, in a Fourth Circuit case[165] a prisoner sued various defendants, including correctional officials, for their failure in violation of federal statutory law to provide a preliminary hearing prior to temporary transfer to another state for the purpose of trying him there on criminal charges. The Fourth Circuit reversed the district court's grant of summary judgment for the defendants and remanded for further consideration of the question of whether defendants should have known they were violating clearly settled law when they transferred plaintiff without a hearing. Twelve days before they did so, the Supreme Court had ruled in *Cuyler v Adams*[166] that a preliminary hearing was in fact required. Thus, the law was clearly settled when the defendants acted. The only issue on remand, according to the Fourth Circuit, would be whether the defendants could show that, because of exceptional circumstances, they neither knew nor should have known of this decision. This would be a hard burden to carry inasmuch as several prior lower court decisions had reached the same result as *Cuyler*. Also, the defendants had a direct interest in learning of and applying *Cuyler*, and 12 days may have been enough time to do so.

Similarly, where the plaintiff inmate sued correctional officials for failure to provide him sufficient access to an adequate law library, the Fourth Circuit[167] observed that the key question was when the law on library or attorney access for prisoners in local jails was so enunciated by the courts that a Virginia official knew or should have known that these rights were established. Plaintiff was incarcerated from January 1976 until May 1978, while the Supreme Court decision apparently on point, *Bounds v Smith*,[168] was not decided until April 1977. Affirming summary judgment in favor of defendants, the court first noted that arguably relevant case law prior to *Bounds* had dealt only with state, not local, jails and was distinguishable. Thus, there was no clearly settled law at that time. Even after *Bounds*, 14 months was not an unreasonable period of time to give the defendants to comply with the requirements of *Bounds*, although the court made this finding "with some reluctance."

Another example of the exceptional circumstances exception is an Eighth Circuit decision[169] where, relying on *Harlow*,[170] the court affirmed the district

---

[164] *Id* 727.

[165] Arebaugh v Dalton, 730 F2d 970 (4th Cir 1984).

[166] 449 US 433 (1981).

[167] Harris v Young, 718 F2d 620 (4th Cir 1983). Judge Murnaghan dissented on this issue.

[168] 430 US 817 (1977).

[169] Green v White, 693 F2d 45 (8th Cir 1982). *But cf* Ware v Heyne, 575 F2d 593 (7th Cir 1978) (per curiam) (rejecting as "sheer nonsense" the argument that defendants should not have known of a circuit decision on point decided two months prior to conduct).

[170] Harlow v Fitzgerald, 457 US 800 (1982).

court's grant of summary judgment in favor of a prison superintendent accused of violating the plaintiff's right to free exercise of his religion. Plaintiff could not show that the defendant had violated any of plaintiff's clearly settled rights through the imposition of reasonable restrictions on the exercise of his religion in connection with holding religious services with other inmates and the distribution of a religious newspaper. As to plaintiff's claim that he was not allowed to grow a beard or have long hair as called for by his religion, at the time these were prohibited by prison regulations for security reasons. Even though the constitutional rules regarding long hair had before that time been changed in the Eighth Circuit, the defendant was not a lawyer, he had to rely on regulations issued by the Missouri Division of Corrections, and he had no reason to know that there had been any change in the law regarding inmates' rights to have long hair. Thus, even though there may have been settled law, there was no duty on the part of the defendant to know it.

It is also important to be sensitive to the primacy of the court's role in the clearly settled law determination and at the same time to distinguish between the elements of the prima facie case and the clearly settled law inquiry so as to avoid inconsistent verdicts. For example, in a Fourth Circuit case[171] where the plaintiff inmate alleged the unnecessary and excessive use of mace against him in his cell in violation of the Eighth Amendment, the court affirmed a jury verdict for the defendant on the ground that, even though he had violated plaintiff's Eighth Amendment rights, he was protected by qualified immunity. It was too late for the plaintiff to argue on appeal that the jury should have been instructed on the objective nature of qualified immunity, since he did not raise that issue at the trial. Furthermore, in distinguishing case law set out by the dissent, the court found that it was not clearly established law that the use of mace against an inmate in his cell was per se unconstitutional: to the contrary, the rule took account of the totality of the circumstances. Thus, the jury could properly have found that the defendant reasonably believed that his conduct was constitutional.

Judge Ervin dissented, arguing first that the court's qualified immunity instruction was plain error, regardless of plaintiff's failure to object at trial. Second, the majority was incorrect in asserting that he was contending that the use of mace was per se unconstitutional. Rather, his position was that it was clearly established law that the excessive use of mace was violative of the Eighth Amendment and that in this case defendant's use of mace was unquestionably excessive. Defendant should have known that, under the circumstances, his use of mace violated plaintiff's Eighth Amendment rights. Thus, the jury should not have been allowed to decide the qualified immunity issue in defendant's favor.

---

[171] Bailey v Turner, 736 F2d 963, 972 (4th Cir 1984). *See also* Lucas v Hodges, 730 F2d 1493, 1506 (DC Cir 1984) ("the absence of a square holding either way by the Supreme Court, this court, or the District of Columbia district court could weigh more heavily in deciding the qualified immunity issue than it does in our decision on the merits of this legal issue").

In a Fifth Circuit case[172] where the defendants were sued for the use of excessive force against a mentally disturbed pretrial detainee while he was arrested and incarcerated, the Fifth Circuit held that jury findings in favor of a deputy sheriff and jailer on qualified immunity grounds were inconsistent with findings that they had used excessive force against the detainee. They were inconsistent because the instructions on the excessive use of force issue required that the jury find that defendants knew they were using such force, while the instructions on qualified immunity required that defendants, to have qualified immunity, neither knew nor reasonably should have known that they were using excessive force. Thus, the finding of excessive force precluded a finding of qualified immunity and the claims against these defendants should be remanded for a new trial.

And in a case involving unconstitutional strip searches by the defendant, the Seventh Circuit[173] stated that a jury was not competent to decide the state of the law in the course of applying *Harlow's* objective qualified immunity test. Whether a legal principle was clearly established was an issue reserved to the court. Only if there were *extraordinary circumstances* might a defendant's actual knowledge be relevant for the jury to consider in connection with the qualified immunity test. However, the defendant did not preserve this issue for appeal by objecting to the immunity instruction to the jury. In any event, there was sufficient evidence to support the jury's rejection of defendant's qualified immunity defense. Defendant acted in disregard of prison regulations and he also acted, the jury found, wantonly and with reckless disregard for plaintiff's rights.

Previously, members of prison disciplinary committees who acted in a quasi-judicial capacity were, in some circuits, protected by absolute judicial immunity[174] while in others[175] they were protected by qualified immunity. The underlying question was whether the functional approach of *Butz v Economou*[176] should be applied to such prison officials and, if so, whether the holding in *Wood v Strickland*[177] that school board members are protected by qualified immunity for their quasi-judicial conduct was thereby threatened.

In *Cleavinger v Saxner*,[178] a recent decision, the Court, finding that such prison officials are not functionally comparable to judges, ruled that they are

---

[172] Lozano v Smith, 718 F2d 756 (5th Cir 1983). *See also* Miller v Solem, 728 F2d 1020 (8th Cir 1984) (same) and Albers v Whitley, 743 F2d 1372 (9th Cir 1984) (same) *revd*, 106 S Ct 1078 (1986); Haygood v Younger, 718 F2d 1472, 1483-84 (9th Cir 1983) (prima facie Eighth Amendment case and qualified immunity).

[173] McKinley v Trattles, 732 F2d 1320 (7th Cir 1984). *See also* Bates v Jean, 745 F2d 1146 (7th Cir 1984) (jury role and inconsistent verdicts).

[174] Ward v Johnson, 690 F2d 1098 (4th Cir 1982) (en banc).

[175] King v Wells, 760 F2d 89 (6th Cir 1985); Saxner v Benson, 727 F2d 669 (7th Cir 1984), *affd sub nom* Cleavinger v Saxner, 106 S Ct 496 (1985).

[176] 438 US 478 (1978), discussed at §7.10.

[177] 420 US 308 (1975), discussed at §8.02.

[178] 106 S Ct 496 (1985). Chief Justice Burger and Justices Rehnquist and O'Connor dissented. *See also* §7.10.

protected only by qualified immunity. In the course of its decision, the Court reaffirmed that the adjudicatory conduct of school board members is protected by qualified, not absolute immunity. A related inquiry, whether parole board officials should in some circumstances be protected by absolute immunity, is discussed later in this chapter.[179]

§8.11   State and Local Law Enforcement Officers

Until *Pierson v Ray* was decided in 1967,[180] the Supreme Court's only decision on individual immunity under §1983 was *Tenney v Brandhove*,[181] which set out an absolute legislative immunity. But in *Pierson* the Court not only held that judges are absolutely immune under §1983, but also held that police officers have an affirmative defense of good faith and probable cause to claims of unconstitutional arrests. The plaintiffs in that case, peaceful sit-in demonstrators, asserted that they had been arrested, first, under a breach of the peace statute subsequently held unconstitutional and, second, under circumstances clearly indicating the absence of any factual basis for their arrest.

The Court noted as to the first claim:

> Under the prevailing view in this country a peace officer who arrests someone with probable cause is not liable for false arrest simply because the innocence of the suspect is later proved. A policeman's lot is not so unhappy that he must choose between being charged with dereliction of duty if he does not arrest when he has probable cause, and being mulcted in damages if he does. Although the matter is not entirely free from doubt, the same consideration would seem to require excusing him from liability for acting under a statute that he reasonably believed to be valid but that was later held unconstitutional, on its face or as applied.[182]

The Court then applied *Monroe v Pape*'s[183] *background of tort liability* approach, described as including the defense of good faith and probable cause, to the police officers and concluded: "We agree that a police officer is not charged with predicting the future course of constitutional law."[184] The Court thus suggested that if the reasonableness of the defendants' conduct in connection with the legal status of the statute had been the only issue before it, it would have ruled as a matter of law that the defendants acted reasonably.

However, the Court held as to the second claim that it was for the jury to determine whether the police officers "reasonably believed in good faith that

---

[179] *See* §8.18.

[180] 386 US 547 (1967).

[181] 341 US 367 (1951). Of course, Monroe v Pape, 365 US 167 (1961) had earlier established governmental immunity under §1983. *See* **ch 6.**

[182] 386 US at 555 (citations omitted).

[183] 365 US 167 (1961).

[184] 386 US at 557.

the arrest was constitutional."[185] If the jury believed the officers' testimony, then they would prevail; if it believed the testimony of the plaintiffs and other witnesses, the plaintiffs would prevail.

The Court also rejected the defendants' argument that plaintiffs had "somehow consented" to their illegal arrest. The Court simply observed that plaintiffs had not "tricked or goaded" defendants into arresting them. Further, plaintiffs had a right to be where they were when they were arrested.[186]

In discussing the defense of good faith and probable cause, the Court in *Pierson* clearly indicated that police officers have the burden of proving this reasonable grounds–good faith defense.[187] Further, while *Pierson* may be criticized for its rather conclusory assertion that such a common law tort defense ought to be fully applicable to police officers in §1983 cases,[188] *Pierson* reflects the Court's concern that a margin for error be given to police officers to allow them to perform effectively.[189]

Regrettably, however, the Court's language in defining the defense was somewhat confusing. Throughout its opinion, the Court frequently referred to good faith and probable cause. Yet, the Court could not in fact have meant probable cause. Otherwise, police officers who arrested a person in good faith but without probable cause, as ultimately determined by a court, would always be liable in damages. Elaborating on this point before *Harlow*,[190] the Second Circuit stated in a much-cited post-*Pierson* case:

> To prevail the police officer need not allege and prove probable cause in the constitutional sense. The standard governing police conduct is composed of two elements, the first is subjective and the second is objective. Thus the officer must allege and prove not only that he

---

[185] *Id.*

[186] For discussion of the seldom raised issue of consent in a §1983 setting, see Nahmod, *Section 1983 and the "Background" of Tort Liability*, 50 Ind LJ 5, 26-28 (1974); *see also* Weatherford v Bursey, 429 US 545, 554 (1977) (§1983 Sixth Amendment case in which the Court asserted that a defendant in a criminal trial does not assume the risk that a third party is an informer); Blackburn v Snow, 771 F2d 556 (1st Cir 1985) (rejecting argument that prison visitor's return to prison after first strip search constituted consent to violation of her Fourth Amendment rights); *cf* Town of Newton v Rumery, 778 F2d 66 (1st Cir 1986), *cert granted*, 106 S Ct __ (1986) (holding invalid as contrary to public policy a covenant not to sue police officers and others for constitutional violations in exchange for their decision not to prosecute him).

[187] For further discussion of who should have this burden see **§8.16.**

[188] *See generally* Nahmod, *Section 1983 and the "Background" of Tort Liability*, 50 Ind LJ 5, 26-30 (1974).

[189] Add to this necessary margin for error the fact that the police officer's employer, such as a municipality or county, is not liable under §1983 through respondeat superior, see **ch 6** on local government liability. Also, the judge who may be involved is absolutely immune. *See* **ch 7.** Thus, the police officer is frequently the sole target.

[190] Harlow v Fitzgerald, 457 US 800 (1982).

believed, in good faith, that his conduct was lawful, but also that his belief was reasonable.[191]

Thus, before *Harlow*, reasonable belief in the legal validity of an arrest and search was a different and less restrictive standard than probable cause. The Seventh Circuit[192] also drew this same distinction. As will be seen, *Harlow's* qualified immunity test has caused some confusion in the circuits on the relation between probable cause and the clearly settled law inquiry.

Those Supreme Court decisions subsequent to *Pierson*, which were discussed earlier,[193] elaborated on the objective part of the *Pierson* test and clearly demonstrated that their qualified immunity test is essentially the same as the affirmative defense in *Pierson*, as modified by *Harlow's* elimination of the subjective part of the test. Thus, police officers, like school officials, mental hospital officials, and prison officials, must prove that they did not know and should not have known they were violating the clearly settled constitutional rights of the plaintiff.

Many of the troublesome post-*Harlow* qualified immunity issues in the circuits involve the Fourth Amendment's requirement of probable cause and its relation to the qualified immunity inquiry, together with the question of the proper roles of judge and jury in such cases. On the one hand, as noted earlier, a police officer should not invariably fail the qualified immunity test just because he or she arrests or searches without probable cause. The Fifth Circuit stated: "The mere fact that a person is wrongfully arrested and charged with an offense whose elements are well-settled does not mean that the arrest itself contravenes 'well-settled' law."[194] On the other hand, the Fourth Amendment's requirement of probable cause for arrest and search is, at the general level, clearly settled law. The Supreme Court thus stated in *Mitchell v Forsyth*[195] that it "[did] not intend to suggest that an official is always immune from liability or suit for a warrantless search merely because the warrant requirement has never been explicitly held to apply to a search conducted in identical circumstances. . . ." But where there is "a legitimate question whether an *exception* to the warrant requirement exists," then, according to the Court, a warrantless search does not violate clearly settled law.

---

[191] Bivens v Six Unknown Named Agents, 456 F2d 1339, 1348 (2d Cir 1972). This case, which involved federal law enforcement officers, is more fully discussed at **§8.12.**

[192] Boscarino v Nelson, 518 F2d 879 (7th Cir 1975). *See also* Brubaker v King, 505 F2d 534 (7th Cir 1974) and Tritsis v Backer, 501 F2d 1021 (7th Cir 1974). The Seventh Circuit's earlier decision in Joseph v Rowlen, 402 F2d 367 (7th Cir 1968), which emphasized probable cause and not reasonableness, is no longer good law. For a view critical of this approach see Theis, *"Good Faith" as a Defense to Suits for Police Deprivations of Individual Rights*, 59 Minn L Rev 991 (1975). For further discussion, *see* Nahmod, *Section 1983 and the "Background" of Tort Liability*, 50 Ind LJ 5, 28 n 95 (1974).

[193] Procunier v Navarette, 434 US 555 (1978), discussed at **§8.09;** Harlow v Fitzgerald, 457 US 800 (1982), discussed at **§§8.03-8.04;** O'Connor v Donaldson, 422 US 563 (1975), discussed at **§8.08;** and Wood v Strickland, 420 US 308 (1975), discussed at **§8.02.**

[194] Saldana v Garza, 684 F2d 1159, 1164 (5th Cir 1982).

[195] 105 S Ct 2806, 2820 n 12 (1985), set out more fully at **§8.05.**

In a relatively easy Fifth Circuit case,[196] where the defendant police officer arrested plaintiff without "one scintilla of evidence" giving rise to probable cause, the defendant failed the qualified-immunity test. It was clearly established as a fundamental proposition in *Terry v Ohio*[197] that a police officer cannot arrest without probable cause simply because a person "acts suspiciously." In this same case, however, where another police officer with time to investigate arrested a different plaintiff without probable cause on the direct order of his superior, he was protected by qualified immunity. A contrary result would have been unfair, even though such reliance on a direct order does not always relieve a subordinate police officer from liability.

In contrast, in a questionable decision[198] where plaintiff was improperly arrested without probable cause for violating a disorderly conduct statute, the Fifth Circuit held that the constitutionality of a related stop-and-identify statute on which the defendant arresting officer *might* have relied was not clearly established at the time of the arrest. Six months *after* plaintiff's arrest, the Supreme Court had overturned a conviction based on this stop-and-identify statute, and two years thereafter a federal court had held it facially invalid. Because the arresting officer passed the qualified immunity test as a matter of law, even though he had not in fact relied on the stop-and-identify statute when he arrested plaintiff for disorderly conduct, the jury's damages award against him was overturned.

In a warrantless arrest setting, the First Circuit[199] distinguished between probable cause and qualified immunity as follows:

> Despite a finding of no probable cause at a later hearing, a police officer should not be found liable under §1983 for a warrantless arrest because the presence of probable cause was merely questionable at the time of the arrest. His qualified immunity is pierced only if there clearly was no probable cause at the time the arrest was made.

However, the Third Circuit,[200] apparently taking a different approach, suggested that if an arrest lacks probable cause, then it violates clearly settled law for that reason alone.

In an important Fifth Circuit case,[201] plaintiff, arrested by the defendant police officers for public intoxication and disturbing the peace, claimed that

---

[196] Vela v White, 703 F2d 147 (5th Cir 1983).

[197] 392 US 1 (1968).

[198] Trejo v Perez, 693 F2d 482 (5th Cir 1982). In another questionable decision, the Eighth Circuit ruled that defendants' warrantless arrest of plaintiff in his home did not violate clearly settled law even though there was at the time an 11-day-old Eighth Circuit decision on point. The court reasoned that the issue was then still open in the Supreme Court.

[199] Floyd v Farrell, 765 F2d 1, 5 (1st Cir 1985).

[200] Deary v Three Un-Named Police Officers, 746 F2d 185 (3d Cir 1984). The Eleventh Circuit may have taken a similar approach in Clark v Beville, 730 F2d 739 (11th Cir 1984).

[201] Saldana v Garza, 684 F2d 1159 (5th Cir 1982).

he was arrested without probable cause and that unreasonable force was used against him. Affirming a directed verdict in favor of one officer and a jury verdict in favor of the other, the Fifth Circuit spoke of the "quiet revolution in the law of official immunities" brought about by the Supreme Court's decision in *Harlow v Fitzgerald*. Plaintiff argued that defendants violated clearly established law because he was neither publicly intoxicated nor disturbing the peace. However, the court rejected this argument, stating: "The mere fact that a person is wrongfully arrested and charged with an offense whose elements are well-settled does not mean that the arrest itself contravenes 'well-settled law.'" The court went on to explain:

> Police officers can be expected to have a modicum of knowledge regarding the fundamental rights of citizens. Lawlessness will not be allowed to pervade our constabularies. However, in holding our law enforcement personnel to an objective standard of behavior, our judgment must be tempered with reason. If we are to measure official action against an objective standard, it must be a standard which speaks to what a reasonable officer should or should not know about the law he is enforcing and the methodology of effecting its enforcement. Certainly we cannot expect our police officers to carry surveying equipment and a Decennial Digest on patrol; they cannot be held to a title-searcher's knowledge of metes and bounds or a legal scholar's expertise in constititutional law.[202]

A related issue is the respective roles of judge and jury in such probable cause cases. According to the Seventh Circuit[203] sitting en banc, the probable cause issue is for the jury where reasonable persons can differ while the qualified immunity–clearly settled law inquiry is ordinarily for the court. This distinction prevents a police officer defendant from getting "two bites at the apple." The Sixth Circuit[204] similarly ruled that whether police officers accused of seizing certain property without probable cause passed *Harlow*'s qualified immunity test was for the court, not the jury. However, where a defendant claims that there were extraordinary circumstances justifying the failure to know clearly settled law, then that question may be for the jury.

There was a split in the circuits regarding the effect of a magistrate's issuance of a warrant on the Fourth Amendment liability of the police officer who obtained it. Thus, in a Fifth Circuit case,[205] the court overturned a jury verdict against a police officer accused of arresting the plaintiff without probable cause, but upheld it against the police department and city. As to the defendant

---

[202] *Id* 1164-65.

[203] Llaguno v Mingey, 763 F2d 1560 (7th Cir 1985) (en banc). There were various concurring and dissenting opinions focusing primarily on the probable cause determination. *See also* Moore v Marketplace Restaurant, 754 F2d 1336 (7th Cir 1985).

[204] Donta v Hooper, 774 F2d 716 (6th Cir 1985) (finding scope of plain view doctrine clearly established).

[205] Garris v Rowland, 678 F2d 1264 (5th Cir 1982).

officer, the jury had found in answers to special interrogatories that the officer reasonably believed that his conduct was lawful and he did not act with knowledge of or reckless disregard for violating plaintiff's constitutional rights. Specifically, even though the affidavit the officer prepared and presented to the magistrate did not *facially* conform to constitutional requirements, there was sufficient evidence to support the jury's finding that he acted with a reasonable good faith belief in its validity. Defendant had taken the affidavit to the district attorney's office for review and approval. Moreover, the officer was not responsible for the magistrate's failure to make an independent evaluation of the existence of probable cause for the issuance of the warrant. Any *subfacial* inaccuracies in the affidavit were at most negligent, and these, standing alone, did not undermine the affidavit. For all these reasons, according to the court, the defendant did not act in violation of settled, indisputable law.

However, the First Circuit's contrary position was recently affirmed by the Supreme Court in *Malley v Briggs*.[206] In this case, the First Circuit had stated, after analyzing *Harlow* and *United States v Leon:* [207]

> We now rule that judicial approval of a warrant cannot serve as an absolute bar to the §1983 liability of the officer who obtained the warrant . . . [W]e hold that only where the officer is "constitutionally negligent," that is, where the officer should have known that the facts recited in the affidavit did not constitute probable cause, will liability attach. Where the sufficiency of the facts fall [sic] into the grey area appropriate for judicial determination, submission of the affidavit to a magistrate will insulate the officer from liability.[208]

In affirming, the Supreme Court similarly held:

> [T]he same standard of objective reasonableness that we applied in the context of a suppression hearing in *Leon* . . . defines the qualified immunity accorded an officer whose request for a warrant allegedly caused an unconstitutional arrest. Only where the warrant application is so lacking in indicia of probable cause as to render official belief in its existence unreasonable . . . will the shield of immunity be lost.[209]

Malley's approach is consistent with the clearly settled law inquiry of *Harlow* in that it does not improperly relieve a police office who submits a probable cause

---

[206] 106 S Ct 1092 (1986), *affg*, Briggs v Malley, 748 F2d 715, 721 (1st Cir 1984). Justices Powell and Rehnquist concurred in part and dissented in part. *See also* BCR Transp Co v Fontaine, 727 F2d 7 (1st Cir 1984). In both cases the First Circuit properly refused to dispose of the issue on causation grounds. *See* §§3.17-3.18. The Seventh Circuit adopted the same rule as the First Circuit in Olson v Tyler, 771 F2d 277 (7th Cir 1985).

[207] 104 S Ct 3405 (1984) ("good faith" exception to exclusionary rule where police officer obtains search warrant from detached and neutral magistrate).

[208] 748 F2d at 721.

[209] 106 S Ct at 1098.

affidavit to a magistrate from the anticipated and often intended consequences of his or her conduct.

A novel Fourth Amendment-related evidentiary issue was presented in a Fifth Circuit case[210] where a mother and son sued police officers alleging illegal searches, an illegal seizure, an illegal arrest, a beating, malicious prosecution, and conversion of an automobile. The Fifth Circuit, after noting that defendants had not asserted qualified immunity, went on to say:

> While we find no reversible error in the admission of the evidence in this case, we wish to make clear that the evidence was not offered to prove a good faith defense. . . . *We express grave reservations about whether, as a matter of law, police officers who illegally obtain evidence may use that evidence to establish a good faith defense to a Section 1983 action.*[211]

Whether a §1983 case involves the Fourth Amendment or another constitutional provision, it is important to distinguish between any subjective state of mind requirement for the constitutional violations and the elimination by *Harlow* and its progeny of the subjective part of the qualified immunity test. This should have been done, but was not, in a Fourth Circuit decision[212] involving the claimed use of excessive force by police officers which resulted in the death of plaintiff's son. The court approved an instruction on qualified immunity allowing the jury to consider the defendants' subjective good faith belief that their conduct was lawful and that they relied in subjective good faith on police department standard operating procedures. The Fourth Circuit went on to read *Harlow* as not eliminating the subjective part entirely, but only as holding that under the qualified immunity test objective factors were *primary*, not exclusive. However, Judge Wister dissented,[213] arguing that the Supreme Court has indicated explicitly that the *Harlow* clearly settled standard is wholly objective. In this case, he contended, the law that police officers cannot subject a person to unreasonable and excessive force was clearly established at the time of defendant's conduct.

While Fourth Amendment and excessive use of force cases predominate in the law enforcement setting, there are often settled law issues regarding other constitutional provisions as well. These include the First[214] and Sixth Amend-

---

[210] Jonas v City of Atlanta, 647 F2d 580 (5th Cir 1981).

[211] *Id* 588 n 12 (emphasis added).

[212] Vizbaras v Prieber, 761 F2d 1013 (4th Cir 1983). *See also* McElveen v County of Prince William, 725 F2d 954 (4th Cir 1984), *cert denied,* 105 S Ct 88 (1984). See generally on the subjective part **§8.15.**

[213] Vizbaras v Prieber, 761 F2d 1013, 1017 (4th Cir 1983). He also argued that the qualified immunity issue should not have been submitted to the jury at all since there was clearly settled law prohibiting the use of excessive force.

[214] *E.g.,* Benson v Scott, 734 F2d 1181 (7th Cir 1984) (right of employees to be free from retaliation clearly settled since Pickering v Board of Education, 391 US 563 (1968)); Zook v Brown, 748 F2d 1161 (7th Cir 1984) (not clearly settled that the application of the *Pickering* balancing test would result in finding of First Amendment violation).

ments,[215] due process,[216] and other constitutional provisions.[217] Here, too, the elements of the prima facie case must be kept distinct from the clearly settled law inquiry.

It is likely, as a District of Columbia Circuit decision[218] demonstrated, that when supervisory police officers order arrests, they will be required under the objective part of the test to know more about the legality of their conduct than the ordinary police officer need know. More frequently, however, the question raised by a §1983 suit against such a defendant is put in terms either of the scope of that defendant's duty to supervise or instruct underlings in connection with their allegedly illegal conduct, or of liability under respondeat superior.[219] In either case, the question is not qualified immunity but rather the scope of the prima facie §1983 cause of action and the proper basis of liability.[220]

Even though police officers and others, such as prosecutors,[221] who engage in law enforcement activities are protected by qualified, not absolute,

---

[215] *E.g.*, O'Hagan v Soto, 725 F2d 878 (2d Cir 1984) (en banc) (unclear in the circuit whether right to counsel attached at time defendant questioned plaintiff); Silverman v Ballantine, 694 F2d 1091 (7th Cir 1982) (unclear whether right to counsel attached upon arrest).

[216] *E.g.*, Coleman v Frantz, 754 F2d 719 (7th Cir 1985) (due process prohibition against detaining person for 18 days without an appearance before a judge or magistrate not clearly settled; Judge Gordon dissented); Losch v Borough of Parksburg, 736 F2d 903 (3d Cir 1984) (regarding plaintiff's §1983 malicious prosecution claim, the law protecting persons from police officer use of official position for private vendetta was clearly settled); McGee v Hester, 724 F2d 89 (8th Cir 1984) (extensive surveillance could become so intrusive as to violate plaintiff's clearly settled property right; Judge Gibson dissented).

[217] *E.g.*, Acoff v Abston, 762 F2d 1543 (11th Cir 1985) (although Supreme Court's decision in Tennessee v Garner, 105 S Ct 1694 (1985) which prohibited the use of deadly force against a nondangerous fleeing felon would be applied retroactively, it did not follow that the law as to such use of deadly force was clearly settled); Creamer v Porter, 754 F2d 1311 (5th Cir 1985) (clearly settled Fourth Amendment law prohibiting police officers from exceeding the scope of their search warrant); Rex v Teeples, 753 F2d 840 (10th Cir 1985) (law regarding involuntary confessions and the ability to knowingly waive constitutional rights clearly settled at time of questioning); Logan v Sheely, 660 F2d 1007 (4th Cir 1981) (strip search in an area exposed to the general view of persons known to be in the vicinity violated clearly settled law).

[218] Dellums v Powell, 566 F2d 167 (DC Cir 1977) (chief of police). In this case, which involved arrests on the steps of the United States Capitol in violation of plaintiffs' First Amendment rights, the court affirmed the jury's finding of liability of the chief of police and observed: "The law here was not highly technical, penetrable if at all only with the help of counsel . . . [Defendant] was fully acquainted . . . with the controlling case. . . ." *Id* 185.

[219] See, e.g., Kostka v Hogg, 560 F2d 37, 40 (1st Cir 1977) where the court, not reaching the qualified immunity test, held that "a police chief is under no general federal constitutional duty to take positive action to reduce the incidence of unconstitutional conduct by police officers on the beat. . . ." The plaintiff's decedent had been killed by a police officer arresting him.

[220] *See* **ch 3.**

[221] *See* §§**7.13-7.14.**

immunity, the Supreme Court held in *Briscoe v LaHue*,[222] applying a functional approach, that absolute witness immunity protects a police officer accused of perjury at a criminal trial. However, there is a split in the circuits regarding the testimony of police officers in other proceedings.[223]

§8.12   Federal Law Enforcement Officers

Section 1983 actions lie only against state law enforcement officers, not against federal law enforcement officers. Still, even before *Harlow v Fitzgerald*,[224] *Davis v Scherer*,[225] and *Mitchell v Forsyth*,[226] a close relationship existed between §1983 qualified immunity law and other federal qualified immunity law.[227] When, for example, the question of the scope of the qualified immunity for federal law enforcement officers arose in the matter of Fourth Amendment actions for damages, the Second Circuit, in *Bivens v Six Unknown Named Agents*,[228] borrowed directly from *Pierson*[229] and held the test from that case applicable. It said: "It would, we think, be incongruous and confusing, to say the least, if we should rule that under one phase of federal law a police officer had immunity [§1983 actions] and that under another phase of federal law [Fourth Amendment actions] he had no immunity."[230]

Similarly, several circuits in other pre-*Harlow*[231] cases relied on §1983 qualified immunity decisions of the Supreme Court regarding the qualified immunity of federal law enforcement officers. For example, the Ninth Circuit[232] applied the §1983 qualified immunity test to Internal Revenue Service agents charged with maliciously destroying the plaintiff's income tax service business. The court found no significant reason to distinguish between federal and state

---

[222] 460 US 325 (1983), set out more fully at **§7.11.**

[223] *Compare* Wheeler v Cosden Oil & Chem Co, 734 F2d 254 (5th Cir), *modified* 744 F2d 1131 (5th Cir 1984) (absolute immunity not applicable to probable cause hearing) *with* Kincaid v Eberle, 712 F2d 1023 (7th Cir 1983) (per curiam) (absolute immunity applicable to grand jury proceeding). *See generally* **§7.11.**

[224] 457 US 800 (1982), discussed at **§§8.03-8.04.**

[225] 104 S Ct 3012 (1984).

[226] 105 S Ct 2806 (1985).

[227] While the pre-*Harlow* cases discussed in **§8.12** deal with the borrowing of §1983 qualified immunity law for application to federal law enforcement officers, occasionally a court in a pre-*Harlow* §1983 case borrowed from other federal qualified immunity law which in turn was originally taken from §1983. *E.g.*, Brubaker v King, 505 F2d 534 (7th Cir 1974), a case involving state police officers, among others, which relied on Bivens v Six Unknown Named Agents, 456 F2d 1339 (2d Cir 1972), a Fourth Amendment federal police officer case.

[228] 456 F2d 1339 (2d Cir 1972).

[229] Pierson v Ray, 386 US 547 (1967).

[230] 456 F2d at 1346-47.

[231] 102 S Ct 2727 (1982).

[232] Mark v Groff, 521 F2d 1376 (9th Cir 1975).

law enforcement officers and emphasized the need for uniformity because of the similar interests involved.

A District of Columbia Circuit[233] decision also applied §1983 qualified immunity law to a federal law enforcement officer, in that case a police chief who ordered the arrest of persons protesting on the United States Capitol steps. The court first stated: "There can be no doubt that state and federal police officers sued under section 1983 and *Bivens,* respectively, have available to them a qualified immunity defense, a privilege based on good faith and reasonableness and that the burden is on the defendant officers to prove it."[234]

It then upheld a jury verdict against the defendant, noting that he was familiar with the ordinance which served as the basis for the arrest of plaintiffs. It further found that reasonable persons could differ as to whether there was a factual basis for the arrests under the ordinance and whether, as defendant claimed, he relied on good faith advice of counsel after making full disclosure to counsel.

The Supreme Court thereafter held that §1983 qualified immunity law is generally applicable to federal executive officials for their constitutional violations. In *Butz v Economou,*[235] defendants, federal executive officials and others, were sued for allegedly wrongful, malicious, and hence unconstitutional enforcement of the Commodities Exchange Act against plaintiffs. The district court dismissed, citing a leading early Supreme Court decision presenting an *outer perimeter of line of duty* test for absolute immunity of executives.[236] Reversing and relying on the Supreme Court's §1983 qualified immunity cases for the proposition that defendants here were similarly protected only by a qualified immunity, the Second Circuit said: "Both types of suits serve the same function of protecting citizens against violations of their constitutional rights by government officials."[237] Agreeing with the Second Circuit, the Supreme Court stated: "[I]n the absence of congressional direction to the contrary, there is no basis for according to federal officials a higher degree of immunity from liability when sued for a constitutional infringement as authorized by *Bivens* than is accorded state officials when sued for the identical violation under §1983."[238]

That the qualified immunity rules for §1983 and *Bivens* actions are now

---

[233] Dellums v Powell, 566 F2d 167 (DC Cir 1977).

[234] *Id* 176.

[235] 438 US 478 (1978), *vacating & remanding* 535 F2d 688 (2d Cir 1976), also discussed at **§7.10.** Chief Justice Burger and Justices Rehnquist, Stewart, and Stevens concurred in part and dissented in part.

[236] Barr v Matteo, 360 US 564 (1959).

[237] 535 F2d at 695 n 7.

[238] 438 US at 500. The Court also held, using an increasingly influential functional approach, that those judges and prosecutors participating in adjudication within a federal administrative agency are entitled to absolute immunity. See generally **§§7.05, 7.10, 8.13, 8.14 & 8.18** on the functional approach.

virtually identical[239] is most clearly evident from *Harlow v Fitzgerald, Davis v Scherer,* and *Mitchell v Forsyth.* In *Harlow,* a *Bivens* case, the Court changed the qualified immunity test by eliminating the subjective part[240] and then made clear that its discussion of qualified immunity also encompassed §1983 actions.[241] Thereafter, in *Davis,* the Court applied *Harlow*'s qualified immunity test in a §1983 setting.[242] Finally, in *Mitchell,* the Court in a *Bivens* case held that *Harlow*'s qualified immunity test applied to the nonadvocacy law enforcement activity of the United States Attorney General. The Court went on in *Mitchell* to rule for the defendant on clearly settled law grounds.[243] Consequently, post-*Harlow* qualified immunity doctrine developed for federal law enforcement officers is equally applicable to state and local law enforcement officers and vice versa.

For example, the Second Circuit[244] characterized as clearly established law that a seizure of property by federal law enforcement officers during the search of a residence pursuant to an arrest warrant must be based on probable cause to believe that the property was connected to the suspected crime. Thus, affidavit testimony regarding the taking of plaintiff's personal property by the defendants established a triable issue of fact precluding summary judgment for defendants.

In a Sixth Circuit case,[245] a district director of the Internal Revenue Service was sued by a taxpayer for an allegedly wrongful tax termination assessment and levy in that, among other things, a deficiency notice required by 26 USC §6861 was never provided. Affirming the district court's grant of summary judgment for the defendant, the Sixth Circuit observed that at the time the defendant acted, "it was uncertain whether the IRS, when assessing and collecting the unreported tax due after the termination of a taxpayer's period, must follow the procedures mandated by 26 USC §6861 for the assessment and collection of a deficiency whose collection is in jeopardy."[246] Defendant could not reasonably have been expected to know the proper procedure, as it had not yet been declared, and therefore did not violate clearly settled constitution-

---

[239] There is still, though, an open question regarding whether and to what extent the functional approach of Butz v Economou, 438 US 478 (1978), *vacating & remanding* 535 F2d 688 (2d Cir 1976), will apply to state and local government executives exercising quasi-legislative or quasi-judicial functions. *See* §§**7.05, 7.10, 8.13, 8.14 & 8.18.**

[240] *See* §**8.15.**

[241] 457 US at 818 n 30.

[242] *See* §**8.05.**

[243] *See* §**8.05.**

[244] Dale v Bartels, 732 F2d 278, 285 n 12 (2d Cir 1984). *Cf* Creighton v City of St Paul, 766 F2d 1269 (8th Cir 1985), *cert granted,* 54 USLW 3851 (Sup Ct June 20, 1986), where the Eighth Circuit held that the meaning of *exigent circumstances,* which justify the warrantless search of a home, was clearly established on November 1, 1983, the date on which the defendant FBI agent searched plaintiff's home. There were "numerous cases" detailing the few exigent circumstances.

[245] Hall v United States, 704 F2d 246 (6th Cir 1983).

[246] *Id* 250.

al or statutory rights. It was also significant that plaintiff relied only on her pleadings to defeat the defense at the summary judgement stage.

And in a Ninth Circuit case,[247] an Internal Revenue Service agent sued by a taxpayer for constitutional violations allegedly stemming from a levy on the taxpayer's wages was entitled only to qualified immunity protection and not to absolute quasi-judicial immunity. The activities of the IRS agent were not subject to the safeguards of formal adjudication. In addition, the intra-agency file forwarded to the agent had little resemblance to a complete and reliable trial-type record. Throughout its discussions, the Ninth Circuit emphasized a functional approach to executive immunity. In ultimately remanding for a determination of whether the defendant passed the qualified immunity test, the court suggested that if defendant knew of plaintiff's protest or was aware of its substance, then defendant would likely not pass the qualified immunity test, because such a protest under existing federal statutory law triggered certain procedural rights of a taxpayer.

§8.13   State Executives

Pierson v Ray[248] dealt only with police officers and relied primarily upon the §1983 action's *background of tort liability.*[249] Moreover, the Supreme Court's decisions on absolute legislative and judicial immunity similarly relied substantially on the tort law background.[250] For this reason, cases following *Pierson* dealing with the liability of a state's higher executive officials under §1983 often extended absolute immunity to the conduct of these officials because that was the common law rule generally accepted in the federal system.[251] It was thus

---

[247] Bothke v Fluor Engs & Constructors Inc, 713 F2d 1405 (9th Cir 1983). In an interesting pre-*Harlow* clearly settled law case, a district director of United States Customs, sued for allegedly violating the plaintiff's Fifth Amendment due process rights by seizing her automobile and failing to refer her case promptly to the United States Attorney for forfeiture proceedings, did not pass the objective part of the qualified immunity test. Although defendant argued, based on two federal district court decisions in the Ninth Circuit, that he could not have predicted that his delay was unconstitutional, the Ninth Circuit pointed out that these two cases were decided *after* the defendant's challenged conduct. At the time he delayed, however, two other federal district courts in the Ninth Circuit had held that such delays *were* unconstitutional. Thus, the law was clearly settled at the time he acted, even if it became unsettled later, despite the fact that only *after* the defendant's conduct did the Ninth Circuit resolve the conflict and hold that such delays were indeed unconstitutional. Seguin v Eide, 645 F2d 804 (9th Cir 1981).

[248] 386 US 547 (1967), discussed at **§8.11.**

[249] This phrase was taken from Monroe v Pape, 365 US 167 (1961). Its implications for the prima facie §1983 cause of action are discussed in **ch 3.**

[250] Pierson v Ray, 386 US 547 (1967) (judicial immunity); Tenney v Brandhove, 341 US 367 (1951) (legislative immunity). Absolute prosecutorial immunity in a §1983 context was established in Imbler v Pachtman, 424 US 409 (1976).

[251] Barr v Matteo, 360 US 564 (1959); Spalding v Vilas, 161 US 483 (1896); Gregoire v Biddle, 177 F2d 579 (2d Cir 1949), *cert denied,* 339 US 949 (1950).

to the surprise of many that the Supreme Court in 1974 held that a state's executive officials, including its highest, the governor, are protected from §1983 liability only by a qualified immunity.

Scheuer v Rhodes[252] concerned §1983 actions against the governor of Ohio, the adjutant general and his assistant, various named and unnamed officers and enlisted members of the Ohio National Guard, and the president of Kent State University, arising out of the death of three students at the university during alleged civil disorders. Reversing the Sixth Circuit which had held that the defendants were absolutely immune, the Court said that they were not. It acknowledged the utility of the common law rule of absolute liability because "the public interest requires decisions and action to enforce laws for the protection of the public."[253] However, in addition to considering this interest and the danger to it stemming from the possibility of §1983 liability, the Court considered the purposes of §1983. It found that to grant absolute immunity to executives would drain §1983 of all meaning. Finally, after discussing *Pierson* and considering the differences in exercise of discretion between law enforcement executives at the police level and those at higher levels, the Court held:

> [I]n varying scope, a qualified immunity is available to officers of the executive branch of government, the variation being dependent upon the scope of discretion and responsibilities of the office and all the circumstances as they reasonably appeared at the time of the action on which liability is sought to be based. It is the existence of reasonable grounds for the belief formed at the time and in light of all the circumstances, coupled with good-faith belief, that affords a basis for qualified immunity of executive officers for acts performed in the course of official conduct.[254]

The Court refused to provide a "definitive exploration" of the scope of this qualified immunity, but simply reversed and remanded. However, the decision did indicate that the governor's declaration of an emergency, while to be given great weight by the fact-finder, was not conclusive as to the existence of reasonable grounds for good faith belief.[255] Conversely, the Court added that executives are entitled to rely on traditional sources for the information on which they act, especially in responding to the "obvious need for prompt action" when "a condition of civil disorder in fact exists."[256] There was, finally, the suggestion that lower executive officials, here the "lesser officers and enlisted personnel of the Guard," have a qualified immunity when they act "in good-faith obedience to the orders of their superiors."[257] Apparently they had no duty to inquire into the legality of their orders; that the orders came from

---

[252] 416 US 232 (1974).

[253] *Id* 241.

[254] *Id* 247-48.

[255] *Id* 250.

[256] *Id* 246.

[257] *Id* 250.

their superiors seemed to constitute grounds for a reasonable belief in the validity of those orders.[258]

Scheuer presented a more general statement of the qualified immunity than *Pierson*, which only dealt with police officers. *Scheuer* suggested what subsequent Supreme Court decisions would thereafter demonstrate: that the qualified immunity set out in *Scheuer* is a unitary standard applicable to virtually all state employees. This unitary standard has since, as noted, been modified by the Supreme Court in *Harlow v Fitzgerald*[259] through the elimination of the subjective part of the qualified immunity test and the emphasis on an *objective* inquiry into the duty to know clearly settled law. Consequently, the major difference in the §1983 litigation process between actions against police officers and higher executives is reflected in the jury instructions given on the duty to know clearly settled law imposed on these very different law enforcement officials.

This difference may cut two ways. On the one hand, the greater the scope of discretion of an executive the more likely the fact-finder is to defer to the executive's assertion that the action taken was accompanied by reasonable grounds for a belief in the legal validity of the conduct. On the other, the greater the scope of discretion, the more the executive's responsibility to be sensitive to questions of legality of conduct engaged in. While neither the police officer nor the executive is charged with predicting constitutional law developments, an executive, unlike a police officer, typically has readier access to counsel and is in a better position to act deliberately. Furthermore, the impact of an executive's conduct is often more wider than is the impact of a police officer's conduct. For these reasons, *Harlow*'s objective qualified immunity test, with its duty to know clearly settled law, should mean in practical terms that a higher executive is charged with knowing a fair amount of relevant constitutional law.

A good example is a Ninth Circuit decision[260] where plaintiff was discharged from her position with a state's department of education in violation of the First Amendment. In reversing the district court's grant of summary judgment in favor of the officials who had fired her, the Ninth Circuit rejected the district court's finding that as a matter of law the defendants were protected by qualified immunity. After *Mount Healthy City School District Board of Education v*

---

[258] Compare Hanna v Drobnick, 514 F2d 393 (6th Cir 1975) where illegal searches by housing inspectors were held to be reasonable in part because the defendants relied on their superiors.

[259] 457 US 800 (1982), discussed at §§8.03-8.04.

[260] Fujiwara v Clark, 703 F2d 357 (9th Cir 1983). *But cf* Snyder v Kurvers, 767 F2d 489 (8th Cir 1985) (no clearly settled law regarding right of privacy and sexual conduct outside marriage where executive secretary of state board of judicial standards engaged in authorized investigation of judicial misconduct); Casines v Murchek, 766 F2d 1494 (11th Cir 1985) (no clearly settled law requiring state probation and parole commission officials to provide pretermination hearing; it was irrelevant that defendants acted in violation of a state regulation); Jensen v Conrad, 747 F2d 185 (4th Cir 1984) (no clearly settled law imposing affirmative duty on officials of state department of social services to intervene and protect children from beatings by guardians).

Doyle[261] there was clearly settled First Amendment law protecting a public employee who speaks out on matters of public concern. Defendants should have known of the applicability of such law as applied to a case where, as here, the firing of an employee is for multiple grounds. The court disagreed with defendants' argument that the *Mount Healthy* standard regarding the appropriate burden of proof—*see* §3.15—was rendered ambiguous to a layman by subsequent lower court applications. For one thing, these lower court decisions were not as ambiguous as defendants contended. For another, the *Mount Healthy* standard itself was clear from the Supreme Court's own opinion. Thus, defendants failed the post-*Harlow* qualified immunity test as a matter of law. Also, in denying defendants' later petition for rehearing, the court asserted that the defendants' error was one of law and did not implicate disputed factual issues.

However, reliance on advice of counsel by an executive, even if erroneous, will often result in a finding that the qualified immunity test was passed as a matter of law. In a Sixth Circuit case,[262] plaintiff sued the executive secretary of a state racing commission for attempting to prohibit him from horse racing at a certain race track in alleged violation of due process. Reversing the district court's judgment against the executive secretary, and assuming that a due process violation had occurred, the Sixth Circuit held that the defendant had passed the post-*Harlow* qualified immunity test as a matter of law. The record indicated that the letter sent by the defendant, which had revoked plaintiff's racing privileges, had received the approval of legal counsel for the racing commission and that the defendant therefore reasonably believed he was acting constitutionally.

Two Eighth Circuit cases make the same point about reliance on advice of counsel. In one,[263] the plaintiff insurance company sued a former state governor for a press release issued by defendant, when he was governor, which directed the state's division of insurance to ban the future sale of cancer policies in Missouri. Among other things, the press release accused sellers of cancer policies of deception and questioned the limited payment of benefits to policyholders. Holding that the defendant was as a matter of law protected by qualified immunity, the Eighth Circuit emphasized that defendant acted with the welfare of citizens in mind, was advised by legal counsel that he had the authority to do what he did, and believed that the directive was within his discretionary executive authority. In addition, it was not clear that defendant legally lacked the authority to issue the directive.

In the other,[264] the Eighth Circuit cautioned that "state employees may not

---

[261] 429 US 274 (1977).

[262] Bier v Fleming, 717 F2d 308 (6th Cir 1983).

[263] American Family Life Assurance Co v Teasdale, 733 F2d 559 (8th Cir 1984).

[264] Wentz v Klecker, 721 F2d 244 (8th Cir 1983). In an interesting case where a prisoner sued a department of corrections administrator for allegedly violating his right to procedural due process in connection with his parole, the Seventh Circuit held that "a state official enjoying qualified immunity may assert the good faith defense [even] when a state statute indemnifies him for any damages liability incurred as a result of

rely on their ignorance of even the most esoteric aspects of the law to deny individuals their due process rights." It nevertheless affirmed the district court's qualified immunity ruling in favor of the defendant director of a state advocacy program for the mentally retarded who fired plaintiff, a resident advocate, without a hearing. Defendant erroneously believed, in reliance on advice of experienced counsel, that plaintiff was an independent contractor not entitled to any hearing. While such reliance was not always dispositive, here plaintiff's unique employment situation warranted defendant's soliciting legal advice from her attorney.

There may be situations where state executives are, under a functional approach,[265] protected by absolute immunity for quasi-judicial or quasi-prosecutorial conduct. The Tenth Circuit[266] so ruled in connection with a governor's failure to appoint replacements to a personnel review board in alleged violation of due process. Also, the First Circuit[267] so held in the alternative regarding the quasi-prosecutorial conduct of members of a state committee on unauthorized practice of law in sending the plaintiff a letter requesting that he discontinue his divorce mediation business.

The question whether absolute immunity should apply to the quasi-judicial or quasi-prosecutorial conduct of state executives is still open in the Supreme Court.[268] The ultimate answer will most likely depend upon policy considerations, not statutory interpretation.[269]

---

his good faith execution of his duties." After judgment in favor of the plaintiff on the constitutional issue, the parties had stipulated that defendant would pass the qualified immunity test if it were applicable. The Seventh Circuit correctly rejected the argument that qualified immunity should be inapplicable because the defendant faced no threat of personal liability. The court reasoned that entitlement to qualified immunity is a matter of federal law, not state law. Jaworski v Schmidt, 684 F2d 498 (7th Cir 1982).

[265] The functional approach is discussed at §§7.05, 7.10, 8.13, 8.14 & 8.18.

[266] Johnston v Herschler, 669 F2d 617 (10th Cir 1982).

[267] Werle v Rhode Island Bar Assn, 755 F2d 195 (1st Cir 1985). The court also held that in any event defendants passed the qualified immunity test. Cf Marion v Michigan Bd of Medicine, 765 F2d 590 (6th Cir 1985) (members of state board of medicine protected by qualified immunity in connection with claimed procedural due process violations; public policy did not require absolute immunity for performance of licensing functions); Richardson v Koshiba, 693 F2d 911 (9th Cir 1982) (members of a state's judicial selection committee protected by qualified immunity for their failure to reappoint plaintiff; defendant performed an executive function).

[268] Compare Wood v Strickland, 420 US 308 (1975) discussed at §8.02 with Butz v Economou, 438 US 478 (1978) discussed at §7.10. See also §8.18 on parole board officials and §7.05 on "regional legislators".

[269] Before Harlow, the Court addressed §1983 immunity in statutory interpretation terms. It was becoming increasingly clear, however, that policy analysis divorced from statutory interpretation—in the sense of discovering legislative intent or purpose—frequently predominated. The reasons were several. Once the Supreme Court considered the common law background in a particular case to be relevant to the existence vel non of some nonabsolute immunity, §1983's language provided no further guidance on the immunity question. Also, §1983's legislative history was of little or no help on the issue of scope of immunity. Indeed, Justice O'Connor made such an observation about §1983 remedy issues in arguing openly that the proper standard for

§8.14 Local Government Executives

There is no sound reason for distinguishing, for qualified immunity purposes, between a state's executive officers and those of a local government entity, and in fact the circuits do not. Thus, for example, the Fourth Circuit[270] in a pre-*Harlow*[271] case applied the qualified immunity test to a city manager who unconstitutionally discharged a fireman for circulating a critical petition. Ruling for plaintiffs, the Fourth Circuit observed: "No preview of an uncertain future was needed to determine that firing one for his participation 'in circulating a letter of complaint' was constitutionally impermissible."[272] The Seventh Circuit[273] in another pre-*Harlow* case applied the test to an acting park district superintendent and others accused of unconstitutionally refusing to grant a permit for a peaceful demonstration. It asserted that "the narrow reading by a public official of a case on constitutional law must be upheld unless patently unreasonable and without arguable support in logic or policy,"[274] but went on to hold as a matter of law that the defendants had acted unreasonably because their reading of a Supreme Court obscenity case was too narrow.[275]

Since *Harlow,* circuit courts have confronted clearly settled law issues in connection with various constitutional violations by local government executives. In a First Amendment case arising in the Eleventh Circuit,[276] a mayor who fired plaintiff in violation of the First Amendment was found liable after a bench

---

an award of punitive damages under §1983 is primarily a question of policy for the Court to resolve. Smith v Wade, 461 US 30, 92 (1983). Justice Brennan contended that §1983's 1871 common law background should not be used to freeze its development. *Id* 34 n 2. Butz v Economou, 438 US 478 (1978), while paying lip service to §1983 qualified immunity as an issue of statutory interpretation, hedged somewhat and spoke also—as it had to, because a *Bivens* action was involved—of weighty policy considerations of a functional nature cutting in favor of all constitutional tort defendants.

If there was any doubt that the scope of §1983 qualified immunity is primarily a function of judicial policy making, it was dispelled in *Harlow.* The *Harlow* Court made no attempt to explain the change in qualified immunity as a matter of statutory interpretation. The Court left little doubt that *Harlow*'s modified qualified immunity test applies to §1983 cases as well as to *Bivens* cases. This frank policy-oriented approach to qualified immunity frees the Court to fashion whatever qualified immunity test it wishes. On the one hand, this provides judicial flexibility to make changes, as shown by *Harlow.* On the other, it provides the opportunity to cut back on the effective scope of §1983 by expanding the protection of qualified immunity.

270 Jannetta v Cole, 493 F2d 1334 (4th Cir 1974).

271 Harlow v Fitzgerald, 457 US 800 (1982).

272 Jannetta v Cole, 493 F2d 1334, 1338 (4th Cir 1974).

273 Slate v McFetridge, 484 F2d 1169 (7th Cir 1973).

274 *Id* 1174.

275 The court observed that defendants "had notice by [the obscenity case] that their prompt resolution of [plaintiffs'] permit request was a dictate of due process in the protection of First Amendment rights."*Id* 1176.

276 Berdin v Duggan, 701 F2d 909 (11th Cir 1983). *Cf* Nekolny v Painter, 653 F2d 1164 (7th Cir 1981) (pre-*Harlow* case where the court held that clearly settled law prohibited the termination of the plaintiff for political reasons). *See* Czurlanis v Albanese, 721 F2d 98 (3d Cir 1983) (post-*Harlow* First Amendment case emphasizing that the existence of clearly settled law is ordinarily a question of law for the court).

trial. Affirming, the Eleventh Circuit asserted that disciplining a public employee in 1974 for exercising his First Amendment right to speak violated law that was clearly settled by 1972. Because defendant should have known this, he was not protected by the post-*Harlow* qualified immunity test.

In another First Amendment case, the Fifth Circuit[277] carefully distinguished between the applicability of *Harlow* "to determine the reasonableness of an official's mistake of *law*" and the need for a subjective inquiry regarding an official's mistake of relevant *fact*. Here, the plaintiff had been discharged for what defendants, members of a city's police review board, contended were intentional falsehoods by plaintiff. The court asserted that if defendants in fact believed, even if erroneously, that plaintiff lied, then his discharge would not violate clearly settled First Amendment law. Only if defendants did *not* believe that plaintiff made intentionally false statements would they have violated clearly settled law in discharging him.

And in an Eighth Circuit First Amendment case,[278] a police department had a chain-of-command policy requiring that misconduct by officers be reported first to the police chief and then to the mayor. The plaintiff was discharged for violating this policy and sued, claiming a First Amendment violation. In holding that the defendants violated plaintiff's First Amendment rights under the circumstances, the Eighth Circuit went on to "accept the district court's finding that [the individual defendants] acted in a reasonably good faith belief that they could legally dismiss [plaintiff] for his partial disregard of the chain of command." Thus, they were protected by qualified immunity.

Two Fifth Circuit cases involved a combination of Fourth Amendment and due process violations. In one,[279] a mayor was sued for causing the arrest and detention of the plaintiff maliciously and without probable cause because of a dispute over a sewer. Holding that defendant was not protected by qualified immunity, the court asserted that defendant should have known that plaintiff committed no crime and consequently should not have been arrested and detained. In the other,[280] where the plaintiff landowners sued a county supervisor for the wrongful removal and destruction of culverts from their property, as well as for the illegal arrest of one of them, the Fifth Circuit affirmed the district court's ruling that defendant was not protected by qualified immunity. Defendant knew or should have known that he did not have probable cause to arrest that plaintiff. Also, he knew or should have known that the "unilateral destruction" of plaintiffs' culverts was a violation of due process.

Procedural due process was dealt with in an Eleventh Circuit case[281] where

---

[277] Neubauer v City of McAllen, 766 F2d 1567 (5th Cir 1985).

[278] Brockell v Norton, 732 F2d 664, 669 (8th Cir 1984).

[279] Thomas v Sams, 734 F2d 185 (5th Cir 1984).

[280] Hart v Walker, 720 F2d 1436 (5th Cir 1983).

[281] Barnett v Housing Auth, 707 F2d 1571 (11th Cir 1983). *See also* Shelton v City of College Station, 754 F2d 1251 (5th Cir 1985) (clearly settled law prohibited arbitrary and discriminatory denial of plaintiffs' requests for zoning variances by members of city's zoning board of adjustment); Davis v Mansfield Metropolitan Hous Auth, 751 F2d

a directed verdict in favor of a housing authority's officials sued for dismissing plaintiff in alleged violation of due process was reversed by the court. Plaintiff's suit was not based on "a novel theory of constitutional entitlement," but was rather based on the deprivation of a property interest without due process of law. Also, state law, by explicitly requiring "cause" for plaintiff's termination, recognized a property interest in him. Thus, defendants failed the qualified immunity test: they violated clearly settled law by discharging plaintiff without cause and without a posttermination hearing. However, without elaboration, the court indicated that on remand, defendants should be permitted to argue that Harlow's exceptional circumstances exception might apply to relieve them of their duty to know this settled law.

Such exceptional circumstances may well include reliance by local government executives on advice of counsel. For example, in an Eighth Circuit case,[282] members of a county board of election commissioners were sued for damages and injunctive relief for their termination of plaintiff's employment in alleged violation of due process. Reaching the qualified immunity issue on interlocutory appeal, the Eighth Circuit reversed the district court and held that defendants passed the objective qualified immunity test. There was no clearly settled due process law applicable to plaintiff at the time the defendants terminated her because it was not clear that the employees' policy manual, which may have created a property interest in continued employment, covered her. There was thus a dispute as to its interpretation. In addition, the defendants relied on counsel who advised them that the plaintiff served at their pleasure.

Purposeful discrimination based on sex has also been held to violate clearly settled equal protection law in certain circumstances. For example, in a First Circuit case,[283] the court held that inasmuch as the district court instructed the jury that the defendant members of a municipal lighting commission, in order to be liable for sex discrimination, must have engaged in purposeful discrimination on that basis, a separate instruction on qualified immunity was unnecessary because it would be superfluous. The Supreme Court case law had been clear

---

180 (6th Cir 1984) (clearly settled law prohibited executive director of housing authority from depriving person of public assistance without some type of hearing); Evers v County of Custer, 745 F2d 1196 (9th Cir 1984) (no clearly settled law prohibiting county commissioner from declaring without a hearing that a road crossing plaintiff's property was public).

[282] Tubbesing v Arnold, 742 F2d 401 (8th Cir 1984). But *cf* a pre-*Harlow* Fifth Circuit case where the court reversed a judgment nov and reinstated a jury verdict against a mayor, chief of police, assistant chief of police, and others in connection with politically motivated arrests of plaintiff. It found that reasonable persons could conclude that defendants acted with malice against plaintiff. It also stated, in rejecting defendants' contrary argument: "Reliance on advice of counsel does not serve as an absolute defense to a civil rights action . . . [A] jury is entitled to evaluate the testimony about advice of counsel and to make a decision concerning its credibility." Crowe v Lucas, 595 F2d 985, 992 (5th Cir 1979).

[283] Stathos v Bowden, 728 F2d 15 (1st Cir 1984).

since *Personnel Administrator v Feeney*[284] that such discrimination was unconstitutional. Further, defendants could show no extraordinary circumstances to justify why they should not have known this law.

Similarly, where a judge was successfully sued for sex discrimination in transferring the plaintiff from one position to another, the Eighth Circuit[285] noted that the possibility of qualified immunity was logically excluded in such a case. The right to be free from sex discrimination was "certainly" clearly established in the same way that the unconstitutionality of racial or ethnic discrimination was clearly established. Hence, the district court did not err in failing to instruct the jury on qualified immunity.

It should be noted that here, as with state executives,[286] there may be situations where local executives are protected, under a functional approach, by absolute immunity for certain conduct. For example, in a Third Circuit case,[287] the court ruled that members of a borough council, the borough's attorney, and its mayor were absolutely immune from damages liability in connection with the discharge of the plaintiff. Defendants had voted for an ordinance abolishing his position, with the borough attorney advising in the drafting of the ordinance. The Third Circuit adopted a functional approach, noting that the plaintiff had charged the mayor with voting to pass the ordinance, a legislative act. Similarly, because the attorney was acting "in direct assistance of legislative activity," he was also entitled to absolute immunity.

Similarly, in a Seventh Circuit case,[288] plaintiffs, bar owners, sued numerous village officials and others for allegedly destroying their business in violation of due process. As to the conduct of the village's mayor in his capacity as local liquor control commissioner, he was acting in a judicial capacity when he suspended and revoked plaintiffs' liquor license, and was thus absolutely immune in this regard. Similarly, the mayor and members of the village's board of trustees were absolutely immune for their legislative conduct in reducing the number of certain liquor licenses in the village.

Note, however, that as mentioned earlier in connection with state executives,[289] the question whether absolute immunity should apply to the quasi-legislative, quasi-judicial or quasi-prosecutorial conduct of local government executives is similarly open for local government executives in the

---

[284] 442 US 256 (1979).

[285] Goodwin v Circuit Court, 729 F2d 541 (8th Cir 1984). Judge Bowman dissented on the merits. See §§7.06-7.11 on the scope of judicial immunity.

[286] *See* §8.13. On the functional approach generally see §§7.05, 7.10, 8.13 & 8.18.

[287] Aitchison v Raffiani, 708 F2d 96 (3d Cir 1983). *Cf* Hernandez v City of Lafayette, 643 F2d 1188 (5th Cir 1981) where the court held that a mayor who allegedly acted unconstitutionally in vetoing two zoning ordinances was entitled to absolute legislator immunity for his "legislative acts."

[288] Reed v Village of Shorewood, 704 F2d 943 (7th Cir 1983).

[289] *See* §8.13.

Supreme Court except for school board members acting in a quasi-legislative or quasi-judicial capacity.[290]

§8.15   The Qualified Immunity Test: The Subjective Part Before and After *Harlow*

In contrast with the objective part of the qualified immunity test, the now eliminated subjective part caused relatively little difficulty in the circuits. It was described as "good faith belief" in *Pierson*[291] and *Scheuer*[292] and as "intentional injury" in *Wood*[293] and *Navarette*.[294] Whatever words were used, the subjective part required an inquiry into the defendant's state of mind. State of mind is adduced both directly by a defendant's testimony as to actual knowledge and indirectly by testimony as to what a defendant said and did. Further, a fact-finder evaluating a defendant's state of mind is certainly not bound by how that defendant describes that state of mind. The fact-finder can use its common sense and evaluate the totality of a defendant's conduct in order to make a finding as to state of mind.[295]

Because the subjective part of the qualified immunity test depended so much on credibility, the jury as fact-finder was particularly well suited to deal with this question. Thus, unlike the objective part of the test, where possible legal complexities would often lead a district court to direct a verdict or grant summary judgment for defendants on the clearly settled law issue, the subjective part would usually raise a jury issue unless the evidence was one-sided. It would therefore be relatively rare for a district court to take the subjective part of the test from the jury.[296] Furthermore, as with the objective part, a defendant had the burden of proving absence of intentional injury and of coming forward initially with evidence to show such absence. Moreover, the subjective part of the qualified immunity test was important not only for

---

[290] Wood v Strickland, 420 US 308 (1975), discussed at §8.02 *reaffirmed in* Cleavinger v Saxner, 106 S Ct 496 (1985) (member of prison disciplinary committee protected only by qualified immunity). See also §8.18 on parole board officials.

[291] Pierson v Ray, 386 US 547 (1967).

[292] Scheuer v Rhodes, 416 US 232 (1974).

[293] Wood v Strickland, 420 US 308 (1975).

[294] Procunier v Navarette, 434 US 555 (1978).

[295] There was a practical connection between the objective and subjective parts. The more unreasonably a defendant was found to act, the greater the likelihood of a finding of intent to bring about the resulting injury. Of course, a defendant had in any event to pass both parts of the qualified immunity test before *Harlow*.

[296] For a questionable pre-*Harlow* approach to the jury's role regarding the subjective part of the qualified immunity test, see McGhee v Draper, 564 F2d 902 (10th Cir 1977) where the Tenth Circuit affirmed the district court's directed verdict for defendant school officials on the subjective part even though defendants had as yet introduced no evidence at all on their own behalf. A possible explanation is that defendants were called by plaintiff and there was thus some testimony on qualified immunity. While the court's desire to conserve judicial resources was commendable, its approach here may have been unfair to the plaintiff.

defense purposes. Because it focused on the defendant's state of mind, it was relevant to the issue of punitive damages as well.[297]

However, as explained in considerable detail earlier in this chapter,[298] the Court in *Harlow v Fitzgerald*[299] eliminated the subjective part—with its accompanying jury role—in order to permit the defeat of insubstantial claims without resort to trial through summary judgment. In this way, the Court reasoned, the costs of defending against §1983 damages actions will be reduced considerably where there is no clearly settled law. While it is true, however, that a defendant's subjective state of mind is not relevant as such to the existence of clearly settled law, it may be important for determining whether the defendant is liable for violating clearly settled law because he knew it even where the *reasonable* defendant would not have known it. This appears to be the point of Justices Brennan, Marshall, and Blackmun in their concurring opinion in *Harlow*.[300] Of course, even for them the law must first be clearly settled before this subjective inquiry is made.

There is another connection in which a subjective inquiry may become relevant: where a defendant claims, pursuant to *Harlow*, that there were exceptional circumstances justifying his or her failure to know and comply with clearly settled law.[301] For example, the defendant may claim that he or she relied on erroneous advice of counsel.[302] In such a case, it may be important to inquire into whether there was such reliance in fact.[303]

Despite *Harlow*, it is extremely important to distinguish between *Harlow*'s elimination of the subjective part of the qualified immunity test and any state of mind requirements for the prima facie case. Where appropriate, an inquiry into a defendant's state of mind must still be made for prima facie case purposes. In an Eleventh Circuit case,[304] for example, the plaintiff sued various

---

[297] *See* **ch 4.**

[298] *See* §§**8.03-8.04.**

[299] 457 US 800 (1982). *Harlow*'s elimination of the subjective part was retroactively applied in Wolfel v Sanborn, 691 F2d 270 (6th Cir 1982) (construing Supreme Court's remand order in same case).

[300] 457 US at 820.

[301] McKinley v Trattles, 732 F2d 1320 (7th Cir 1984) (court, not jury, to determine the existence of clearly settled law; however, state of mind may be relevant where defendant can show no knowledge or reason to know clearly settled law).

[302] See the cases at §**8.06.**

[303] Only in the ways described here is it possible to assert, as the Fourth Circuit has twice done, that *Harlow* did not entirely eliminate the subjective part of the qualified immunity test and that the *Harlow* test does not turn exclusively on objective factors but only "primarily" on them. Vizbaras v Prieber, 761 F2d 1013 (4th Cir 1985); McElveen v County of Prince William, 725 F2d 954 (4th Cir 1984). However, it is not clear that the Fourth Circuit meant to distinguish, as done in this section, between the existence of clearly settled law and actual knowledge of, or the duty to know, clearly settled law.

[304] Dykes v Hosemann, 743 F2d 1488 (11th Cir 1984), *revd in part on other grounds,* 776 F2d 942 (11th Cir 1985) (en banc). See generally **ch 3** on state of mind requirements for particular constitutional violations. Compare the need to distinguish between the probable cause issue and qualified immunity in a Fourth Amendment setting, as discussed at §**8.11.**

defendants, including an official of a state health and rehabilitation services department, for conspiring to deprive her of the right to raise her child in alleged violation of due process. Reversing the district court's grant of summary judgment for the official on qualified immunity grounds, the court observed that the issue was *not* whether defendant was expected to know that adjudicating plaintiff's right to custody without notice would violate her constitutional rights; it was clear that he should have known. Rather, there were material issues of fact in dispute regarding the official's participation in the alleged "understanding" to violate plaintiff's rights. Even if defendant did not have a statutory duty to notify plaintiff, he could still be held liable for conspiracy.

§8.16 The Burden of Proof

Before *Harlow v Fitzgerald*[305] eliminated the subjective part, a defendant in §1983 cases had and, as a matter of policy, should have had the burdens of pleading and proving qualified immunity by a preponderance of the evidence. To say that these were plaintiff's burdens was to confuse the prima facie §1983 cause of action with the §1983 qualified immunity.[306] In practical terms, this meant at least three things. First, where the defendant introduced no evidence as to reasonableness and good faith belief after the plaintiff established a prima facie §1983 claim, then the defendant lost.[307] Second, where the evidence as to compliance with the qualified immunity test was in equipoise (50-50), then, again, the defendant lost. And third, and of considerable significance, the defendant, because of having the burden of proof, also had the initial burden of coming forward with evidence to establish a qualified immunity.[308]

Before the subjective part was eliminated by *Harlow,* there were cases ruling that where a defendant acted intentionally in connection with the constitutional violation alleged, the defendant thereby failed the subjective part of the test. *See e.g.,* Williams v Board of Regents, 629 F2d 993 (5th Cir 1980) (First Amendment and malicious intent) and Flores v Pierce, 617 F2d 1386 (9th Cir 1980) (equal protection and discriminatory intent).

[305] 457 US 800 (1982).

[306] See **ch 3** on the importance of distinguishing between the prima facie §1983 claim and qualified immunity.

[307] *E.g.,* United States *ex rel* Tyrrell v Speaker, 535 F2d 823 (3d Cir 1976) where the court affirmed a judgment for plaintiff against the defendant warden and observed that the warden apparently introduced no evidence on qualified immunity at all. *Compare* Morris v Travisono, 528 F2d 856 (1st Cir 1976), where state correctional officers sued for their use of tear gas as an alleged Eighth Amendment violation were precluded from raising the issue of settled rights because they failed to object to the instructions given on this point.

[308] This burden shifts back and forth in the course of a trial depending on the evidence introduced by the parties. The failure to rebut exposes a party to the possibility of a directed verdict.

However, the Fifth Circuit[309] read *Wood v Strickland*[310] as establishing "the principle that an individual school board member is not personally liable for damages under §1983 unless the plaintiff can establish a 'malicious intention to cause a deprivation of constitutional rights or other injury to the student'."[311] It relied on the following language in *Wood:* "A compensatory award will be appropriate only if the school board member has acted with such an impermissible motivation or with such disregard of the student's clearly established constitutional rights that his action cannot reasonably be characterized as being in good faith."[312]

This pre-*Harlow* approach to the burden of proof was also expressly taken initially by the First Circuit[313] but thereafter rejected.[314] It was also implied by the Tenth Circuit,[315] despite an earlier Tenth Circuit case which seemed to place the burden of proof on the defendant.[316] In contrast, the District of Columbia Circuit, the Third Circuit, the Sixth Circuit, and the Eighth Circuit explicitly placed these burdens on the defendant after consideration of the question, and the Second Circuit apparently did so as well.[317]

The language in the *Wood* opinion, which was rather loose to begin with, was, moreover, taken out of context by the Fifth Circuit. The Court's last quoted statement applies where both parties have already introduced evidence both as to the existence of the prima facie claim and the qualified immunity. The Court in *Wood* was not addressing the burdens issue, but only the scope of the qualified immunity. Also, the discussion in *Wood* occurred against the background of *Pierson* and *Scheuer*, both of which placed the burden of proof on the defendant. A Supreme Court change in the burden of proof would surely

---

[309] Hander v San Jacinto Junior College, 519 F2d 273 (5th Cir 1975). *See also* Barker v Norman, 651 F2d 1107, 1121 (5th Cir 1981) and Gullatte v Potts, 654 F2d 1007, 1014-15 (5th Cir 1981). *But cf* Barratt v Thomas, 649 F2d 1193, 1201 (5th Cir 1981).

[310] 420 US 308 (1975), discussed at **§8.02.**

[311] 519 F2d at 277 n 1.

[312] 420 US at 322. The much more extensive quote is set out in **§8.02.**

[313] Kostka v Hogg, 560 F2d 37 (1st Cir 1977), relying on Gaffney v Silk, 488 F2d 1248 (1st Cir 1973) and Stadium Films Inc v Baillargeon, 542 F2d 577 (1st Cir 1976).

[314] DeVasto v Faherty, 658 F2d 859, 865 (1st Cir 1981).

[315] McGhee v Draper, 564 F2d 902 (10th Cir 1977); Prebble v Brodrick, 535 F2d 605 (10th Cir 1976). The Tenth Circuit nevertheless conceded that the defendant has the burden of pleading and of going forward initially with the evidence on qualified immunity. *See also* Freed, *Executive Official Immunity for Constitutional Violations: An Analysis and a Critique,* 72 Nw UL Rev 526, 562-63 (1977).

[316] Smith v Losee, 485 F2d 334 (10th Cir 1973) (en banc), *cert denied,* 417 US 908 (1974).

[317] Davidson v Scully, 694 F2d 50 (2d Cir 1982) ("affirmative defense"); Reese v Nelson, 598 F2d 822 (3d Cir 1979); Landrum v Moats, 576 F2d 1320 (8th Cir 1978); Dellums v Powell, 566 F2d 167 (DC Cir 1977); Skehan v Board of Trustees, 538 F2d 53 (3d Cir), *cert denied,* 429 US 979 (1976); United States *ex rel* Tyrrell v Speaker, 535 F2d 823 (3d Cir 1976); Laverne v Corning, 522 F2d 1144 (2d Cir 1975); Glasson v City of Louisville, 518 F2d 899 (6th Cir), *cert denied,* 423 US 930 (1975).

have addressed the issue much more directly than *Wood* supposedly did. In short, as Judge Seitz of the Fifth Circuit said:

> Although *Wood* establishes a qualified immunity for school board members, I see nothing in that opinion which would reorder the burden of pleading and proving that immunity. Thus, I am unable to agree that plaintiff's failure to allege facts in his complaint negativing a potential defense makes the complaint susceptible to a motion to dismiss for failure to state a claim.[318]

The Supreme Court expressly addressed the pleading aspect of this affirmative defense issue in *Gomez v Toledo*,[319] a pre-*Harlow* decision. It held in *Gomez* that a §1983 defendant has the burden of pleading qualified immunity and, correspondingly, a §1983 plaintiff need not allege bad faith in order to state a cause of action. Plaintiff had sued a police superintendent for damages under §1983, alleging a violation of procedural due process in plaintiff's discharge from employment. Granting defendant's motion to dismiss for failure to state a cause of action, the district court concluded that plaintiff "was required to plead as part of his claim for relief that, in committing the actions alleged, [defendant] was motivated by bad faith." The First Circuit affirmed.

Resolving the conflict among the circuits, the Supreme Court reversed in an opinion by Justice Marshall. The Court emphasized the following:

1. Neither the language nor legislative history of §1983 indicates that a §1983 plaintiff must allege bad faith in order to state a cause of action

2. The qualified immunity test is an affirmative defense and as such is not relevant to the existence of a prima facie §1983 cause of action

3. Whether a qualified immunity exists in a particular case depends on facts peculiarly within the knowledge and control of the defendant which a plaintiff cannot ordinarily be expected to know

Justice Rehnquist concurred, noting that the Court's opinion addressed only the burden of pleading issue. However, especially before *Harlow* eliminated the subjective part of the qualified immunity test, the reasoning in *Gomez* was equally applicable to the burden of proof. The important question, though, is what effect *Harlow*, decided *after Gomez*, has on the burden of proof issue. As to the question of the existence of clearly settled law, to speak of a burden of proof with its evidentiary emphasis appears misplaced. After all, whether clearly settled law existed at the time a defendant acted is an issue of law for the court.

Nevertheless, it is still meaningful to speak about an evidentiary burden of

---

[318] Zeller v Donegal School Dist Bd of Educ, 517 F2d 600, 611, 612 (3d Cir 1975) (dissenting opinion). For a similar view see Kattan, *Knocking on Wood: Some Thoughts on the Immunities of State Officials to Civil Rights Damage Actions*, 30 Vand L Rev 941, 986-89 (1977).

[319] 446 US 635 (1980).

proof to be imposed on the defendant in at least one situation: where there is clearly settled law and the defendant claims *exceptional circumstances* justifying his or her failure to know and comply with it.[320] As stated by the Fourth Circuit,[321] the burden of proof as to this question is and should be on the defendant, even after *Harlow.*

Thus, *Gomez* is still good law on the burden of pleading issue, and its reasoning, even after *Harlow,* should apply to the burden of proof respecting the qualified immunity test as well. As of this writing, the Fourth Circuit,[322] Sixth Circuit,[323] and Eighth Circuit[324] have so stated, while the Seventh Circuit left the question open,[325] and the Eleventh Circuit[326] apparently follows the Fifth Circuit's questionable approach.

Regardless of this burden of proof issue, a plaintiff who seeks *punitive* damages must allege in the complaint the state of mind of the defendant which is appropriate for the recovery of such damages—*see* Chapter 4. Similarly, it is part of the plaintiff's prima facie case burden to plead and prove the requisite state of mind for the constitutional or federal statutory violation claimed.

§8.17   The Coverage of The Qualified Immunity Test: Government Officials and Private Persons

The decisions of the Supreme Court and the circuits demonstrate that the qualified immunity test covers all state and local government officials at all levels of responsibility with the exception of those who have an absolute immunity.[327] There is in effect a national unitary standard which governs the conduct of such officials for qualified immunity purposes.[328] Consistent with such wide coverage, the circuits have, for example, applied the qualified

---

[320] See **§8.15** on the now eliminated subjective part. Another example relates to the defendant's burden of proving that he or she did not actually know that clearly settled law existed.

[321] Arebaugh v Dalton, 730 F2d 970 (4th Cir 1984).

[322] *Id.*

[323] Alexander v Alexander, 706 F2d 751 (6th Cir 1983). *See also* Wolfel v Sanborn, 691 F2d 270 (6th Cir 1982).

[324] Bauer v Norris, 713 F2d 408, 411 n 6 (8th Cir 1983).

[325] Crowder v Lash, 687 F2d 996, 1002-03 (7th Cir 1982) (question "unsettled" but court assumed arguendo that plaintiff had the burden). *But cf* Chavis v Rowe, 643 F2d 1281, 1288 (7th Cir 1981) (burdens of pleading and proof on defendant).

[326] Zeigler v Jackson, 716 F2d 847 (11th Cir 1983) (per curiam).

[327] See **ch 7** and the discussion of the functional approach. See also **§§8.13, 8.14 & 8.18.**

[328] *See generally* Kattan, *Knocking on Wood: Some Thoughts on the Immunities of State Officials to Civil Rights Damage Action,* 30 Vand L Rev 941 (1977).

immunity test to housing inspectors accused of unconstitutional inspections,[329] to parole officers charged with improperly arresting a parolee without a hearing,[330] to a city's beer board members who allegedly violated plaintiff's rights by granting a beer license to a third party on condition that the licensee not employ the plaintiff,[331] to a court reporter accused of altering a trial transcript under instructions of a judge,[332] to a probation officer who mistakenly caused the arrest and incarceration of a person on probation,[333] to a county health administrator, county planning director, and county commissioner in connection with the initiation of civil commitment proceedings against plaintiff,[334] to a court clerk accused of concealing the entry of a judicial decision,[335] and to a department of welfare's family counselor charged with participating in an extensive conspiracy to frame plaintiff.[336]

Whether state legislative employees, local legislators, judicial employees, those subject to judicial orders, and certain defense counsel are protected by either an absolute immunity or a qualified immunity is discussed elsewhere.[337] Similarly discussed elsewhere[338] is the rule that governmental entities which are held to be persons under §1983 are not protected by qualified immunity.

As set out in Chapter 2,[339] there may be situations where private persons act "under color of law" and thereby become liable under §1983.[340] The question is whether such private persons are protected by qualified immunity or no immunity at all. In *Folsom Investment Co v Moore*,[341] an important Fifth Circuit case, the court held that a private party who invokes a presumptively valid state attachment statute later held to be unconstitutional is entitled to a good faith immunity from monetary liability under §1983. The test is whether the private defendant knew or should have known that the statute was unconstitutional, the same objective test made applicable by *Harlow v Fitzgerald* to state officials performing discretionary functions. The court relied on the following considerations: (1) the public interest in permitting ordinary citizens to rely on presumptively valid state law and in protecting them from damages liability when the state statute is later held to be unconstitutional; (2) the public interest in protecting private citizens from damages liability when their role in unconstitutional action is marginal; and (3) the existence of a common law

---

[329] Hanna v Drobnick, 514 F2d 393 (6th Cir 1975); Laverne v Corning, 522 F2d 1144 (2d Cir 1975).

[330] Wolfel v Sanborn, 555 F2d 583 (6th Cir 1977).

[331] Burnett v McNabb, 565 F2d 398 (6th Cir 1977).

[332] Green v Maraio, 722 F2d 1013 (8th Cir 1983).

[333] Galvan v Garmon, 710 F2d 214 (5th Cir 1983) (per curiam).

[334] Reese v Nelson, 598 F2d 822 (3d Cir 1979).

[335] Lowe v Letsinger, 772 F2d 308 (7th Cir 1985).

[336] Slavin v Curry, 574 F2d 1256 (5th Cir 1978).

[337] *See* ch 7.

[338] *See* §6.18.

[339] *See* §2.10.

[340] See §§2.04-2.10 on state action and color of law.

[341] 681 F2d 1032 (5th Cir 1982).

defense of probable cause to malicious prosecution actions which "convinces us that Congress in enacting §1983 could not have intended to subject to liability those who in good faith resorted to legal process."[342] However, the court cautioned that it was not holding that a private defendant's degree of knowledge is always the same as that attributed to a public official.

Similarly, where plaintiffs sued certain creditors and others claiming a violation of due process in their use of an unconstitutional state garnishment statute, the Eighth Circuit[343] ruled, after finding action under color of law, that the private defendants were protected by qualified immunity. Relying on *Folsom Investment Co v Moore,* the court spoke of the common law background of the tort of malicious prosecution with its requirement of the absence of probable cause, and the strong public interest in permitting private individuals to rely on presumptively valid state laws. The court also asserted that qualified immunity protection accommodated the competing interests in compensation for constitutional deprivations on the one hand and the protection of private creditors seeking redress under presumptively valid state laws on the other. It was significant as well that several Supreme Court justices had made a similar suggestion in *Lugar v Edmundson Oil Co.*[344] Finally, on the qualified immunity merits the Eighth Circuit remanded. It could not rule for the defendants as a matter of law because the relevant state garnishment statute had been declared unconstitutional *prior to* their use of it in this case.

Where, however, private persons engage in *conspiracies*[345] to deprive others of clearly settled constitutional rights, then such defendants will likely fail the *Harlow* qualified immunity test.

§8.18   Parole Board Officials

The broad argument that all defendants who act in a quasi-judicial capacity should have an absolute judicial immunity was rejected in *Wood v Strickland*[346] where the defendant school board members had disciplined students in an adjudicatory proceeding. The nature of the challenged conduct—whether it might be characterized as quasi-legislative or quasi-judicial—was relevant in *Wood* only with respect to the defendants' compliance with the qualified immunity test. This also appears to be the thrust of the Court's decisions in *O'Connor v Donaldson*[347] and *Procunier v Navarette*[348] which applied the qualified immunity test to hospital and prison officials.

Despite this, and even before the recent spread of the functional approach

---

[342] *Id* 1038.

[343] Buller v Buechler, 706 F2d 844 (8th Cir 1983).

[344] 457 US 922 (1982).

[345] *See* §2.10.

[346] 420 US 308 (1975).

[347] 422 US 563 (1975).

[348] 434 US 555 (1978).

to immunity,[349] the Fourth and Fifth Circuits extended absolute quasi-judicial immunity to parole board members.[350] Their decisions, which did not consider *Wood*, relied on a leading pre-*Wood* Ninth Circuit case, *Silver v Dickson*[351] which had concluded: "State officials are, while employed in the processing of applications for parole, performing quasi-judicial functions . . . [which are] closely related to the operation of a state judicial and penal system."[352] However, this reliance on *Silver*'s approach was misplaced after *Wood*. Moreover, there are other officials whose work is closely related to the judicial and penal system who are nevertheless protected only by a qualified immunity.[353] Further, *Silver*'s decision had an alternative ground: that parole officials perform *discretionary governmental functions* which entitle them to absolute immunity. However, *Scheuer v Rhodes*[354] undercut this second ground just as *Wood* undercut the first.

The real question in such cases is not whether parole board officials are judicial or excutive officials, for they "are in reality executive officers carrying out the policy of the state in respect to probation and parole.[355] It is instead whether—through application of the functional approach of *Butz v Economou*[356] —these parole board officials should be found to function in a quasi-judicial capacity in the context of decision making which has some of the attributes of a judicial proceeding. In an influential post-*Wood* Ninth Circuit case,[357] an inmate sued parole officials alleging they had unconstitutionally given him a parole release date that required him to serve an excessively long prison sentence. After an extensive discussion of the case law and relevant policy considerations, the Ninth Circuit held that parole officials are functionally similar to judges and should therefore be protected by absolute immunity in connection with decisions to grant, deny, and revoke parole. It also emphasized the existence under California law of habeas corpus through which the length of a prison term could be challenged.

The same functional approach was used by the Seventh Circuit[358] in a case

---

[349] *See* §§7.05, 7.10, 8.13, 8.14 & 8.18.

[350] Douglas v Muncy, 570 F2d 499 (4th Cir 1978); Franklin v Shields, 569 F2d 784, 798 (4th Cir), *cert denied,*435 US 1003 (1978); Johnson v Wells, 566 F2d 1016, 1018 (5th Cir 1978). *See also* Pate v Alabama Bd of Pardons & Paroles, 409 F Supp 478 (MD Ala), *affd,* 548 F2d 354 (5th Cir 1976).

[351] 403 F2d 642 (9th Cir 1968), *cert denied,* 394 US 990 (1969).

[352] *Id* 643-44.

[353] *E.g.,* court clerks and prison officials. *See* **ch 7**.

[354] 416 US 232 (1974), discussed at **§8.13**.

[355] Thompson v Burke, 556 F2d 231, 237-38 (3d Cir 1977) (applying qualified immunity test to nonadjudicatory conduct but stating that absolute immunity is applicable to adjudicatory conduct).

[356] 438 US 478 (1978), set out at **§7.10**.

[357] Sellars v Procunier, 641 F2d 1295 (9th Cir 1981). *See also* Anderson v Boyd, 714 F2d 906 (9th Cir 1983) (reaffirming absolute immunity rule).

[358] United States *ex rel* Powell v Irving, 684 F2d 494 (7th Cir 1982). *See also* Trotter v Klincar, 748 F2d 1177 (7th Cir 1984) (applying absolute immunity to revocation of parole). Even more recently the Seventh Circuit rejected a distinction between

involving an action for damages brought by the plaintiff, who had repeatedly been denied parole, against state parole board officials who allegedly discriminated systematically against blacks. The Seventh Circuit used what it called a *functional comparability* test and held that the defendants were protected by absolute judicial immunity. Relying heavily on the Ninth Circuit's decision to the same effect,[359] the court found that the defendants, in the processing of parole applications, performed an adjudicative function comparable to that of judges. Just as the decision-making process by judges "must be kept free from fear, so must that of parole board officials." The Seventh Circuit also observed that there were state law safeguards protecting prisoners seeking parole, as well as possible federal habeas corpus review.

As of this writing, the question whether parole board officials are protected by absolute immunity for their quasi-judicial conduct is open in the Supreme Court.[360] However, in *Cleavinger v Saxner*[361] the Court held that members of a prison disciplinary committee are not functionally comparable to judges and are thus not protected by absolute immunity. In the course of so doing, the Court asserted that parole board officials are very different from members of prison disciplinary committees. This may suggest that parole board officials, who serve on a "neutral and detached" professional hearing body which is required to provide many due process protections, will eventually be protected by absolute quasi-judicial immunity.

In the circuits, in addition to the Seventh and Ninth Circuits, the Fifth[362] and the Eighth Circuits[363] have also recently either reaffirmed or adopted an absolute immunity rule for the quasi-judicial conduct of parole board officials. It is thus fair to say that this is the trend in the circuits.

"adjudicatory" and "administrative" acts of parole board officials. Walker v Prisoner Review Bd, 769 F2d 396 (7th Cir 1985).

[359] Sellars v Procunier, 641 F2d 1295 (9th Cir 1981).

[360] Martinez v California, 444 US 277 (1980).

[361] 106 S Ct 496 (1985).

[362] Hilliard v Board of Pardons & Paroles, 759 F2d 1190 (5th Cir 1985). But see Fowler v Cross, 635 F2d 476 (5th Cir 1981), holding that state parole officials, accused of due process violations in connection with a parolee's transfer from a county prison to the state system, were protected by qualified immunity.

[363] Evans v Dillahunty, 711 F2d 828 (8th Cir 1983).

APPENDIX A
Table of Leading
Constitutional Law
Cases

Certain substantive constitutional law issues arise in frequently recurring §1983 litigation involving educational institutions, prisons, mental institutions, and the police. This table is designed to get the lawyer quickly into such specific issues which are otherwise beyond the intended scope of this book. The cases collected are for the most part those of the Supreme Court (current through the 1985-86 Term) although there are other federal decisions as well. They are presented in reverse chronological order, with the most recent decisions first. However, this table is not all-inclusive. Further research and the use of Shepard's/McGraw-Hill, Inc's Citator system are strongly recommended. Also, use of this table should be accompanied by study of Chapter 2 which deals with state action and the relationship between the Fourteenth Amendment and §1983, and of Chapter 3 which deals with state of mind requirements for different constitutional provisions.

Public Educational Institutions: Teachers and Students

Academic Freedom and Freedom of Speech

Teachers

Minnesota State Board for Community Colleges v Knight, 465 US 271 (1984)(statutorily required conferral with professional employees' exclusive representatives)

Perry Education Association v Perry Local Educators' Association, 460 US 37 (1983) (preferred access of organization to teachers' mailboxes)

Abood v Detroit Board of Education, 431 US 209 (1977) (non-union teachers required to pay fee to union)

Mount Healthy City School District v Doyle, 429 US 274 (1977) (teacher reinstatement after nonrenewal in violation of First Amendment)

Madison, City of, Joint School District No 8 v Wisconsin Employment Relations Commission, 429 US 167 (1976) (teacher speaking at school board meeting)

Russo v Central School District No 1, 469 F2d 623 (2d Cir 1972), *cert denied*, 411 US 932 (1973) (teacher's refusal to salute flag)

James v Board of Education, 461 F2d 566 (2d Cir 1972), *cert denied,* 409 US 1042 (1972), *rehg denied,* 410 US 947 (1973) (wearing of black arm band)

Mailloux v Kiley, 448 F2d 1242 (1st Cir 1971) (teacher discussion of four letter words in class)

Connell v Higginbotham, 403 US 207 (1971) (loyalty oath)

Keefe v Geanakos, 418 F2d 359 (1st Cir 1969) (teacher assignment to students of controversial article)

Epperson v Arkansas, 393 US 97 (1968) (teaching evolution in public schools)

Pickering v Board of Education, 391 US 563 (1968) (teacher speaking on public issue)

Keyishian v Board of Regents, 385 US 589 (1967) (loyalty oath)

Baggett v Bullitt, 377 US 360 (1964) (loyalty oath)

Cramp v Board of Public Instruction, 368 US 278 (1961) (statute requiring teachers to swear no affiliation with communist party)

Shelton v Tucker, 364 US 479 (1960) (requirement that teachers reveal organizational affiliations)

Beilan v Board of Public Education, 357 US 399 (1958) (teacher dismissal for incompetency based on refusal to answer questions)

Slochower v Board of Higher Education, 350 US 551 (1956) (loyalty oath)

Adler v Board of Education, 342 US 485 (1952) (loyalty oath)

Meyer v Nebraska, 262 US 390 (1923) (teaching German language in public schools)

Students

Bethel School District v Fraser, 106 S Ct 3159 (1986) (right of school to discipline student for language used at student assembly)

Board of Education v Pico No 26, 457 US 853 (1982) (right of school board to remove books from school library)

Widmar v Vincent, 454 US 263 (1981) (free speech right of students to use school facilities for religious purposes)

Trachtman v Anker, 563 F2d 512 (2d Cir 1977) (distribution by student newspaper of sex questionnaire)

Minarcini v Strongsville City School District, 541 F2d 577 (6th Cir 1976) (removal of books from school library)

Nitzberg v Parks, 525 F2d 378 (4th Cir 1975) (independent student newspapers)

Healy v James, 408 US 169 (1972) (student organizations)

Eisner v Stamford Board of Education, 440 F2d 803 (2d Cir 1971) (prior approval requirement for distribution of independent student newspaper)

Tinker v Des Moines Independent School District, 393 US 503 (1969) (wearing of black arm band)

West Virginia State Board of Education v Barnette, 319 US 624 (1943) (flag salute)

For additional cases see **§3.03** on basis of liability for First Amendment violations; § **4.06** on compensatory damages; **§4.12** on punitive damages; and **§8.07** on qualified immunity of school officials.

Procedural Due Process

Teachers

Cleveland Board of Education v Loudermill, 105 S Ct 1487 (1985) (process due to terminated school district employees)

Migra v Warren City School District Board of Education, 465 US 75 (1984) (preclusive effect of state court judgment)

Perry v Sindermann, 408 US 593 (1972) (when teacher is entitled to a hearing)

Board of Regents v Roth, 408 US 564 (1972) (when teacher is entitled to a hearing)

Students

Carey v Piphus, 435 US 247 (1978) (damages for procedural due process violations)

Board of Curators of University of Missouri v Horowitz, 435 US 78 (1978) (what kind of hearing)

Ingraham v Wright, 430 US 651 (1977) (procedural due process and corporal punishment)

Wood v Strickland, 420 US 308 (1975) (qualified immunity of school board members for procedural due process violations)

Goss v Lopez, 419 US 565 (1975) (when student is entitled to a hearing; what kind of hearing)

For additional cases see §§**3.08-3.11** on basis of liability for due process violations; **§4.05** on compensatory damages; **§4.11** on punitive damages; and **§8.07** on qualified immunity of school officials.

Substantive Due Process

Students

Regents of University of Michigan v Ewing, 106 S Ct 507 (1985) (right to retake examination)

Racial Discrimination and Equal Protection

Grove City College v Bell, 465 US 555 (1984) (regulation of private college's financial aid program under Title IX)

Martinez v Bynum, 461 US 321 (1983) (residency requirement denying admission to minors living apart from parents)

Mississippi University for Women v Hogan, 458 US 718 (1982) (man's right to attend all-female nursing school)

Crawford v Los Angeles Board of Education, 458 US 527 (1982) (state constitutional amendment reducing state's obligations for pupil assignment and transportation to equal protection minimum)

Washington v Seattle School District No 1, 458 US 457 (1982) (state statute removing school board's power to implement voluntary remedial busing scheme)

Plyler v Doe, 457 US 202 (1982) (illegal alien children's entitlement to free public education)

Board of Education v Harris, 444 US 130 (1979) (discriminatory teacher assignments)

Dayton Board of Education v Brinkman, 443 US 526 (1979) (duty to disestablish dual school system)

Columbus Board of Education v Penick, 443 US 449 (1979) (school board's continuing affirmative duty to disestablish dual school system)

Harrah Independent School District v Mary Jane Martin, 440 US 194 (1979) (school board-imposed continuing education requirement for teacher)

Bustop, Inc v Board of Education, 439 US 1380 (1978) (staying enforcement of school desegregation order)

Regents of University of California v Bakke, 438 US 265 (1978) (affirmative action program for admission to state medical school)

Pasadena City Board of Education v Spangler, 427 US 424 (1976) (annual student reassignments and racial balance)

Washington v Davis, 426 US 229 (1976) (intentional, purposeful discrimination required for equal protection violation)

Milliken v Bradley, 418 US 717 (1974) (judicial remedy which crosses school district boundaries)

Keyes v School District No 1, Denver, Colorado, 413 US 189 (1973) (distinctions between de jure and de facto segregated schools)

Swann v Charlotte-Mecklenburg Board of Education, 402 US 1 (1971) (broad scope of judicial remedy for de jure segregated schools)

Green v County School Board, 391 US 430 (1968) (freedom of choice plan)

Griffin v County School Board, 377 US 218 (1964) (closing of public schools to avoid integration)

Brown v Board of Education, 347 US 483, (1954) (de jure segregated schools violative of equal protection)

For additional cases see §**3.14** on basis of liability for equal protection violations; §**4.07** on compensatory damages; and §**4.13** on punitive damages.

Free Exercise and Establishment of Religion

Witters v Washington Department of Services for the Blind, 106 S Ct 748 (1986) (financial aid to blind student at private Christian college)

Aguilar v Felton, 105 S Ct 3232 (1985) (public funding of parochial school programs)

Grand Rapids School District v Ball, 105 S Ct 3216 (1985) (public funding of parochial school programs)

Wallace v Jaffree, 105 S Ct 2479 (1985) (one-minute period of silence in public schools for meditation or voluntary prayer)

Mueller v Allen, 463 US 388 (1983) (state tax deduction for costs of tuition, textbooks, and transportation of parochial school children)

Bob Jones University v United States, 461 US 574 (1983) (tax-exempt status of private school with religiously based racially discriminatory policies)

Larkin v Grendel's Den, Inc, 456 US 913 (1982) (authority of churches and schools to veto liquor license applications)

Widmar v Vincent, 454 US 263 (1981) (free speech right of students to use school facilities for religious purposes)

Stone v Graham, 449 US 39 (1980) (posting of Ten Commandments on classroom walls in public schools)

Committee for Public Education & Religious Liberty v Regan, 444 US 646 (1980) (state statutory scheme providing direct cash reimbursement for church-sponsored and secular nonpublic schools for performing various secular functions mandated by state law)

New York v Cathedral Academy, 434 US 125 (1977) (state aid to sectarian schools)

Wolman v Walter, 433 US 229 (1977) (state provision of textbooks, diagnostic and testing services, instructional materials and equipment)

Meek v Pittenger, 421 US 349 (1975) (loan of instructional materials and equipment)

Sloan v Lemon, 413 US 825 (1973) (tuition grants to parents)

Committee for Public Education & Religious Liberty v Nyquist, 413 US 756 (1973) (grants to schools and parents)

Hunt v McNair, 413 US 734 (1973) (revenue bonds benefiting Baptist-controlled college)

Wisconsin v Yoder, 406 US 205 (1972) (compulsory public education for Amish children)

Tilton v Richardson, 403 US 672 (1971) (state aid to sectarian schools)

Lemon v Kurtzman, 403 US 602 (1971) (state aid to sectarian schools)

Epperson v Arkansas, 393 US 97 (1968) (teaching evolution in public schools)

Board of Education v Allen, 392 US 236 (1968) (public loan of books to sectarian schools)

School District v Schempp, 374 US 203 (1963) (school prayer)

Engel v Vitale, 370 US 421 (1962) (school prayer)

Zorach v Clauson, 343 US 306 (1952) (release time for sectarian classes)

McCollum v Board of Education, 333 US 203 (1948) (release time for sectarian classes)

Everson v Board of Education, 330 US 1 (1947) (public funding of sectarian school bussing service)

Pierce v Society of Sisters, 268 US 510 (1925) (right to establish and attend sectarian schools)

Fourth Amendment

New Jersey v TLO, 105 S Ct 733 (1985) (school authorities' search of student on school premises)

For additional cases see §3.04 on bases of liability for Fourth Amendment violations.

Eighth Amendment and Corporal Punishment

Ingraham v Wright, 430 US 651 (1977) (corporal punishment not violative of the Eighth Amendment)

For additional cases see §3.07 on basis of liability for Eighth Amendment violations.

Prisons

First Amendment: Speech, Press, and Religion

Speech and Press

Bell v Wolfish, 441 US 520 (1979) (receipt of books by pre-trial detainees)

Procunier v Navarette, 434 US 555 (1978) (qualified immunity of prison officials in connection with interference with outgoing mail)

Jones v North Carolina Prisoners' Labor Union Inc, 433 US 119 (1977) (union activity)

Saxbe v Washington Post Co, 417 US 843 (1974) (press interviews)

Pell v Procunier, 417 US 817 (1974) (press interviews)

Procunier v Martinez, 416 US 396 (1974) (censorship of mail)

For additional cases see §3.03 on basis of liability for First Amendment violations; §4.06 on compensatory damages; §4.12 on punitive damages; and §§8.09-8.10 on qualified immunity of prison officials.

Religion

Teterud v Burns, 522 F2d 357 (8th Cir 1975) (refusal to have hair cut on religious grounds)

Remmers v Brewer, 494 F2d 1277 (8th Cir 1974) (per curiam) (new religion protected by the free exercise clause)

Cruz v Beto, 405 US 319 (1972) (free exercise of religion by Buddhist inmate)

Cooper v Pate, 382 F2d 518 (7th Cir 1967) (inmate religious communications and visits by clergymen)

Procedural Due Process

Davidson v Cannon, 106 S Ct 668 (1986) (negligent failure to protect inmate from attack)

Daniels v Williams, 106 S Ct 662 (1986) (negligent deprivations of life, liberty or property; Parrott v Taylor overruled in part)

Superintendent, Massachusetts Correctional Institute at Walpole v Hill, 105 S Ct 2768 (1985) (revocation of inmate's good time credits)

Black v Romano, 105 S Ct 2254 (1985) (alternatives to incarceration before revoking probation)

Ponte v Real, 105 S Ct 2193 (1985) (prison officials' refusal to call requested witnesses in a disciplinary hearing)

Block v Rutherford, 104 S Ct 3227 (1984) (cell searches)

Hudson v Palmer, 104 S Ct 3194 (1984) (intentional deprivation of prisoner's property by state employee)

Olim v Wakinekona, 461 US 238 (1983) (no deprivation of liberty as a result of interstate prison transfer)

Hewitt v Helms, 459 US 460 (1983) (procedure for confining prisoner to administrative segregation)

Parratt v Taylor, 451 US 527 (1981) (negligent deprivation of property)

Cuyler v Adams, 449 US 433 (1981) (pre-transfer hearing before prisoner transferred to another jurisdiction)

Wood v Georgia, 449 US 341 (1981) (revocation of probation for failure to pay probation fines in installments)

Hughes v Rowe, 449 US 5 (1980) (prisoner's confinement to segregation without prior hearing)

Vitek v Jones, 445 US 480 (1980) (transfer of state prisoner to state mental institution)

United States Parole Commission v Geraghty, 445 US 388 (1980) (class action challenging parole release guidelines)

Portley v Grossman, 444 US 1311 (1979) (revocation of parole)

United States v Addonizio, 442 US 178 (1979) (post-sentencing change in policies of United States Parole Commission)

Greenholtz v Nebraska Penal Inmates, 442 US 1 (1979) (parole release)

Bell v Wolfish, 441 US 520 (1979) (due process and Fourth Amendment rights of pre-trial detainees)

Meachum v Fano, 427 US 215 (1976) (transfer of inmate to maximum security prison)

Wolff v McDonnell, 418 US 539 (1974) (prison disciplinary proceedings)

Marshall v United States, 414 US 417 (1974) (addict participation in drug rehabilitation program)

Gagnon v Scarpelli, 411 US 778 (1973) (parole revocation proceedings)

Morrissey v Brewer, 408 US 471 (1972) (parole revocation proceedings)

For additional cases see §§3.08-3.11 on basis of liability for due process violations; §4.05 on compensatory damages; §4.10 on punitive damages; and §§8.06-8.07 on qualified immunity of prison officials.

Access to the Courts, Lawyers, and Legal Materials

Nix v Whiteside, 106 S Ct 988 (1986) (effective assistance of counsel and defense attorney's response to client's intention to commit perjury)

Hill v Lockhart, 106 S Ct 366, 54 USLW 4006 (1985) (effective assistance of counsel in habeas corpus proceeding)

Evitts v Lucey, 105 S Ct 830 (1985) (right to effective assistance of counsel on first appeal)

United States v Gouveia, 467 US 180 (1984) (entitlement to counsel prior to adversary judicial proceedings)

Waller v Georgia, 467 US 39 (1984) (closure of entire suppression hearing over defendant's objections)

Strickland v Washington, 464 US 501 (1984) (effective assistance of counsel)

United States v Cronic, 466 US 648 (1984) (effective assistance of counsel)

McKaskle v Wiggins, 465 US 168 (1984) (standby counsel's participation)

Press-Enterprise Co v Superior Court, 104 SCt 819 (1984) (guarantee of public criminal trial extends to voir dire examinations)

Rushen v Spain, 464 US 114 (1983) (unrecorded ex parte communication between trial judge and juror)

Cuyler v Sullivan, 446 US 335 (1980) (state prisoner retaining defense counsel representing potential conflicting interest)

Bounds v Smith, 430 US 817 (1977) (assistance for "jailhouse lawyers")

Ross v Moffitt, 417 US 600 (1974) (counsel for discretionary review)

Johnson v Avery, 393 US 483 (1969) (inmate as "jailhouse lawyer")

Lane v Brown, 372 US 477 (1963) (free transcript for post conviction hearing)

Douglas v California, 372 US 353 (1963) (counsel on appeal)

Griffin v Illinois, 351 US 12 (1956) (free transcript on appeal)

For additional cases see §3.13 on basis of liability for access to court violations; and §§8.09-8.10 on qualified immunity of prison officials.

Eighth Amendment

Whitley v Albers, 106 S Ct 1078 (1986) (prison authorities' infliction of pain upon inmate while attempting to stop prison disturbance)

Rhodes v Chapman, 452 US 337 (1981) (double celling of inmates)

Carlson v Green, 446 US 14 (1980) (damage action in federal court against federal officials for violation of deceased inmate's Eighth Amendment rights)

Estelle v Gamble, 429 US 97 (1976) (inadequate medical care)

Inmates of Suffolk County Jail v Eisenstadt, 518 F2d 1241 (1st Cir 1975) (prison conditions)

Inmates of Attica Correctional Facility v Rockefeller, 453 F2d 12 (2d Cir 1971) (official brutality)

Holt v Sarver, 442 F2d 304 (8th Cir 1971) (prison conditions)

Jackson v Bishop, 404 F2d 571 (8th Cir 1968) (use of strap to whip prisoners)

For additional cases see **§3.07** on basis of liability for Eighth Amendment violations; and **§§8.09-8.10** on qualified immunity of prison officials.

Reforming the Prisons

Cunningham v Jones, 567 F2d 653 (6th Cir 1977) (overcrowding and one meal a day)

Rhem v Malcolm, 527 F2d 1041 (2d Cir 1975) (per curiam) (conditions of confinement)

Inmates of Attica Correctional Facility v Rockefeller, 453 F2d 12 (2d Cir 1971) (official brutality)

Sinclair v Henderson, 435 F2d 125 (5th Cir 1970) (unsanitary living conditions)

See also Eighth Amendment cases above.

Mental Institutions

Right to Treatment

Pennhurst State School & Hospital v Halderman, 465 US 89 (1984) (Eleventh Amendment prohibitions when the state is a real, substantial party in interest)

Youngberg v Romeo, 457 US 307 (1982) (rights to safe conditions, to freedom from bodily restraint and to adequate treatment)

O'Connor v Donaldson, 422 US 563 (1975) (confinement without treatment)

Burnham v Department of Public Health, 503 F2d 1319 (5th Cir 1974), *cert denied,* 422 US 1057 (1975) (right to treatment)

Wyatt v Aderholt, 503 F2d 1305 (5th Cir 1974) (minimum standards of treatment)

Jackson v Indiana, 406 US 715 (1972) (indefinite confinement of robbery suspect where no training facilities)

Rouse v Cameron, 373 F2d 451 (DC Cir 1966) (right to treatment)

For additional cases see **§8.08** on qualified immunity of mental institution officials.

Procedural Due Process

Jones v United States, 463 US 354 (1983) (indefinite commitment of acquitted insane defendant)

Secretary of Public Welfare v Institutionalized Juveniles, 442 US 640 (1979)

(commitment of children to mental institution at request of parent or guardian)

Parham v JR, 442 US 584 (1979) (commitment of children to mental institution by parent)

Addington v Texas, 441 US 418 (1979) (standard of proof in state involuntary commitment proceedings)

Jones v Robinson, 440 F2d 249 (DC Cir 1971) (per curiam) (hearing required before transfer of patient to maximum security facilities)

For additional cases see §§3.08-3.11 on basis of liability for due process violations; §4.05 on compensatory damages; §4.11 on punitive damages; and §8.08 on qualified immunity of mental hospital officials.

Eighth Amendment

Knecht v Gillman, 488 F2d 1136 (8th Cir 1973) (vomiting inducing drug)

Wheeler v Glass, 473 F2d 983 (7th Cir 1973) (binding patients in spread-eagle position for long periods)

For additional cases see Right to Treatment cases above, and §3.07 on basis of liability for Eighth Amendment violations.

Reforming Mental Institutions

New York State Association for Retarded Children Inc v Carey, 393 F Supp 715 (EDNY 1975) (consent decree approved regarding conditions)

Wyatt v Aderholt, 503 F2d 1305 (5th Cir 1974) (minimum standards of treatment)

See also Right to Treatment cases above.

The Police

Fourth Amendment

New York v PJ Video, Inc, 106 S Ct 1610 (1986) (probable cause standard for warrant authorizing seizure of materials presumptively protected by First Amendment)

New York v Class, 106 S Ct 960 (1986) (viewing vehicle identification number on car's dashboard)

California v Ciraolo, 106 S Ct 1809 (1985) (warrantless aerial observation of fenced-in backyard)

United States v Montoya de Hernandez, 105 S Ct 3304 (1985) (investigative detention at border on reasonable suspicion of smuggling contraband in alimentary canal)

Maryland v Macon, 105 S Ct 2778 (1985) (police officer's examination and purchase of materials offered for sale)

California v Carney, 105 S Ct 2066 (1985) (warrantless search of mobile motor home)

Tennessee v Garner, 105 S Ct 1694 (1985) (use of deadly force to prevent escape of felony suspect)

Hayes v Florida, 105 S Ct 1643 (1985) (investigative detention at police station for fingerprinting purposes)

Winston v Lee, 105 S Ct 1611 (1985) (surgical intrusion into suspect's body to recover bullet)

United States v Sharpe, 105 S Ct 1568 (1985) (20-minute delay during investigative stop)

Shea v Louisiana, 105 S Ct 1065 (1985) (*Edwards v Arizona* applies to cases pending on direct appeal at time *Edwards* was decided)

United States v Johns, 105 S Ct 881 (1985) (three-day delay in warrantless search of lawfully seized packages suspected of containing contraband)

Thompson v Louisiana, 105 S Ct 409 (1984) (no murder scene exception to search warrant requirement)

Florida v Rodriguez, 105 S Ct 308 (1984) (seizure during airport search based on articulable suspicion)

Massachusetts v Sheppard, 104 S Ct 3424 (1984) (good faith exception to exclusionary rule for search warrants)

United States v Leon, 104 S Ct 3405 (1984) (good faith exception to exclusionary rule for search warrants)

Segura v United States, 104 S Ct 3380 (1984) (independent source exception to the exclusionary rule)

United States v Karo, 104 S Ct 3380 (1984) (monitoring electron beepers in the home)

Welsh v Wisconsin, 466 US 740 (1984) (warrantless entry of home to arrest for civil, nonjailable offense)

Massachusetts v Upton, 466 US 727 (1984) (reaffirmation of the totality of the circumstances test for probable cause determinations)

United States v Jacobsen, 466 US 109 (1984) (exceeding the scope of a private search or seizure and field testing of contraband)

Illinois v Gates, 458 US 1127 (1983) (informant's tip as establishing probable cause for warrant)

United States v Place, 462 US 696 (1983) (90-minute detention of luggage without probable cause)

Illinois v LaFayette, 462 US 640 (1983) (warrantless inventory search at stationhouse of arrestee's shoulder bag)

United States v Villamonte-Marquez, 462 US 579 (1983) (search and seizure by customs officials upon vessel in waters providing ready access to open sea)

United States v Johnson, 457 US 537 (1982) (retroactive effect of Fourth Amendment rulings)

United States v Ross, 456 US 798 (1982) (warrantless search of closed container in car; *Robbins v California*, 453 US 420 (1981) overruled; *Arkansas v Sanders*, 442 US 753 (1979) discredited)

Washington v Chrisman, 455 US 1 (1982) (search and seizure of contraband in plain view)

New York v Belton, 453 US 454 (1981) (search of passenger compartment of automobile including containers found)

Robbins v California, 453 US 420 (1981) (opening of closed containers without search warrant during lawful search of automobile)

Michigan v Summers, 452 US 692 (1981) (effect of warrant to search for contraband on authority to detain occupants on premises)

Steagald v United States, 451 US 204 (1981) (search for subject of arrest warrant in home of third party)

United States v Cortez, 449 US 411 (1981) (investigative stop to search for illegal aliens)

United States v Mendenhall, 446 US 544 (1980) (consent to search for drugs)

Payton v New York, 445 US 573 (1980) (warrantless, nonconsensual entry into suspect's home to make routine felony arrest)

Ybarra v Illinois, 444 US 85 (1979) (search of customer on premises which were subject to search warrant)

Brown v Texas, 443 US 47 (1979) (requiring identification upon a police stop where the officer had no reasonable suspicion of criminal activity)

Arkansas v Sanders, 442 US 753 (1979) (search of luggage without warrant)

Torres v Puerto Rico, 442 US 465 (1979) (search of luggage without warrant and probable cause)

Lo-Ji Sales Inc v New York, 442 US 319 (1979) (search pursuant to an open-ended warrant)

Dunaway v New York, 442 US 200 (1979) (custodial questioning on less than probable cause for arrest)

Delaware v Prouse, 440 US 648 (1979) (random stop of auto and detention of driver for check of driver's license)

Franks v Delaware, 438 US 154 (1978) (challenge to probable cause affidavit)

Zurcher v Stanford Daily, 436 US 547 (1978) (search of newspaper premises)

United States v Chadwick, 433 US 1 (1977) (warrantless search of luggage)

South Dakota v Opperman, 428 US 364 (1976) (warrantless search of car)

United States v Santana, 427 US 38 (1976) (warrantless arrest)

United States v Watson, 423 US 411 (1976) (warrantless arrest)

Texas v White, 423 US 67 (1975) (warrantless search of car)

Cardwell v Lewis, 417 US 583 (1974) (warrantless seizure of car)

United States v Matlock, 415 US 164 (1974) (third party consent to warrantless search of living quarters)

Gustafson v Florida, 414 US 260 (1973) (search incident to valid arrest for traffic violation)

United States v Robinson, 414 US 218 (1973) (search incident to valid arrest for traffic violation)

Katz v United States, 389 US 347 (1967) (electronic eavesdropping)

Pierson v Ray, 386 US 547 (1967) (qualified immunity of police officers in connection with unlawful arrest)

Schmerber v California, 384 US 757 (1966) (blood test)

Preston v United States, 376 US 364 (1964) (warrantless search of car)

Mapp v Ohio, 367 US 643 (1961) (search of premises)

Monroe v Pape, 365 US 167 (1961) (search of person and premises)

For additional cases see **§3.04** on basis of liability for Fourth Amendment violations; **§4.04** on compensatory damages; **§4.10** on punitive damages; and **§8.11** on qualified immunity of police officers.

Fifth Amendment

Moran v Burbine, 106 S Ct 1135 (1986) (waiver of Fifth Amendment rights)

Wainright v Greenfield, 106 S Ct 634 (1986) (use of post-*Miranda* warning silence as evidence of sanity)

Miller v Fenton, 106 S Ct 445 (1985) (voluntariness of confession as issue of law)

Oregon v Elstad, 105 S Ct 1285 (1985) (voluntariness of second statement where initial inculpatory statement was made in response to unwarned yet uncoerced questioning)

Berkemer v McCarty, 104 S Ct 3138 (1984) (roadside questioning pursuant to routine traffic stop)

New York v Quarles, 467 US 649 (1984) (public safety exception to *Miranda* warnings)

Nix v Williams, 467 US 431 (1984) (inevitable or ultimate discovery exception to the exclusionary rule)

Solem v Stumes, 465 US 638 (1984) (*Edwards v Arizona* should not be applied retroactively)

Minnesota v Murphy, 465 US 420 (1984) (probation officer's warning to probationer)

Oregon v Bradshaw, 462 US 1039 (1983) (arrestee's conversation as waiver of *Miranda* rights)

South Dakota v Neville, 459 US 553 (1983) (police inquiry regarding blood-alcohol test as "interrogation" under *Miranda;* admission into evidence of suspect's refusal to submit to such test)

Taylor v Alabama, 457 US 687 (1982) (admissibility of confession after illegal arrest)

California v Prysoch, 453 US 355 (1981) (per curiam) (content of *Miranda* warnings)

Edwards v Arizona, 451 US 477 (1981) (waiver of right to counsel)

Estelle v Smith, 451 US 454 (1981) (right to remain silent prior to in-custody court-ordered psychiatric examination)

Rhode Island v Innis, 446 US 291 (1980) (what constitutes permissible interrogation)

California v Braeseke, 444 US 1309 (1980) (state must carry burden of showing that defendant had waived his *Miranda* rights)

Tague v Louisiana, 444 US 469 (1980) (need for state evidence as to knowing and intelligent waiver of *Miranda* rights)

Fare v Michael C, 442 US 707 (1979) (request for probation officer during interrogation)

North Carolina v Butler, 441 US 369 (1979) (implied waiver of *Miranda*)

Brewer v Williams, 430 US 387 (1977) (what constitutes impermissible interrogation)

Michigan v Mosley, 423 US 96 (1975) (length of time in which police may not question)

Oregon v Haas, 420 US 714 (1975) (*Miranda* warnings as procedural devices)

Michigan v Tucker, 417 US 433 (1974) (bad faith in connection with disclosure of rights)

Harris v New York, 401 US 222 (1971) (use of statements to impeach testimony)

Miranda v Arizona, 384 US 436 (1966) (disclosure of rights to arrested suspects)

For additional cases see §3.05 on basis of liability for Fifth Amendment violations.

Substantive Due Process and Privacy

Bowers v Hardwick, 105 S Ct 2841 (1986) (state sodomy statute as applied to private homosexual conduct)

Paul v Davis, 424 US 693 (1976) (circulation of flyer with names of "suspected shoplifters")

York v Story, 324 F2d 450 (9th Cir 1963) (circulation among police officers of photographs of female crime victim in the nude)

For additional cases see §§3.08-3.11 on basis of liability for due process violations; §3.12 on basis of liability for right of privacy violations; §§4.05 & 4.11 on compensatory and punitive damages for due process violations; and §8.11 on qualified immunity of police officers.

Reforming Police Practices

Rizzo v Goode, 423 US 362 (1976) (police brutality)

Gilligan v Morgan, 413 US 1 (1973) (training and discipline of national guard)

APPENDIX B
Forms

These forms, and others for which they may serve as a model, should only be used after careful study of the checklists in Chapter 1 and relevant textual references.

Form 1   Class Action for Declaratory and Injunctive Relief and Damages Challenging School Procedures for Suspension and Expulsion [one count]

Form 2   Plaintiffs' Motion for Determination of a Class in Connection with Challenge to School Procedures for Suspension and Expulsion

Form 3   Complaint for Damages Against Prison Officials for Failure to Send Inmate's Outgoing Mail [two counts]

Form 4   Class Action Complaint for Declaratory and Injunctive Relief Challenging Continuing "Deadlock" at Prison [three counts]

Form 5   Complaint for Damages Against City, Supervisory Personnel and Police Officers for Police Brutality and Unlawful Arrest [three counts]

Form 6   Complaint for Damages Against Police Officers for Unlawful Arrest, Search and Seizure [four counts]

Form 7   Complaint for Declaratory and Injunctive Relief Challenging Ordinances Regulating Public Assembly on First Amendment Grounds [two counts]

Form 8   Motion for Preliminary Injunction in Connection with Challenge to Ordinances Regulating Public Assembly on First Amendment Grounds

Form 9   Motion for Attorney's Fees Award Under Civil Rights Attorney's Fees Awards Act of 1976 and For Costs Incurred

Form 10   Class Action Complaint for Injunctive Relief and Damages against City, Its Police Department, and Various Individuals Challenging "Strip Searches"

Form 11   Defendant's Request for Production

Form 12   Defendant's Interrogatories to Plaintiff

Form 1   Class Action for Declaratory and Injunctive Relief and Damages Challenging School Procedures for Suspension and Expulsion

1. This is a civil action for declaratory and injunctive relief and for damages for violation of the Constitution and laws of the United States. Plaintiffs, individually and on behalf of all others similarly situated, seek a declaration that the actions of defendant school officials in suspending a student for *[describe conduct]* without a proper hearing and pursuant to un-published rules and regulations violate the plaintiff's right to procedural due process of law, guaranteed by the Fourteenth Amendment to the United States Constitution and the right to be free from arbitrary and unreasonable suspensions and expulsions.

2. Jurisdiction is based on 28 U.S.C. §§1343 and 1344 and 42 U.S.C. §1983 and arises under the Fourteenth Amendment to the United States Constitution. Declaratory relief is authorized by 28 U.S.C. §§2201 and 2202 and Rule 57, F.R.C.P.

3. The named Plaintiff _____ is a _____ year old male residing in the City of _____ who is presently enrolled at _____ Elementary School in _____. _____ is the mother of _____ and is serving as next friend and guardian ad litem for purposes of this action.

4. _____ and _____ bring this action pursuant to Rule 23 of the Federal Rules of Civil Procedure, individually and on behalf of all other persons who have been or will be suspended or expelled from full-time public school attendance in the City of _____ under the statutes and rules complained of herein without (a) adequate notice to them and their parents of the charges against them, (b) a reasonable opportunity to prepare for a hearing on those charges, (c) a hearing and a fair, impartial decision on those charges, and (d) published rules pursuant to which charges are brought which are lawful and reasonable. The class is so numerous that joinder of all members is impractical; there are questions of law and fact common to the class; the claims of the representative parties are typical of the claims of the class; the representative parties will fairly and adequately protect the interests of the class. In addition, the defendants and their agents have acted on grounds generally applicable to the class, thereby making appropriate declaratory and injunctive relief with respect to the class as a whole.

5. Defendants _____, _____, and _____ are members of the Board of Education of the City of _____ and are charged with the responsibility of administration of the public schools within _____ pursuant to *[statutory reference]* and are empowered to oversee the disciplining of pupils.

6. Defendant _____ is the General Superintendent of Schools of the City of _____ and as such is the chief administrative officer of the school board of the City of _____ responsible for the administration of the public schools and the overseeing of the disciplinary process.

7. _____ is a principal of _____ School located near _____ in the

City of _____. Defendant _____ is responsible for the administration of discipline and the expulsion and suspension of all students in _____ School.

8. On or about _____, 19____, Plaintiff _____, who was duly enrolled as a full-time regular student in the _____ grade at _____ Elementary School in the _____ Public School System, *[describe conduct]*. At that time, he was asked on several occasions by defendant _____ and his agents to desist. Plaintiff refused to do so.

9. On _____, 19____, subsequent to arriving at school in the morning, Plaintiff _____ was called into the school office by Defendant _____ and Assistant Principal _____ and told to _____ or he would be suspended.

10. Plaintiff _____ declined to so act. Defendant _____ said he would suspend plaintiff _____ from school immediately if he did not comply.

11. Plaintiff _____ persisted in his refusal and Assistant Principal _____ then left the immediate area apparently for the purpose of telephoning _____'s mother and for the purpose of writing up the report of suspension.

12. Shortly thereafter Plaintiff _____ received a phone call at her home from defendants requesting her to appear at the school immediately because of a problem with _____.

13. Plaintiff _____ promptly went to the school where she was informed by Defendant _____ that _____ would be suspended from school if he did not comply. Plaintiff _____ informed Defendant _____ that she had no objections to her _____'s refusal to comply.

14. Defendant _____ thereupon completed a "Report of Suspension" which he delivered to Plaintiff _____.

15. At no time prior to Plaintiff _____'s arrival at school on _____, 19____, was Plaintiff _____ or his mother given (a) adequate notice of the charges against him and informed of the disciplinary sanctions of removal from full-time school attendance that day, (b) reasonable opportunity to prepare for a hearing on those charges, (c) a hearing at which the burden of proof was on the defendants to show Plaintiff _____ had created a material disruption, (d) an impartial decision on the charges, and (e) notice of a promulgated rule on which the charges were based.

16. Plaintiff's present suspension was preceded by a previous suspension last semester for the same reason, also without a hearing.

17. The current suspension was imposed pursuant to *[statutory references]* which provide that "[T]he general superintendent of schools shall prescribe and control, subject to the approval of the board . . . discipline in . . . the schools . . ." and further, that board shall establish rules "for the proper maintenance of a uniform system of discipline . . . It may expel, suspend, or otherwise discipline any pupil found guilty of gross disobedience, misconduct, or other violation of the . . . rules. . . ."

18. The suspension was further imposed pursuant to the rule of the _____ Board of Education which states as follows:

> "For gross disobedience or misconduct a pupil may be suspended temporarily by the principal for a period not exceeding one school month

for each offense. Suspension shall be reported immediately to the District Superintendent and also to the parent or guardian of the pupil, with a full statement for such suspension. The District Superintendent shall have authority to review the action of the principal and to return the suspended pupil.''

19. Defendants' action to suspend Plaintiff _____ from school violates the Fourteenth Amendment to the United States Constitution in that he is being and has been threatened with being (a) punished pursuant to a Board of Education rule and State statute which are invalid on their faces and as applied; (b) punished without reference to promulgated rules and regulations; (c) denied a proper hearing prior to the punishment which includes adequate prior notice of charges, and opportunity to prepare for a hearing, a proceeding in which the burden of proof is on the school board to show a material disruption has occurred; (d) denied a fair and impartial decision; (e) treated differently from other pupils in the school; (f) punished arbitrarily without reasonable basis; and (g) denied access to public education. Such punishment is arbitrary and improper in violation of the Fourteenth Amendment to the United States Constitution.

20. The suspension of Plaintiff _____ interferes with his education in the public schools by preventing him from keeping pace with the instruction given to the rest of his class at school. Plaintiff _____'s education is threatened with further interference in that Plaintiff will again be suspended for *[describe conduct]* when he returns to school.

21. Plaintiff class members are presently being subjected to a denial of fundamental civil rights for which there is no adequate remedy at law in that they are presently being denied their right to a public education and threatened with a repetition of the denial in the future.

22. Defendants are engaged in a widespread pattern of long-term suspensions and expulsions of public school students without (a) published rules, (b) notice of charges and an opportunity to prepare for a hearing, (c) a hearing in which the burden of proof is on the defendants to show a material disruption has occurred, and (d) a fair and impartial decision. Such suspensions and expulsions have occurred in the past and will continue to occur in the future. A return of Plaintiff class members to school will not remedy the effects of this pattern which is likely and capable of repetition in the future.

WHEREFORE, Plaintiffs pray that this Court:

1. Declare *[statutory references]* and _____ of the Rules of the _____ Board of Education to be unconstitutional and void on their faces and/or as applied;

2. Preliminarily and permanently enjoin defendants from suspending or expelling Plaintiff _____ from attending school without a proper hearing;

3. Permanently order that all records of the suspensions and other punishment complained of herein be expunged from [his or her] school record;

4. Preliminarily and permanently order defendants to provide tutors to enable Plaintiff _____ to make up work missed as a result of the suspension;

5. Preliminarily and permanently enjoin defendants from punishing in-

dividual Plaintiffs or members of the class which they represent in any way for the actions complained of herein;

    6. Award $_____ actual and punitive damages; and

    7. Award any other relief which is necessary and just under the circumstances.

Form 2 Plaintiffs' Motion for Determination of a Class in Connection with Challenge to School Procedures for Suspension and Expulsion

Plaintiffs, by their attorneys, hereby move that this Court enter an order determining that the individual Plaintiffs are proper representatives of the class of all present and future students enrolled in _____ Public Schools pursuant to Rule 23, F.R.C.P., so that this case may proceed as a class action. In support of this motion Plaintiffs state as follows:

(1) The members of the class of all _____ Public School students, present and future, number in excess of _____ and are so numerous that joinder of all of the members as individual plaintiffs would be impracticable.

(2) Questions of law and fact common to the members of the class predominate over any questions affecting only individual members.

(3) The claims of the representative parties are typical of the claims of the entire class.

(4) The representative parties will adequately and fairly protect the interests of each and every member of the class.

(5) The defendants in this action have acted on grounds generally applicable to the class, thereby making appropriate final injunctive relief and corresponding declaratory relief with respect to the class as a whole.

Form 3 Complaint for Damages Against Prison Officials for Failure to Send Inmate's Outgoing Mail

COUNT I

1. Plaintiff, _____, is a citizen of the State of _____, and a resident of this judicial district.

2. Defendants _____, _____, and _____ are all citizens of the State of _____.

3. This action arises under Title 42 of the United States Code, Section 1983, and the Court has jurisdiction of the action under Title 28 of the United States Code, Section 1343.

4. At all times pertinent to this Complaint, Defendant _____ was Director of the _____ State Department of Corrections (hereinafter "Department of Corrections") and was responsible for promulgating and maintaining statewide departmental regulations regarding the rights and privileges of prisoners at penal facilities under the authority of the department; Defendant _____ was employed by the Department of Corrections as Superintendent of the _____ Correctional Training Facility, and was responsible for implementation of all applicable laws and regulations at _____; Defendant _____ was employed by the Department of Corrections as Associate Superintendent of _____, and was responsible for assisting in implementation of all applicable laws and regulations at _____; Defendants _____ and _____ were employed by the Department of Corrections as correctional counselors at _____, and were responsible for supervising certain prisoners, including Plaintiff; Defendant _____ was employed by the Department of Corrections as a member of the prison staff at _____, and was in charge of handling incoming and outgoing prisoner mail.

5. Plaintiff was incarcerated at _____ from approximately _____, 19__ to approximately _____, 19__, at which time Plaintiff was discharged.

6. Defendants _____, _____, and _____, [subordinate personnel] acting both individually and jointly, failed to mail a considerable amount of correspondence which Plaintiff properly submitted to them for mailing during the period of this incarceration at _____. The various pieces of such correspondence dealt with legal, political and personal matters. None of such correspondence threatened, contemplated, or included plans for any criminal activity whatsoever; none threatened or posed any clear and present danger of physical harm of violence to any person; none was obscene; and none was written in any form of code. Said unmailed correspondence includes but is not limited to the following: [describe in detail, giving dates if possible]

7. Defendants, _____, _____, _____, [subordinate personnel] and each of them, acting both individually and in concert, refused to send as registered mail numerous items of correspondence of legal character which Plaintiff duly

presented to said Defendants for posting. As a proximate result of such refusals, none of said letters was ever received by addressees.

8. Correspondence described in Paragraph 6 above failed to reach the addressees to whom destined as a proximate result of interference or confiscation by Defendants _____, _____, _____, *[subordinate personnel]* and each of them, acting both individually and in a concert of action wherein each said Defendant acquiesced, condoned, encouraged, and assisted the actions of the others in a deliberate effort to single out Plaintiff for harsh, arbitrary, and discriminatory treatment with regard to his correspondence, in knowing disregard of applicable statewide prisoner mail regulations then in effect as set forth in *[specify source]*. Said correspondence was in fact permitted by the aforesaid mail regulations.

9. Defendants _____, _____, and _____ *[supervisory officials]* encouraged, directed, ratified and knowingly acquiesced in the actions of Defendants _____, _____, and _____ *[subordinate personnel]* as described above, and did so both individually and in pursuance of a common plan or design, deliberately singling out Plaintiff for harsh, arbitrary, and discriminatory treatment with regard to his correspondence, in knowing disregard of the fact that Plaintiff's constitutional rights were thereby violated.

10. The above described actions by Defendants, and each of them, deprived Plaintiff of his civil rights, including his rights to free speech and due process, as guaranteed by the First, Fifth, and Fourteenth Amendments to the United States Constitution, and by Title 42 of the United States Code, Section 1983. Said actions have caused actual damage to Plaintiff in the amount of $_____, and, due to their aggravated, callous, and malicious character, as well as to the critically important character of the rights herein infringed upon, further entitle Plaintiff to punitive damages in the amount of $_____.

COUNT II

1–7. Plaintiff herein realleges and incorporates by reference Paragraphs 1 through 7 of the First Count in this Complaint, and each and every allegation contained in such Paragraphs, as though fully set forth herein.

8. Such correspondence failed to reach the persons to whom destined as the proximate result of interference or confiscation of said correspondence by Defendants _____, _____, _____, *[subordinate personnel]* and each of them, acting both individually and in concert, in bad faith disregard of the prisoner mail regulations then in effect as embodied in the *[specify source]*, and in each such act of confiscation of or interference with Plaintiff's correspondence, said Defendants lacked probable cause to believe that such correspondence was in violation of said prisoner mail regulations. Said correspondence was in fact permitted by said mail regulations.

9. Defendants _____, _____, and _____ *[supervisory officials]* encouraged, directed, ratified, participated, and knowingly acquiesced in the actions of Defendants _____, _____, and _____, *[subordinate personnel]* as described in Paragraph 2 above, and did so in bad faith disregard of Plaintiff's constitutional rights, and without probable cause to believe that such correspondence exceeded the bounds of constitutional protection enjoyed by

Defendant. As a proximate result thereof, said correspondence failed to reach the persons to whom destined.

10. Plaintiff herein realleges and incorporates by reference Paragraph 10 of the First Cause of Action of this Complaint, and each and every allegation contained therein, as though fully set forth herein.

WHEREFORE Plaintiff, under both Counts of this Complaint, prays this Court award actual damages of $_____, punitive damages of $_____, against each and every Defendant jointly and severally, costs, and such other relief as the Court deems just.

Form 4 Class Action Complaint for Declaratory and Injunctive Relief Challenging Continuing "Deadlock" at Prison

1. This is a civil action for declaratory and injunctive relief, to redress the continuing deprivation of rights secured by the First, Fifth, Sixth, Eighth, and Fourteenth Amendments to the United States Constitution and Title 42 U.S.C. §1983. Jurisdiction is conferred on this Court by 28 U.S.C. §1343 and §2201.

2. Plaintiffs _____ and _____ are prisoners incarcerated at the _____ State Prison at _____.

3. Plaintiffs _____, _____, and _____ are family members and loved ones on the visiting list of prisoners incarcerated at _____. These Plaintiffs continue to be denied all visits with their imprisoned relatives and loved ones at _____ since _____, 19___.

4. Defendant _____ is the Governor of the State of _____. He is the chief executive officer of the State and has the ultimate authority over the operations and policies of the _____ Department of Corrections and the _____ Department of Law Enforcement. He is sued individually and in his official capacity.

5. Defendant _____ is the Director of Corrections of the State of _____. He was appointed by the Governor, and is the chief administrative officer of the _____ Department of Corrections (hereinafter "DOC") which maintains and administers, and has under its control all _____ correctional institutions and their prisoners. He is sued individually and in his official capacity.

6. Defendant _____ is the Director and chief administrative officer of the _____ Department of Law Enforcement (hereinafter "DLE"), the statewide department charged with criminal investigation and identification. He is sued individually and in his official capacity.

7. Defendant _____ is the Warden of _____ Prison and is responsible for the administration of the prison and the custody of prisoners incarcerated therein. He is sued individually and in his official capacity.

8. Plaintiff prisoners bring this action on their own behalf and on behalf of all other prisoners similarly situated who are committed to the _____ DOC and incarcerated in _____.

9. Plaintiff family members and loved ones on the visiting lists of prisoners also bring this action on their own behalf and on behalf of all other persons similarly situated who suffer the total denial of visiting at _____.

10. Each of the above groups of Plaintiffs and those similarly situated constitutes a class in accordance with the provisions of Rule 23(a) and (b) of the Federal Rules of Civil Procedure. The persons who constitute each class are so numerous that joinder of all members is impractical. There are questions of law and/or fact in common to each class; the claims of the Plaintiffs are typical of the claims of each class; the Plaintiffs will fairly and adequately protect the interests of each entire class; prosecution of separate actions by individual members of each class would create a risk of inconsistent or varying

adjudications and would establish incompatible standards for the Defendants, their agents and subordinates; and Defendants have acted and refused to act on grounds that are generally applicable to all members of each class, making declaratory and injunctive relief with respect to each class as a whole appropriate.

COUNT I

1. On _____, 19____, a disturbance occurred at _____ Prison, in which _____ prison guards were killed, and some prison facilities were damaged.

2. Prisoners residing in the _____ Cell House and Segregation Unit at _____ were locked in their cells at the time this disturbance took place.

3. Within hours of the inception of the disturbance at _____, prison authorities had regained total control of the affected areas of the prison, and had secured the entire institution.

4. As part of the process of securing the institution, prisoners were forced to strip naked and remove all their jewelry and other personal belongings and dump them into large piles, thus becoming lost and irretrievable.

5. All the prisoners at _____ were then returned to and locked in their cells, and the prison was placed on "deadlock" status on the orders of Defendants _____, _____ and _____.

6. During, and as part of, the above mentioned "deadlock" at _____, Plaintiff prisoners have been deprived of such basic human necessities as nutritious and appetizing meals, showers, adequate clean clothes and bedding, adequate available medical and dental care, sufficient skin soap and laundry detergent, towels, toilet paper and toothpaste.

7. Plaintiff prisoners have been, almost without exception, locked 24 hours per day, with two and sometimes three men in tiny cells designed to hold only one person. They continue to be denied all out-of-cell activities such as school, worship, exercise, commissary and access to the law library.

8. Plaintiffs at _____ continue to be denied all family visits and visits with other loved ones.

9. The emergency situations which may have existed at the inception of the "deadlock" at _____ have long since ended because *[set out reasons]*.

10. All of the above deprivations suffered by Plaintiff prisoners and those similarly situated as a result of the imposition and continuation of the "deadlock" have been without benefit of any due process protections, or findings of violations of any statute or regulation by Plaintiff prisoners.

11. The continuation of the "deadlock" at _____, long after the termination of any emergency situation which may have existed at the inception of the deadlock, and in the absence of any due process protections, is over-extensive, unreasonable and arbitrary; the "deadlock" has now existed long enough to constitute a grievous loss to Plaintiff prisoners, in violation of all Plaintiffs' First Amendment rights of association, and Plaintiff prisoners' Fourteenth Amendment rights to due process of law.

COUNT II

1–11. Plaintiff prisoners allege and incorporate paragraphs 1 through 11 in Count I above, as if fully set forth herein as Count II.

12. The prison at _____ is massively overcrowded, originally designed to hold far fewer than the number of men now kept inside them.

13. Because of the overcrowding, Plaintiff prisoners are kept two, and sometimes three men in tiny cells designed to house only one person.

14. In _____, the square feet of living space per prisoner is below the _____ square feet set for new facilities by the DOC, and far below the 70 square feet recommended by the American Correctional Association.

15. The oppression resulting from such overcrowding, and other conditions such as inoperable plumbing, the presence of rats and vermin, and the stench resultant from failure to provide cleaning materials, all cruel and unusual in and of themselves, become intolerably aggravated under "deadlock" conditions.

16. Human beings cannot remain in such circumstances without being harmed. Many Plaintiff prisoners have already begun to experience mental anguish, anxiety and depression, in addition to symptoms of various physical ailments, as a result of the "deadlock."

17. The above intolerable conditions at _____, both before the "dead-lock" and since its commencement, have been and are known by the Defendants who, despite this knowledge, have intentionally and wilfully failed, and continue to fail, to alleviate such conditions, in violation of the Eighth Amendment rights of Plaintiffs to be free from cruel and unusual punishment.

COUNT III

1–17. Plaintiff prisoners allege and incorporate paragraphs 1 through 11 in Count I above, and paragraphs 12 through 17 in Count II above, as if fully set forth herein as Count III.

18. Soon after the commencement of the "deadlock" at _____, an investigation was undertaken, and is still being engaged in, by the _____ DLE.

19. This investigation includes individual interrogation of prisoners, for which they are removed from their cells, brought to interrogation rooms, and questioned by law enforcement officials.

20. During these interrogation sessions, many prisoners are discouraged from exercising their Fifth Amendment right against self-incrimination and their Sixth Amendment right to the assistance of counsel.

21. This discouragement takes the form of promises of early paroles or transfers to minimum security institutions if prisoners cooperate with the investigation, and threats of indictment and reminders of the death penalty if they do not cooperate.

22. Many prisoners have been informed by law enforcement officials at the interrogation sessions that the "deadlock" at _____ would be maintained until every prisoner had fully cooperated with the ongoing criminal investigation, and that no prisoners would be allowed to see their families and other loved ones until all prisoners had so cooperated.

23. The continuation of the "deadlock" at _____, while this massive criminal investigation is being conducted, is done by these Defendants in bad faith; the "deadlock" is being used by Defendants as a pretext to intensify and aggravate an already existing psychologically and physically coercive atmosphere within which the Plaintiff prisoners exist in total isolation from their families and loved ones, and within which they face individual interrogation by state law enforcement officials.

24. The use of the "deadlock" status to coerce, intimidate and threaten Plaintiff prisoners into cooperating with criminal investigators is violative of Plaintiff prisoners' rights guaranteed by the Fifth, Sixth, and Fourteenth Amendments to the United States Constitution.

WHEREFORE, for all the above and foregoing Counts, Plaintiffs pray:

A.   That this Court declare that any further continuation of the "deadlock" and attendant restrictions on family and other visitation, is violative of Plaintiffs' First, Fifth, Sixth, Eighth, and Fourteenth Amendment rights;

B.   That this Court issue a Preliminary and Permanent Injunction, enjoining Defendants, their agents, employees, and successors:

   1.   From continuing to bar totally visits by family members at
   _____.

   2.   From continuing to deprive Plaintiff prisoners of such necessities as nutritious and appetizing meals, showers, adequate clean clothes and bedding, adequate available medical and dental care, sufficient skin soap and laundry detergent, towels, toilet paper and toothpaste;

   3.   From continuing to deny Plaintiff prisoners such out-of-cell activities as school, worship, exercise, commissary and access to the law library;

C.   That Plaintiffs be awarded costs and attorney's fees for this action.

D.   For such other and further relief as this Court deems just and necessary.

Form 5 Complaint for Damages against City, Supervisory Personnel and Police Officers for Police Brutality and Unlawful Arrest

1. This is a civil action seeking damages against Defendants for committing acts, under color of law, which deprived Plaintiff of rights secured under the Constitution and laws of the United States; for conspiring for the purpose of impeding and hindering the due course of justice, with intent to deny Plaintiff equal protection of laws; and for refusing or neglecting to prevent such deprivations and denials to Plaintiff. The Court has jurisdiction of this action under 42 U.S.C. § 1983 and 28 U.S.C. § 1343.

2. The Court also has jurisdiction under 28 U.S.C. §1331.

3. Plaintiff _____ is a citizen and resident of the City of _____, State of _____, and the United States of America.

4. Defendant City of _____ is a Municipal Corporation, organized under the laws of the State of _____.

5. Defendant _____ was Superintendent of Police for the City of _____ at all times relevant to this Complaint.

6. Defendant _____ was District Commander of the _____ District of the Police Department of the City of _____ at all times relevant to this Complaint.

7. Defendants _____ and _____ were police officers employed by the Police Department, _____ District Patrol Division, of the City of _____.

8. Plaintiff sues each and all Defendants in both their individual and official capacities.

9. At all times material to this Complaint, Defendants _____, _____, and _____, _____ acted under color of the statutes, customs, ordinances and usage of the State of _____, the City of _____, and the _____ Police Department.

COUNT I

1. On or about _____, 19___, at approximately _____, Plaintiff was seated at the bar inside _____ tavern located at _____ Street, City of _____.

2. Defendants _____ and _____ entered said tavern, told Plaintiff he was under arrest, and refused to tell Plaintiff why he was under arrest.

3. At no time, either in said tavern or at any later time and place, did Plaintiff attempt to resist arrest by _____ or _____ or offer violence to them.

4. Defendants _____ and _____ bodily removed Plaintiff from his seat, without provocation, need, or explanation, dragged Plaintiff from said tavern, and transported him to the _____ District Police Station, located at _____, City of _____, arriving there at approximately _____, _____, 19___.

5. While at the _____ District Police Station, Defendants _____ and

_____ and Defendant _____ assaulted and beat Plaintiff brutally, Plaintiff then being in close custody, unarmed, and unable to resist Defendants.

6. As a result of the assault by Defendants, Plaintiff suffered lacerations about his eyes which left permanent visible scars; lost two teeth which permanently disfigured him; and suffered a fractured ankle, a dislocated hip, cuts, abrasions, and contusions. As a result of said injuries, Plaintiff was unable to work for approximately six weeks.

7. Defendant _____, accompanied by another police officer, took Plaintiff to the _____ Hospital, _____, City of _____, and then returned him to the _____ District Police Station.

8. Plaintiff was received at the lock-up _____, _____, 19____. He appeared in the *[state court]*,was charged as set out in paragraph 9 below, posted bond and was released at approximately _____, _____, 19____. Plaintiff then was taken by his wife to _____ Hospital, _____, City of _____, to seek treatment for his injuries.

9. Defendant _____ swore out a complaint against Plaintiff, alleging battery on the arresting officers, resisting arrest, and being under the influence of intoxicants. Said complaint alleged the stated offenses occurred at _____, _____, 19____, on the street at _____, City of _____. Said charges were Dismissed for Want of Prosecution on _____, 19____ before the *[state court]*, the Honorable _____ presiding. The dismissal was the final determination of said charges.

10. As a result of their concerted unlawful and malicious physical abuse of Plaintiff, Defendants _____, _____ and _____ deprived Plaintiff of his right to equal protection of the laws and impeded the due course of justice, in violation of the Fifth and Fourteenth Amendments of the Constitution of the United States and 42 U.S.C. §1983,

WHEREFORE, Plaintiff _____ demands judgment against Defendants _____, _____, and _____, jointly and severally, for compensatory damages in the amount of $_____ and further demands judgment against each of said Defendants, jointly and severally, for punitive damages in the amount of $_____, plus the costs of this action and such other relief as the Court deems just and equitable.

COUNT II

1–6. Plaintiff realleges paragraphs 1–4, and 8–9 of Count I as paragraphs 1–6 of Count II and hereby incorporates them as though fully set forth herein.

7. There was no warrant for the arrest of Plaintiff on _____, 19____. The arrest of Plaintiff by Defendants _____ and _____, as stated in paragraph 2 above, was without reasonable grounds for said Defendants to believe Plaintiff had committed an offense and Defendants knew they were without probable cause to arrest Plaintiff.

8. Neither at the time of the arrest, as stated in paragraph 2 above, nor at any other time was Plaintiff informed of the grounds for said arrest. No complaint, information, or indictment was ever sworn against Plaintiff alleging offenses occuring prior to the moment Defendants _____ and _____ announced to Plaintiff that he was under arrest.

9. Plaintiff was transported to the _____ District Police Station, as stated in paragraph 4, where he was incarcerated for approximately _____ hours and was not allowed to post bond until approximately _____, 19___.

10. As a result of their concerted unlawful and malicious arrest of Plaintiff, Defendants _____ and _____ deprived Plaintiff of his liberty without due process of law and deprived him of equal protection of the laws, in violation of the Fifth and Fourteenth Amendments of the Constitution of the United States and 42 U.S.C. §1983.

11. As a result of their concerted unlawful and malicious detention and confinement of Plaintiff, Defendants _____, _____, _____, and _____ deprived Plaintiff of his liberty without due process of law and deprived him of equal protection of the laws, in violation of the Fifth and Fourteenth Amendments of the Constitution of the United States and 42 U.S.C. §1983.

WHEREFORE, Plaintiff _____ demands judgment against Defendants _____, _____, _____, and _____, jointly and severally, for compensatory damages in the amount of $_____, and further demands judgment against each of said Defendants, jointly and severally, for punitive damages in the amount of $_____, plus the costs of this action and such other relief as the Court deems just and equitable.

COUNT III

1–15. Plaintiff realleges paragraphs 1–10 of Count I and paragraphs 7–11 of Count II as paragraphs 1–15 of Count III and hereby incorporates them in this Count as though fully set forth herein.

16. At all times relevant to this Complaint Defendants _____, _____, and _____, as police officers of the _____ Police Department, were acting under the direction and control of Defendants _____, *[names of supervisors]* and Defendant City of _____.

17. Acting under color of law and pursuant to official policy or custom, Defendants _____ *[names of supervisors]* and City of _____ knowingly, recklessly, or with gross negligence failed to instruct, supervise, control and discipline on a continuing basis Defendant police officers in their duties to refrain from: (1) unlawfully and maliciously harassing a citizen who was acting in accordance with his constitutional and statutory rights, privileges, and immunities; (2) unlawfully and maliciously arresting, imprisoning and prosecuting a citizen who was acting in accordance with his constitutional and statutory rights, privileges and immunities; (3) unlawfully and maliciously assaulting and beating a citizen or otherwise using unreasonable and excessive force before, during, or after the making of an arrest, whether the arrest was lawful or unlawful; (4) conspiring to violate the rights, privileges and immunities guaranteed to Plaintiff by the Constitution and laws of the United States and the laws of the State of _____; and (5) otherwise depriving Plaintiff of his constitutional and statutory rights, privileges, and immunities.

18. Defendants _____, *[names of supervisors]* and City of _____ had knowledge or, had they diligently exercised their duties to instruct, supervise, control and discipline on a continuing basis, should have had knowledge that

the wrongs conspired to be done, as heretofore alleged, were about to be committed. Defendants _____ *[names of supervisors]* and City of _____ had power to prevent or aid in preventing the commission of said wrongs, could have done so by reasonable diligence, and knowingly, recklessly or with gross negligence failed or refused to do so.

19. Defendants _____, *[names of supervisors]* and City of _____, directly or indirectly, under color of law, approved or ratified the unlawful, deliberage, malicious, reckless, and wanton conduct of Defendant police officers heretofore described.

20. As a direct and proximate cause of the negligent and intentional acts of Defendants _____, *[names of supervisors]* and City of _____ as set forth in paragraphs 17–19 above, Plaintiff suffered physical injury, loss of income, medical expenses, and severe mental anguish in connection with the deprivation of his constitutional and statutory rights guaranteed by the Fifth and Fourteenth Amendments of the Constitution of the United States and protected by 42 U.S.C. §1983.

WHEREFORE, Plaintiff _____ demands judgment against Defendants _____, *[names of supervisors]* and City of _____, jointly and severally, for compensatory damages in the amount $_____, and further demands judgment against each of said Defendants (except for Defendant City), jointly and severally, for punitive damages in the amount of $_____, plus the costs of this action and such other relief as the Court deems just and equitable.

Form 6 Complaint for Damages against Police Officers for Unlawful Arrest, Search and Seizure

1. This is a civil action seeking damages against defendants for committing acts under color of law, and depriving plaintiff of rights secured by the Constitution and laws of the United States. Defendants, while acting in their capacities as policemen in the City of _____, County of _____, State of _____, deprived plaintiff of his liberty without due process of law, made an unreasonable search and seizure of the property of plaintiff, and deprived plaintiff of his property without due process of law, thereby depriving plaintiff of his rights, privileges and immunities as guaranteed by the Fourth, Fifth and Fourteenth Amendments to the Constitution of the United States. The Court has jurisdiction of this action under 42 U.S.C. Section 1983 and under 28 U.S.C. Section 1343.

2. The jurisdiction of this Court is further invoked pursuant to 28 U.S.C. Section 1331.

3. Plaintiff _____ is a citizen and resident of the State of _____ and a citizen of the United States.

4. Defendants _____, Badge Number _____, and _____, Badge Number _____, were, at all times material to this Complaint, duly appointed police officers of the City of _____, assigned to _____ District _____ of the _____ Police Department. At all times material to this Complaint, these defendants acted toward plaintiff under color of the statutes, ordinances, customs and usage of the State of _____, City of _____, and the _____ Police Department.

5. Defendant JOHN DOE and others not presently known to the plaintiff were, at all times material to this Complaint, duly appointed police officers of the City of _____. At all times material to this Complaint, these defendants acted toward plaintiff under color of the statutes, ordinances, customs and usage of the State of _____, City of _____, and the _____ Police Department.

6. Plaintiff sues all defendants in their individual capacities.

COUNT I

1–6. Plaintiff alleges and realleges Paragraphs 1 through 6 as Paragraphs 1 through 6 of this Count, with the same force and effect as if fully set forth herein.

7. On the evening of _____, 19____, at approximately _____, plaintiff _____ was driving an automobile owned by him in the vicinity of _____ Avenue and _____ Street in the City of _____. At all times on that evening, _____ operated this vehicle in accordance with all applicable traffic statutes and ordinances of the State of _____ and the City of _____.

8. On the evening of _____, 19____, at approximately _____, defen-

dants _____ and _____, who were dressed in plain clothes and traveling in an unmarked car, stopped plaintiff. Plaintiff had violated no law, and defendants had seen no evidence or probable cause that plaintiff had committed an offense, nor did defendants have any justification or authority whatever for stopping plaintiff.

9. When plaintiff stepped from his automobile, in full cooperation with defendants _____ and _____, said defendants searched his person twice, abused him both physically and verbally, and searched his automobile. At no time before or during this interrogation and search of plaintiff did defendants see or find any evidence or probable cause that plaintiff had committed any offense against the laws of the State of _____ or the City of _____.

10. Although defendants _____ and _____ had found no evidence of any violation of law by plaintiff, they placed plaintiff in custody, refused to inform him of any charge against him, and transported him to the _____ District Station of the _____ Police Department.

11. At the _____ District Station, defendants detained plaintiff for further interrogation and a further search of his automobile, although they still had seen no evidence or probable cause that plaintiff had committed any violation of law.

12. During the course of the interrogation of plaintiff at the District Station by defendants _____ and _____, defendants conducted a further illegal search of plaintiff's automobile. Neither before, during, nor after this search did defendants have probable cause to conduct this search, nor did they have permission from the plaintiff to conduct it.

13. During this search, said defendants discovered a locked box in the trunk of plaintiff's automobile. By threats to damage plaintiff's property by breaking open the box, defendants coerced plaintiff to surrender the key to said box, over plaintiff's continued and strident objections. Defendants then opened the box and seized from it private property belonging to the plaintiff, although they had no probable cause to search the box for anything.

14. Without probable cause or any justification whatever, defendants _____ and _____ agreed to and did maliciously charge plaintiff with the following offenses: Possession of marijuana under the laws of the State of _____, and obstructing traffic under the laws of the City of _____.

15. Because of defendants' malicious charges against plaintiff, plaintiff was detained without cause by the police for approximately twelve hours.

16. By means of these wholly unfounded charges, defendants _____ and _____ directly caused plaintiff's automobile to be impounded. Said defendants subsequently refused to complete the proper release forms when duly requested to do so by plaintiff. These actions deprived plaintiff of the possession, use and enjoyment of his automobile for approximately six weeks, and caused plaintiff to make numerous inconvenient trips to the Police Department in repeated attempts to regain his own automobile.

17. After plaintiff's automobile was wrongfully and unlawfully impounded, defendants _____, _____ and others not presently known to plaintiff intentionally removed or allowed to be removed the following items of personal property from plaintiff's automobile: one wristwatch, two transistor

radios, one tool box containing tools, one popcorn popper, several school textbooks, one flashlight, one box containing important papers, and other personal effects, all of a total value of approximately $_____.

18. Defendants _____, _____, DOE and/or others not presently known to the plaintiff either sold the aforesaid property at auction without notice to plaintiff, or otherwise intentionally converted that property to their own personal use.

19. On _____, 19____, plaintiff was brought to trial before the Honorable _____, a Judge of the _____ Court of _____ County, _____, upon the charge of possession of marijuana, and the charge was stricken with leave to reinstate on motion of the State, which disposition became a final discharge of plaintiff on said charge.

20. On _____, 19____, plaintiff appeared before the Honorable _____, a Magistrate of the _____ Court of _____ County, _____, upon the charge of obstructing traffic and was discharged on that charge, which discharge was final disposition of said charge against plaintiff.

21. By means of their unlawful detention of plaintiff and the malicious charges they placed against him, defendants _____ and _____ deprived plaintiff of his liberty without due process of law, in violation of the Fifth and Fourteenth Amendments to the Constitution of the United States and 42 U.S.C. Section 1983.

WHEREFORE, plaintiff _____ demands judgment against defendants _____ and _____, jointly and severally, for compensatory damages in the amount of $_____, and further demands judgment against each of said defendants, jointly and severally, for punitive damages in the amount of $_____, plus the costs of this action and such other relief as to this Court seems just, proper, and equitable.

COUNT II

1–9. Plaintiff alleges and realleges Paragraphs 1 through 9 of Count I as Paragraphs 1 through 9 of this Count, with the same force and effect as if fully set forth herein.

10. Defendants' illegal search and abuse of plaintiff, committed intentionally, either with malice or without malice, deprived plaintiff of his right to be free of unreasonable searches and seizures as guaranteed by the Fourth and Fourteenth Amendments to the Constitution of the United States and protected under 42 U.S.C. Section 1983.

WHEREFORE, plaintiff _____ demands judgement against defendants _____ and _____, jointly and severally, for compensatory damages in the amount of $_____, and further demands judgment against each of said defendants, jointly and severally, for punitive damages in the amount of $_____, plus the costs of this action, and such other relief as to this Court seems just, proper, and equitable.

COUNT III

1–20. Plaintiff alleges and realleges Paragraphs 1 through 20 of Count I as Paragraphs 1 through 20 of this Count, with the same force and effect as if fully set forth herein.

21. As a result of the malicious charges placed against plaintiff by defendants _____ and _____, and as a result of the further tortious acts of some or all of defendants _____, _____, DOE and others, including the seizure of his automobile, plaintiff was deprived of his property and the use of his property, both the automobile and its contents, without due process of law, in violation of the guarantees of the Fourth, Fifth and Fourteenth Amendments to the Constitution of the United States and 42 U.S.C. Section 1983.

WHEREFORE, Plaintiff _____ demands judgment against defendants _____, _____, JOHN DOE, and others not presently known to him, jointly and severally, for compensatory damages in the amount of $_____, and further demands judgment against each of said defendants, jointly and severally, for punitive damages in the amount of $_____, plus the costs of this action and such other relief as to this Court seems just, proper, and equitable.

COUNT IV

1–13. Plaintiff alleges and realleges Paragraphs 1 through 13 of Count I as Paragraphs 1 through 13 of this Count, with the same force and effect as if fully set forth herein.

14. Defendants' second illegal search of plaintiff's automobile at the District Station, and the illegal seizure of plaintiff's property, deprived plaintiff of his right to be free from unreasonable searches and seizures as guaranteed by the Fourth and Fourteenth Amendments to the Constitution of the United States and protected under 42 U.S.C. Section 1983.

WHEREFORE, Plaintiff _____ demands judgment against defendants _____ and _____, jointly and severally, for compensatory damages in the amount of $_____, and further demands judgment against each of said defendants, jointly and severally, for punitive damages in the amount of $_____, plus the costs of this action and such other relief as to this Court seems just, proper, and equitable.

Form 7 Complaint for Declaratory and Injunctive Relief Challenging Ordinances Regulating Public Assembly on First Amendment Grounds

COUNT I

1. This is a suit brought by plaintiffs who seek to hold a peaceable public assembly in front of the city hall in _____, _____, against defendant municipal officials and municipal corporation on grounds that the defendants have passed and are enforcing ordinances which bar such assemblies in violation of the First and Fourteenth Amendments to the United States Constitution.

2. This action arises under the Constitution of the United States and the provisions of 42 U.S.C. §1983, as hereinafter more fully appears. The jurisdiction of this court is invoked pursuant to 28 U.S.C. §§1331 and 1343, and 42 U.S.C. §1983.

3. Plaintiff _____ *[organization]* is organized to disseminate ideas through the permissible, non-violent exercise of the rights of free speech guaranteed to it and to the individual plaintiffs by the First and Fourteenth Amendments to the United States Constitution.

4. Defendants _____, _____, _____, and _____, are _____, _____, _____, *[positions]* respectively, of the City of _____, _____. Defendant City of _____ is a _____ municipal corporation.

5. After learning of plaintiffs' plans to hold a peaceable public assembly in front of the _____ city hall, defendants, on _____, 19____, responding solely to the unpopularity of and controversy generated by plaintiffs' plans, caused to be passed two ordinances intended to prohibit or restrict the dissemination of plaintiffs' ideas. *[attach copies]*

6. On _____, 19____, plaintiffs made application for a permit to hold a brief, peaceable public assembly in the City of _____ on _____, 19____, at _____ [a.m. or p.m.] in front of the city hall to consist of less than _____ demonstrators. [Copy of letter of application attached as Exhibit _____.]

7. On or about _____, 19____, plaintiffs received a letter from defendant _____ informing them that their application for a permit had been denied on grounds that the application did not comply with the ordinances herein complained of.

8. Plaintiffs plan to hold an assembly as soon as they are permitted to do so without the restrictions imposed by the ordinances herein complained of.

9. The conduct above complained of constitutes unreasonable and unconstitutional interference with and infringement on plaintiffs' exercise of their rights of free speech guaranteed under the First and Fourteenth Amendments to the United States Constitution. Among other things:

   a) Ordinance _____, which purports to prohibit the dissemination of materials which "promote" or "incite" group hatred, is vague, unintelligible, overbroad, and totally unrelated to the constitutional standards which must be observed before governmental bodies can regulate the exercise of First Amendment rights.

b) Ordinance _____, which purports to regulate parades and public assemblies, is vague, overbroad and, by requiring public liability insurance of $_____ and property damage insurance of $_____ as a condition for obtaining a permit for activities set forth therein unless said conditions are waived at the unfettered discretion of the Board of Trustees, constitutes a restriction on the exercise of First Amendment rights which is totally unrelated to any legitimate public purpose or to the reasonable exercise of the police power of the City of _____.

10. Plaintiffs have been informed by defendants that defendants will employ the ordinances above complained of to arrest plaintiffs and to interfere with, disrupt and suppress the proposed peaceable exercise by plaintiffs of their rights guaranteed under the First and Fourteenth Amendments. Plaintiffs have no adequate remedy at law, and unless this Court grants the injunctive and declaratory relief herein requested, plaintiffs will be unable to exercise their rights and will be irreparably damaged.

COUNT II

1–5. Plaintiffs repeat and reallege Paragraphs 1 through 5 of Count I as Paragraphs 1 through 5 of Count II.

6. The enactment and enforcement of the foregoing ordinances are arbitrary, capricious, and particularly directed against plaintiffs and their ideas and concepts in violation of plaintiffs' rights to equal protection of the laws guaranteed by the Fourteenth Amendment to the United States Constitution.

7. Plaintiffs repeat and reallege the allegations of Paragraph 10 of Count I as Paragraph 7 of Count II.

WHEREFORE, plaintiffs pray that this Court will issue:

1. Preliminary and permanent injunctions enjoining and restraining the enforcement of the ordinances above complained of;

2. Preliminary and permanent injunctions enjoining and restraining defendants from further interference with plaintiffs' exercise of their rights to freedom of speech and assembly;

3. A declaratory judgment adjudging said ordinances null and void;

4. Such other and further relief as to this Court shall seem just and equitable.

Form 8 Motion for Preliminary Injunction in Connection with Challenge to Ordinances Regulating Public Assembly on First Amendment Grounds

Plaintiffs, by their attorneys, hereby move this Court for a preliminary injunction restraining defendants, their agents, employees and others working in concert with them from enforcing City Ordinances *[citations]*, pending final disposition of this cause. In support thereof, plaintiffs submit the attached Memorandum of Law.

Form 9 Motion for Attorney's Fees Award under Civil Rights Attorney's Fees Awards Act of 1976 and for Costs Incurred

Now comes plaintiff's attorney _____, pursuant to the Civil Rights Attorney's Fees Awards Act of 1976, 42 U.S.C. §1988, and moves the Court to award attorney's fees in the amount of $_____ to plaintiff's attorney and against defendants herein. Plaintiff's attorney further moves this Court to order defendants to pay $_____ in costs remaining unpaid from the original trial of this case. In support of said motion, plaintiff's attorney states as follows:

1. This fee is based upon plaintiff's attorney's hours of work multiplied by an hourly rate of $_____ for _____. This hourly rate is reasonable and appropriate in light of relevant factors as will be more fully set out in plaintiff's memorandum in support of this Motion for Attorney's Fees.

2. The Attorney's Fees Motion Affidavit, attached hereto and made a part hereof, itemizes the number of hours worked, at a minimum, by _____. The total number of hours is _____. *[attach exhibit itemizing]*

3. Plaintiff incurred costs of $_____ at the original trial of this case which were never paid, notwithstanding the timely filing of appropriate documents and the absence of any objections by defendants. *[attach bill of costs pursuant to 28 USC Sections 1920 and 1924]*

4. Reimbursement is not sought for the following:

    a) Motions and hearings on motions of plaintiff's attorney for extension of time in which to file briefs

    b) The time of law students in researching various issues of law.

    c) Any higher rate for in-court time or general percentage premium despite defendant's persistent enforcement of an invalid _____ requirement notwithstanding the Court's earlier injunction.

5. As used in the Attorney's Fees Motion Affidavit:

    a) "Date" refers to the date the work was performed.

    b) "Description" characterizes work for which fees are claimed.

    c) The "Hours" for specifically "described" work includes the total number of hours for the activity or memorandum or motion described.

Respectfully submitted,

_____

Attorney for Plaintiff

AFFIDAVIT

I, _____, being duly sworn, hereby state as follows:

555

1. I am and have been one of the attorneys for the plaintiff in the above case.

2. I am a graduate of *[state college and law school]*

3. Since _____, 19____, I have worked as an attorney for _____. Since _____, 19____, my practice has been, in primary part, devoted to federal court litigation of civil liberties and civil rights cases, including those arising under the First Amendment.

4. Major litigation for which I have had or have primary responsibility includes: *[list, describe cases briefly]* and many other cases brought both as class and individual actions in the _____ District of _____ in civil liberties matters.

5. At a minimum, the total number of hours I spent in connection with the litigation in this case is _____ as set forth in Exhibit _____.

Further affiant sayeth not.

_____

SUBSCRIBED AND SWORN to before me this _____ day of _____, 19____.

_____

(Notary Public)

Form 10 Class Action Complaint for Injunctive Relief and Damages against City, Its Police Department, and Various Individuals Challenging "Strip Searches"

NOW COME plaintiffs, by their attorneys, and for their class action Complaint against defendants, allege and state as follows.

NATURE OF THE ACTION

1. This is an action brought by and on behalf of females who, under color of law, were subjected by the _____ Police Department to searches, in which they were forced to undress and spread apart their rectal and vaginal areas, and, in some instances, to rectal and vaginal cavity searches, in which one of the defendants placed a finger or hand on or inside the rectal or vaginal area (hereinafter referred to as "strip searches"). These strip searches were conducted without reason or cause to believe that weapons or contraband were being concealed on or in the body of the female involved and in violation of her constitutional rights.

JURISDICTION AND VENUE

2. This action seeks injunctive relief and monetary damages for violations of the rights, privileges and immunities secured under the Fourth, Fifth, Eighth, Ninth and Fourteenth Amendments to the Constitution of the United States and Title 42 U.S.C. §1983.

3. Jurisdiction of this Court arises under Title 28 U.S.C. §1343 and Title 28 U.S.C. §1331.

4. Venue is proper in the _____ District of _____ since the acts and transactions complained of herein all occurred within this District.

CLASS ACTION ALLEGATIONS

5. (a) Plaintiffs bring this action as a class action pursuant to Rule 23(b)(2) and Rule 23(b)(3) of the Federal Rules of Civil Procedure.

(b) The class consists of all female persons who were detained by the _____ Police Department for an offense no greater than a traffic violation or a misdemeanor, including all females who were never charged with any offense and who were subjected to a strip search in situations where there was no reason to believe that weapons or contraband had been concealed on or in their bodies.

(c) The class is so numerous that joinder of all persons is impracticable. Plaintiffs are informed and believe that at least most or all females detained in custody at the _____ Police Districts, and probably those detained at other Districts, were subjected to strip searches. Based upon that information, plaintiffs believe that the class probably numbers well over _____ persons.

(d) Plaintiffs will fairly and adequately protect the interests of all class members as they are members of the class and their claims are typical of the claims of all class members. Each of the plaintiffs is incensed at the treatment accorded the class members and will aggressively pursue the interests of the entire class. Plaintiffs' interests in obtaining injunctive relief and monetary damages for the violations of constitutional rights and privileges are consistent with and not antagonistic to those of any person within the class.

(e) The common questions of law and fact include:

(i)   whether defendants had a policy and practice to strip search all females detained in custody, regardless of the gravity of the offense and regardless of the lack of any reasonable belief that matter had been concealed upon their persons;

(ii)   whether the supervisory defendants had knowledge of the conduct alleged herein;

(iii) whether the conduct alleged herein is in violation of the Fourth, Fifth, Eighth, Ninth or Fourteenth Amendments to the United States Constitution and Title 42 U.S.C. §1983;

(iv) whether plaintiffs and the members of the plaintiff class are entitled to an award of compensatory or punitive damages.

(f) The wrongful conduct alleged herein has been conducted generally upon all members of the plaintiff class in that the strip searches were conducted pursuant to a long-established plan, policy or procedure of the _____ Police Department.

(g) The common questions of fact and law predominate over questions affecting only individual class members.

(h) A class action is superior to other available methods for the fair and efficient adjudication of the controversy in that:

(i)   A multiplicity of suits with consequent burden on the courts and defendants should be avoided.

(ii)   It would be virtually impossible for all class members to intervene as parties-plaintiff in this action.

(iii) Upon adjudication of defendants' liability, claims of the class members can be determined by this Court.

THE PARTIES

6. Jane Does are all female citizens of the United States who were detained in custody by the _____ Police Department for offenses no greater than traffic violations or misdemeanors, or were detained without ever being charged with an offense and who were subjected to a strip search in situations where there was no reasonable belief or indication that weapons or contraband had been concealed on their persons. Because of the intimate and personal nature of their Complaint, Jane Does have sued under assumed names. Plaintiffs stand ready to reveal their true identities in such manner and at such time as the Court deems appropriate.

7. Defendants are as follows:

(a) THE CITY OF _____ is a _____ municipal corporation and, as such, is responsible for the policies, procedures and practices implemented through its various agencies and agents and for injury occassioned thereby.

(b) _____ are members of the Police Board of the City of _____ (hereinafter collectively "The Police Board"). Their duties, as defined by law, include the promulgation and adoption of rules and regulations and general and special orders for the governance of the _____ Police Department and including the policies, procedures and practices described herein.

(c) Defendant _____ is the Superintendent of the Police Department of the City of _____ and, as such, is and has been responsible for the promulgation and implementation of police policies, procedures and practices in the City of _____, including the policy, procedure and practice of strip searching female persons in the custody of the _____ Police Department.

(d) Defendant _____ is the Commander of the _____ District, which includes the police station located at _____ Street and _____ Street (hereinafter "_____ District") and, as such, is responsible for instituting and implementing police policies, procedures and practices within the _____ District.

(e) Defendants *(insert names)* are the Watch Commanders of the _____ District and, as such, are responsible for implementing police policies, procedures and practices within the _____ District during their respective watches.

(f) Defendant _____ is the Commander of the _____ District, which includes the police station located at the _____ Street and _____ Avenue (hereinafter "_____ District") and, as such, is responsible for instituting and implementing police policies, procedures and practices within the _____ District.

(g) Defendants *(insert names)* are the Watch Commanders of the _____ District and, as such, are responsible for implementing police policies, procedures and practices within the _____ District during their respective watches.

(h) Defendant _____ is the Commander of the _____ District, which includes the police station located at _____ Avenue and _____ Avenue (hereinafter "_____ District") and, as such, is responsible for instituting and implementing police policies, procedures and practices within the _____ District.

(i) Defendants *(insert names)* are the Watch Commanders of the _____ District and, as such, are responsible for implementing police policies, procedures, and practices within the _____ District during their respective watches.

(j) MAX MOES 1-50 are the Commanders and Watch Commanders of Districts of the _____ Police Department other than the _____ District, _____ District and _____ District and, as such, are responsible for implementing police policies, procedures and practices in their respective Districts.

(k) MAXINE ROES 1-50 and MAX ROES 1-50 are officers or employees of the _____ Police Department who participated in the strip searches of members of the class of plaintiffs at the police stations and whose names are presently unknown to plaintiffs, except that plaintiffs are informed and believe that one such defendant was _____.

(l) MAXINE ROES 51-100 and MAX ROES 51-100 are officers or employees of the _____ Police Department whose names are presently unknown to plaintiffs, except that plaintiffs are informed and believe that _____ and _____ are two of such persons, and who knowingly caused members of the class plaintiffs to be subjected to strip searches or rectal and vaginal cavity searches by causing such persons to be taken to police stations or by refusing to cause the release of such persons when bail was properly posted before the searches took place.

(m) MAXINE ROES 101-150 and MAX ROES 101-150 are officers or employees of the _____ Police Department whose names are presently unknown to plaintiffs and who observed the strip searches of members of the class of plaintiffs in person or by video camera but did not participate in such strip searches.

(n) MAX ZOES 1-100 and MAXINE ZOES 1-100 are persons whose names are presently unknown to plaintiffs, who formerly served in positions presently held by other defendants named herein and who, while in those positions, promulgated, instituted or implemented police policies, procedures and practices relating to strip searches conducted on members of the class of plaintiffs, who participated in such strip searches, who caused members of the class of plaintiffs to be arrested or otherwise taken to the police stations in the _____, _____ or _____ Districts, whereupon plaintiffs were strip searched, or who observed the strip searches of members of the class of plaintiffs in person or by video camera but did not participate in the strip searches.

ALLEGATIONS OF WRONGFUL CONDUCT

8. For at least five years prior to and continuing at the time of the filing of this Complaint, defendants City of _____, the Police Board, the Superintendent and certain of the Max Zoe defendants have created, authorized, maintained, permitted and enforced a policy or procedure in which most or all female persons in the custody of the _____ Police Department are routinely subjected to a strip search without a search warrant and in situations where it was not reasonable to believe that any contraband or weapons had been concealed on their person. Male persons in similar situations are not subjected to strip searches.

9. Jane Does 1-5 were detained for an offense no greater than a traffic violation or misdemeanor, or where they were not charged with any offense, and subjected to a strip search in situations where it was not reasonable to believe they had concealed any contraband or weapons upon their person, to wit:

(a) Jane Doe #1, a resident of the State of _____, was subjected to a strip search on or about _____, 19__. She had followed an arrested male companion to a police station where, despite the fact that she had not been arrested or charged, she was instructed to remove all her clothes and to squat three times. Immediately after the strip search, she was released; no charges were made against her. The male companion was not subjected to a strip search, and the charges against him were dismissed on _____, 19____.

(b) Jane Doe #2, a resident of the state of _____, was subjected to a strip search on or about _____, 19____. She had been stopped by a _____ policeman for an improper left turn. She had left her driver's license at home and was told to follow the policeman to a police station in her own car unaccompanied by police personnel. The _____ Police Department confirmed that Jane Doe #2 had a valid _____ driver's license. A female companion, who had accompanied Jane Doe #2 to the police station, advised police that she would pick up Jane Doe #2's license and return to the police station. Jane Doe #2 was then subjected to a strip search, being told to "pull down your pants, squat three times, and spread your vagina." When Jane Doe #2 protested, she was told, "if you don't cooperate, six guys will come in and do it for me." She was then released on the bond of her driver's license. The charges of an illegal left turn were subsequently dismissed.

(c) Jane Doe #3, a resident of the State of _____, is a minor and sues by her next friend and mother, Sally Doe. On or about _____, 19____, Jane Doe #3 was arrested for disorderly conduct when she was discovered in the hallway of her high school without a hall pass. At the police station, Jane Doe #3 was taken to a hallway in front of a cell and told to remove her clothing, squat three times and spread her vagina. She was later released on _____ bond. The charges against Jane Doe #3 were subsequently dismissed.

(d) Jane Doe #4, a resident of the State of _____, was arrested at her place of work on _____, 19____, and charged with assault and battery stemming from a fight with a girlfriend of the arresting officer in a restaurant six hours earlier. The sister of Jane Doe #4 followed the paddy wagon to the police station with bond money. Prior to being allowed to post bond, Jane Doe #4 was told to remove her clothes, squat three times, and spread her rectum and vagina. The charges against Jane Doe #4 were subsequently dropped.

(e) Jane Doe #5, a resident of the State of _____, voluntarily went to a _____ police station on or about _____, 19____, at the instructions of the police personnel to post bond for unpaid parking tickets and retrieve her impounded vehicle. Jane Doe #5 was taken to an open cell, told to remove her blouse, her brassiere and her pants, and then told to squat three times, bend over and spread her cheeks. A male officer came to the cell before the search was completed. Shortly thereafter, she was allowed to post bond on the unpaid parking tickets and was released.

10. Defendants _____ and Max Moes 1-50 and certain of the Max Zoe and Maxine Zoe defendants have instituted and implemented the policies and procedures identified in paragraphs 8-9 above by engaging in the following acts and practices toward the named plaintiffs and the plaintiff class:

(a) Females who are taken into custody are subjected to strip searches without regard to whether it was reasonable to believe that any contraband or weapons may have been concealed on the person of the female.

(b) The acts and practices described in subparagraph (a) of this paragraph 10 are engaged in even where the female in question has not been charged with any crime or informed of any reason for detention prior to the strip search.

(c) The acts and practices described in subparagraph (a) of this paragraph 10 are engaged in even where the female in question has been charged only with a motor vehicle violation under _____ of the Municipal Code of the City of _____ and is taken into custody only because she does not have on her person a _____ driver's license.

(d) The acts and practices described in subparagraph (a) of this paragraph 10 are engaged in even where the female in question has bond available when she arrives at the police station or where bond or a valid _____ driver's license is presented to the police officers prior to the strip search taking place.

(e) The acts and practices described in subparagraph (a) of this paragraph 10 are engaged in even where the female in question has been permitted, after arrest for a motor vehicle violation, to drive in her own vehicle to the police station unattended and unguarded by any officer or employee of the police department, so that no reasonable person could believe that the female would keep any incriminating material on her person.

(f) The acts and practices described in subparagraph (a) of this paragraph 10 are engaged in even where the female in question has not been taken into custody until she voluntarily came to the police station alone, solely to post bond under such circumstances that no reasonable person could believe that the female would keep any incriminating material on her person.

11. The acts and practices described in subparagraphs (a)-(f) of paragraph 10 are engaged in with respect to most or all females taken into custody, even though males taken into custody under identical circumstances are not subjected to strip searches. Furthermore, where a male and female companion are taken or directed jointly to the police station, and the female is charged with the same or an even lesser offense than the male, the female is subjected to strip search and the male is not.

12. When rectal and vaginal cavity searches are made, the police matron making the search is not trained in such techniques, does not wash her hands or use gloves, and generally proceeds with a vaginal search after the rectal search and after the search of outer clothing and searches performed on other persons in custody.

13. It was the policy, procedure and practice of at least certain of the police stations, including that of the _____ District, to conduct the strip searches in the presence of police officers, employees and other persons not conducting the searches. In addition, at certain stations there existed the capability to photograph and transmit photographs of the strip searches to the central information and processing desk in the lobby by closed-circuit television for viewing by policemen and policewomen not in the area where the searches were performed and, on occasion, by the public waiting in the lobby of the police station. There was no policy prohibiting such photographing and transmission of photographs. Max Roes 101-150, Maxine Roes 101-150 and certain of the Max Zoe and Maxine Zoe defendants observed such searches in this manner.

14. The acts and practices described in paragraphs 8-13 including but not

limited to the fact that females in custody were being forced to undergo strip searches whereas males in identical situations were not, were made with the approval, authorization, knowledge, ratification and consent of defendants City of _____, _____, _____, and Max Moes 1-50. Plaintiffs specifically allege that these defendants had been made aware of the policy, procedure, acts and practices alleged by virtue of complaints filed with certain of the defendants, filed with the _____ Police Department and filed in court. Nonetheless, defendants named in this paragraph continued to enforce and to give the appearance of approving of all of the policies, procedures and practices alleged above.

15. Each of defendants _____ and Max Moes 1-50 has the duty to command, regulate and control the actions of police officers and employees under their supervision so as to prevent those subordinate officials from acting in a manner that deprives female persons in custody of their rights under the Constitution and laws of the United States, but has failed to, and is failing to do so, in the following respects:

(a) Each has failed to exercise adequate supervision over subordinates and failed to take steps to regulate and control the discretion of subordinate officers so as to prevent the conduct alleged in paragraphs 9-13 above which were known to exist.

(b) Each has failed to provide or enforce lawful and proper guidelines and procedures to assist subordinates to engage in only lawful acts.

16. The policies, procedures, practices and acts of defendants alleged above have continued unchanged for many years. Upon information and belief, defendants promulgated a written policy directive in _____, 19____ (attached hereto as Exhibit A), which was vague and has been enforced and known by all defendants to have been enforced in a manner consistent with those policies, procedures, practices and acts previously in effect and alleged herein. Upon information and belief, defendants have recently issued a new policy directive (attached hereto as Exhibit B), which is also vague and overbroad and is continuing to be enforced against female arrestees in a discriminatory and offensive manner.

THE VIOLATIONS

17. The policies, procedures, practices and acts of defendants alleged in paragraphs 8-16 above violated the rights of plaintiffs and members of the class under the Fourth, Fifth, Eighth, Ninth and Fourteenth Amendments to the Constitution of the United States and, therefore, are violative of Title 42 U.S.C. §1983 as follows:

(a) The strip searches were conducted without probable cause or reason to believe that any contraband, dangerous materials or incriminating objects would be found and thereby constituted unreasonable searches and seizures in violation of the rights, privileges and immunities of plaintiffs and members of the class under the Fourth Amendment and Fourteenth Amendment.

(b) The strip searches constituted gross invasions of the rights of plaintiffs and members of the class to privacy and due process under the Fifth Amendment, Ninth Amendment and Fourteenth Amendment.

(c) The photographing and transmission of photographs of strip searches constituted gross invasions of the rights of plaintiffs and members of the class to privacy under the Fifth Amendment, Ninth Amendment and Fourteenth Amendment.

(d) The strip searches without due process constituted cruel and unusual punishment under the Eighth Amendment and Fourteenth Amendment where no charges greater than traffic violations or misdemeanors were filed.

(e) The strip searches constituted compulsory disclosure of self-incriminating testimony without due process in violation of the rights, privileges and immunities of plaintiffs and members of the class under the Fifth Amendment and Fourteenth Amendment.

(f) The performance of rectal and vaginal cavity searches without proper medical supervision, training and practices constituted cruel and unusual punishment and a violation of the rights of plaintiffs and members of the class to due process under the Eighth and Fourteenth Amendments.

(g) The policies, procedures and practices of defendants relating to strip searches were only applied to females and not to males taken into custody in identical or more incriminating circumstances in gross violation of the rights, privileges and immunities of plaintiffs and members of the class to due process and equal protection of the laws under the Fourteenth Amendment.

18. Defendants Max Roes 51-100 and Maxine Roes 51-100 and certain of the Max Zoe and Maxine Zoe defendants conspired with and aided and abetted the defendants described in paragraphs 8-16 above to violate the rights, privileges and immunities of plaintiffs and members of the class as alleged in paragraph 17 above by providing substantial assistance to such other defendants in carrying out the policies, procedures and practices of subjecting females to strip searches by forcing such females to go to the police stations or by failing to secure release of such females prior to the performance of such searches when bail had been presented, all with knowledge that such strip searches would occur in violation of the constitutional rights of plaintiffs as alleged in paragraph 17 above.

19. The policies, procedures, practices and acts alleged in paragraphs 8-16 and 18 above were undertaken, aided, authorized, supervised or consented to by each defendant with malice, with willful and wanton desire and design to violate, and with deliberate indifference to and reckless disregard of the rights, privileges and immunities of plaintiffs and members of the class under the Fourth, Fifth, Eighth, Ninth and Fourteenth Amendments to the Constitution of the United States as set forth in paragraph 17 above.

20. As a result of the policies, procedures, practices and acts of defendants, Jane Does 1-5 and members of the class have suffered violations of their rights, privileges and immunities under the Constitution and have suffered severe emotional and psychological distress, anguish, anxiety and injury and pain and suffering due to the willful, wanton and deliberate misconduct of defendants.

21. Unless immediately, preliminarily and permanently enjoined from continuing to subject females taken into custody to strip searches, defendants will continue to engage in the willful, wanton and deliberate violation of the constitutional rights of females, and plaintiffs and members of the class will

continue to suffer gross violations of their constitutional rights and gross indignities, each of which constitutes irreparable injury for which plaintiffs have no adequate remedy at law.

WHEREFORE, plaintiffs pray that this Court enter an order:

1. Finding that this action should proceed as a class action under Rule 23, Federal Rules of Civil Procedure;

2. Preliminarily and permanently restraining, enjoining and prohibiting defendants from undertaking, enforcing, maintaining or adopting any policies, procedures, practices or acts by which any person not charged with any offense no more serious than a traffic violation or misdemeanor is subjected to a strip search without a warrant, except where the person has been detained for an offense other than a violation relating to the operation of a motor vehicle or possession of a motor vehicle operator's license, and where there is probable cause to believe that contraband or weapons are being concealed on the person;

3. Preliminarily and permanently restraining, enjoining and prohibiting defendants from undertaking, enforcing, maintaining or adopting any policies, procedures, practices or acts by which any person not charged with any offense or charged only with a traffic violation or a misdemeanor is subjected to any rectal or vaginal cavity search, except where such search is made by a physician licensed by the State of _____ and upon a warrant issued by a court;

4. Preliminarily and permanently restraining, enjoining and prohibiting defendants from undertaking, enforcing, maintaining or adopting any policies, procedures, practices or acts by which any person charged with a misdemeanor is subjected to a strip search or rectal or vaginal cavity search in the presence of police officers or employees not necessary for such search to be performed (and in no event in the presence of more than one additional such officer and/or employee), or of the opposite sex, or in such a manner that the search is being recorded or transmitted in any manner by videotape or other visual means to or for any person;

5. Preliminarily and permanently restraining, enjoining and prohibiting defendants from undertaking, enforcing, maintaining or adopting any policies, procedures, practices or acts by which any female charged with a misdemeanor is subjected to any strip search if a male arrestee is not or would not be subjected to the same search in the same circumstances;

6. Awarding damages to each plaintiff and member of the class and against defendants jointly and severally in the amount of _____ as actual damages for emotional and psychological distress, severe mental anguish, anxiety, humiliation, degradation and pain and suffering of body and mind, and _____ as punitive damages for the willful and wanton misconduct of defendants, together with such other amount of special compensatory damages as may be shown to exist;

7. Awarding plaintiffs and the class their costs of suit and their attorney's fees under Title 42 U.S.C. §1988;

8. Awarding such other and further relief that this Court may deem just and proper.

Form 11   Defendant's Request for Production

Now comes the defendant, _____, by and through his attorney, _____, and pursuant to Federal Rules of Civil Procedure requests the plaintiff to produce the following articles and information:

1.   Any and all statements, reports, photographs, investigative reports, and/or opinions and statements of Plaintiff and/or Defendants regarding the incident alleged in the Complaint.

2.   All physical evidence regarding the incident alleged in the Complaint.

3.   A list giving the names and addresses of all witnesses to the occurrence alleged in Plaintiff's Complaint.

4.   A list giving the names of all witnesses listed in No. 3 (above) who will be called to testify at trial.

5.   The name and address of Plaintiff's employer on the date of the incident alleged in his Complaint.

Form 12 Defendant's Interrogatories to Plaintiff

NOW COMES defendant, _____, by his attorney, _____, and requests that the following Interrogatories be answered by the plaintiff, _____, under oath, within thirty (30) days after service, in accordance with Rule 31 of the Federal Rules of Civil Procedure.

1. Please state your full name, present residence address, your date and place of birth, your Social Security number, your driver's license number and, if you have ever been known by any other name, please state all the names by which you have been known, the dates of use of each such name, and the reasons for any change of name.

2. For each occupation or job held during the last ten (10) years, please state the full name and address of each employer, the dates of commencement and termination of each such employment, a brief description of the services or work performed in each such employment, the weekly average wages or earnings in each such employment, whether a physical examination was required prior to employment and if so, the place, date and person giving any such examination, the name of your immediate foreman, supervisor or superior at each such place of employment, and the reason for termination of each such employment.

3. If you have ever pleaded guilty to or been convicted of a crime punishable as either a misdemeanor or felony, the date of each prosecution or conviction, the name of each court and the location of each court where the prosecution or conviction took place, and a full description of any and all sentences imposed.

4. If you have ever been involved in any civil legal action (workmen's compensation claims included), either as defendant or plaintiff, state the date and place each such action was filed, including the name of the court and parties involved, the court file number of all such actions, the names of attorneys representing each party, a description of the nature of each such action, including the disposition of each such action, whether or not there was an appeal and, if so, the result thereof, including the name and citation of each case reported, and the amount of any settlement or judgment obtained in each such case.

5. If you are presently married, state the name and address of your spouse, the date and place where your marriage took place, the full names, birth dates, and present residence addresses of any and all children born of said marriage; if you and your spouse are presently separated, please list your spouse's present address and the date when the separation occurred or, if you or your spouse have filed for divorce, the county and state where the divorce action is pending and the date upon which the complaint for divorce was filed.

6. Prior to _____, had you ever been admitted to any hospital or other medical institution, or been under the treatment and care of any physician? yes _____ no _____ If so, please state:

    a.   The full name and address of each such hospital or other medical institution and each such physician.

b.   The inclusive dates of confinement at each such hospital or medical institution and the dates of treatment by any such physician.

c.   The reason for your confinement in such hospital or medical institution, and the condition or conditions for which you were treated by such physician.

7. Prior to _____, had you ever suffered any personal injury or been involved in any accident of any kind, nature, or description whatsoever? If so, please state:

a.   The date and places where each such injury or accident occurred.

b.   The names and present addresses of any other person or persons involved.

c.   The names and addresses of any and all doctors who attended you, examined or rendered treatment to you, or hospitals, medical institutions, or clinics to which you were confined or where you received medical attention for each such personal injury or accident.

d.   The nature of the injury or injuries suffered.

e.   The approximate date of your recovery from each such injury.

f.   If you did not recover fully, the date your condition became stable and a description of your condition at that time.

8. Have you been examined medically, received any kind of medical care and/or treatment, or have you been admitted to any hospital or medical institution since _____ for the injuries allegedly sustained as a result of the occurrence involved in this case? Yes _____ No _____ If yes, please state:

a.   The names, addresses, and telephone numbers of any and all physicians or other health care practitioners, hospitals, or medical institutions who or which rendered services to you.

b.   The date or dates of examination, care, or treatment by each such physician or other health care practitioners, the date or dates of admission and discharge as to each hospital or medical institution.

c.   The nature of the care or treatment rendered by each such physician or other health care practitioner, hospital, or other medical institution and the reason or reasons for such treatment or hospitalization.

d.   List any expenses incurred, the portion of the expenses which has been paid, and the name and address of each person paying a portion or all of said expenses.

e.   Did you have any form of medical insurance or reimbursement which covered any of the medical expenses arising out of the occurrence involved in this litigation? If so, please state the name and address of the insurer or other person who reimbursed you and the amount so paid.

9. Have you or your attorney received any written report by any physician

or other health care practitioner or by any hospital or health care facility concerning your mental condition as a result of the occurrences involved in this litigation? If so, please state:

    a.   The date each report was made.

    b.   The name, address, and profession or occupation of the person making the report.

    c.   The name and address of the person who has present custody of the report or any copy of it.

    d.   A description of the contents of the report.

    e.   If you will do so without a motion to produce, please attach a copy of each such report to your answers to these Interrogatories.

10. State whether you filed income tax returns with the Director of Internal Revenue and/or with any State tax authority or department for each of the ten (10) years immediately preceding the date of the accident which is involved in this litigation. If so, please state:

    a.   The office of the Director of Internal Revenue with which such federal return was filed.

    b.   The amount reported as earned income on each such federal return.

    c.   The amount of tax shown to be due on each such federal return.

    d.   The State tax authority or authorization with whom each such tax return was filed.

    e.   The amount reported to each such State tax return as earned income.

    f.   The amount of tax shown to be due on each such tax return.

    g.   If you will do so without a motion to produce, please attach a copy of all such federal and state tax returns listed above to your answers to these Interrogatories.

11. Have you been employed since _____? If so, please state:

    a.   The name and address of each of your employers.

    b.   Your present work title; whether you have had this work title since the date of this accident, including any changes in specific work duties and the reasons for any such changes.

    c.   The date during which you worked for each employer.

    d.   The weekly average wages or earnings in such employment.

    e.   The reason you left or changed from any employer's service.

    f.   If applicable, list all periods of time you were off work and all the reasons why you were off work during this period.

12. Set forth any loss in income which you claim as a result of the occurrences involved in this litigation, stating the following:

    a.   The total gross and net income claimed lost.

    b.   The claimed source of any alleged lost income, including name and address of each such source.

    c.   The manner, that is, by daily rate, weekly, monthly, etc. in which you compute the amount of any claimed loss.

    d.   If you have any documents which substantiate your claimed loss of earnings, state:

        1.   A full description of each such document.

        2.   The name and address of the person or persons now in possession of each such document or any copy of the same.

        3.   If you will do so without a motion to produce, please attach copies of any substantiating documents to your answers to these Interrogatories.

13. What are the names and addresses of all persons known to the plaintiff having any information whatsoever with respect to the happening of the occurrences involved in this litigation and the causes thereof? Further, were any statements obtained from these persons that you have listed having information with respect to the happening of the occurrences involved in this litigation and the causes thereof? If so, would you kindly attach a copy of same to these answers to Interrogatories?

14. a.   State the name and addresses of all witnesses that you expect to call as an expert witness at trial.

     b.   State the subject matter on which the expert is expected to testify.

     c.   State the substances of the facts and opinions to which the expert is expected to testify and a summary of the grounds for each opinion.

15. State whether you or your attorneys or agents or anyone acting on your behalf have taken any statements, signed or unsigned, oral or written, or have in their possession any such statements, or know of the existence of any such statements, from or by any person who has, or claims to have, knowledge of the facts concerning the occurrence complained of, or who were, or claim to have been, witnesses to the occurrence complained of; if so, state the identity and present or last known location of each such person together with the present whereabouts and number of such statements.

The foregoing interrogatories shall be deemed continuing in nature from the time of this cause, and if any further information comes to the knowledge of the plaintiff or his attorney, or agent, or employee in this regard, you are hereby requested without further notice to file and serve supplemental answers.

Table of Cases

F

H

Haines v Kerner, 404 US 519 (1972) §§**1.01, 1.16, 1.17**

Haldane v Chagnon, 345 F2d 601 (9th Cir 1965) §**2.10**

Halet v Wend Inv Co, 672 F2d 1305 (9th Cir 1982) §§**2.09, 5.04, 5.05**

Hall v Beals, 396 US 45 (1969) §**5.04**

Hall v Borough of Roselle, 747 F2d 838 (3d Cir 1984) §**1.26**

Hall v Hall, 738 F2d 718 (6th Cir 1984) §**1.19**

Hall v Quillen, 631 F2d 1154 (4th Cir 1980) §**2.09**

Hall v Tawney, 621 F2d 607 (4th Cir 1980) §**3.10**

Hamilton v General Motors Corp, 606 F2d 576 (5th Cir 1979) §**4.17**

Hamlin v Warren, 664 F2d 29 (4th Cir 1981) §**5.11**

Hamner v Rios, 769 F2d 1404 (9th Cir 1985) §**1.26**

Hampton v City of Chicago, 484 F2d 602 (7th Cir 1973), *cert denied*, 415 US 917 (1974) §**7.14**

Hampton v Hanrahan, 600 F2d 600 (7th Cir 1979), *denying cert but revg on attorney's fee issue*, 446 US 754 (1980) §§**1.19, 2.11, 3.10, 7.14**

Hander v San Jacinto Junior College, 519 F2d 273 (5th Cir 1975) §§**6.17, 8.16**

Hanna v Drobnick, 514 F2d 393 (6th Cir 1975) §§**6.01, 8.11, 8.13, 8.17**

Hanrahan v Hampton, 446 US 754 (1980), *denying cert on other issues but revg on attorney's fees issue*, 600 F2d 600 (7th Cir 1979) §**1.19**

Hans v Louisiana, 134 US 1 (1890) §**5.08**

Hansen v Ahlgrimm, 520 F2d 768 (7th Cir 1975) §**2.10**

Hanson v Circuit Ct of First Judicial Dist, 591 F2d 407 (7th Cir 1979) §**5.11**

Hardwick v Hurley, 289 F2d 529 (7th Cir 1961) §**3.05**

Haring v Prosise, 462 US 306 (1983), *affg* 667 F2d 1133 (4th Cir 1981) §§**5.17, 5.18**

Harkless v Sweeney Indep School Dist, 427 F2d 319 (5th Cir 1970), *cert denied*, 400 US 991 (1971) §§**1.17, 6.04**

Harley v Oliver, 539 F2d 1143 (8th Cir 1976) §**7.07**

Harlow v Fitzgerald, 457 US 800 (1982) §§**1.16, 7.10, 8.01, 8.03, 8.10, 8.15**

Harper v Merkle, 638 F2d 848 (5th Cir 1981) §**7.08**

Harrington v DeVito, 656 F2d 264 (7th Cir 1981) §**1.19**

Harris v City of Canton, 725 F2d 371 (6th Cir 1984) §§**4.17, 6.16**

Harris v City of Fort Myers, 624 F2d 1321 (5th Cir 1980) §**1.19**

Harris v City of Roseburg, 664 F2d 1121 (9th Cir 1981) §§**2.09, 8.11**

Harris v Harvey, 605 F2d 330 (7th Cir 1979) §§**2.09, 3.14, 4.07, 4.13, 7.08, 7.14**

Harris v Hubbert, 588 F2d 167 (5th Cir 1979) §**2.09**

Harris v Pirch, 677 F2d 681 (8th Cir 1982) §**3.15**

Harris v Young, 718 F2d 620 (4th Cir 1983) §**8.10**

Harrison v NAACP, 360 US 167 (1959) §**5.16**

Hart v Walker, 720 F2d 1436 (5th Cir 1983) §**8.14**

Hathaway v Worcester City Hosp, 475 F2d 701 (1st Cir 1973) §**6.03**

Havens Realty Corp v Coleman, 455 US 363 (1982) §**5.05**

Hawaii v Standard Oil Co, 405 US 251 (1972) §**1.08**

M

McCausland v Mason County Bd of Educ, 649 F2d 278 (4th Cir 1981) **§4.17**

McCaw v Winter, 745 F2d 533 (8th Cir 1984) **§7.10**

McCord v Bailey, 636 F2d 606 (DC Cir 1980) **§2.09**

McCray v Burrell, 516 F2d 357 (4th Cir 1975) **§1.17**

McCray v Maryland, 456 F2d 1 (4th Cir 1972) **§§3.13, 7.10**

McCulloch v Glasgow, 620 F2d 47 (5th Cir 1980) **§4.08**

McCune v Frank, 521 F2d 1152 (2d Cir 1975) **§5.15**

McCurry v Allen, 606 F2d 795 (8th Cir 1979), *revd,* 449 US 90 (1980) **§§5.13, 5.15, 5.19**

McDonald v City of West Branch, 466 US 284 (1984) **§§5.17, 5.19**

McDonald v Doe, 748 F2d 1055 (5th Cir 1984) **§1.19**

McDonald v Hall, 610 F2d 16 (1st Cir 1979) **§3.18**

McDonald, Sommer & Frates v County of Yolo, 54 USLW — (S Ct June 25, 1986) **§3.10**

McElveen v County of Prince William, 725 F2d 954 (4th Cir 1984) **§8.15**

McFadden v Sanchez, 710 F2d 907 (2d Cir 1983) **§§3.19, 4.09**

McFerren v County Bd of Educ, 455 F2d 199 (6th Cir), *cert denied,* 407 US 934 (1972) **§1.17**

McGarvey v Magee-Womens Hosp, 340 F Supp 751 (WD Pa 1972), *affd,* 474 F2d 1339 (3d Cir 1973) **§1.07**

McGhee v Draper, 564 F2d 902 (10th Cir 1977) **§§8.07, 8.15, 8.16**

McGillicuddy v Clements, 746 F2d 76 (1st Cir 1985) **§2.11**

McGovern v Sullins, 676 F2d 98 (4th Cir 1982) **§2.13**

McGruder v Phelps, 608 F2d 1023 (5th Cir 1979) **§1.16**

McKay v Hammock, 730 F2d 1367 (10th Cir 1984) **§§3.08, 4.17, 6.10**

McKee v Heggy, 703 F2d 479 (10th Cir 1983) **§§3.10, 3.16**

McKeever v Israel, 689 F2d 1315 (7th Cir 1982) **§1.16**

McKinley v City of Eloy, 705 F2d 1110 (9th Cir 1983) **§§6.09, 6.13**

McKinley v Trattles, 732 F2d 1320 (7th Cir 1984) **§§4.10, 8.10, 8.15**

McKinnon v City of Berwyn, 750 F2d 1383 (7th Cir 1985) **§§1.25, 3.16**

McKinnon v Patterson, 568 F2d 930 (2d Cir 1977), *cert denied,* 434 US 1087 (1978) **§8.10**

McKinnis v Mosely, 693 F2d 1054 (11th Cir 1982) **§5.11**

McKnight v SouthEastern Pa Transp Auth, 583 F2d 1229 (3d Cir 1978) **§5.16**

McLaughlin v Alban, 775 F2d 389 (DC Cir 1985) **§3.17**

McLaughlin v City of LaGrange, 662 F2d 1385 (11th Cir 1981) (per curiam) **§3.16**

McLaurin v Fischer, 768 F2d 98 (6th Cir 1985) **§1.11**

McLean v Arkansas Bd of Educ, 723 F2d 45 (8th Cir 1983) **§1.19**

McNaff v United States, 318 US 332 (1943) **§8.04**

McNeese v Board of Educ, 373 US 668 (1963) **§§2.02, 5.10**

McSurely v McCellan, 753 F2d 88 (DC Cir 1985) (per curiam) **§7.03**

McVarish v Mid-Nebraska Community Mental Health Center, 696 F2d 69 (8th Cir 1982) **§2.09**

Mears v Town of Oxford, 762 F2d 368 (4th Cir 1985) **§5.19**

Members of Bridgeport Hous Auth Police Force v City of Bridgeport,

P

Rainey v Jackson State College, 551 F2d 672 (5th Cir 1977) §§1.19, 1.24, 1.25

Raley v Fraser, 747 F2d 287 (5th Cir 1985) §1.19

Ramie v City of Hedwig Village, 765 F2d 490 (5th Cir 1985) §§3.12, 6.10

Randall v Goldmark, 495 F2d 356 (1st Cir 1974), *cert denied*, 419 US 879 (1974) §2.12

Rankin v City of Witchita Falls, 762 F2d 444 (5th Cir 1985) §3.10

Rankin v Howard, 633 F2d 844 (9th Cir 1980) §§2.11, 7.08, 7.09

Raskiewicz v Town of New Boston, 754 F2d 38 (1st Cir 1985) §3.10

Rawlings v Ray, 312 US 96 (1941) §4.15

Raymond Motor Transp, Inc v Rice, 417 F Supp 1352 (WD Wisc 1976), *revd*, 434 US 429 (1977) §1.08

Redd v Lambert, 674 F2d 1032 (5th Cir 1982) §§1.21, 5.03

Redding v Fairman, 717 F2d 1105 (7th Cir 1983) §§7.10, 8.10

Reed v Village of Shorewood, 704 F2d 943 (7th Cir 1983) §§7.05, 7.10, 8.14

Reel v Arkansas Dept of Correction, 672 F2d 693 (8th Cir 1982) §1.19

Reese v Nelson, 598 F2d 822 (3d Cir 1979) §§8.16, 8.17

Reeves v City of Jackson, 608 F2d 644 (5th Cir 1979) §3.10

Reimer v Smith, 663 F2d 1316 (5th Cir 1981) §§3.17, 5.17

Rendell-Baker v Kohn, 457 US 830 (1982), *affg*, 641 F2d 14 (1st Cir 1981) §§2.05, 2.07, 2.08

Reproductive Health Servs v Freeman, 614 F2d 585 (8th Cir 1980) §1.19

Rex v Teeples, 753 F2d 840 (10th Cir 1985) §§7.14, 8.11

Reynolds v Abbeville County School Dist No 60, 554 F2d 638 (4th Cir 1977) §6.04

Reynolds v Coomey, 567 F2d 1166 (1st Cir 1978) §1.24

Rey v City of Fredericktown, 729 F2d 1171 (8th Cir 1984) §1.15

Rheuark v Shaw, 628 F2d 297 (5th Cir 1980) §§6.07, 7.10

Rhoads v Horvat, 270 F Supp 307 (D Colo 1967) §4.10

Rhoades v Penfold, 694 F2d 1043 (5th Cir 1983) §§1.10, 5.15

Rhode v Denson, 776 F2d 107 (5th Cir 1985) §§6.09, 6.10

Richardson v City of Conroe, 582 F2d 19 (5th Cir 1978) §§8.11, 8.16

Richardson v City of Indianapolis, 658 F2d 494 (7th Cir 1981) §§3.16, 3.17

Richardson v Fleming, 654 F2d 366 (5th Cir 1981) §2.11

Richardson v Koshiba, 693 F2d 911 (9th Cir 1982) §§5.16, 7.08, 8.10

Ricks v Sumner, 647 F2d 76 (9th Cir 1981) §2.13

Riddell v National Democratic Party, 712 F2d 165 (5th Cir 1983) §1.25

Rittenhouse v DeKalb County, 764 F2d 1451 (11th Cir 1985) §§3.10, 3.11

Rivera v Green, 775 F2d 1381 (9th Cir 1985) §4.17

Riverside, City of v Rivera, 106 S Ct 2686 (1986), *affg* 763 F2d 1580 (9th Cir 1985) §1.25

Rizzo v Goode, 423 US 362 (1976) §§3.15, 3.18, 5.13, 6.06

RJ Williams Co v Fort Belknap Hous Auth, 719 F2d 979 (9th Cir 1983) §2.09

Roadway Express, Inc v Piper, 447 US 752 (1980), *affg* 599 F2d 1378 (5th Cir 1979) §§1.23, 1.24, 1.27

Rymer v Douglas County, 764 F2d 796 (11th Cir 1985) §3.10

Rzeznik v Chief of Police, 374 Mass 475, 373 NE2d 1128 (1978) §1.13

S

Safety Harbor, City of v Birchfield, 529 F2d 1251 (5th Cir 1976) §§1.08, 7.03

Saffioti v Wilson, 392 F Supp 1335 (SD NY 1975) §7.04

Saldana v Garza, 684 F2d 1159 (5th Cir 1982) *cert denied*, 460 US 1012 (1983) §§8.03, 8.11, 8.16

Sampley v Ruettgers, 704 F2d 491 (10th Cir 1983) §§3.07, 3.10

Samuel v University of Pittsburgh, 375 F Supp 1119 (WD Pa 1974), *modified*, 538 F2d 991 (3d Cir 1976) §6.20

Samuels v Dist of Columbia, 770 F2d 184 (DC Cir 1985) §2.13

Samuels v Mackell, 401 US 66 (1971) §§5.12, 5.13

Sanchez v Schwartz, 688 F2d 503 (7th Cir 1982) §1.19

Sanders v Conine, 506 F2d 530 (10th Cir 1974) §2.12

San Diego Gas & Elec Co v San Diego, 450 US 621 (1981) §3.10

San Filippo v United States Trust Co, 737 F2d 246 (2d Cir 1984) §§2.11, 7.11

Santiago v City of Philadelphia, 435 F Supp 136 (ED Pa 1977) §3.15

Sapp v Renfroe, 511 F2d 172 (5th Cir 1975) §8.07

Sargeant v Sharp, 579 F2d 645 (1st Cir 1978) §§1.18, 1.22

Sassi v Breier, 584 F2d 234 (7th Cir 1978) §4.17

Saxner v Benson, 727 F2d 669 (7th Cir 1984), *affd sub nom* Cleavinger

v Saxner, 106 S Ct 496 (1985) §4.05

Scheuer v Rhodes, 416 US 232 (1974) §§3.01, 3.02, 5.08, 7.04, 7.05, 7.10, 7.13, 8.01, 8.02, 8.03, 8.09, 8.13, 8.15, 8.18

Schiff v Williams, 519 F2d 257 (5th Cir 1975) §8.07

Schilb v Kuebel, 404 US 357 (1971) §2.03

Schmerber v California, 384 US 757 (1966) §3.08

Schmidt v Oakland United School Dist, 662 F2d 550 (9th Cir 1981) §8.07

Schulman v Huck Finn, Inc, 472 F2d 864 (8th Cir 1973) §1.12

Schultz v Baumgart, 738 F2d 231 (7th Cir 1984) §3.15

Schultz v Sundberg, 759 F2d 714 (9th Cir 1985) §7.03

Schultz v Wellman, 717 F2d 301 (6th Cir 1983) §2.09

Schweiker v McClure, 456 US 188 (1982) §8.04

Scott v Dixon, 720 F2d 1542 (11th Cir 1983) §7.10

Scott v Greenville County, 716 F2d 1409 (4th Cir 1983) §§5.05, 7.05

Scott v Hayes, 719 F2d 1562 (11th Cir 1983) §7.08

Scott v Plante, 691 F2d 634 (3d Cir 1982) §§8.01, 8.08

Scott v Roseberg, 702 F2d 1263 (9th Cir 1983) §2.10

Screws v United States, 325 US 91 (1945) §2.04

Seaton v Sky Realty Co, 491 F2d 634 (7th Cir 1974) §§4.07, 4.13

Security & Law Enforcement Employees v Carey, 737 F2d 187 (2d Cir 1984) §8.10

Segarra v McDade, 706 F2d 1301 (4th Cir 1983) §§4.03, 7.10, 8.10

Seguin v Eide, 645 F2d 804 (9th Cir 1981) §8.12

Thomas v Younglove, 545 F2d 1171 (9th Cir 1976) §7.05

Thompson v Burke, 556 F2d 231 (3d Cir 1977) §§4.05, 7.10, 8.18

Thornton v Buchmann, 392 F2d 870 (7th Cir 1968) §3.05

Timmerman v Brown, 528 F2d 811 (4th Cir 1975) §§5.15, 7.12

Toa Baja Dev Corp v Garcia Santiago, 312 F Supp 899 (DPR 1970) §1.09

Todd v Baskerville, 712 F2d 70 (4th Cir 1983) §5.11

Toledo Peoria & Western RR v Illinois Dept of Transp, 744 F2d 1296 (7th Cir 1984) §6.20

Tollett v Henderson, 411 US 258 (1973) §5.18

Tomko v Lees, 416 F Supp 1137 (WD Pa 1976) §7.14

Torres v Sachs, 538 F2d 10 (2d Cir 1976) §1.24

Tovar v Billmeyer, 609 F2d 1291 (9th Cir 1980) §§5.15, 5.16

Tower v Glover, 467 US 914 (1984) §§2.01, 2.05, 2.09, 5.13, 7.01, 7.12

Trafficante v Metropolitan Life Ins Co, 409 US 205 (1972) §5.05

Trainor v Hernandez, 431 US 434, (1977) §§5.12, 5.13, 5.14

Traver v Meshriy, 627 F2d 934 (9th Cir 1980) §§1.11, 2.09

Trejo v Perez, 693 F2d 482 (5th Cir 1982) §8.11

Trigg v Ft Wayne Community Schools, 766 F2d 299 (7th Cir 1985) §2.13

Tritsis v Backer, 501 F2d 1021 (7th Cir 1974) §8.11

Trotman v Board of Trustees, 635 F2d 216 (3d Cir 1980) §§3.03, 4.02

Trotter v Klincar, 748 F2d 1177 (7th Cir 1984) §§7.10, 8.18

Trudeau v Wyrick, 713 F2d 1360 (8th Cir 1983) §§3.17, 4.06

Trujillo v Board of City Commrs, 768 F2d 1186 (10th Cir 1985) §3.10

Tubbesing v Arnold, 742 F2d 401 (8th Cir 1984) §§1.16, 8.03, 8.14

Tuley v Heyd, 482 F2d 590 (5th Cir 1973) §3.15

Turman v Tuttle, 711 F2d 148 (10th Cir 1983) §1.24

Turner v Raynes, 611 F2d 92 (5th Cir 1980) §7.08

Turpin v Mailet, 579 F2d 152 (2d Cir 1978), *vacated & remanded sub nom.* City of West Haven v Turpin, 47 USLW 3234 (US Sept 1, 1978) §§6.01, 6.16

Tuveson v Florida Governor's Council on Indiana Affairs, 734 F2d 730 (11th Cir 1984) §5.08

T&W Inv Co v Kurtz, 588 F2d 801 (10th Cir 1978) §7.10

Twining v New Jersey, 211 US 78 (1908) §2.02

Tyler v Mmes Pasqua & Tolosa, 748 F2d 283 (5th Cir 1984) §§1.10, 2.13

Tymiak v Omodt, 676 F2d 306 (8th Cir 1982) §7.10

U

Uniformed Firefighters Assn v City of New York, 676 F2d 20 (2d Cir 1982) §2.13

United Air Lines v Evans, 431 US 553 (1977) §4.17

United Carolina Bank v Board of Regents, 665 F2d 553 (5th Cir 1982) §5.08

United Church v Medical Center Commn, 689 F2d 693 (7th Cir 1982) §5.15

United Farmworkers Hous Project, Inc v City of Delray Beach 493 F2d 799 (5th Cir 1974) §§6.03, 6.20

V

Ward v Dearman, 626 F2d 489 (5th Cir 1980) §1.19

Ward v Johnson, 690 F2d 1098 (4th Cir 1982) §§7.10, 8.10

Ware v Heyne, 575 F2d 593 (7th Cir 1978) §8.10

Warren v Byrne, 699 F2d 95 (2d Cir 1983) §5.19

Warth v Seldin, 422 US 490 (1975) §5.05

Washington v Davis, 426 US 229 (1976) §§3.14, 4.08

Washington v Texas, 388 US 14 (1967) §2.03

Watkins v Mobile Hous Bd, 632 F2d 565 (5th Cir 1980) §§1.23, 1.24

Watson v Interstate Fire & Casualty Co, 611 F2d 120 (5th Cir 1980) §§3.15, 7.08

Watts v Graves, 720 F2d 1416 (5th Cir 1983) §5.19

Weatherford v Bursey, 429 US 545 (1977) §§3.02, 3.06, 8.11

Webb v County Bd of Educ, 105 S Ct 1923 (1985) §§1.21, 1.25

Webster v City of Houston, 689 F2d 1220 (5th Cir 1982), *vacated,* 735 F2d 838 (5th Cir), *reinstated,* 739 F2d 993 (5th Cir 1984) §§6.11, 6.19

Weigel v McCloskey, 113 Ark 1, 166 SW 944 (1914) §3.08

Weise v Syracuse Univ, 522 F2d 397 (2d Cir 1975) §2.08

Weisenberger v Huecker, 593 F2d 49 (6th Cir 1979) §1.26

Wellington v Daniels, 717 F2d 932 (4th Cir 1983) §§6.09, 6.13

Wells v Doland, 711 F2d 670 (5th Cir 1983) §4.05

Wells v Hico Indep School Dist, 736 F2d 243 (5th Cir 1984) §4.12

Wells v Ward, 470 F2d 1185 (10th Cir 1972) §3.02

Welsh v Kinchla, 577 F2d 767 (1st Cir 1978) §3.10

Wentz v Klecker, 721 F2d 244 (8th Cir 1983) §8.13

Werch v City of Berlin, 673 F2d 192 (7th Cir 1982) §5.03

Werle v Rhode Island Bar Assn, 755 F2d 195 (1st Cir 1985) §§7.14, 8.13

Westberry v Fisher, 309 F Supp 12 (D Me 1970) §6.04

Western Food Plan, Inc v MacFarlane, 588 F2d 778 (10th Cir 1978) §5.16

Weston v Bachman, 682 F2d 202 (8th Cir 1982) §4.17

Whalen v Roe, 429 US 589 (1977) §3.12

Wheatley v Ford, 679 F2d 1037 (2d Cir 1982) §§1.25, 1.26, 4.04

Wheeler v Cosden Oil & Chem Co, 734 F2d 254 (5th Cir), *modified,* 744 F2d 1131 (5th Cir 1984) §§3.10, 3.17, 7.11, 8.11

Whirl v Kern, 407 F2d 781 (5th Cir), *cert denied,* 396 US 901 (1969) §§3.08, 3.13, 8.10

White v Bloom, 621 F2d 276 (8th Cir 1980) §§2.11, 7.15

White v New Hampshire, 455 US 445 (1982), *revg.* 629 F2d 697 (1st Cir 1980) §§1.18, 1.23

White v Rochford, 592 F2d 381 (7th Cir 1979) §3.10

White v South Park Indep School Dist, 693 F2d 1163 (5th Cir 1982) §4.02

White v Walsh, 649 F2d 560 (8th Cir 1981) §3.19

Whitehurst v Wright, 592 F2d 834 (5th Cir 1979) §3.19

Whiting v Jackson State Univ, 616 F2d 116 (5th Cir 1980) §4.03

Whitley v Albers, 106 S Ct 1078 (1986) §§3.07, 3.08, 8.10

Whitley v Seibel, 676 F2d 245 (7th Cir 1982) §§4.03, 4.04

Table of Statutes and Rules

INDEX